THE PURSUIT OF THE
Heiress

THE PURSUIT OF THE
Heiress

ARISTOCRATIC MARRIAGE
IN IRELAND
1740–1840

A.P.W. MALCOMSON

Anthony Malcomson

ULSTER HISTORICAL
FOUNDATION

for
Emily Villiers-Stuart
and in memory of
her late husband
James Villiers-Stuart

ENDPAPERS
The first plate in Hogarth's famous series, *Marriage à la Mode*, published in 1745.
See page 45.

FRONTISPIECE
George Grenville, 1st Marquess of Buckingham, with his wife, their elder son and a blackamooor page, painted by Sir Joshua Reynolds, c.1783. Lady Buckingham was an heiress, and was also the daughter of the Irish peerage's most notable heiress-hunter, Robert Earl Nugent (National Gallery of Ireland).

Ulster Historical Foundation is pleased to acknowledge support for this publication from the Esme Mitchell Trust, the Belfast Natural History and Philosophical Society and Belfast Buildings Preservation Trust. All contributions are gratefully acknowledged.

First published in 2006
by Ulster Historical Foundation
Unit 7, Cotton Court, Waring Street, Belfast, BT1 2ED
www.ancestryireland.com

Except as otherwise permitted under the Copyright, Designs and Patents Act 1988, this publication may only be reproduced, stored or transmitted in any form or by any means with the prior permission in writing of the publisher or, in the case of reprographic reproduction, in accordance with the terms of a licence issued by The Copyright Licensing Agency. Enquiries concerning reproduction outside those terms should be sent to the publisher.

© A.P.W. Malcomson, 2006
Printed by The Bath Press
Design by Dunbar Design
ISBN 10: 1-903688-65-5
ISBN 13: 978-1-903688-65-6

Contents

	LIST OF ILLUSTRATIONS	vi
	PREFACE AND ACKNOWLEDGEMENTS	ix
ONE	Law, terminology and the nature of the evidence	1
TWO	'Collateral calculation': the constraints of the marriage settlement	26
THREE	The superior bargaining power of the heiress	54
FOUR	Collateral damage: the lure of the younger son	83
FIVE	The 'marriage of affection'	112
SIX	Elopements, mésalliances and mis-matches	155
SEVEN	'Speculations and castle-buildings': the identification of an heiress	186
EIGHT	The safer and surer routes to riches	217
	CONCLUSION	241
	NOTES	247
	BIBLIOGRAPHY	273
	INDEX	285

LIST OF ILLUSTRATIONS

ENDPAPERS: *Marriage á la Mode* (p.45)	
FRONTISPIECE: The 1st Marquess of Buckingham and his family, by Sir Joshua Reynolds, c.1783	ii
Lord Brabazon and Lady Mary Maitland, 1868	xii
Aldborough House, Amiens Street, Dublin, 1836	2
The 1st Earl of Carysfort from a portrait by John Hoppner, c.1800	11
The 2nd Earl of Aldborough from a portrait by Thomas Gainsborough, c.1780	14
'The Wedding Night' of the Princess Royal and the Hereditary Prince of Wurttemberg, 1797	16
Viscount Pery by Hugh Douglas Hamilton, c.1790	20
The 1st Marquess of Donegall by Thomas Gainsborough, c.1780	22
Robert, Earl Nugent, 1782	23
Viscount Crosbie and the Hon. Diana Sackville by H.D. Hamilton, 1777	28
The 1st Marquess of Abercorn after Sir Thomas Lawrence, c.1793	33
Emily, Duchess of Leinster after Sir Joshua Reynolds, 1754	40
Caricature of William Ogilvie, by his son-in-law, c.1800	43
Hogarth's *Marriage à la Mode*, Plate 1, published in 1745	45
The Rt Hon. Thomas and Lady Louisa Conolly by H.D. Hamilton, c.1775	48
The 1st Viscount Sackville, 1785	49
Caroline, Countess of Kingston, 1810	55
'A sketch of St Albans': Harriot Mellon and her youthful second husband, the 9th Duke of St Albans, 1827	57
General Lord Hutchinson, 2nd Earl of Donoughmore, 1809	59
Curraghmore, Co. Waterford, c.1800	61
Elizabeth, Countess Grandison, c.1763	69
Pre-nuptial survey of the heiress, Margaret Hamilton's, Caledon estate, 1737	76
The 2nd Earl of Glengall and his heiress-wife, Margaret Lauretta Mellish, 1834	78
Caricature of the 2nd Marquess of Londonderry by Richard Dighton, 1821	82
Anne Eyre, Countess of Massereene, by William Hoare of Bath, c.1750	84
Shortgrove, Newport, Essex, English seat of the earls of Thomond	88
Sir Laurence Parsons, 5th Bt, 2nd Earl of Rosse, 1810	90
Lady Gertrude Villiers by Angelica Kauffman, 1794	92
Katherine Fitzgerald Villiers, Viscountess Grandison, c.1690	94
Anne Catherine McDonnell, Countess of Antrim, by H.D. Hamilton, c.1800	96
Glenarm Castle by William Vitruvius Morrison, 1824	97
Charlotte McDonnell, Lady Mark Kerr, afterwards Countess of Antrim, c.1805	98
Lord Mark Kerr by Margaret Carpenter, c.1810	99
Two caricatures satirising Irish fortune-hunters, 1779 and 1794	101, 103
Frances Anne, Marchioness of Londonderry, c.1825	104
John Hely-Hutchinson and his heiress-wife, Lady Donoughmore, by Reynolds, c.1780	106, 107
John Proby, 1st Lord Carysfort, by Reynolds, 1765	108
Sir Henry Cairnes, 2nd Bt, c.1720	114

LIST OF ILLUSTRATIONS

The 1st Earl of Hardwicke, author of the Marriage Act of 1753	117
Speaker Foster and his family by John James Barralet, 1786	124
Lady Caroline Creighton and her mother, Lady Erne, by H.D. Hamilton, c.1789	130
The 2nd Duke of Leinster, 1802	132
The 2nd Earl of Egmont and his (first?) wife, c.1750	133
The 5th Earl of Orrery, c.1740	135
Mary Bermingham, Countess of Leitrim, and her daughter, Maria, after Sir Thomas Lawrence's portrait of 1805	138
The long gallery, Adare Manor, Co. Limerick, where portraits of 1840 of the 2nd Earl of Dunraven and his heiress-wife are prominently displayed	141
Tête à tête engraved portraits of the 7th Earl of Cork and his mistress, 1782	144
Lady Belmore in bed with her lover, Lord Ancram, 1790	148
Lady Cloncurry being seduced by Sir John Piers in 1806	151
The 1st Marquess of Hertford, 1791	154
The 1st Earl of Limerick, c.1815	157
The Countess of Rosse and her daughters, Jane and Alicia, by Thomas Foster, c.1825	158
Henry Villiers-Stuart, Lord Stuart de Decies, c.1832	163
Pauline Theresia Ott, Lady Stuart de Decies, c.1826	164
Baroness Burdett-Coutts, 1883	167
Joshua Sharpe after Reynolds, 1785	170
The 1st Earl of Donoughmore, 1810	171
The 1st Marquess of Abercorn's mistress, Mrs Maguire, and one of their sons, after Lawrence's portrait of 1805	173
Ralph Bernal Osborne, 1870	176
The 2nd Viscount Mountjoy, later Earl of Blessington, c.1810	179
Frances Cairnes Murray, Countess of Clermont, after a Reynolds portrait of c.1775	189
The 2nd Earl of Buckinghamshire by Gainsborough, c.1780	192
General the 10th Lord Cathcart by James Gillray, 1800	194
Silhouette of Jane, Countess of Rosse, 1838	195
The 7th Viscount Fitzwilliam of Merrion, pre-1816	197
The 12th Earl of Pembroke, c.1830	203
Charles Smyth and his daughter, Juliana Vereker, by H.D. Hamilton, c.1770	208
Colonel Charles Vereker, 2nd Viscount Gort, 1811	209
The 12th Viscount Dillon by Edward Mawbrye, c.1787	214
Portraits of Theodosia Magill, heiress-wife of the 1st Earl of Clanwilliam, by Gainsborough and Reynolds, 1765	219, 220
General the 2nd Earl of Moira, 1804	222
The 1st Earl of Bessborough by Charles Jervas?, 1727?	226
Bust of the 2nd Earl of Belvedere by Thomas Kirk, 1816	231
The 8th Earl of Abercorn by John Giles Eckhardt, c.1760	235

PREFACE AND ACKNOWLEDGEMENTS

The previous edition of this book was published, also by the Ulster Historical Foundation, in 1982, which means that the research on which it was based was completed almost twenty five years ago. Since then, new archival sources have come to light (or, at least, to my knowledge), a number of books and articles bearing materially on the subject have been published, and – to be frank – a number of errors and omissions have become apparent in the text as it stood.

Moreover, the 1982 version was deliberately confined to the Irish context and did not participate in the wider debate over aristocratic marriage and inheritance strategy in England which was then beginning to develop. Since its publication, the 1982 version has in fact been drawn into that debate because of the notice taken of some of its conclusions by two of the main combatants, the late Professor Lawrence Stone and Professor Eileen Spring; the former, in particular, made favourable mention of the notion of 'cadet inheritance' which was tentatively advanced in *Pursuit of the Heiress* Mark One. So, it is appropriate that any republication of my book should place it more overtly in the context of the wider debate, and broaden the book's perspective by drawing on the views of Stone, Spring and others.

Accordingly, when approached by the Ulster Historical Foundation in 2003 with the proposal that the book, now out of print for some years, should be reprinted, I was flattered (especially at the thought that there were people wanting to buy it) but reluctant to agree to a reprint when I knew well that a re-write was called for. This has proved a fairly lengthy business and had to wait until other projects then under way had been completed. But I hope that the effort and the delay are thought to be justified by results.

In this completely new, and much longer, version, I have not departed significantly from the basic ideas propounded by the younger and more diffident scholar of c.1978-82. But I have corrected errors and reassessed interpretations, I have added a considerable body of further evidence to support those ideas, and I have shown far greater awareness of the sometimes corroborative, sometimes complementary, sometimes contradictory ideas of others. I have also, where necessary, updated the locations of the surprisingly itinerant archives drawn upon before, and the names of a number of institutions which have been changed – never for the better – in the intervening period. Finally, I have adjusted the covering dates of the study to accord more accurately, not just with the new material introduced this time round, but with the actual time-frame of the 1982 book. In spite of this change, I have treated the new dates of 1740–1840 as cavalierly as the old 1750–1820.

For permission to draw upon unpublished material, whether for the first or second time, I should like to record my debt of gratitude to the following individuals and institutions: the Marquess of Abergavenny; the Archbishop of Armagh; the Earl of Arran; the Trustees of the Bedford Estates; the Earl Belmore; Mr G.H. Boyle; the British Library Board; Rosemary, Viscountess Brookeborough; the Brynmor Jones Library, University of Hull; the Lady Mairi Bury; the Cambridge University Library; the Marquess Camden; Mrs Ian Campbell; the Trustees of the Chatsworth Settlement; Mr and Mrs Charles

Clements; Mr and the Hon. Mrs Alec Cobbe; Lady Coghill; the Comptroller of HM Stationery Office (in respect of the Chancery Masters Accounts and Chatham and Home Office Papers in The National Archives, Kew); Mr Adrian Cosby; the Marquess of Donegall; the Marchioness of Dufferin and Ava; the Viscount Dunluce; the Earl of Dunraven; the Lord Egremont; the Earl Erne; Sir Adrian FitzGerald, Bt, Knight of Kerry; the Trustees of the Fitzwilliam Wentworth Estates; the Lord Hotham; the Keele University Library; the Centre for Kentish Studies, Maidstone; the late Capt. D.J.R. Ker; Mr James King; the Limerick University Library; Miss F.M. Martin; Messrs Martin & Henderson, solicitors, Downpatrick; the Viscount Massereene and Ferrard: Mr Simon Meade; the Earl of Meath; the Viscount Midleton; the Director of the National Archives of Ireland; the Board of the National Library of Ireland; Mr Thomas Pakenham; the late Mrs Hales Pakenham-Mahon; the Earl of Pembroke and Pembroke Estates Management Ltd. (Dublin); the late Major J.R. Perceval-Maxwell; Mr J.D. Pollock; Sir William Proby, Bt; the Deputy Keeper of the Records, Public Record Office of Northern Ireland; the Registry of Deeds, Dublin; the Royal Irish Academy; the Earl of Rosse; P. & B. Rowan (antiquarian booksellers, Belfast); the Earl of Shannon; Sheffield Archives, Sheffield; the late Dr T.A.P. Smythe Wood; the Earl of Stradbroke; the Hon. G.R. Strutt; the Ipswich Branch of the Suffolk Record Office; the Surrey History Centre, Woking; the East and West Sussex Record Offices; Mr and the Hon. Mrs Jonathan Sykes; Major-General M.E. Tickell; the late Rear-Admiral W.G.S. Tighe; the Tipperary County Library; Mme P. Trasenster; the Board of Trinity College, Dublin; Miss R.W. Verner; the late Mr James Villiers-Stuart; and the Marquess of Waterford.

The bibliography at the end of the book records my debt to the numerous scholars whose books and articles I have drawn on in this text. In addition, I should like to acknowledge the more active assistance of some of them and of a number of other historians, archivists, colleagues, acquaintances and friends: the late Angela, Countess of Antrim; Dr T.C. Barnard; Dr John Bergin; Dr David J. Butler; Professor B.M.S. Campbell; Dr Anne Casement; Dr Jonathan Cherry; Mrs Brigid Clesham; Mr and especially the Hon. Mrs Alec Cobbe; Professor S.J. Connolly; Dr W.H. Crawford; Professor L.M. Cullen; Mr and Mrs Alan Dalton; Mr Desmond FitzGerald, Knight of Glin; Dr D.A. Fleming; Mrs John Grieve; Mr R.C. Guinness; Mr Robin Harcourt-Williams; Professor D.W. Hayton; Mr David Huddleston; Dr Arnold Hunt; Ms Aideen Ireland; Mrs Catherine Jessel; Ms Hannah Jones; the late Professor P.J. Jupp; the late Mr Edward Keane; Dr James Kelly; Mr Peter Kenny; Mrs Thomas Long; Mr Gerard Lyne; Mr John McCabe; Mrs Alison McCann; Mr Timothy J. McCann; Dr Trevor McCavery; Mr James I. McGuire; Dr Edward McParland; Dr W.A. Maguire; Mr Peter Marson; Mr Ian Montgomery; Mr Christopher Moore; Ms Eliza Pakenham; Mr and Mrs Thomas Pakenham; Dr A.P. Ryan; Dr G.J. Slater; Mr Martin Smyth; Ms Joanne Stone; Mr Kieran Thompson junior; Dr W.E. Vaughan; the late Mrs Anne Warren; Mr Christopher Whittick; and Dr Deborah Wilson.

Many of the illustrations are taken from my own collection, which means that my acknowledgements under this head are fewer than would otherwise be the case. Nevertheless, I am under obligations to numerous individuals, institutions and organisations for granting me permission to reproduce illustrative material and for providing me with images of appropriate quality. These include: the sale-rooms Adam's, Christie's, Colnaghi's and Sotheby's; the Deputy Keeper of the Records, PRONI, and the Trustees of the Abercorn Heirlooms Settlement, of the National Museum of Northern Ireland (in

PREFACE AND ACKNOWLEDGEMENTS

respect of portraits in the Ulster Museum collection), of the National Gallery of Ireland and of the National Portrait Gallery (London); Dr David J. Butler; Mrs Ian Campbell; the Churchill House Press (Tralee); Mr and Mrs Charles Clements; Mr Alec Cobbe; Dorinda, Lady Dunleath; the Viscount Dunluce; Desmond FitzGerald, Knight of Glin; Dr D.A. Fleming; Mr William Laffan; Dr Ann McVeigh; the Viscount Massereene and Ferrard; Mr and Mrs J.A.D. Nesbitt; the Earl and Countess of Rosse; Mrs Charles Scott; Dr R.W. Strong; and Mr Joe Walsh.

During some of the trickier stages in the writing of this book, I have gone – as is my wont – into retreat in two of my favourite places, to Murvey Lodge, Roundstone, for seclusion, and to Newport House, Co. Mayo, for shameless cosseting. I should like to record my debt to my respective hosts at these locations – Mr and Mrs Robert Molony and their family, and Mr and Mrs Kieran Thompson, Mrs Catherine Flynn and the staff of Newport House.

In the preparation of the text for publication, I have received unstinting assistance from those employed or engaged by the UHF to carry out the various stages of the work. To Fintan Mullan, Joe Armstrong, Wendy Dunbar and, above all, the always goodnatured and usually humorous Frances Brennan, I offer my thanks.

The production of a book like this has been an expensive undertaking. It would not have been possible without the generous sponsorship of a benefactor who insists on being anonymous, of the Belfast Buildings Preservation Trust, of the Esmé Mitchell Trust, and of the Belfast Natural History and Philosophical Society.

While the labours involved in researching, writing and even indexing *The Pursuit of the Heiress* have been mostly pleasurable, I have two deep regrets to express. The first is the untimely death of my friend and colleague of many years' standing, Professor P.J. Jupp. Peter and I worked together long ago on some of the 'big house' archives which form the basis for this study, notably those at Birr Castle, Co. Offaly, Castle Forbes, Co. Longford and at that time still at Knocklofty, Co. Tipperary. As I re-read those parts of the text which I particularly associate with him, I am reminded of the loss he is to archives, history, teaching and his friends.

The dedication, too, reflects another, less recent loss, that of James Villiers-Stuart, who died in 2004. I might never have started to think about heiresses if I had not encountered, at the formative age of twenty-five, the remarkable series of female successions which the Dromana archive revealed. In my work of sorting, listing and making historical sense of it, I was greatly assisted by James's knowledge, and cheered by the enthusiasm (and hospitality) displayed by his wife, Emily, and himself. Moreover, almost the only shortcut I have been vouchsafed during the long and sometimes tortuous research which has led to this book, was James's previous enquiries into the still mysterious Stuart de Decies peerage case. Since his death, Emily has helped me with a variety of other problems and queries, so that I have been enabled in this new *Pursuit of the Heiress* to give due centrality to Dromana in my study of female inheritance and aristocratic marriage. On archival, historical and personal grounds, James and Emily Villiers-Stuart are highly appropriate dedicatees.

A.P.W. MALCOMSON
DECEMBER 2006

Lord and Lady Brabazon, later 12th Earl and
Countess of Meath: an engagement
photograph of 1868 with watercolour tinting

AUTHOR'S COLLECTION

ONE

Law, terminology and the nature of the evidence

In 1787, Edward Stratford, 2nd Earl of Aldborough, married, as his second wife, a well connected and well dowered English lady. In the following year he announced to his agent his imminent arrival in Ireland with the

> new Lady Aldborough and the Duchess of Chandos [her aunt] and Sir John and Lady Henniker [her parents].... A more amiable, accomplished, and united family than those I am connected with can't be. I wish I could say as much for mine.... My wife brings me £50,000 hard cash down, and will at her father's and aunt's death succeed to £150,000 more. She is certainly the first match in England, and I'm happy enough to be preferred to English noblemen, one of [them of] higher rank and fortune.[1]

His first wife, too, who had died in 1785, had been English, and a considerable acquisition. According to the Aldborough entry in Debrett's *New Peerage* of 1784 (which clearly was contributed by Lord Aldborough himself), she was 'the heiress of Mrs Herbert, otherwise North, heiress to her brother, Dudley North' of Great Glemham, Suffolk, and as a result of her marriage to Lord Aldborough, the Suffolk estate of Aldborough-Tunstall, Stratford-upon-Alde, etc., which had been alienated long ago through female succession, would 'be properly reinvested in the Stratford' family.[2] It is easy – and facile – to conclude from such evidence that Lord Aldborough 'married successively two English heiresses'.[3]

In matters of family history Lord Aldborough was wont to carry embellishment to the point of embezzlement – notably the embezzlement of the Butler family's ancient title of Ormonde.[4] Because his mother's maiden name happened to be Oneal, he saw no difficulty in tracing his maternal descent from 'Oneal, head of the Oneals, King of Ulster and for a time of all Ireland'. On the Stratford side, he was 'fortieth in descent from Edward Stratford, who lived in the reign of Alfred'; 'the name of Stratford [was], however, clearly of Grecian import ... the rather as the arms of the noble peer are the same as those of Alexander the Great'; there was also a pre-Conquest, Norman ancestor who came from Amiens

Alsborough House, Amiens Street, from an engraving in the *Dublin Penny Journal*, 13 February 1836.

in Picardy, and whose place of origin was commemorated in Lord Aldborough's subsidiary title of Viscount Amiens of Mount Amiens. (Amiens Street, Dublin, which is often erroneously derived from the Peace of Amiens of 1802, is actually a continuing commemoration of his boasted Norman descent.) His boasts about his wives and their inheritances were somewhat better-founded. There is no reason to doubt that his first wife was, at least potentially, an heiress; and there is no particular reason to doubt that his second wife brought him a fortune of £50,000: with a landed income reckoned at nearly £13,000 a year in 1792, he was rich enough to aspire to such a dowry.[5] All the same, since his first marriage was childless (as indeed was his second), it is likely that the first Lady Aldborough's Suffolk estate passed to collaterals of her own family, rather than to collaterals of his. Moreover, the expectations of a further £150,000 with the second Lady Aldborough are suspiciously great, for she was not an heiress, either of her father (who had three other children, all male), or of her aunt, the Duchess of Chandos (who had a daughter).

Inexact use of the word 'heiress', inflated estimates of the size of inheritances, and exaggerated ideas of the scope for financially advantageous marriage, are not peculiar to 'that strange madman, Lord Aldborough'.[6] They are commonplaces of much other contemporary correspondence and of apparently sane and sober *Peerages, Landed Gentrys*, and family and other histories. In 1736, for example, the debt-laden 5th Earl of Orrery was seriously advised, 'You have no possibility of retrieving yourself but by marrying'.[7] As recently as 1979, a modern Irish historian discerned still wider possibilities in advantageous marriage: 'about 60 of the [144] resident Irishmen who were created peers during the eighteenth century, were the sons or husbands of an heiress (some indeed were in the happy position of being both), the creation of a peerage setting a seal on the merger of two landed fortunes.'[8] Clearly, some attempt needs to be made to bring the possibilities of aristocratic marriage in Ireland within at least the bounds of common sense.

In making the attempt, this study does not seek to involve Ireland in the wider English debate, inaugurated by Professor Habbakuk back in 1940, about marriage as a major factor in the rise of the great estate.[9] Not surprisingly, some of the conclusions which it reaches, though independently arrived at, are similar to those brought up and used in evidence against Habbakuk.[10] However, this is simply because common sense operated on both sides of the Irish Sea. In other respects, the Irish context is different, because no one has yet extended to Ireland Habbakuk's thesis that marriage was the main cause of large estates getting larger: indeed, it is not clear that they were getting larger in Ireland. In the Irish context it is therefore easier to focus on marriage as an object of investigation in its own right; to inquire to what extent it was, and was regarded as, an agent of general dynastic aggrandisement; and to give due emphasis to factors of a personal, human and non-economic kind. Moreover, Ireland and its more-or-less resident aristocracy are sufficiently small for it to be possible in the Irish context to convey, within the confines of one book, some impression of the *mores* of aristocratic marriage on a country-wide basis and over a significant period of time.

The materials for such an examination are fairly abundant, but not entirely straightforward. Wills, the most obvious source, are usually uninformative. Their scope generally does not extend beyond the testator's personal estate, any real estate acquired by him and not subsequently placed under settlement, and any discretion reserved to him by previous settlements (e.g. in the matter of apportioning a global sum among individual younger children); sometimes it does not extend beyond bequests to the Church and to domestic servants. Thus, the will of the 8th Earl of Abercorn, who died in 1789, specified bequests to the value of some £30,000, but did not give any details about the rest of the testator's personal estate (popularly reckoned at £200,000), or mention at all his real estate, which had a rental of between £20,000 and £30,000 a year.[11] Casual, gossipy letters often state that A has died and left his estate to B, and sums of money charged upon it to C and D,[12] but this probably means no more than that the death had given effect and publicity to a settlement made years previously.

In the cases where wills are informative (e.g. when they dispose of a significant amount of real estate), their provisions still need to be interpreted in light of previous settlements and other hard evidence about the family property. Otherwise, the evidence of the will alone may be seriously misleading. For instance, the will of the Rt Hon. Nathaniel Clements, made in 1775 with two codicils added between then and 1777, disposes of a great deal of real estate and other assets. But it falls far short of being a complete statement of what the testator was worth because it omits everything which he had *settled* on someone during his lifetime.[13] He might retain all or most of the income from such settled assets while he lived, but the legal ownership of them was vested in trustees and he was not free to dispose of them by will.

Equally misleading are the near-contemporary dispositions made by Bernard Ward, 1st Viscount Bangor (will dated 30 August 1779; codicils 11 February 1780 and 7 May 1781),[14] particularly his bequest of his Bangor estate, Co. Down, to his third son, Robert Ward. This is usually regarded as the point at which the Ward estates at Strangford and Killough, Co. Down, were separated from the Ward estate in Bangor. But what happened is, as usual, more complicated. In 1709, Lord Bangor's father had married the co-heiress to the Bangor estate, Anne Hamilton (who was Lord Bangor's mother). Soon after, her sister, Margaret, the other co-heiress, had married the 6th Viscount Ikerrin. In 1779 Lord Bangor purchased the Ikerrin interest in Bangor (for £12,337) – a transaction not mentioned in the will.[15] It was this half of the estate which he was free to bequeath, and which he did bequeath, to his third son, Robert: the other half of the estate, which had come into the possession of the Ward family through the marriage of 1709, passed at Lord Bangor's death to his eldest son, being part of the family's settled estates. His will, however, is silent about the settled estates, because they lay outside its scope.

Lord Bangor and Nathaniel Clements had real estate to dispose of by will because both had been purchasers of land. Clements, indeed, though born into a landed family, was a fifth son and had had to buy every acre he owned. So had an earlier entrepreneur of humbler origins, Charles Campbell of Dublin. By the time of his death, which took place in 1725, Campbell had made no settlement of any part of his estates, so his will is an abnormally comprehensive document. It is accessibly glossed in a letter written at the time by one of his trustees:

> Charles Campbell has left his real estate to his grandson Burton for life with remainders to his issue male, and for want of such to some of his nephews in like manner, and for want of such issue to his granddaughter Burton, to whom he has left £6,000, which with the fortune she is to have from her father, will be £13,000. He has left his wife £300 a year jointure, and £50 to buy her mourning, at which she is displeased. He has ordered all his personal estate and leases to be sold, and money arising thereby to be laid out in purchasing an estate in fee to be settled as his real estate is. His real estate is betwixt £1,100 and £1,200 per annum, and his leases about £800 per annum. What money debts or personal estate he had we can't yet certainly know till his accounts are made up, for he had abundance of other people's money laid out in his name.[16]

By the standards of testamentary evidence, this is a complete and clear résumé of what seem to have been the total assets of the individual concerned.

Campbell's actual will was probably a long and elaborate rigmarole; for, no other will of this period disposed of as large a landed property in as short and simple a fashion as the will of Charles Moore, one and only Earl of Charleville (d.1764).[17] Lord Charleville's will, made on 13 August 1762 and proved on 18 August 1764, runs to only two smallish membranes of parchment. He had a great deal to dispose of by will because his only son had died, his marriage had failed to produce any female issue, and the family settlements had either not provided for this eventuality or had been overridden by some earlier act of Lord Charleville's. So his will proceeds, after bequests of two annuities and some sums of money and the furniture, books and plate in his two houses, to bequeath his Tullamore estate in Co. Offaly (the largest in that county) to John Bury, eldest son of his sister Jane and her husband, William Bury of Abbey Street, Dublin (and Shannongrove, Co. Limerick), and settles it on John Bury's issue male, with remainder to Jane Bury's other sons and their issue male, and so forth. There is no recital of previous settlements and events, and no itemising of the townlands comprising the estate – the two exercises which usually add length, bulk and apparent complexity to documents of this kind. Significantly, there is also no stipulation – very general in cases of inheritance on the female side – that the Bury inheritor should assume the name and arms of Moore. This raises the suspicion that Lord Charleville was an old and disappointed man, whose own line had failed and who was mainly concerned to make a tidy exit from this world. Something of the kind is surely necessary to account for the very untypical succinctness of his dispositions.

The case of Lord Charleville is also very untypical in that he had a huge estate to dispose of by will. It is hard to think of another of comparable size and value which was so disposed of in the period under review – or, indeed, until 1878, when the 3rd Earl of Leitrim bequeathed estates with a 'nett income of … about £19,000 a year and … funded property [of] £150,000'.[18] Normally, a settlement was the vehicle for dispositions of this magnitude. For this reason, settlement documents are a more frequent, reliable and comprehensive source of information than wills. But they, too, are not free of difficulties of interpretation. For one thing, because the remuneration of attorneys was partly calculated on an acreage basis, these documents always enter into the repetitious detail which is so happily absent from Lord Charleville's will, and often run to immense and unnecessary length. In addition, they often fail to state what is most important. Where casual, gossipy letters are apt to give an inflated version of the 'fortune' which a bride brought with her on marriage, marriage settlements run to the opposite extreme. In particular, they never identify a woman as an heiress, co-heiress, heiress apparent, etc, or indeed use the term 'heiress' at all. This was because, in the eyes of the law, nobody was an heiress until everyone who stood between the inheritance and her was dead, and dead childless.

In 1810, a prospective father-in-law observed: 'the lady's fortune … is only £5,000, without pledge or security for more, [but] with such a moral probability as perfectly satisfies.' Settlements, however, were based on legal certainty, not moral probability. The settlement made on the marriage of the lady in question, Harriet Skeffington, is a case in point. It took no account of, and did not even mention, her position as heiress presumptive to the Massereene family estate: two older brothers of her father, one of them the 3rd Earl of Massereene, and both bachelors in their mid-sixties, were still alive in 1810; and even after her father succeeded as 4th Earl in the following year, although it was highly probable that she, as his only child, would succeed him in due course, this was not certain until his death, without subsequent issue, in 1816.[19] Like her, a number of great heiresses whose cases are documented in this study had an actual marriage portion of a mere £5,000 or £10,000. If things went according to plan, this would be a mere token: if they did not, it was all their husbands were going to get – unless, that is, some monetary consolation were given to the lady for the disappointment of her expectations.

Another bride who, at a much earlier period, 1733, had brought her husband a marriage portion of only £5,000 with a 'moral probability' of more to follow, was Lady Anne Wentworth, eldest daughter of the British Earl of Strafford. Her husband, William Conolly junior, was the nephew and principal heir of William Conolly of Castletown, Co. Kildare (1662–1729), Speaker of the House of Commons, 1714–29, and Ireland's most remarkable, recent example of a 'rags-to-riches' success story. William Conolly junior gladly accepted Lady Anne on these indefinite terms, and made a lavish settlement on her and on the children of the marriage. However, his mercenary and matriarchal aunt, Katherine Conolly, the Speaker's widow, was doubtful: 'English wives ought to bring large portions, which I never heard was our case, for it's all to come.' Fortunately for William Conolly, it did come. In 1739 Lady Anne inherited landed property which later sold for £16,000. Beyond that, her expectations depended solely on chance (her only brother's continuing childlessness). But chance favoured her – to the eventual extent of something like £200,000 (inclusive of the original £5,000 and the £16,000), of which c.£115,000 went to the Conollys' only son, Thomas, and the rest to their daughters or their daughters' children.[20]

Compared to Lady Anne Conolly's, Harriet Skeffington's expectations were gilt-edged, and were realised only six years after her marriage. Nothing could have prevented their realisation except her death and/or her having no children. But recent Massereene family history had underlined the necessity for caution. This was because of the 'extraordinary career' of her father's eldest brother, the 2nd Earl of Massereene (1743–1805), who had come close to alienating the entire family estate in counties Antrim and Monaghan. After his coming-of-age he had taken up residence in Paris where, either as a result of feeble-mindedness or of extreme fecklessness, he was bamboozled into running up a large volume of debt. Refusing to pay any of these fraudulently incurred obligations, he spent the years 1771–89 in a series of Paris prisons, from the last of which he escaped during the early days of the French Revolution. After a brief sojourn at the family seat, Antrim Castle, he moved to London, where once again he fell into the hands of sharpers and found himself imprisoned for debt.

Just before this, he had encountered a woman called Elizabeth Lane or Blackburn, who 'was a menial servant in a house immediately opposite his lodgings. She possessed a particular dexterity in twirling her mop and his Lordship admired her dexterity so much that he fell in love with this fair twirler',[21] whom he lived with from 1796 and married in 1802. From 1797 until his death in 1805, they lived at Antrim, where the new Lady Massereene gradually succeeded in secluding him from communication with his mother, brothers and sister. Eventually, she obtained such a complete ascendancy over him that she prevailed upon him to make a will leaving all his real and personal property to her and not to the brother who was due to succeed him in the earldom. This will remained

LAW, TERMINOLOGY AND THE NATURE OF THE EVIDENCE

a secret until after his death, when the 3rd Earl of Massereene took proceedings to have it invalidated on grounds of undue influence. The only thing certain about this litigation was that it was going to cost a great deal of money. So, in May 1809, the parties joined in a compromise agreement whereby Lady Massereene waived her claims under the will in return for a down payment of £15,000 and an annuity of £800. This latter ran until her death in 1838.

The Massereene case, divested of its sensational features, is of considerable, general significance. First, it is another example – however extreme – of a will which disposed of a sizeable estate (worth c.£5,000 a year nett). Second, it is an example of the near-frustration of the expectations of the heir presumptive. Third, it marks the dangers inherent in any settlement which legally fell short of being a strict settlement. At the time of the marriage of Lord Massereene's parents, in 1741, the Antrim and Monaghan estates had been settled on the sons of the marriage in order of seniority. A strict settlement would have gone further, and limited the estate to the second and other sons of the marriage, and to their issue male, on failure of issue male to the eldest son (who would have been made a '*tenant* in tail male'): unlike the Massereene settlement, it would have circumscribed the power over the estate which the eldest son could exercise once his father was dead and he himself was of age. The 1st Earl of Massereene died in 1756; the 2nd Earl came of age in 1763; and in 1770 the latter 'suffered a recovery' of the estates[22] – the term for a fictitious legal transaction whereby an inheritor of landed property established his unfettered ownership thereof. Because he had gone through these motions, the 2nd Earl was legally entitled to do what a strict settlement would have prevented – to deprive 'an ancient and most respectable family ... of a valuable and extensive property which had descended from their fathers'.[23]

At about the same time, a similar upset deranged the affairs of another Ulster family, the Annesleys of Castlewellan, Co. Down, and threatened the prospects of the heir presumptive. In November 1795, the 1st Earl Annesley, a childless widower of fifty-five, came to dine with his brother and heir presumptive, with whom he was on the most affectionate terms. On the way up the drive, he was 'much struck with the appearance' of one Sophia Connor, the wife of his brother's gardener, and

> remained for some time in conversation with her...; in the short time that such conversation lasted, the said Sophia was so dazzled by the rank and splendour of the said Earl ... that, in violation of her marriage vow, she consented to elope from your suppliant [as the gardener was termed in a subsequent legal case paper] with the said Earl on his return to Dublin that evening, which promise she accordingly fulfilled, and was on the evening of the said day taken off by the said Earl in his phaeton to Dublin.

Two years later, in 1797, Lord Annesley married Sophia Connor – illegally, in view of her pre-contracted marriage to the gardener; and although his brother offered 'to concur in any act that might meet the wishes of Lord A. to make a provision for the woman he co-habited with and for any children he might have by her', Sophia said she 'would not agree to it, but would take her chance'. She took her chance, after Lord Annesley's death in 1802, by endeavouring (unsuccessfully) to prove the legitimacy of her son by him, and her son's consequent right to the Annesley earldom and the family estate of nearly £5,500 a year. The ensuing litigation lasted until 1819, when Sophia settled for an annuity of £400. She nevertheless had the effrontery to complain that this was insufficient to enable her to 'resume her splendid appearance in Paris, where she had ... [previously] kept her *barouche* and servants in green and gold liveries, with her box at The Opéra, and moved in the first circles'. She died at a Rue de Rivoli address in 1850.[24]

More usually, settlement arrangements were upset, or threatened with upset, by unexpected events of a less sensational kind. In 1804, the 1st Marquess of Thomond (and 5th Earl of Inchiquin) recalled how

> his uncle, the late [4th] Earl of Inchiquin, who was married to the Countess of Orkney and had two daughters but no son by her, sent for him from Ireland when he was quite a youth, and proposed to him to marry the eldest of the daughters. This he did [in 1753], though she was both deaf and dumb, and lived with her in a manner so proper that he can reflect upon it with satisfaction. Lord Thomond was then presumptive heir to his uncle's title.... Lady Orkney had bad health and died ... after which Lord Inchiquin [in 1761] married again to a handsome young woman of thirty.... Happily, she had no children, and [in 1777] Lord Inchiquin died.

The virtue of Lord Inchiquin's nephew, who now succeeded to the title and estates, was accordingly rewarded.[25]

Another strange tale, which this time ended less happily for the heir presumptive, is that of the 3rd Earl of Darnley, an eccentric bachelor who suffered from the delusion that he was a teapot. In 1766, when he was nearly fifty and had held the family title and estates for almost twenty years, Lord Darnley suddenly and unexpectedly married; and between 1766 and his death in 1781, he fathered at least seven children, in spite of his initial alarm that his spout would come off in the night.[26] The heir presumptive did not, however, go empty away. He was Lord Darnley's nephew, William Tighe of Rosanna, Co. Wicklow; and because he married the year before his uncle, and was still 'considered one of the best matches in Ireland' at the time, he obtained the hand of 'a great heiress', Sarah Fownes, only child of Sir William Fownes, 2nd Bt, of Woodstock, Co. Kilkenny. The Tighes' daughter was sure that 'Sir William would not have consented to ... the match ... had he known that Lord Darnley was on the point of being married.... [Sir William had] always intended that she should marry a nobleman, and she had already refused several, some of whom she had sense enough to perceive were fortune-hunters.'[27]

These examples demonstrate the unpredictability of the marriage market. They also explain why settlements and other legal documents eschew all mention of heirs or heiresses, far less heirs or heiresses apparent, presumptive or whatever.

They are uncommunicative in this respect, not only because of the legal impossibility of predicting the future, but also because of the legal device of swathing heiresses, and ownership generally, unrecognisably in trusteeships. Such trusteeships were deemed necessary because, as one English heiress was bluntly reminded in 1792: 'Women having power [over their own property] is in general of little avail – they are either kissed or kicked out of it.'[28] The effect of trusteeships is to make settlement documents difficult to interpret: to the point that they often do not make the identity of the present, far less the future, owner of the estate immediately apparent. The purpose of these elaborate arrangements was that all the parties to the settlement, including those yet unborn, should be protected against each other, and against all eventualities. The protection of the interests of those yet unborn is an important consideration. In 1759, Viscount Conyngham roundly declared that any settlement which left the (unborn) eldest son 'totally in the power of their father ... is nugatory', and that 'a provision for younger children ... [is to no] purpose ... if the father can defeat it the next day'.[29]

The eventualities so far considered have all been the unexpected marriages – of varying degrees of suitability – made by old or fairly old male heads of families, most of which did not actually contravene the family settlement then in operation. The possibilities for actual contravention were also numerous. Those open to the head of the family/beneficial owner[30] of the family estate included the following: failing to pay punctually the jointure of his predecessor's widow; failing to pay the portions of all or some of his younger children, or dividing the provision for younger children among them in a way which contravened the settlement; exceeding the limits imposed by the settlement on his leasing or borrowing power; shifting a settlement charge from one property to another, particularly if this made the security for the charge inadequate or in some other way counteracted the objects of the settlement; etc, etc. Of these, failure to pay jointures was the most open and shut case of contravention. For this reason, settlements went into some detail in prescribing the precise mode of legal redress to be followed by aggrieved dowagers (and other species of annuitant). A good example of an aggrieved dowager was Margaret, Viscountess Mountjoy, whose jointure of £1,000 a year was stated to be £7,000 in arrears in 1820.[31] She is also, therefore, a good example of a patient and forbearing dowager.

Some of the other forms of contravention exemplified above may, on investigation, turn out to be more technical than real. For example, the principal of portions often remained unpaid for many years, either because younger children had no particular need for the lump sum and were content with the income from it, or because they did not want to exacerbate the financial difficulties which the head of the family might be experiencing. Often the rate of interest payable on portions was specified in settlements, which implied an assumption that the principal was not going to be paid when it fell due at coming-of-age or marriage. Two of the sisters of Thomas Conolly (1738–1803) of Castletown, Co. Kildare, did not receive the principal of their portions (£8,000 each) for many years after their respective marriages, one of them not in her lifetime. There was major litigation between Conolly and his surviving sisters between 1797 and 1801, but not over their portions.[32] In 1798–9, during the negotiation of the settlement to be made on the marriage of his eldest daughter, the 2nd Duke of Leinster made it clear that her portion, of £10,000, was not going to be paid in a hurry;[33] and in 1799, during the negotiation of the settlement for the eldest daughter of the 12th Viscount Dillon, it was actually stipulated that her portion, also of £10,000, would not be paid until after his death.[34]

In the case of daughters who remained unmarried, it seems to have been almost a legal presumption that they would not need the principal. This is strongly suggested by the terms of the bequests respectively made by the Earl of Farnham in 1798 and the Earl of Blessington in 1823 to an unmarried daughter and an unmarried sister of mature years; the first was to receive the income from £9,000 and the second from £5,000, but neither was to be paid the principal unless she married. It is also strongly suggested by contemporary jokes about 'old maids on annuities'.[35] Only if the annuities, or the interest on the principal sum of the portion, were paid tardily or not at all, was litigation likely to ensue. This seems to have been what happened in the case of Juliana Prendergast, Countess of Meath, and with the portion she brought to the 6th Earl of Meath on their marriage in 1731. She was the eldest daughter of Sir Thomas Prendergast, 1st Bt, who had been killed at the battle of Malplaquet in 1709. Her two sisters and she were endowed with £2,000 apiece. But, in Lady Meath's case, neither principal nor interest seems to have been paid in her lifetime; for, her husband's successor, the 7th Earl, was obliged to take legal proceedings against the then representatives of the Prendergast family, and over the period 1767–71 painfully extracted from them the large sum of £6,547.[36]

Except in cases where failure to pay principal was compounded (in both senses) by failure to pay interest – particularly over a prolonged period – matters could usually be amicably adjusted more-or-less to the satisfaction of all parties. A reasonable degree of flexibility could also be expected over the observance of other stipulations of the settlement. For example, a father who was 'only tenant for life' could not borrow money on the security of the settled estate over and above a maximum laid down in the settlement. Rather than leave him to pay an usurious rate of interest to some unscrupulous lender, the eldest son would – usually and within reason – agree to 'open' the estate to allow some additional debt incurred by the father to be charged upon it. In 1726, for example, James Stopford, later 1st Earl of Courtown, stated that he had paid debts of his late father's, amounting to less than £2,000, for which Stopford was not legally liable because they exceeded his father's borrowing power under the latter's marriage settlement. On the other hand, John Browne of The Neale, Co. Mayo, later 1st Lord Kilmaine, declined when his marriage settlement was being negotiated in 1764 to allow his father's additional debts to become a charge on the estate; the father had held out the inducement of an allowance of £1,000 a year for the newly weds during his lifetime, but the son thought this was no equivalent for the £12,000 of debt with which it was proposed to burden the estate.

Another restriction commonly imposed by settlements on a tenant for life was on the length and tenure of the leases he was empowered to grant; and here again an eldest son might be called upon to agree to a relaxation. In 1783, for example, after the 11th Viscount Dillon had explained to Sir Neale O'Donel, a tenant of part of the Dillon estate in Co. Mayo, that Dillon 'was under settlements on ... [his eldest son's] marriage and could give me but 31 years', O'Donel asked the son to join with the father in granting a longer term. If the son or other remainderman under the settlement, were unborn or not of age at the time it became desirable to lift such a restriction, a private act of parliament would have to be obtained for that purpose, and this would not be passed until evidence had been heard or produced from all the interested parties signifying their consent. In 1783, for example, it was thought desirable for the development of the 2nd Lord Carysfort's urban estate at Blackrock and Stillorgan, Co. Dublin, and his seaside property at Arklow, Co. Wicklow, that he should be empowered to grant building leases for lives renewable forever (i.e. in perpetuity) or 99 years. This, however, he was precluded from doing by his marriage settlement of 1774, which limited his leasing power to three lives or 31 years. Since his eldest son was not of an age to enter into a re-settlement (he was four), an act of parliament was obtained in 1784.[37] Parliament might also be called in to alter other settlement terms – e.g. to release land from entail so that it could be sold to pay debt. Strictly speaking, there was no such thing as a strict settlement.

In general, however, these things would usually be adjusted by the less expensive means of inter-familial arrangement; and, in the nature of things, such adjustments often became necessary during the long period of roughly a generation which usually elapsed between one major settlement and the next. Some settlements actually allowed for them. In 1759, Viscount Conyngham reminded his lawyer: 'The marriage settlement of my father ... had a power of revocation in it, by consent of parties and trustees.' Such things were not

John Joshua Proby, 2nd Lord and 1st Earl of Carysfort (1751–1828), reproduced from a portrait of c.1800 by John Hoppner in Borenius and Hodgson, *Elton Hall Pictures* ...(London, 1924), p.78

contraventions of the previous settlement provided they had the consent of *all* the interested parties, sometimes including very remote remainderman. For example, during the 2nd Earl of Massereene's long incarceration in Paris, his widowed mother and younger siblings had to join in a deed which provided for the raising of the latter's portions (off the Derbyshire estate which she enjoyed in her own right) in a way which dispensed with his participation.

This deed of variation or re-arrangement must have had the consent of all the interested parties except the unavailable Earl. But when such consent was obtainable and was not asked and obtained, a serious situation had arisen. Even then, however, litigation could often be averted by negotiation: lawyers could be instructed to get together to hammer out a compromise, or the points in dispute could be put out to 'a reference' (i.e. arbitration) on the part of one or more private gentlemen who were mutual friends of or selected by the contending parties. But, if all else failed, the dispute/s would have to be resolved via the courts. This is what happened at a later stage in the troubled history of the Massereene family. In the years (1812–33) between the birth and coming-of-age of the future 10th Viscount Massereene, his father, the 2nd Viscount Ferrard, greatly exceeded the maximum sum he was empowered by settlement to raise on the security of the family estate in Co. Louth. On coming of age, the son refused to enter into a re-settlement which would retrospectively have allowed the father's excess borrowing to become a charge on the estate, and litigation raged between them from 1838 until Lord Ferrard's death in 1843.[38]

For all their apparent precision, the dispositions made by Charles Campbell (which, as has been seen, were embodied in a will, not a settlement, though that does not signify in the present discussion) contained one element which was fatally open to conflicting interpretations. In 1737, by which time Campbell's son-in-law, Samuel Burton (1687–1733), was dead, a dispute broke out over the additional portion of £6,000 which Campbell had left to Burton's daughter, Catherine (1712–84), now Viscountess Netterville. The £6,000 had been left to her on condition that she married with her father's consent, and it was this condition which caused the trouble. When she married in 1732, Burton had refused his consent, possibly because her husband, the 5th Viscount Netterville, was 'a fop and a fool', but more probably because Burton desperately needed the money to reduce his impending losses in the famous failure of Burton's Bank.[39] All attempts to settle the dispute amicably proved unavailing, and three-cornered litigation ensued between and among Burton's executors, Campbell's nephews and nieces, and Lord and Lady Netterville.

A more celebrated, and savage, dispute arising out of a settlement was that of c.1765 to c.1785 between Simon Luttrell, 1st Lord Irnham and Earl of Carhampton, and his eldest son, Colonel Henry Lawes Luttrell, later 2nd Earl of Carhampton. This originated in Lord Irnham's illegal sale of certain lands which his marriage settlement of 1735 had settled on his eldest son, and which were part of the security for the financial provisions of that settlement. Matters were eventually compromised between them by a series of legal acts, all dated May 1769. Irnham paid the most pressing of Luttrell's debts, settled on him the manor of Luttrellstown, Co. Dublin, and the rest of his Irish estates, together with the reversionary interest which Lady Irnham enjoyed in a plantation in Jamaica, charged the Luttrellstown estate with an annuity of £600 payable to Luttrell, and granted Luttrell a seven-year lease of the house and demesne of Luttrellstown at a rent of £400 a year.[40] This re-settlement, broadly speaking, represented a restoration of Luttrell's expectations under the settlement of 1735, the annuity of £600 being the compensation given him for the earlier sale of settled lands. It was, as Luttrell later described it dramatically, the consideration 'for which Lord Irnham made me convey to him my birthright'.[41]

Unfortunately, it proved insufficient to keep Luttrell out of debt. In March 1771 he borrowed £2,000 and used as part-security the estates and money which would come to him under the re-settlement of 1769 once both his parents were dead.[42] This was, in effect, borrowing 'post-obit.' – a method unfailingly offensive to the parents whose deaths were anticipated, and detrimental to the 'character' of the borrower. Accordingly, Irnham withheld payment of the £600 a year. The precise terms of the offending loan were submitted to 'the investigation of competent persons', and Irnham seems to have joined Luttrell in March 1772 in raising another loan, this time for £4,000, and with no element of the 'post-obit.'[43] A quarrel then broke out on some other issue (perhaps Irnham regarded his assistance in raising the £4,000 as absolving him from the necessity of paying the £600 a year). In August or September 1773, this, too, was put out to 'a reference', which petered out in October 1774. A lawsuit followed. This was complicated by the fact that, at the end of his seven-year tenancy of the house and demesne of Luttrellstown in 1776, Luttrell refused to give up possession to his father. Litigation dragged on until 1778, when the outcome was pretty much a draw. Lord Irnham regained possession of Luttrellstown, but lived there in 'terror … from a lawless banditti armed with clubs, bludgeons, etc, and headed by Colonel Luttrell with his sabre'.[44] In 1785, he joined with Luttrell in another deed rationalising the latter's debts,[45] so perhaps there had been some kind of *rapprochement* by then. In January 1787, he died suddenly – 'to the great concern of his affectionate son'.[46]

Both Luttrells were popularly regarded as a bad lot. 'Junius' (who excoriated Colonel Luttrell because of the part he famously took against John Wilkes in the Middlesex election of 1769) declared that 'the son has regularly improved upon the vices of his father and has taken care to transmit them pure and undiminished'.[47] Righteous indignation is, however, the tone of the letters which both father and son wrote to the exhausted arbitrator in 1774 – though, of course, each was concerned to demonstrate the justness of his cause and to present himself in a favourable light. Luttrell stressed that he would 'proceed at law with reluctance, happy if at last even that undesirable course of proceeding should convince his Lordship that he has been for some years past in error as to my conduct. A victory over a father is scarcely to be distinguished from a defeat, but I cannot give up my honour and probity.' Irnham, for his part, observed sententiously: 'When my son in his latter days shall take a view of all the ruin he had occasioned to his family, the prospect ... will be most dreadful.'[48] Then as now, outraged rectitude and extreme bitterness characterised family quarrels. In another contemporary instance of c.1777 – one of the recurrent 'contests' in the Stratford family – Lord Aldborough's sister, Lady Hannah Stratford, wrote to their mother, the Dowager Lady Aldborough:

> I know not who is right or who is wrong in the originating of this contest, yet I must say that in continuing it the parties must be *all* wrong. Even you, my dearest Mother, still carry on your resentment and litigation, and look upon your children as aliens. The fruit of your body stinks in your nostrils, and your time is spent among vile attorneys and solicitors, who counsel you against your own blood.[49]

Edward Stratford, 2nd Earl of Aldborough, c. 1780, reproduced from a print (after Gainsborough) in E.M. Richardson ed. *Long-forgotten Days ... an Aldborough Family History* (London, 1928), p.212

The Luttrell lawsuit was a contemporary *cause célèbre* and by the same token was an exceptional occurrence. Nevertheless, it is important in two respects. It provides a practical demonstration of what elaborate settlements were trying to guard against, and some justification for the detail and length to which they ran. Second, it shows – as do the Massereene and Annesley lawsuits – what a wealth of evidence is thrown up when things went wrong and a reference or a lawsuit or both ensued.

Such evidence is invaluable. It would be impossible to reconstruct the financial history of aristocratic families on the basis of settlement documents alone, unaccompanied by correspondence, wills and testamentary papers, legal case papers, rentals, accounts, and so on. Each of the various forms of documentation has its limitations. But they are mutually corroborative and/or corrective, and there is need for them all. The financial situations of great landed families were constantly shifting, in the light of births and deaths, marriages and mortgages, inheritances and bequests. Landownership itself was not as static as is commonly supposed. And even where nominal ownership remained in the hands of the original proprietary family, effective ownership could have been alienated by devices such as the fee farm grant or the perpetuity lease (lease for lives renewable forever); under such circumstances, while the acreage of the estate would remain static, so would the rental. There could also be a considerable discrepancy between gross and nett rental, or rather, between gross rental and disposable income. As the early-nineteenth century agriculturist, Edward Wakefield, remarked: 'There are owners in Ireland of very large estates who have not a shilling of income, the whole of their fortune being absorbed ... by ... debts contracted by themselves or left them by their predecessors.'[50]

A striking contemporary example of this last phenomenon – and one which, again, is revealed by rentals, accounts and family correspondence and not by settlement documents – was the vast Co. Tipperary estates of the Earls of Dorchester, with a gross rental of over £8,000 in about 1790 and £22,225 in 1848.[51] The 2nd Earl of Dorchester died unmarried in 1808 and, in the words of *The Gentleman's Magazine*, was succeeded 'by his only sister, the Lady Caroline Damer, on whose decease they devolve to the [2nd] Earl of Portarlington, whose grandmother, Mary Damer, Viscountess Carlow, was sister to the 1st Lord Dorchester'. But the succession was by no means as cut-and-dried as the obituary notice made out. The youthful heir presumptive, Lord Portarlington, was warned by his mother that he must not count on or boast of

> the supposed acquisition of a great fortune, ... as I should be sorry it should come to Lady Caroline's ears; it being entirely in her option to give it to the Churchills [of Henbury, Dorset, still more remote cousins], if she pleases.... [The affairs of the late Lord Dorchester and his late brother] were so much deranged that Lady C.'s income will be very little increased for some years to come. The debts of both brothers, especially the last, were enormous, as he trusted everything to his agents, and they never could get him to look at an account.... The people in Ireland, if you will believe them, such as Kemmis [the Portarlington family's lawyer], etc., will tell you their estates amount to £50,000 or £60,000 a year; but supposing it were so, if they are swallowed up with debts, the advantage to his heirs may not accrue till they are quite old.[52]

Lady Portarlington might be suspected of exaggerating the bleakness of the situation, in an effort to keep an impressionable first-born on the straight and narrow. But it is a fact that the Dorchester, along with the Portarlington, estate was sold up in the Landed Estates Court in the years 1857–8. The 2nd Earl of Portarlington's nephew, the 3rd Earl, bought back a considerable proportion of both estates, thus using the Court – after the fashion of several landowners of the day[53] – as a cheaper and less laborious means of establishing a clear title to his own property than the time-honoured procedure of 'fine and recovery'.[54] But the rest seems genuinely to have been sold, and sold for the purpose of paying off debts. The chaos of the Dorchester inheritance is particularly relevant to present purposes; for, next to the huge Burlington estate in counties Cork and Waterford and the plum Dublin City property of the Fitzwilliam family of Merrion,[55] the Dorchester was probably the most considerable Irish estate in terms of size and gross rental to come down through an heiress in the period under review. It is therefore a revelation that, for some years to come, Lady Caroline Damer's inheritance would exist mainly on paper.

THE PURSUIT OF THE HEIRESS

A more general cause of misconception about the extent of the wealth possessed by and transmitted through women than the tittle-tattle of 'the people in Ireland…, such as Kemmis, etc.', is the popular contemporary use of the word 'fortune' as a synonym for the precise contemporary term 'portion'. The modern 'dowry' seems to have had no contemporary currency except in the context of royal marriages – almost certainly because the mediaeval, Common Law concept of 'dower' had not yet faded from memory and meant something quite different (see below). 'Fortune' has an inflationary ring about it, which 'portion' and 'dowry' lack. But that was not how it seemed to contemporaries. Indeed, Lord Aldborough wrote to his nephew, George Hartpole, in 1794 complaining that 'Mrs Hartpole's fortune' was 'extremely small', and there are other examples of the conjunction of this adjective and noun.[56] A 'fortune' did not make a woman an heiress: rather, it was the necessary minimum to make her marriageable. This was true in both practical and legal terms. In practical terms, no man was likely to marry a portionless woman, and in canon law (as interpreted in the late mediaeval period) a dowry of some sort was almost always requisite if the marriage were to be valid.[57]

It was equally necessary if a woman remained single, as spinsters were expected to finance at least the basics of board and lodgings out of the interest of their portions.[58] They could not aspire to full independence for the simple reason that

Contemporary caricature of the wedding of Charlotte Augusta, the Princess Royal, and the enormously fat Hereditary Prince of Wurttemberg on 18 May 1797; the bride's parents, George III and Queen Charlotte, lead the procession into the bedchamber, while the Prime Minister, William Pitt the Younger, struggles under the weight of the bride's dowry of £80,000.

AUTHOR'S COLLECTION

their portions were most unlikely to be large enough to make this possible. A portion of £10,000, which in England was the usual provision for a duke's daughter, would produce – 'at the usual safe rate of interest' – an income of only £300 or at most £350 a year; which was not enough to pay for a house in London or Dublin, an establishment of servants and a carriage. 'It was never intended that women should be provided with sufficient to allow them to live independently; they were always intended to be dependent on father, husband, brother or son' – or else to pool resources with another woman, either as an equal partner or as an unpaid companion. 'Only the luckiest of unattached [gentle]women could have afforded … to live in comfort on their own': most 'were to be found in braces or swarms',[59] whether in Dublin, London or in fashionable English resorts like Bath, Cheltenham, Clifton or Tunbridge Wells. A good example of a trio of unattached ladies who lived together and pooled their considerable resources was the Dowager Countess of Leitrim and her two unmarried daughters, Ladies Elizabeth and Louisa Clements. Lady Leitrim was widowed in 1804 and died in 1817; her daughters then went on living together until 1836, when Lady Louisa died and – partly because of this economical mode of living – left £40,000–£50,000 in her will.[60]

Those whose fortunes and other attractions obtained them husbands did not necessarily fare better than the unattached. A married woman's fortune was the only one she was ever likely to see; she had one, and only one, bite at the matrimonial cake. Her fortune was paid over to her husband or into the hands of the trustees of their marriage settlement, and was non-returnable. If her husband died, she would receive the jointure (or widow's annuity) stipulated in the settlement. Even if this were generous in relation to her fortune, it was not particularly attractive to a second husband because it ran only for her life; and if her first husband had provided her, by post-nuptial arrangement or by will, with an addition to her jointure, with a life-interest in one of the family houses or with some other asset over and above her original entitlement, it would almost certainly be on condition that she did not re-marry, and would be forfeited if she did.

Unless some such post-nuptial arrangement had been made for her, a widow would have to use part of her jointure to cover the cost of the house she lived in during widowhood. There seems to have been no such thing as an Irish dower house in the period 1740–1840, and perhaps until the twentieth century, and therefore nowhere where a dowager could reside rent-free. Dowagers would usually want to make a beeline for a metropolis or a watering-hole, and would not want to live close to and overshadowed by their daughters-in-law in some isolated part of rural Ireland where few others of their class and kind were to be found. But it would have been of benefit to them to have had a country retreat to which they could return in order to economise, or which they could swop with their eldest son for something more suitable. As things were, only dowagers who had been specifically left a retirement home by their husbands, were in a position to bargain with their eldest sons. The Dowager Lady Leitrim is a good example (and also of a dowager who declined to live in the country). Her husband had left her for her life the family seat, Killadoon, Celbridge, Co. Kildare (not far from Dublin), but she exchanged it with her son for a house in Grosvenor Square, London. Likewise, the Dowager Lady Mountjoy (widow of Luke Gardiner, 2nd Viscount Mountjoy, who had been killed at the battle of New Ross in 1798), was only too glad to extricate herself profitably from the wilds of rural Ulster in 1804 by conveying to her stepson her life-interest in the house, furniture and demesne at Rash, Co. Tyrone, in return for an annuity of £700.[61] These were two fortunate widows: most had to pay for their accommodation out of their jointures.

The lot of married women whose marriages did not last until widowhood was harder still. If a marriage failed and ended in separation – even if it failed because of cruelty, adultery or other misconduct on the part of the husband – his wife would be left to subsist on whatever annual allowance was awarded her by a private deed of separation or by an ecclesiastical or criminal court; and she was still incapacitated from doing any legal act without the participation of her husband, who also retained control of her personal estate and over all components of her real estate as were not ring-fenced by will or settlement. If the marriage failed on grounds of simple incompatibility, and the husband did not agree to a separation, she got nothing.[62] Whatever the basis of the failure, she was precluded from re-marriage, since access to divorce was effectively denied to women until the successive reforms in the divorce laws which took place between 1835 and 1885, particularly the Divorce Act of 1857.[63] Her husband, if he had grounds (e.g. adultery), could divorce her. But she could not divorce her husband – for adultery or almost anything else. The only justification which existed for the glaringly double standards by which female and male adultery were judged was the fact that the former threatened the whole system of inheritance. Dr Johnson attacked female adultery because of 'the confusion of progeny which might result', and declared that 'all the property in the world depended on female chastity'.[64]

If 'fortune' is a word which misleads because of its implicit magnitude and because it belies the bleakness of its possessor's situation, 'heiress' is one which equally requires definition and reflection. Heiresses loom large in the historiography of seventeenth and eighteenth century Britain because of the role assigned to them by Habbakuk, his disciples and his critics as a factor in other developments, notably the rise of the great estate. As a phenomenon in their own right, and in absolute numerical terms, heiresses were less important and fewer in the seventeenth and eighteenth centuries than they had been in the Middle Ages. In the latter period and under Common Law rules, it was normative that a man's daughter would inherit his estate in preference to his brother, his nephew or another collateral male relation. The cumulative effect of legal developments of the sixteenth and early seventeenth centuries in this area of inheritance was to replace Common Law with statute law and, moreover, with a number of statutes which shifted the norms of inheritance from daughters to collateral males and empowered individuals to devise and entail estates in accordance with this shift. Under the legal device of the strict settlement which dates from c.1650, 'inheritance by women [gradually] fell to less than one-third of what it had been'.[65]

In parallel, a new legal concept of the 'postponed' heiress emerged. This, as applied to a daughter whose pretensions were set aside in favour of those of a collateral male heir, is an unhelpful term – a 'by-passed' heiress would surely be more meaningful? Initially, there seems to have been some assumption that, in consideration of or in compensation for being by-passed, she was entitled to a sum equivalent to roughly one-third of the value of the estate. This was a sizeable consideration, worth an estimated seven or more times the annual rental.[66] It was a not-unheard-of provision in the period under review. In 1802, Lady Grace Maxwell, only daughter of the 1st Earl of Farnham (of the second creation) by his second marriage, was given a marriage portion of (allegedly) £40,000. At this date the family estate in Co. Cavan, which was destined to pass to her cousin if (as looked increasingly likely) her brother had no son, had a rental of c.£9,400 a year.[67] So the £40,000 was indeed a portion which approached in value a figure of seven times the annual rental of the estate. An even more spectacular, though much later, example is Lady Mary Maitland, only daughter and by-passed heiress of the 11th Earl of Lauderdale, whose marriage in 1868 to the future 12th Earl of Meath brought something like £250,000 into the far-from-affluent Meath family[68] – a sum which must have been worth far more than seven times the then rental of the Lauderdale estate.

These inheritances, however, which approached or exceeded the one-third/sevenfold paradigm, were a matter of luck rather than lien. Lady Grace Maxwell's fortune, which was actually only £12,000 at the time of her marriage, did in all probability reach a total of c.£40,000 after the deaths of her unmarried half-sister and of her mother; but the money came almost entirely from Lord Farnham's personal estate or from lands far from Co. Cavan which he had inherited from his mother; it was not a multiple of the Cavan estate rental.[69] Likewise, the provision made by Lord Lauderdale for Lady Mary Maitland probably had little to do with the value of the Lauderdale estate and much to do with the fact that he was a retired admiral and had no doubt picked up a great deal of naval prize money.

More usually, by-passed heiresses of the period 1740–1840 had to make do with a much scaled-down level of compensation. When Edmond Sexten Pery, one and only Viscount Pery, died in 1806, his personal fortune passed to his two daughters and co-heiresses, while the settled Pery estates passed to his brother's son, the 1st Earl of Limerick. *In toto*, the ladies seem to have received c.£20,000 each, £5,000 of which represented their original (and still unpaid) marriage portions.[70] (These figures are belied by the usual family anecdotage, according to which one daughter got £60,000 in cash and the other the equivalent in land.)[71] In other words, they received £15,000 each, over and above their marriage portions, in compensation for being by-passed by a previous settlement in favour of the collateral male heir. Since the settled estates of which Lord Limerick now took possession were plausibly reckoned to be producing £8,000 a year,[72] the by-passed heiresses were not compensated lavishly. Nor, probably, would they have got even £15,000 if Lord Pery had not left a considerable personal estate.

In most instances in the period under review, the compensation for the by-passed heiress was confined to the provision earmarked by settlement for *all* her parents' younger children, particularly that earmarked for non-existent sons. This seems to have been the lot of Selina Elizabeth and Letitia Charlotte Brooke, only children and by-passed co-heiresses of Sir Arthur Brooke, Bt, of Colebrooke, Co. Fermanagh (d.1785). Under his marriage settlement of 1751, Sir Arthur was empowered to charge the Brooke estates with a maximum of £10,000 for younger children. He used up the whole of this on his daughters' marriage portions. Additionally, he must have had power to charge the estates with a further £6,000, which he did – either for the benefit of his daughters or to finance his own extravagant lifestyle (or a mixture of the two). The estates were not huge, and Francis Brooke, the nephew who succeeded to them, and Francis Brooke's descendants considered themselves aggrieved and impoverished by the open-handedness of Sir Arthur.[73] This is typical of the male whingeing of the period and of the bias of family history written by men. It would be more to the point to suggest that the two by-passed heiresses, with a maximum provision of £8,000 apiece, were not well done by.

An extreme instance of male chauvinism is the will of Acheson Moore (1691–1770) of Summerhill, Dublin, and Ravella, Aughnacloy, Co. Tyrone, an aged and eccentric Jacobite, who left an estate of '£5,000 per annum … from his daughters to a Mr Stuart, whom he supposed heir to the crown of England'. Although this was a good story, it was not the whole truth. 'Mr Stuart', who was Andrew Thomas Stuart, subsequently 1st Earl Castle Stewart (1725–1809), was a relation of Acheson Moore, whose mother seems to have been a sister of Stuart's great-grandmother. So, this was not so much a piece of Jacobite eccentricity as a striking case of by-passing close female relations in favour of a distant male.[74]

The erosion of the position of women did not apply to daughters alone. A widow whose Common Law 'dower' had amounted to a life-interest in one-third of the income from her husband's estate, payable from the date of his death to the date of her own, found herself reduced under the strict settlement to a jointure which almost never exceeded 20 per cent per annum of the fortune she had brought to her husband on marriage, and was gradually falling – along with

Edmond Sexten Pery, Viscount Pery (1719–1806); from a pastel portrait of c.1790 by Hugh Douglas Hamilton
AUTHOR'S COLLECTION

interest-rates – until it settled at a norm of ten.[75] Thus, Francis Burton of Buncraggy, Co. Clare, who was described as one of the 'few gentlemen in this kingdom' with a rental of £3,000 a year in 1720, was paying out of it a jointure to his widowed mother of only £400 a year: under Common Law rules, she would have been entitled to £1,000. Contemporaries were not unaware of this historical development. In 1729, an Irish judge commented, *apropos* a recently married woman of fortune, that 'she certainly must have had a jointure settled on her in lieu of all thirds and dower'. In 1741, the settlement on the marriage of the 2nd Earl of Massereene's parents stated that an annuity of £800 settled on his mother if she survived his father, was 'in full of her jointure and in lieu, bar and satisfaction of her dower and thirds at Common Law'. And in 1769, the marriage settlement of Selina Elizabeth Brooke 'declared' her jointure of £700 a year 'to be in full satisfaction and bar of dower'.[76] Wording to this effect remained a common feature of settlements right up to the end of the period under review.[77]

Misleadingly, some anachronistic echoes of the old Common Law entitlement to one-third continue to be heard in legal documents or found in inheritance practice. In 1752, Admiral Sir Peter Warren left his (recently purchased) Irish estate to his three daughters, and one-third of the income from it to his widow until they married or came of age. In c.1790, the Countess of Granard found herself, for a time, 'entitled to the possession of the third of ... [her husband's] landed property for her life', if she survived him, because the existing entail of the Granard family estates had a legal flaw in it. In 1799 the 3rd Earl of Strafford's widow, because he left no current will and their marriage settlement long ante-dated his succession to the Strafford titles and estates, became entitled to his personal estate and to one-third of the income from his real estates for her life. And, throughout the eighteenth century, private estate acts (at any rate of the British parliament) continued almost absent-mindedly to empower landowners to provide jointures worth up to one-third of the rental income of their estates.[78] Landowners, however, very rarely did anything of the kind.

The major downturn in the level of provision made for widows is belied by a number of instances, many of them to be encountered in the course of this study, of women who were generously provided for in their widowhood. For example, Grace, Countess of Farnham (mother of Lady Grace Maxwell and second wife/widow of the 1st Earl of Farnham), and Barbara, Marchioness of Donegall (third wife/widow of the 1st Marquess of Donegall), both of whom were widowed c.1800, enjoyed large jointures which were out of all proportion to the portions they had brought with them at marriage. This, however, may be attributed to the aberrant generosity of elderly and doting husbands whose circumstances, or the size of whose personal estates, gave them the flexibility to be lavish. Generally speaking, widows who were exceptionally well provided for fall into one of two categories. Either they were heiresses who were entitled, under their marriage settlements or by some other legal dispensation, to receive in

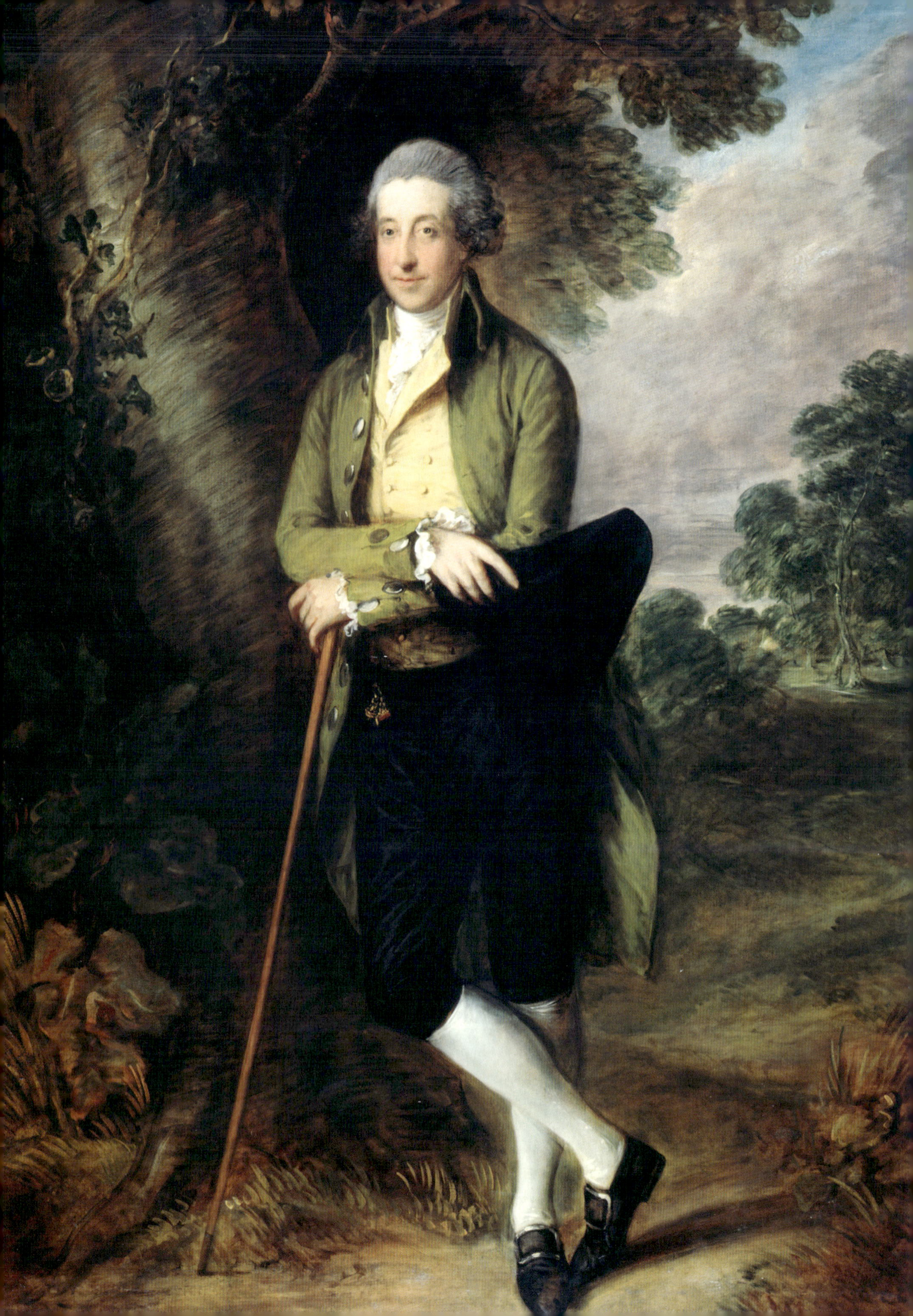

widowhood all or a proportion of the income from their own estates; or they were the widows of husbands who had no son or no children whatever, and who had been succeeded in their estates by a daughter or daughters or by a collateral male relation.

In the case of widows in the first category, there seems to have been a convention that, in addition to a perhaps token jointure, they should either retain their own estate for life or enjoy a life-interest in all or part of its income. One such lady was described in 1798 as the 'heiress of an estate which she now ... enjoys as a widow'.[79] Examples who will occur frequently in these pages are Mary Sandys, Marchioness of Downshire, Caroline Wyndham, Countess of Dunraven, and Frances Anne Vane-Tempest, Marchioness of Londonderry. Widows in the second category usually did not have an estate of their own and so received their exceptional provision out of their husbands' estate. This was because a loving husband whose direct male line had failed, was likely to want to benefit his widow at the temporary expense of someone who had not expected to succeed to the estate in the first place. This was a genuine case of 'postponement'. How generous a husband might be, depended on various things: his feelings for his wife, his feelings for his heir, the size of his personal estate, the proportion of the family estate which was unsettled, and the latitude allowed him by settlement in the event of his having no son. In one instance which will be encountered later, that of the 3rd Earl of Burlington (d.1753), the estate was settled on the heir (his one surviving daughter and her issue), but Burlington was free to leave a life-interest in the income from it to his widow – which he did.[80]

Robert Nugent of Carlanstown, Co. Westmeath (c.1720–1788), one and only Earl Nugent, married as his third wife a widow who was in category one. But his main achievement had been to marry, as his second wife, an heiress-widow who was even better-circumstanced than that and possessed money and an estate which were hers outright and not just for life. Her inheritance included Gosfield Hall and the Gosfield estate in Essex and the parliamentary borough of St Mawes in Cornwall, both of which became Lord Nugent's absolute property at her death in 1756. Not for nothing was he described by a contemporary as 'a jovial and voluptuous Irishman who had left popery for the protestant religion, money and widows'.

OPPOSITE

The 1st Marquess of Donegall, from the portrait of c.1780 by Thomas Gainsborough

ULSTER MUSEUM

'A jovial and voluptuous Irishman': Robert Nugent, Earl Nugent, from a contemporary caricature published on 14 May 1782

AUTHOR'S COLLECTION

Horace Walpole thought that a word 'nugentise' – meaning to marry widows for their money – should be added to the language.[81] In short, Lord Nugent was a master of matrimony whose success-story flies in the face of most of the arguments advanced in this book. It is, however, a story which gives a misleading and inflated idea of the wealth of widows. It was, in fact, most unusual for a widowed heiress, or any other form of heiress, to have her inheritance at her own absolute disposal.

The second Lady Nugent was English: the most covetable Irish widow of the period 1740–1840 was not an heiress at all but the lavishly dowered (in the mediaeval sense of the term) Jane, Countess of Belvedere, second wife and widow of the 2nd Earl of Belvedere (1738–1814). Lord Belvedere had no children by either of his marriages; his two younger brothers had no children either; the heir to the settled part of the family estate was his sister, the Countess of Lanesborough; and approximately half of the entire estate was unsettled. He had married a young second wife in 1803, and presumably doted upon her; and he may not have been fond of his sister who had re-married controversially after Lord Lanesborough's death. Perhaps for this reason, Belvedere left Lady Belvedere the whole of the unsettled estate, and not just for life but *outright*. It comprised at least 2,500 Irish acres at a rental in 1822 of £3,844 a year, rising to £4,666 in 1844. A year after Belvedere's death, in 1815, Lady Belvedere married Abraham Boyd, KC (1760–1822), the Dublin barrister who had acted for Belvedere; their eldest son was christened George Augustus after Belvedere, and succeeded to the estate at her death in 1836. The Belvedere family name was Rochfort; so the issue of her second marriage double-barrelled their name to Rochfort Boyd, later inverted to the more familiar Boyd Rochfort. They had, of course, not a drop of Rochfort blood in them.[82]

It may be that the example of Lady Belvedere and some of these other widows-in-clover, together with the notoriety of Lord Nugent's 'nugentising' and of the bigamous Duchess of Kingston's inheritance in 1773 of most of the fortune of her late husband, the 2nd Duke, blinded contemporaries to the reality of the general downturn in the level of provision made for widows. For whatever reason, the usual perception of contemporaries, particularly as expressed in literary evidence, is that dowagers were parasites, if not bloodsuckers, and their jointures a drain on estate income and a major cause of insolvency in the landowning class. As recently as the middle of the twentieth century, one landed gentleman reported callously that 'the widow of my father's elder brother ... [has] died after 46 years' jointure'. This is also the tenor of most modern historical writing on the finances of the landed class.[83] The present study presents a somewhat different picture. It comes to conservative conclusions about the impact of women on inheritance and on aristocratic finances generally, because it starts from the premiss that in 1740–1840 the fortunes (in all senses) of women were, comparatively speaking, at a low ebb, and that the fairly recent interventions of statute law in this sphere had all conduced to a patrolineal pattern of succession.

Heiresses still existed in 1740–1840, when there was no close patrolineal alternative to them and sometimes even when there was; but their incidence had been reduced. In a sense, eighteenth century heiresses resemble the many and much-vaunted 'centres of excellence' of the present day. The term obtains its commonest currency when the essence of the thing has gone.

TWO

'Collateral calculation'[84]

THE CONSTRAINTS OF THE
MARRIAGE SETTLEMENT

'Major landowners had … been resorting to the strict settlement before the end of the seventeenth century (usually incorporating it in the eldest son's marriage settlement)…. The most significant shift in practice during the eighteenth century was the increasing tendency' from early in the century for landowners to provide for their younger children in cash rather than endow them – particularly the younger sons – with land. By 1750, 'marriage settlements (the most usual instrument for effecting a strict settlement) appear to have been very commonly resorted to by families in many walks of life among the Protestant nation; one comes across them being made, not only by peers and country gentlemen, but also by merchants, clergy and what appear to be modestly endowed farmers'.[85] In 1742, a spoof pamphlet purportedly written by an Irish fortune-hunter who had hoped to reap his harvest in England, railed against 'that mercenary, ridiculous custom of a settlement, which has made more bad and undutiful wives in England than in any nation besides'.[86] The spoof pamphleteer's real grievance was, of course, that the existence of a settlement greatly circumscribed the practice of fortune-hunting.

In this as in other respects, the objects of the strict settlement were essentially defensive and protective. Calculation was certainly involved, but it was 'collateral' – indeed multilateral. It was not usually the purpose of either of the principal protagonists – the negotiators on behalf of the bridegroom and of the bride – to try to over-reach the other. Driving so hard a bargain that it was doubtful if the other party could deliver on it, was not in the best interests of anybody, and would not conduce to the success of the marriage or to harmony between the contracting families. In 1738, the cautious and conscientious guardian of an unmarried young woman of fortune gave a revealing explanation of his role. 'There have been many offers rejected for want of a sufficiency,' he wrote, 'for, though parents may dispose of their children without suspicion, yet the guardian who does not regard equality of fortune is generally supposed to have sold his ward for his own interest'.[87] This emphasis on 'a sufficiency' and an 'equality of fortune' is telling; the most that could be expected even of a guardian was that he get good value for his ward's 'fortune' and obtain an equivalent in the marriage market.

From the point of view of those negotiating on behalf of the bridegroom, the objects of the settlement were: to preserve intact, for another generation and beyond, the capital of the bridegroom's family (usually represented in whole or in part by a landed estate); to prevent the bridegroom from selling or encumbering (beyond specified limits) the lands comprised in the settlement; to impose upon the eldest son of the forthcoming marriage a similar restraint by making him a 'tenant in fee' or a 'tenant in tail male' until the next settlement (probably his own marriage settlement) could be put in place; and to provide portions for the younger children of the forthcoming marriage, 'present maintenance' for the newly weds if the bridegroom's father was still alive, 'separate maintenance' or 'pin money' (an independent allowance) for the bride during her husband's life, and a widow's jointure for her if she outlived him. The portions, present maintenance, pin money and jointure were secured on the estate of the bridegroom's father (or of the bridegroom himself, if he had already inherited). Usually they bore a relationship to the marriage portion which the bride brought with her, the jointure being calculated as a percentage per annum of the portion. While the level of the jointure was negotiable, the level of the bride's portion usually was not. This was because it had already been determined by prior considerations: the provision made in the marriage settlement of her parents, their rank, the number and sex of her siblings, and so on.

To begin with jointures: these, as has been seen, were commonly calculated at 20 per cent per annum of the portion in the early eighteenth century, falling – with the overall fall in interest-rates – to a norm of 10 per cent by the last third of the eighteenth century or earlier. In 1780, Simon Digby of Landenstown, Co. Kildare, a member of the substantial gentry and a kinsman of the 1st Earl Digby, was 'willing to settle a hundred per annum present maintenance for every thousand he shall receive [with his eldest son's bride], and the like for jointure, but must have at least £3,000 now deposited'.[88] In 1824, General Lord Hutchinson, who was advising his younger brother, Francis Hely-Hutchinson, on a marriage negotiation, stated: 'The usual bargain is £100 a year for every £1,000 given. According to this rule, your daughter would only be entitled to £300 a year.... A woman who has only £3,000 for her fortune is not entitled to anything more.' Nevertheless, Hutchinson did 'not suppose that Sir Samuel [Hutchinson, the prospective bridegroom's father] will offer less than £500'.[89] Much the same had been said during a marriage negotiation of nearly seventy five years earlier. In 1751, Gustavus Handcock of Waterstown, Co. Westmeath, the father of the prospective bridegroom, wrote to the 1st Lord Knapton: 'my son ... tells me ... that you purposed to give [a] portion with Miss [Vesey] of £3,000 and expected a settlement of a larger jointure than £300 a year.'[90]

These examples suggest that 'the usual bargain' was often just the starting-point for a negotiation, to be adhered to or departed from according to the

THE PURSUIT OF THE HEIRESS

outcome of negotiations over other aspects of the settlement, including the present maintenance and pin money and the size and source of the provision for younger children. In 1743, for example, the settlement on the marriage of the second son of John Foster of Dunleer, Co. Louth, shows a textbook adherence to 'the usual bargain': the bride's portion was £3,000 and her jointure was to be £300 a year. There was no reason for Foster to 'offer' more. The settlement went on to stipulate that, depending on the number and sexes of the children, their portions would cost a total of anything between £3,000 and £6,000. If there was a difference to be paid, Foster was going to have to pay it.[91]

Some over-ambitious fathers of bridegrooms or over-eager bridegrooms proved incapable of balancing these various elements in the settlement, or perhaps disdained to bother with such calculations. In 1777, Viscount Crosbie, son and heir of the 1st Earl of Glandore, agreed to provide his well-connected English bride-to-be with a jointure which was 20 per cent of her portion and roughly one-third of the then annual rental of his father's Co. Kerry estate. He argued, speciously: 'It can never affect myself, as it must take place after my death, and then, if I should have a son, by the time he can be of age, the estate will be very well able to afford such a jointure.'[92] In 1777, Lord Crosbie was within a few years of succeeding to the family titles and estates: another similarly situated and equally impetuous bridegroom was Lord Delvin, who married in 1812 and succeeded as 8th Earl of Westmeath in 1814. His bride was another well-connected Englishwoman, Lady Emily Cecil, second daughter of the 1st Marquess of Salisbury, with whom he obtained a portion of £15,000, and upon whom he settled a jointure of £3,000 a year. In response to less than searching inquiries on Lord Salisbury's part, Lord Delvin stated with magnificent vagueness that his estate would, on the falling-in of old leases, be re-let for £10,000 a year. By 1828, however, its gross rental still stood at only £4,800 (or so he then stated on oath), subject to £1,650 a year in interest payments and £840 in annuities to relatives. In other words, unless he lived to a great age, there was little possibility that a jointure of £3,000 a year would be payable out of income.[93]

Lords Glandore and Westmeath were both pre-deceased by their wives (the former by only one year). So their over-ambitious marriages (the first of which was not a success and the second a catastrophic failure) did not entail financial ruin, though they certainly straitened the borrowing-power of both husbands. Unless the fathers of both were in their dotage in 1777 and 1812 respectively, it is surprising that, in the interests of their other children and of the solvency of their estates, they did not resist this reckless over-jointuring. Presumably they, too, were dazzled by English rank and connections at Court. (The 7th Earl of Westmeath had the additional motive that he wanted to win

A pair of engagements portraits of Lord and lady Crosbie, by Hugh Douglas Hamilton, 1777; reproduced from a Sotheby Irish Sale catalogue, 16 May 2003

'COLLATORAL CALCULATION'

Lord Delvin's consent to making better provision for Westmeath's son and daughters by a second marriage, and possibly to 'opening' the estate to more of Westmeath's debts.) More usually, such recklessness occurred when the bridegroom had already come into his estate and was as much his own master as settlements permitted anyone to be. It was particularly likely to occur in the case of oldish men who had built up sizeable personal estates – e.g. the already-mentioned 1st Earl of Farnham, whose second wife and widow received a jointure to the enormous amount of £4,900 a year at his death in 1800.[94] The over-jointuring in this instance did not have the potentially fatal consequences of Lord Crosbie's. But it did deprive the Farnham estate of something which was always wanted and wanting – liquidity.

Some families avoided the danger of over-jointuring by going to the other extreme: the figure of eight per cent, for example, is to be found in one settlement of the mid-1760s and in an intended settlement of the 1780s.[95] Some settlements deprived the next generation of any discretion in the matter by stipulating that the unborn eldest son of the marriage was empowered to provide a jointure of no more than eight or at most 10 per cent.[96] The settlement made in 1722 on the marriage of the Hon. Hayes St Leger, second son of the 1st Viscount Doneraile, explicitly established a relativity between the level of jointure and the number of children subsequently born to the marriage (15 per cent if there were no children or only one, and 10 per cent if there were two or more).[97] In 1725, the 4th Lord Bellew proposed 'to settle £1,000 a year' on a wife, 'in case she has a son, £1,500 a year in case of failure of issue male'; and the settlement made many years later, in 1834, on the marriage of the 2nd Earl of Glengall provided a jointure of £1,200 a year for his widow if the £20,000 earmarked for younger children were needed, and £2,000 a year if it was not. In another, perhaps unique instance, the second marriage of the 2nd Lord Carysfort in 1787, the provision for the widow was not only to vary in accordance with the number of children she had had, but was expressed as a lump sum (£12,000 or £17,000) which was to provide for her widowhood regardless of how long it lasted.[98] Such ingenious attempts to set up a sliding scale, place settlement provision on an empirical footing and set limits to the cost of widows, seem not to have been widespread. So jointures representing 10 per cent per annum of portions became established as the rough yardstick, to be varied upwards to 12.5 or even 15 per cent if other aspects of the settlement seemed to justify such expansiveness.

The relationship between the portion which the bride brought with her and the future portions of the younger children of the marriage was even less standardised, although traditionally there was supposed to be one. Often, the total provision for younger children coincided with the bride's portion in amount; often, whether the amounts coincided or not, the intention was declared that the wife's portion should be used for the benefit of the younger children; and theoretically, had the financial circumstances of the bridegroom and/or his father enabled them to put the bride's portion out at compound interest, or otherwise to apply it to the operation of the settlement, the marriage should have been from their point of view self-financing. In 1774, the 1st Earl of Belvedere stipulated in his will that the provision for younger children which his still unmarried son and heir, Lord Belfield, was expowered to charge on the family estate should be in the ratio of £1,000 for every £1,000 which Belfield received on marriage, up to a limit of £20,000; and in 1820, the recently mentioned Francis Hely-Hutchinson, who was not similarly tied down, voluntarily committed himself to making prudent use of the portion he was to receive with his eldest son's bride. 'In order to facilitate the arrangement,' Hely-Hutchinson declared, 'I shall not desire any part of the lady's fortune..., though it would be somewhat convenient to me..., which may all be applied to the settlement, both as present maintenance and jointure, in such way as may be agreed upon.'[99] He was exceptional. Very few fathers of bridegrooms, or bridegrooms themselves, applied the bride's portion to the settlement; almost no settlement proved to be self-financing; and in practice means usually had to be found to exceed the settlement's stipulations. Luck sometimes endorsed the intentions of the settlement by ordaining that the marriage produced no more younger children than were affordable (this was a matter of luck, because the practice of contraception within marriage does not seem to have been common in the period 1740–1840.[100]) In situations, however, where there were more younger children than were affordable under the settlement, and the family's financial circumstances did not permit (if legal means for the purpose could have been found) any exceeding of the stipulated provision, real difficulty and even hardship ensued.[101]

This applied particularly to some high-ranking families whose wealth was on the wane. Rank (in the sense of title), when originally conferred by the crown, bore a close correlation to landed wealth; but subsequent bearers of the family title could, through misfortune or improvidence, find themselves burdened with 'an empty rank'. Such individuals would indeed find it difficult to make suitable matches for their younger children. In 1751, the Lord Chief Justice of the Common Pleas (who must have had considerable professional experience of the terms of marriage settlements) observed that honours were an embarrassment, especially to women, in the absence of a fortune adequate to keep them up; even dukes' daughters, he added cynically, were little regarded after their fathers' death. In 1794, the debt-encumbered 1st Earl Ludlow lamented: 'So small are the settlements on my younger children that I dread leaving them to such a pittance as £12,000 divided amongst five.' In 1799, the 1st Marquess of Bute, writing of his sister, a widowed Irish countess, and her daughters, observed: 'Ladies of quality without fortunes are perhaps worse off than any other class.' And in 1819, the 6th Viscount Ranelagh, in a letter to the Prime Minister soliciting pensions for Ranelagh's sisters, besought him 'to reflect on the melancholy situation of two ladies, one of them with three children, with rather less than £80 a year [each] to exist on'.[102]

'COLLATORAL CALCULATION'

The number and, to a lesser extent, the sex of the younger children were important factors in determining whether a settlement worked or imposed hardship. The more younger children there were the greater, obviously, the financial strain of portioning them. This had not been obvious to the 1st Duke of Leinster, who confessed to his wife in 1766 that his expenditure on Carton, Co. Kildare, the family seat, was 'a folly, considering the number of children we have'. He should have considered sooner than this the consequences of a marriage which brought him a portion of only £10,000 and seventeen children, of whom ten survived to majority.[103] The Duke's sole, and small, consolation was that six of the ten children were male. Male children did not absolutely require cash portions; more important, they could earn their own living in one of the approved professions. The great Co. Down magnate, the 2nd Marquess of Downshire, made this point explicitly in his will, which was dated 1797 (four years before he actually died). This document is the more interesting because, clearly, it was written in Lord Downshire's own, down-to-earth language and not sanitised by a lawyer:

> My wish is, having by my settlements the power to divide £40,000 as I may think fit, and as my boys will serve their country and have many ways of providing for themselves, and as the dear girls have not such opportunities but must patiently wait the caprice, the love or perhaps the avarice of some man to obtain a settlement, I, having considered the subject to the best of my judgment, do advise, ordain and fix that the division of the said £40,000 shall be and is to be divided [sic] in proportions equal to the proportion of 7 to 10 or thereabouts, the boys to have the lesser, the girls the larger, number.[104]

Of the professions which the boys might pursue, only the army was expensive. In 1790, one of the Duke of Leinster's younger sons expected to raise £4,000 by the sale of his commission; and in 1796 an anxious mother was informed that the price of the lowest commission, an ensigncy, 'in quiet times is £500 in an old regiment, £400 in a new'.[105] Entry into the Church, the Law and the civil and diplomatic service, by contrast, cost nothing except a good education; and entry into the Navy did not cost even that. The rewards from these professions varied and to a considerable extent were a matter of luck: most naval officers, for example, sooner or later obtained substantial sums in prize money, whereas only a minority of military engagements – e.g. the storming of Seringapatam in 1799 – yielded booty more valuable than naval prizes. All these professions could be pursued without loss of caste, although the Hon. Charles Dillon-Lee, who was not a younger son but still needed paid employment, thought that the lower reaches of the diplomatic service were beneath him and that 'It would be better to live upon bread and water than commit such a mean action as to become a petty Minister at a petty Court' like Brussels or Ratisbon. This was an eccentric view – and a surprising one for Dillon-Lee to take: other financially 'ruined' men were only too glad to become diplomats and live abroad out of reach of their creditors.[106] In general, young men of aristocratic birth eagerly embraced the variety of professional outlets open to males. Females were not so lucky. So, if settlement provision were tight and were divided equally among the younger children of both sexes, the outcome was likely to be that 'the daughters lived in greater penury than their brothers'.[107]

Because daughters were solely reliant on their portions, it was the increasing practice for them to be treated equally as to level of portion. The exceptions to this rule tend to be exceptional in other respects also. In 1740, the 6th and last Earl of Anglesey provided for his three daughters according to a sliding scale of £10,000, £8,000 and £7,000. But this was probably a characteristic, though uncharacteristically harmless, piece of eccentricity; in the following year, he repudiated his wife, daughters and the settlement, and when one of his daughters went to visit him on his deathbed, in 1760, endeavoured to shoot her.[108] Another exception to the rule of equal provision for all daughters was the will of the 2nd Earl of Kingston in 1799, by which he appointed '£8,000 apiece to his daughters, except Lady Mary – to her £300 a year annuity'; this must have been because 'the unhappy Lady Mary' had been the victim of a notorious abduction and was deemed unmarriageable (though she did later marry).[109] These dispositions, plainly, were supplemental to the provisions of his marriage settlement, which must also have reserved to him a discretion to portion his daughters unequally and on a different basis.

A similar, but not identical, case is the will, made in 1730, of George Rochfort of Gaulstown, Co. Westmeath, father of the 1st Earl of Belvedere. This recited that his three (surviving) daughters, Alice, Thomasine and Anne (all of them still unmarried), had been allocated portions of £2,500 each under his marriage settlement of 1704, and augmented this provision unequally by making Anne's portion up to £4,000 and the portions of the other two up to only £3,000.[110] The significant point is that these women had started off on level pegging, and that it was paternal favouritism, the need to compensate for a physical disadvantage or some other afterthought or development which led to the inequality of their treatment. The same applied to the seven daughters of William Conolly junior of Castletown, who died in 1754. Under his marriage settlement of 1733, the portion of each had been set at £4,000, but by codicil added in 1754 to his will he increased this to £8,000 except in the case of the eldest, who was to have £10,000. The preferential treatment given to the eldest daughter may not, in this instance, have been her father's doing. The eldest was the god-daughter of, and had been called after, Conolly's formidable aunt, Katherine. The elder Katherine (Speaker Conolly's widow) had died only two years previously, naming Katherine junior in her will as one of her residuary legatees; so the additional £2,000 was probably the result of that bequest.[111] Unless some special circumstance like this existed, it was very unusual to observe either primogeniture or any other distinction among daughters. Therefore, where they were concerned, numbers were of particular importance in determining the level of portion.

That level having been predetermined by all or some of the above considerations (and not usually by the particular match in prospect), negotiations over the terms of the marriage settlement would focus on other matters which still left plenty of room for manoeuvre: obviously, on the level of the jointure, and – less obviously – on whether all, part or none of the portion should be paid into the hands of the bridegroom's father; on the other points which had exercised Francis Hely-Hutchinson in 1820; and on the key question of what contribution, if any, was to be made by the bridegroom's father towards the provision for the younger children. For example, during the negotiation of a marriage treaty between the 1st Marquess of Abercorn's daughter (portion: £10,000) and the son and heir of the 3rd Earl of Wicklow (rental: £16,000–£20,000 a year charged with £40,000 for younger children), Lord Abercorn's go-between reported to him in January 1816:

> Thus circumstanced, he [Lord Wicklow] said he thinks he cannot give his son more than £4,000 annually [in present maintenance], and £2,000 jointure for any lady he may marry. At the same time, he does not desire one shilling of the fortune of such lady – let that be settled on herself and her issue. He is ready to make this present provision, and to settle his whole estate on his son and the issue of his marriage. A considerable objection was raised by … Lord Wicklow's lawyer … on the point of jointure given – that is, 10 per cent on the fortune. Lord Wicklow said he did not wish to be regulated at all by what was or is the custom, or to appear making a bargain, and he felt no objection to make it £2,000 and the interest of her own fortune; that fortune to be settled, together with another £10,000, on his estate, for younger children of the marriage. However it seemed the intention … that the interest of both sums of £10,000 should, in case of issue more than one son, be a present provision for that younger issue, and in that case the jointure would be but £2,000 per annum.

John James Hamilton, 1st Marquess of Abercorn (1756–1818), reproduced from a portrait of c.1793 by Sir Thomas Lawrence in Borenius and Hodgson, *Elton Hall Pictures*, p.85

In the end, Lord Abercorn – possibly to obtain a higher jointure – took the unusual step of increasing the portion to £15,000, the additional £5,000 to be paid at his death. Since the daughter in question was his only surviving younger child he could afford both the provision and the precedent.[112]

All the same, it is clear that, in spite of this increase, the marriage in all human probability could not prove financially advantageous to the Wicklow family and estate. The usual effect of such negotiations was to make a dear bargain of the bride. This could be the case even if her portion were generous: even if it were so generous that, considered in isolation from the rest of the settlement, it made her superficially resemble an heiress. In the already-mentioned instance of the second Lady Aldborough, the portion of '£50,000 hard cash down' may well have been counter-balanced by a jointure of £5,000 a year. As things turned out, Lady Aldborough, though at least ten years younger than her husband, survived him by only a year – a stroke of luck from the point of view of the heirs to the Stratford estates. No such luck favoured Thomas Conolly of Castletown and his successors. Although they did unexpectedly well out of Lady Anne Conolly's Wentworth inheritance, the c.£115,000 which they received fitfully and over a long period (1739–c.1817) from that source, was actually exceeded by the steady drain of her jointure. This had been set in 1733 at the high level of £3,000 a year (largely in recognition of her then nebulous expectations); and as her husband, William Conolly junior, died when not quite fifty in 1754, and as she did not die until 1797, aged eighty-four, the £3,000 a year contributed materially to the mounting financial difficulties of their son.

The facts and figures of the Conolly case have only recently been established; but other cases of long-lived, well jointured widows have long been familiar and have led to the conclusion that

> maintaining dowagers was an expense incurred more generally and for a good deal longer by heads of families than might be expected. Out of 101 Irish peers in 1783 ... (the whole Irish peerage at this time, excluding first-generation peers), 72 either were or had been supporting dowagers, and the average period during which jointure income had to be found was as high as 21 years.... The classic Irish example of a dowager burdening an estate appears to be the case of the widow of the 1st Earl of Milltown, who survived his death in 1783 for 58 years.[113]

The argument that the cost of jointures was rising is valid only if no regard is had to the ampler provision for widows which had been normative in an earlier age.[114] There was, however, a genuine rise, admittedly from a low base, in the period 1740–1840. This was not just a matter of increased provision; it was also the effect of demographic change.

The classic study of 'The Demography of the British Peerage'[115] for most purposes treats the aristocracy of the British Isles as a whole, and does not give separate figures for the aristocracy of Ireland. This probably matters little because, although 'the Irish are consistently the least accurately recorded of the three national aristocracies..., there is evidence that demographic rates varied little between the three'. In any case, it is hard to regard the Irish as a national aristocracy at all, not so much because of intermarriage with English and British peers and their children, as because of the large number of non-Irishmen who were peers of Ireland, and the number of Irishmen in the Irish peerage who also held peerages of England, Great Britain and the United Kingdom.[116] If, then, demographic conclusions about the aristocracy as a whole are valid for the Irish aristocracy as a part, it would seem that the period 1740–1840 was the heyday of the Irish dowager:

> The mortality of women over 40 showed one sharp decrease at the beginning of the eighteenth century…; a second decrease may be dated around 1750–65.… Since the mid-eighteenth century (or 1761, perhaps, for a specific date), women have drawn well ahead of men, and currently [1959] enjoy an expectation of life at the age of 40 that is almost 15 per cent higher than their brothers'.… During the eighteenth century, the mortality of middle-aged [40–65] women, declined sharply, but the men were slow to improve *[sic!]* until the latter part of the century. Up to about 1757, males had the lower mortality rates; from then until about 1827 there was little difference between the sexes; and in the cohorts born after 1775 [1775–99 and 1800–25] the woman's relative position improved greatly.

Demography thus contributed to make jointures payable in more cases and for longer in this period than had been the situation prior to the middle of the eighteenth century; and obviously, if a dowager lived for a long time, the jointure-provision for her could cost a great deal more than she had originally brought her husband's family in portion, even assuming that the jointure had been calculated in the first place 'according to the fortune given – that is, 10 per cent on the fortune', and that the portion had duly been 'applied to the settlement'.

To the problems of demography were added those of inflation. In the years up to the 1780s, and particularly in the third quarter of the century, Ireland experienced a genuine economic boom. But, from the outbreak of war with Revolutionary France in 1793 until c.1815, a boom of a more deceptive, artificial, unsustainable and inflationary kind supervened. Irish farmers were now supplying a British market which was increasingly dependent on imported food for a variety of reasons: population increase, industrialisation, shortages occasioned by a series of bad harvests in the early nineteenth century, the cutting-off by war of traditional sources of supply from abroad, and the requirements of Admiralty victualling contracts. The increased economic activity engendered by the growth, processing and export of Irish agricultural produce was financed by a necessary expansion of credit and banking activity. On top of this came increased military expenditure in the 1790s and consequently greater government borrowing. When the Bank of Ireland suspended specie payments in 1797, it was enabled to continue discounting to the merchants and lending to the government on an extended scale. Moreover, private banks were now authorised to hold Bank of Ireland notes as well as specie as a reserve. The result of this credit expansion was a rapid increase, especially after 1797, in the issue of Bank of Ireland notes, which further fuelled the inflation.[117]

There was also, in Ireland as in Great Britain, a marked increase in the rate of peerage-creations and of promotions in the peerage in the last third of the eighteenth century. The exertions of patronage required to maintain the government's control of the Irish Parliament, particularly in the struggle over the Act of Union in 1799–1800, were an important element in this aspect of the contemporary inflation, although the swelling of the peerage was, for the most part, no more than a recognition of the new wealth of many old gentry families. Nevertheless, all these developments, in conjunction with demographic change, were bound to place a strain on settlement provision which had seemed adequate a generation earlier. They created a strong inducement to increase the level of jointure (and portions) established by the previous settlement, in order to take account of intervening rises in the cost and standard of living, in the rental of the estate, and in the rank and/or status of the family. The cost of any such increase would of course fall unilaterally on the estate of the husband/father.

An (admittedly extreme) instance of this phenomenon was the settlement-provision made for Mrs John Foster, subsequently Viscountess Ferrard, whose jointure was increased tenfold during this period, all at the expense of John Foster's estate. When she married the future Speaker of the House of Commons, in 1764, her portion of £2,000, entitling her to a jointure of only £200 a year, was inadequate even to the expectations of the heir of a substantial country gentleman. That was John Foster's then status and lot. In 1766, however, his father became one of the lord chief justices; in 1777 John Foster himself became, effectively, Chancellor of the Irish Exchequer; and in 1785, he became Speaker. In 1777, when the Fosters were re-settling their estate, it was decided to augment Mrs Foster's £200 with £600 from Foster sources. By 1810, however, the date of the next settlement, even this was judged inadequate. In the intervening years she, too, had signally risen in rank and status, having in consideration of her husband's political services been created a baroness in 1790 and a viscountess in 1797. In 1810, therefore, it was decided that Viscountess Ferrard (as she now was) would require a jointure of £2,000 a year (the difference of £1,200 coming once again from Foster sources) to support her rank in the peerage with becoming dignity after her husband's death. Between 1777 and 1810 the rental of the Foster estate had more than doubled, to about £10,000 a year. Nevertheless, the burden was going to be heavy, and the more so because almost wholly unilateral. 'Happily', Lady Ferrard did not live to widowhood.[118]

The provision for younger children, like the provision for dowagers, often proved inadequate in the light of the changed circumstances of a generation after. For example, the 5th Viscount Grandison obtained with his wife a portion of £2,000 in 1707: in 1739, when their daughter and only surviving younger child married, her portion was £8,000. In the intervening years Lord Grandison had been promoted to an earldom, the rental of his estate had risen, and he had been relieved by death of the extensive claims of his mother (an heiress) and his mother's grasping second husband. This case is instructive: first, because the most obvious reason for the inadequacy of the mother's portion to cover the portions of her younger children (that there could only be one mother, and there was likely to be more than one younger child) did not apply; second, because Lord Grandison does not seem to have been the man to give his daughter a penny more than was necessary. Previous correspondence, at a time when he had at least three daughters and one younger son to dispose of, show him to have been a very calculating father. In 1728, he was asked by his agent 'whether a[n Irish] gentleman of a good family, without a title, of £1,000 yearly estate, would be agreeable for any of them [the daughters]'. The agent reckoned 'that it were better even to dispose of one so, than to let her wait for a better...; and England in my poor opinion is not so proper a place to match daughters of moderate fortunes, as it is to get a great deal of money for sons'.[119] The case of Lord Grandison will recur,[120] because further deaths in his family had the effect of making another daughter, who was married ten years later, in 1739, an heiress.

This heavy mortality in the Grandison family ran counter to current demographic trends, which were towards increased family size and stepped-up 'replacement rates' among the aristocracy (trends as unwelcome, from the financial point of view, as the contemporary trend towards more and longer-lived dowagers):

> The principal picture is one of ... high mortality and fertility, which balanced each other until the middle of the eighteenth century, after which ... the rate of replacement was above unity.... For some reason, the desire to limit the size of the family seems to have become weaker during the eighteenth century, only to become stronger again during the nineteenth.

The 1st Duke of Leinster was thus only an extreme manifestation of a widespread phenomenon.

It is possible to assess this phenomenon in the context of the Irish aristocracy only (bearing in mind all the imperfections of that concept), and in terms of the mean family size and the replacement rates exhibited in the families born to children of Irish peers and of the eldest sons of Irish peers. In this group, a peak of 4.50 (mean family size) and 1.445 (replacement rate) was achieved around 1815 – as compared to 3.33 and 0.829 around 1750:[121] figures which for some reason were higher in the case of the Irish aristocracy than in that of the British and the Scottish. (A possible reason is that the Irish aristocracy may have had a slightly greater propensity than the British and the Scottish to marry within its own class; and it can be proved statistically, at any rate from about 1750, that 'marriages between two members of the nobility' result in 'higher fertility'.)[122] Whatever the reason, it is clear that the aristocracy was not unaffected by the population explosion in pre-Famine Ireland of which the peasantry was the most spectacular victim. The aristocracy did not starve. But it was hard-hit financially by the necessity to provide portions for a larger number of younger children, as well as to provide each with a portion of a larger amount, than had been anticipated a generation earlier.

If providing the portion was likely to run the bride's family into difficulty, receiving the portion was likely to lead the bridegroom's family into temptation. One temptation has already been mentioned: submitting to the future evil of a burdensome jointure in return for the present benefit of a large portion. Another temptation (which the terms of only a minority of marriage settlements resisted) was to misapply the money. In 1825, for example, it was reported: 'Lord Clare is certainly to be married to Miss Burrell ... with some say £30,000, some £60,000; 'tis wanted.'[123] And in 1784, Lady Southampton was supposed to be 'inexorable' about her eldest son's economically unsatisfactory marriage, 'for she has thirteen other children, and a fortune was very requisite'. (Lady Southampton, though the wife of a British peer, was herself Irish and the co-heiress to an Irish estate; she sold her share of it in 1790, presumably to help with the portioning of her thirteen other children.)[124] In both these instances, the large marriage portions which were 'wanted' or 'requisite' were intended for purposes other than those of the eldest son's marriage settlement. Instead of being ring-fenced and put out at compound interest to accumulate for the benefit of his widow and younger children, they were going to be hi-jacked to provide short-term relief for other financial problems.

The most obvious mode of misapplication was to use the bride's portion to liquidate or reduce existing debt on the estate of the bridegroom or his father. This, pretty clearly, was what Lord Clare was going to do. In three, better-documented instances, it was what the bridegroom proposed explicitly to do. In 1720 Francis Burton of Buncraggy, Co. Clare, father of the 2nd Lord Conyngham, admitted in the course of negotiations for his marriage that he owed 'some money', and baldly stated that it was a sum which his intended wife's 'fortune will very near, if not quite, clear'; in 1724 the recently married Sir Henry King, 3rd Bt, declared that he had spent half the fortune he obtained with his wife in 1722 clearing his own and his late brother's debts[125]; and in the already-mentioned Carysfort-Grenville marriage settlement of 1787, it was specifically provided that the bride's portion of £19,000 was to be used to pay off mortgages to that amount on the bridegroom's Elton Hall, Huntingdonshire, estate. If the financial pressure were great (which it was in King's case, since he still owed the very large sum of £15,000), this might be the only option. But it was an option fraught with danger for the future, unless a plan were immediately made to deal with the problem of debt either by retrenchment or by the sale of assets. One settlement, that of Lord Oxmantown and his heiress-bride, Mary Field, in 1836, specifically stated that £15,700 of her portion of £20,000 was to be applied to the liquidation of the debt affecting the estate of his father, the 2nd Earl of Rosse. But, ingeniously, it settled the £20,000 on the younger children and stipulated that the income from it should be earmarked to the present maintenance of the newly weds during Lord Rosse's lifetime. So Lord Rosse, instead of paying interest on the £15,700 to a third party, would be paying it to the trustees of his daughter-in-law's fortune and to serve the purposes of the marriage settlement.[126] This was probably an unusual device. More usually, the indebted father-in-law pocketed the portion and was not even legally tied up to use it to liquidate or reduce his debts.

The other mode of misapplying the bride's portion was what Lord and Lady Southampton had intended to do until stymied by their son's improvident choice: this was to use it to pay the portions of younger children of the present generation, instead of reserving it for the younger children of the next, and of the marriage. Thus, Lord Crosbie in his near-sighted calculations of 1777 pointed out that the portion of the prospective Lady Crosbie would 'exactly provide for my two sisters an equal portion with Lady Anne Talbot' (the eldest and already-married sister); and the 1st Earl of Egmont noted in 1737 that, of the £12,000 received with the wife of his son and heir, '£7,000 must be reserved for my daughter, Helena's, portion'. Earlier, in 1732, Lord Egmont had pithily observed: 'Sell or borrow I must, to satisfy daughters' portions.'[127] This was the inevitable consequence of running one generation in arrear.

It was also the inevitable consequence of a more important and general phenomenon: the landed class's lack of liquidity. In 1817, the 2nd Earl Belmore was warned that 'The main piece of prudence is to have £10,000 or £12,000 for emergencies';[128] but the warning went unheeded, by Lord Belmore and most of his peers. To the great majority of the class, the idea of saving did not occur. On coming into his inheritance in 1789, Lord Belmore's Co. Tyrone rival, Lord Abercorn, noted with satisfaction: 'To speak in round numbers, I have reason to suppose my annual income, to spend, will be nearer thirty than twenty thousand pounds.' People like Lord Abercorn always did speak in round numbers.[129] His fellow Ulster marquess, the 1st Lord Londonderry, was as will be seen,[130] one of the most prudent managers of his day; but even Lord Londonderry allowed himself, under a resettlement of 1816, £12,350 a year for personal and household expenditure, out of a gross rental of £31,350 and a disposable income of £17,350.[131] Since he was then an old gentleman of seventy-seven who never stirred from his Co. Down seat, Mount Stewart, and was no longer carrying on building operations there, the £12,350 a year was an enormous sum. The already-quoted Lord Egmont had admitted in 1737 that, until obliged to settle £1,500 a year on his son and daughter-in-law for present maintenance, he had had his 'whole estate at my command and lived up to it'.[132]

By no means all landowners had their whole estate at their command; but nearly all lived up to what they had, or lived beyond it. From the early 1790s, during the years of artificial, wartime prosperity and of inflation, it was common for landowners to assume that the price of agricultural products and consequently the level of their rentals were ever-rising, and to calculate, behave and spend accordingly. Instead of rising in the post-war period, the Abercorn rental, for one, fell and by a dramatic amount – from £37,000 a year in 1815 to £26,000 in 1832.[133] In 1809, a lesser magnate than the Abercorns, the 1st Earl of Glengall, had anticipated (in all senses of the word) a rental which was going to rise to £36,000 a year: the chronic indebtedness of his son and successor the 2nd Earl forty years later probably had much to do with the fact that the Glengall rental in 1848 was actually only £15,000.[134] Obviously, landowners

Emily, Duchess of Leinster, c.1754; a mezzotint after
a portrait by Joshua Reynolds

AUTHOR'S COLLECTION

'COLLATORAL CALCULATION'

who spent up to the hilt of their income possessed greater freedom of manoeuvre than those who anticipated it. But the former were still in a poor condition to withstand the sudden stroke of a portion or the slower paralysis of a jointure. The late eighteenth- and early nineteenth-century 'systems of protecting and reproducing wealth ... were predicated on the rash assumption that the good times of rising rent rolls would last forever. And they did not.'[135]

None was in a poorer condition than Ireland's highest-ranking nobleman and only duke, the 2nd Duke of Leinster, elder brother of the famous Lord Edward Fitzgerald, and the eldest of the ten children of his parents who survived to majority. The 2nd Duke succeeded his father in 1773, and to a rental which had been £12,000 a year a decade earlier. He also succeeded to a burden of debt amounting to no less than £148,000, exclusive of the annual and first-priority demands made on him for jointures. His grandmother's jointure (of approximately £3,000 a year) had to be paid from her widowhood in 1744 until her death in 1780; and his mother's jointure, which had been set at the even higher sum of £4,000 a year, had to be paid from 1773 until her death in 1814, ten years after his own.[136] Of the £4,000 a year, £3,000 derived from his parents' marriage settlement: the additional £1,000 derived from his father's will, which also included staggering bequests of a life interest to the Dowager Duchess in 'Leinster House [Dublin] and Carton, with plate, furniture, horses, stock, etc., etc. ... if she does not marry or live in England; £2,000 a year estate to his [the late Duke's] third and to his fourth sons each, and £10,000 to all his younger children.... It is said the present Duke has not £7,000 a year to live on now.'[137] With his other debts of c.£150,000 it is probable that he did not have anything like '£7,000 a year to live on'.

His mother did in fact remarry. But she took care to exchange Carton and Leinster House for Frescati, a seaside villa at Blackrock, Co. Dublin, and for a sum which may have been as much as £40,000, before she acknowledged that she had made a second, and hitherto secret, marriage to her children's tutor, William Ogilvie.[138] Ogilvie, it was scurrilously reported in 1785 (by John FitzGibbon, the future Earl of Clare).

> was originally a drummer in a Scotch regiment. From the drum, he was preferred to a writing-school in a village in the county of Kerry, from whence he was translated to a writing-school in Dublin, from whence he was preferred to the [1st] Duke of Leinster's nursery in the capacity of private tutor to his children. Whilst in this station, he did his Grace the honour to get three or four bastards on the person of his Duchess, to which said bastards the present Duke has the honour to pay £10,000 each [in portions], and now, Mr Ogilvie having made an honest woman of his mother, that worthy and sagacious nobleman, his stepson, repays the many obligations which he had conferred upon him, by submitting himself wholly to his [Ogilvie's] management and direction.[139]

Instead of giving financial assistance to the overburdened Duke, the Dowager Duchess and Ogilvie busied themselves in founding a family of their own – or, rather, an acknowledged family of their own; and with such success that one of their daughters, Cecilia Ogilvie, nearly married the son and heir of the 1st Marquess of Donegall in 1790, and ended up marrying into the rich, though illegitimate, Lock family of Norbury Park, Mickleham, Surrey.[140]

The Duke, meanwhile, had indeed to provide portions of £10,000 each for the three of his sisters who married, and at least the interest on the £10,000 of the fourth, who did not. In effect therefore, his sisters alone cost him £40,000. The figure could hardly have been set at less; but the provision made for his brothers was ludicrously generous. The four who lived to marry, Lords Charles, Henry, Edward and Robert, pursued careers in the navy, army and diplomatic service, from which they derived a comfortable income, and in which they were considerably advanced by the Duke's political influence. On the strength of this influence, the eldest, Lord Charles, also held between 1792 and 1806 a semi-sinecure office producing an estimated £4,000 a year in 1797. In addition, the four brothers were provided for, in kind or in cash, on a scale which falls little short of the already-quoted contemporary résumé of the terms of their father's will. Lords Charles and Henry were endowed with the detached, northern part of the family estates, in the barony of Lecale, Co. Down; Lord Charles's share, on the strength of which he was raised to the Irish peerage in 1800 as Lord Lecale, consisted of over 2,000 Irish acres at a rental in 1808 of over £2,500.[141] Lord Edward was provided for out of the main family estate in Co. Kildare with a property at Kilrush which was producing £839 a year in 1798 (when he was attainted and it was temporarily forfeited to the crown).[142] Lord Robert was probably provided for in cash, as in 1801 he had £11,000 in the Funds, independent of a diplomatic pension of some £440 a year and income of a further £550 from some unspecified source.[143]

The consequences of the reckless settlement policy and the general financial ineptitude of the 2nd Duke's father and his grandfather would have been fatal but for one thing: the 2nd Duke's own marriage. It is one principal purpose of this study to demonstrate that marriages so brilliant, from the husband's point of view, hardly ever happened; but the 2nd Duke of Leinster's is certainly a case in point. His wife, whom he married in 1774, was the only child of Lord St George of Headford Castle, Co. Galway. She was not his sole heiress, as the St George estates were destined for a tripartite division. Her share of the inheritance excluded Headford itself and the accompanying landed property, but included the whole St George estate in Co. Roscommon, which passed to her on terms compatible with its being sold for the ultimate advantage of the eldest son of her marriage. This sale raised £68,000, and enabled the Duke to reduce the capital debt on his patrimonial property to the bearable level of 'only' (as he put it) £80,000.[144] Yet, not even a windfall of this magnitude could compensate for the financial follies of the two previous generations, to say nothing of those of the Duke himself.[145] Indeed, it barely sufficed to provide for the seven younger children born to the Duke and Duchess. Their eldest child, the 3rd Duke, who came into possession of a heavily encumbered gross rental standing at £36,320 in 1822,[146] was not really rich enough to support a dukedom.

Meanwhile, the descendants of Emily, Dowager Duchess and that 'sad old rogue', Ogilvie,[147] flourished – ironically, at Ardglass Castle, Co. Down, the sometime seat and estate of Lord Lecale. Lord Lecale's step-father, more provident than he, had bought it from him in 1806, presumably with money saved out of the Dowager Duchess's jointure. That jointure alone, over the forty-one-year period for which it was payable, cost the 2nd and 3rd Dukes of Leinster £164,000. When it expired with the death of the Dowager Duchess in 1814, Ogilvie even had the effrontery to write to her grandson, the newly-of-age 3rd Duke, seeking financial recompense for all Ogilvie's services to the Fitzgerald family over the years![148]

Had the 1st Duke, back in the early 1770s, been a more alert and suspicious husband, he would not have provided so generously for his wife. Indeed, he would possibly have divorced her. Had this happened she, in common with the small but growing number of divorcees during this period, would have forfeited her entitlement to the jointure stipulated in her marriage settlement (not just to the additional provisions for her made by the Duke). Yet, paradoxically, even in this final phase of a marriage, the provisions of the marriage settlement played a significant part in protecting the interests of the wife (and children). In cases of judicial separation, a court would fix the sum to be paid in alimony (often with an eye to the provision made for the wife in her marriage settlement). In cases of private separation and divorce, this provision was really the only available guideline. Divorce, the only means of legally ending a marriage and freeing both parties to re-marry, was obtained by private act of parliament, in the consideration and drafting of which almost all the work was done by the House of Lords. However, as the chairman of committees in the British House of Lords explained in 1798, it was 'not the present usage in the House of Lords to insert any allowance to the lady in divorce bills...: it is left to the injured party [the husband] to make such allowance as they think fit'.[149]

Since every divorce, by the one-sided rules then applied, was founded in some element of misconduct on the part of the wife, the husband would almost always retain her portion. But the divorce settlement would ensure that she (and her family) received some value for it; she would otherwise become a charge on her family, unless whisked off into a second marriage. The English divorcees, Viscountess Bolingbroke (best-known as Lady Di Beauclerk), the Duchess of Grafton and Mrs Henry Cecil received annuities of £800, £2,000 and £1,200 a year in 1767, 1769 and 1791 respectively, and Lady Belmore (who was English, but whose husband and divorce act were Irish) received in 1793 £1,000 a year during her ex-husband's life and her full jointure of £2,000 a year after his demise.[150] This

The 'sad old rogue' William Ogilvie, c.1800; a caricature by Charles Lock, the husband of Ogilvie's daughter, Cecilia, reproduced from the Duchess of Sermoneta, *The Lock's of Norbury* (London, 1940), p.84

last settlement was exceptionally generous. But, harsh or generous, a settlement bore some relationship to pin money and jointure; it could not be less than the former and it could not be more than the latter. Likewise, in any deed of separation the allowance settled on the wife to enable her to live apart from her husband had to be more than the pin money settled on her while they lived together. As for the children of the marriage, they might well be glad of the provision made for them by their parents' marriage settlement while they were still unborn. A cuckolded father might 'take against' the children whom his divorced or separated wife had borne him, especially if there were the slightest, even unfounded, doubt about their paternity.

Divorce settlements are an exception to the usual give and take of marital arrangements, the usual tendency of which was for the husband's family to give and the wife to take. So far, these have been discussed in purely, and at times brutally, financial terms. Occasionally, however, at least part of what was given or taken was not calculable on such a basis. In one freak instance in 1721, for example, it was reported that 'Leeson, the brewer' had given his daughter '£5,000 portion, which as times go is a smart fortune for this place [Dublin]; and he has besides, to encourage the bridegroom from being idle, promised another £1,000 on the birth of the first child'.[151]

Since Joseph Leeson had made his money in trade, and was in the process of founding a landed and titled family (the earls of Milltown), it might be expected that he would have used the £1,000 premium to purchase the 'condescension' of a better-born and preferably a titled son-in-law. But premiums seem seldom to have been payable for 'condescension', simply because it was not very common

> for a landowner's eldest son to take as his wife the daughter of an ambitious and wealthy merchant or financier prepared to portion his daughter on a lavish scale in order to see her acquire rank.... Such men were not numerous in Ireland, and social custom militated against such matches – hence their infrequency. For instance, of 151 matches contracted by the Irish peerage as it was constituted in 1783, only six can with certainty be described as alliances between commercial wealth and landed property, although another eight may just possibly have fallen into this category.[152]

A complicating factor in any such analysis is the rapidity with which wealthy merchants distanced themselves from their source of wealth, bought land, entered landed society and even joined the ranks of the peerage. 'Leeson, the brewer's' only son did all of these things, built the magnificent mansion of Russborough, Co. Kildare, and was raised to the peerage in 1756. Nicholas Lawless, a highly successful woollen manufacturer in Dublin, did much the same, and was created a baronet in 1776 and a baron in 1789. Both families were also inventive in finding a French derivation for their surnames and a Norman origin for their ancestors. Such misleading inventiveness was not peculiar to the period under review, and nor was it a peculiarly Irish phenomenon.

In 1886, an English radical wrote mischievously about the bearer of the newly created UK barony of Hindlip, Sir Henry Allsopp, who 'brewed beer and by so doing acquired a fortune', and was first made a baronet and next a peer.

> What was the first step Sir Henry Allsopp took when he became a peer? He wrote to *The Times* complaining that he had been described as a brewer and saying that he had ceased brewing; and at a bucolic festival which occurred in the country shortly afterwards, ... some gentleman present suggested that Lord Hindlip (*née* Allsopp) was descended from one of the Plantagenet kings.... Now will the future Lord Hindlip [his son] prove a useful member of the Upper House in connection with commerce? Will he allude to the paternal butt? In all probability he will think a great deal of his Plantagenet ancestors, and the respected vendor of intoxicating liquor to whom he owes his title will be entirely forgotten.[153]

Bankers, unlike brewers, were usually in no great hurry to forget, and encourage others to forget, the source of their new wealth. However, precisely because they saw no social derogation in combining landownership and ennoblement

The first plate in Hogarth's famous series, *Marriage à la Mode*, published in 1745; on the right, two fathers (one of them a wealthy merchant or financier and the other a hard-up earl) assisted by a lawyer, huckster over the marriage settlement, while on the left the groom shows more interest in himself than in his bride, and the bride more interest in another lawyer than in her husband-to-be. Note the pictorial family tree held by the earl at the bottom right.

with their original calling, they too are an obstacle to sociological analysis. In Ireland, the link between landownership and banking was if anything closer than in England, particularly after 1756, when an act of the Irish parliament prohibited merchants from engaging in banking. Practically, and now legally, Irish banking was the near-monopoly of the landed class, who used their estates as the credit-base for their banking partnerships. For two generations, the Dawson family of Dawson's Grove, Co. Monaghan, combined banking in Dublin with ownership of the largest estate in Monaghan; in the second generation, Thomas Dawson married the daughter of a British earl, was raised to the Irish peerage in 1770, and did not retire from banking until 1771.[154] He retired by choice, not under social duress. In the early nineteenth century, at least two Irish peers, the 2nd Lord Ffrench and the 2nd Lord Newcomen, were active bankers. As for the famous banking family of Latouche: they were major landowners in at least three counties, might have had a peerage (or more than one, granted their genealogical ramifications) for the asking, and emphatically belonged to what used to be called 'the untitled aristocracy'.

Since class distinctions among the titled and untitled *élite* were fuzzy, and in some instances deliberately fudged, the interactions between peerage and beerage were probably more numerous than the bare statistics would suggest. But clear-cut cases of marriage between possessors of titles and possessors of commercial wealth are not easy to find. The most remarkable is the marriage of the 2nd Earl of Glengall in 1834 to the daughter and co-heiress of an army contractor and London docklands landlord. Other, earlier examples are the 4th Lord Carbery, who married in 1792 the daughter and heiress of a Bengal engineer,[155] and the Luttrells who, in their willingness to ally themselves with commercial wealth, as in other things, stand apart. Lord Irnham (created 1st Earl of Carhampton in 1785) married endogamically (i.e. within the titled and landed class). But the basis of his wife's fortune was, effectively, commercial. She was Judith Maria Lawes, daughter and eventual heiress of Sir Nicholas Lawes, Governor of Jamaica, 1718–22, and she inherited from him (many years later and after the expiration of a life-interest, c.1790) the plantations of Snow Hill, Swallow Field, etc, in the parish of St Andrews, Jamaica, comprising over 2,000 acres with all the negroes, slaves, etc, belonging to them. The Irnhams' son, Colonel Henry Lawes Luttrell, later 2nd Earl of Carhampton, married incontrovertibly outside his own caste (although he is not counted among the six peers of 1783 who had done so, since he did not inherit the family peerage until 1787). His wife, whom he married in 1776, was Jane, daughter of George Boyd, a Dublin merchant, who provided her with a very generous portion of £20,000. There is no reason to think that this was the cash-strapped Luttrell's principal motive for marrying her – and for marrying out of caste. It was noted at the time that Luttrell, though a notorious womaniser, had 'liked her for above three years, which I hope is a good omen for his constancy hereafter'.[156]

The already-mentioned Lord Conyngham would be a more striking example of marriage into the mercantile class but for the technical disqualification that, at the time of his marriage in 1744, he was a great landowner but neither a peer nor the heir to a peerage: he was created Baron Conyngham in 1753, Viscount Conyngham in 1756 and Earl Conyngham (just before his death) in 1781. The Conynghams had a seat and small estate at Slane, Co. Meath, and huge (if unproductive) estates in Co. Donegal. But through his mother Henry Conyngham had also inherited a seat and estate at Minster-in-Thanet, Kent, and property and other interests elsewhere in that county, notably in the ports of Sandwich and Ramsgate. This English base, and the partially commercial nature of his English interests, may explain Conyngham's unusual (for an Irish landed magnate) choice of marriage partner. His wife, Ellen Merrett, was the only daughter and heiress of one Solomon Merrett of St Olave's, Hart Street, London, a 'merchant', by his wife, Rebecca, daughter of Charles Savage, also of St Olave's, a 'packer'. From a cryptic reference in one of Conyngham's letters, it appears that her portion was £25,000. Following her father's death, c.1760, Conyngham also laid claim to 'the fortune left my wife' in the form of Merrett's London property and other assets, and of legacies from members of the Savage family. He made good his claim to a substantial house in Hammersmith and other house property, but some of Lady Conyngham's inheritance was thought to be 'out of my power' and was still the subject of litigation at the time of his death.[157]

Nevertheless, his enterprising and unusual marriage strategy would have yielded a satisfactory return if the £25,000, the real estate and whatever else was eventually extricated from 'the fortune left my wife', had been pure gain to Conyngham and his heirs and successors (who were his sisters' sons, his marriage having been childless). This, however, was not the case. The first offset to their gain was that Lady Conyngham lived to be 97, dying in 1816 and drawing from the Conyngham estate for some thirty-five years a jointure which cannot have been less than £1,000 a year. The second offset derived from the childlessness of the marriage. Because the Conynghams had no son, one component of Conyngham's Irish estates, the Limavady estate in Co. Londonderry, devolved at his death on Thomas Conolly of Castletown, who was the collateral male heir under a previous settlement. Since this estate must have been worth c.£40,000, subject to a mortgage for £15,000,[158] Conyngham lost more by producing no son than he gained from his marriage to the rich merchant's daughter.

When every allowance has been made for the imprecision of the statistics, it remains incontrovertible that the Conyngham-Merrett marriage was exceptional and that, in general, the pattern of marriage among Irish aristocrats was endogamic: 'Many young, noble heirs married daughters or close relatives of peers: [in 1783] 55 per cent of the matches analysed were of this kind.' This is hardly surprising, and also accords with the evidence for the contemporary British peerage.[159] Most of these marriage partners would have been known to each other from an early date, through kinship, parental friendship, exchanges

THE PURSUIT OF THE HEIRESS

of visits in town and country, etc, etc, and as they approached marriageable age they would have been thrown together ever more frequently in country society, 'Parliament winter' in Dublin and, in the case of the highest-ranking and/or richest, the London season. In 1774 one substantial country gentleman was chidden for his failure to give his daughters their chance in the well established

> [Dublin] Castle market, where there has been a greater number of the female sex [at] the Queen's Birthday [ball] than has been known for many years. The Castle, you must judge from thence, was extremely brilliant, and why would you not make it more so by the addition of those who, by their genteel education and behaviour (and the fortune[s] you intend them), add to the number?[160]

Marriages made in Dublin Castle were unlikely to be *mésalliances*.

Because marked disparity of rank and status was not a common occurrence among marriage partners at this level of society, it cannot have been a common element in the calculation of settlement provisions. Indeed, the remarks quoted earlier about the special difficulties encountered in the marriage market by ladies of rank without fortunes to match, suggest that rank alone counted for little. This also seems to have been true when the rank was the prospective husband's and the money the prospective wife's. In 1738, the 18th Lord Athenry proposed for the hand of Frances Ingoldsby, a modest Co. Limerick heiress (modest, that is, in fortune: there proved to be nothing modest about her behaviour). Since she was a minor, it fell to her guardians to respond to the proposal. As one of them reported to another: 'His chief recommendation was the ancient nobility of the family, but not one word of the estate. Our answer to him was that Miss Fanny did not want gentility and that we feared Lord Athenry's fortune … would not be sufficient to support his dignity and the dignity of the young lady.'[161]

The Rt Hon. Thomas and Lady Louisa Conolly; a pair of pastel portraits of c.1775 by Hugh Douglas Hamilton, reproduced from an Adam sale catalogue, 28 September 2005

One young lady who greatly out-ranked her husband was Lady Louisa Lennox, sister of an English duke, the 3rd Duke of Richmond, and wife of Thomas Conolly of Castletown, the only son of William and Lady Anne, and the great-nephew and heir of the self-made Speaker Conolly. The couple met because she was a sister of the Duchess of Leinster, and Thomas Conolly a friend and Co. Kildare neighbour of the Duchess's husband, the 1st Duke. In spite of the disparity of rank between them, Lady Louisa brought Conolly on their marriage in 1758 the same size of portion as her sister had brought the Duke of Leinster, £10,000. (As has been noted already, levels of portions were generally pre-determined by a previous settlement, and were not adjusted to take account of a particular marriage negotiation; also, it was usual to treat all daughters the same.) Nor was Conolly called upon to pay dearly for his high-ranking wife in terms of jointure: Lady Louisa's jointure was set at £2,500, which, though generous in relation to a portion of £10,000, was not as generous as the Duchess of Leinster's £3,000.[162] The widow of a commoner was presumably supposed to live more modestly than the widow of a duke. What is particularly significant about the example of Lady Louisa Conolly is that her high rank was English: if any cash was going for 'condescension', it is likely to have been paid by Irishmen or Irishwomen marrying into English high society.[163]

Such marriages, like marriages involving marked disparity of rank and status, were not usually made by members of the Irish aristocracy. But Lord Crosbie is a case in point: his intended of 1777 was the daughter of the notorious Lord George Sackville/Germain, and the granddaughter of an English duke; and in view of her Englishness and ducal descent, Lord Crosbie noted with surprise and gratification that she would bring him '£10,000, which indeed is more than I thought her fortune would be, for the daughters of these great families have seldom more than six'.[164] In the same period, the 1st Earl, later 1st Marquess, of Hertford, head of another great English family, was indeed offering only some £6,000 with each of his daughters.[165] This discrepancy may, however, be partly explained by the fact that there were six of them, whereas Diana Sackville had only one sister. It is interesting to note how Lord Hertford's daughters fared: one married the heir to a British dukedom, two married Irish earls, two married Irish commoners (the first of them decidedly a social inferior, and the second a 'poor' match), and another remained unmarried.[166] At least one of Lord Hertford's Irish sons-in-law, Lord Grandison, accepted very hard financial terms – a jointure of £2,000 a year, or 33.3 per cent per annum on the portion. Yet it is doubtful if these particular examples prove more than that Lord Crosbie, a provincial from remote Co. Kerry, was easily impressed by English rank, and that Lord Hertford had 'taste ... for nothing ... but to get money'.[167] The more usual pattern was that discount for rank was neither given nor asked, and the more typical example that of Lady Louisa Lennox and Thomas Conolly.

Lord George Sackville/Germain, later 1st Viscount Sackville, from an engraving in the *European Magazine* for 1785.

AUTHOR'S COLLECTION

Besides, it may not have been rank so much as political influence which rendered Lord George Sackville and Lord Hertford desirable to their Irish sons-in-law. Political influence is generally less definable than rank. But in the present instances it is capable of fairly precise definition: when Diana Sackville married Lord Crosbie, her father was Secretary of State for the American Colonies; and when two of Lord Hertford's daughters married Irishmen, in the years 1765–6, their father was Lord Lieutenant of Ireland. It might well be imagined that possession of the colonial secretaryship of state would have made Lord George Sackville a more desirable father-in-law to an American loyalist than to an Irishman. However, Lord George was a known intimate of the Lord Lieutenant of the day,[168] so that the marriage could reasonably have been expected to pay dividends in Irish political terms – which it actually did not. With the fall of Lord North's ministry in Great Britain, and the loss of the American colonies, Lord George Sackville became not only redundant but unemployable. His remaining influence was purely English, and was exerted on behalf of his other son-in-law, who was a member of the British parliament. Ironically, in view of Lord Crosbie's unconcealed glee back in 1777 that 'my marrying in this manner will mortify the narrow, envious people of Kerry', this other son-in-law, Henry Arthur Herbert of Muckruss, was another Kerryman, who presumably had met his wife through her sister.[169]

As Lord Lieutenant himself, Lord Hertford's political influence was directly applicable to Ireland. Indeed, one of the last acts of his lord lieutenancy was to recommend the second of his Irish sons-in-law (actually, without success) for an Irish peerage.[170] Moreover, his political influence in Ireland was not solely of an impermanent, official kind: he owned a very valuable estate round Lisburn, Co. Antrim, and controlled the parliamentary borough of Lisburn. His second Irish son-in-law, Robert Stewart (later 1st Marquess of Londonderry) was the one best situated in geographical terms to profit from Lord Hertford's influence as a great Irish landowner, for Stewart's own Irish property was in the adjoining county of Down ('Ardes' had been his abortive choice of title in 1766). Stewart's only son by this marriage, another Robert (later 2nd Marquess of Londonderry, but better known as Lord Castlereagh), was subsequently given charge of the Hertford 'political interests in this country'. Lord Castlereagh also profited from his Hertford ancestry in more general respects: in the post-Union period his career in British politics was significantly advanced by Hertford family influence – notably by the then Lady Hertford's influence with the Prince Regent.[171] The terms of the 1766 marriage settlement had been financially disadvantageous to the Stewarts. Not only was the separate maintenance of £300 and jointure of £1,000 which it provided for Lord Hertford's daughter high in relation to her portion; it was high in relation to the increased jointure of £3,000 provided at the same time for the elder Robert Stewart's mother, an heiress whose wealth had brought almost the whole Stewart estate into the family.[172] Moreover, in comparison to the size of their mother's portion, the £25,000 provided for the younger children (rising to a maximum of £100,000, should there be four daughters and no son and heir) can only be described as astronomical. Yet, from the political point of view, the marriage was to prove a resounding triumph.

Actually, the ill-effects of the generous provision made for Lord Hertford's daughter and her children were not felt by the Stewarts, as she died young, in 1770, soon after the birth of Lord Castlereagh, who was the only child of the marriage. This left her widowed husband free to marry again, which he did in 1775. His choice of second wife, and the again disadvantageous financial terms which he made, suggest that he was consciously pursuing political advantage. His wife was the Hon. Frances Pratt, daughter of the 1st Lord Camden, an ex-Lord Chancellor of England; her portion was a mere £5,000, and her jointure £1,000 (ultimately increased by £2,500 from Stewart sources); their eldest (and only surviving) son was to have £400 a year settled on him (and ultimately received a great deal more); and their younger children, who in the end amounted to seven daughters, were to have the sum of £15,000 divided among them (and ultimately received portions of £5,000 each).[173]

This provision for the children of the second marriage was of course exclusive of and additional to the allowance which had to be paid to their half-brother, Lord Castlereagh. He came of age in 1790, and an annuity of £5,000 a year was settled on him at his marriage in 1794. It is some measure of the weight of the financial burden which Stewart had thus shouldered, that the rental of his entire Co. Down estate was only £6,500 a year in 1790, and that other land in family possession at the time of the marriage settlements of 1766 and 1775 had a rental of barely £1,000 by that date. In 1779, however, either his father or he had somehow raised enough money to acquire a long leasehold estate in Co. Londonderry. The income from this estate, £2,500 in 1791 and £4,500 in 1795, and the fact that the income from his other estates was also rising rapidly, saved him from disaster. As things were, sheer weight of settlement charges (not, incidentally, the legendary cost of the Co. Down election of 1790, which seems to have been only a little over £11,500 to him), forced him to make unseemly sacrifices. These included the raising of £1,950 in 1791–2 by the sale of family portraits.[174]

Although the second marriage was much costlier than the first, it was an even more striking political success. Lord Camden was recalled to political life in 1784, and sat in Pitt's Cabinet until his death in 1794. He took on the role of political mentor to his step-grandson, the young Lord Castlereagh, and in 1790 he obtained for the elder Robert Stewart what Lord Hertford had failed to obtain in 1766, an Irish peerage. In 1795, Lord Camden's son and successor, the 2nd Earl Camden, was appointed Lord Lieutenant of Ireland, and in 1798 he made Lord Castlereagh his acting Chief Secretary; substantive rank was conferred on Castlereagh by Camden's successor at the beginning of 1799. Though his subsequent achievements are fairly to be attributed to his own ability, integrity and hard work, there can be little doubt that the foundation of his political career was laid by his father's marriage connections. Moreover, insufficient account has been taken of the debt he owed his father for what the 1st Marquess of Londonderry himself described as 'the discretion which has always marked my conduct in the management of family affairs'.[175] In 1816, on the eve of another major purchase of land, Lord Londonderry's financial situation was un-aristocratically sound: the total rental income of the family estates was over £28,000, of which land producing £11,000 a year had been acquired by him; all his children had been satisfactorily married and provided for – his daughters' portions had even been paid; and his debts amounted to no more than £32,000, all but £10,000 of which could be attributed to land purchases since the previous family settlement of 1794. In 1816, therefore, both Lord Londonderry and Lord Castlereagh could contemplate more than the outcome of the Congress of Vienna with satisfaction.

The example of the Londonderrys is striking, but isolated. It is difficult to think of another aristocratic Irish family which played the marriage market by making great financial sacrifices for great non-financial gains. The 2nd Earl of Lucan undoubtedly gained a good deal, in terms of Co. Mayo political patronage, from the fact that his sister was married to the 2nd Earl Spencer, Home Secretary (with overall responsibility for Ireland), 1806–7,[176] but this marriage connection lay in the opposite direction – it was between an Irish lady and a British lord – and, in any case, the details of the financial arrangements underpropping it have not so far been ascertained. A closer parallel with the Stewarts is to be found in the marriage in 1743 of the Hon. John Ponsonby, second son of the 1st Earl of Bessborough (an Irish earl), with a daughter of the then Lord Lieutenant, the 3rd Duke of Devonshire (an English duke). But this connection, though it obliged Lord Bessborough to go to great expense in endowing John Ponsonby's cadet line,[177] was not the first between the Bessborough and the Devonshire families; and arguably it was not decisive in conferring on the former the benefit of most of the latter's political influence in Ireland.

The family which most resembles the Stewarts is the very differently circumstanced Cobbe family of Newbridge, Donabate, Co. Dublin.[178] Its founder in Ireland was the Rev. Charles Cobbe (1686–1765), who came over as a viceregal chaplain in 1718, was archbishop of Dublin, 1743–65, and built Newbridge, c.1747, as a family not an episcopal seat. His ambitions to found an Irish dynasty became focused on his one surviving son, Thomas Cobbe (1733–1814), who made a politically promising marriage in 1755 to Lady Elizabeth Beresford, sister of the increasingly powerful 2nd Earl of Tyrone. She brought him a marriage portion of £6,000 which – though substantial – was dwarfed by the settlement which the Archbishop made on the young couple. Being a widower, almost seventy years of age and in enjoyment of two palaces and an income of between £7,000 and £10,000 a year as archbishop of Dublin, he could afford to be generous. So he made over to the trustees of the marriage settlement Newbridge House and estate, his other privately owned estates, and a large lump sum of £18,000.[179] His object, plainly, was to harness the Beresford family's political influence to the advancement of the Cobbes; and in 1767, two years after the Archbishop's death, Thomas Cobbe was described as 'a man of fortune, … married into the Tyrone family…, [and] seeking a peerage'.[180] At this point, however, the resemblance to the Stewarts ceases. No peerage was forthcoming; Thomas Cobbe and his only son were extravagant and ran into debt (partly as a result of supporting the Beresford political interest in the nearby borough of Swords, Co. Dublin); and by the 1790s the Cobbes were hardly rich enough to support a peerage if one had been offered.

The case of the Cobbes helps to highlight what was remarkable about the Stewarts. Not many families produced three generations of financially astute men – Lord Londonderry's father, Lord Londonderry himself, and his two sons. Not many dynasts became widowers in time to make a second marriage which was as advantageous as their first. Not many fathers were prepared to make financial sacrifices for their children of the magnitude made by Lord Londonderry (and Archbishop Cobbe). And not many families remained as happily united as the Stewarts,[181] in spite of the interposition of half-blood. It is therefore permissible to regard Lord Londonderry's two wives as unique examples of what can only be called the 'political heiress'. This does not mean that other husbands did not make more modest gains, in terms of political influence, out of their marriages, or that political influence did not weigh something in the scale of other marriage settlements. For example, at least one more of Lord Hertford's Irish sons-in-law derived significant political advantage from the marriage connection with him.[182] So it is necessary to interpret 'collateral calculation' widely and to include within it a variety of considerations of a non-financial kind.

THREE

The superior bargaining power of the heiress

What has so far been suggested is that the fortunes possessed by the great majority of brides were fortunes in the special marriage-settlement sense, not the general sense, of that word. According to the complex rules of the marriage-settlement game, value would ultimately have to be given for the fortunes thus received, and usually given in the form of younger children's portions and widow's jointures. If subsequent developments rendered the settlement obsolete and necessitated an adjustment of the arithmetic, it was likely to be the bridegroom's family which was the loser; and in some cases the bridegroom's family was actually the loser from the outset, because its objective in making the marriage was, not fortune, but political connection or some other non-financial benefit.

While all this helps to clarify what an heiress (in the conventional, financial sense of the word) was not, no definition has as yet been offered of what such an heiress was. The only meaningful definition is, surely, that she was a bride who brought with her assets which far outweighed any return that her husband's family was obliged to make. In other words, the term, like the heiress herself, is to be approached warily. No means test had to be passed to qualify as one; the only common denominator among heiresses was that they had no brother; and it might well be more advantageous to marry an ordinarily well portioned girl than the heiress of a small squire or the heiress to a large but heavily encumbered estate. For example, Catherine and Frances Ingoldsby, daughters and co-heiresses of the late Henry Ingoldsby of Carton, Co. Kildare, and Ballybricken, Co. Limerick, who had died young and in embarrassed circumstances in 1730, were each of them worth less than a very well portioned woman with £20,000 in cash. (Because the younger co-heiress, Frances, was the victim of a now famous abduction in 1743, her financial circumstances will be discussed in greater detail later in this chapter.) Likewise, *The Complete Peerage* describes Jane, Countess of Belvedere, as 'the daughter and eventually sole heiress' of an obscure Co. Dublin clergyman. It is unlikely that her inheritance amounted to much, and more than likely that she invented this form of words herself, as some sort of justification for the disproportionately lavish provision made for her by Lord Belvedere. The

THE SUPERIOR BARGAINING POWER OF THE HEIRESS

most important, single fact about the term 'heiress' is that it is relative, and must be defined in relation to the extent of her father's wealth and also in relation to the extent of her husband's sacrifices. Subjected to this rigorous assay, many heiresses that glister prove not to be gold.

To begin with, only brides of eldest sons are in the running; for, if a younger son married an heiress or an unusually well portioned girl, the result would almost certainly be that his father would be obliged to increase his portion accordingly or deviate from the principle of primogeniture – as happened in the already-quoted instance of the Hon. John Ponsonby in 1743. The eldest son, on the other hand, was due to inherit all or almost all his father's estate in any case; so that if he married an heiress, the most his father could be expected to do was make a particularly generous provision for him during the father's own lifetime. However, this could well be more than the father was prepared for. During the marriage negotiations of 1737, Lord Egmont appears to have declined to accept £8,000 of his daughter-in-law's very large portion of £20,000 because the consequence would have been a commensurate increase in the present maintenance he was called upon to provide for the newly-weds.[183] Instead, he presumably 'applied' the £8,000 'to the settlement'. Few fathers were as selfless in their dynastic planning as Lord Londonderry and Archbishop Cobbe.

Furthermore, if the fathers of only averagely portioned girls approached the question of their matrimonial future in the calculating spirit of a Lord Grandison, it was not to be expected that the fathers, trustees or guardians of known heiresses would have failed to exploit the full potential of their strong bargaining position. There were, of course, exceptions. Lord Londonderry's father had allegedly married his heiress-wife, Mary Cowan (in 1737) 'before she was aware of what man or money was',[184] and had had easy access to her because they were first cousins, because her half-brother and the source of her inheritance suddenly died, and because it had probably not been her half-brother's intention that she should inherit all his wealth. Cousinhood, too, facilitated a family-arranged match in 1769 between Caroline Fitzgerald, granddaughter and heiress to the Co. Cork estate of the 4th Lord Kingston (of the first creation), and Robert King, Lord Kingsborough, son and heir of the 1st Lord Kingston (of the second creation); the purpose and effect of the match was to set the clock back and reunite the Cork estate to the Kingston title. However, cousinhood notwithstanding, Caroline Fitzgerald retained in her own hands control of her own estate, which did not merge with the Kingston estates when her son succeeded as 3rd Earl of Kingston in 1799, nor till she died in 1823.[185]

Caroline Fitzgerald, Countess of Kingston, heiress-wife of the 2nd Earl; from an engraving published in *La belle Assemblée* for 1810

AUTHOR'S COLLECTION

In circumstances more usual than the Stewart-Cowan marriage, plenty of legal means existed to protect the interests of the bride.[186] When the immensely rich, 73-year-old banker, Thomas Coutts, married the Irish-born, 37-year-old comedy-actress, Harriot Mellon, in January 1815, the terms of the settlement show

55

what safeguards could be provided against the general legal presumption that a married woman's property belonged to her husband:

> The said Harriot Mellon, being now possessed in her own right of certain real, copyhold and leasehold estates and personal property in the counties of Essex and Middlesex and at Cheltenham in Gloucestershire, and of stock in various public stocks or funds in her own name, jewels, silver, plate and securities for money and money in the hands of her bankers in London, ... shall still continue to hold and enjoy the same, and it is hereby agreed between the parties that all the property of the said Harriot Mellon aforesaid shall be always and entirely at her own sole disposal and command the same as if she was still unmarried; and that she may, as often as she pleases to change the securities, ... sell and dispose of the same and convey the same to purchasers and reinvest the money in any manner she pleases without any consent or concurrence being necessary or required from her husband.[187]

Almost all this property and these assets had been given to Miss Mellon by the adoring Coutts during the ten years which preceded their marriage. His objective in the settlement was to establish her independent right to them and, in the probable event of his pre-deceasing her, to secure them against any possible claim on the part of his three daughters by his first marriage.[188] So this was an exceptional and perhaps one-off situation. However, in a situation where the bride was genuinely possessed of inherited wealth in her own right, her marriage settlement would not be less foolproof in protecting her interests.

The case of Harriot Mellon demonstrates this too. Her marriage to Coutts was a resounding success. Her devotion to him and, later, to his memory, showed that his characteristically good judgment had not failed him when he fell in love with her and – more particularly – when he made a will leaving her the disposal of his entire fortune at his death in 1822. She was now the richest woman in the United Kingdom. Not surprisingly, after her years of domestic seclusion with the aged Coutts, she began to have a good time, and took up with a titled toyboy, the 9th Duke of St Albans (1801–49), whom she married in 1827. The Duke was not well off, and she undoubtedly showered cash and other presents upon him. But she was no more an infatuated old fool than her own benefactor, Coutts, had been. The Coutts fortune remained under her own exclusive control, and altogether independent of her second husband. At her death in 1837, she left the latter a life interest in their London house and out-of-town villa and £10,000 a year for his life. Almost all the rest of her Coutts inheritance, amounting to a reputed £1,800,000, she left to the descendant of Coutts who she (sensibly) decided was worthiest of him and most likely to use the fortune wisely. Interestingly, she chose another woman, Coutts's granddaughter, Angela Burdett-Coutts.[189]

It was not unheard-of for an heiress's fortune to be settled, in the event of her marriage proving childless, on the surviving partner in the marriage. But it was

A Sketch at St ALBANS or Shaving the new maid DUTCHESS!!!

much more usual for the remainder in fee (as it was called) to be settled on the heiress herself, with 'contingent remainders' either to specified members of her own family or to whomsoever she should appoint.[190] Thus, Hester Coghill, heiress to the Coghill estates in counties Dublin, Kildare, Meath and Tipperary, had inherited them on the basis that, unless she had children, they would revert to the descendants of a Coghill cousin. In 1737 she married the one and only Earl of Charleville, by whom she had no children and after whose death in 1764 she 'reserved to herself the sole power over all her real and personal estates'. She next contracted a love match with a certain Capt. John Mayne, whom she met at the viceregal court in Dublin and who was 'a peculiar favourite with the ladies'. This marriage, too, proved childless, and there was no possibility of her having children at the age she was when she made it. Mayne was supposed to have 'got a large fortune with this lady'; and, like Lord Charleville before him, was joined with her in all leases of and other legal acts affecting her estates. But this derived simply from the legal convention that a married woman could not dispose of property in her own name alone. Her will, which she made in 1784, revealed the true situation. It made a life-provision for her husband if he survived her (in the event he died in 1785 and she in 1789), but recited that her estates had long since been settled on her right heirs, 'notwithstanding my coverture and as if I were sole and unmarried'.[191]

Harriot Mellon being 'shaved' (or fleeced) by her second husband, the 26-year-old Duke of St Albans; from a contemporary caricature of June 1827 (the date of their marriage). The head on the wig-stand on the left is that of Thomas Coutts; the double portrait above the Duke is of his ancestor Charles II and Nell Gwyn. The masked clerical figure on the right must be the Duke's uncle, the Rev. Lord Frederick Beauclerk.

COURTESY OF MR AND MRS J.A.D. NESBITT

THE PURSUIT OF THE HEIRESS

Less specific detail is available for the basis on which the estate of an earlier heiress, Mary, daughter of Sir John Williams of Minster-in-Thanet, Kent, was settled. But the subsequent descent of the Williams estate shows that it was well secured against unforeseen and unwelcome contingencies. Mary Williams's first marriage, which took place in 1690, was to John Petty, Lord Shelburne, a wealthy Irish peer with a vast estate in Co. Kerry. In spite of this, the terms of the settlement favoured the heiress. The marriage was childless, Lord Shelburne died young in 1696, and later in the same year Lady Shelburne married another Irishman, Brigadier Henry Conyngham. Though the Shelburne estate remained saddled with the payment of a jointure to her, and though she continued, as was the fashion of the day, to use her first husband's title, this young widow was free to carry the Williams estate into the Conyngham family.[192] Brigadier Conyngham and she had three children: Williams (invariably misspelt as 'William'), their heir, who succeeded to the Conyngham estates after his father's death in the battle of Almanza in 1706 and to the Williams estate after Lady Shelburne's death in 1710; Henry (the already-mentioned Lord Conyngham), who succeeded to both estates in 1738 when Williams died in that year without surviving issue; and Mary, wife of Francis Burton of Buncraggy, whose two sons succeeded Lord Conyngham in different parts of the combined inheritance in 1781 and the elder of them to the barony of Conyngham. In 1816 a grandson of Brigadier Conyngham and Lady Shelburne was created Marquess Conyngham. He later, in recognition of the part the Williams inheritance had played in his rise, chose Minster as his title when made a peer of the United Kingdom in 1821.

Another Kentish heiress who retained full control of her own estate was 'Jane Roberts..., sole heiress of Sir Walter Roberts [6th Bt] of Glassenbury'. According to the early nineteenth-century Ulster King-of-Arms, Sir William Betham, writing in 1807, Jane Roberts had 'no issue or near relative', so that, when she 'accidentally heard that the arms of Roberts had been painted on a carriage ordered by a[n Irish] gentleman of that name', Thomas Roberts (1736–1817), a banker and small landowner in Cork, she 'commenced a correspondence, the result of which was that she bequeathed the estate to his family'. This sounds a little far-fetched, although it is more plausible than the version given by Betham's still-more-inventive successor, Sir John Bernard Burke, according to which the two Robertses had bumped into each other at an inn.[193] The important fact is that Jane Roberts did have a 'near relative', her husband, the 3rd Duke of St Albans, whom she had married in 1752, and whom she pre-deceased in 1776. The couple had, indeed, 'no issue'. But the Duke is delicately described by *The Complete Peerage* as dying in 1786 '*s.p. legit.*' (without legitimate children) – a form of words which generally imports that he had had some illegitimate ones. From this it is permissible to infer that the marriage had not perhaps been a happy one, and indeed to suggest that Thomas Roberts was the very accident which the Duchess had been waiting to happen. By making him her heir she asserted her independence of, and also punished, the errant Duke.

THE SUPERIOR BARGAINING POWER OF THE HEIRESS

Something similar occurred in the more important English instance (which also had an Irish sequel)[194] of Isabella, Duchess of Manchester. In 1723, when the 2nd Duke of Manchester married her, she was co-heiress apparent to her father, the 2nd Duke of Montagu. The marriage was dynastically appropriate, because both bride and groom were Montagus, and it seems to have been a love-match too (though it did not remain so). Disaster followed from the Manchesters' point of view. The marriage was childless, the Duke of Manchester died young in 1739, and the widowed Duchess was at liberty to redeploy her half of her father's estate in her next marriage settlement. The Manchester family held on to her marriage portion, which was probably as token as the portions of great heiresses usually were, and was saddled with a jointure of £2,000 a year (charged on a rental of no more than c.£4,000) for the next forty-seven years.[195]

In this instance, there had at least been a good chance that the Manchesters would have children to inherit the Duchess's estate: in other instances, the estates/fortunes of heiresses of child-bearing age remained unsettled when they married a husband of similar years. This happened in the case of the already-mentioned Sir Samuel Hutchinson,[196] who had married in 1801 the daughter and co-heiress of a well-known attorney and land agent, John Hatch (d.1797), of Lissen Hall, Co. Dublin, and Harcourt Street, Dublin City. In 1824, when negotiations were afoot for the marriage of the Hutchinsons' only son to a daughter of the Hon. Francis Hely-Hutchinson, the unsettled status of Lady Hutchinson's Hatch property in Co. Dublin was something of a stumbling-block, since it was 'by far the most considerable in point of value' of the different Hutchinson estates (which had a combined rental of c.£10,000 a year). Francis Hely-Hutchinson fretted that 'Lady Hutchinson is most likely to survive her husband, and ... [if] this estate of hers should remain unsettled, ... she might choose to give it to her daughter instead of her son'. However, his brother, Lord Hutchinson, was of the view that 'The mother will never agree to put that out of her power over which she has now the perfect dominion.... Women generally speaking on such subjects are a great deal more tenacious than men.'[197] Lord Hutchinson, a worldly-wise and cynical old bachelor, clearly did not subscribe to the view that 'Women having power is in general of little avail'.

Mary Cairnes, Lady Blayney (c.1703–1790), a much greater heiress than Lady Hutchinson, and a much more amiable individual, took the opposite view of having 'perfect dominion' over her estate: she could not wait to put her 'very easie [*sic*] fortune' out of her own power. In 1743, she had inherited on the death

General the Hon. John Hely-Hutchinson (1757–1832) created Baron Hutchinson in 1801, succeeded as 2nd Earl of Donoughmore in 1825; from an engraving of 1809 after a portrait by Thomas Phillips.

AUTHOR'S COLLECTION

of her uncle, Sir Henry Cairnes, 2nd Bt, an extensive landed property comprising the town and neighbourhood of Monaghan, Co. Monaghan. This had been bought in 1696 by another uncle, William Cairnes (d.1706), who had settled it on his brothers, Alexander and Henry, and their issue male, in failure of which it was to pass to their issue female. Alexander Cairnes (1665–1732), the eldest brother, who was created a baronet in 1708 and flourished as a banker in London until the South Sea Bubble burst, had one short-lived son and a daughter, Mary Cairnes, Lady Blayney. At Sir Alexander's death in 1732, the estate (and the baronetcy) passed to the youngest brother, Henry, who died childless in 1743. Under the settlement made by William Cairnes, Lady Blayney, who now inherited the Monaghan estate, was 'entirely my own mistress' and had it 'in my power to cut off the entail and give it to whom I pleased'. Her first husband, the 7th Lord Blayney, was long dead and she had had no children by him. Her second husband, Colonel John Murray, by whom she had had five daughters (later reduced by death to four), 'was in so declining a state of health [in 1743] that he was not likely to live'. She herself was still young enough to marry again and perhaps have a son. However, she decided to enter into a deed by which she would 'oblige myself to settle my estate on my children' by Colonel Murray. This still left her 'as rich as if it [the estate] was in my own power, only I shall not be so much in the way of doing an indiscreet thing'.[198]

Lady Blayney was unusual among heiresses in being exposed to the risk of indiscretion: most were well protected in this respect either by a previous settlement or by the vigilance of parents or guardians. A good example of parental vigilance (carried to the point of officiousness), and more generally of the strong bargaining position of the heiress, is the to-ing and fro-ing between 1765 and 1769 over the marriage of Elizabeth Monck. She was the only daughter of Henry Monck of Charleville, Bray, Co. Wicklow, the by-passed heiress to the Monck patrimonial property, and the heiress-apparent to her father's large and growing personal estate. Her prospective husband, the 2nd Earl of Tyrone, was an ostentatiously eligible young man. He was politically influential, held the ancient barony of La Poer (to which, admittedly, his right was dubious), and had a rental of some £8,000 a year, subject to debts of some £40,000. On her side, Miss Monck had a portion of £8,000, and expectations, after the death of both her parents, of £32,000 more (only half of it actually guaranteed to her by previous settlements). Significantly, it was not Lord Tyrone, but Henry Monck, who was unenthusiastic about the proposed match: 'Though the fortune the young people may probably have be sufficiently ample, yet [they] are not at present circumstanced for each other, and [it would be] difficult to accommodate the plan for a settlement to the satisfaction of both parties.' Accordingly, he broke off negotiations.

They were renewed, this time successfully, four years later, in 1769. But Monck was still grudging in his approval. He endeavoured to bind Lord Tyrone to a plan of economy, under which the latter would have reduced both his capital debt and the rate of interest payable on it, deferred and circumscribed the

THE SUPERIOR BARGAINING POWER OF THE HEIRESS

building of his mansion at Curraghmore, Co. Waterford, and in the meantime taken up his abode with his in-laws, the Moncks. When Lord Tyrone evaded these intrusive stipulations, Monck was grieved:

> Now, alas, ... my Lord is to pay at the rate of five per cent or six per cent on the £40,000, besides what other money he may have borrowed lately, which would be the difference of more than £2,000 a year, besides the loss of the pleasure of living in harmony with a virtuous, discreet and good-natured couple; and then the money that periodically comes in for the wood, might be applied to make bricks, buying up cut-stone and timber as such materials offered cheap.... A fine, elegant house [at Curraghmore] of eleven windows in front would not cost above £10,000, with the old materials and the new procured in the above prudent way; and the impatience to be at it to put them together would prompt the young people, when they come to their full fortune, to live genteely, but prudently, so as sooner to effect the building, the habit of which economy may be of great advantage.[199]

It is not hard to see how Monck amassed sufficient money to make his daughter a very considerable heiress.

In the end, her inheritance, including her original portion, seems to have amounted to little less than £110,000, plus some property of unspecified value.[200] However, the maximum which she had to offer, present and future, in 1769 was £40,000 – which was no more than Lord Tyrone's rental income over a five-year period, and the exact amount needed to free that rental income from all the then encumbrances. It is a striking illustration of the bargaining position

Curraghmore, Co. Waterford: a pen, ink and wash drawing of c.1800 showing the house as built in the late 1760s. The anonymous artist has portrayed the garden front (half hidden by trees); the entrance front, with its famous forecourt, was wider and probably did contain more than the eleven windows recommended by Monck. For a fuller description of this picture and of Curraghmore, see W. Laffan (ed.), *Painting Ireland: Topographical Views from Glin Castle* (Churchill House Press, Tralee, 2006), pp.26–7.

COLLECTION OF
THE KNIGHT OF GLIN

of heiresses that Monck, even though he did not press his reservations to the point of imposing co-habitation 'with a virtuous, discreet and good-natured couple' on Lord Tyrone, clearly did not think him much of a match. However, for all his moaning and interference, Monck was not a hard bargainer: the generality of heiresses were better protected than Lady Tyrone, and their husbands made to pay more dearly for them than Lord Tyrone.

In view of the publicity given to the practice of heiress-abduction, particularly in the writings of Sir Jonah Barrington and J.A. Froude,[201] it is necessary to advert to protection in the physical as opposed to the legal sense of the word. A recent study of 'The Abduction of Women of Fortune in Eighteenth-Century Ireland'[202] suggests that Ireland's evil reputation in this regard was not altogether undeserved. It was not for want of legislation or even for want of law-enforcement (though this latter could be patchy and half-hearted) that the practice remained prevalent, particularly in Dublin City and County, Co. Galway and in parts of south Leinster and most of Munster:[203] the problem was, rather, the reluctance of victims to prosecute their abductors. Since the motive behind most abductions was economic, it is not surprising that throughout the eighteenth century more than 50 per cent of abductees belonged to the gentry – almost always the lesser gentry – class. About 27 per cent of abductors also came from this class, although this percentage dropped considerably in the last four decades of the century. Sir James Cotter, a baronet, and Sir Henry Hayes, a knight, who abducted rich women in 1718 and 1797 respectively, are the only abductors who can loosely be described as aristocratic. Four or five of the victims can also be so described.

Of these last, the most aristocratic was Miss Charlotte Newcomen of Carrigglas, Co. Longford, whose abduction was unsuccessfully attempted by an aspiring suitor in 1772. Miss Newcomen belonged to an ancient baronetal family in Longford; her estate in the county was supposed to be producing between £4,000 and £5,000 a year;[204] she was engaged at the time of the abduction to, and subsequently married, William Gleadowe of Killester, Co. Dublin, a prominent Dublin banker, who was created a baronet in 1791; and she herself was created a peeress in 1800.[205] Moreover, two leading local aristocrats feature prominently in the tale, as friends and protectors of the victim – the 5th Earl of Granard, and the 1st Lord Annaly (who was also lord chief justice of the King's Bench). Of the abductor, little seems to be known, except that he was called Thomas Johnston, was a member of the local gentry, and had just finished his studies at Trinity College, Dublin.

The abduction took place from a house in Longford town, whither Miss Newcomen had been brought for safety and where she was staying with friends called Webster.

> Miss Newcomen ... made all the resistance that woman could do. She was dragged downstairs. On the first flight Miss Webster met her and caught her in her arms; then both held fast by the banister of the stair. Johnston, they say, cried out 'Break their arms!' ... William Edwards, on a horse of Mr Robert

THE SUPERIOR BARGAINING POWER OF THE HEIRESS

Featherstone's with a pillion behind him, stood near Mr Webster's doorway, ready to receive her. As Johnston came out of the door, a Miss Cornwell, niece to Mr Webster, who lived next door, struck him on the head with an iron pin which fastened his window. He raised his sword, looked about, but said nothing....

The poor soul [Miss Newcomen] ... scratched Johnston's face, cuffed Edwards, tore his hair, and kept herself so stiff by the help of an iron that was to the pillion, that they could not get her fixed to the horse, though they ... dragged [her] barefoot through a street as dirty as possible, and in their attempts to put her on horseback used her with as much roughness and as little delicacy as if she had been a common hussy. On seeing Mr Webster, she held out her arms and begged for assistance ... Mr Webster ... fired, and Johnston fell on his knees. Owen Dougherty at that instant would have stabbed Mr Webster with a sword, but before he made good his thrust, Mr Thomas Webster saved his father by shooting him with a blunderbuss ...

They were pulling Miss N. on horseback when the shots went off. The horse started, and she fell.... Although the street was full of men and women who heard her cry, no one had mercy on her but ... [a] poor woman, who stuck by her and endeavoured to keep down her petticoats, for which good office she was knocked down, but still persisted. Johnston was mortally wounded in the breast.... The clergyman ... asked him, had he any encouragement from Miss N., and why he would undertake so rash an action. He said villainy, ambition and bad advice had prompted him to it (as her estate lay amongst his friends)...; that he deserved his fate and had no one to blame but himself.

For all the oddities of this account (written by a female friend of Miss Newcomen), and its firm grasp of inessentials, the circumstantial details which it provides only underline the atrociousness of the crime.

For present purposes, the more important consideration is its pointlessness. As a very considerable heiress, Charlotte Newcomen was well protected by a family settlement and by trustees. She seems also to have been a sensible young woman, who was fully aware of the premium she could command in the marriage market. Earlier in the year of the abduction, her trustees had rejected a proposal made on behalf of the fairly eligible heir to a Co. Westmeath estate; the reason given was that 'the settlement Mr Smyth [of Barbavilla] proposed to give to his son was not agreeable to Miss Newcomen or her friends, to whom Miss Newcomen had left it'.[206] It may well be that the real reason was the attachment she had formed to William Gleadowe. Even so, it does not sound as if Gleadowe was going to find her easy prey. Nor would Thomas Johnston have done so, had he succeeded in abducting her. She was spirited as well as sensible, unlikely to acquiesce for long in a forced marriage, and too rich for her chances of making a subsequent, more suitable marriage to be seriously imperilled by abduction or even rape. Clearly, Johnston had acted on very 'bad advice' indeed.

Two other *causes célèbres*, the first of which resembles that of Miss Newcomen, are the murder of Miss Mary Anne Knox of Prehen, Londonderry, shot 'in the side, below her stays' by John Macnaghten of Benvarden, Co. Antrim, in 1761; and the abduction in 1797 of Miss Mary Pike, a Cork Quakeress with a fortune of £20,000 (some said £80,000), by a Co. Cork knight of mercantile Cork City background, Sir Henry Hayes. Both perpetrators were tried and convicted. Macnaghten (best-known as 'half-hanged Macnaghten') was executed; Sir Henry Hayes was sentenced to death, but the sentence was commuted to transportation because, in the view of Lord Chancellor Clare, the trial judge entertained 'a silly doubt ... on a point of law'. Macnaghten, who claimed to be precontracted to Miss Knox, may have shot her in mistake for her father, towards whom his feelings were less tender; and Hayes's failure actually to rape Miss Pike was variously attributed to gentlemanly finer feelings and to the fact that 'the cock would not fight'.[207] Whatever the details, none of the protagonists belonged, strictly speaking, to the aristocracy, though the Knoxes did to the major gentry. Miss Knox's father, Andrew, was a county MP and, although she was not an heiress, her fortune of £6,000 put her on a par with the daughter of many a contemporary peer. Miss Pike may or may not have been an heiress but, granted the size of her fortune, this is a technicality.

Other cases involving women with distinguished connections and/or ample fortunes include that of Miss Frances Ingoldsby in 1743. She was co-heiress with her sister to their late father's embarrassed and depleted estate in Co. Limerick, each sister receiving as her share a portion of £3,000 (which may have been more than could be raised off the remaining property) and land with a rental of £870 a year. Frances Ingoldsby's abductor, Hugh Fitzjohn Massy, though a landless younger son, was as well connected as she was; and other features of the case suggest that she was no great acquisition in personal terms and more than acquiescent in her own abduction.[208] Moreover, those with long memories would have been struck by the irony of her case: thirty years earlier, in 1709, during the heyday of her family's prosperity and influence, when her grandfather, General Sir Richard Ingoldsby, was actually one of the lords justices of Ireland, he had

> committed a rape on the body of Miss Hawkins, the King-at Arms' daughter, which she swore before Judge Coote.... Her father was going over to England to lay the matter before the Queen, but he now says 'twas a false report...; which some think owing to a good round sum.[209]

Obviously, the 'good round sum' had been paid him in hush-money by General Ingoldsby.

A case of abduction which took place after Frances Ingoldsby's, in 1777, involved a thirteen-year-old girl called Mary Wax, whose fortune – of allegedly £30,000–£40,000 – was much larger than Frances Ingoldsby's and certainly of a size to place her among the more significant heiresses. Her abductor, Samuel Phillips, sounds like a member of at least the minor gentry, since he is described as 'of Foyle, Co. Kilkenny'. But this episode is shrouded in ambiguity. Phillips was a distant cousin of Miss Wax; the upshot seems to have been a marriage, or at any rate a betrothal; and it does not look like a straight case of abduction.[210] Another essentially family affair was the abduction of the already-mentioned Lady Mary King,[211] daughter of the 2nd Earl of Kingston, in 1797. This took place under circumstances peculiar to that most extraordinary family; and she was not an heiress.

A case too celebrated to be passed over in silence, but really a one-off and not entirely relevant to the present discussion, is that of Elizabeth Lady Cathcart (c.1691–1789).[212] Though undoubtedly an aristocrat, she was the widow of a Scottish, not an Irish, peer; her wealth, deriving mainly from property in Hertfordshire and the City of London, was English; being mostly in the form of an income for life (of £1,600–£1,800 a year)[213], it made her a rich woman, but not actually an heiress; and although her fourth husband was an Irishman, Colonel Hugh Maguire (c.1710–1766), they were not married in Ireland nor did she have anything to do with Ireland until he carried her off there by stratagem and force in October 1746. She is, incidentally, the only abductee in the sample who was already married to her abductor.

From 1746 to 1754, she seems to have lived, as an ostensibly free woman and as the hostess at Maguire's entertainments, in a house at Carra, near Magheraveely, Co. Fermanagh. From then until his death in 1766, she appears to have been re-located to Castle Nugent near Edgeworthstown, Co. Longford, a house and estate which he acquired out of the surplus from her income; and for at least the latter part of the time she lived there, she seems actually to have been imprisoned in an attic room (probably as a means of coercing her into divulging the whereabouts of her jewellery). Granted the then legal presumption that a woman's property vested in her husband in the absence of specific provisions to the contrary, and granted the situation of durance and duress in which she found herself, it is hardly surprising that he made free not only with her income but with her capital of over £8,000. On the other hand, she is supposed to have entered into a settlement of her property in 1745, prior to her marriage, whereby she vested it in trustees of her own appointing and with the proviso that it was to be 'in no wise subject to the debts, or to be under the power or at the disposal, of' Maguire.[214] In other words, the Lady Cathcart saga becomes a test case of the truth or otherwise of the argument that heiresses and other women of fortune were fully protected by law long before 1872.

What in fact happened is that the settlement of 1745 contained a fatal let-out clause: the trust established by it was 'for her separate use, [but] with a power of disposal and appointment reserved to herself'.[215] This power she exercised just before her abduction to Ireland,[216] when she was in sexual thraldom to a handsome, virile man eighteen years her junior, but probably under no other form of duress. By this second deed (of 3 October 1746) she surrendered 'all the interest that she had in the premises' to two new trustees, established various trusts of an unsuspicious kind, assigned half her annual rents and other income to Maguire, reserving the other half to herself, and provided that her whole estate should revert to herself if Maguire pre-deceased her, or vest in Maguire if she pre-deceased him.[217] None of these provisions was sinister or unusual. Nor were the new trustees of obviously dubious character. One was called 'Mr Taaffe' and sounds like an Irish 'Wild Goose' who had served in the Imperial army (as Maguire had done in earlier days);[218] the other was the 6th Lord Ward, a wealthy crypto-Jacobite and former member of the British House of Commons, who was promoted to the viscountcy of Dudley and Ward in 1763.[219] Taaffe may have been privy to Maguire's intentions, but there is no reason to think that Ward was, or that he would have approved and abetted them had he known what was going on.

The problem for Lady Cathcart was that she 'was for twenty [years] deprived of all correspondence with any person'[220] while shut up in Ireland, so that it was effectively impossible for her trustees or her friends, all of whom were in England, to know what was happening or that she was not an entirely free agent when she made further use for Maguire's benefit of the power she had rashly reserved to herself. She later, in 1775, asserted that he obtained receipt of the half of her income which she had retained 'under the authority of a letter of attorney which Colonel Maguire prevailed upon me to join him in signing without ever having read it to me'.[221] Presumably he obtained control of her capital by the same means. It is significant that she did not allege a higher degree of coercion, which by 1775 she had every motive for doing since she was trying to invalidate her own legal acts. This suggests that she had been actuated by infatuation rather than intimidation.

The received versions of the Lady Cathcart story suggest that she thought she had protected herself and her interests adequately by making herself of greater value to Maguire alive than dead: in fact, because of the clause in the deed of 1746 vesting all her estate in him if she died first, she gave him some reason to kill her, or at least to encourage her to die through maltreatment. His inducement to keep her alive was intrinsic to the nature of her income, which was a life interest only (her capital was hers outright). He not only kept her alive, but administered what had become their joint property with colourable legality, presumably so that the trustees would have no cause for suspicion. He invested her capital in buying up a mortgage and other debts affecting his family estate at Tempo, Co. Fermanagh, then in the possession of his elder brother, Robert, and by 1755 was in a position, if he so desired, to foreclose and acquire the property for himself and his heirs.[222] This was not itself an objectionable use to which to put Lady Cathcart's money – indeed, since a family property was at stake (and Castle Nugent was also a family property, on his mother's side), it might have seemed logical and meritorious. True, it temporarily disabled the trustees from making a payment of £1,500 to a beneficiary of both the original settlement of 1745 and the deed of trust of 1746; but this sum was successfully extracted from Maguire (ever law-abiding) by a decree of the English Court of Chancery in 1763.[223]

Unquestionably, circumstances of an extra-legal and even illegal nature strengthened Maguire's hold on Lady Cathcart's property. His removal of her from one jurisdiction to another and from all her friends and relations; his reputation as a deadly duellist, which had the effect of discouraging awkward enquiries; and a censorious society's disposition to think that an ageing woman (she was 53 in 1745 and he about 35) who had flouted convention and succumbed to carnal desires, was good value for whatever happened to her – all of these factors operated in his favour. But, essentially, he succeeded in maintaining control of her property and her, and probably would have inherited all if he had outlived her, because he kept up a colour of legality almost to his dying day. In his will, made in March 1766, he even left to Lady Cathcart 'all the jewels and plate of which she was possessed at the time of her intermarriage with me'. This sounds like black humour, since her jewels seem to have been the one valuable asset which she had saved from falling into his clutches.[224]

Following his death later in 1766 and her release from captivity at Castle Nugent, she took legal proceedings (which were hopelessly and indeed fraudulently mismanaged)[225] against his executors for the recovery of her property. In the end, and ten years after her own death in 1789, her heir obtained restitution of the money invested in the Tempo mortgage, probably with all the arrears of interest then due, by forcing a sale of that estate.[226] Whether she or her heir recovered the estimated £20,000 which Maguire had received over the years out of her half of her income,[227] is a moot point. What, however, is fairly clear is that she did not succeed in disputing and invalidating any of the legal instruments he had allegedly coerced her into signing during their marriage.[228] The money recovered by Lady Cathcart or her heir was recovered on the basis that, by the deed of 1746, Maguire's and her joint property became the sole property of the survivor. Indeed, were it not for the testimony of the Edgeworth family and other Co. Longford neighbours (part of it used in Maria Edgeworth's novel, *Castle Rackrent*, first published in 1800), there would be good reason to suspect that the dramatic aspects of Lady Cathcart's abduction and incarceration were invented by herself in order to support her case against Maguire's executors.[229]

There was a sequel to her escape. At the time of her marriage to Maguire she is reputed to have quipped: 'If I survive, I will have five.'[230] The fifth, whom she did not actually marry, may have been her 'servant' or steward at her Hertfordshire seat, Tewin Water.[231] He was called Philip Cosgrave (which sounds as if he, like Maguire, was a crypto-Catholic Irishman). When she died in 1789, she left legacies of £3,000 to various people, some annuities to servants, and the rest of her estate which might (depending on how much she recovered from the Maguires) have amounted to £25,000 or more, to – Philip Cosgrave. This was a lot to leave to a steward and, as Cosgrave unctuously put it, 'far beyond my expectation or merit'.[232] It is known that Lady Cathcart 'danced at Welwyn assembly when she was 95';[233] so she may, in spite of her experiences at Castle Nugent, have remained a silly, randy old woman to the end of her days.

THE PURSUIT OF THE HEIRESS

What is more important for present purposes is that her story, rightly interpreted, does not throw doubt – quite the contrary – on the view that heiresses and women of fortune were well protected against their husbands by the legal devices available to them in this period. Indeed, in the two cases which will now be examined – those of Lady Elizabeth Villiers, daughter and ultimately sole heiress of the already-mentioned Lord Grandison, and Susan, Lady Carbery, a late eighteenth-century 'nabob's' daughter and heiress – the terms of the marriage settlement were such that it was not the wife but the husband who, in crucial respects, was unprotected.

Lord Grandison, as the representative on his mother's side of the ancient family of FitzGerald of the Decies, Co. Waterford, and on his father's side of the Irish branch of the ducal family of Villiers, had name as well as landed wealth to transmit. In 1739 Lady Elizabeth Villiers, who was then a younger child, not an heiress, had married Aland Mason, a rich resident of Waterford City. In spite of the disparity of rank between the couple, the marriage was funded according to the 10 per cent relativity between portion (£8,000) and jointure (£800)[234] – a further indicator of the worthlessness, in the marriage market, of rank. Apart, however, from the fact that it was non-noble, there was nothing socially amiss with Mason's family. His background was not mercantile (as his place of residence would suggest); his estate, which had a rental of £2,500 a year in 1739, consisted of land, as well as of urban property in Waterford City; and his grandfather had sat in parliament for the county of Waterford – actually, alongside Lord Grandison's step-father. Subsequent deaths in the Grandison family, one of them later in 1739, resulted in Lady Elizabeth's becoming in 1746 sole heiress-apparent to her father. Accordingly, a distinct viscountcy of Grandison (later advanced to an earldom) was conferred on her, with remainder to the heirs male of her body, of which there was one by then, her only child by Mason.[235]

Mason might not have been allowed to marry the new Lady Grandison, had it been known in 1739 that she would inherit the Grandison estate and that her son would be the next Lord Grandison; and the Masons seem to have been much overawed by the length of the Grandison lineage, and snobbishly proud of the connection.[236] This presumably explains why, in 1747, Mason was prepared to execute an ignominious resettlement, 'in gratitude for having the good fortune to match himself with her [Lady Grandison] and into her noble family'. Under the terms of this re-settlement, his own, Mason estate was to pass on his death (which took place in 1759) to his and Lady Grandison's son; 'in case he [the son] fails, … to any other children, male or female, that Lady Grandison may have by any other husband; in failure of all children, to her Ladyship; and, should she fail, the whole to the present Earl of Grandison [her father] and his right heirs'.[237] In other words, he cut his own collateral Mason relations (apart from the possible children of an actually childless uncle) out of the succession to the Mason estate.

The extent of this concession can best be expressed in rental terms. In 1765,

Elizabeth, Countess Grandison in her own right, painted by an unknown follower of the English portrait-painter, Thomas Hudson, possibly at the time of her second marriage in 1763. The staff she holds is a 'sprug', which denotes that she is meant to be a shepherdess.

PRIVATE COLLECTION

ABETH
Countess of Grandison
Died 1782

before parts of both estates were sold to pay what can reasonably be described as Grandison debts, the Mason estate was producing £3,765 a year, and the Grandison estate in Ireland just over £7,000, with another £1,000 from a smallish Grandison property in Hertfordshire. Had Mason's son died, the Mason estate would have passed, either to a child of the second marriage which Lady Grandison made in 1763 or, more probably, to a Villiers kinsman of Lord Grandison. Even as things turned out, the Mason name and inheritance were subsumed: in 1771, before he actually succeeded to the Grandison estates and as 2nd Earl Grandison, Mason's son added the name Villiers to his patronymic.[238] In a sense, therefore, although Mason had secured an heiress, he effectively extinguished his own line, and risked actually extinguishing it, in the process.

A more bizarre example of the risks attending marriage to an heiress is the settlement terms conceded to, or extorted by, Susan, Lady Carbery, who married the 4th Lord Carbery in 1792. The Carbery estates in Ireland, mainly in Co. Limerick, had a rental of roughly £7,000 in the mid-eighteenth century, and through a fortunate early eighteenth-century marriage to the co-heiress of the Blatherwycke estate in Northamptonshire and Rutland, the family had also acquired an English seat and property, Laxton Park. By the later 1750s, family finances were in palpable disarray. In 1758, the 2nd Lord's creditors were receiving £4,000 a year out of the estate (probably the Irish estate only) and the 2nd Lord only £1,000. Settlement charges seem to have been at least partly to blame for this situation, as the 3rd Lord complained in 1760, just after his succession, that out of his first half year's rent, he had to pay £1,000 to his mother and £400 to his brother and sister.[239] By 1791, the rental of the Irish estate stood at a little over £5,000 a year, roughly £4,000 of which appears to have been consumed in the servicing of debt. It must therefore have been a considerable relief to the 4th Lord when he fell in with the heiress of a dead 'nabob', one Colonel Henry Watson, a sometime engineer in the East India Company's service, whose fortune of something like £100,000 apparently derived from a feat of engineering performed at Calcutta Harbour.[240] In the following year, 1792, Lord Carbery duly married Miss Watson.

In his eagerness to make this alliance, Lord Carbery submitted to settlement terms by which his wife was entitled, not only to a large jointure of £2,000 but, in the event of their having no children, to the complete disposal of her own fortune and of Laxton as well.[241] Over three years later, the Irish agent wrote encouragingly to him: 'I am rejoiced to find the India business is going on so well. A little patience and a very few years will, I trust, give your Lordship one of the most independent fortunes in Ireland. Lands have risen since your Lordship was here 10 per cent, and [this] is likely to go on.'[242] Both encouragement and patience were requisite. Colonel Watson's fortune was in rupees, and conversion to sterling led to complications. Moreover, there had been other women in the Colonel's life than Lady Carbery's mother, and one of them was still disputing the inheritance in 1820. Most alarming of all, no son – no child of any kind – had yet been produced by Lord and Lady Carbery. Since sufficient of her fortune could not be disengaged to discharge his debts, it was doubtful if, in the event of his death, the nett income from the estate would cover her £2,000 a year; the more so because his father, the 3rd Lord, had made an eccentric will under which the 4th Lord's sister was to inherit the unentailed part of the Irish property (a large part, producing nearly £5,500 a year in 1815), should the 4th Lord die without issue male.[243]

This is what happened, in 1804. The Carbery title and most of the Irish estate now passed to an elderly uncle; Laxton and her own fortune, to Lady Carbery; and the rest of the Irish estate to the late Lord's sister. In the following year, 1805, the elderly uncle's only son died, followed by the elderly uncle in 1807. His successor in the entailed lion's share of the Irish estate was George Freke Evans, a second cousin of the 4th Lord Carbery, and a younger brother of the new bearer of the title. George Freke Evans was also – and this was no coincidence – the second husband of the widowed Lady Carbery, whom he had married in 1806. Their marriage settlement states her fortune as almost £80,000 in cash, and presumably in hand, with a further £33,000 locked up in a Chancery suit;[244] all of which George Freke Evans, who was an enthusiastic litigant over matters great and small, seems ultimately to have recovered on her behalf. On her death, in 1828, she left it to him, together with Laxton. On his death, in 1829, he in turn left his wife's fortune and Laxton to his elder brother, the 6th Lord Carbery, who now also succeeded to the entailed Carbery estate in Ireland. In this extraordinary and circuitous manner, the Carbery estate in England, swelled by the spoils of the Bengal engineer, was reunited with the entailed Carbery estate in Ireland and the Carbery title; and the disastrous consequences of the 4th Lord's over-eagerness to marry an heiress were averted.

In more usual circumstances, the heiress's fortune brought with it trouble, inconvenience, risk, but not positive danger. This was the experience of Sir Robert Tilson Deane, 6th Bt, formerly of Dromore Castle, Co. Cork, who made a runaway marriage in 1775 with Anne Fitzmaurice, sole heiress to Springfield Castle, Dromcollogher, Co. Limerick, and to the accompanying Fitzmaurice estates, and who was created Lord Muskerry in 1781. This was not, however, the success-story (from Lord Muskerry's point of view) that it sounded. The Fitzmaurice estate was beset with encumbrances and lawsuits, the former of which stood at £35,000 in 1802, which it was reckoned was more than the whole estate was worth. So, Lord Muskerry derived little benefit from it and appears to have been dependent on his pay as colonel of the Co. Limerick Militia; and his heiress-wife, who survived him by twelve years, dying in 1830, remained in straitened circumstances for the duration of her widowhood. The main advantage of the marriage from the point of view of the husband was that his own family, the Deanes, had already run through their patrimonial estate, including Dromore itself, and needed an alternative seat. This, if little else for years to come, was provided by Springfield Castle.[245]

THE PURSUIT OF THE HEIRESS

Trouble, inconvenience and not much to show for it in the short term, were also the experience of Lord Clements, later (1804) 2nd Earl of Leitrim, who married in 1800 Mary, elder daughter and co-heiress of the late William Bermingham (d.1798) of Rosshill, Co. Mayo. Apart from 'the beautiful villa and demesne of Rosshill',[246] the extensive Bermingham estate lay in Joyce Country, Co. Galway. As so frequently happens, its existence and Mary Bermingham's half-share of it (which had come to her under her father's will), are not mentioned in the marriage settlement, in this instance because the Rosshill estate was settled by a separate deed of the same date, 24 July 1800. Confusingly, neither document makes any mention of the other. The marriage settlement concentrated on establishing trusts to secure the bride's meagre portion of £5,000 and her pin money of £300 a year and jointure of £800. The £5,000 was settled on the younger children of the marriage, but was to revert to the bride and her 'right heirs' if the marriage was childless, a most unusual provision, as a bride's portion was almost always non-returnable. The settlement of the Rosshill estate was similarly weighted against the bridegroom. The estate was settled on Lord and Lady Clements for their lives and the life of the survivor, with power to charge it with another (and very necessary) £5,000 for younger children and with an additional £3,000 for any other purpose, and then on the eldest son of the marriage. In the event of their being no son, the estate was to revert, after the deaths of Lord and Lady Clements, to Lady Clements's heirs and assigns.[247]

The estate was surveyed as comprising 22,543 statute acres in 1857 and 13,593 Irish acres in 1860, but it was wild, woolly and westerly, and the rental was low in relation to the acreage: £2,229 in 1804, £3,089 in 1816 and £3,152 in 1860. This was the gross rental. From it had to be deducted nearly £350 a year for chief rent, agent's fees, etc.[248] Between 1798 and her death in 1826, it was also liable to a charge of £1,000 a year for the jointure of Mrs William Bermingham, the mother of the co-heiresses.[249] In addition, the house at Rosshill, which had been damaged in the 1798 Rebellion and lay empty for most of the time, was kept in good order, as was the demesne, both of them at some recurrent expense.[250] There was a fleeting prospect of there being mineral resources on the estate, but no more is heard of this after 1812.[251] The rental, clearly, peaked during the wartime boom and fell back thereafter, probably after being further depressed by abatements granted during the Famine. The estate was valued (i.e. if out of lease) at £3,465 a year in 1857, which does not suggest much progress since 1816. And this in spite of the achievement of Alexander Nimmo and his team of engineers in opening up Connemara and north-west Galway by road-, bridge- and harbour-building from c.1820 onwards.

In 1802, Lady Clements' younger sister, Anne Bermingham, married the 2nd Earl of Charlemont, whose estates were in Counties Armagh and Tyrone (principally the former); Lord Clements/Leitrim's estates were in the county of that name and in Donegal. In c.1804, the husbands of the co-heiresses, with their wives' concurrence, resolved to get the Rosshill estate valued for purposes of partition, and to obtain a private act of parliament empowering them to break the stipulations of William Bermingham's will and sell it for the purpose of buying two properties of equivalent value in counties Leitrim and Armagh. The valuation, which proved inconclusive, cost Lords Leitrim and Charlemont c.£350 each, and the act of parliament, which passed in 1808, also put them to 'a considerable expense'.[252] Moreover, when the plan was unfolded to old Mrs Bermingham, she wrote to Lord Leitrim expressing her surprise and disappointment:

> Though I never imagined, trifling as the estate of Rosshill is, that the division of it would be as easily accomplished as you all seemed to expect, I own the sale of it never once entered my calculations, ... land in that remote, wild country never within my knowledge selling for anything near its value. The last I recollect being sold in that neighbourhood was the property generally known by the name of the Cong estate, which after being advertised for years was at length purchased ... for less than half its value....
>
> If Mary and her sister, who are of age to judge for themselves and their children, after mature consideration have made up their minds to it, it shall *not* meet with any opposition from me. But ... what income will they have to look forward to in place of that of their estate? Naturally, one would suppose, that of the lands purchased with its produce in the counties of Leitrim and Armagh. But I am very much deceived indeed if any purchases made in either of these counties would return anything near the income they are likely to have and may expect from Rosshill, if properly and judiciously managed, being doubtless a very rising property.[253]

Mrs Bermingham's objections prevailed. She was wrong in thinking Rosshill 'a very rising property' (at least in the longer term), but she may have been right in thinking that, unless what she called 'the difficulty of access' to it were removed, it would not sell for a capital sum which bore any relation to its income.

Lady Leitrim had probably, from the beginning, been reluctant to sell 'dearest, loveliest Rosshill', for which she had 'a very animated affection'. Lady Charlemont's affection for it was less 'animated' but she was not insensitive to its attractions. She was also disposed to defer to her sister's wishes. Lady Leitrim's mental equilibrium was uncertain (she suffered some kind of mental breakdown in 1830–32), and none of the family wanted to disturb it.[254] Even her death, which took place in 1840, made no difference. Shortly after that event, Lord Leitrim expressed his feelings to Lady Charlemont:

> More than thirty years have elapsed since the act of parliament passed, and nothing has occurred in that period to change the opinion I then formed as to the advantage that would have accrued to our families if the estate had been sold.... But ... having, in compliance with the wish of her to whom upon this point I was bound to pay every deference, given up a plan which I had then much at heart, I feel myself still bound by every principle of honour as well as

of good feeling and consistency to preserve my moiety of the estate during my life.[255]

Since he lived until 1854, this resolution deferred the question of sale for nearly fifteen years, and nothing in fact happened until 1860. Even then, because his son, the 3rd Earl of Leitrim, was devoted to his mother's memory, had 'great taste for the wild and picturesque' and by disposition was a preserver and buyer rather than a seller of land, only the Charlemont half of the estate was sold (most of it actually to Lord Leitrim).[256]

The case of the Rosshill estate and the Bermingham co-heiresses illustrates a number of things (and will be referred to again in other contexts). Obviously, it illustrates the expense, the inconvenience and the strings attached to marrying a landed heiress. Usually the strings were legal: in the Bermingham case, they were personal and emotional. Actually, they were apron strings, which still tied the son long after the mother was dead. The other and, for present purposes more important, thing which this case illustrates is the strong bargaining power of the heiress, particularly when she was a landed heiress, and the risks incurred by the man who succeeded in marrying her and by his family. The Clementses did not run the risk, as the Masons and Carberys had done, that their own estates would be sucked into the possession of the heiress's family should the marriage be childless. But, in that event, the Clements estate would have been saddled with a charge of £300 a year during the joint lives of Lord Clements and the heiress, and £800 a year if she survived him, and her portion of £5,000 would have reverted at his death to herself, her heirs and assigns and been lost altogether to the Clementses. Likewise, if the marriage had produced no son, Mary Bermingham's half share of the Rosshill estate would have passed, on his death, to *her* representatives, not his.

Generally speaking, such stipulations were typical of the settlement terms which a landed heiress was in a position to dictate. This is why it is inherently improbable that Lord Aldborough's childless first marriage should have brought him an acre of his wife's Suffolk property. Two better-documented examples, one with an unhappy and one with a happy ending, will serve to illustrate contemporary thinking and practice with regard to estates in the possession of heiresses who lacked heirs male to inherit them.

In 1776, Colonel John Maxwell of Falkland, Co. Monaghan, a kinsman of the earls of Farnham and a future Governor of the Bahamas, married a landed widow, Mrs Grace Corry. Her property, in counties Fermanagh, Monaghan and Tyrone, was settled on the issue of their marriage, with remainder to herself. There was no issue. As she later complained in 1779, when seeking a divorce, Colonel Maxwell, in spite of 'repeated efforts for the purpose', had 'never consummated the said marriage, but appears totally impotent'. She also complained that, in the previous year, he had induced her to re-settle her estate on him, in failure of issue; and that she had subsequently discovered that he had

THE SUPERIOR BARGAINING POWER OF THE HEIRESS

made a will by which he had left his remainder in fee in her estate to his nephews and nieces, leaving to her nothing but 'a small island on the coast of North America at ... [that] time ... actually in the hands of the insurgents'. Presented with these alleged facts, counsel drily commented:

> It is pretty extraordinary that the lady should have executed her power in the Colonel's favour at the time when she did, and considering what had passed in the interim between the marriage and the execution of the power. However, extraordinary as that was, I should think she had a right to expect relief from a court of equity, provided the grounds for a divorce should be made out in the ecclesiastical court and a divorce obtained.[257]

The sequel is unclear, and in any case not particularly important. What is important is that the estate was originally settled on the issue of the marriage with remainder to the heiress; and that even after the subsequent re-settlement of the remainder on the husband, it was unlikely that he or his heirs would in fact succeed to it if it could be proved that the childlessness of the marriage was his fault. Clearly, 'women having power' were not so easily to be 'kissed or kicked out of it' after all[258] – although in this instance there was some doubt about the effectiveness of the kissing.

The second instance is uncomplicated by bad marital relations between the heiress and her husband. The already-mentioned 1st Earl Annesley appears not to have resorted to gardeners' wives and other mistresses until after the death (in 1792) of his own wife, Mary Grove, heiress to the Grove estate of Ballyhimmock, near Castletownroche, Co. Cork. Ballyhimmock had presumably been settled on the issue of their marriage, which was childless. However, she

> had power under her marriage settlement to dispose of her said estate by will as she should think fit; and ... by her will, made in 1784, she in execution of such power devised the same to ... the use of her husband during his life, the remainder to ... [a series of aunts and female cousins for their lives], remainder to General Annesley [a younger son of her husband's younger brother and heir presumptive] in fee.[259]

It is possible to reduce these complex and seemingly mindless arrangements to some sort of sense. In 1784, when Lady Annesley's will was made, her husband's nephew, the future General, was about to come of age. Some sort of provision was therefore going to have to be made for him, and probably the terms of the Annesley settlements placed the obligation to provide for him on his uncle, Lord Annesley, as the then head of the family and possessor of the Annesley family estate. A remainder in fee, however remote, would have been an advantage to the young man in the marriage market. So Lady Annesley presumably consented that her own Ballyhimmock estate should be employed for this purpose, in order to reduce correspondingly the burden on the Annesley estate; the expectations

THE PURSUIT OF THE HEIRESS

of her own family were to be satisfied by the various intervening life-interests which her will created.

The gain to the Annesley estate from the arrangement is obvious: the gain to Lady Annesley, and her object in making the arrangement, are less so. In effect, what Lady Annesley, and Ballyhimmock, gained was a man to succeed there and carry on the Grove name and line. When the life interests at last fell in and the estate came into his actual possession – which cannot have been until the mid-1840s – the General duly double-barrelled his name to Grove-Annesley; and his son and successor went two better, by dropping the Annesley and punningly re-christening Ballyhimmock 'Annesgrove'. It would have been more logical for Lady Annesley to have chosen the man from among her own blood relations; but presumably she wanted to help her husband and plant a Grove at the one stroke. However, the help to her husband did not extend to putting the Grove estate into his disposable power. Instead, she tied it up in remainders which would and did last for half a century.

On the whole, therefore, it was more prudent for a landowner who sought to improve his financial position by marriage, to seek out an heiress whose fortune was in money than in land. Quite apart from the complications and conditions attending land, there was one simple economic fact to be borne in mind. Most

Portion of a 'Map and survey of part of the estate of Caledon, lying in the county of Tyrone, belonging to, and surveyed at the instance, of the Hon. Miss Hamilton, surveyed in autumn 1737 by John Reed'. Since it was made the year before Margaret Hamilton's marriage to Lord Orrery, it can perhaps be described as a pre-nuptial survey.

PRONI CALEDON PAPERS, D/2433/A/13/1

landowners would be paying interest on debts secured on their estates; and since the rate of interest payable for borrowed money was usually higher than the return on capital tied up in land, the liquidation of debt would be of greater advantage to them, in purely financial terms, than the acquisition of another estate.[260] In 1736 the 5th Earl of Orrery was reminded by his agent of the pressing importance of cash in hand: 'Your Lordship must not hold out for too much fortune, if you can get enough to make you easy. It will not be prudent to run the most manifest hazard of being under at present, and indeed forever, because it is possible you may get ten or twenty thousand more.' Lord Orrery ignored this advice, by holding out for another two years, and by securing at the end of it a landed, not a drily, heiress. The lady, Margaret Hamilton of Caledon, Co. Tyrone, was reputedly worth £80,000, but this must have been a guess at the capital value of the Caledon estate (which did in fact fetch £96,400 when sold many years later, in 1776). In the short term, however, the marriage if anything exacerbated Lord Orrery's financial difficulties: by 1751, he had reverted to his old habit of borrowing, this time £20,000 at one stroke.[261]

In 1747, the co-heiress to 'a good part of Colonel Paul's estate in the Counties Kildare and Carlow', summed up this classic dilemma in a surprisingly modern turn of phrase when she declared 'that the person for whom she formerly intended the land will have more occasion for the ready'. In 1788, regret was expressed that the 2nd Earl of Arran's recently-married son and heir had not likewise opted for 'the ready': 'He has certainly done very well for himself in point of [landed] income, but I much doubt whether £30,000 in cash, of which he might have had the disposal, would not have produced advantages equal at present and greater in future.' The emphasis of the remark almost certainly fell on the phrase, 'of which he might have had the disposal'; a modest, but disposable, sum was usually of more practical benefit than either land or a larger sum with strings attached.[262]

In general, money – in whatever quantity – was less likely to have strings attached than land. There were exceptions. One, obviously, is Susan, Lady Carbery's supposed £100,000. Another is the £37,378 which Mrs David Ross ultimately brought to her husband, the younger brother of a financially embarrassed Co. Down squire. By the terms of their marriage settlement, made ten years before she inherited her £37,378, the money had to be divided equally among her children, and when her husband used it almost exclusively for the benefit of the eldest son, the Court of Chancery declared his action null and void.[263] Miss Monck's/Lady Tyrone's fortune was likewise mainly earmarked for younger children, although her husband and she seem to have received £24,600 of it in the acceptable form of 'presents'.[264] But, even assuming that all the rest of her fortune, some £85,000, was so earmarked, this was probably the use to which her husband would have put it had he been a free agent: her original portion of £8,000 was obviously inadequate, particularly to provide for a family which in the end ran to two younger sons and four daughters, and for a family

THE PURSUIT OF THE HEIRESS

whose head was raised a step in the peerage, to the marquessate of Waterford, in 1789, twenty years after the marriage. As things were, the family estates were burdened, apparently at the time of the 1st Marquess's death in 1801, with a capital debt of £130,000 and annual interest charges of £7,000; and things would have been a great deal worse if Lady Waterford's fortune had not been large enough to portion the younger children.[265]

In this case, the conditions annexed to the wife's fortune were reasonably appropriate to the husband's financial circumstances – as conditions in favour of younger children were likely to be in a period characterised demographically by dramatic increase in family size. In the case of the even larger fortune which Lord Londonderry's mother had earlier, in 1737, brought into the Stewart family, the conditions were fairly nominal, although this was partly because the accidents of birth, death and fertility also favoured the Stewarts.[266]

One example of a very large fortune in cash which was, by any reasonable standards, unfettered and free, was the £100,000 which Margaret Lauretta, younger daughter and co-heiress of the recently deceased William Mellish of Woodford, Essex, a shady English army contractor who owned a valuable estate in the London docklands, brought with her on her marriage to the 2nd Earl of Glengall in 1834. Lord Glengall's financial situation had for some time past been dire, as it was reckoned that his estate (with an already-mentioned gross rental of only £15,000 a year) 'owes more than it could pay if brought to the hammer tomorrow'.[267] Lady Glengall's trustees, however, were apparently prepared to spend the whole of her marriage portion redeeming the estate, and it was thought that most of the creditors would allow time for appropriate arrangements to be made.

It was Lord Glengall who frustrated these generous intentions. Carried away by his dazzling marriage and by the knowledge that Lady Glengall was worth much more than the £100,000 initially settled, he embarked from 1839

The 2nd Earl and Countess of Glengall at the time of their marriage; from a pair of engravings of c.1874.

NATIONAL PORTRAIT GALLERY

78

THE SUPERIOR BARGAINING POWER OF THE HEIRESS

onwards on a highly ambitious and uneconomic programme of estate improvement, which included the restoration of the old and ruinous Cahir Castle and the rebuilding of much of much of the town of Cahir. Eventually, a combination of the Famine, a lawsuit over the Mellish fortune between Lady Glengall and her elder sister and co-heiress, Lady Elizabeth Thynne, and the mounting alarm of Lady Glengall's trustees, forced him to abandon this in 1847. By 1848, his debts amounted to £250,000–£300,000. He was declared bankrupt in 1849 and was still a bankrupt when he died in 1858. (In the interim, the townspeople of Cahir kept the bailiffs at bay, because they were determined not to lose Lady Glengall's spending power and charitable handouts.) With him relegated to the sidelines, the trustees moved to clear the entangled thickets of debt by putting the whole estate up for sale through the Encumbered Estates Court, which they did in 1853. As a result of these sales, most of the property (9,769 Irish acres at a rental of £12,800 in 1864), now disencumbered from the debts of the 1st and 2nd Earls of Glengall, was re-acquired by the trustees at a cost of £200,000. The exceptions included some outlying mountainous lands, much of the town of Cahir, and the family seat in the town, Cahir House, with its accompanying demesne of Kilcommon. The town estate and Kilcommon demesne were bought back in 1876 by the 2nd Earl's and Margaret Lauretta's only child and heiress, Lady Margaret Butler Charteris.[268]

Lady Glengall's fortune was enormous and the way in which it saved the Glengall estate from ruin dramatic. But because the Irish aristocracy and its sons and heirs tended to marry within the ranks of the landed class, examples of great mercantile windfalls like this, or even of the more-than-useful £25,000 and £20,000 which Lord Conyngham and Colonel Luttrell received when they married merchants' daughters in 1744 and 1776 respectively, are few and far between. Another potential source of 'the ready' is fortunes made in the East or West Indies. An East India Company fortune financed the purchase of the Caledon estate, founded the Alexander family who bought it and funded the earldom of Caledon to which they were raised in 1800; but as that family is still going strong in the male line, it never produced an East Indian heiress. Mention has already been made of two West Indian heiresses who married into the Irish aristocracy, Colonel Luttrell's mother and Lady Altamont. Another was Martha Bayley, who married Joseph Leeson, nephew of the 2nd Earl of Milltown, in 1793. Their engagement in the previous year had given rise to the quip 'When Leeson, without sixpence, gets a wife of £4,000 a year, any man may hope', and to the rumour that Lord Milltown himself was going in pursuit of Miss Bayley's sister and co-heiress (which was improbable, since he was notoriously homosexual). In any case, the ladies being 'West Indians, the property [was] therefore something precarious'.[269]

One further potential source of ready-money windfalls is fortunes made from office-holding and/or 'venality' (the buying and selling of certain types of office). For at least the first half of the period under review, office was an important element in the wealth of the political *élite*.[270] However, it is not easy to find in Ireland examples of, and figures for, fortunes derived from office alone, since many office-holders were also landed men, and since successful office-holders (such as Nathaniel Clements) were quick to invest their profits in landed estates.

To locate heiresses to fortunes made exclusively or almost exclusively through office-holding, it may be necessary to look to England. One such is Mary Robinson, only daughter and heiress of John Robinson, Lord North's patronage secretary to the treasury (1770–82) and 'political rat-catcher'. Robinson had inherited an estate in Westmorland, which he had sold, and his resources mainly derived from the pickings of office[271] plus the proceeds of that sale. The only property he still possessed c.1780 were his town house and country villa and some houses in the borough of Harwich in Essex which he had bought for electioneering purposes. When, therefore, his daughter made a 'good' marriage to the Hon. Henry Nevill, later Lord Nevill and 2nd Earl of Abergavenny, in 1784, Robinson gave her a marriage portion of £25,000 in cash, and attached no strings to it. At his death in 1802, more money and some land were added to the settlement.[272] Robinson's friend and fellow bureaucrat, Anthony Todd, the secretary to the General Post Office, was similarly situated. In 1782, when Todd's only daughter and heiress, Eleanor, married Lord Maitland, son and heir of the 7th Earl of Lauderdale, Todd transferred '£30,000 three per cents, worth in cash now about £30,000' and yielding £1,500 a year, to the trustees of the marriage settlement. All that Lord Lauderdale was required to do in return was pay the young couple £1,500 a year in 'present maintenance' during his own life and provide a jointure of £1,500 should Lady Maitland survive her husband.[273]

Fortunes of similar size, though not from the same source, are not infrequently encountered in aristocratic marriages in Ireland. Indeed, the resources of Mary Robinson and Eleanor Todd roughly equate to the £30,000 in cash of which Lord Arran's son and heir 'might have had the disposal'. In Ireland, the likeliest source in the aristocratic marriage market of a disposable fortune of this level was a by-passed heiress or just an exceptionally well portioned young lady. Two such brides have already been mentioned in other contexts – the Hon. Elizabeth Burrell, who brought the 2nd Earl of Clare somewhere between £30,000 and £60,000 in 1825, and Lady Grace Maxwell who brought her husband c.£40,000 in and after 1802.[274] The former lady had two brothers and originally two older sisters (who may have died young, thus increasing her share of the provision made for younger children); she was not an heiress, but her mother was; and her father, the 1st Lord Gwydyr (d.1820), had been a very rich man.

Lady Grace Maxwell was the by-passed heiress of Lord Farnham and, since her father was dead, was represented in the negotiations with her husband-to-be, Sir Ralph Gore, 7th Bt, by her redoubtable mother. Gore was in a weak bargaining position, since his predecessor had run through almost the whole of the family estate.[275] However, when 'Lady Farnham endeavoured to settle a *part* of her [Lady Grace's] fortune *only* in her own disposal, in the event of her having no children, ... Sir R.G. resented it and stopped the proceedings and would have relinquished the match rather than have consented'. Lady Farnham persisted, and Gore, 'after a tough battle', gave in to her, so that 'a part of Lady Grace's property [was] left to her own disposal'. Gore could console himself with the thought that he had 'a certain value for money, and was not very likely from personal accomplishments to obtain soon a similar fortune'.[276] Since he had fared so well, the implication is that a bridegroom with a stronger bargaining position would have had no difficulty in engrossing the whole fortune without any strings attached except pin money and jointure.

Emily, Dowager Duchess of Leinster, took the view that her third son, Lord Henry Fitzgerald, was in just such a bargaining position during the protracted negotiations in 1791 over his proposed marriage to Miss Charlotte Boyle Walsingham. Lord Henry, though a younger son, had been endowed (as has been seen)[277] with half of the remaining family estate in the barony of Lecale, Co. Down, his half comprising land in and around Strangford. Charlotte Boyle Walsingham was the sole heiress of her brother, who had died young in 1788, and she possessed an Irish estate worth some £600 a year and a fortune in cash of c.£80,000, subject to her late brother's debts of c.£20,000. She was therefore worth over £70,000 nett. According to Emily, Duchess of Leinster, 'the point in dispute' in the marriage negotiations was

> whether her property, failing of issue, shall be settled on her relations [and away from] Henry, to whom the law would give it if she did not dispose of it otherwise by settlement or will. Her trustees insist on this. His friends and he himself think it very unreasonable, and very dishonourable to Henry, as they have offered her a full power to dispose of her property as she pleases; which is surely a very handsome offer and what they ought to be contented with.[278]

The point in dispute became academic because the marriage, which went ahead later in the year, was blessed with children. But it is unlikely that Charlotte Boyle Walsingham's property would have been left unsettled if it had been mainly in land.

The Ladies Henrietta and Emily Hobart were not actual heiresses at the time of their respective marriages (although both subsequently became such); but they were very amply portioned brides. Lady Henrietta who (with fatal results) married the 1st Earl Belmore in 1780, brought him £5,000 down with £15,000 more to come on the death of her father, the 2nd Earl of Buckinghamshire, which took place in 1794.[279] The £15,000 was part of the large fortune of her mother, an heiress or by-passed heiress. (Usually, when an aristocratic bride had a fortune of £20,000 or more and was not herself a by-passed heiress, this was the result of a bequest from a mother, grandmother, unmarried aunt or some other benefactor.) Lady Henrietta Hobart's mother was Lord Buckinghamshire's first wife; his second wife, Caroline Conolly, was also a considerable heiress. As a result, Lady Emily Hobart, Lord Buckinghamshire's only child by her, had a

THE PURSUIT OF THE HEIRESS

large portion and great expectations when she married Robert Stewart, the future Viscount Castlereagh, in 1794. Emily, Lady Castlereagh, who is principally remembered for her eccentric habit of wearing her husband's Garter ribbon in her hair, blushes unseen among the brasher matrimonial successes of Lord Castlereagh's grandfather, father (the 1st Marquess of Londonderry) and half-brother (the 3rd). However, her portion at their marriage in 1794 was £30,000, and at her mother's death in 1817 she inherited an income from sundry estates which amounted to £3,500 a year.[280] This £3,500 a year must have been warmly welcomed by her husband, because for almost all of his life and Foreign Office career he was only heir apparent to the Londonderry estate in Co. Down and the Londonderry titles. He was to enjoy them for only a year and a half: the 1st Marquess died in January 1821 and Castlereagh, the 2nd Marquess, in August 1822.

These fortunes of £20,000–£70,000 mainly in cash, some of them deriving from women who technically were not even heiresses, seem superficially small when set beside the broad acres of the Bermingham co-heiresses. However, it is more than doubtful if the whole Rosshill estate would have fetched £40,000 in c.1800, and if it had, the income from the money would largely have been consumed by Mrs Bermingham's jointure, which had twenty-five years to run. When the estate was valued with a view to sale in 1857, the probable price – at 22 years' purchase (a generous assumption) of a nett valuation of c.£3,100 a year[281] – was c.£68,000. If regard is had to the regular and the one-off expenditure which the possession and administration of remote Rosshill required during the intervening period, and to the risk and liabilities which the marriage settlement with the Rosshill co-heiress involved, there can be little doubt that the 2nd Earl of Leitrim would have done better to marry a well portioned woman with c.£30,000 of which he 'had the disposal', than to do what he did and marry a landed heiress.

Heiresses whose fortunes were in money were much more likely to bring them, untrammelled, into the possession of their husband and his family than heiresses whose fortunes were in land. The main drawback with monied heiresses was that they were not necessarily any richer than well portioned women who technically were not heiresses at all.

'A view of Londonderry': an engraved portrait of Lord Castlereagh in 1821, just after his succession as 2nd Marquess of Londonderry, by Richard Dighton

AUTHOR'S COLLECTION

FOUR

Collateral damage

THE LURE OF THE YOUNGER SON

This chapter takes one stage further the argument that, when the heiress's fortune was in land, it was almost certain that there would be conditions attached to the inheritance, and highly probable that they would be anything from inconvenient to intolerable (from the husband's point of view). This was because a particular mystique attached to land. Hence the otherwise inexplicable preparedness of the landed class to encumber their land up to (and in the case of Lord Glengall beyond) its capital value, rather than sell an acre of it. All landed families were 'of' somewhere, the somewhere being usually their country seat. It was a mark of distinction, not a mere postal address. Every effort was made to ensure that, should the misfortune of a break in the direct male succession occur, the name and the land would continue to go together: either through the succession of a collateral male (in which case any by-passed daughters would be provided for by specially large portions charged on the land), or through the succession of a daughter's male child, usually on condition that he assumed his mother's maiden name, and with 'contingent remainders' to specified people and their issue, if the first-named heir should 'fail'. Developments in the law of property uniformly tended towards the first alternative; but the second retained the attraction that it harmonised parental affection for a daughter with the paramount dynastic consideration of continuing the name and line.

The importance attached to continuing the heiress's name and line cannot be sufficiently emphasised. The usual device for accomplishing this, assuming that the heiress's marriage produced more than one son, was to remainder her estate on a younger son. For example, when Earl Nugent's daughter and heiress married the nephew and heir of the 2nd Earl Temple, in 1775,[282] it was reported that Lord Nugent '*settles £8,000* a year on Miss Nugent's marriage with Mr Grenville'. The £8,000 must have referred to Lord Nugent's entire property – his Gosfield estate in Essex as well as his larger estates in Ireland, mainly in Co. Westmeath; and even then the figure sounds inflated. However, the report was correct as to the essential point that the estates were *settled*: when Lord Nugent died in 1788, his son-in-law, by then Marquess of Buckingham, assumed the name Nugent before that of Grenville; and in 1800, Lady Buckingham was created Baroness Nugent in the Irish peerage, and in 1812 was succeeded in that title and in the Nugent estates by their second son. Lord Buckingham summarised his role succinctly when in 1794 he described himself 'as holding in trust for my family a great situation in Ireland'. Likewise, Buckingham's younger brother, Lord Grenville, whose wife unexpectedly succeeded to the Cornish and Dorset estates of her brother in 1804, described himself in the same year as 'steward' of this newly acquired inheritance.[283]

Other such examples abound, because it was instinctive in landowners whose direct heirs male had failed, to try to ensure, by whatever means, that their estates became an appanage not an appendage. The examples would, in fact, be still more numerous if plans for cadet inheritance had not sometimes been pre-empted by circumstances, or subsequently reversed by further failures of heirs male. The Massereene family is a case of plans pre-empted by circumstances. Anne Eyre, Dowager Countess of Massereene and mother of the weak-minded 2nd Earl, was the only daughter and sole heiress of Henry Eyre of Row Tor in Derbyshire, and her father and she had both intended that the Row Tor estate should pass to a younger son of her marriage rather than be submerged in the Irish estates of the Massereene family. However, the debts run up by the 2nd Earl of Massereene in the end made it necessary for her to sell it in order to provide portions for the younger children and a supplement to her own erratically paid jointure. The Wicklow family is a case of how cadet inheritance could subsequently be reversed by further failure of heirs male. In 1755, Ralph Howard of Shelton Abbey, Arklow, Co. Wicklow, married Isabella Forward, daughter and sole heiress of William Forward of Castle Forward, St Johnstown, Co. Donegal. He was created Viscount Wicklow in 1785 and died in 1789; she was created countess of Wicklow in her own right in 1793 and died in 1807. Their respective estates had rentals of £6,000 and £3,500 a year in 1781. The Co. Wicklow estate passed in 1789 to the eldest son, Robert, and the Co. Donegal in 1807 to the second son, who had been christened William after his maternal grandfather. However, this arrangement was reversed in 1815, when the 2nd Earl of Wicklow died unmarried and the Castle Forward brother succeeded to the earldom and the Co. Wicklow estate.[284]

An interesting example of a cadet inheritance which lasted for a hundred years and then was reversed, is the Barry of Newtownbarry (Bunclody) estate,

Anne Eyre, Countess of Massereene: a pastel portrait by William Hoare of Bath, c.1750

KILLADOON COLLECTION, COURTESY OF CHARLES AND SALLY CLEMENTS

COLLATORAL DAMAGE: THE LURE OF THE YOUNGER SON

Co. Wexford, which was settled on the issue of the marriage of its heiress, Judith Barry, to John Maxwell of Farnham, Co. Cavan, in 1719. For a hundred years it was kept separate from the Cavan estate by the device of settling and re-settling it on a younger son, who then changed his name from Maxwell to Barry. In 1823, however, when the representative of the cadet line, Colonel John Maxwell Barry of Newtownbarry, succeeded to the Farnham estate and as 5th Baron Farnham, he retained Newtownbarry in his own possession. This was the second time that a Barry had succeeded to Farnham. But this time special circumstances obtained. First, the 5th Baron's younger brother was a wastrel and not the man to carry on a cadet line at Newtownbarry. Second, the Farnham estate had been heavily encumbered over the past two generations to provide extra-large portions for by-passed heiresses. So family finances no longer permitted a hiving-off of Newtownbarry. The Cavan and Wexford estates remained united until 1852 when what James Barry, the father of the Newtownbarry heiress, had feared in 1719 finally came to pass: the 7th Baron Farnham decided that Newtownbarry was so remote an appendage that it would be of more value to Farnham if converted to hard cash. He sold it to a property developer from Manchester.

This is by no means an isolated example. Indeed, when inheritance patterns are studied on a regional basis, as Dickson has the greater Cork region, it begins to look as if devoting the heiress's estate to the founding of a cadet dynasty was not so much an idea which occurred independently to numerous families appropriately circumstanced, as an unwritten rule or norm, and one so widely understood and accepted that settlement documents often do not make specific provision for it. Dickson's illustrations of this point are the more significant in that they begin before the start-date of the present study:

> John Bayly of Castlemore (Muskerry), when leaving his estate to an only daughter in 1718, specifically settled the reversion on the second son of her marriage. The 1st Viscount Doneraile married an English heiress in 1690, and their fortune was destined for their second son, Hayes St Leger; in 1720 Doneraile sold £10,000 held in the Funds, presumably part of his wife's fortune, and purchased the manor of Liscarrol. It was said at the time that thereby he 'designs to make a second family', an enthusiasm no doubt strengthened by the fact that he was on extremely bad terms with his elder son.[285]

As in the Doneraile instance just mentioned, cadet inheritance of the maternal estate sometimes wears a misleading appearance of having been inspired by paternal (or maternal) favouritism. Younger sons were more likely to become objects of favouritism than their elder brothers, because they left the parental nest later and were not so soon exposed to the kind of temptations which would bring them into disfavour. One mother among many who adored her second son, 'a most pleasing young man', and came to detest her first-born, was Theodosia, Countess of Clanwilliam, heiress to the Magill family estates of her father at Gilford and Rathfriland, Co. Down.[286] But these feelings may well have had nothing to do with the decision that Rathfriland, which was much the more valuable part of the Down estates, should pass to the second son and his issue.

Her plans at the time of her marriage in 1765 to the great Tipperary landowner, Sir John Meade, 4th Bt, subsequently created Earl of Clanwilliam, are unclear. It looks as if she intended that the eldest son should have Gilford, where the Magill family seat and haunted house of Gill Hall was located, in addition to the Clanwilliam estates in Counties Tipperary, Cork and Kilkenny. In 1787 and again in 1794 it became necessary to revise dramatically the terms of the 1765 settlement. This was because the Clanwilliam estates in the south were dwindling to nothing under pressure of the debts which the feckless and dissolute Lord Clanwilliam had loaded upon them. In 1793, Lady Clanwilliam quarrelled with her eldest son over his choice of a wife. The effect of the quarrel was that she did nothing, under the re-settlement of 1794, to compensate him in Co. Down for the loss of effectively everything he had expected to inherit in the south. The Gilford estate was formally settled upon him and upon the issue of his stigmatised marriage, but future earls of Clanwilliam were going to be much smaller and poorer landowners than the junior branch of the Meade family upon whom Lady Clanwilliam now settled the estate at Rathfriland. This founding of a cadet dynasty had probably been her plan from the beginning: the significance of her quarrel with the next Lord Clanwilliam was that it disinclined her to change the plan following the disappearance of the southern estates.[287]

In the same decade, the 1st Marquess of Donegall's entirely justified preference for his younger over his elder son caused him to leave to the former at his death in 1799 every square inch of property within his disposable power. But this does not fully explain how and why the younger son had come into possession of one part of his inheritance, the southern estate of Dunbrody Park, Co. Wexford. Dunbrody had come into the Donegall family through marriage with the heiress of its then owners, the Itchinghams, back in 1660. Since then, it had been reserved for cadet branches, who had added Itchingham to their patronymic. At one point it seems to have reverted to the main branch and in the next generation been employed again for the endowment of a younger son. The son of that younger son inherited the family estates and title in 1757 and was created marquess of Donegall in 1791. Not surprisingly, he followed the family tradition and inheritance pattern by employing Dunbrody as an endowment for his own younger son, on whom he settled it when the younger son married in 1795.[288] These developments were obviously too remote and too complicated to have been anticipated by the original Donegall-Itchingham marriage settlement of 1660. Rather, the explanation lies in the fact that an estate brought into a family by or through a woman acquired a life, and its descent a momentum, of their own.[289]

There is no clearer instance of this than the extraordinary descent of the large Thomond estate in counties Clare and Limerick and in Essex, Cambridgeshire and Northamptonshire. In 1707, Henry O'Brien (1688–1741), 7th and last

Earl of Thomond, married Lady Elizabeth Seymour, eldest of the four daughters of the 6th Duke of Somerset. Soon afterwards, her next sister, Catherine, married Sir William Wyndham, 3rd Bt, of Orchard Wyndham, Somerset. The Wyndhams had two sons, Charles, the heir, who also succeeded in 1748 as 2nd Earl of Egremont and to estates in Sussex, Cumberland and Yorkshire, and Percy, a landless younger son. Meanwhile, the Earl and Countess of Thomond, whose marriage had proved childless, were casting about them for an heir. The logical choice, in dynastic terms, would have been the 4th Earl of Inchiquin, a friend, a distant kinsman, a resident Irish landlord, and the sharer with Lord Thomond of a common descent from the ancient kings or princes of Thomond. This was the choice which Lord Thomond made, but in an ineffectual way. Though he must have known that two of Lord Inchiquin's sons had already died young, he willed the estates to the third and only surviving one, Lord O'Brien, a boy of ten. In the event of Lord O'Brien's death, the next heir designated by the will was not Lord Inchiquin or Lord Inchiquin's heirs and successors, but *Lady* Thomond's nephew, who had of course no O'Brien blood in him whatever. The one precaution which Lord Thomond took against the possible submergence of the Thomond inheritance in the still greater estates of the Egremonts, was cadet inheritance. The Wyndham nephew who was placed in remainder to the Thomond estates was Percy, the younger son, and if he inherited them he was to assume the name O'Brien. These dispositions would be more explicable if they had been made by, or under the influence of, Lady Thomond. But she pre-deceased her husband, dying in 1734. So it was Lord Thomond himself who left the reversionary interest in the estate to a man who was not a blood relative.

In the event, the reversionary clause became operative. Lord Thomond died in April 1741 and Lord O'Brien five months later in September. 'The interest of this noble family', the O'Briens, was now split in two. Lord Inchiquin's new heir was his nephew (who, as has been seen, also became his son-in-law in 1753), while Lord Thomond's new heir was Percy Wyndham, who double-barrelled his name to Wyndham O'Brien, and was created earl of Thomond (for British party-political reasons) in 1756. Percy Wyndham O'Brien contemplated standing for Co. Clare in 1744, took some initial interest in his huge Irish inheritance and at least did not milk it for English purposes. But the Dublin-based head agent for the estates, Edmond Hogan, was soon complaining of Wyndham O'Brien's 'indolence' and inactivity. Nor was much help forthcoming from Lord Inchiquin who – surprise! surprise! – had 'lately neglected us strangely'. Once Wyndham O'Brien was raised to the Irish peerage, the possibility of his standing for Co. Clare ceased to exist; he resided constantly in England, either in London or at the Thomond seat of Shortgrove, Newport (near Saffron Walden), Essex; and his main contribution to Irish affairs in later life was to join in the opposition to the proposed absentee tax in 1773. He died, unmarried, in the following year, 'possessed' according to Horace Walpole 'of near £10,000 a year and £50,000 in money'.

Shortgrove, Newport, Essex, from a postcard of c.1890. The house has since been demolished.

COURTESY OF MRS IAN CAMPBELL (a descendant of its purchaser in 1801)

Percy Lord Thomond had intended to repeat the device of cadet inheritance in the next generation by leaving the Thomond inheritance to his younger nephew, the Hon. Percy Charles Wyndham (1757–1833). But he died intestate. This meant that his real estate passed to his eldest nephew and heir-at-law, the 3rd Earl of Egremont, the youthful head of the Wyndham family. Egremont voluntarily gave the Thomond estates in England to Percy Wyndham (who sold Shortgrove in 1801), but retained the Irish estates in his own hands and assumed the name of O'Brien. This was probably for the good and generous reason that he knew that managing the Irish side of the inheritance would be attended with heavy responsibility, labour and expense. But it meant that, as far as the lands in the homeland of the O'Briens were concerned, cadet inheritance was at an end. In 1798, Egremont was loftily informed that, 'compared with your English property, your property in Ireland is of little consideration'. It still amounted to 44,000 statute acres as late as 1879.[290]

The descent of the Thomond estate to a younger son of the Wyndhams, its alienation from the great Irish family of O'Brien, and its subsequent submergence among the greater estates of the Egremonts, made no sense in either dynastic or geographical terms. There had been geographical rationale in the separating of Dunbrody from the Antrim and Donegal estates of the Donegalls – although such considerations did not inhibit the 1st Marquess of Donegall from leaving his younger son in 1799 parts of the northern estates as well. There was also geographical rationale for cadet inheritance in the Clanwilliam-Magill and Annesley-Grove instances, because in all of them the heiress's estate was in a different province from her husband's. In another case of cadet inheritance, the Naper/Dutton estates, the geographical rationale was stronger still, because the estates were in different kingdoms. In 1743 James Dutton Naper of Loughcrew, Oldcastle, Co. Meath, inherited via his mother the estate of an English cousin, Sir John Dutton, 2nd Bt, of Sherborne, Gloucestershire. When Naper died in 1776, he practised cadet inheritance in reverse: i.e. he settled the more prestigious and probably more valuable Gloucestershire estate on his eldest son, who changed his name to Dutton and was created Lord Sherborne in 1784, and the Meath estate on his second son, William Naper.

However, it was not geography which really decided such things. The 'teapot' Lord Darnley, for example, when at last he married, secured an adjacent heiress called Stoyte, whose Co. Westmeath inheritance was well situated to form an adjunct to his own Meath/Westmeath estate. Her property, however, appears to have passed to the second son. The same thing happened in the case of the Petty estate in Co. Kerry. In 1751, when it passed into the family of Anne Petty (d.1737), wife of Thomas Fitzmaurice, 1st Earl of Kerry, geography would have suggested – since both estates were in the same county – that they be united in the one person. But this did not happen. Instead, the Petty estate passed to a younger son of the 2nd Earl of Kerry who became the 1st Earl of Shelburne of a second creation and founded a separate dynasty of Petty-Fitzmaurices.[291]

In another instance, too, that of the Ormonde and Wandesford estates in Co. Kilkenny, united in 1784 in the persons of the 17th Earl of Ormonde and his wife, Lady Frances Susan Wandesford (sole heiress of her father, the 5th Viscount Castlecomer and only Earl Wandesford), considerations of geography and county electioneering would have suggested that the two should remain united ever after. The Ormonde estate had a rental of over £14,000 a year in 1760, and the Wandesford a rapidly rising rental of £2,395 at about that time plus the income from the famous Castlecomer collieries. One contemporary, referring to the combined income of the two families, exclaimed: 'Some German princes are obliged to support standing armies with less.'[292] Nevertheless, the Ormonde and Wandesford estates were settled on different sons. When the 17th Earl of Ormonde died in 1796, he was succeeded in the Ormonde estate by his eldest son, who died without issue in 1820, and was succeeded by his next brother. When the Dowager Lady Ormonde died in 1830, having retained the Wandesford estate as a separate entity for the whole period from 1784 to then, she was succeeded in it by the fourth, but third surviving, son, who assumed the name Wandesford. He also assumed the name Southwell, because his maternal grandmother, Countess Wandesford, had been the heiress of a minor Co. Limerick family of that name. So, regardless of geography, the younger son succeeded to the female part of the inheritance, which itself had no geographical rationale.

Geography mattered a lot to those far lower down the social scale than the aristocracy. They might well marry into the neighbouring farm or the next-door field, especially in periods of receding population; and, if they lacked capital, that might be the only mode of annexation open to them. But, except in a few instances, marriage to the neighbour's daughter was not an aristocratic habit,[293] simply because the aristocratic marriage-market was country-wide, or rather Dublin-, and after 1800 increasingly London-, orientated. One apparent exception, the heiress who in 1678 annexed an adjacent estate in Donegal to the Abercorn family's estate in Tyrone, turns out on closer examination to be an exception who proves the rule; for she was an English lady whose inheritance was in cash, and whose trustees used it to buy this Donegal estate when it came on the market seventeen years after her marriage to an Abercorn.[294] Another apparent exception is provided by the aristocratic marriage pattern in Co. Cork at the end of the eighteenth century. At that time, eight heads 'of the twelve ennobled families [resident in the county] ... were married [in]to other Cork titled or "county" families, three more had married into other Munster families, and the exception, the 2nd Earl of Shannon', had married the daughter of a non-resident Cork landowner.[295] However, this interesting and, in all senses, provincial marriage pattern did not lead to the dynastic aggrandisement of any of the families concerned, because none of the ladies seems to have been an heiress. Perhaps it was peculiar to Cork, or Munster?

More commonly, marriage to a lady who either was or became a landed heiress, involved her husband in the trouble and responsibility of running an estate which, if not ultimately lost to his family by cadet inheritance, was remote from and inconvenient to the rest of his landed interests, and which, if near and convenient, was no less liable to cadet inheritance for that.

An estate which passed, again more or less under its own momentum, through two heiresses, without coming to rest in the family of the husband of either of them, was the Harman estate of Newcastle near Ballymahon, Co. Longford. In 1742, Anne Harman, ultimate heiress to the Harman estate, married – as his second wife – Sir Laurence Parsons, 3rd Bt, of Parsonstown (Birr), Co. Offaly. Parsons's son by his first marriage succeeded to the baronetcy and the Parsons estate, while his surviving son by the second marriage succeeded in 1784 to the Harman inheritance (amounting, by repute, to nearly £8,000 a year and £50,000 in cash) and assumed the name Harman in lieu of Parsons.[296] The new Mr Harman and his half-brother's son and successor, Sir Laurence Parsons, 5th Bt, were closely allied politically; so much so that in 1792 the Lord Lieutenant successfully recommended Harman for an Irish peerage as 'Lord Oxmantown, with remainder to Sir L. Parsons..., as by that means ... we got the goodwill of Sir L. Parsons, who is a very troublesome debater'. Another contemporary commentator added: 'Mr Harman has one daughter and is one of the richest men in the kingdom; I suppose he will marry her to Parsons.'[297] This was a somewhat strained supposition (reminiscent of the arranged match within the Inchiquin family to which reference has already been made). But, since the title of Oxmantown, and the earldom of Rosse to which Lord Oxmantown was promoted in 1806 with the same collateral remainder, had formerly been held by another branch of the Parsons family, it might reasonably have been supposed that Lord Oxmantown intended to unite his estates and titles in the person of Sir Laurence Parsons.[298]

Even this supposition, however, was unwarranted. In 1799, Lord Oxmantown's daughter and heiress married, not his own nephew, but his wife's,

Sir Laurence Parsons, 5th Bt, who in 1807 succeeded his uncle as 2nd Earl of Rosse, from an engraving of 1810 by J. Heath after John Comerford.

AUTHOR'S COLLECTION

the Hon. Robert King. Having already (in effect) obtained a peerage for Sir Laurence Parsons, Lord Oxmantown now set about obtaining another for his King nephew and son-in-law, whom he described in his letter of recommendation as

> grandson to Edward, [1st] Earl of Kingston, and in possession of all his properties (and I flatter myself, of all his virtues), amounting to £11,000 a year. He has also above £1,500 a year by his wife [Lord Oxmantown's daughter]. On the death of his uncle, Colonel King, he will get near [?£2,000] a year in landed property, and I daresay £50,000 in money.... I have above £8,000 a year at my own disposal, which I have no doubt will belong to him or his children.

Yet, notwithstanding his eagerness to secure the advancement of both his nephews, and the geographical appropriateness of the '£8,000 a year at my own disposal' to the estate of either of them, it was not Lord Oxmantown's intention that the Harman inheritance should be merged in the King estate any more than in the Parsons. The guarded reference to its belonging ultimately to King's children, meant a younger son. On Lord Oxmantown's death in 1807, it passed to his widow, and on her death in 1838 to the Kings' second son, who duly double-barrelled his surname to King-Harman.[299]

The striking features of this complicated case are that Lord Oxmantown, who had shown such anxiety to preserve the Harman name and the separate identity of the Harman estate, had not himself been born a Harman, and had been sufficiently alive to his Parsons ancestry to revive in his person the extinct Parsons peerages; also, that neither of the heiresses to the estate (Lord Oxmantown's mother and daughter), far less the husbands of either of them, ever seems actually to have owned it.

The examples so far considered of marriage to landed heiresses show, therefore, that the result was, not to provide adjuncts to the Annesley, Grenville, Clanwilliam, Donegall, Darnley, Farnham, Fitzmaurice, Naper, Ormonde and Parsons estates, but to provide the Grove, Nugent, Magill, Itchingham, Stoyte, Barry, Petty, Dutton, Wandesford and Harman estates with male heirs. It was the heiress's, not her husband's or son's, estate which was the beneficiary of these alliances. In the male-orientated and -dominated world of this period, an estate needed a man: it needed one to reside upon it at least periodically; to provide employment for, and otherwise to spend money among, some of its inhabitants; to protect its interests as a local magistrate and perhaps county grand juryman; and, if it was big enough, to represent in parliament the county constituency in which possession of it conferred electoral influence. In 1800, the second husband of a British dowager announced that in consequence 'of the alliance which has taken place between me and the Duchess of Newcastle, the management of all the Duke of Newcastle's [her son] affairs and interests of course devolves upon me, jointly with the Duchess, during his minority'.[300] The baldness of the assumption and especially the use of the phrase 'of course', are striking.

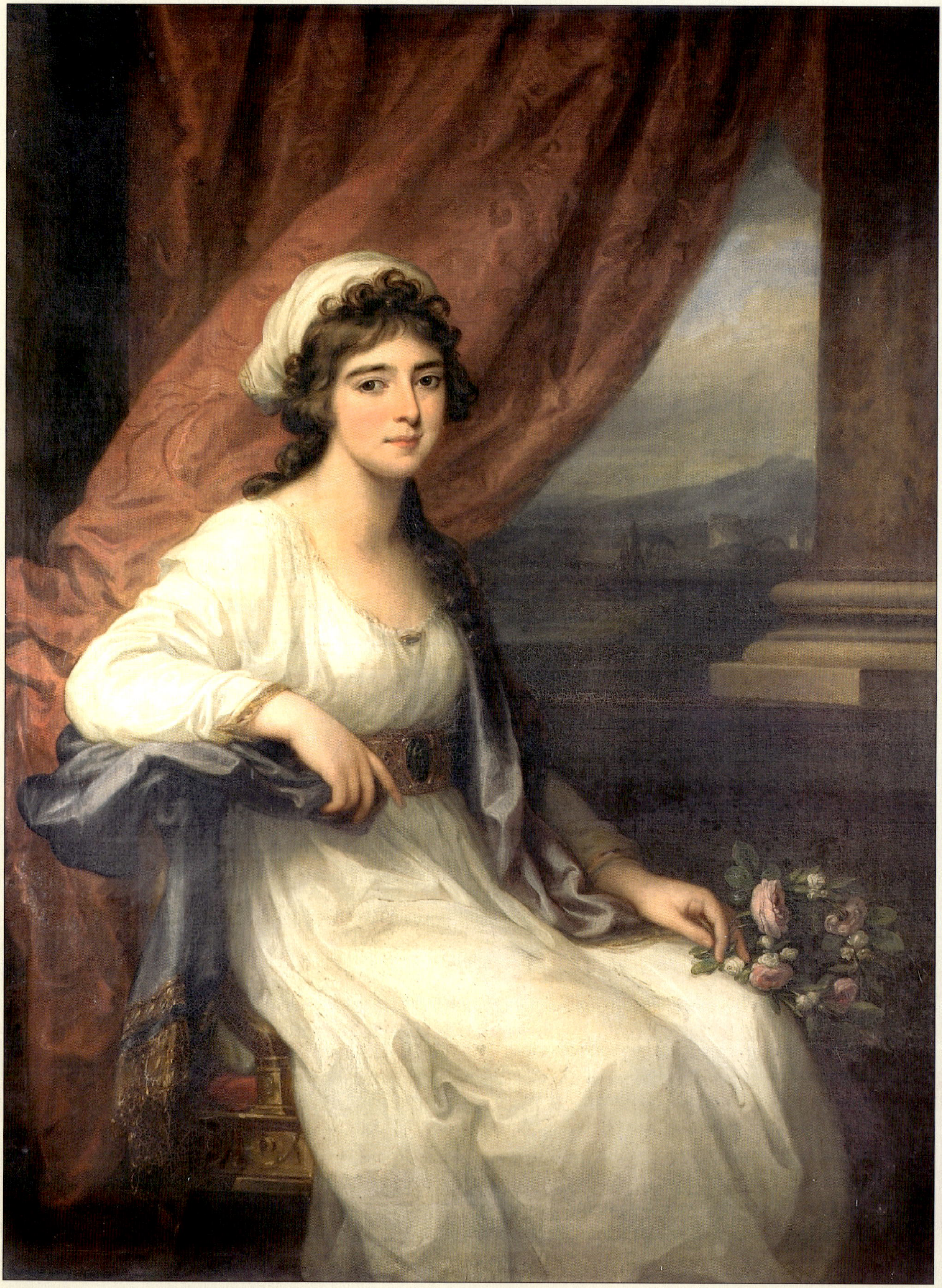

COLLATORAL DAMAGE: THE LURE OF THE YOUNGER SON

No Irish family more frequently lacked the benefits of male management of its 'affairs and interests' than the Grandison family; for, on three different occasions in the period 1662–1800 male heirs failed and the family estate passed to and through a woman. In 1782, when the 2nd Earl Grandison succeeded his mother, Lady Grandison, the second of these women, after a fourteen-year period of absenteeism as well as female possession, the family agent declared:

> My ambition would be fulfilled if I had once the happiness of seeing you fixed at Dromana [the family seat in Co. Waterford], where you would be adored, and [I] am convinced your residence there, even for a few months, would most materially contribute to the final adjustment of your affairs.[301]

Unfortunately, there proved to be nothing adorable about the 2nd Earl Grandison. He had always been 'inclined to be wild', and ten years earlier had been described as 'very ingenious in the art of wasting the most possible money in the least possible time'.[302]

He died, unlamented, in 1800, and was succeeded by the third woman to inherit Dromana since 1662, his only child, Lady Gertrude Amelia Villiers. With a rental income of almost £8,000 a year (it had been c.£9,000 before her father inherited), Lady Gertrude must have been one of the biggest catches of the day, in British as well as Irish terms: indeed, she had earlier numbered among her suitors the eldest son of an English duke, the 5th Duke of Leeds.[303] The condition of her marriage to the heir of this or any other great family would presumably have been that the Grandison estate would pass to a second son, since not even the 2nd Earl Grandison would have been so foolish as to allow it to be forgotten among the broader English acres of the dukes of Leeds, and perhaps eventually disposed of as an inconvenient addendum. After 1800, however, the Grandison family needed a full-time male head and the Grandison estate a man, more urgently than the slow process of remainder on a younger son would have permitted.

This is probably why Lady Gertrude made, in 1802, a far from splendid marriage to a ready-made, up-and-running younger son. Her choice fell on Lord Henry Stuart, the impecunious fifth son of a British marquess, the 1st Marquess of Bute. Interestingly, at roughly the same time and for roughly the same reason, a similar match was made by another great heiress (to whom reference will shortly be made), Lady Charlotte McDonnell, daughter and co-heiress of the Marquess of Antrim. Neither lady needed to seek for acreage in a husband, although ready money would have been welcome to both. But what both needed above all was a man, of suitable social status and sufficiently free from commitments of his own, to assume the headship of their respective families and to act as a rallying point for their respective family interests. Indeed, Lady Gertrude was willing to pay handsomely for such a man: the marriage settlement provided for Lord Henry Stuart what can only be described as a widower's jointure, and of the large amount of £3,000 a year.[304] In co-operation with Lady Gertrude's

Lady Gertrude Amelia Mason Villiers, painted by Angelica Kauffman in Rome in 1794. When every allowance is made for Kauffman's propensity to flatter, it is clear that Lady Gertrude was a beauty as well as an heiress.

PRIVATE COLLECTION

Katherine Fitzgerald, later Fitzgerald Villiers (1652–1725), Viscountess Grandison in her own right, the first of the Dromana heiresses; from a portrait of c.1685–90 by a follower of Sir Peter Ledy.

PRIVATE COLLECTION

trustees, Lord Henry immediately set to work 'to curb present irregularities' and raise the Dromana rental, by an estimated £1,500 a year from March 1803.[305] It was a considerable misfortune for the Grandison family that he (and Lady Gertrude) died young, in 1809. Well before then, however, his brother-in-law, Sir William Homan, Bt, had been installed at Dromana in the capacity of agent for the trustees; and Homan's rank, relationship and residence proved sufficient to tide things over until Lord Henry's and Lady Gertrude's eldest son, another Henry, who had assumed the name Villiers before his patronymic, came of age in 1824.

The need for a man was felt most strongly in that essentially male preserve, local politics and administration; and here the effects of the Stuarts' coming to

COLLATORAL DAMAGE: THE LURE OF THE YOUNGER SON

Dromana were strikingly felt. Traditionally, the Grandison family's great rivals for the highest county offices and the county representation in parliament, were the earls of Tyrone/marquesses of Waterford. This dynastic rivalry dated from at least the 1670s, when the first of the Dromana heiresses, Katherine FitzGerald of the Decies, had been rescued from an enforced marriage to the 2nd Earl of Tyrone by her second marriage to Edward Villiers, the first of the Grandisons to reign at Dromana. After the death of their son, the 1st Earl Grandison, in 1766, there followed the next female interregnum at Dromana; and during these years, the Earl of Tyrone of the day (who has already featured as Henry Monck's son-in-law) obtained for himself the county governorship and came to dominate the county representation. On his succession, in 1782, the 2nd Earl Grandison made a determined effort to challenge Lord Tyrone's political monopoly; but without success.[306] His only success was in the social sphere. In 1785, one visitor to both Dromana and Lord Tyrone's seat, Curraghmore, pronounced the latter to be 'a noble place and a fine house' (though externally plain, it was not the economy-edifice which Monck had recommended); but she found Dromana much the more 'charming' and 'pleasant' place to stay.[307] Immediately on marrying the Dromana heiress in 1802, Lord Henry Stuart sought to assert its political as well as social pre-eminence over Curraghmore. He laid plans to 'wrest the county out of the hands of all antagonists', and was contemplating offering himself as a candidate for the next vacancy, when death intervened in 1809.[308]

It was left to his son, Henry Villiers-Stuart, to carry these plans into execution, by standing for the county in 1826, shortly after his coming-of-age, and defeating the Curraghmore candidate, an uncle of the 3rd Marquess of Waterford. There was another dimension to this election campaign, Henry Villiers-Stuart's espousal of Catholic Emancipation and adoption by the Catholic Association.[309] But this has been given undue prominence relative to the older, dynastic dimension. Although Henry Villiers-Stuart lost the seat at the general election of 1830, he soon afterwards made a longer-lasting gain at the expense of Curraghmore. The change of government later in that year, the coming-to-power of his political friends, the Whigs, and the minority (by a matter of months) of the 3rd Marquess of Waterford, a Tory, made possible his appointment as Lieutenant of the City and County of Waterford in 1831, when lieutenancies on the English model were introduced into Ireland in place of the old Irish county governorships.[310] The governorship of Co. Waterford had not belonged to Dromana since 1766. Finally, in 1839, Henry Villiers-Stuart was created a baron of the United Kingdom, as Lord Stuart de Decies. His grandiloquent choice of title sounds absurd out of context. But in the context of the FitzGerald family of the Decies's long search for a male heir and representative to re-live their former glories and discomfit their old rivals, it is singularly appropriate.

Viewed in this perspective, the Stuarts appear to have fairly earned the Dromana inheritance – particularly Lord Stuart de Decies, to whom most of the work fell because of Lord Henry's early death, and who had the further

'The quarrelling Countesses': detail of a portrait of Anne Catherine, Countess of Antrim (1775–1834), painted by Hugh Douglas Hamilton, c.1800; and *overleaf* a cut-down head and shoulders portrait of her younger sister and successor as countess of Antrim.

COURTESY OF VISCOUNT DUNLUCE

incentive of being the actual owner of the estate. This, Lord Henry never would have been; and nor was his similarly situated contemporary, Lord Mark Kerr, third son of the 5th Marquess of Lothian, and husband of the already-mentioned Lady Charlotte McDonnell.

Lady Charlotte was co-heiress with her elder sister, Lady Anne Catherine, Countess of Antrim in her own right, of their late father, the 6th Earl and only Marquess of Antrim.[311] Lord Antrim had died without issue male in 1791. Well before his death, in anticipation of a female succession, he had obtained a new creation of his earldom of Antrim, specially remaindered on the issue male of his daughters, in order of seniority. At that stage there were three daughters. The second of them, Lady Letitia, died young and unmarried in 1797. This left Lady Anne Catherine, who succeeded as Countess of Antrim, and produced one daughter and no issue male; and Lady Charlotte, who produced a large family of four sons and six daughters, and whose eldest surviving son ultimately succeeded to the specially remaindered earldom of Antrim. What confused matters and led to ill-blood between the sisters, was that Lord Antrim's disposition of his estates – mainly in the north Antrim baronies of Cary, Dunluce and Glenarm (where his seat, Glenarm Castle, was) – did not coincide with the remainders in his new earldom, even though his will was made in 1789 and the earldom had been conferred in 1785. Instead of entailing all his landed property on the bearer of the title for the time being, he had divided it equally among his (then) three daughters.

In 1799, the two surviving daughters and co-heiresses both married: Anne Catherine, Countess of Antrim, married Sir Henry Vane-Tempest, 2nd Bt, and Lady Charlotte married Lord Mark Kerr. Sir Henry was a rich Co. Durham proprietor, but the potential (in terms of coal) of his property had not yet been fully grasped, so he was far from uninterested in his wife's Co. Antrim estate. Lord Mark Kerr had much more reason to be interested in the Antrim estate; as a younger son and a landless seaman, he was mainly dependent on the income from it to feed, clothe and educate his growing family. Between two brothers-in-law thus situated, litigation inevitably ensued. It raged until 1803, when the Irish Court of Chancery decreed

> Sir Henry and his wife … to be entitled to one-third part of the Antrim estates, including the barony, castle and park of Glenarm, as tenants-in-tail [male],[312] and to a half of one other third [Lady Letitia's] of the estate as tenants-for-life; and Lord Mark Kerr and his wife … [to] be entitled to the remainder of the estate being one half of the entire estate, as tenants-for-life.… It was … supposed that the Chancellor would decree differently as to the division of the estates, and the will as it is framed would warrant him to do so. But … in this

A first design for Improvement & Restoration of Glenarm Castle. by William Morrison. Esqr. Archt.

case, if the Countess should die without male issue, the issue male of Lady Mark Kerr would take the *entire* of the Antrim estate and exclude the female issue of the Countess – and you know this circumstance is very likely to happen. And therefore … according to the decree, … if it shall happen that the Countess shall die without male issue and that Lady Mark Kerr shall leave a son, such son on his coming of age will be entitled to two-thirds of the Antrim estate [plus half of Lady Letitia's third].

Although the worst of the litigation ended in 1803, disputes continued over the implementation of the decree and over which parts of the estate should be sold to raise the £70,000-odd required to pay off the debts of the late Lord Antrim. The unsold property was eventually partitioned between the two co-heiresses in 1814, after protracted surveying and valuing, which caused much trouble and led to much expense.

Relations between the two sisters during the time of Lady Antrim's first marriage were strained. But they became even more strained when, four years after Sir Henry Vane-Tempest's death in 1813, Lady Antrim married as her second husband one Edmund Phelps, who was 'five years her junior, his birth as low as possible' – his father had been an auctioneer and his mother a milliner[313] – and who now assumed the name McDonnell in right of his wife. Lady Mark Kerr inveighed against the marriage because it was morganatic. But at the back of her mind was probably the fear that even at this late stage Lady Antrim might have a son, who would succeed to all Lady Antrim's half of the estate, as well as to the earldom of Antrim. This fear proved groundless. When Lady Antrim died, in 1834, her only issue was her daughter by her first marriage, Frances Anne Vane-Tempest, now Marchioness of Londonderry (wife, since 1819, of Lord

'A first design for improvement and restoration of Glenarm castle by William [Vitruvius] Morrison Esq., architect', c.1824. One of the positive benefits of Lady Antrim's second and morganatic marriage was that Edmond Phelps/McDonnell persuaded her to undertake this 'improvement and restoration' of the family seat to Morrison's designs.

PRONI, D/3560/1

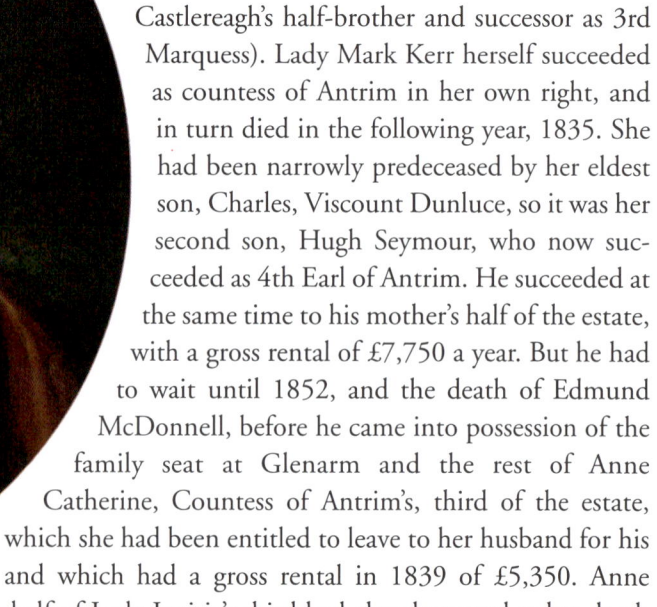

Charlotte, Lady Mark Kerr (1779–1835), painted by an unknown artist, c.1805.
COURTESY OF VISCOUNT DUNLUCE

Castlereagh's half-brother and successor as 3rd Marquess). Lady Mark Kerr herself succeeded as countess of Antrim in her own right, and in turn died in the following year, 1835. She had been narrowly predeceased by her eldest son, Charles, Viscount Dunluce, so it was her second son, Hugh Seymour, who now succeeded as 4th Earl of Antrim. He succeeded at the same time to his mother's half of the estate, with a gross rental of £7,750 a year. But he had to wait until 1852, and the death of Edmund McDonnell, before he came into possession of the family seat at Glenarm and the rest of Anne Catherine, Countess of Antrim's, third of the estate, which she had been entitled to leave to her husband for his life, and which had a gross rental in 1839 of £5,350. Anne Catherine's half of Lady Letitia's third had already passed at her death in 1834 to her daughter, Frances Anne, Marchioness of Londonderry, and was entailed on Frances Anne's issue male. This last part of the estate, with a gross rental in 1839 of £2,450 a year, was thus permanently divorced from the Antrim title, in accordance with the Marquess of Antrim's will of 1789, as interpreted by the Chancery decree of 1803.[314]

From his marriage in 1799 to his death, which took-place in 1840, Lord Mark Kerr, the husband of the co-heiress who ultimately inherited five sixths of the estate, and the father of the inheritor of the Antrim title, was in the thick of this protracted legal and family conflict. His portrait at Glenarm Castle, and his surviving letters, show him to have been a warm- and big-hearted man. He even died on affectionate terms with Edmund McDonnell. To such a man, the position of husband and legal representative of the co-heiress to a disputed inheritance, was 'painful'. Moreover, even in financial terms, it was unprofitable to him personally. In spite of this, he found it necessary in 1838 to provide 'a detailed account ... of all I had done on the Antrim estate since it was bestowed upon me', for the purpose of refuting 'vile reports' that his extravagance and too-great regard for his younger children had impoverished the 4th Earl of Antrim. The 'detailed account' merits extensive quotation:

Lord Mark Kerr (1776–1840), wearing naval uniform with a tartan slung over his shoulders to emphasise his (Lowland) Scottish origins. Painted by Margaret Carpenter, c.1810.
COURTESY OF VISCOUNT DUNLUCE

> I have the innate satisfaction of knowing and feeling that, whatever was expended or whatever is now expending, was so done for the benefit of the person who gave me the power, for her estate or for her children. The difficulties we had in

living on our means and supporting and educating and bringing forward into the world so many children, was [*sic*] indeed beyond expression. The pains I took to keep to *myself alone* many and many great anxieties I had on this account, that her heart might not be scathed, caused me hundreds and hundreds of sleepless nights....

When I came to the estate, nearly as I can recollect we had about £1,600 a year after paying the [Dowager] Marchioness's jointure, but I think I might then possess about £7,000 of [naval] prize-money – fortunately, as out of this principal I was under the necessity of furnishing or adding to the comforts we required at the different homes we rented. They were, however, our means being small, small also – generally about £70 per annum. The first thing I recollect was the sale of estates for the payment of Lord Antrim's debts. Amongst others, £14,000 Irish currency was allotted to me, it being part of a portion allotted to his daughters. I immediately put it out of my power, by settling it on my younger children. I was young at the time, and performed this deed, that I might not be tempted to expend it extravagantly on other matters, and as it was my own....

From year to year (and subjecting us to great difficulties) did we pay for many things beneficial to the estate – law expenses, etc, for the various commissions [for their sons in the army] and other expenses – and it was then said, of course, our first son that comes of age will repay you these out-goings which press you so hard; and it was done. As near as I could, I calculated what would repay me, and £12,000 was raised, out of which I was to take £7,000. This I did take, though I considered that it was not enough, and I still was in debt about £2,000. But, relieved from so much, I thought I could find means from our increasing estate and increasing frugality to overcome it. The remaining £5,000 was applied for other purposes, £2,000 for the estate, [£3,000 for more commissions, etc]....

I can only add that in the whole of my life, as connected with this estate, I have never spent one farthing in extravagance. Everything was expended for her comfort and happiness or for her children.... I had £7,000 of my own in the first instance, I reaped additional prize-money to the amount of more than £4,000 more, and I got a legacy at my father's death of £3,000. Such portion of these sums, I expended in indulgences to ourselves, in collecting a few books and in purchasing such matters of curiosity or pictures as may now be seen in the possession of [the writer].

However incredible these assertions may be, when made by the husband of a countess of £7,750 a year, and the father of an earl of £13,000, nothing that is known about Lord Mark Kerr gives reason to doubt his word. Besides, in this instance he was writing to Edmund McDonnell, who was in the best possible position to detect misstatement.

Obviously, there were special circumstances affecting the Antrim family estate, notably the 'almost ruinous'[315] expenses of litigation, arbitration and partition; but these were to some extent offset by the bonus that the dowager and the burden of her jointure were fairly short-lived. It is perhaps fair to conclude that Lord

Mark Kerr's role, compared to that of other husbands of landed heiresses, was disagreeable, but not especially difficult, not especially ill-remunerated, and not especially invidious. This last characteristic, the invidiousness, derived from the failure of contemporary, like subsequent, commentators to grasp that the husband was, essentially, a male *locum tenens* for his son, the rightful heir. Provided the husband was socially qualified for his situation (which Lords Henry Stuart and Mark Kerr manifestly were, and Edmund McDonnell manifestly was not), nothing else was required – and indeed an estate of his own, with its concomitant duties and preoccupations, was arguably a positive disqualification. Perversely, however, not even possession of an estate of his own would protect him against the imputation of being an adventurer.

This was the imputation levelled in 1865 at Fulke Southwell Greville (1821–83) by his own father-in-law, the 8th Earl and only Marquess of Westmeath. The marriage of Lord Westmeath and Lady Emily Cecil, which had taken place in 1812 on the basis of considerable misrepresentation by the bridegroom of the size of the income from his estate,[316] had produced two children by 1818, when the couple finally parted beds. Of these children, the son and heir died in infancy in 1819, leaving only the Westmeaths' one daughter, Lady Rosa Nugent. In the early stages of a twenty-five-year battle between the Westmeaths arising from the catastrophic failure of their marriage, Lady Westmeath coerced Lord Westmeath into settling the Westmeath family estates in counties Westmeath and Roscommon on Lady Rosa, to the exclusion of his half-brother and of any male child he himself might have by a subsequent marriage. This made Lady Rosa a significant heiress, even though the property was still encumbered and was now feeling the additional strain of her parents' continuous and expensive litigation (in which she took the part of her father, who had custody of her, in spite of the fact that it was to her mother that she owed her status as an heiress).

In 1839 Lady Rosa became engaged to Greville, whom she married in 1840. The engagement, of which her mother was merely notified after the event, found favour with her father, who may even have had a hand in the choosing of Greville. The latter came from a long line of younger sons, had no landed commitments of his own, and was well suited socially to take charge of her inheritance. However, unlike Lords Henry Stuart and Mark Kerr, he must have had money. In 1858 he bought, for something like £125,000, the 7th Earl of Granard's estate in and around Mullingar, the county town of Westmeath, with a rental of £5,270 a year. In 1866, he double-barrelled his name to Greville-Nugent, in 1869 he was created Lord Greville of Clonyn Castle, Co. Westmeath, and from 1871 onwards (when Lord Westmeath died) he flattened the old, decaying castle of that name and built an ugly new one on an adjacent but better site. No husband of an heiress could have done more.

Nevertheless, these achievements won him no immunity from the cantankerousness and irascibility for which Lord Westmeath was increasingly notorious.

COLLATORAL DAMAGE: THE LURE OF THE YOUNGER SON

They quarrelled over Greville's candidature at the Co. Westmeath election of 1865, when Westmeath wrote letters to *The Westmeath Guardian* denouncing Greville as a sham Conservative and the catspaw of the Roman Catholic priesthood. Another cause of offence was Greville's claim in an election address that he had a 'long connection' with Co. Westmeath, which Lord Westmeath hotly contradicted on the grounds that Greville's claim, if it meant anything, 'means a connection through me'. Granted the importance of Greville's contribution to their combined landownership in that county, this was quite unfair. It also imperilled what Lord Westmeath ought to have promoted – a Greville-Nugent victory in county politics. (In the event, Greville was elected, but as a Liberal, not any form of Conservative, and sat for Co. Westmeath until raised to the peerage by the Liberals in 1869.) Nevertheless, this controversy, and the fact that contemporaries and subsequent commentators failed to distinguish between what was Greville's own land and what he inherited via marriage to Lady Rosa Nugent, have left the impression that he was just another man of straw married to an heiress. Ironically, the Greville motto, still to be seen at the foot of the Greville coat of arms on the hotel and market house in Mullingar, is '*Vix ea nostra voco*'.[317]

'Paddy on horseback' (1779), the earliest dated caricature of James Gillray (1757–1815), which depicts a dishevelled Irish adventurer, riding backwards towards London on a galloping Irish bull, carrying a sack of potatoes and a list of ladies with great fortunes living in London. Reproduced from L. Fitzpatrick and R. Teehan, 'Caricature at Churchill', in W. Laffan, *A Year at Churchill* (Churchill Press, Tralee, 2003)

CHURCHILL HOUSE COLLECTION

PADDY on HORSE-BACK.

THE PURSUIT OF THE HEIRESS

A more celebrated example of the prejudice against, and the misrepresentation of, the husband of an heiress is the mid-eighteenth century case of Edward Hussey, Earl of Beaulieu, although it is complicated by national prejudice against Hussey, who was not only the husband of an heiress, but the Irish husband of an English heiress. Hussey's wife, whom he married in 1743, was the already-mentioned Isabella, daughter and ultimately (1749) co-heiress of the 2nd Duke of Montagu, and childless widow of her kinsman, the 2nd Duke of Manchester.[318]

Hussey's engagement to her, which seems to have taken place in the previous year, inspired a witty pamphlet entitled *The Irish Register, or a List of the Duchess Dowagers, Countesses, Widow Ladies, maiden Ladies, Widows and Misses of large Fortunes in England, as registered by the Dublin Society for the Use of Members ...* (Dublin printed: London reprinted ... 1742). The pamphlet begins with a spoof 'President's speech to the Hibernian Society, advising a speedy draught of their members to be imported into England for the service of the English ladies'. This will 'redress our present calamities by cultivating those valuable talents which nature has kindly provided us with', thus counteracting 'the miserable state our dear nation is reduced to by the great number of absentees now residing in England, who spend their fortunes there ... regardless of their country's ruin'. England has to offer 'hundreds of widows and maiden ladies of very great fortunes [who] lie unoccupied and neglected', and who might 'by the most prevailing means' be married and forced 'to come and settle among us.... And that you may flourish according to the dimensions of your different parts and capacities, they [the ladies – not the parts!] are distinguished by their classes.' The classes comprise 11 dowager duchesses (including Manchester), two dowager marchionesses, 15 dowager countesses, 27 widow ladies (all peeresses), 34 baronets' widows, 62 maiden ladies (all titled), 106 widows (all commoners), and 538 misses. Addresses, mainly in London, are provided for all, which justifies Horace Walpole's description of the pamphlet as 'one of the most impudent things that ever was printed'.[319] It concludes with 'Orders and resolutions of the Brave and Heroic Society of Adventurers at Dublin for incorporating ... British commodities'.[320]

Worse was to follow. Following Hussey's marriage to the Dowager Duchess in 1743, the well-known English diplomat and wag, Sir Charles Hanbury-Williams, wrote a poem lampooning him both for his Irishness and his alleged lack of any visible assets except a pair of shapely legs:

> [Since] careful Heaven designed her Grace
> For one of the Milesian race, ...
> I'll sing the conquered Duchess;
> I'll sing of that disdainful Fair,
> Who, 'scaped from Scotch and English snare,
> Is fast in Irish clutches ...

AN IRISH ATTACK ON AN ENGLISH SURLOIN.

Look down, St Patrick, with success,
Like Hussey, all the Irish bless!
May they do all as he does! …
Nature, indeed, denied them sense,
But gave them legs and impudence …
To comfort English widows.[321]

'An Irish attack on an English sirloin', by the Irish caricaturist, William O'Keefe, showing an overweight, overdressed English heiress being wooed by an Irish adventurer. Published by S.W. Forres, 1794 (ibid.).

CHURCHILL HOUSE COLLECTION

Hussey at least accomplished what the Duchess's first husband had not, by fathering an heir to her share of the estates of the dukes of Montagu, in right of which Hussey assumed the name of Montagu on the death of his father-in-law in 1749 and was created Baron Beaulieu in 1762 and earl of Beaulieu in 1784 (both in the peerage of Ireland). However, the son and heir died young, the Duchess died without further issue in 1786, and Hussey died in 1802. Her estates then reverted to the descendants of her sister and co-heiress, one of whom likewise assumed the name of Montagu, and was created Baron Montagu of Beaulieu in 1885. This last attempt at providing Beaulieu with a male heir had much in common with the first attempt by which, presumably, it would have descended to a younger son of the Duchess by her first husband, the Duke, on whom a specially remaindered peerage would previously have been conferred.

The second attempt, involving Hussey, was not the *mésalliance* which the lampoonists misrepresented it as being. As the Duchess pointed out in an (unsuccessful) petition to George II in 1752, she had 'no unreasonable foundation to

THE PURSUIT OF THE HEIRESS

hope' for a barony for 'Mr Montagu', derived from his claims as well as her own. 'His family lost the same rank in Ireland' for supporting the crown against Cromwell, 'and if a fortune can be a motive for restoring an ancient family to what they lost, we have both in England and Ireland estates to support the honour we entreat'.[322] The estates in Ireland were of course Hussey's. Arthur Young computed their rental at £2,500 in 1779; Hussey's estate in Co. Laois (and he owned land elsewhere) was surveyed at over 3,000 Irish acres in 1766; and after his death, in 1810, his 'great possessions' in Ireland were popularly reckoned as bringing in £7,000 a year.[323] Only his invidious position as the husband of an heiress, combined with his Irishness, exposed him to the imputation of being an adventurer.

The same charge was, more surprisingly, brought against the 3rd Marquess of Londonderry, then Lord Stewart, when he married in 1819 the already mentioned Frances Anne, daughter of the Countess of Antrim and Sir Henry Vane-Tempest. One of Lord Londonderry's tormentors, Tom Moore, himself of course an Irishman, sang of young ladies being so mad as 'To marry old dandies who might be their daddies'.[324] But most of the other contemporary criticism was anti-Irish as well as anti-adventurer in sentiment: in spite of her mother's indisputable Irishness, Frances Anne counted as an English heiress. In 1819, Lord Londonderry enjoyed an income of £2,000 a year, charged on the Londonderry family estates; he was heir to part of those estates, with a gross rental of £10,500, and heir presumptive to nearly £21,000 more; and he held ambassadorial, military and Household appointments with salaries totalling £15,500.[325] Adventurers should be made of slighter stuff. The £1,000 a year jointure he settled on her was ludicrously disproportionate to the great possessions in Co. Durham which she had inherited from Sir Henry Vane-Tempest (although it was precisely proportioned to the £10,000 which she brought him in token fortune). But she was already amply provided for out of her own inheritance.

What she lacked was issue male to succeed to the Vane-Tempest estates, and also to her expectations out of the Antrim family estate. Lord Londonderry provided the issue male; he used his political influence to obtain a United Kingdom earldom of Vane and viscountcy of Seaham for himself, with remainder to their sons; and he developed the collieries on the Durham estates with an efficiency, tempered with humanity, which has recently been accorded the complimentary description of 'entrepreneurial paternalism'.[326] These were Vane-Tempest progeny, Vane-Tempest peerages and Vane-Tempest pits: Lord Londonderry's son by

Frances Anne, Marchioness of Londonderry, c.1825, from an engraving of 1838 by Thomson after Chalon
AUTHOR'S COLLECTION

COLLATORAL DAMAGE: THE LURE OF THE YOUNGER SON

a previous marriage was due to inherit his own marquessate of Londonderry and his own estates in Ireland. This separation of the two portfolios applied to the present as well as the future: the incomes from the Stewart and the Vane-Tempest estates were kept distinct, and there was no subsidising of Co. Down by Co. Durham.[327] It was accident – the death, childless, of the 4th Marquess of Londonderry, in 1872, and the succession as 5th Marquess of his Vane-Tempest half-brother, the 2nd Earl Vane – which united the Vane-Tempest name and estates to the marquessate of Londonderry on a permanent basis.[328] Up to that point, the arrangements made following the 3rd Marquess's marriage to the Vane-Tempest heiress had conformed to the usual pattern of cadet inheritance.

Cadet inheritance was not invariably incompatible with the aggrandisement of the husband's family and estate: they could be made compatible when the landed inheritance of the wife was sufficiently great, or perhaps sufficiently scattered, to permit some freedom of manoeuvre. A good example is the landed inheritance of Caroline Wyndham (1790–1870), who married the Hon. Windham Quin, later 2nd Earl of Dunraven, in 1810, and in 1814 inherited the Dunraven Castle estate, Bridgend, Glamorganshire, and a less valuable property at Clearwell Court, near Coleford in Gloucestershire. When she died in 1870, she left Clearwell to their younger son, while the elder, who had already succeeded to his father's earldom and the Quin family estate at Adare and elsewhere in Co. Limerick, received the Glamorganshire estate and, more important, its coal mines. In 1926, by which time the Irish estate had been reduced to very little by Land Purchase, the process was reversed when the Clearwell Court line succeeded to the earldom of Dunraven.[329]

In the case of the dukes of Devonshire, it was no serious loss to the bearer of the dukedom and family head when part of the northern English estates of the Burlington family, whose sole heiress the 4th Duke had married in 1748, were hived off on a younger son, the 1st Earl of Burlington of a new creation (made, when he was 77, in 1831). Meanwhile, the Burlington estates in Ireland, with a rental of £17,000 a year in the late 1790s,[330] remained annexed to the dukedom of Devonshire, as did the jewel of the Burlington inheritance, Chiswick Villa. Likewise, it was no serious loss to future marquesses of Downshire when Mary Sandys, who married the 2nd Marquess in 1786 and was heiress of three different families and to more than half a dozen different properties, settled one of the latter, Ombersley Court, Droitwich, Worcestershire, on a younger son, the 2nd Lord Sandys (and at the same time perpetuated her own family name by getting herself created Baroness Sandys with remainder to him). Notwithstanding this hiving-off of the Sandys estate, subsequent marquesses of Downshire still inherited through her the large Blundell family estates in Down and Offaly, and the Trumbull family estate of Easthampstead Park, Berkshire. Easthampstead, in particular, was the jewel of Mary Sandys's inheritance, since it boasted a more venerable seat than Ombersley, and one better situated from the point of view of access to parliament in London and royalty at Windsor.

THE PURSUIT OF THE HEIRESS

By the standards of 'leviathans' like the Devonshires and the Downshires, these were sentimental gestures towards cadet inheritance, although it may be significant that Lady Downshire did not make hers until 1802, just after her husband's death. They were mere gestures, not just because the heiresses' acres were broad and far-flung, but because the husbands were, in their own right, landowners on an even greater scale than their wives. As Lord Downshire loftily observed, in another context, '*ex nihilo, nihil fit*'.[331]

Successful dynastic marriage was not simply a matter of like marrying like, and money making money. Henry Monck hit on a truth of very wide bearing when he observed, *apropos* the first attempt at a Monck-Tyrone marriage alliance, that the couple were not 'circumstanced for each other, and [it would be] difficult to accommodate the plan for a settlement to the satisfaction of both parties'.[332] A correspondence of financial circumstances was essential if a marriage alliance was to be a bilateral success from the dynastic point of view. Success was easily attained when the husband was a landless younger son and the wife a landed heiress with no man to fulfil the social, political and administrative needs of her estate; but such a marriage cannot be called a dynastic marriage, or a 'merger of two landed fortunes', because the husband had come empty-handed. When the two contracting dynasties had independent assets and distinct interests, accommodating the 'settlement to the satisfaction of both parties' became extremely difficult – as, for example, was apparent in the marriage of Lord Orrery, who needed money, to the Caledon heiress, who brought him land. Actually, just such an accommodation was achieved in the Monck-Tyrone instance: Lord Tyrone's family was advantaged because Monck's loose cash was plentiful enough to portion the Tyrones' younger children; and Monck's family was not disadvantaged, because Monck's landed property (which was already settled on his nephew, the collateral male heir) was large enough to entitle the nephew to be raised to the peerage (in 1797), and the nephew's son to be further advanced to an earldom (in 1822).

John Hely-Hutchinson, in his robes as Provost of Trinity, and *opposite* his heiress-wife, Christian Nickson; non-contemporary engravings of 1866, after portraits by Sir Joshua Reynolds of c.1780, in the possession of the then Lord Donoughmore.

AUTHOR'S COLLECTION

No couple can have been better 'circumstanced for each other' than were John Hely of Gortroe, Co. Cork, an up-and-coming Dublin barrister and a man on the make, and Christian Nickson, whom he married in 1751. Neither name means much, because both were changed. The bride was the great-niece, adopted daughter and heiress of Richard Hutchinson of Knocklofty, near Clonmel, Co. Tipperary, and on succeeding to his estate in 1759 her husband and she double-barrelled their name to Hely-Hutchinson. John Hely-Hutchinson, the future provost of Trinity, was to prove one of the most successful politicians of his day, whose political services earned for his wife, in 1783, an Irish peerage as

106

Baroness Donoughmore of Knocklofty. But skilful operator though he was, not even he found the marriage market a bridegroom's market or an heiress easy prey.

The terms of the settlement of 1751 are complex. But what seems to have happened is that Hely agreed to assume, not only the name Hutchinson, but liability for Richard Hutchinson's debts, totalling some £12,000. Hutchinson, for his part, was not called upon to give any portion with the bride, but instead settled the Knocklofty estate on Hely for life (after Hutchinson's own death), with remainder to the children of the marriage, then to the bride's children by any subsequent marriage, then to Hutchinson's right heirs.

How good or bad a bargain this was from Hely's point of view depends on an unknown quantity, the value of the Knocklofty estate at the time. Since its gross rental was only £4,000 a year in 1790, it could hardly have been producing more than £2,000 a year in 1751, subject to head rents of £438. On this assumption, and on the further assumption that Hely could reasonably have expected a marriage portion of £2,000, and in fact received nothing, the estate cost him £14,000, or roughly half its capital value. This was if anything dear at the price, since he acquired only a contingent, reversionary and life interest. Hutchinson, on the other hand, had greater reason for self-congratulation, having relieved himself of annual interest payments of nearly £700, and having thus increased his disposable income from £850 to over £1,550 a year. However, since Hely needed a position in landed society as much as Hutchinson needed relief from his debts, since Knocklofty was an ideally situated property for a man whose interests were divided between Dublin and Cork, and since the Hely-Hutchinsons had more than enough children to secure the succession to it, the striking retrospective feature of the marriage is how mutually beneficial it was.[333]

Christian Nickson, Lady Donoughmore.
AUTHOR'S COLLECTION

By contrast, the almost contemporary (1758) descent of half of the Co. Dublin and Co. Wicklow estates of the Viscounts Allen of Stillorgan to the Proby family of Elton Hall, Peterborough, Huntingdonshire, can at best be called only a qualified success in dynastic terms. The 2nd Viscount Allen (d.1742) had one son and two daughters. The son died young and unmarried in 1745, the viscountcy passed to a cousin, and the estates went for life to the 2nd Viscount's widow, Margaret (d.1758), with remainder to the Allen daughters and co-heiresses. The elder of these, Elizabeth, married John Proby, the heir to

Elton, in 1750, on which occasion half of the Allen estate, comprising Stillorgan and Blackrock, Co. Dublin, and the manor or lordship of Arklow, Co. Wicklow, with a rental of £2,208 a year, was settled on the issue male of the marriage. The other half of the estate, comprising lands in and around the parliamentary borough of Carysfort and elsewhere in Co. Wicklow, and in counties Carlow, Dublin and Kildare and Dublin city, was settled in 1758 on the issue male of the marriage of the younger sister and co-heiress, Frances, later Lady Newhaven. Both marriage settlements contained 'remainders over' from a sister who had no son to a sister who did. In the event, this meant that almost all of Lady Newhaven's half-share passed to the Probys when she died childless in 1801. Although the Carysfort property was not on his half of the estate, John Proby was raised to an Irish barony of Carysfort in 1750, and his only son by Elizabeth Allen was created earl of Carysfort in 1789. Ten years later, the rental of Lord Caryfort's half-share was £6,668 a year and, in view of the advanced age of Lady Newhaven, would he reckoned 'very shortly amount to £14,000 or £15,000'.

Meanwhile, his by now remote kinsman, the 5th Viscount Allen (1728–1816), whose collateral branch of the Allen family had succeeded to the viscountcy in 1745, was left with only a tiny fraction of the Allen family property, at Punchestown, Co. Kildare, whence derived his nickname of 'the Bog'. To maintain his rank in the peerage, he was dependent on a pension from the government. His situation improved markedly in 1801 when, following the death of Lady Newhaven, he inherited an annuity of £500 under the will of Margaret, Viscountess Allen. But in c.1820 his son and successor, the 6th and last Viscount Allen (d.1845), and other family members were still in receipt of 'aristocratic dole' (in L.B. Namier's famous phrase) in the form of government pensions to a combined value of £1,000 a year. From the point of view of the Allen family, it was dynastically and financially disastrous that the family title had become divorced from the family estate.

Nor, more surprisingly, were the Probys entirely satisfied. The Proby estates in Huntingdonshire and Northamptonshire had a (badly paid) rental of £5,678 a year in 1823, which was a good deal less than half the income the 2nd Earl of Carysfort derived from the Allen estates in Ireland at that date. But the 1st Earl of Carysfort, when urged to devote more time to Ireland and his Irish concerns, roundly declared in 1790: 'My lot is irrevocably cast in this country [England], and it is impossible for me to pursue any political line in Ireland with effect [i.e. by living there], unless I could bring myself to sacrifice Elizabeth's [his English

John Proby, 1st Lord Carysfort (1720–72), decked out in the then fashionable Van Dyck costume. Reproduced from a portrait of 1765 by Sir Joshua Reynolds in Borensius and Hodgson, Elton Hall Pictures, *p.66.*

second wife] domestic happiness and my own at the same time.' From the mid-nineteenth century, the 3rd, 4th and 5th Earls of Carysfort developed a peripatetic pattern of residence which harmonised the interests of their English and Irish estates; but for most of the period under review there was a tension between the two.[334] This was because, back in 1750, the Proby heir and the Allen co-heiress had not been 'circumstanced for each other'. Cadet inheritance within the Proby family would at least have preserved the Allen family name, and relieved the 1st Earl of Carysfort from the difficulty of having to be in two places at once. But cadet inheritance was not possible in this case, because the Allen-Proby marriage produced no second son, and because in the next generation the eldest son died young, the second son succeeded to the title and estates but never married, and the third son then succeeded his elder brother as 3rd Earl of Carysfort.

Moreover, had a cadet line been available, the further difficulty would have arisen that the maternal estate, which would logically have gone to the younger son, was much more valuable than the paternal. This was particularly the case after the accession of the Newhaven share in 1801, which more than compensated for the disfranchisement of Carysfort borough at the Union and the loss of the political clout deriving from its two seats. This question of the relative values of the paternal and maternal estates is probably of crucial importance. Marriage to a landed heiress was likely to be successful, from the husband's dynastic point of view, either if the estates of both the husband and the heiress-wife were so large that cadet inheritance or partial cadet inheritance could be practised without much mattering, or if the heiress-wife's estate was too small for cadet inheritance to be an option.

Heiresses of the latter kind and scale are not easy to recognise because their marriages tend not to create much comment, their estates merge unobtrusively with those of their husbands, and if it is observed that an additional estate has come in, there can be no certainty that it was not acquired by purchase. The Bermingham co-heiresses are perhaps a case in point. Even if Mrs Bermingham was being huffy and sardonic when she described the Rosshill estate as 'trifling',[335] the fact remains that it was low in rental income by comparison with the estates owned by the co-heiresses' husbands, Lords Leitrim and Charlemont. A half-share of it each was hardly a major acquisition. Nor was any attempt made by the Bermingham family and their trustees to perpetuate the Bermingham name and line by cadet inheritance or any other means. (Lord and Lady Leitrim called their eldest son Robert Bermingham Clements, and Lord Leitrim was later to appear, rather unflatteringly, as 'Lord Birmingham [sic]' in Trollope's *The Macdermots of Ballycloran*.) So, in spite of the broadness of their acres, Mary and Anne Bermingham may be regarded as heiresses whose estates were too small for cadet inheritance to be an option.

Another, less-well-known example is Juliana Warter Wilson, daughter of Edward Wilson of Bilboa, Co. Limerick, and sole heiress to his estate on the

Limerick/Tipperary border. Her father died in 1762, so she was already in possession of the estate at the time of her marriage in 1788 to Sir John Rous, 6th Bt, of Henham Hall, Suffolk, subsequently created Earl of Stradbroke in the peerage of the United Kingdom. In 1800, at the time of the Union, Rous applied (unsuccessfully) to the Prime Minister for an earldom in the peerage of Ireland, on the strength of his 'considerable property in the counties of Limerick and Tipperary (extending over more than 14,000 English acres, which, though now little productive, may in the event of the Union be of large value)'. This seems to have been an optimistic statement, as the capital value of the estate was reckoned at only £63,618 forty years later.[336] The point is that, had the estate been as large and valuable as Rous claimed, his marriage settlement would have attached strings to its descent which, as things were, appear to have been lacking. Certainly, it descended, not to Rous's daughter and only child by the Wilson heiress, but to the 2nd Earl of Stradbroke, his eldest son by a subsequent marriage. The flexibility of the terms presumably derived from, and certainly made up for, the modestness of the inheritance.

The same was true of the Hely-Hutchinson family's inheritance of the estates of the Nixons of Belmont, near Enniscorthy, Co. Wexford, through the marriage of Francis Hely-Hutchinson, third son of the Provost and Lady Donoughmore, to the Nixon heiress in 1785. At the time of the marriage, the Nixon estates were worth £1,000 a year, but 'encumbered with more than £6,000'; so, as Francis himself remarked: 'I believe I shall not be very rich for some time.' Presumably because of this, the marriage and marriage settlement were unusually informal, no sacrifices were exacted from the Hely-Hutchinson family (the Provost and Lady Donoughmore did not even know about the wedding until it was over), and Francis acquired unfettered control of his wife's estates. The Nixon rental in fact rose gratifyingly, to £1,525 in 1814 and £2,820 in 1820. But it was still possible for Francis, a firm believer in primogeniture where landed property was concerned, to ensure that the Nixon estate went to his eldest son, even after it had become apparent that the eldest son was also going to succeed to Knocklofty, all the Hely-Hutchinson estates of Francis's eldest brother, and to the earldom of Donoughmore.[337]

The landed property of the already-mentioned Emily, Viscountess Castlereagh,[338] was rather more valuable than the Wilson and Nixon estates. Moreover, the location of most of it at Bellaghy, Co. Londonderry[339] – a county where the Londonderrys had estates and political interests and where their title came from – made it a useful adjunct to the family portfolio for as long as she lived (which she did until 1829). Because the Castlereaghs had no children, she left it to members of her own family rather than to her late husband's half-brother and successor, the 3rd Marquess of Londonderry. So it has never featured alongside the collieries in histories of the rise of the Londonderry family.

Like many another dazzling match, the 3rd Marquess's marriage to an heiress contained elements of loss as well as gain from the husband's point of view. Only in the extreme case of Lord Carbery did the loss, or rather near loss, extend to the husband's property. More commonly, the husband's loss was one of time, effort, peace of mind, identity, reputation. His corresponding gains were considerable – increased consequence and perhaps status, enhanced life style, and so on. But since he often did not acquire control of his wife's money, and almost never of her land, he was not free to rationalise the affairs of the combined families, or even to regard the families as combined. Such rationalisation would have to wait until the next generation, probably until both husband and wife were dead. Moreover, it very often was not possible even then, because of the prevalence of cadet inheritance; and, should cadet inheritance take place, the husband's family and estate would probably have nothing to show for the connection. Indeed, the cost of the heiress's jointure, which would fall on the husband's estate, would probably outweigh the saving on the portion of the younger son who was to inherit the estate of his mother. In short, cadet inheritance and the other forms of collateral damage had the effect that the heiress ceased to be an heiress, as already defined: a woman who brought into her husband's family assets which far outweighed any return which it was obliged to make.

FIVE

The 'marriage of affection'[340]

Since the late 1970s there has been a vigorous debate among historians of the British aristocracy about the supposed rise, in the course of the eighteenth century, of what have been called 'the affective family' and the 'affective' or 'companionate' marriage.[341] The first thing to be said about this change, if change there were, is that it must have been one only of degree. Implicit or explicit in most of the marriages discussed in the preceding chapters is an important element of 'affectiveness', or more simply love, mixed up with which, also as an ingredient in most marriages, was 'collateral calculation'. The change postulated by Stone, Trumbach and others can only be an adjustment of the *recipé* which strengthened the existing element of affectiveness and reduced that of calculation. Had it been more sweeping, it would have been reflected in the financial provisions of marriage settlements, it would have greatly increased the incidence of exogamic marriage, and it would have led to more frequent runaway marriages than Chapter Six will argue actually took place. All the same, any change – no matter how subtle and slight – is important for its potential impact on the conventions of aristocratic marriage and on the position of heiresses.

Apart from the difficulty of tracing anything subtle and slight, there is a practical and methodological obstacle to dating 'too precisely' the rise of the affective marriage and family, and other, similar 'changes of attitude or practice': analyses of marriages 'commonly take as their basic unit cohorts according to dates of birth … [but] the marriages of a particular decadal cohort may be scattered over 40 years'.[342] However, the present study spans 100 years, which ought to be long enough to document the extent of any change; and this chapter takes as its starting point the beginning of the period 1740–1840 and, in particular, two marriages which took place just before 1740, in 1733 and 1734 respectively. Both of these give a well documented, contemporary focus to the issue of affectiveness.

The first is that of the already-mentioned William Conolly junior and Lady Anne Wentworth. The Conollys were a fashionable, trend-setting couple whose marriage and early married life not only illuminate, but must have influenced, the attitudes of the extensive social circle in which they moved. William Conolly junior was heir to Ireland's largest fortune and greatest mansion (though he did not come fully into his inheritance until the expiration of his aunt, Katherine

Conolly's, life-interest in 1752); Lady Anne Wentworth was a goddaughter of Queen Anne, the eldest daughter of a British earl, and a prospective heiress – even though her expectations – over and above her meagre marriage portion of £5,000 – were as yet undefined. Socially, she was Conolly's superior. Before she met him, she had been pursued unsuccessfully by English and Scottish noblemen, at least one of whom had probably been regarded by her father, the 1st Earl of Strafford, as a better bet than Conolly. Her marriage to Conolly was plainly a love-match as well as a dynastic alliance. Writing to his new father-in-law in May 1733, Conolly declared: 'You have made me as completely happy as my wishes could have done in giving me dear Lady Anne, and though this is wrote in the hunnymoon [*sic*], I believe I shall be able to say as much seven years hence.'[343]

In the following year, a small problem arose over part of her potential inheritance from the Wentworths, which had not been settled on Conolly in 1733 because she had not then been of age. When Lord Strafford made difficulties about this, Lady Anne showed that, in her scale of values, affectiveness weighed more than calculation. She regarded compliance with Conolly's wishes 'as the only return in my power to make him for the innumerable obligations I have to him...; and as to my jointure, as 'tis what I hope never to enjoy, it never gives me the least anxiety, for I am too much assured of his honour in every particular to doubt it in anything'. This might be interpreted as an example of a woman's having been successfully 'kissed out of' her entitlements. But other contemporary correspondence establishes beyond doubt that theirs was an affective marriage. Katherine Conolly, for example, described Conolly as 'the very most indulgent husband in the world'.[344]

The next marriage to be scrutinised is that of the already-mentioned Mary Cairnes, Lady Blayney, and her second husband, Colonel John Murray, which took place the year after the Conolly marriage, in 1734. Born c.1703, Lady Blayney was a contemporary of William Conolly junior. But, where his one and only marriage was a combination of calculation and affectiveness, her two marriages seemed to mark a progression from the one to the other. Her first, made in 1724, appears to have been arranged between her father and her husband, and her second, made in 1734, was avowedly made by herself for love.

The family of her first husband, the 7th Lord Blayney, had become proficient in arranged marriages. They represented the old nobility of Co. Monaghan, and with two estates, one in and around Monaghan town and the other in and around the eponymous Castleblayney, they were the leading landowners in the county. However, the financial and other pressures of the Civil War had compelled the 3rd Lord Blayney to sell each estate in turn to a London merchant called Richard Vincent. A calculated marriage to Vincent's daughter in 1653 (the year of the second sale) ultimately brought both estates back to the 5th Lord Blayney. But he then fell into financial difficulties himself, and was compelled first to mortgage and then to sell the Monaghan estate, which was bought by William Cairnes in 1696. The 5th Lord's nephew, the 7th Lord, decided to attempt a repetition of the earlier successful tactic of marrying the purchaser's heiress. This time round, the situation was more complicated. In 1724, when Lord Blayney married her, Mary Cairnes was heiress to her father's large personal estate but was not due to inherit at Monaghan unless her father's younger brother died without a son. Nor, even if all went according to plan, would any son born to Lord Blayney and Mary Cairnes inherit both the Monaghan and the Castleblayney estates, since Lord Blayney, a widower, already had a son and heir to the Castleblayney by a previous marriage. Nevertheless, there was always a chance that future events might bring about a second reunification.

Nothing of the kind took place, for the reasons stated in the frank and forthright account which Lady Blayney has left of her two marriages:

Sir Henry Cairnes, 2nd Bt, c.1670–1743, of London and Donoughmore, Co. Donegal, owner of the Monaghan estate, 1732–43; from a portrait of c.1720

COURTESY OF DORINDA, LADY DUNLEATH

I was married to my Lord Blayney against my own opinion. He had an agreeable outside, but there was a terrible inside. I endured all sorts of indignity for several years, even frequent blows. After bearing this longer, perhaps, than many others would, … at last I went back to my father at Monaghan, and … never had a child by a man I could not love.… [Both her father and Lord Blayney died in 1732, and in 1734] I married a relation of my own, Colonel Murray. He was the choice of my reason as well as my heart, and my expectations were fully satisfied.… I had children very soon, which gave me great pleasure, as I loved the father.… [But] some years ago he grew sickly.… [When] my uncle, Sir Harry, died [in 1743, and] his whole estate came to me…, I saw my friend [Colonel Murray] could not live many weeks, and to show him that I had been sincere in my regards to him, I told him the day I heard of my uncle's death that I would … by a deed oblige myself to settle my estate upon my children by him [all of whom were daughters]. He was overcome with it.… We came to Dublin, made the settlement, and in a week he died in my arms in the coach going home.

This is a moving story, which seems almost to be a paradigm for the rise of the affective family. But other conclusions, too, may be drawn from it and from Lady Blayney's subsequent role as matriarch of the Cairnes inheritance. First, Lord Blayney was a most ineffective dynast because he failed to win the affections of his wife and indeed treated her very badly. There might have been some point in this if she, like Lady Cathcart, had already come into her inheritance and if he were trying to break her spirit and induce her to settle the reversion to the Monaghan estate on the son of his previous marriage. But since this was not the case, no mercenary, dynastic purpose was served by his ill-treatment. Second,

Lady Blayney showed by her behaviour that she was a sensible as well as loving woman. She knew the strength of her own emotions, and she decided to put herself out of the way of temptation by tying her estate up by settlement. She then devoted herself (as will be seen) to the upbringing of her daughters and, when they came to marry, 'had the great comfort' of finding that ... 'my sons-[in-law] are like affectionate friends and brothers to me' and also to each other. The story of Lady Blayney does not so much mark a transition from calculation to affectiveness as demonstrate that the two were co-existent and inseparable in successful marriages and in successful dynastic planning.[345]

The Conolly marriage of 1733 and Lady Blayney's second marriage of 1734 together demonstrate that by 1740 the affective marriage was an established fact in Ireland. Granted this, two further questions arise: was it as recent a development as the proponents of 'the rise of the affective family' have argued; and was the phenomenon universal, widespread, or patchy in its incidence.

Two scholars, both writing with particular reference to Ireland, have questioned the proposition that affectiveness was a recent thing which manifested itself only from the end of the seventeenth century onwards. In his study of Richard Boyle (1566–1643), the 1st and 'Great' Earl of Cork, Nicholas Canny concludes:

> While it would not be permissible to argue ... that relationships among the Boyle family were companionate, the evidence ... does make it clear that Richard Boyle was familiar with and attracted towards the concept of a companionate relationship, as he was also attracted by the concept of individuality.... What was true of the Earl of Cork was equally true of his contemporaries ... [and] pending further detailed studies of particular families at different social levels, one must consider works such as those of Lawrence Stone ... as but highly stimulating hypotheses on the character of familial relationships in the early modern period.

S.J. Conolly takes the argument one stage further:

> Canny's case study of Richard Boyle indicates that there had been major changes in the course of the seventeenth century. Relations between husbands and wives, parents and children, if by no means egalitarian, had become less formal and authoritarian and more overtly affectionate. Whether this reflected a fundamental restructuring of people's emotions and personal relationships, or only a change in manners and customs, remains to be more fully explored, though Canny's conclusions would certainly support the latter view.... [It is also possible] that both the extent and the significance of changes in the character of family relationships during the early modern period have been greatly exaggerated.[346]

It may be suggested that Katherine Conolly is one example of the unchanging, and affective, character of family relationships. Born, probably, in the first half of the 1660s, she was in many respects a hard, mercenary, worldly old woman who did not change willingly with the times. In 1750, for example, it was undutifully observed by the Conolly family's head agent that 'Old Steel (I mean Mrs Conolly) ... is as well as she was eighty years ago'.[347] She was not fazed by the affective marriage made by her nephew (b.1706) and Lady Anne (b.1713), as she surely would have been had this been a 'new' phenomenon. Her attitude to children, it is true, was not redolent of the affective family. When William and Lady Anne proposed to her that their newly born son and heir should be called William (after her late husband, the Speaker), she consented, 'but not till I had a promise that, if it died, I should have another William'. (Of the offspring of another nephew and niece she remarked still more brutally: 'I think so likely and healthy a father and mother never had so rotten, miserable creatures: fine, handsome children till they come to three or four years old, and then they die like so many rotten sheep.')[348] Perhaps, however, this was just her characteristically outspoken version of what was common form in an age of high infant mortality – a self-protecting refusal to become emotionally involved with those whose time on earth might be short.

A truer indication of the depth of feeling of which she was capable, was her extravagant grief at the death of her husband in 1729. Some of this extravagance took the literal form of an ostentatious mourning designed to demonstrate that the Conolly family was now 'of the first quality'. But her closest relations, who worried that this might bring her into ridicule, never doubted the genuineness of her grief and worried even more that it was endangering her own life.[349] There is no reason to doubt the sincerity of her love for Speaker Conolly. Later in their marriage, these feelings became mixed up with a less amiable pride in his (and her) new wealth, status and power. But at the time of their marriage, in 1694, it had been Katherine Conolly who had condescended to Conolly in all these respects; he was then an obviously rising man, but Katherine Conolly, her marriage portion of £2,500 and her family connections helped him essentially in his rise. Though it may be difficult to view 'Old Steel' in this soft and romantic light, there is every likelihood that her own marriage had been a love-match.

This may explain why she entered into the spirit of her nephew's marriage to Lady Anne – a momentous dynastic event about which she seems barely to have been consulted in advance. She complained, not unreasonably, that too little of Lady Anne's fortune was cash down; she criticised the restlessness and peripatetic life-style of the young couple; and she faulted William Conolly for his failure to save money. But she liked and admired Lady Anne. Her remark that Conolly was 'the very most indulgent husband in the world' was not meant critically, as she herself indulged Lady Anne to a fault, going to lengths which were thought unsuitable to provide amusement for her at Castletown. She paid Lady Anne the supreme compliment (for Mrs Conolly) of calling her 'a good woman'.[350]

From the undoubted affectiveness of the Conolly family, including the redoubtable Katherine, which conveys the impression that the phenomenon was nothing new, it is now necessary to pass to some evidence of a contrary tenor, which suggests that affectiveness, whether new or old, had made only a limited impact on familial relationships by even the end of the eighteenth century. In 1739, Anne Granville (sister of the future Mrs Delany) wrote – *apropos* English high society:

> There is not a couple in London but grow happily indifferent [to each other] in six months! And if they drag the chains as many years, *what joy it is to part*. A present instance is the Duchess of Manchester. Her duke is dying and do you think she'll spoil her eyes with crying? No, no. She has better employment for them.[351]

Lord Hardwicke's Marriage Act of 1753, which passed the British House of Commons without undue difficulty, flew in the face of affectiveness and was a major step in the strengthening of patriarchal authority,[352] and the Royal Marriage Act of 1772 gave to the king control over the marriages of other members of the royal family. In Ireland, too, patriarchy was still, in the 1780s and 1790s, an active force in the regulation of affairs of the heart. In a private and soon-to-be ennobled Irish family, the Bernards of Castle Bernard, Bandon, Co. Cork, James Bernard overruled his daughter's choice of marriage partner in 1785, and in another Co. Cork instance, that of the Rev. Edmond Lombard, an eldest son was disinherited in 1798 because of objections to his choice.[353]

It has recently been argued that one very important aristocratic group, the Whigs of the period 1760–1837, who were mainly English but had many Irish ramifications, did not allow affectiveness to play much

> part in the choice of a husband or wife…. Whigs … liked to marry their cousins. Quite simply, too much was at stake to do anything else. Marriage was regarded as the union of great fortunes. Its purpose was to produce an undisputed heir…. Once that task had been accomplished, the marriage was counted a success in Whig eyes, and husband and wife could then do as they pleased.

This would seem to be an oversimplified view, based narrowly on the activities of a few fornicating great ladies – Georgiana Duchess of Devonshire, Lady Bessborough (her sister), Lady Melbourne and Lady Elizabeth Foster. They, and their husbands, were not representative of all Whigs. Charles James Fox, for example, married his mistress of many years' standing. The 3rd Earl of Egremont (1751–1837) did not trouble to do even that, but left his vast possessions among

Philip Yorke, 1st Earl of Hardwicke, Lord Chancellor of England, 1737–56; reproduced from an illustration specially designed by Richard Bentley for Horace Walpole's *Memoires of the last ten years of the Reign of George II*. Walpole, who was hostile to Hardwicke, specified that the illustration should feature the Marriage Act, so it shows Hymen in fetters with her torch extinguished by Law.

AUTHOR'S COLLECTION

the three illegitimate sons whom his devoted and long-serving mistress had borne him. And George Byng of Wrotham Park, Barnet, the advanced Whig MP for the prestigious constituency of Middlesex, 1780–84, enjoyed an affective marriage himself and had firm views 'on the subject of my children's marriage[s]. Let them judge for themselves. I would rather they should see with false eyes than act under control from me.'[354] Nevertheless, the great fornicating Whig ladies, particularly the Duchess of Devonshire, who stood at the pinnacle of society, constitute an important qualification to the theory that affectiveness was in the ascendant as a factor in aristocratic marriage.

Lady Elizabeth Foster, the Duchess's friend and rival for the favours of the Duke, had entered the rarified sphere of the Whig grandees by accident and only because of the failure of her first marriage. Born Elizabeth Hervey, she was the second daughter of the Hon. Frederick Hervey who, as Bishop of Derry, held the Church of Ireland's second-richest preferment, but who was so immersed in his own selfish extravagances that he declined to give her a marriage portion appropriate to his wealth and position. He therefore pushed her, in 1776, into an ill-assorted and ill-fated marriage with John Thomas Foster, an obscure Irish squire.[355] Four years later, in 1780, in a similar exercise of unwarranted paternal control, the already-mentioned Lady Henrietta Hobart was pushed by *her* father, Lord Buckinghamshire, into marriage with Armar Lowry Corry, later 1st Earl Belmore, whom 'she did not even know … by sight'; she consented to the marriage, with great misgivings, only because she considered 'the time in which she ought to have been consulted as past'.[356] Elizabeth Hervey and Lady Henrietta Hobart were under-age women when these matches were proposed to them, and not really in a position to hold out against parental authoritarianism. But the fact that it was exercised at such a late period of the eighteenth century, is again a qualification to the theory that affectiveness was in the ascendant.

The tender-hearted Lady Louisa Conolly believed in affectiveness, but thought that she was in a minority. In 1764, she expressed the view that 'marrying the person you like is so much the first thing to be considered that everything else ought to give way to that'; but she added that this view was 'not an usual one' and not agreeable to 'the common ways of doing well in the world'.[357] In expressing it, she was not so much stating an abstract view of marriage as finding an excuse for the recent elopement of a friend, Lady Susan Fox-Strangways, with – of all people – an Irish actor. An earlier event in her immediate family circle, the elopement of her eldest sister with Henry Fox in 1744, had pre-disposed her to such views. (She was also to get much more practice in later life when her younger sister, Sarah, committed adultery and ran off with her lover, and her older sister, Emily, did the same with, and then married, Ogilvie.) In the present context, the most significant thing about her attitude is her consciousness that it was 'not an usual one'.

John FitzGibbon, 1st Earl of Clare, Lord Chancellor of Ireland, 1789–1802, was a friend and admirer of Lady Louisa and, somewhat surprisingly, shared her companionate idea of marriage. With long forensic and judicial experience of settlements and family affairs, he certainly did not think that this was a usual view or that affectiveness (not that he would have used or understood the term) had gained much ground over baser motives and feelings. Writing in June 1800, following the defeat of a bill to reform the law of divorce in England and Wales, which had included a controversial provision bringing British law into line with Scottish by preventing an adulterous and divorced woman from marrying her partner in adultery, Clare declared with characteristic trenchancy:

> My opinion is unaltered that you are to look for the root of the evil which must alarm every sober man, to the dissolute habits of the higher ranks of men, who consider marriage as a mere traffic for private or political purposes, and that they are therefore fully at liberty to treat their wives with the most contemptuous neglect at best. I am quite satisfied that it is the nature of womankind to behave well to every husband who treats his wife as becomes him, and therefore I shall always feel reluctant in agreeing to any law which is to bear hardest upon the party who in most instances has the first and most cruel injuries to complain of.[358]

In Clare's view, it was husbands who had reduced marriage to 'a mere traffic for private or political purposes': in the view of a somewhat earlier English pamphleteer, writing in 1789, the fault lay with worldly and ambitious parents who promoted adultery by obliging their children to marry for gain or advantage:

> Where laws, prejudices and customs are in opposition to nature, it will seek a kind of indemnification in gallantry, libertinism or debauchery.... How can it be expected a son or daughter who is instructed by his family that all inclinations and all principles must give way to authority or interest, and who is forced or deceived into a disagreeable connection for life, should on a sudden assume all the virtues of a moral character...? The abuse of parental authority and of the laws respecting marriage are the general causes of infidelity to the marriage vow.[359]

Although the pamphleteer and Lord Clare were not precisely agreed as to the reason for this, they were certainly agreed that upper-class marriage was governed by 'interest', not affectiveness.

Both Clare's letter and the 1789 pamphlet were written in reaction – perhaps over-reaction – to a new and disturbing phenomenon, divorce (a topic which will recur later in the present chapter). Both writers subscribed to the idea of affective marriage (indeed the pamphleteer thought that it was in accordance with the laws of nature), and both were emphasising the 'arranged' and mercenary elements in marriage in an endeavour to explain the rising divorce-rate, just as Lady Louisa Conolly had emphasised the affective element in an endeavour to justify her friend's elopement. In these instances the context is clear. But in many others, whether they undermine or adorn the idea of the rise of the affective family, the context is far from clear and it would be unwise to base firm conclusions upon them. What may be plausibly suggested is that affectiveness in marriage and in family relationships was known and practised among the ruling *élite* in Ireland by the middle of the seventeenth century, was widespread by the middle of the eighteenth century and, *pace* Lord Clare, was probably the norm by 1800. In all periods, the extent to which it influenced attitudes and behaviour varied according to circumstances and the views of individuals, so that intermediate fluctuations are a complicating presence on the graph of its rise.

Although the term 'companionate marriage' is often used as a synonym for 'affective marriage', they are not actually the same thing and may not have followed the same trajectory. Companionability implies community of tastes and interests, intellectual sympathies and a near-equality of education. The affective marriage of William and Lady Anne Conolly, for example, may not have been companionate: as a young couple they were always on the tear; later, when Lady Anne was slowed down by the bearing and rearing of nine or ten children, William Conolly continued to dash about from one of his scattered properties to another or to attend parliament in either Dublin or London; and they did not have the chance to settle into a companionate old age because he died in 1754, before he was fifty. By contrast, the senior Conollys' marriage was companionate as well as affective. Katherine Conolly entered warmly into Speaker Conolly's political life, quarrelled with close relations who failed to follow the Conolly party line, acted as Conolly's political hostess, hobnobbed with vicereines as his representative as well as spouse and, it has recently been suggested, provided much of the impetus behind the building of the symbolic power-base of Castletown.[360]

Katherine Conolly was not a particularly well educated woman; and there are some indications that the ruling *élite* in Ireland were slow to attach due importance to the education of their daughters. In 1728, for example, a member of an important clerical and landed family notable for the number of spiritual peers in its recent history, came to the realisation that he had 'too long neglected' the education of his daughter, Anne; as long as she continued to reside with her parents on his benefice in the wilds of north Antrim, it was

> impossible she can improve ... except it be in the dialect of Scotland. I have been informed of a very good boarding-school for young gentlewomen in Drumcondra Lane [Dublin] where she may be happily accommodated and learn to dance.... I would bestow something more upon her education than I formerly intended, hoping at the same time that a year or thereabout may be sufficient.

By the sound of this, his daughter's schooling in Dublin was going to be neither protracted nor profound. Lack of rudimentary education was also – and more surprisingly – imputed to her higher-ranking near-contemporary, Lady Elizabeth Ponsonby (1719–78), better-known by her married name of Lady Betty Fownes. Many years later, c.1800, Lady Betty's clever and accomplished granddaughter, Caroline Hamilton (1777–1861), marvelled that Lady Betty, 'though an earl's daughter, could write only a short letter containing a few kind sentences, in a very large hand, spelling very ignorantly; and yet she was considered a sensible woman'.[361]

It is possible that Caroline Hamilton, who could have had no first-hand recollection of her grandmother, was unfamiliar with the orthography of an earlier age or judged from too small a sample of Lady Betty's letters. Certainly, the most frequently quoted authority for the illiteracy of Irishwomen of rank in the middle of the eighteenth century – Horace Walpole's strictures on the illiteracy (and brogues) of the Gunning sisters – needs to be taken at a huge discount. The beautiful Miss Gunnings, Maria (later-Countess of Coventry), born in 1731, and Elizabeth (successively Duchess of Hamilton and Argyll), born in 1732, arrived in London from Co. Roscommon in 1750 and proceeded to take Court and Society by storm and make brilliant marriages. The sensation they created inspired Walpole to waspish flights of fancy. In particular, he either did not know, or suppressed the fact, that they were born in England and had not taken up residence in Ireland until c.1740, after their father had unexpectedly inherited his elder brother's remote and run-down estate.

> [Their mother] was the daughter of a peer [the 6th Viscount Mayo] and … however culpably she may have neglected the education of her children in some respects, took care that they avoided the provincial brogue of their Irish neighbours.… The suggestion that … [they], who had never heard English spoken with the brogue of the native Irish until they were eight or nine years of age, spoke the tongue of the stage Irish peasant, … [is] ridiculous.… The Gunning girls had practically neither more nor less of that form of education to be acquired from the study of books or 'lessons' than the average young woman of their own day who[se education] had been neglected.[362]

Horace Walpole's strictures on the Gunnings are therefore no proof that young Irish ladies of good class were still ill-educated to the point of illiteracy in the middle of the eighteenth century. It may well be that Ireland lagged behind England in the matter of female education. But a number of letters, written from the 1720s onwards and quoted in this and other chapters, make plain the importance given to education in the catalogue of the attributes possessed by young ladies for whom a husband was being sought. More significantly, there are references – one dated 1725, the other 1734 – to education being a sales point in favour of young men who were seeking a wife. In the 1725 instance, the prospective husband was described as a 'well educated … [and] most promising young gentleman', and in the 1734 he had 'an agreeable person, an exceeding good humour, has had a good education and is a man of sense'. For women, a 'genteel education' (usually with a strong musical emphasis) had become a matrimonial *sine qua non* by the mid-1770s, and probably for many years earlier.[363]

Some aristocratic wives rose well above this minimum standard. Emily,

Duchess of Leinster (b.1731; m. 1747), read Rousseau, which was what gave her the unfortunate idea of employing Ogilvie as her younger children's tutor. Two country house libraries – probably the two best in eighteenth-century Ireland – were founded by blue-stocking women: the library at Castle Forbes, Co. Longford, co-founded by Lady Elizabeth Hastings (1713–1808), third wife of the 1st Earl of Moira, and her favourite daughter, Selina (1759–1827), wife of the 6th Earl of Granard; and the library at Pakenham Hall, alias Tullynally Castle, Co. Westmeath, founded by Elizabeth Pakenham (*née* Cuffe), Countess of Longford in her own right (1719–94).[364] Of these highly educated and cultured women, the Duchess of Leinster and Lady Moira were English by birth; but Lady Granard was born and brought up in Ireland, and Lady Longford was wholly Irish by birth and parentage.

People are much less likely to have written about their routine domestic life with their spouses than they are to have written about courtship, marriage and marriage settlements. To that extent, the graph of the companionate marriage is harder to draw than that of the affective – not that the latter is easy. But if a near-equality of education between men and women be regarded as an essential element in, and perhaps a touchstone of, the companionate marriage, then there is some reason to think that the first half and particularly the second quarter of the eighteenth century was the period when the phenomenon became widely diffused in aristocratic circles in Ireland. By the second half of the eighteenth century it was not uncommon to find wives (for example, the Lennox sisters and Lady Longford) who were better-educated than their husbands.

What bearing, then, did the diffusion of ideas of affectiveness and companionability have on the content of marriage settlements and on inheritance patterns? In this connection, it is an important consideration that affectiveness was known and practised by at least the mid-seventeenth century. This means that it was not a subsequent intrusion on the strict settlement, but evolved alongside it and over approximately the same period of time – which makes perfect sense. For, had it been a superimposition on a system which was well underway, it would have made a marked or at least noticeable alteration in the terms of marriage settlements. For example, it would have significantly increased the level of provision made for younger children and for widows. It might also have improved the position of heiresses by reversing the fifteenth-to-seventeenth-century tendencies of statute law to favour the collateral male heir, and by restoring the heiress (and the widow) to something like their Common Law heyday. Clearly, there were no such reversals of the previous trends towards male primogeniture. Provision for younger children and widows went up in the period 1740–1840, but this for the most part was in line with inflation and with other economic circumstances, and was not a rise in real terms. Nor is there any evidence that in this period heiresses made gains at the expense of their old enemy, the collateral male relation.

Extreme proponents of the rise of the affective family have taken the opposite view. They have argued that the provision made for younger children (which in their view was rising in real terms) under the strict settlement is proof of how affectiveness had undermined male primogeniture. This is surely mistaken? The strict settlement, rightly regarded, was an instrument for reinforcing male primogeniture. It made male primogeniture possible by making reasonable concessions to the interests of the younger children, but it circumscribed affectiveness by laying down the level of provision for the younger children before they were born and before they had a chance to engage parental affection. Contemporaries were certainly of the view that 'the future feelings of a father', if given rein, would lead to an exceeding of the provisions of a settlement; and George Rochfort of Gaulstown has been cited as an example of a father who did just that by augmenting in his will the portions provided for his daughters by his marriage settlement.[365]

Generally speaking, ways could be found by fathers, and/or mothers, to effect such an augmentation. It was usual to leave part of the family estate unsettled, so that it could be sold or mortgaged to answer some emergency. Sometimes additional land would be acquired by purchase or inheritance, or a cash legacy would be received from some collateral quarter. Often a father would live long enough to effect a re-settlement of the estate on his son's coming-of-age or to be a party to his eldest son's marriage settlement; in either of which cases he could, if his eldest son agreed, augment his younger children's portions or his wife's jointure. In the already-mentioned case of Speaker Foster, both opportunities arose. When his eldest surviving son (who died young in 1792) came of age in 1777, a re-settlement which benefited mother and younger children was effected; and when the next son, now the heir, married in 1810, the mother benefited still more. However, while these flexibilities existed, they were minor variations on a theme of male primogeniture. There can be no doubt that the purpose of the strict settlement was to pre-empt sentiment.

The previous discussion[366] of the two successive increases in the jointure provided for Speaker Foster's wife, Lady Ferrard, was in the context of the late eighteenth-century inflation of prices and peerage honours and its tendency to render inadequate the settlement provision made a generation earlier. There was, however, more to it than inflation – in the Foster case and in many others. Everything about Foster's marriage in 1764 to his cousin, Margaretta Burgh, including the fact that they were cousins and possibly childhood sweethearts, is indicative of a love-match. Angelica Kauffman was prone to flattery, but her 1771 portrait of Mrs Foster depicts a serenely beautiful woman. Barralet's group-portrait of the Fosters on the steps of Oriel Temple, Collon, Co. Louth, in 1786 would serve as the cover illustration for a book about the affective family. Even the inscription on the commemorative urn which Foster placed in the garden of the Temple after Lady Ferrard's death in her mid-eighties in 1824, is a moving declaration of love. A considerable increase in the jointure of £200 a year allotted to her under their marriage settlement of 1764 was definitely required to

John Foster, his wife and their children, on the steps of Oriel Temple, Collon, Co. Louth, a mock temple built on top of the hill in the Foster demesne, 1786; from a watercolour by John James Barralet

COURTESY OF VISCOUNT MASSEREENE AND FERRARD

enable her to live as a dowager viscountess. But she did not need £2,000: £1,000 or at most £1,250 would have done her (particularly in view of the embarrassed state of Foster finances in 1810). The difference may confidently be ascribed to affectiveness. The same goes for the lion's share of Grace, Countess of Farnham's, £4,900 a year – except that in her case it is to be ascribed, not only to affectiveness, but to the effect of her domineering personality.

One aspect of affectiveness which is not much mentioned in discussions of this topic is brotherly love. Yet, examples of this are not uncommon. In 1769, the 2nd Lord Knapton and 1st Viscount de Vesci took advantage of the drawing up of his own marriage settlement to make an irrelevant provision for his only unmarried sister, Jane, whose portion he doubled to £3,000; and in 1778, when the 2nd Lord Longford came into a large, windfall inheritance, he shared his good fortune with his younger brother, Thomas, by making over to the latter the Coolure estate, near Castlepollard, Co. Westmeath, producing £200 a year in rent, and by adding £4,000 to Thomas's existing portion of £2,000.[367] As far as is known, these were voluntary acts and not the result of any obligation placed on the doer by will, settlement or unwritten undertaking.

The main scope for conflict between settlement and sentiment was the provision for younger children, particularly daughters. Unless their jointures were as ludicrously inadequate as Lady Ferrard's £200 a year, widows could always be subsidised in kind by a bequest of the right to occupy, rent-free, a house in town or, sometimes, country; younger sons could also be assisted, at no cash cost to their fathers or to the next head of the family, by exertions of family influence to obtain from the government jobs and promotions of various kinds. But daughters were dependent on their portions, and in their case parents might be moved to augment the provision stipulated in their marriage settlement. Alternatively, parents might be provoked into rewarding a dutiful and obedient daughter at the expense of one considered to be undutiful and disobedient.

The suspicion that the strict settlement could be used as an agent of patriarchy as well as male primogeniture arises out of the presence in many settlements of clauses which stipulated that portions were not payable unless younger children married with the consent of parents or guardians, or which specified an overall sum for the provision of portions and left it to parents or guardians to decide how this was to be divided among the younger children. (Parental consent or discretion was never required in the case of the marriage of the eldest son, because such a stipulation would have made the settlement 'nugatory' by placing him 'totally in the power of ... [his] father'.[368] For this reason, the Rev. Edmond Lombard, who disinherited his eldest son in 1798 for marrying unsuitably, cannot have been under settlement.) It is probable that, c.1740, only a minority of settlements included such a stipulation. This was the view taken by Aland Mason in 1739, and he was insistent that a requirement of parental consent should be written into the marriage settlement to which he was about to become a party. Likewise, the settlement made on the first marriage of the future 1st Earl of Farnham (of the second creation) in 1757, gave him discretion to apportion an overall provision of £4,000 for younger children in such shares as he thought fit.[369]

The presence in or absence from marriage settlements of a stipulation or discretion of this kind might be deemed a reasonable test of the affectiveness of the family concerned and, more generally, of the prevalence or otherwise of the affective family. However, expensive computer-analysis of a statistically valid and therefore extensive sample of marriage settlements would be required before conclusions could be reached as to what proportion of them contained such provisoes and whether it was going up or down. Even then, as with many exercises of this kind, the results might not be particularly informative. For example, it is clear that Aland Mason wanted to use the parental consent clause in his marriage settlement as an agent of patriarchal control over the marriages of his younger children, but it is not clear that Lord Farnham had the same object in view. The discretion reserved in the Farnham settlement may in fact have been conceived as a simpler alternative to a complex sliding scale whereby the portion of each younger child was fixed according to the number and sexes of the younger children. This was certainly how Lord Downshire intended his executors to interpret the discretion he gave them in the very affective will he made in 1797.[370]

In 1816, the future 1st Earl of Dunraven mentioned that he did not know whether he had or had not power to apportion the £10,000 provided for younger children under his marriage settlement of 1777, and did not seem to attach much importance to the matter.[371] There were good reasons for his apparent indifference. For one thing, a daughter would often have ways of kissing her father out of his opposition to a marriage which the daughter wanted to make. For another, when there was serious doubt about the financial, as opposed to the personal, eligibility of a prospective son-in-law, the trustees of the parents' marriage settlement would not be warranted in releasing a daughter's portion unless it could be fully secured for the purposes of the new settlement. If the estate of the prospective son-in-law was already too heavily burdened to bear the charge, or was held by a lease too short to be reliable security for it, the settlement would not be good in law in any case. Parental consent or discretion was therefore helpful, but not always necessary, to the exercise of parental control.

Lady Blayney's views on the legitimate extent of parental control, like her views on most things, are worth quoting:

> It is hardly possible to imagine any behaviour in a child to justify the disinheriting them, though very allowable to make a difference if their behaviour deserves it. For this reason, I only obliged myself to give my estate to my children…, but I could divide or charge it among them as I pleased. I always intended to give the estate to the eldest, with good fortunes however to the others, as by this method she might marry so well that she and her husband might be a protection for the others…. If my eldest daughter made a choice for herself which was improper, but without doing it clandestinely, I should have told her … 'If you do not choose it [the estate], the second shall be in your place and you shall have the fortune intended for her.' This scheme should have gone through [i.e. dealt with] any disappointment I might have met [with] from

them, and at the same time prevented my doing a hardship from sudden resentment. But I had the great comfort of everything happening as I could wish.[372]

These sentiments strike such a nice balance between calculation and affectiveness, love and lucre, that it is not easy to distinguish between them; kindness to one child might, in Lady Blayney's sensible view, mean unfairness to the others. Such a balance, rather than the rise of the affective element at the expense of the other, would seem to be the keynote of aristocratic marriage in Ireland in the period under review.

In short, Lord Clare did less than justice to the motives and feelings of husbands, and the English pamphleteer of 1789 to those of parents; the latter also exaggerated the submissiveness of children. Lady Catherine Cecil, who married in 1737 and whose views on whom she was prepared to marry will be quoted below, is a good example of the independent-mindedness of children. But matters did not usually come to a rupture between parents and children because both were agreed on the essentials of what was likely to prove a 'good' (in all senses) marriage. 'There is no reason to believe that most aristocratic sons and daughters did not subscribe to the prevailing ethic in favour of marriages of equal rank, nor that they did not attach similar importance to considerations of status and fortune.' George Byng was probably extreme in the view that it was better for his children to 'see with false eyes than act under control from me'. However parents in general probably 'gave their children considerably more freedom of choice in the eighteenth century' than they had done in an earlier era, provided it was understood that this was 'a freedom within acceptable limits'. As for the children, since they – particularly the girls – had been brought up to obey their parents, to do what they were meant to do and to marry within their caste, since their 'choice itself had been constrained by the restricted circles' in which they had moved, it is hardly ever appropriate to call their marriages 'arranged'.[373]

Moreover, it is simplistic to assume that parents were always on the side of prudence, and children on the side of romance. It was the niece of Horace Walpole (he who coined the phrase 'the spirit of collateral calculation'), and not her father on her behalf, who jumped at an offer of marriage in 1760 on the ground that she was 'likely to be large and to go off soon'. The mother of the future 4th Duke Devonshire opposed his marriage to the Burlington heiress tooth-and-nail on the ground that the proposed bride was too young, and urged him instead to marry another lady, who was decidedly less rich. Still more remarkably, the family of the Countess of Antrim deplored her marriage to the rich Sir Henry Vane-Tempest, and applauded her younger sister's contemporary marriage to the hard-up Lord Mark Kerr, on the sensible ground that Sir Henry was a notorious drunk, and Lord Mark a young man whose character had no black mark against it. Lord Downshire, a friend of the family, and himself no teetotaller, commented: 'The Countess of Antrim is going to marry herself to Sir Harry Vane-Tempest, a rich man, but not very favourably spoken of. It is a match of her own making ... [and] if she is not happy, she can blame no one but herself.'[374] Parents who were themselves in the enjoyment of an affective and companionate marriage may reasonably be credited with some understanding of such matters. So, the objections which the 2nd Earl of Rosse and his wife entertained in 1837 to their daughter, Alicia's, attachment to Edward Conroy,[375] were quite possibly to his unsuitability as a husband rather than to his poorness as a match. If so, they were amply to be borne out by events.

In a great many, probably a majority of, cases the concern of parents was to ensure that any marriage entered into by a child was soundly based financially. They were usually motivated by prudence rather than greed. Sometimes they entered fully into the romantic spirit of a young couple's attachment, but had the wisdom and experience to see that it might not endure if subjected to severe financial strains. In 1780, the Dowager Lady Massereene aptly expressed these different concerns in a letter to the 1st Earl of Roden, the prospective father-in-law of her fourth son, the Hon. Chichester Skeffington: 'Though both reason and experience show me that love and a *cottage*, however pleasing in idea, will not do when reduced to practice, yet I am equally persuaded that happiness does not depend on affluence, though it does on a competence, nor can the greatest riches purchase it.' Soon afterwards, when the young couple had been united, his sister added:

> Chichester is as happy as possible in his wife. They adore each other. 'Twas an attachment of years. He has got an employment [in the revenue service, which family influence had obtained for him in order to enable them to marry] and [they] live as comfortably as possible on about £1,000 a year, which for the youngest of four brothers is I think very well to begin upon.... Lady Harriet (Chitty's wife) is the best of all beings.... Her fortune was but small, but she is highly connected.[376]

Over forty years later, the 2nd Earl of Leitrim echoed these sentiments in the course of the very well documented negotiations which took place over the marriage of his third and youngest daughter, Caroline, to John Ynyr Burges of Parkanaur, Castlecaulfield, Co. Tyrone. The whole correspondence repays study and is not without entertainment value. For present purposes, it suffices to quote from three letters he wrote to his wife in February 1833. In the first he reports on a visit from Burges, who he thinks is 'a very plain man and I should suppose above seven- or eight-and-thirty years old [Lady Caroline was about twenty-nine] – in short, not at all the kind of person that I should have thought any girl could have taken a fancy to. But there is no accounting for taste.' In the second letter, he lamented that

> they will be miserably poor. £400 a year with the interest of her fortune, which may be calculated at about £250 a year, is all that they will have to live upon at present, which she, poor girl, says she considers an affluence and that she does not in the least desire to have more. Mr B. has expectations which, if they should be realised, may some day or other give him a considerable fortune. But

> the only thing he can look to as certain is an estate of about £1,500 a year, which he must inherit if he survives [his great-aunt] Lady Poulett. But she will give him nothing in her lifetime.... I will ... only add that, ... from all that I have been able to learn of him, I believe he is a man of extremely good character, of perfect good temper and, what is very essential in his circumstances, extremely prudent and economical in his expenses.

And finally:

> Caroline being of an age to judge for herself, it appeared to me that I could not do more than *advise* her against, which I did, but that I should not be justified in putting a veto upon it. I have endeavoured therefore to make the best of it, to make in short a virtue of necessity and to get the best settlement for her that the case admitted of.[377]

While most of the worries expressed by Lord Leitrim related to money, it is obvious that he would have been more enthusiastic about the match if Burges had been younger, more dashing and more fun. The father was a greater romantic than the daughter.

Because financial negotiations were concomitants of virtually every aristocratic marriage, they are easily mistaken for causes, not concomitants; the details of any marriage settlement would be dictated by 'the spirit of collateral calculation', but that does not mean that the same spirit had dictated the initial choice of marriage partners. For example, it was popularly believed that the father of the Lennox sisters, the 2nd Duke of Richmond, had married a daughter of the 1st Earl Cadogan in 1719 in settlement of a gambling debt to her father.[378] But, for all that, the marriage was one of the love-matches of the century. Likewise, Lord Belfast, later 2nd Marquess of Donegall, probably met his future wife, Anna May, because he was hopelessly indebted and her father was a moneylender and an expert at fending off creditors by devices of doubtful legality; and Lord Belfast certainly obtained relief from his most pressing embarrassments and release from debtor's prison in 1795, when he married her. But Lady Belfast was a good-looking, agreeable and gracious lady, with manners so charming that they disarmed criticism of her shady antecedents and associations.[379] There is therefore no reason for doubting that this, too, however financially convenient at the time, was a love-match.

A letter describing the negotiations in 1799 over the marriage of James Stuart-Wortley, later 1st Lord Wharncliffe, heir to large estates in Yorkshire, Cornwall and Scotland, and the only daughter of the Donegal and Fermanagh proprietor, the 1st Earl Erne, establishes the due proportion between financial and non-financial considerations:

> Lady Caroline Creighton's marriage is declared with S. Wortley.... He will have a property of £18,000 a year from his father, besides Mackenzie's [his great-uncle]. He is highly spoken of, and they are much attached. There has been a difficulty, owing to old Wortley's [his father] fears about Lord Creighton, her half-brother, who is confined [i.e. insane]. But Lord Erne, who is in England,

Lady Caroline Creighton as a girl, with her mother, the Countess Erne, painted by Hugh Douglas Hamilton, c.1789, and reproduced in Christie's Irish Sale catalogue, 14 May 2004.

cleared it up to the family, as Lord Creighton's illness was owing to cold bathing in a course of mercury, which disordered his head. She was to have £15,000 from Lord Erne, but I believe he does more in point of present income, as old Wortley has a large establishment. I am very glad, for she is a very worthy girl and the Wortleys seem quite to adore her.[380]

Clearly, reciprocal regard was the deciding factor in a match which was barely satisfactory to the Wortleys from the financial point of view. Their principal misgiving was, not that the bride's portion was beneath the reasonable expectations of their eldest son, but that the insanity in her family might be of an hereditary kind.

This same misgiving arose in the near-contemporary but non-Irish instance of the marriage of Lady Louisa Gordon, daughter of the 4th Duke of Gordon, to the son and heir of the 1st Marquess Cornwallis in 1797. To overcome Lord Cornwallis's fears of the strain of insanity which dogged the ducal House of Gordon, the matchmaking Duchess of Gordon assured him that her daughter had not a drop of Gordon blood in her.[381]

THE 'MARRIAGE OF AFFECTION'

In 1803, a marriage was negotiated between the 2nd Marquess of Waterford (eldest son of the 1st Marquess and the heiress Elizabeth Monck) and one of the daughters of the 1st Marquess of Abercorn. The portion of Lord Abercorn's daughter, like that of her younger half-sister, was £10,000: a sum which Lord Abercorn with characteristic loftiness pronounced to be 'an object totally unworthy of consideration with whoever is in a situation to marry her'. When, on the eve of the marriage, the bride-to-be died, Lord Abercorn's letter to Lord Waterford on the occasion suggests that reciprocal regard between the young people and their families, and certainly not objects of financial consideration, had been the basis for the projected alliance. Another interesting feature of this episode is its sequel. Lord Waterford, who had been perfectly happy to marry Lord Abercorn's unexceptionally portioned daughter, then went on to marry an heiress, through whom the Waterford family acquired the Ford Castle and Seaton Sluice estate, Northumberland, and one seat for the parliamentary borough of Berwick-upon-Tweed.

The importance of reciprocal regard was explicitly stated during negotiations over the marriage of yet another Abercorn daughter in 1805: 'I confess', wrote an adviser of the bridegroom, 'it appears quite impossible to propose anything in any degree satisfactory to the views Lord Abercorn may entertain respecting a provision for his daughter. I suspect it will end in a marriage of affection.'[382] Want of such affection was the reason for the failure of another negotiation. In 1796, the prospective match between the great heiress, Lady Gertrude Villiers, and the heir to the dukedom of Leeds was pronounced 'entirely off, after an ineffectual attempt to fall in love with each other at Weymouth, and which was rather an awkward business for both'.[383]

The earlier, successful negotiations of 1751 over the marriage of Robert, son and heir of Gustavus Handcock of Waterstown, Co. Westmeath, to Elizabeth, daughter of John Denny Vesey, 1st Lord Knapton, are a model of affectiveness. Gustavus Handcock wrote as follows to Lord Knapton:

> Upon his last leaving home, my son told me he was greatly enamoured with [sic] Miss Vesey, your daughter, and that the obtaining her for a wife would make him the happiest person in the world.... As I have the highest respect for your Lordship's and your Ladyship's families and [for] the most amiable character of the young lady, I could not but approve his inclinations....
>
> He tells me ... [that, having laid a statement of the Handcock family's finances] before your Lordship, ... [he] had your leave to pay his addresses to Miss [Vesey].... When your Lordship and I shall meet and treat upon this affair, I hope every objection will be got over, assuring your Lordship with the utmost sincerity that my wife and I have no other views or dispositions than to make our son happy, who is our only child, and that upon this consideration alone much must be allowed to contingencies. The character of the young lady stands in my view in the place of many thousands, and the gratification of my son's warm and passionate desires ... will carry me as far in bringing this affair to a happy issue as can be reasonably expected I should go.[384]

Miss Vesey was neither an heiress nor a well portioned young woman; so Gustavus Handcock had no ulterior motive for being so eager to bring the negotiation to a successful conclusion. The marriage went ahead and, though happy, was short-lived. The couple had one son, Gustavus junior, and Robert Handcock died in 1754.

At the end of the century a similarly affective marriage was negotiated between Lady Mary Fitzgerald, eldest daughter of the 2nd Duke and recently deceased Duchess of Leinster, and Sir Charles Lockhart Ross, 7th Bt, of Balnagowan, Rosshire, a widower with one surviving daughter by his first wife. In December 1798, the Duke wrote to him:

> I feel much flattered by the opinion you have formed of my daughter and the preference you show her.... My daughters being of an age to look forward to their future settlements in life, you may well imagine I was not unmindful of their situation. Previous to the death of their beloved mother, it was her object, as it is mine, to consult the feelings of her children. Though our expectations might be great, yet we always agreed how little that signified if it was not accompanied with other questions. I trust we never encouraged them to aspire too high but to consider their future happiness, which is not always to be found in the highest circles.... That being the case, unless some unforeseen circumstances should arise in arranging matters for her future destination, there can be no objection to your making yourself more acquainted with her amiable and good qualities, which I think are such as will do credit to the education she has received under the auspices of her most valuable and departed mother. Her fortune will be a charge for the present on my estate of £10,000.

William Robert Fitzgerald, 2nd Duke of Leinster (1749–1804), engraved by J. Heath after an original full-length portrait of 1802 by Martin Archer Shee
AUTHOR'S COLLECTION

Undeterred by these sententious and condescending remarks, Sir Charles Ross pressed his suit, and the couple were married in April 1799. Three months later, he wrote fulsomely to the Duke: 'However sanguine my expectations of happiness were, and however perfect your daughter was in my estimation, they have both been infinitely surpassed by the reality.'

Apart from the reference to the £10,000, this negotiation gives every impression of having been conducted without regard to financial considerations and of affording clear proof of the dominance of affectiveness. The impression is misleading. Ross must have been aware that a Highland baronet who already had a child by a previous marriage was doing well to obtain a portion of that amount (even though, plainly, it was not going to be paid over for a long time to come) and with it the eldest daughter of a duke. Leinster, on his side, had said nothing about Ross's financial situation for the simple reason that he had already found out about it by previous, private communication with the banker, Thomas Coutts. Coutts had reported:

THE 'MARRIAGE OF AFFECTION'

Sir Charles ... has three estates – and properly three names. Lockhart is his born name. His mother was Baillie and an heiress of an estate which she now, I believe, enjoys as a widow. Ross he succeeded to as heir of entail to the estate of Balnagowan.... His father's estate is in Clydesdale, nearer to Ireland. I have always understood his [i.e. the Lockhart] estate to be £5,000 or £6,000 a year. The Balnagowan estate is I know strictly entailed upon the male heir, and if he dies without a son would go to his brother. His mother's estate, I suppose, as it came by the female line, would go to his daughter.[385]

Leinster had therefore done his homework before embarking on the hifalutin sentiments of his letter to Ross; this marriage, like most others, represented a balancing of personal and financial considerations; and its true nature cannot be understood until the full context of the marriage negotiations has been explored.

A similar balancing is evident in the very multilateral negotiations which led to the marriage of Lord Perceval, son and heir of the 1st Earl of Egmont, in 1737. Lord Egmont, significantly, placed her portion of £20,000 last among the attributes of his prospective daughter-in-law, Lady Catherine Cecil, sister of the 6th Earl of Salisbury. 'Her age', Egmont noted, was 'eighteen, her health good, her face and person beautiful and graceful, her education virtuous and careful, her sense and temper remarkably good'. On the Cecil side of the negotiation, Lord Salisbury's attorney spent a whole morning examining the Egmont rentals

The 2nd Earl of Egmont and his wife (probably his first wife, Lady Catherine Cecil, who died aged 33 in 1752); from a non-contemporary engraving of 1876 after a portrait by Reynolds. In the background is Egmont's mediaeval-revival castle at Enmore in Somerset, on which work began in 1751.
AUTHOR'S COLLECTION

and estate accounts, and was entirely satisfied with what he found. But the deciding factor in the negotiation was the bride, whose temper may have been 'remarkably good' but who had a mind of her own. She later told her husband that she would never have married against her own will and 'would have refused the Earl of Berkeley and the Duke of Leeds if they [had] offered'. These two, it should be noted, were English peers of superior rank to Egmont.[386]

In 1786 the 1st Marquess of Downshire described *his* prospective daughter-in-law, the already-mentioned Mary Sandys, one of the greatest heiresses of the day with a reputed '£60,000 in ready money and £3,000 a year, besides her expectancies', in similar terms to those used by Egmont.

> Miss Sandys, Lord Sandys's niece, ... is a genteel, agreeable little girl; not a beauty, but as nearly being so as a wise man would choose his wife to be; of a cheerful, sweet disposition, and a very proper age for him [the future 2nd Marquess, then 33], 22. Her fortune is more than he wants or wished for, though it will do him no harm.

The concluding remark about her fortune is not to be taken at face value. Nevertheless, the place which her 'fortune' is given in the catalogue of her virtues is most revealing. In other instances where 'fortune' was placed first, it was almost always accompanied by personal accomplishments: in 1725, Miss Hamilton, an Irish heiress 'that has £2,000 a year', was further described as 'not handsome, but very sensible, and carefully educated'.[387]

What the Egmont and Downshire marriages both demonstrate – in spite of the fact that they are separated from each other by a period of fifty years – is that love, or at any rate mutual attachment, were important elements in the choice of partners even when families of the highest rank and greatest wealth were the parties to the settlement. The 2nd Earl of Egmont's marriage to Lady Catherine Cecil probably continued to be 'a marriage of affection': she bore him five sons and a daughter in the comparatively short time which elapsed between 1737 and her early death in 1752. The 2nd Marquess of Downshire's marriage to Mary Sandys was an undoubted success, as their even larger family and other evidence indicate. Lord Downshire was not entirely faithful; but Lady Downshire was so far from being alive to this possibility that it came as a great shock to her to discover, after his death, that he had three illegitimate, teenage children living, whom his will commended to 'the kindness and protection of my beloved wife'. With a loyalty and a high-mindedness which few people would have shown under the circumstances, and which must have been the product of deep devotion, she declared: 'It wounds me to the soul that my dearest Lord should have been so infatuated by such a creature.... I am convinced it caused him, poor dear soul, many an unhappy hour.' More practically, she set about badgering the Prime Minister for a government employment for the son.[388] Likewise, Lady Louisa Conolly, whose marriage to the endearing if infuriating Thomas Conolly was a huge success, was distressed to discover, after his death in 1803, that he had a mistress and an illegitimate child.[389]

These two examples suggest that it is unwise to assume that the success of an aristocratic marriage was purchased by the wife's connivance at the husband's infidelities. In this connection, it is worth recalling the case of the 1st Marquess of Thomond, who conducted himself as husband to his deaf and dumb cousin 'in a manner so proper that he can reflect upon it with satisfaction'.390

In other words, lots of aristocratic husbands were not as 'dissolute', calculating, and indifferent to the charms of their wives as Lord Clare alleged. Two examples of amorous bridegrooms may be given. In 1728, the future 5th Earl of Orrery, then Lord Boyle, joked that, as 'soon as my father will find a woman whose person shall please me and whose fortune will please him, she shall be heartily welcome to the arms of [himself]'; and in 1747 a young Kerryman called Frederick Mullins, possibly a younger brother of the 1st Lord Ventry, complained that the trustees of his marriage settlement were unnecessarily delaying 'my taking possession of the charming Phoebe' because they were 'not so eager for a f – k as I am'.391 The strong, but finer, feelings of other bridegrooms – William Conolly junior, Robert Handcock and James Stuart Wortley, for example – have already been recorded, along with the reciprocal affection of their brides.

These instances all concern young or comparatively young couples. It might be expected that second marriages or late marriages would be actuated to a greater extent by the spirit of calculation. In 1816, when the 4th Earl Poulett married, as his second wife, John Ynyr Burges's great-aunt, he was marrying both an heiress and a wealthy widow, and was thought to have been motivated by 'the hope of getting back from her a mortgage which she had on his estate, in which hope he was disappointed. The old lady held it fast and would not give it up.'392 But clear instances of affection are to be found in the older age-group too. In 1798, the near-octogenarian General Eyre Massy, younger brother of the 1st Lord Massy, applied for an Irish peerage for his wife (by the title of Lady Niagara, the scene of one of his youthful exploits in the Seven Years War), and justified the request on the ground that she was 'a virtuous, good wife, and a most excellent mother, ... who[m] I adore'.393 General Massy had married at the age of almost fifty: unusually late even by the standards of aristocratic males, who tended to marry later than the common man. He is one of a number of striking instances of a late marriage being a love-match – or, in the case of Lady Cathcart, of there being no fool like an old fool.

In the instance of Lord Sydney, a Co. Laois magnate and retired diplomat in his mid-forties, who married in 1774 a lady half his age, the folly had fatal consequences. Lord Sydney, in order

The 5th Earl of Orrerry, who married the heiress to the Caledon estate, Co. Tyrone, in 1738; from a non-contemporary engraving of 1807
AUTHOR'S COLLECTION

> to render himself agreeable to his lady upon their marriage, stopped two issues he had in his thighs, but found no ill-effects until..., after a night of great exercise by dancing, his temper and reason, as appears since, was in some sort affected.... He complained of indisposition, and sent for a physician.... After which, being disappointed in an attempt to shoot himself and one to poison himself, he took ... the dose [of Danish poison] which was sufficiently strong to carry him off in a few hours.[394]

It may be added, though not relevant to the present purpose, that Lady Sydney survived her two months of marriage to Lord Sydney by sixty-two years; so that her jointure was payable for an even longer time than Lady Milltown's and for almost as long as Lady Rosse's.[395]

This was Lord Sydney's first (and, obviously, last) attempt at matrimony: others who were married more than once seem to have lost, rather than gained, prudence as they went their matrimonial way. The 1st Marquess of Donegall, father of the much-indebted Lord Belfast, had shown great prudence (some would have said, to the point of heartlessness) in all his affairs, matrimonial and otherwise, up to the time of his third marriage. This took place in 1790, when he was fifty-one. His wife was a young beauty, who can have brought him little in portion and who (as might reasonably have been anticipated) survived his death in 1799 by thirty years. In 1793, because his jointuring power was limited by the existing family settlement, he agreed to acknowledge his son's then debts in return for his son's agreement to settle a larger jointure on the new Lady Donegall; and by his will, he further increased her jointure, and made other bequests to her for which his heart, not his head, had its reasons.[396]

Another magnate whose matrimonial and general grasp slackened with age was Sir Richard Quin of Adare, Co. Limerick, 1st Earl of Dunraven. Between 1800 and 1822, Quin climbed the full flight of stairs from commoner to earl. When still a commoner, in 1777, he had made an upwardly mobile and financially far from onerous marriage to the daughter of a British earl (portion, £10,000: jointure, £1,000). After her death, he married, in 1816, when he was sixty-four, a twice-married widow of no particular social status or wealth. Within a year, they had separated, Lord Dunraven commenting ruefully: 'She got more when I left her than I got from her when I married her.' This did not take into account the alimony of £150 a year which he settled on her at their parting. In spite of his generosity, he was subjected for some years to 'the puerile and unjustifiable menaces of Colonel Coghlan [her brother], which ... [Lord Dunraven] holds in the utmost derision and contempt', and which were aimed at extorting a further £150 a year out of him. These spirited expressions of his 'derision and contempt' nearly led to a duel.[397]

In short, second or late marriages are not to be equated with calculation, or even prudence, unless it is demonstrable that they were based on the sound sense exhibited by the septuagenarian 1st Lord Glentworth in 1792:

> I am determined to marry…, for I can no longer live alone, and want a nurse to take care of me in my decline of life, and a proper person to manage my family. The lady … is Mrs Crump, to whom I have been strongly attached for many years, and whose fortune is much better than I could expect. She is past 50 years old, and therefore there is no danger of [her] bringing me any children…. Her advanced age will not require much conjugal endearments, which I am nearly past the time of giving.[398]

Significantly, the order in which Lord Glentworth placed Mrs Crump's merits – his strong attachment to her first, and her satisfactory fortune second – is the order in which (as has been seen) the endowments of younger brides were commonly placed.

These examples of the nice balancing of financial and personal considerations in the negotiations preceding a marriage have included one heiress, Mary Sandys – or two, if the earlier instance of Lady Anne Wentworth, a potential heiress, be included. Evidence of the personal feelings of courting, engaged or married couples for each other is, understandably, not all that easy to come by. But it does survive in the cases of some relationships involving heiresses, including those of William Conolly junior and Lady Anne Wentworth, Lady Blayney and Colonel Murray and the young Lord Leitrim and his heiress-wife, Mary Bermingham. The Bermingham sisters were both great beauties, highly accomplished and remarkable for the sweetness of their dispositions. (Sir Thomas Lawrence painted them separately in 1805, and in their case had no need to resort to his meretricious skill in falsifying the record.) In the early years of their marriage, c.1800–09, the young Lord and Lady Clements/Leitrim wrote tender and charming letters to each other, and would have written more but for the simple and romantic fact that the two of them were almost inseparable. Unless she was about to have one of their numerous children, she accompanied him to whatever uncomfortable posting had been assigned to his regiment, the Co. Donegal Militia, or on electioneering visits to Co. Leitrim, where she helped him in the canvass. It is therefore from her surviving letters to her mother, 1800–02 and 1825, that the best picture of the young Leitrims' early married and family life is to be obtained.[399] Clearly, their marriage was and remained an affair of the heart, to which her material attractions were irrelevant.

Later, when Lady Leitrim's mental illness put strains on her relationship with her husband and some of their children, he did not falter in his devotion. After one of a number of rows and recriminations, all attributable to her unhappy mental state, he wrote to her in February 1836:

> The first object of my life has ever been to do everything in my power that could contribute to your comfort and happiness. For many years I succeeded, and I enjoyed as perfect happiness myself as perhaps falls to the lot of any man in this world. I was grateful to you for it, and I hope I was grateful to the Almighty. It is but too true that that happiness has of late years been but too

Mary Bermingham, Lady Clements, afterwards Countess of Leitrim, with her eldest child, Maria, 1805; from a mezzotint after the original portrait by Sir Thomas Lawrence

KILLADOON COLLECTION
COURTESY OF CHARLES AND SALLY CLEMENTS

frequently and most severely interrupted, and you little know, and never *can* know, what I suffered upon those occasions. Religion alone supported me under the trials I have experienced....
The Almighty graciously heard my prayers. You were restored to your former good feelings and affection for me.... Often and often have you told me ... that I was the most affectionate person you had ever known in your life, that I was the only man in the world that could have made you happy, the only person that ever appreciated you or understood your character. The delight which I felt as often as you spoke in this manner is only to be equalled by the pain I now feel at the different language which you have lately held to me....
I am now, alas!, a miserable, broken-hearted old man. But old and broken-hearted as I am, I love you still, notwithstanding all that has passed, to distraction.... May God Almighty bless and preserve you, and may he return you to your former love and affection for your most unhappy husband.[400]

Another marriage involving an heiress which (though it did not last into old age because of the premature deaths of both partners) began on the same footing as that of the Leitrims, was Lord Hartington's (the future 4th Duke of

THE 'MARRIAGE OF AFFECTION'

Devonshire) marriage to Lady Charlotte Boyle. There survive among the Devonshire Papers at Chatsworth some charming notes written on the back of playing cards and passed between them during their courtship over the years 1746–8; presumably, this was their only mode of communication granted the strict surveillance under which the courtship must have been conducted. When Lady Hartington died young in 1754, the stricken Hartington wrote to her mother, Lady Burlington:

> The loss that I have had and the affliction that I undergo, teaches me to feel what you must suffer, and every consideration prompts me to lend all my assistance to alleviate your concern. But there is one motive which is far above all the rest, which is the relation you bear to the poor, dear creature that is gone. For as long as I live, Madam, everything that belonged to her or that she had regard for, shall be dear to me.

Although he was only 34 in 1754, he did not re-marry during the ten years which remained to him.[401]

The courtship of the Hon. Windham Quin, later 2nd Earl of Dunraven, and Caroline Wyndham, his future wife, whom he was later actually to describe as 'a great heiress', did not begin quite so romantically. Indeed, for the first two years of its unusually long duration, Quin seems to have been motivated by calculation rather than affection. Writing to his father in March 1810 (the couple were married in December), he recalled:

> I continued the pursuit [of Caroline Wyndham] in 1818 [*sic* – 1808?], because I did like the girl, and you were so convinced of it that you joked me for being over head and ears in love with her. I contradicted that. I was not what is called in love. I discontinued, because ambition mastered the liking, as I thought I might form a great match perhaps, where the fortune would be *present*. I resumed, because as I told you, I know no person who is a fit match for me whom I think more amiable and hold so high … [and because], if I did not take this opportunity, I might long wait for another. I suppose it was reflection, and not suddenly conceived fancy, led me to this conclusion, for I had not seen [her] for nine months.

Once, however, he had committed himself to 'the pursuit', it was his 'natural temperament' to do it 'with ardour and … vehemence'.

This is reflected in the love letters he wrote to her during the remainder of 1810, which she carefully cherished, as she did his subsequent, more sombre and more moving communications. In January 1825, when he thought he was dying, he wrote her a farewell note, and assured her: 'You have merited and maintained my affection and my esteem through life.' In May 1830 he 'opened this letter … only [to] say, my dear wife, that time has only shown you more and more excellent, and made me love you more and more'. In June 1840, he took another farewell, and thanked 'God for having given you to me, for having given

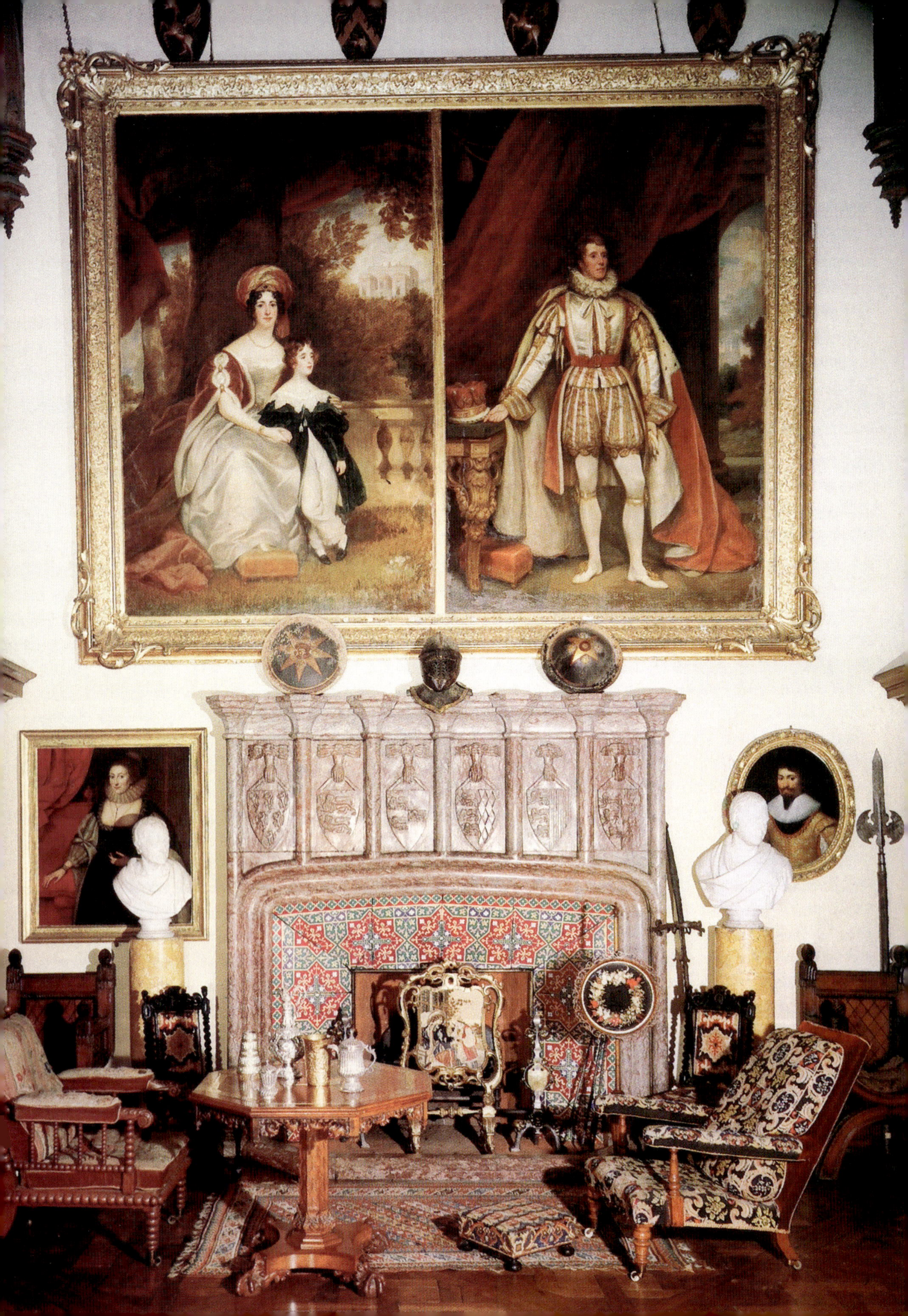

THE 'MARRIAGE OF AFFECTION'

me so many blessings, and left them to me so long'.[402] Since she did not receive these cumulative tributes until he really did die, on 5 August 1850, she had no opportunity to record her feelings in reply. These feelings can, however, be divined from the idealised, youthful portrait of him which she had painted in 1840 (when he was actually nearly 60), and which hung until c.1980 alongside a somewhat more realistic portrait of herself, in the long gallery at Adare Manor, their Co. Limerick seat.

The extraordinary nature of the Newcomen case provided scope for a much more explicit display of feelings. When reunited to her proper *fiancé*, Mr Gleadowe, Miss Newcomen threw 'off all reserve and the joy she expressed at seeing him showed how well she loved'; to which he responded by going 'quite mad for an hour'.[403]

The Fitzgerald family, in the generation of the 2nd Duke of Leinster himself, provides two further, and final, examples of affective marriages to heiresses. His mother thus described to the Duke in 1791 the personal qualities of Charlotte Boyle Walsingham, the *fiancée* of his younger brother, Lord Henry Fitzgerald:

> Finding herself entirely her own mistress with such a fortune at one-and-twenty would have turned many girls' heads, but she mixes great prudence and discretion with her love of pleasure, and will I hope and believe make him an excellent wife. Henry is really excessively fond of her and she is much in love with him, and seems to know all his little ways already, rallies him about his laziness continually in a very pretty manner, without a possibility of his being displeased at it.... I think them perfectly well suited.

The Duke himself received in 1795 the following letter from his own wife, Emilia Olivia St George, an heiress roughly on a par with Charlotte Boyle Walsingham as to fortune, written after they had been married some twenty years:

> My dear friend, since I saw you I have lost my two front teeth and have suffered much in body and mind. I hope you will not think me *quite* a fright. I have so long experienced your attachment to me, I cannot suspect it to be capable of change from the loss of any *outward* advantage.[404]

All these examples conform to the 'affective' model. However, without benefit of surviving personal correspondence, they would all – because of the worldly suitability of the marriage partners one to another – look like 'a mere traffic for private or political purposes' or like marriages dictated by 'authority or interest'. Of the heiresses in the sample, the only one who might (in purely material terms) have got better value for her fortune than she did was Charlotte Boyle Walsingham; she obtained the younger brother of a duke for roughly the same sum as Emilia Olivia St George obtained the duke! On the other hand, because of the over-portioning of the 1st Duke of Leinster's younger children, Lord Henry Fitzgerald owned an estate of his own at Strangford, Co. Down, and was

The chimneypiece in the Long Gallery at Adare, over which hang Thomas Phillips' portraits of Lord and Lady Dunraven in the costumes they had worn at George IV's coronation twenty years earlier, in 1821; reproduced from Christie's Adare Manor sale catalogue, 9–10 June 1982 in a position to provide a seat and territorial base for his wife – and for the ancient, English barony of de Ros, which was called out of abeyance in her favour in 1806.[405]

On this admittedly impressionistic evidence, plenty of young ladies, heiresses included, made marriages which were suitable in worldly terms and which were happy and successful in emotional terms as well. This is not a surprising conclusion given the view of aristocratic marriage propounded in the preceding chapters of the present study. But it runs counter to the view of Lord Clare and the pamphleteer of 1789, neither of whom used the term 'arranged marriage' (because it was not in contemporary usage), but both of whom thought that most upper-class marriages were imposed on the partners, with disastrous consequences in many instances for the future. Clare may have been influenced in his views by the experiences of his niece, Marianne Jeffereyes, who married the 7th Earl of Westmeath in 1784, committed (or perhaps was driven to) adultery and was divorced by him in 1796: the 1789 pamphlet was certainly written in response to an earlier case of adultery, this one involving an heiress (which Lady Westmeath was not), Mrs Henry Cecil, wife of the nephew and heir-presumptive of the 9th Earl of Exeter.

The Cecil marriage had taken place in 1776, thirteen years before Mrs Cecil committed adultery with the local curate, the Rev. William Sneyd (whose involvement gives the story a slight Irish association, as he was the brother of two of Richard Lovell Edgeworth's wives). The marriage had produced children, none of whom survived infancy, and for years was as contented as the shallow, pleasure-loving natures of Henry Cecil and Emma Vernon permitted. Nor had it been particularly 'arranged': both were 22 years of age in 1776, and although Emma Vernon's mother, a silly, socially ambitious woman, leant heavily upon her to marry Henry Cecil, and Lord Exeter also favoured the match, another of Emma Vernon's trustees and guardians was opposed to it and would have backed her up if she had offered resistance. So, the circumstances of the Cecil-Vernon marriage did not fit the stereotype propounded by the pamphleteer – unfortunate young couple with nothing in common coerced into an uncongenial marriage by match-making parents or guardians.

The consequences of the adultery, however, did bear with undue severity on Mrs Cecil. She was divorced two years later, in 1791. In the meantime, she had lost the consolation of her relationship with Sneyd, whose mind had given way under the weight of guilt and remorse. The financial cost of her misconduct was also severe. Her marriage settlement had placed her house and estate, Hanbury Hall, Worcestershire, under the sole control of her husband for their joint lives; and, if the marriage were childless (which it was), only £4,000 a year of her income of £6,000 would revert to her or her right heirs at his death. Her adultery and divorce meant that she lost her pin money of £1,000 a year and her entitlement to a jointure of £1,500 a year, and continued to be locked out of Hanbury Hall and any income from her own estate. The £1,200 which she received as a separate maintenance (and which at least was a larger sum than her pin money) was an annuity granted her by Lord Exeter. There was a further aggravation of her situation, which came to light only in the 1960s. Just before Henry Cecil divorced her, he contracted a bigamous 'marriage' to one Sally Hoggins of Bolas, Shropshire, whom he married a second time on 3 October 1791, after the divorce had taken place and who became 'the cottage countess' of Exeter in 1793.[406] To this day, the date of Henry Cecil, 10th Earl of Exeter's, second marriage is falsified in Burke's and other *Peerages*.

Although the bigamous aspect of the case did not transpire, the other circumstances of it were more than sufficient to excite moral outrage and create alarm, the more so as high-society scandals like the Cecil, Belmore and Westmeath adulteries were symptomatic of a general increase in the number of divorces (and of separations, whether judicial or by private deed). In the case of divorces, each of which required an act of parliament and therefore is recorded in the *Commons' Journals*, it is possible to quantify the increase with precision. In the period 1700–49, there were only thirteen successful petitions for divorce to the British House of Lords, while in 1799 there were ten in that one exceptional year alone.[407] In Ireland, divorce was much less common among the class of people who alone were able to afford it than it was in Britain: there were only seven divorce acts of the Irish parliament prior to the 'Constitution of 1782', and only seven between then and the Union.[408] The Constitution of 1782 did nothing to prevent Irishmen from divorcing their wives via an act of the British parliament, provided only that non-Irish property or a non-Irish peerage was concerned. Nevertheless, if divorce acts of both parliaments initiated by Irish peers over the course of the eighteenth century are reckoned together, the total comes to only five:[409] Ligonier (1771), Tyrconnel (1777), Belmore – Lady Henrietta Hobart's husband – (1793), Westmeath (1796), and Abercorn (1799). Of these, Ligonier and Tyrconnel had no more than a titular connection with Ireland, Abercorn had property, peerages and residences in all three kingdoms, and only Belmore and Westmeath were exclusively Irish in property and peerage and obtained their divorces from the Irish parliament.[410] Since the figure is as low as five, it is obvious that divorce alone cannot be used as a touchstone of the frequency of marital breakdown.

One obvious reason for this, and for the infrequency of divorce, is dread of the publicity which always accompanied it. While the parliamentary stage of the divorce procedure would largely be conducted in camera, the preceding stages, which were an action in an ecclesiastical court for separation from bed and board, and a separate action in a criminal court (usually the King's Bench) for 'criminal conversation' (known as 'crim. con.') – i.e. for damages against the wife's seducer – would both of them be attended with publicity in the form of newspaper reports. If the evidence was sufficiently salacious, it might be reprinted in pamphlet form, and – worst of all – it might find its way into a compendium such as *The Cuckold's Chronicle: being select Trials for Adultery, Incest,*

Imbecility, Ravishment, etc (two volumes, London, 1793). The court proceedings in the Belmore divorce, for example, which took place in 1792, were recorded in the newspapers, a pamphlet and *The Cuckold's Chronicle*. Proceedings in an ecclesiastical court for the purpose of obtaining a formal separation, would potentially attract the same amount of publicity as the preliminaries to divorce, and therefore were similarly distasteful to the individuals and families concerned. For this reason, they usually preferred to proceed by private, informal deed of separation so that the estranged couple's 'differences would be kept from the world'.[411]

Another reason for the infrequency of divorce was that, until the Divorce Act of 1857, it was exceedingly difficult for a woman to obtain one (or a judicial separation) unless she had been subjected to cruelty of an aggravated nature. The Marchioness of Westmeath eventually succeeded in obtaining a judicial separation in 1827, but this was a 'freak' verdict, since the degree of cruelty which she had experienced fell well below the usual criteria of aggravation. Divorce, therefore, was in practice almost the exclusive prerogative of men. But even they had little hope of obtaining a divorce except on grounds of adultery. The 'wars of the Westmeaths' provide an illustration of this point too. From c.1840 Lord Westmeath, who up to the 1830s had strenuously opposed all his wife's efforts to obtain a separation, changed his tune and sought to divorce her so that he would be free to marry his mistress. However, since Lady Westmeath had not misconducted herself in any way (beyond an innocent but indiscreet friendship with that great lover, the Duke of Wellington), there was no possible ground for divorce. Only her death, which took place in 1858, released Lord Westmeath from her and allowed him to re-marry, which he immediately did at the age of seventy-three.[412]

No adultery was committed by the wife in this case; and in a great many others – where a married woman's name was coupled with that of an active philanderer like the Duke – the smoke was without fire. To judge from the tittle-tattle

Edmund Boyle, 7th Earl of Cork and Orrery (1742–98), and his mistress, Miss Greenhill, reproduced from *The Town and Country Magazine* of 1 April 1783. This is given as an example of the *tête à tête* series, but it is indicative of the prevailing double standard that a 'suspicious husband' (who had separated from his wife in 1773 and unsuccessfully tried to divorce her in 1782) thought nothing of going about openly in company with a mistress.

AUTHOR'S COLLECTION

THE 'MARRIAGE OF AFFECTION'

of Horace Walpole and his like, the famous '*tête à tête*' series published in *The Town and Country Magazine* in the 1770s and 1780s, and even Lord Clare's letter about the 'traffic' of marriage, which includes a reference to 'the tribe of cuckold-makers' – adultery on the part of the wife was a routine fact of upper-class life and was practised on an extensive scale. It may actually have been more prevalent in Britain than in Ireland: in 1804, crim. con. 'was said … to be "novel in this country" [Ireland] and in 1816 to be still "very rare"'[413] – although in the period between those dates there had in fact been at least three sensational cases of it in the Irish courts. Nevertheless, even in Britain it was not nearly as common as the published and private tittle-tattle would suggest. There was a good deal of *amitié amoureuse* and a little light dalliance, but they usually went no further than 'a business on the sofa at worst'.[414]

Nor is this surprising, granted the way in which the laws of marriage were biased against women. A woman taken in adultery would lose much of the financial security which she enjoyed under her marriage settlement; she would be parted from her children and might never see them again; and unless she was particularly well connected (like Lady Elizabeth Foster, Lady Sarah Lennox/Bunbury/Napier and Elizabeth Vassall, Lady Holland), she would be permanently excluded from good society. In the a-moral world of 'the Grand Whiggery', it is true, some latitude was allowed to wives who had done their duty and produced the proverbial 'heir and spare'; but it should be remembered that the easy-going and enormously rich 5th Duke of Devonshire almost divorced his wife, Georgiana, in 1791–2, for having a child by another man. Although Lord Clare was 'perfectly certain that, at the outset of an intrigue, the lady's great argument to herself is that she will escape detection', this was actually a rather far-fetched assumption (both of Lord Clare and the lady). Granted the quantity of servants employed in country houses, town houses, lodgings and even inns,[415] it was simply a matter of time before an adultery was detected.

The infrequency of adultery on the part of the wife was therefore one good reason for the infrequency of divorce; and a further and final reason was that a husband who had successfully proceeded against his adulterous wife and her adulterous lover, or who had good legal grounds for doing so, might not be anxious or even willing to go the full distance of divorcing her. Some cuckolded husbands, particularly those who had already sired an heir, had no wish to re-marry: they might be too old or too tired, have a perfectly satisfactory mistress, be in a financial situation which made it impossible to provide for a further family, etc, etc. Some may have been eager to deprive their adulterous wives of the pleasure of marrying the adulterer. Some may have baulked at the heavy cost of divorce. All were at liberty to stop short, because if they were separated from their wives by private deed or by decree of an ecclesiastical court, and if they were able to prove that the separation had continued without interruption, there would be little danger of their becoming financially liable for any children their wives might have by another man.

THE PURSUIT OF THE HEIRESS

Since no study of aristocratic marriage, and of 'the marriage of affection' in particular, is complete without some consideration of the causes and circumstances of marital breakdown, it is necessary to probe a little deeper than divorce and judicial separation in order to come to some sort of conclusion on the matter. This is not easy. Unless it resulted in publicity or scandal, marital breakdown usually passes unnoticed – certainly by *The Complete Peerage* and other *Peerages*. The aristocratic lifestyle was peripatetic, and peerage families maintained a variety of houses and establishments in town and country. Prolonged sojourns by wives in a different house from their husbands, or in one of the fashionable watering-holes, could obviate the need for even a private separation, and can conceal the temporary or permanent collapse of the marriage. What, for example, is to be made of the marital status of 'that mysterious personage', the 1st Earl Erne (1731–1828)? His wife's brother paid tribute to Lord Erne's 'kind, affectionate, steady heart', but Lord Erne, though he professed the deepest affection for Lady Erne and their daughter, Lady Caroline Creighton, 'lived entirely separate from them and very rarely saw them'.[416] In many instances, marital breakdown was concealed by the fact that the wife (unlike Ladies Downshire and Louisa Conolly) knew that the husband was unfaithful, but continued to live with him. Many wives even continued to live with husbands who were promiscuously unfaithful and liable to infect them with venereal disease.

In general, infidelity was regarded as a venial sin unless committed by the wife: infidelity on the husband's part was much less dangerous (except to health), because it did not bring into question the succession to property and perhaps peerages. It also cost less in financial terms. A small annuity would satisfy the needs of a husband's mistress and illegitimate children, whereas a wife's illegitimate children would have to be portioned as generously as her children by her husband for as long as husband and wife continued to live together.[417] However understandable this double standard was, it was still a double standard. It made it additionally difficult for a faithful wife to obtain a separation from an unfaithful husband, and so contributes to a false impression that more marriages were successful – particularly from the point of view of the wife – than in reality was the case. Even if it were statistically possible to add to the five divorces the number of formal and informal separations involving Irish aristocrats, the figure would still fall vastly short of the true incidence of marital breakdown.

It might be expected that marriages with heiresses would be the ones most liable to marital breakdown, because they were more likely than most to have been 'arranged'. The English instance of Henry Cecil and Emma Vernon seems superficially to bear out this hypothesis, although the reality was rather different: it is worth repeating that each of them was twenty-two at the time of the marriage in 1776 and therefore well able to judge for himself/herself; also that they lived together, and produced children who died in infancy, for nearly fifteen years before disaster struck. In Ireland, the hypothesis is more plausibly borne out by the outcome of the arranged marriage between Lord

THE 'MARRIAGE OF AFFECTION'

Kingsborough, the future 2nd Earl of Kingston, and the heiress to the former Kingston estate in Co. Cork, which took place in 1769, was soon on the rocks and ended in an informal separation in the early 1790s. Later in that decade, the separation resulted in disgraceful exhibitions of sexual depravity and of abuses of his power as colonel of the North Cork Militia on the part of the now unfettered husband, who 'exultingly owned' in July 1798

> that a number of pretty women had come to him in behalf of their husbands, fathers or brothers [arrested or captured United Irishmen]; that he always said to them 'If you'll grant me one favour, I'll grant you another'; that very few eventually refused these terms; and, he added, 'I have been very unfortunate, since out of all these I have hitherto had only two maidenheads'.[418]

The only other marriages to an heiress or potential heiress which ended in dramatic marital breakdown were those of Lord Blayney and Mary Cairnes in 1724, of Sir John Meade, later Lord Clanwilliam, and Theodosia Magill in 1765, of Armar Lowry-Corry, later Lord Belmore, and Lady Henrietta Hobart in 1780, and of Count Alfred d'Orsay and Lady Harriet Gardiner in 1827. The first has been fully discussed in the present chapter and the last will be fully discussed in Chapter Six.

The marriage of Lord Clanwilliam and Theodosia Magill was certainly a 'merger of two landed fortunes': his Cork and Tipperary estates were yielding £10,000 a year at the time of the marriage in 1765, and hers in Co. Down must have been yielding something similar by the time of his death in 1800. The couple were of full age when they married. They cannot have been wholly averse to each other, because they produced five sons and five daughters between 1765 and 1782. Some years before the latter date, however, Lord Clanwilliam had started to take mistresses and to indulge in all sorts of debauchery. His wife and he never seem to have separated formally – he even came back to live with her for a while just before his death in 1800 – but they increasingly lived and drifted apart. Her grandson later asserted that she had been 'soured by the misconduct of a dissolute husband', which implies that the marriage had begun on a happy footing. Beyond this, nothing is known of the circumstances which brought them together in 1765, and whether they entered willingly into the marriage or were cajoled or coerced into it by ambitious relations.

Much more is known about the outset of the Belmore marriage in 1780. Indeed, it has already been cited as an example of how a loveless, arranged marriage could still be perpetrated at a time when the affective marriage is supposed to have been in its heyday. Following the marriage, Lord Belmore 'behaved to his wife ... with the greatest love and attention, and appeared to try everything possible to win and retain her affection, but ... without success, for she ... behaved in such a manner towards ... [him] as to convince ... every person who saw her behaviour that she had a total aversion to him'.[419] In 1781, six weeks after the birth of their only child, Louisa, the Belmores separated by private

THE PURSUIT OF THE HEIRESS

deed. For nine years they lived apart, he in Ireland and she, in compliance with the terms of the separation, elsewhere. Then, in the summer of 1790, she formed a *liaison* with the Earl of Ancram, son and heir of the 5th Marquess of Lothian (and, incidentally, eldest brother of Lord Mark Kerr). This was conducted with increasing flagrancy until, in 1792, Lord Belmore felt that his honour required that he divorce her. Following the divorce, she married Lord Ancram in 1793, and on the death of her father, Lord Buckinghamshire, in the following year, inherited Blickling Hall and his Norfolk estate. It will be suggested in Chapter Seven that it was the distant prospect of this inheritance which had been a principal inducement to Belmore to marry a woman with whom he was only slightly acquainted.

The Blayney, Kingsborough, Belmore (and d'Orsay) marriages conform to the stereotypical view of marriage 'by authority or interest'. But the others in an admittedly haphazard sample of unsuccessful marriages among the Irish aristocracy are of a quite different tenor. For one thing, none of them involves an heiress.

The first is 'the melancholy amour of Lady Belfield and Arthur Rochfort, which is of so shocking a nature that it is not to be paralleled'.[420] In 1736, Robert Rochfort (son and heir of George Rochfort of Gaulstown), who was later created Baron and Viscount Belfield and earl of Belvedere, married as his second wife Mary, eldest daughter of the 3rd Viscount Molesworth. It was later stated that Lord Belvedere had married her 'for love, she being very handsome, though no fortune, and used her in the tenderest manner'. (As usual, 'no fortune' is not to be taken literally: in fact, she had a modest £3,000, which was not proportionate to her jointure of £500 a year, but still was a respectable sum.) They lived together – some said happily, others unhappily – until 1743, by which time she had borne him three sons and a daughter. In March 1743, however, he was informed that she was having an affair with his younger brother, Arthur, which she first confessed (possibly under duress) and thereafter denied. His brother, who had a wife and children, also denied the charge, but deemed it prudent to flee the country.

It was reported that Belvedere, 'resolving to be divorced, is now prosecuting her as an adulteress, and we are told that, when separated, she will be transported

Lady Belmore in bed with Lord Ancram, reproduced from The Trial of Viscountess Belmore (formerly Lady Henrietta Hobart, and Daughter to John Earl of Buckinghamshire) for Adultery with the Earl of Ancram ... *(London, 1792)*

THE 'MARRIAGE OF AFFECTION'

to the West Indies as a vagabond'. In fact, Belvedere did not trouble to obtain a judicial separation, far less a divorce, but instead locked her up in Gaulstown, where she remained until he died in 1774.[421] He had no reason to go to the expense and through the opprobrium of a divorce: he already had an heir and two spares; he had a second, and preferred, country residence where he could live apart from his wife (Belvedere, near Mullingar); and, to judge from his will, he had the consolation of a 'housekeeper', Mary Turner, to whom and to whose son he left £6,000 and more besides. Since the law would not have allowed him to transport Lady Belvedere to the West Indies, unofficial imprisonment for life was the harshest punishment he could have inflicted upon her. His revenge was a case of Shakespeare's 'Sweet Love..., changing his property/Turns to the sourest and most deadly hate'. As for Arthur Rochfort, Belvedere seems to have been willing to leave him alone, until he persisted in returning to Ireland. In 1759, during one of Rochfort's provocative return visits, Belvedere prosecuted him for crim. con., obtained the enormous sum of £20,000 in damages against him, and left him to rot in debtors' prison in Dublin.[422]

The next separation in point of time was much more under-stated and even amicable. In 1766 or 1767 Bernard Ward, later 1st Viscount Bangor, separated by private deed from his wife, Lady Anne Bligh/Magill, daughter of the 1st Earl of Darnley, widow of Robert Hawkins Magill (d.1747) and mother, by her first marriage, of Theodosia, Countess of Clanwilliam. The Wards had married in 1748. They must have known each other well, since Lady Anne had been associated with Co. Down since her first marriage in 1742. Her two husbands had been friends, and Bernard Ward had succeeded Robert Hawkins Magill as MP for the county in 1747. The Wards stuck together for almost twenty years, and had three sons and four daughters. However, Lady Anne was 'domineering and erratic', 'whimsical' and had 'a shade of derangement in her intellects, an hereditary malady' which she may have been responsible for transmitting to her eldest son by Bernard Ward. As for Bernard Ward, he was so notoriously promiscuous that the Rector of Ballyculter (the local living of which Ward was patron) later (c.1776) admonished him privately on the subject and then pointedly preached a sermon against 'whoremongers and adulterers'. Ward's extra-marital adventures, rather than the probably apocryphal quarrel between Lady Anne and him over whether their new house at Castle Ward should be Gothick or Classical, may have precipitated the separation. It was sufficiently un-acrimonious for Lady Anne's daughter, Lady Clanwilliam, to remain on very good terms with her errant stepfather.[423]

The next instance of marital breakdown, which was caused by adultery on the part of the wife, though it terminated in divorce, was also surprisingly un-acrimonious. Indeed, it was a case of sweet love which never changed his property but remained touchingly constant in spite of all. Richard Martin (1754–1834) of Dangan and Ballynahinch, Co. Galway, MP for that county, 1800–27, may loosely be described as an aristocrat on account of the princely status accorded him in the wilds of Connemara, of which he was the ground landlord. He had married his wife, Elizabeth, daughter of George Vesey of Lucan, Co. Dublin, for love, and she certainly was not an heiress. In 1791, she quite unexpectedly eloped with a small, ugly Englishman called William Petrie, whom Martin successfully sued for crim. con. He divorced Mrs Martin in 1792, and she promptly married her seducer. Since Petrie

> was known to be a great savage, capable and likely to use her ill, Mr M. wrote to him as follows: 'Sir, I scorn to remind you of past events – the law has settled that question [by awarding Martin £10,000 in damages]. But, if ever I hear that you treat the lady who once had the honour to bear the name of Martin with anything but the strictest respect, you may be assured you shall answer [for] it to me.'[424]

The next startling case of marital breakdown – excluding the Belmore divorce, which has already been dealt with – was the divorce of the 7th Earl of Westmeath from Lord Clare's niece. During the earlier crim. con. proceedings in 1795, a sensation was created by the graphic descriptions which witnesses gave of the sexual acts performed in a carriage by Lady Westmeath and her seducer and, later, second husband, the Hon. Augustus Cavendish Bradshaw. However, the more important fact (for present purposes) to emerge from the proceedings was that this, too, had been a love-match. 'The ... counsel for the plaintiff [Lord Westmeath] emphasised at some length that the match was "purely the result of love to the lady", reciprocated by her, and that no "compulsion of parental authority" had been used on her.'[425] Nor could Lord Westmeath have had any mercenary motive for marrying her, since she was not an heiress and indeed came from a family which was in parlous financial circumstances.

The next divorce was that of Lord Abercorn from his second wife, Cecil Hamilton. She was his first cousin, and prior to their marriage in 1792 had always lived under his roof – as a kind of mistress of the robes to the first Lady Abercorn and, it was rumoured, mistress to himself. She rapidly became notorious for the sumptuous and *décolleté* character of her entertainments. Soon, however, 'the scandalous world' was 'occupied with ... [Lady Abercorn's] adventures' of an altogether more serious nature. She had an affair with Capt. Joseph Copley (who happened to be a disreputable brother of her predecessor), and in 1798

> found herself with child by Copley; which was the more awkward as Lord Abercorn had parted beds and could not be the father.... She went down to the country, where Lord Abercorn was, and called him out and told her story.... He took it very coolly, though with great surprise, and behaved with sufficient temper and liberality.... She meant to return to her hack chaise, but Lord Abercorn insisted on her going like the Marchioness of Abercorn and taking his coach and servants.

They were divorced in 1799. Clearly this had been a love-match, probably to an

THE 'MARRIAGE OF AFFECTION'

ex-mistress and certainly to a poor relation who can have had little in the way of fortune.[426]

Much the same – at least as to love and little fortune – could have been said of Lady Cloncurry, who was divorced by her husband in 1811. She was Elizabeth Georgiana Morgan, first wife (1803) of Valentine Lawless, 2nd Lord Cloncurry (1773–1853), and a woman 'whom he adored'. In 1806, Lady Cloncurry was seduced by a hardened philanderer, Sir John Piers, 6th Bt, at the Cloncurry seat, Lyons, Co. Kildare, where what passed was observed by an Italian mural-painter called Gaspar Gabrielli, who was working (unobserved by the preoccupied couple) at the top of a ladder in the very same room. Lord Cloncurry brought an action for crim. con. against Piers in 1807, and secured damages of £20,000. Granted the dramatic and, from the point of view of those not involved, humorous circumstances of the adultery, the case attracted great publicity, was celebrated in contemporary caricatures, and in more recent years inspired some poorish verse by John Betjeman. Cloncurry, immediately on receiving from Lady Cloncurry a confession of her guilt, had sent her back to her father, and the couple lived apart until he obtained a divorce act in 1811. In his *Personal Recollections*, published in 1849, he described the years 1806–11 as a time when 'my quiet was painfully disturbed by occurrences that ended in the year 1811 in a dissolution of my hasty and imprudent marriage'. He remarried in 1811, and lived with his second wife 'in uninterrupted happiness and affection for thirty years'. Despite the gloss he put upon his first marriage long after the event, there is no reason to doubt that while it lasted it too had been characterised by 'happiness and affection'.[427]

Lady Cloncurry seduced by Sir John Piers in 1806, in full view of the mural-painter, Gabrielli: a contemporary caricature. The '12 connoisseurs' were the jury and the £20,000 was the damages they awarded to Cloncurry.

COLLECTION OF THE KNIGHT OF GLIN

After the stir caused by the Cloncurry divorce, Co. Kildare was further excited in 1816 by an action for crim. con. brought by Christopher Taaffe of Rookwood, Co. Galway, against Lord William Fitzgerald (1793–1864), younger brother of the 3rd Duke of Leinster. Taaffe was a substantial country gentleman with an estate supposedly worth £5,000 a year. Mrs Taaffe, *née* Honora Burke of Glinsk, Co. Galway, was his second wife, to whom he had been married in 1806. She was a poorly portioned bride, who brought him only £2,000 (his short-lived first wife had brought him £5,000). There is therefore every reason to assume that the couple had married for love. They lived together 'in a state of the most enviable felicity' from 1806 to 1813, when Lord William entered their lives. After repeated acts of adultery with Mrs Taaffe, starting in the latter year, Lord William ran off with her, and with the Taaffes' two children, in 1814. Taaffe claimed damages of £20,000, but was awarded only £5,000 – possibly because he had been so credulous and trusting that it almost looked as if he had condoned the adultery. (The same objection must have been raised in Richard Martin's crim. con. proceedings, since the £10,000 damages awarded to him was low in relation to the sums received by other plaintiff husbands.) Lord William did not marry Mrs Taaffe, was not deemed fit to fulfil the primary function of a cadet Fitzgerald by representing Co. Kildare in parliament, and lived and died abroad.[428]

Finally, 'the wars of the Westmeaths'. These were fought through various courts over the long period 1819–34 and then broke out afresh in pamphlet form in 1857. The contending parties were George Nugent, Lord Delvin (later 8th Earl and only Marquess of Westmeath), only son of the 7th Earl and the latter's divorced first wife, and the 8th Earl's first wife, Lady Emily Cecil. Lord Delvin, as has been seen, had falsified the size of his father's rental in order to obtain Lady Emily's hand in 1812. He had done so partly because of the rank and prestige of the Cecil family and the desirability of a connection with Hatfield House. But there is no reason to doubt that he was in love with Lady Emily (and that he remained so, in spite of their violent quarrels, until about 1820). Lady Emily, on her side, was of a colder temperament and, as the evidence generated by the quarrels would later demonstrate, prudish in her attitude to sex. But there is again no reason to doubt that initially – though not for long – she was in love with the handsome Lord Delvin. Otherwise, it is hard to see why she would have wanted to marry a man who, for all the antiquity of his family, was a backwoods earl by Hatfield House standards and the son of a divorced and disgraced woman. The match was certainly of the couple's own making; nobody arranged it for them; and Lady Emily, though a wealthier woman than Lord Delvin could reasonably have expected (especially if he had told the truth about his rental), was not an heiress. The passion with which both pursued their quarrels, and the obsessiveness with which Lady Westmeath pursued them long after Lord Westmeath had decided to put his failed marriage behind him, also suggest that this was another case of sweet love turning to the sourest and most deadly hate.

What sense, if any, can be made of this small, haphazard sample of divorces and dramatic marital breakdowns? Writing specifically about England, Stone suggested: 'The unions most likely to break down in the eighteenth century seem to have been..., statistically, sudden love-matches [contracted] at a very early age without consent or advice of parents and friends, or marriages arranged by parents and friends without any consultation about the wishes of the spouses.'[429] None of the Irish instances in the sample falls into the first category; the Blayney, Belvedere, Kingsborough, Belmore and d'Orsay marriages fall into the second, though with the qualification that the wishes of one of the two spouses had been consulted. Four of the same five marriages also involved heiresses (or in Lady Belmore's case what will be called in Chapter Seven a 'speculative heiress') – the exception is of course Lady Belvedere. Two other marriages which did not involve heiresses were also, if the term has any meaning at all, 'arranged': those of Lady Elizabeth Foster and Lady Erne (who was her sister), both of whom were married in 1776 to inappropriate husbands because their selfish father wanted to dispose of them on the cheap. On this showing, love-matches contracted by couples of full age under no duress of 'authority or interest' were at least as likely to go wrong as marriages made under duress which involved heiresses.

This analysis relates solely to the basis on which the marriage was made, which is not the only way in which to look at the problem. For example, although Lord Westmeath and Lady Emily Cecil chose each other and married for love, they were as blind to the sexual and other incompatibilities which wrecked their marriage as any match-making parents could possibly have been. Perhaps the reason for marital breakdown is to be sought in how the couple related to each other during their married life together, rather than in the basis on which they married. In this regard, Lord Clare may have been old-fashioned in his assumption that a wife would expect no more of her husband than that he treat her as became him. Perhaps affectiveness had spread too widely for this to be a reasonable assumption. In 'a society [which believed] it was the natural order of things for a [married] woman … not to expect, as an entitlement, affection and respect from that relationship', married women would be prepared to put up with much. But 'the ideal of the companionate marriage, as a new and romantic alternative to the family-arranged model, tended to lead to more tension and unhappiness … [and] higher rates of divorce, since the expectations of the participants were unreasonably high'.[430]

This explanation may be a little too convenient, and may lean too heavily on the shaky premiss of the rise of the affective family. The course of wisdom is not to seek for models and patterns at all, but to allow human nature to run its empirical course. Human nature would not be human nature if it did not leave room for surprises such as the failure of Lord Abercorn's love-match with a lady who was probably an erstwhile mistress, and the success of Lord Downshire's dynastic marriage with a great heiress. Most of the empirical evidence supports the view that aristocratic marriages in Ireland were often and perhaps usually 'marriages of affection', and that financial considerations did not prevent men and women, heiresses included, from finding partners who were at the very least companionate. This was because the conventions of aristocratic marriage were sufficiently flexible to accommodate all but the most perverse. If the five married daughters of the proverbially mercenary Lord Hertford are taken as a sample, what is very striking is the wide diversity, in worldly terms, of the matches they made, ranging from the heir to a British dukedom at one extreme, to the younger brother of an Irish squire of £2,000 a year, at the other.[431]

Similar diversity is apparent if all the heiresses so far mentioned are taken as a sample; their husbands range from dukes to commoners, and from eldest sons far wealthier than they, to younger sons with nothing but portions of a few thousand pounds. Granted such diversity, it was easily possible for most men and women to find partners to their liking, and even to their loving, without positive *mésalliance* on either side.

'The rise of the affective family', like all great theories and great debates, has generated as much heat as light, and has encouraged interpretations which are both adversarial and reductionist. It may well be that no objective measure of affectiveness can be found, nor one decade or generation to which the rise of this allegedly new phenomenon can plausibly be pinned, simply because it had always been there, as a factor of varying importance, in familial relationships and in the choosing of marriage partners. The present study, therefore – though it throws up much evidence which supports the affectiveness cause – stays firmly on the sidelines. It must, however, take issue with one argument advanced by proponents of that cause – the argument that it is a proof of affectiveness that there was 'a large decline in the proportion of sons of peers married to heiresses'.[432] If this decline took place, which it may or may not have done, it is unlikely to have had much to do with affectiveness. For one thing, as Chapters One to Four have argued, heiresses were not what they used to be and not all they were cracked up to be; there were some sound, practical, worldly reasons for giving them a miss. For another, as the present chapter has argued, affectiveness was an element in more relationships than might be imagined. A man may fall in love with an heiress as easily as, or – since it is more convenient – more easily than, a milkmaid.[433] But if he marries the milkmaid, it is called a love-match; and if he marries the heiress it is called an arranged marriage. There is preconception and there is prejudice, but no logic, in the distinction.

Lord Hertford:
an engraving of 1791
after a drawing from life by
W.H. Brown
AUTHOR'S COLLECTION

SIX

Elopements, mésalliances and mis-matches

Thus far, the tendency of the present study has been to play down the sensational in aristocratic marriage (with particular reference to marriages involving heiresses) and play up the more prosaic and commonsense elements of 'collateral calculation' and mutual affection. Edward Hussey has been shown to have had greater assets than 'legs and impudence', and Lord Stewart/Londonderry to have been much more than an 'old dandy'. The duress under which Lady Cathcart acted has been lightened, and the period and conditions of her durance shortened and softened. Love has been discerned in some of the most dynastically advantageous marriages, and the benefits of others have been shown to be more evenly balanced and distributed than at first sight had appeared. Finally, it has been demonstrated that, insofar as it was possible to predict the future (which marriage settlements went to great lengths, in both senses of the term, to do), it was unlikely that one contracting party would gain significantly at the expense of the other. Nevertheless, there remained a certain amount of scope for surprises and even sensations. Much of Chapter Seven will be devoted to a consideration of events which occurred subsequent to the marriage settlement and were unforeseeable at the time it was drawn up. The present Chapter, as its title makes plain, is devoted to events of a more dramatic kind.

Elopements (and clandestine marriages) have much in common with abductions. This is, firstly, because after the event they were often acquiesced in by the bride's family (even when she was much the better-endowed in terms of fortune) because her reputation had been so tarnished by the escapade that she was unlikely, if legal means could be found to 'break' the marriage, ever to find an alternative spouse. Secondly, elopements – like abductions – often received before the event at least some covert support from members of the bride's family or of the families of both bride and groom. In the purely English case of the Hon. Cassandra Twistleton in 1790, her mother complained that 'more of the family *winked* at this continued attachment (if *not* the *elopement*) than we were aware of'; her elder daughter, Julia, and Julia's husband, in particular, were never 'in their *hearts* against the alliance'. Actually, this was not surprising. The eloping couple were socially well matched, and the main obstacles to their union were that the bride's fortune was small and that the bridegroom's wealthy father was mean. The marriage went ahead on English soil after the two of them had been intercepted at Dover and prevented from proceeding to France.[434]

Like abductions, elopements which led to clandestine marriage came under the cognisance of the criminal law. In Ireland, this was embodied in the already-mentioned series of acts passed by the Irish parliament between 1707 and 1749 to curb such practices. Scotland was, literally, a law unto itself. In England and Wales, Lord Hardwicke's Marriage Act held sway from 1753 until the early 1820s though, for all its much criticised draconianism, it may actually have been less effective than the Irish code of statutes.[435] For example, Lord Hardwicke's act could usually be circumvented by any couple who had both the leisure and the means to obtain a marriage license by taking up temporary residence in a parish where they were not known.[436] Where the act was draconian was in the technical safeguards which it specified. These mainly related to the form of consent required (on the part of parent/s or guardian/s) when the bride was under the age of twenty-one. But they also included – among the proofs of clandestiness – such things as the locking of the church door while the marriage ceremony was in progress. Since church doors might well be locked in the interests of privacy not secrecy, and since it was also easy for innocent parties to neglect or infringe the technicalities of consent, the act invalidated many marriages which should never have fallen into its toils in the first place.

Ironically, in view of the fact that Lord Hardwicke's act did not apply to Ireland, the greatest *cause célèbre* arising out of its provisions, and probably the highest-ranking couple of the many caught in its net, were Lord Belfast and Anna May, who married in 1795 and became 2nd Marquess and Marchioness of Donegall in 1799. This was ironic in another respect. The act was intended to protect young women, particularly under-age heiresses, from being married clandestinely without the consent of parents and/or guardians and/or the lord chancellor. However, Anna May, though under-age, was not an heiress, and it was not she but Lord Belfast who needed protection (from the designs of her unscrupulous father, Edward May). The marriage fell within the provisions of Lord Hardwicke's act because it took place in England, Lord Belfast being incarcerated at the time in the Marshalsea debtors' prison in London. Although this did not come to light until twenty years later (1819), the marriage was invalid because Anna May was illegitimate as well as a minor. Under the terms of the act an illegitimate child could not legally marry under-age with the consent of only one parent, and Anna May's mother was long discarded or dead, and either way was not involved.

The effects of the technical invalidity of the marriage were wide-ranging: the Donegalls' seven children were illegitimised, the settlement provision made for them was nullified, and the eldest son of Lord Donegall's younger brother became next-in-line for the marquessate and the Donegall estates. There had

ELOPEMENTS, MÉSALLIANCES AND MIS-MATCHES

been a number of other instances of property being set adrift by the technicalities of Lord Hardwicke's act, and public sympathy and even the sympathy of a majority of the members of the House of Lords, were on the side of the Donegalls. So, matters were retrospectively rectified by an act of parliament passed in 1822 – an act which, along with a sequel measure passed in the following year, contained provisions which relaxed the rigours of Lord Hardwicke's act and presaged its supersession.[437]

Irish men and women unwilling, pre-1822–3, to run the gauntlet of that act or of the Irish legislation on the same subject, took advantage of the thriving matrimonial business which Hardwicke had started up in Scotland, particularly at the main point of entry into Scotland, Gretna Green. (It had been intended that Scottish law in regard to marriages should be brought into line with British, but this never happened.[438]) There are at least two documented cases of Gretna Green marriages contracted by members of Irish peerage families. In 1808, Dublin was agog at the first of them,

> the case of Lord Limerick whose son, Lord Glentworth, a lad of 19 [and therefore a minor], has been inveigled to marry a niece of Sir Jonah Barrington without any fortune. The mother has been attached by the Chancellor, and Lord Limerick is determined to take every possible step to break the marriage. They have been married here by a Mr Murphy which marriage Lord Limerick will certainly be able to break; but they were also married at Gretna Green, and it is not so clear that that marriage can be broken. Lord Limerick, however, is determined to try, and thus the validity or invalidity of Scotch marriage will be legally determined.[439]

Edmond Henry Percy, 1st Earl of Limerick (1758–1844): an engraving of c.1840 after a portrait of c.1815

AUTHOR'S COLLECTION

If Lord Limerick tried to break the marriage, he did not succeed, since Lord Glentworth remained married to his Gretna Green partner. It is possible, however, that Lord Limerick did not even try. Fathers had considerable scope for 'squeezing' eldest sons, but when the estate was settled (as it almost always was) eldest sons also had considerable bargaining power against fathers. This has already manifested itself in the cases of Lord Irnham and Colonel Luttrell, Lord Donegall and Lord Belfast, and Lord Ferrard and Lord Massereene.[440] Perhaps Lord Limerick and Lord Glentworth were another case in point?

The second Gretna Green marriage involving a member of the Irish aristocracy is much more revealing. In late May 1837, Edward Conroy (1809–69), son and heir of the Duchess of Kent's comptroller and favourite, the Irish-born Sir John Conroy, eloped to Gretna Green with the 20-year-old Lady Alicia Parsons, second daughter of the 2nd Earl of Rosse. She was not an heiress. But she had a substantial marriage portion of £16,000, made up as follows: £10,000 under her parents' marriage settlement, and a further £6,000 added by Lord Rosse's aunt-by-marriage, the Dowager Lady Rosse, to the portions of his three younger children as some compensation to him for his disappointment of the Harman inheritance.[441] The bridegroom's father was an adventurer, and the marriage connection to that extent was undesirable. But the expectation, as William IV's years mounted and his health declined, was that 'at loyal dinner parties in the next reign, we … [will] be obliged to toast Sir John Conroy and the rest of the Conroyal family'.[442] So, from the point of view of political influence, the marriage connection seemed to have much to recommend it. In fact, Sir John lost all his influence after the accession of the Duchess's daughter, Queen Victoria, in the following month (June 1837). But that was not how things looked in May, when Edward Conroy, as his eldest son, seemed to be a young man of promise and considerable expectations.

Perhaps uniquely among elopers, Conroy kept a journal.[443] It is not a blow-by-blow record of events as they occurred, but it was written fairly soon after the elopement, and certainly too soon for afterthoughts and hindsight. He describes Lady Alicia as 'gay and very handsome, sought-after and admired, … [with] rank and £16,000', and adds: 'My affection for … [her] had been long known and commented upon, and the harshness of her family in rejecting me.' What brought matters to a head was Lady Rosse's discovery that he had gone to church on the morning of Sunday 28 May for the purpose of catching a glimpse of, and perhaps snatching a word with, Lady Alicia. This meant, he knew, that the 'storm of her mother's anger would break upon her dear head … and her health [would be] destroyed by inches'. He also suspected that it would induce Lord Rosse to close up the Rosses' London house at 4 Belgrave Square and immure Lady Alicia in Birr Castle, the family seat in Ireland. Accordingly, when she made a pre-arranged signal at 3.15 p.m. that she was ready to run away with him that very night at 11 p.m., he ran about the town making hasty preparations. (What follows is, in effect, an elopers' *vade mecum*, and repays study.)

In the midst of all this, he still found time to write a letter to Lord Rosse which would not be delivered until the following morning, and in which he stated that

> Alicia and I were seriously attached upon the conviction that our happiness depended on each other, and that he had been misinformed as to my dissipated habits of life…; that on the score of fortune I was unworthy of his daughter, but that I had enough to keep her *as a lady* and enough for *no wants*; as to my blood, it was better than his own; and as to my character, it was spotless…. [I reminded him of] the intimacy he and Lady Rosse had allowed Alicia and me in his house, and the unkind manner I had been treated in the moment it was found I aspired to her hand, because I *was poor*…. [I also complained of the]

The Countess of Rosse with her young daughters, the
Ladies Jane and Alicia Parsons, c.1825,
by Thomas Foster, reproduced from the original portrait
at Birr Castle, Co. Offaly

COURTESY OF THE EARL AND COUNTESS OF ROSSE

THE PURSUIT OF THE HEIRESS

determined hostility of Lady Rosse and Lord Oxmantown [the Rosses' elder son], who had been reputed to have said 'that he would rather see Alicia in her coffin than married to me'. I therefore asked him, what hope had we of better things.

The escape from Belgrave Square and the headlong dash to Gretna both passed off without incident. Had Lord Oxmantown 'pursued and succeeded in overtaking me, he should not have stopped me, for I had resolved to adopt the bold act of Lord Westmorland[444] and to have destroyed one of the horses of the pursuing carriage by a pistol shot'. Arrived at Gretna, Conroy was relieved to find that there was no truth in the 'cock-and-bull stories' he had heard about the village 'blacksmith and the marriage being solemnised in a forge'. He also noted with satisfaction that the marriage register contained 'the names of several lords and ladies'. Having been warned that 'the "parson" made people pay for marrying them according to their apparent wealth and flourishing appearance', Lady Alicia and he were as unforthcoming as possible about their identities. However, the minister, 'a tall, gaunt, ill-looking, middle-aged man...: with ... [a] canting, hypocritical look', at once saw through this pretence and charged them £50. So they 'were married in proper form before the landlady, the postboy and my servant, who then signed the paper as witnesses'. After breakfast, Conroy wrote again to Lord Rosse, and also to his own father, asking forgiveness and declaring his and Lady Alicia's intention of being married a second time according to the rites of the Established Church.

Back in London, the Rosses' initial reaction to the elopement, predictably, was one of outrage. 'Lady Rosse was first violent, then hysterical and then bilious, and went to bed.' Lord Rosse, 'a choleric old gentleman', was somewhat calmed by Conroy's pre-elopement letter. Lord Oxmantown descended on Kensington Palace (residence of the Duchess of Kent and Princess Victoria), where 'my father received him so coldly and proudly that the fat Lord was awed'. Meanwhile, Lord Rosse had decided that the marriage should be announced in the newspapers, a decision with which Sir John Conroy concurred. Next week, 'at Almack's ball nothing else was talked of, and Alicia and I were the lions of the day.... No person (except a dowager or two) spoke against me.... For nine days all London rang with our escapade and then we were forgotten.'[445] All this time, they had been lying low in the Lake District where, some weeks after the 'escapade', they received a letter of forgiveness from Lord Rosse. He was 'most kind' when they called at Belgrave Square, but 'her ladyship still sulked'. A couple of days later, she too came round. Lord Rosse later 'praised me and said it was "the best done and most spirited thing he had ever known"'. Meanwhile, 'By the kind liberality of my father, I was enabled to make as good a settlement on Alicia, in [the] event of my death, as my brother-in-law, Knox, heir to £11,000 a year, made upon Lady Jane, his wife [who was Lady Alicia's elder sister].'[446] On 25 July 1837, Conroy and Lady Alicia were married for the second time in an Anglican church in Kensington.

ELOPEMENTS, MÉSALLIANCES AND MIS-MATCHES

Conroy's journal is a fascinating document, written with jauntiness and self-assurance, reading in places like a novel, and yet full of minute and practical detail. It does, however, omit a number of important circumstances which all contributed to make the marriage more acceptable than it had been on 28 May. On 20 June, while the newly-weds were still in the Lake District, William IV died. Gossip and speculation about his last illness and about the doings of his youthful successor contributed to the rapid subsidence of interest in the elopement. Queen Victoria's immediate declaration of hostility towards Sir John Conroy meant that his hopes of acquiring a commanding influence in the new reign were finally dashed. But, as he was compensated with a baronetcy and a pension of £3,000 a year and continued to have opportunities to plunder the Duchess of Kent,[447] his financial future at least was secure, and Edward Conroy was now next in succession to a title. The settlement which Sir John was enabled to make on Lady Alicia and the issue of the marriage was more 'liberal' than would have been possible prior to the granting of the pension. It comprised a Conroy family property in Co. Roscommon which provided ample security for her £16,000; and this still left a villa and small property in Berkshire and an estate in Montgomeryshire, both of which had been acquired by Sir John and would be likely to descend to Edward Conroy at his father's death.[448] Edward Conroy was no longer 'poor'.

It may be doubted, however, if the Rosses' pre-elopement objections to him had been primarily on the score of lack of means. There was also the question of his 'character' and allegedly 'dissipated habits of life'. For all the tenderness which he expresses towards Lady Alicia in his journal, and no doubt sincerely felt at the time, he was not constant in his affections, and 'the romance did not endure. Soon after the birth of their only child [the future 3rd baronet, in 1845] they parted, probably because Conroy had a wandering eye.' He had had extra-martial affairs and, almost certainly, an illegitimate daughter. In the last year of his life, 1869, he addressed 'a passionate plea of forgiveness' to Lady Alicia, which it looks as if she was on the point of accepting when he suddenly died.[449] As the journal makes plain, it was not Lord Rosse – whose business it was to take care of his daughter's financial future – but Lady Rosse who had been strongest in opposing the marriage. Perhaps, with a woman's intuition, she had sensed Conroy's shallowness from the start. According to Conroy, Lady Rosse declared soon after the marriage that he was 'an excellent husband ... and that they [the Rosses] were delighted to have got me as a son-on-law'. But this assertion has a hollow ring.

The Conroys' elopement started from London. For couples eloping from Ireland, Portpatrick was a more accessible bolt-hole than Gretna Green. However, the marriage register for the parish of Portpatrick records few possible instances of marriages involving Irish 'lords and ladies'. Of the 208 Irish people entered during the period 1752–1820, only thirteen can with reasonable certainty be identified as aristocrats. (Among the uncertainties is the daughter of a dame styled – possibly self-styled – 'the Rt Hon. Lady Catherine O'Toole of Great George Street', Dublin.) The figure of thirteen is made up of: one peer (the 3rd Lord Massy); two future peers (the Hon. Barry Bingham and Arthur French of Frenchpark, Co. Roscommon); seven younger sons/brothers of peers (the Hons. Randal Plunket, John Browne, George Massy, Frederick Forbes, Peter Boyle Blaquiere, Hamilton Ralph Crofton and Henry Caulfeild); one younger brother of a future peer (Percy Freke); and one sister and one daughter of future peers (Eliza Blake of Ardfry, Co. Galway, and Lyne Crosbie, daughter of the future 3rd Lord Branden).

Not only is the figure of thirteen low; most of the marriages concerned are to apparently suitable spouses.[450] The Hon. Henry Caulfeild, for example, who at the time of his marriage (1819) was heir presumptive to his brother, the 2nd Earl of Charlemont, married Margaret Elizabeth Browne, daughter of Dodwell Browne of Rahins, Co. Mayo. She was not yet 21, and he was twice her age (having been born in 1779). Apart from her minority and the disparity between the couple's ages, there does not seem to have been any reasonable objection to the marriage. As well as belonging to an old gentry family, Mrs Caulfeild – to judge from her letters[451] – was an intelligent, articulate, politically sophisticated woman, and well qualified to bring up the heir to the Charlemont earldom (which her son succeeded to in 1863). It looks as if her parents were in Canada in 1819; so this circumstance, coupled with her minority, may explain this Gretna Green marriage. Others, too, seem to have been made for similarly technical reasons.

This is not to say that runaway marriages were not an issue in this period. Indeed, the incidence of them was sufficiently heavy for the Irish Lord Chancellor to lament in 1804, in strains which anticipate his Gilbertian successor in England: 'My wards are continually carried off, and whether married or not I frequently find [it] difficult to discover.'[452] But they do not seem to have been marriages which, because of the gross disparity in rank and/or fortune of the partners, can reasonably be described as marriages beyond the pale of the conventions. Rather, they were marriages made to extort an *ex post facto* consent from over-ambitious, over-protective, prejudiced or plain unreasonable parents. The marriage of Edward and Lady Alicia Conroy falls loosely into this category. So, possibly, does that of Lord and Lady Glentworth, and definitely the previously mentioned marriage of Lady Southampton's eldest son, George Ferdinand Fitzroy, later 2nd Lord Southampton, who in 1784 ran off to Gretna Green with the daughter of the Hon. and Rev. Frederick Keppel, Bishop of Exeter and younger brother of the 3rd Earl of Albemarle.[453]

The other, even more important (for present purposes) characteristic of these elopements and/or clandestine marriages was that none of them seems to have involved an heiress. Lady Alicia was no more than a well portioned young woman. In many of the other cases it was the man who had advantages of wealth and rank over the woman, not the other way round. In this respect, an even

ELOPEMENTS, MÉSALLIANCES AND MIS-MATCHES

more striking case than Lord Belfast was the Prince of Capua, brother of King Ferdinand II of Naples, who eloped in 1836 with a beautiful Irish girl called Penelope Smyth, and married her at Gretna Green; although the marriage ceremony was later repeated in London, the King – unlike Lord and Lady Rosse – never accepted the *fait accompli* and never gave his consent.[454] In 1779, the facetious Lord Buckinghamshire jokingly advised 'a most … beautiful [Irish] girl … that she should never listen to any man, whatever he may offer with one hand, unless he brings his rental in the other'.[455] This pleasantry, combined with the evidence just now cited of eligible men succumbing to the charms of less affluent women, are reminders that such old-fashioned figures of melodrama as the adventuress and the designing female did in fact exist.

Next to Lord Belfast, the most important contractor and victim of a clandestine marriage in the period under review was the already-mentioned Henry Villiers-Stuart, one and only Lord Stuart de Decies (1803–74).[456] In 1826 or 1827, about the time of his victory in the Co. Waterford election and the dynastic comeback of the Dromana family, he married either at St James's Roman Catholic church, Spanish Place, London, or in a private house in London, an Austrian Roman Catholic whose maiden name was Pauline Theresia Ott (and who is still disrespectfully called 'the hot Ott' by their descendants). The ceremony was performed by a Roman Catholic clergyman, which meant that it was of doubtful validity under English law at that date. So, the Villiers-Stuarts seem to have gone through two subsequent marriages, in Scotland in 1827 and in England c.1835–6.

Henry Villier-Stuart, Lord Stuart de Decies, in his uniform as lieutenant of Co. Waterford: detail of an original, full-length portrait of c.1832

PRIVATE COLLECTION

Because of her religion, Mrs Villiers-Stuart would have been a political liability to her husband and a propaganda gift to his anti-Emancipationist opponents in Co. Waterford. This mattered much less after he lost his seat in 1830, but still she stayed or was kept away from Ireland. Until 1842, the couple lived mainly in London (particularly during the years 1827–34), Scotland, or travelled on the Continent. When his younger brother, William, married in 1833, Henry Villiers-Stuart allowed him to reside at Dromana, which he continued to do until c.1845.[457] Henry Villiers-Stuart, who had been returned to parliament for an English constituency, Banbury, in 1831, also encouraged William to stand and be returned on the family interest for Co. Waterford in 1835; and William continued to represent Co. Waterford until 1847. When Lord and Lady Stuart (as the Henry Villiers-Stuarts became in 1839) came to live in Ireland with any permanency, in 1842, they settled first at a rented villa called Maretimo at Blackrock, outside Dublin. Late in 1843, they took up residence at Dromana,[458] but always alternated between it and a subsequent Dublin villa, Fortfield, Rathfarnham, and continued to travel a good deal.

In 1840, Lord Stuart had given a written promise to William that William would inherit Dromana and the family estate; and in 1848, Lord Stuart, who was a remainderman to the vast and increasing estates and wealth of his cousin, the (late) 2nd Marquess of Bute, subscribed to a private act of parliament relating to the Bute estate in Cardiff by describing himself as having *no issue* in spite of the fact that Lady Stuart and he had had a son, Henry (b.1827), and a daughter, Pauline. The promise of 1840 and the disclaimer of 1848 show that Stuart considered that his marriage(s) were invalid for more than technical reasons. In fact, he had come to think that, unwittingly, he had committed bigamy.

In 1826, at the time of her marriage to him, Lady Stuart had claimed to be the widow of one Leopold Gersch, an officer in the Austrian Imperial Archer Guard, by whom she had had two children, a daughter called Leopoldine (b.1821), who made a prestigious marriage to an Austrian baron and (later) field-marshal, and a son, Emil (b.1823), who went to the bad and died in 1864. On this basis, Lord Stuart married her (the secrecy and repetitions of the ceremony being explicable on the grounds that she was a devout Roman Catholic and he a fervent Anglican). Subsequently, however – probably c.1833 – Gersch proved to be very much alive and, hearing that his former 'wife' had married a rich foreigner, began to 'touch' Lord Stuart for money. The latter yielded to blackmail and paid Gersch to stay dead until he actually did die, c.1852. Throughout these years, neither Lady Stuart nor Gersch told Lord Stuart the truth, viz. that they had lived as man and wife but had never actually been married. Lady Stuart's motives for this deception were, obviously, the interests and marriage prospects of her children by Gersch; and Gersch presumably realised that he could extract

Pauline Theresia Ott, Lady Stuart de Decies, from a miniature of c.1826
PRIVATE COLLECTION

more money from Lord Stuart by representing himself as a husband than as an ex-lover.

Lord Stuart, although he was prepared to pay to avoid distressing publicity, was too religious and honourable a man to practise deception within his own family, and particularly in his relations with his younger brother, William, whom he now acknowledged as heir presumptive to the estates. Accordingly, his only son, Henry, was brought up, not precisely as an illegitimate, but certainly as a younger, son. Like all younger sons, he was prepared for a profession, and in the end had careers in both the army and the church. He was a cadet in Prince Liechtenstein's Regiment (the 5th Regiment of Light Horse) of the Austrian Imperial Army, 1844–6, was then an ensign in the 26th (British) Regiment, 1846–7, and then took holy orders and was appointed Vicar of Bulkington, Warwickshire, 1852, and of Napton, Warwickshire, in 1855. Towards the end of Lord Stuart's life, however, his attitude towards Henry changed dramatically. Lady Stuart (who was thirteen years older than her husband) died in 1867, and Lord Stuart in 1874. It is possible that, on her deathbed, she confessed to him for the first time that she had not been married to Gersch; which meant that the Stuarts' marriage was not bigamous and that Henry Villiers-Stuart was not illegitimate.

Whatever happened, from the late 1860s onwards Lord Stuart treated Henry as his successor. The insertion of 'Windsor' among Henry's Christian names, which seems to have taken place about this time, was probably an assertion of the son's legitimacy and of the transfer to him of his father's by-now-remote rights of succession to the Bute estates (Windsor being the family name of the heiress who brought Cardiff into the Bute family). In 1870, Lord Stuart endeavoured, without much success, to get his brother, William, to release him from the promise that William would inherit Dromana and the family estate. In 1871, Henry Windsor Villiers-Stuart resigned holy orders (in accordance with the Clerical Disabilities Act of 1870) in order to stand for parliament, and was MP for Co. Waterford, 1873–4 and 1880–85. And in 1872, Lord Stuart went into an elaborate negotiation to have him made vice-lieutenant of Co. Waterford, on the ground that his own failing health disabled him from exercising the lieutenancy (but clearly with a view to giving status to Henry Windsor).

Following Lord Stuart's death in 1874, Henry Windsor's claim to the barony of Stuart de Decies was referred to the Committee for Privileges of the House of Lords, whose slow and suspicious examination of the evidence made it obvious that this was no open-and-shut case. In 1876, fearful of the outcome, he withdrew his petition to succeed as 2nd Lord Stuart (although he continued to be addressed locally as Lord Stuart until at least 1880 and made unsuccessful attempts to have a new barony of Stuart conferred on him in reward for his services as a Liberal MP). In order to succeed in the peerage claim, Henry Windsor would have had to prove that his mother had not been married to Leopold Gersch, thereby in all probability ruining the lives of his half-sister, Leopoldine, and her family in status-obsessed Austria. In the event of his failing and therefore being proved illegitimate, there was a danger that his cousin (William Villiers-Stuart's son, Henry John), who was playing an increasingly hostile part in the peerage case, would claim the estates. In the event of his being proved illegitimate, he would at the very least incur, in addition to unwelcome publicity, a higher rate of succession duty (10 per cent instead of one per cent) on that part of his father's estate which had passed to him by willl – at that date, succession duty on legacies from father to son was charged at a much lower rate than on legacies from father to remoter relations, including illegitimate children. So, Henry Windsor played safe and allowed the hard-won barony to expire quietly.

It was not he but his father who, by one incautious leap in the matrimonial dark, had forfeited the dynastic gains made in the 1820s and the 1830s. More important, Lord and Lady Stuart's marriage caused a great deal of personal unhappiness to all concerned – her children, their children and themselves.

It can certainly be described as a *mésalliance* (in the sense that one partner greatly outranked the other in wealth and status), as can others in the 'runaway' and 'clandestine' category already discussed – Lord Belfast and Anna May, the Prince of Capua and Penelope Smith, possibly Lord and Lady Glentworth, etc. But the number of *mésalliances* in the category is, as has been noted, surprisingly small. Indeed, the most glaring cases of *mésalliance* so far considered in this study, Lord Annesley and the gardener's wife and Lord Massereene and the mop-twirler, were neither of them runaway or clandestine marriages. Writing about England, not Ireland, Professor Cannon concludes that *mésalliances*, in whatever circumstances contracted, were 'rare' and only seem to be more frequent because, when they occurred, they gave 'vast pleasure to letter-writers and commentators'.[459] Upbringing, conditioning and ingrained respect for the conventions combined to reduce them to small proportions.

Curiously, the Annesley case illustrates this point; for, subsequent to his second marriage, Lord Annesley went to great trouble to fabricate a story that Sophia Connor was a gentlewoman with a fortune of £2,000 left her under the will of her long-lost father; he even went through the rigmarole of raising the £2,000 and paying it to himself.[460] The thinking behind all this must have been that possession of a portion distinguished the honest from the kept woman. Lord Annesley's lip-service to the conventions is the more remarkable for the fact that he was the head of his family and a free agent: younger men and women, for whom flouting the conventions meant displeasing parents or guardians and perhaps incurring financial penalties, did not enjoy the same degree of freedom.

One old woman (and great heiress) who was not free to marry anyone she liked was Angela Burdett-Coutts, created Baroness Burdett-Coutts in 1871. Under the will of Harriot Mellon, whose elaborate succession-planning seemed to anticipate all eventualities, Lady Burdett-Coutts was to forfeit most of her inheritance if she married an alien, which was just what she proceeded to do in 1881 at the age of sixty-seven. Her husband was William Ashmead Bartlett, a

ELOPEMENTS, MÉSALLIANCES AND MIS-MATCHES

28-year-old, 'good-looking, very impudent snob of American parentage'. This, of course, gave 'vast pleasure to letter-writers and commentators', including the Countess of Dartrey, wife of the leading landed proprietor in Co. Monaghan:

> The chief social topic is the to be or not to be of Lady B. Coutts's marriage…. She is 66, and has I hear grown more monstrous than ever the last two years, and enhances her hideousness by her extraordinary dress and love of glaring colours and contrast…. She denies the marriage, but I hear on authority that it seems difficult to doubt, that it is to be and that the settlements are actually being drawn up, and she goes out riding with her youthful swain…. On her marrying, £80,000 a year of the fortune will pass to Mrs Money and her son, but Lady Coutts will still have over £100,000 a year, so she will not starve….
>
> She consulted the Archbishop of Canterbury as to the likelihood of her having a family, saying she was precisely the same age as Sarah when Isaac was born! Mr A. Bartlett is … [to receive] £350,000 in cash on the wedding day. Lady B. Coutts says he is the only perfectly disinterested affection she has ever met with.[461]

Lady Dartrey's figures are exaggerated: Lady Burdett-Coutts' reduced income worked out at only some £16,000 a year, and the capital sum she was in a position to make over to Ashmead Bartlett was much smaller than £350,000 and was transferred over a long period.[462] But the scale of the financial sacrifice and of the *mésalliance* was still colossal.

Because of the precautions taken by Harriot Mellon back in 1837, the dynastic consequences of Lady Burdett-Coutts' marriage were minor, because her shares in the bank were preserved to her sister, Clara Coutts (Mrs Money). In the case of James Dutton Naper (d.1776) of Loughcrew, Co. Meath, and Sherborne, Gloucestershire, the consequences were comparatively minor, because the marriage and property in dispute were those of a cousin, to whom Naper/Dutton was heir-at-law; had he been more successful in the litigation, he would have received a substantial addition to the Naper estate, but the Naper estate itself was

Baroness Burdett-Coutts, from *Vanity Fair*, 3 November 1883

AUTHOR'S COLLECTION

not in jeopardy. The cousin concerned was Major-General William Naper (d.1773) of Littleton, Co. Westmeath, who owned estates in the counties of Westmeath, Cavan and Dublin and in Dublin City. While serving in Germany towards the end of the Seven Years' War, the General formed a *liaison* with 'Ann Fitzgerald, who was a woman of notoriously bad character [and] a regular follower of the camp', and afterwards married her under dubious circumstances. 'The chief witnesses to establish the marriage ... were Edward Bell, who was a trooper in the carbineers, and Mary Swayne, the wife of Matthew Swayne, another trooper in the same regiment..., [who] swore that they were present at the marriage, which took place in the General's tent at Markholendoff in Germany.' The General and his 'wife' had one son, another William Naper (1764–1834), who succeeded to all the General's property at the General's death in 1773. The heir-at-law, James Dutton Naper, had little time to contest these dispositions, because he died in 1776. But his eldest son, the 1st Lord Sherborne, resolved to challenge the legitimacy of William Naper by every means in his power and thus to establish his own title to the Naper of Littleton estates.

There followed, between c.1785 and 1790, a succession of trials and re-trials for ejectment, heard before special juries of the counties where the estates were located and of Dublin City. 'The public was so occupied and excited by the case as to become divided into two parties: one for the wealthy peer, the other for the injured and persecuted child [who was 21 in 1785!]. No means were left untried to obtain verdicts, and scenes of the most infamous corruption, bribery and perjury were frequently brought to light by the astuteness and perseverance of the most eminent lawyers of the day.' One of the witnesses to the 'marriage', Mary Swayne, who 'cried hysterically ..."Oh no! I swore enough already. I'll swear no more"', was convicted of perjury. The 'bad character' of Ann Fitzgerald/Mrs Naper was further developed in the course of the various proceedings. It was, for example, deposed that, following the General's retirement from the army and return to Littleton, his 'wife' and he had attended the assizes in Mullingar, where 'Mrs Naper drank a little too freely, *regularly broke loose,* and acted in a very unbecoming manner: so much so ... [that] General Naper said "...What can I do? She is my wife; I am sorry for it", and burst into tears.' In the end, the special juries with one exception found in favour of the validity of the marriage, so that: 'William Naper was the legitimate son of Major-General Naper in the counties of Cavan [and] Westmeath and in the city of Dublin, and an illegitimate son in the county of Dublin.' It may be doubted if the value of the Co. Dublin estate which was now adjudged to him compensated Lord Sherborne for the cost of all the litigation. As for William Naper, he was later forced to sell a large part of the Westmeath estate to his attorney for £22,800 in satisfaction of the attorney's bill of costs.[463]

From the point of view of the Littleton branch of the Naper family, the General's *mésalliance* had fatal consequences, as potentially did the *mésalliances* contracted by Lords Annesley and Massereene. All three originated in the widespread practice of forming *liaisons* with lower-class mistresses (by no means all of whom, it should be said, were women 'of notoriously bad character'). But, although the practice was widespread, most Irish noblemen who indulged themselves in it took care that such relationships did not get out of hand and/or assume the proportions of matrimony. Lord Abercorn, if in fact he married an ex-mistress as his second wife, had taken care that she was a woman of good family – his own. His other liaisons filled gaps in his marriages or were discreetly conducted alongside them. The mistress who bore him children, and the two sons in question, were suitably provided for with annuities. As has been seen, Lord Downshire's and Thomas Conolly's mistresses and illegitimate children were such a well kept secret that the adoring Lady Downshire and Lady Louisa Conolly did not find out about them until widowhood.[464]

Henry Conyngham, Baron, Viscount and Earl Conyngham (1706–81), was probably estranged and separated from his wife before he took mistresses, which he did from 1768 onwards, if not earlier. In his case, therefore, there was no reason for concealment, and he actually gave some publicity to his activities by documenting them as precisely as possible in a series of non-marriage settlements. (In this, he anticipated the present Marquess of Bath's arrangements with his 'wifelets' at Longleat, Wiltshire.) In July 1768 he instructed Joshua Sharpe, his attorney in Lincoln's Inn, to

> draw a short deed of annuity for life of £26 a year payable to Elizabeth Bulstrode, spinster, provided she lives with me in the station of housekeeper during my life or her power to serve, to be void in case she marries without my consent or if she has carnal communication with any person but me. The consideration [i.e. the value she had given] is her having given her character of virtue to me.[465]

Lord Conyngham was not a believer in monogamy, and a month later he instructed Sharpe to draft another deed of annuity, this time 'from me to Mrs Mary Perfect, spinster, of £100 a year for her life, ... secured by £1,000 vested in the Funds..., provided she lives with me for my life ... wherever I shall appoint either in England or Ireland'. The larger amount, and the omission of any mention of domestic service, reflected Conyngham's nice sense of class distinction, Miss Perfect being the 'daughter of the Rev. Mr Henry Perfect of Bedfordshire'.[466] She was street-wise as well as genteel; for she took counsel's opinion about the terms of the agreement, objected to various aspects of it, and demanded that a large legacy be secured to her. At this point Sharpe tried to warn his client off; but Conyngham was not to be deterred:

> I ... am much obliged to you for your hints relative to the lady. But, as she refused many young persons of quality and others with three, four and five times the settlement she accepted from me in preference to them, I am bound

in honour to make it up to her as a voluntary gift.... The bond for £2,000 payable a month after my decease is nothing to me, as I have no child and have mended my fortune £10,000 since I got it. This bond should be..., I suppose, [subject to] the provisoes that she lives with me during my life ... either in England or Ireland, ... that she shall not contract matrimony without my consent, that she shall not alienate or dispose of the bond, and that she shall keep no company but such as I approve of.[467]

Meanwhile, he had not forgotten his earlier annuitant, Elizabeth Bulstrode, whose trustingness compared very favourably to the rapacity of Miss Perfect, and whom 'I have had ... for several months past. She behaved well. I therefore would have you draw a deed or bond to secure her £40 a year at my decease, provided she goes to no man without my consent.'[468] He was soon back in Elizabeth Bulstrode's arms, because Miss Perfect committed matrimony with a man called Gardiner, left the kingdom, and still demanded the performance of Conyngham's legal and financial obligations to her. Sharpe was instructed to take proceedings against her, and Conyngham even contemplated bringing the matter before the Irish House of Lords – a proceeding which would have exposed him to great ridicule.[469] Sharpe must have succeeded in calming him down, and seems also to have fought off the claims of Mrs Gardiner. But Conyngham was incorrigible. In January 1771, Sharpe was desired to 'draw an annuity from me to Miss Ann Barker, daughter of the Rev. Thomas Barker, late of Grettleton, Wilts., of £50 a year English money'.[470]

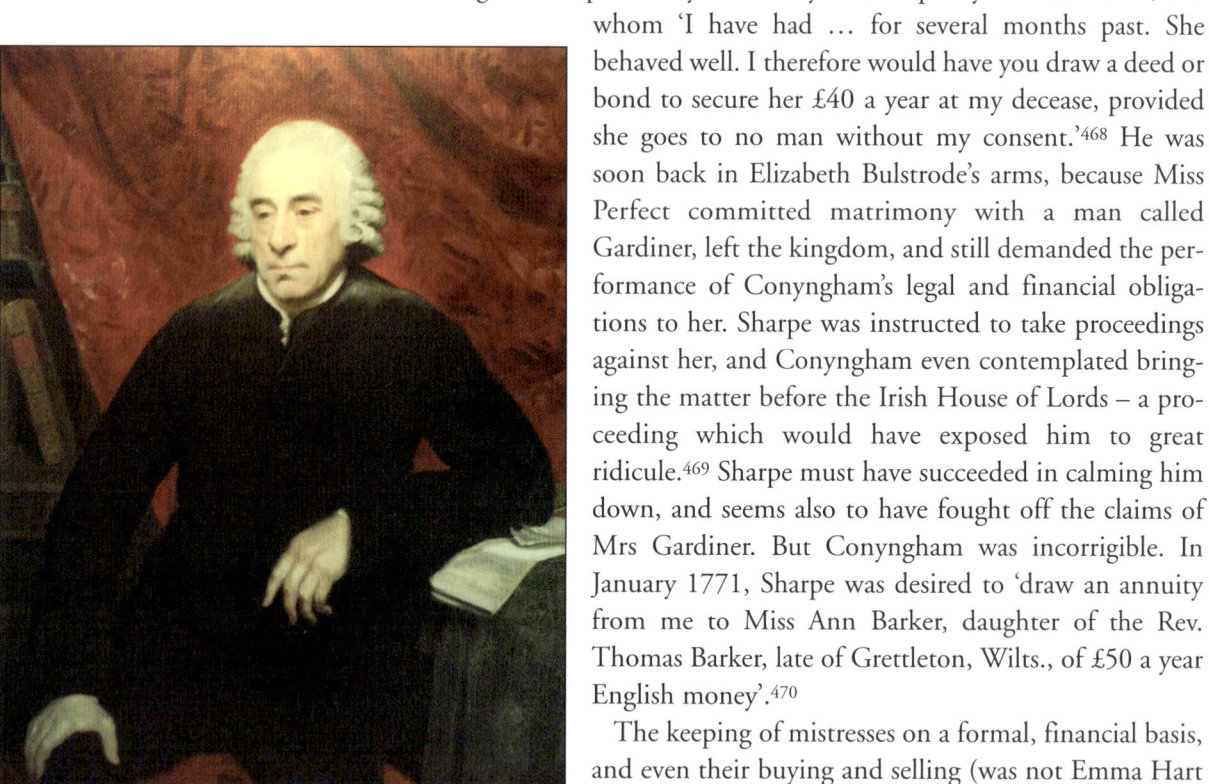

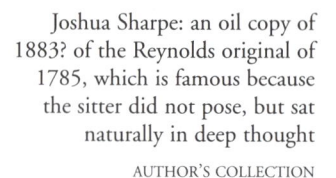

Joshua Sharpe: an oil copy of 1883? of the Reynolds original of 1785, which is famous because the sitter did not pose, but sat naturally in deep thought

AUTHOR'S COLLECTION

The keeping of mistresses on a formal, financial basis, and even their buying and selling (was not Emma Hart sold to Sir William Hamilton in 1786 by his nephew, Charles Greville?), were established practice for most of the period under review. Indeed, a failure to provide decently for a regular mistress, and particularly for any children she might bear, would have been considered *infra dig*. For this reason, evidence of such financial provision, though rare, is not unheard of, and the Conyngham letters – though they are perhaps uniquely explicit as to the conditions which the mistresses are to observe – are not in other respects unique. Some form of evidence would have been necessary to executors in the administration of the affairs of the deceased, in the fulfilment of his obligations and in the protection of his estate from imposition. Usually, the evidence would have been destroyed, from motives of delicacy, once its legal usefulness was spent. But this did not always happen. Another Irish nobleman whose archive still retains evidence of this kind is Thomas Pakenham, 2nd Earl of Longford (1774–1835).

ELOPEMENTS, MÉSALLIANCES AND MIS-MATCHES

Lord Longford inherited early, in 1792, and married late, in 1817.[471] Prior to his marriage, he had at least three illegitimate children by three different women, all of whom he provided for. In addition, he took care of the personal and financial needs of the illegitimate children of his brother, General Sir Edward Pakenham, killed at the battle of New Orleans in 1815.[472]

Both Lords Conyngham and Longford were married men: other Irishmen of rank devoted themselves to mistresses and never married. Field-Marshal Lord Ligonier (1680–1770), an Irish Huguenot who became commander-in-chief of the British army, 1757–66, and an Irish viscount and a British earl, brought some respectability and even lustre to the fathering of illegitimate children. He kept a very long-standing mistress, one Penelope Miller of Southwark, who was the mother of his only (acknowledged) child, another Penelope, and the recipient of an annuity under his will. Their relationship was well known, but discreet (she had a different address and her own establishment), and their daughter made a good marriage into an Irish gentry family.[473] Ligonier was also guardian (from 1746) of his younger brother, Francis's, illegitimate son, Edward, following Francis Ligonier's death in the '45 Rebellion. Lord Ligonier, who was Ranger of the Phoenix Park, Dublin, 1733–51, at one point seems to have intended that Edward should succeed him in that office; he took care that Edward's illegitimacy should not retard his rise in his chosen profession, the army; and in 1762 he obtained a second Irish viscountcy for himself with a special remainder to Edward (in spite of George III's reluctance to allow peerages to descend to illegitimate children). Edward succeeded to this title in 1770, and was further advanced to an Irish earldom of Ligonier in 1776.[474]

The one and only Lord Callan (1751–1815) and the 1st Earl of Donoughmore (1756–1825) are two further examples of Irish peers who were unmarried but left children. In 1809, the former made a will in which he acknowledged sixteen surviving illegitimate children by two different mistresses; to the children he left £1,000 apiece and a share, along with their mothers, in the interest from a trust fund of £70,000.[475] The dispositions, and the identity of the illegitimate children, of Lord Donoughmore were less easy to unravel. He had one favourite son, John, to whom he left £1,900 a year, which at the time was more than the nett rental of his Co. Tipperary estate, so that 'there would have been nothing left for anybody'.[476] Fortunately for Donoughmore's brother and heir, this son died young, c.1814. However, Donoughmore's will still contained un-lapsed legacies 'of £60 a year to a common strumpet in this neighbourhood [Clonmel, Co. Tipperary], which she may call on the executors to redeem on the payment of £600, … £300 to a supposed natural daughter of his by Parker's daughter (no more his child than she was mine), … [and] £700 to a second, supposed natural daughter of his, whom he calls Mary Long'.

Richard Hely-Hutchinson, 1st Earl of Donoughmore, from an engraving in *The Hibernian Magazine* of 1810. This highlights his position as Grand Master of the Freemasons of Ireland, but the sensual – not to say lecherous – expression on his face is also apparent.

AUTHOR'S COLLECTION

In life as in death Donoughmore's private life had been an embarrassment to his family. He was not discreet in his amours and the provision he made for some of his bastards was as stingy as that for his son, John, had been over-generous. In 1821, his exasperated brother complained that Donoughmore had

> lately got himself into a disgraceful, contemptible scrape which has made him outrageous beyond all bounds. Two infamous women of the lowest description charged him with having got each of them with child, and I believe left the children at his gate or at least somewhere near the house. He desired an under-steward ... to put them out to nurse, which was accordingly done, and they were regularly paid for during two years. But for the last two he has refused to give anything ... [and, having won on a technicality at Cashel petty sessions, has got away with robbing] the poor people of what was justly due to them.... There is neither common honesty nor commonsense in such proceedings.[477]

A similar neglect of illegitimate children had been one of the many sins laid to the charge of Williams Conyngham of Slane nearly a century earlier. Following his death in 1738, his aunt, Katherine Conolly, reported that Conyngham's long-suffering wife/widow had taken his 'two bastards ... from the slut of a mother, ... had clothed them, for they were quite naked', and had lodged them with 'a decayed gentlewoman, who will teach them to read and say their prayers'.[478]

The 1st Lord Ligonier's behaviour also – though for different reasons – fell short of the standards expected of a gentleman and especially of a nobleman. His admiring biographer refers coyly to 'constant gossip ... that Ligonier liked his girls almost indecently young.... The author of the scurrilous satire, *Chrysal*, published in 1763, devoted a whole chapter to "the General's" method of employing his manservants to procure young girls for him.'[479] An author hostile to Ligonier describes him as 'an old rogue' still dedicated in his late seventies to a 'quest for nymphets' (which, apparently, was what he called his victims).[480] On this evidence, the first soldier of the British Empire, had he lived 250 years later, would have done time for child-abuse.

Even the very grand and rank-conscious Lord Abercorn offended against the proprieties. He had his best-known mistress, Mrs Maguire, and one of his two children by her, painted by Sir Thomas Lawrence in 1805, and allowed the picture to be exhibited at the Royal Academy in 1806. This was considered an error of taste, and Lawrence's handling of the delicate subject still more so. 'The woman looked like a [whore] ... and, what was worse, he had infused a similar expression into the countenance of the boy which, at least for his age, was unnatural. He looked as if he had been bred among the vices of an impure house.'[481] In the foreground of the composition lies a Newfoundland dog; and when the picture was engraved c.1840 for a volume devoted to Lawrence's best-known portraits, it was evasively captioned 'The faithful friend', it being left to the beholder to decide whether this referred to the dog or the lady.

Mésalliances conducted with the sordidness of Lord Donoughmore's, particularly when compounded by Lords Annesley's and Massereene's disinheritance of the legitimate, collateral heir, inevitably created a great stir and resulted in the social derogation of the perpetrator. But, without such aggravating circumstances, *mésalliance* per se did not entail either social disgrace or financial disaster. In the case of Lord Callan, the legitimate, collateral heir was a somewhat distant cousin, who had no rights of inheritance and for whom there was a great deal of land and money left after due provision had been made for the mistresses and their issue.[482] As for Lord Conyngham, the £100 a year and the legacy of £2,000 promised to Miss Perfect, even in conjunction with his other sex expenditure, was 'nothing' to him, 'as I have no child'. He did have nephews and heirs, and he also had a wife whose jointure – though he was not to know this – would run for thirty-five years. But in the context of the wealth of the Conyngham family, his extra-marital engagements had cost little, the more so as Miss Perfect's claims seem to have been successfully resisted.

'The faithful friend.' The 1st Marquess of Abercorn's mistress, Mrs Maguire, and one of their sons, after Lawrence's portrait of 1805

AUTHOR'S COLLECTION

THE PURSUIT OF THE HEIRESS

When the *mésalliance* was persevered in to the point of matrimony, the consequences were apt to be more serious (even in instances by no means as extreme as the Annesley and the Massereene). For younger children like Lady Alicia Parsons, a poor marriage meant that they got poor value for their portions and were in danger of sinking in the social scale. For this reason, the formidable Dowager Lady Downshire (who lived until 1836) put up a tougher resistance than Lord and Lady Rosse to the 'courtship of eight years' standing' between her generously portioned fifth son, Lord George Hill, and Jane Knight, the younger daughter of Edward Knight of Godmersham Park, Kent. In September 1834, Lady Downshire 'at last consented', though it was still a case of 'No money – all charms'.[483]

Eldest sons were in a somewhat better position to survive a marriage which was 'No money – all charms'. For them, such a *mésalliance* was undoubtedly a misfortune in the short term: it meant that the entire – as opposed to a considerable part of – the cost of the marriage fell upon their or their father's estate, and that the outside chance of gaining significantly by marriage was lost to them for one whole generation. There was, however, the compensation that a woman with little or no portion was entitled to no more by way of jointure than the bare minimum appropriate to her husband's rank. In the purely English and admittedly one-off instance of the 'cottage Countess' of Exeter, the bride's lack of fortune did not matter, because Henry Cecil had already made quite unreasonable financial gains out of his first marriage and at the expense of his divorced heiress-wife. (The more serious cost to the Exeters was of another kind: the cottage Countess's humble origins and rural accent proved socially awkward in later years and exposed her to humiliation.[484] However, the breed of that branch of the Cecils was no doubt the sturdier for the infusion of her new blood.) In general, a marriage portion which fell well below the reasonable expectations of an eldest son – however much parents like Lord Limerick and Lady Southampton might bewail its inadequacy – would not bring about a dynastic disaster unless family finances were already in a desperate plight. One bad marriage never, on its own, ruined a family.

It is therefore more useful to think in terms of 'mis-matches', not mere *mésalliances*. A mis-match was the marriage of a couple who were seriously ill-circumstanced[485] for each other. Lady Emily Cecil and the 8th Earl of Westmeath are a case in point. She was accustomed to the best of everything, to the grandeur of Hatfield and, during the London season, to Court life in the metropolis: his tastes and pastimes were inexpensive (as perforce they had to be because of his limited means), and centred on country life in a fairly remote part of Ireland and on the historic but tumbledown and uncomfortable Clonyn Castle on the outskirts of Delvin. A couple who were ill-circumstanced for each other might be socially and even financially on a par, but the terms of the marriage settlement might be unequal or the respective assets, locations of estates, places of residence, backgrounds, religions, etc, of the contracting parties might not accord. Of the marriages already discussed in other contexts, the Allen-Proby, Carbery-Watson and Crosbie-Sackville, as well as the Westmeath-Cecil, were all mis-matches (and none of them *mésalliances*), because they endangered the dynastic and/or financial future of the first-named families. The *mésalliances* between Lord Belfast and Anna May, Lord Stuart and Pauline Ott, and Lords Annesley and Massereene and their respective spouses, were also mis-matches of a dangerous order, and significant for that reason and not for the disparities between the partners. Some other mis-matches will be discussed, again in a different context, in the next Chapter. So the remainder of this Chapter will confine itself to two major examples of the phenomenon, Ralph Bernal and Catherine Osborne, and Count Alfred d'Orsay and Lady Harriet Gardiner, both of which involved great heiresses.

Catherine Osborne (c.1818–1880) became heiress (in 1824) to the Osborne estate in counties Waterford and Tipperary under peculiar circumstances. Her father, Sir Thomas Osborne, 9th Bt (1753–1821), was an ageing bachelor when he met, by accident, a young Englishwoman called Catherine Smith, the daughter of a major in the Royal Engineers. They married in 1816, when he was sixty-three and she was twenty. She was a total stranger to Ireland, and her modest family background had done nothing to prepare her for the role of mistress of Newtown Anner, near Clonmel, the Osborne family seat, which she thought 'immensely large', nor for the running of Sir Thomas's 'very large ... establishment'. The estate, too, was large: over 13,000 statute acres, almost all of it (apart from the Newtown Anner demesne) in Co. Waterford, and producing a rental of at least £6,000 a year. The Osbornes had two children: a son and heir called William, born in 1817, and their daughter, Catherine.

In the course of nature it was likely that Lady Osborne would long survive her husband and probable that she would find herself presiding over a minority. But Sir Thomas, an autocratic *paterfamilias* of the old school, did nothing to induct her into financial business and estate management. Instead, she was 'withered' by the boredom and solitude of her life at Newtown Anner.[486] In May 1821, when he died (sooner, presumably, than he had expected), she suddenly found herself in a situation for which she had not been prepared – that of an executor of his will, a trustee of his estate and a guardian of their children. Although others were joined with her in these responsibilities and she had the good legal advice of Thomas Lefroy, a future lord chief justice of Ireland, she found herself somewhat at sea, and sometimes at variance with her fellow-executors, trustees and guardians.[487] In 1824, her isolation was intensified by the death of her young son, William, the 10th Baronet. The title now passed to Sir Thomas's younger brother, Henry, but under the terms of Sir Thomas and Lady Osborne's marriage settlement of 1816, not an acre of Osborne land went with it: the sole heiress to the estate was their daughter, Catherine. As Stone observes, in another but contemporary instance, the re-settlement of the estates of Lord Westmeath in 1817: 'This was a very unusual arrangement, since it ...

separated the descent of the property from that of the title.'[488] It would have been more usual for the daughter to be compensated with a large cash portion and by-passed in favour of Sir Henry, 11th Bt. The exclusion of Sir Henry (and his four sons) suggests that Sir Thomas and he had been on less than fraternal terms. Indeed, Sir Thomas's action in marrying an unknown young woman late in his life smacks of a deliberate plan to 'dish' his younger brother.

His young widow, Catherine Lady Osborne, could certainly expect no help from her Osborne in-laws in managing business affairs during her daughter's minority, and particularly in the selection of a suitable husband to take on the Osborne inheritance. Ralph Bernal (1808?–1882) was certainly not an obvious, and in the event not a fortunate, choice.[489] He was a Dublin Castle aide-de-camp in the second half of the 1830s, which may have been how he met the young Catherine Osborne (whom he did not marry until 1844). But his background was Jewish and mercantile, he was a Londoner rather than a countryman, and the fast-receding wealth of his family derived from plantations in Trinidad. His main recommendations were personal. He was an elegant man-about-town, a wit and raconteur, and (from 1841) a promising young MP whose radical politics sat not too uneasily with the Whig tradition of the Osbornes. Lady Osborne may have looked kindly on him simply because he was, like her, an outsider to Irish county society; and, since he was only ten or twelve years younger than she was, he may have dazzled the mother quite as much as the daughter.

Ralph Bernal Osborne, from *Vanity Fair*, 28 May 1870. The accompanying thumbnail sketch includes the sentence: 'There is no subject on which … [he] is not prepared to form and enunciate an opinion at five minutes notice or less'.

AUTHOR'S COLLECTION

For whatever reason, Lady Osborne's attitude to him was always one of uncritical admiration, though she did try, gently and with little success, to point his political talents and ambitions towards Ireland. In 1846 or 1847, she told her daughter that it was 'quite natural that Mr O. [Bernal had assumed the name Osborne in 1844] should continue [as MP] for Wycombe, but I would rather see him an Irish member – and there is such a lack of Irish members!' A little later she returned to this theme. 'If Mr Osborne fails for Middlesex [which he represented from 1847 to 1857], I hope he will try for Tipperary…, [where the gentry] would be glad of a gentleman and a man of talent in preference to a blockhead; and, besides, I think it would be serving the cause of liberalism to take it out of the hands of the priests.' However, after he had been elected for Middlesex, she gave up on Tipperary and contented herself with following his parliamentary performances, which 'justified the good opinion I had formed of his talents'.[490] Long after her death in 1856, he did, in fact, represent an Irish constituency (Waterford City, 1870–74). But his superciliousness of manner and disdain for intellectual inferiors were disqualifications for the rough and tumble of Irish electioneering. Nor – though he held office between 1852 and 1858 – was he altogether serious in his political pursuits or steadfast to any one party. As he himself remarked: 'No one knows what my jokes have cost me.'[491]

He is supposed to have been an active Irish landlord and country gentleman. This may just mean that he hunted hard and entertained well. Certainly, it is difficult to reconcile with the tactless and ungrateful sentiments he expressed in 1865: 'It is grievous to reside in a country where one has so few sympathies.... How much I should prefer a small cottage near Rogate to a mansion in this country, you may imagine!'[492] In c.1855, Lady Osborne had been concerned to hear that the Bernal Osbornes 'seriously think of selling Newtown [Anner].... If you spend all the summer in London, I don't see the use of a country house to you.'[493] In other words, although Bernal had assumed the name Osborne, he had made not much effort to assume the role which the name implied – no doubt to the considerable vexation of the then Osborne baronet, who was still living in Tipperary, not precisely in a small cottage, but definitely not in Newtown Anner.

Nor does the marriage seem to have been much more successful personally than it was dynastically. In her naïve *Memorials of the Life and Character* of her mother, Catherine Bernal Osborne noted that, even after her marriage, she and her mother were almost 'never separated'.[494] This, it may be suspected, had more to do with Bernal Osborne's indifference than his indulgence. He was happy to park his wife with her mother so that he would be free to pursue his own more sophisticated and metropolitan lifestyle. Early in their marriage, he had refused to participate in family holidays at Kilkee, Co. Clare. Many years later, in the 1860s or 1870s, his relations with his wife were still marred by his selfishness and egotism:

> He and Mrs Osborne lived in Ireland, and I once stayed in their house.... He had a pungent wit and ready repartee, but he generally made a butt of some innocent person at the table.... Though they entertained together in the house and with the fortune which belonged to Mrs Bernal Osborne, they did not hit it off well. When we arrived we were asked by the major domo, *whose* guests we were, was our invitation from Mr or Mrs Bernal Osborne? We replied the former, and at dinner we sat at the top of the table with some other friends near our host. We had special wine served us, the best I imagine, and the friends of the hostess fared worse. Mrs Bernal Osborne would not speak to Mr Bernal Osborne's friends and Mr Bernal Osborne did the same. I never spent a more unpleasant time, and was thankful when the visit was over.[495]

His wife's death in 1880 followed by his own in 1882, left no opening for the by-passed 15th Baronet, Sir Francis Osborne, who had succeeded to the title in 1879. The Bernal Osbornes had two daughters, both of whom married and had children. The elder probably received her share of the inheritance in cash. The younger married the 10th Duke of St Albans. Their son, the 12th Duke, inherited Newtown Anner and the Osborne estate,[496] where he spent much of his time. At his death without issue in 1964, Newtown Anner passed to his sister's daughter, the Marchioness of Salisbury, and until recently was the property of her grandson, the 7th Marquess.[497] Meanwhile, the Osborne baronetcy still exists in the person of Sir Peter George Osborne, 17th Bt, who lives in London.

The consequences of the second mis-match in the sample, that of Count Alfred d'Orsay and Lady Harriet Gardiner in 1827, were yet more dire. The two cases had it in common that Catherine Osborne and Lady Harriet Gardiner had only become heiresses because of the deaths at a young age of their respective brothers; so, to that extent, their marriages were not the first or only misfortune which befell their families. There, however, the resemblance ceases, because the downfall of the Gardiners is wholly without parallel and would be an incredible story if it were not based on evidence which, in essentials, is clear.

The Gardiners had risen to prominence in the eighteenth century as the purchasers and developers of a large estate in north Dublin where, to this day, a number of streets and squares still bear Gardiner-associated names. Their origins were fairly modest (though not as humble as envy and tittle-tattle among contemporaries alleged). Their founder, as a major family, was Luke Gardiner (c.1675–1755), who was a very important Irish Treasury official as well as a builder and town-planner.[498] He was succeeded by a feckless son, Charles, who died, before he could do much harm, in 1769. (In the four generations for which the male line of the Gardiners lasted, the head of the family was alternately 'good' and 'bad', the good ones being called Luke and the bad ones Charles.) Luke Gardiner II (1745–98) was the popular, independent MP for Co. Dublin, 1773–89, and is best-remembered as the sponsor of the Catholic Relief Acts of 1778 and 1782. He married twice. His first wife died in 1783, the year after she had borne him a son and heir, Charles John Gardiner. He married again in 1793, and was long survived by his second wife. In 1789 he was created Lord Mountjoy and was promoted to the viscountcy of Mountjoy in 1795.[499] This title had previously been held by the Stewart family of Newtownstewart, Co. Tyrone, who were now extinct in the male line and from whom Luke Gardiner had a female descent. In 1797 he also inherited the Newtownstewart and other Co. Tyrone estates of the Stewart family, which in conjunction with his north Dublin estate and smaller properties elsewhere placed him in the first rank of Irish landowners. In the following year he was killed fighting at the head of the Co. Dublin Militia at the battle of New Ross, Co. Wexford.

Charles John Gardiner, 2nd Viscount Mountjoy (1782–1829), succeeded to the title and estates at the age of sixteen. Because the Dowager Lady Mountjoy was his stepmother, not his mother, he was effectively divested of parental guidance and restraint. No young man needed them more. He was feckless, rudderless, extravagant, susceptible to the charms of the wrong sort of woman, and too rich for his own good. In 1804, he established himself as an at least part-time resident on his Tyrone estates,[500] where he began to build and or/enlarge houses at Rash and at Mountjoy Forest. He involved himself in Tyrone politics and amateur theatricals, in both cases following the lead of his grand but louche neighbour, Lord Abercorn. In 1809 he fell in love with a great beauty called Mary Campbell, the first of two such *liaisons* with married women who were unfree to marry him until their husbands obligingly died, and both of whom were portionless. Mary Campbell, by whom he had two illegitimate and two legitimate children, died in 1814, after only two years' marriage to him. Her successor, whom he was eventually able to marry in 1818, was Margaret or Marguerite Power, the daughter of a disreputable squireen from near Clonmel, Co. Tipperary. She was to become famous as 'the most gorgeous Lady Blessington' (Lord Mountjoy having been advanced to the earldom of Blessington in 1816), the image of her beauty still being preserved in a well-known portrait by Lawrence in the Wallace Collection.[501]

On her first appearance in Co. Tyrone, a local baronet reported (quaintly) to Lord Abercorn: 'If she is one day to be a countess, as far as beauty goes he has not made a bad choice. She seems about 25 and in size and shape about what his former wife was when he first met with her.'[502] This suggests a remarkable consistency in Blessington's taste in women. However, what became increasingly doubtful was whether his taste lay wholly in the direction of the opposite sex. As the down-to-earth Thomas Conolly had remarked in 1786, when he was shown the Earl-Bishop of Derry's art-collection at Downhill, Co. Londonderry: 'from the frequent appearance of Ganymede, I should suppose his Lordship much fonder of boys than of girls.'[503] Lord Blessington's marriage to a 'gorgeous' woman would seem to militate against such a supposition in his case. But Lady Blessington is generally supposed to have been made frigid by her experiences when very young at the hands of a brutal first husband. Rather, the touchstone of Blessington's sexuality is the extraordinary relationship which developed between him and Count Alfred d'Orsay (1798–1852), a penniless French adventurer whose birth was less noble than it sounded.

They first met in London in August 1821, when d'Orsay was twenty-three. He was handsome, dandified, narcissistic and supremely self-confident, the very embodiment of *ton* and taste, and just the person to captivate the aimless and impressionable Blessington. D'Orsay's own sexuality remains an enigma. Jane Walsh Carlyle's first impression, formed in 1839, was that 'his beauty is of that rather disgusting sort which seems to be, like genius, "of no sex"'. The best guess so far made is that he was impotent, which would certainly explain why the

Charles John Gardiner, Earl of Blessington, c.1810, after the [miniature?] by [James?] Holmes, reproduced from Michael Sadleir, *Blessington-D'Orsay ...* (London, 1933), p.12

sexually damaged Lady Blessington was drawn to him almost as strongly as her husband, and why d'Orsay and she were to remain inseparable for as long as they both lived. By whatever chemistry, the two Blessingtons and d'Orsay settled into a perfect *ménage à trois*. They were wandering the Continent in this threesome (accompanied, however, by a huge retinue of servants), when news reached them that Blessington's only legitimate son, Lord Mountjoy, had died in March 1823 at the age of nine. Since the possibility of his having children by Lady Blessington had by this stage been tacitly ruled out – if indeed it had ever existed – this meant that Blessington was now without an obvious heir. It may also have meant that some of the emotional attachment he had hitherto focussed on the young Lord Mountjoy was transferred to d'Orsay.

This was the background to the fateful will which Blessington made while the *ménage à trois* was in Genoa in the spring of 1823, and which he ratified and slightly altered (to Lady Blessington's disadvantage) in London in August. Although it took the form of a will, it was in effect a settlement since the most important of its provisions was put into operation during his lifetime. By the terms of this will/settlement he divided his landed property, producing a heavily encumbered income of c.£23,000 a year, into two unequal shares. His estate at Newtownstewart, Mountjoy Forest and elsewhere in Co. Tyrone, producing about £9,300 a year, he left to his illegitimate son and namesake, Charles John Gardiner, who had been born in 1810, before Blessington had married the boy's mother, Mary Campbell. To his legitimate daughter, Lady Harriet (1812–69), he left his more valuable estate in Dublin City and County, producing c.£13,400 a year,[504] 'provided she intermarries with my friend and intended son-in-law, Alfred d'Orsay'. If she did not, he bequeathed her 'the sum of £10,000 only'. His illegitimate daughter, Mary (b.1811), was left £20,000, but would receive the Dublin estate if Harriet declined to marry d'Orsay and Mary agreed to do so.[505] This will, even in the London version, was so badly drafted that it was not clear what was to happen if neither daughter was prepared to marry him. But this problem did not arise. In December 1827, the fifteen-year-old Harriet became Countess d'Orsay, although it was privately agreed, on account of her youth, that they should not live as man and wife for the next four years. Blessington presumably expected to have plenty of time to reconcile her to the mis-match and smooth relations between the less-than-happy couple. But it was not to be. He died suddenly in May 1829 at the age of forty-six.

His death not only disabled him from marriage guidance, but gave unwelcome publicity to the heavy load of debt which burdened his estates – most of it the result of his and Lady Blessington's wildly extravagant lifestyle. All told, the debts amounted to a principal sum of £161,069 plus annuity payments to the value (as late as 1846) of £7,887 a year, including Lady Blessington's jointure of £2,000.[506] Of the £161,069, £40,000 was attributable to the marriage portion paid or to be paid, in two instalments, to the trustees of d'Orsay's and Lady Harriet's marriage settlement. The income of the £40,000 (at six per cent)[507] and whatever was left of the income from the Dublin estate when the annual liens upon it had been met, were d'Orsay's to enjoy during their joint lives; the estate itself was settled on their issue male, with remainder (should there be none) to the issue male of Charles John Gardiner. Thus circumstanced, and granted d'Orsay's indifference to Lady Harriet and her aversion to him, d'Orsay had no incentive to make the marriage work – quite the contrary. For, if she formed a *liaison* with another man or otherwise misconducted herself, the £40,000 would belong outright to him and, depending on the outcome of the ensuing divorce proceedings, the Dublin estate might also fall into his absolute possession. It even looks as if he quietly encouraged her to have an affair with a mutual friend.[508]

In the event, Lady Harriet out-manoeuvred him (in August 1831) by running away and putting herself under the protection of Blessington's step-mother, the Dowager Lady Mountjoy, and of his sister, the Hon. Miss Harriet Gardiner. Soon afterwards, and probably by collusion with Lady Mountjoy and Miss Gardiner, Charles John Gardiner instituted a lawsuit to challenge the validity of Blessington's will. Lady Harriet could not as yet institute proceedings on her own account because she did not come of age until 1833 and, until then, had been placed by the will under the uncongenial guardianship of Lady Blessington, who was on intimate terms with d'Orsay (they were widely, though improbably, supposed to be lovers) and was providing him with a home in her own London house in Seamore Place. But it was obvious that Lady Harriet would contest the will and the legality of her marriage and marriage settlement as soon as she was legally free to do so.

In the meantime, the problem for all concerned was how to support themselves financially when the Blessington estates were producing very little income nett of interest charges. Charles John Gardiner, who initially received an allowance of £1,000 a year out of the Tyrone estate (reduced to £600 in 1834), was as spendthrift as his father, and having run up debts of over £35,000 was ultimately (by 1842) declared bankrupt.[509] D'Orsay was even less capable of living within any income, however large. Between 1829 and 1834 he must have received some small part of the rents of the Dublin estate, and he certainly received £2,400 a year from the marriage portion of £40,000. But he borrowed large sums by annuity on the security of the latter, until by 1832 the £2,400 a year had ceased to exist.[510] Lady Blessington's £2,000 a year was a first charge on the estates, and was punctually paid until 1847, when the effects of the Famine forced a reduction. Although she struggled to augment it by literary earnings which in a good year could amount to £1,000, her income proved inadequate to support her lifestyle and to enable her to subsidise d'Orsay's.[511]

As for Lady Harriet, though notionally a great heiress, she had no income at all between 1831, when she separated from d'Orsay, and 1834, when the Court of Chancery ordered that she be paid an allowance of £400 a year out of the estate (and d'Orsay £550). Neither her father's will nor her marriage settlement seems to have provided her with pin money or any income independent of her husband's, and £400 a year was obviously inadequate to her needs. So she too ran up debts (totalling over £20,000 by 1846),[512] and would no doubt have run up more if she had not been subsidised by the comparatively affluent Dowager Lady Mountjoy and Miss Gardiner.[513]

To financial stalemate was added legal impasse. While Charles John Gardiner's proceedings might assist Lady Harriet in the short term by straitening d'Orsay's resources, in the longer term 'the persons between whom the serious questions exist as to the construction of the will are Mr Gardiner and Lady H.; their interests under the will are completely opposed to each other and must be stoutly contested for each, since on the result of these contests will depend the extent of burthen each estate is to bear'.[514] To that extent, it behoved Count and Countess d'Orsay to join forces against Charles John Gardiner. Nor could husband and wife, even if either could have afforded the cost of the contest, hope for decisive victory one over the other. Lady Harriet's increasingly irregular private life (she became the mistress of among others, the Duc d'Orléans, who was killed in 1842),[515] gave d'Orsay grounds for divorcing her; but she might have been able to counteract such a proceeding by alleging that the non-consummation of her marriage was not solely due to the four-year moratorium agreed upon in 1827.

Neither had therefore much to gain by pushing matters to extremities. In April 1832 d'Orsay proposed a compromise whereby the Dublin estate would be sold and the proceeds divided between them in the ratio of two-thirds to d'Orsay and one-third to Lady Harriet.[516] Such a ratio probably corresponded to contemporary estimates of the respective values of a husband's and a wife's interests in jointly owned property. But it may well not have satisfied Lady Harriet. In any case, other legal obstacles interposed to prevent the further consideration of this or any other proposal for a compromise. Eventually, in February 1838, Lady Harriet entered into a private deed of separation with d'Orsay whereby his concurrence was no longer required to validate any legal act done by her, and by another deed of the same date (16 February) compelled him to accept a phased monetary payment for his interest, under their marriage settlement and Lord Blessington's will, in the Dublin estate. All told, he was to receive £93,000, inclusive of the £40,000 provided by the marriage settlement, payable as and when the proceeds from sales of parts of the estate permitted; in the meantime, he was to be allowed interest, of which his Court allowance of £550 per annum was to count as part.[517] Michael Sadleir was therefore not far wrong when he reckoned that 'between 1838 and the final sale of the Blessington lands in 1851, d'Orsay (or rather his creditors) received something over £100,000'.[518]

By the deed of separation Lady Harriet also confirmed an earlier deed of 1836 (whose validity had been questioned) whereby she had settled the reversion of the Dublin estate (in the event of her being childless) on Charles John Gardiner and his sister, Mary, one half of it to be enjoyed by each.[519] This presumably 'squared' Charles John Gardiner and purchased his assent to the compromise arrangement with d'Orsay.

Even with Gardiner and d'Orsay bought off, sales of the Blessington estate proceeded slowly. They were complicated by the competing claims of the different creditors, and also by the bankruptcy of Gardiner. So much property in two concentrated locations (north Dublin and the Omagh/Newtownstewart area of Tyrone) did not readily attract buyers in sufficient numbers. Later, the Famine squeezed credit, and the Encumbered Estates Act glutted the market. In 1846 a Blessington Estates Act was passed (9 Victoria, cap. 1) to facilitate the process of sale, having been petitioned for by all the interested parties. The act authorised the raising of a sum not exceeding £350,000 to satisfy all demands (including those of d'Orsay), and £344,342 was accordingly raised,[520] probably by 1851. D'Orsay died in 1852.

In January of the following year,[521] Lady Harriet married the man with whom she had been living in France for some years past. He was the Hon. Spencer Cowper (1818–79) of Sandringham Hall, Norfolk,[522] third son of the 5th Earl Cowper. This well connected Englishman (the nephew of one prime minister, Melbourne, and the stepson of another, Palmerston) had no previous association with Ireland and presumably no interest in an Irish estate except as a source of revenue. This is implicit in the terms of the marriage settlement. It settled the estate on the issue of the marriage and, should there be none (a likely eventuality, since Lady Harriet was forty-three at the time), on Cowper and his right heirs if he survived Lady Harriet. (Both Charles John Gardiner and Mary Gardiner must presumably have been dead without issue by now: otherwise it is hard to see how their reversionary interest could have been overridden.) In the event, there was one child of the marriage, a daughter, who died in infancy in 1854. Following this bereavement, Lady Harriet turned religious and died in 1869, pre-deceasing Cowper by ten years. He remarried, and at his death left the estate to his widow, who probably sold it c.1885. More sales of freeholds had taken place after Lady Harriet's death, and property values in north Dublin were falling. But, amazingly, the Gardiner estate was still worth £120,000 in 1882, subject only to a mortgage for £10,800.[523]

On these figures, it would appear that Lady Harriet had netted rather more than d'Orsay out of the estate and a great deal more than the two-thirds to one-third ratio which he had proposed to her in 1832. It is also clear that she had husbanded her resources much more efficiently than her brother, Charles John Gardiner, whose Tyrone estate had been reduced to a mere £600 a year by 1855.[524] At the time of her second marriage three years earlier, Lady Harriet's remaining fortune was impressive. In 1873 Lord Rosebery, whose standards and expectations were high, spoke of £100,000 as the minimum amount necessary to qualify a woman as an heiress.[525] If so, Lady Harriet still qualified. The wonder is that the settlement made on her second marriage did not reflect this fact. Possibly this was because of Cowper's grander family and connections. Possibly it was because there were no Gardiners left to whom she might have secured the contingent reversion to the Dublin estate. Possibly – and this is the likeliest explanation – poor Lady Harriet, having been denied affection by the dashing d'Orsay when she was in her prime, now fell with some desperation upon (the far from prepossessing) Cowper before all hope of bearing children was lost.

This is the human aspect of the Blessington disaster. The dynastic aspect was that in the sixty or so years which elapsed between the making of Lord Blessington's unjust and absurd will in 1823 and the probable date of the sale of the last of the Blessington estate, well in excess of £450,000 worth of land had come under the hammer and the very name of Gardiner had disappeared. On the Tyrone estate this extinction was visible to all. A neighbour who visited the Blessingtons at Mountjoy Forest in 1818, soon after their marriage, had written:

> The park is supposed to contain 12,000 trees ... and commands bold mountain views. A wide-flowing river glides through the grounds, sheltered by magnificent specimens of the old Irish ash and sycamore.... There is a picturesque oak wood and a plantation of the rarest kinds of trees, through which you ride or drive for miles ... [until you come] to a door of a small irregular, thatched cottage, which ... opened ... into an apartment ... as handsome in size and fitting-up as you would see in any castle or mansion – very large Louis XIV gilt tables, family portraits and pier glasses, a magnificent chimneypiece and cabinet.

'These magnificent grounds' he added half a century later, in 1855, 'are now all turned into farms. The cottage has been let and the princely furniture sold. I am the only one alive of that party.'[526]

The downfall of his family and the dispersal of his estates and treasures were not inevitable at the time of Lord Blessington's death in 1829. The estates were very heavily, but not inextricably, encumbered. The main problem was that, until the annuity-creditors died off, very little income would be forthcoming. Under these circumstances, it was crazy for Blessington to separate the Tyrone from the Dublin estate and to try to provide a landed inheritance for more than one of his children. Admittedly, there was historical rationale for the division, in that the Tyrone estate had been inherited through marriage into the Stewart family, while the Dublin estate was the patrimonial property of the Gardiners; Blessington seems to have been observing this distinction, since he enjoined in his will that Charles John Gardiner should call himself *Stewart* Gardiner. However, the mountain of debt which Blessington had piled on both estates left no room for such refinements.

Had he been serious and single-minded in his dynastic purpose, he would have left cash legacies to Gardiner and, if he must, to d'Orsay, and pitched upon Lady Harriet as the sole heiress to his landed property. If placed under the care of sensible guardians, she could have found a rich husband whose independent income would have supported them while the estates recovered, or a younger son like Lord Henry Stuart or Lord Mark Kerr who would have been prepared to live frugally and manage carefully for the future benefit of their children. The name of Gardiner, or if Blessington preferred, Stewart Gardiner, could have been perpetuated by the usual name and arms clause, and might once again have been borne with pride when his own depredations on the estates had been made good. Instead, by allowing his infatuation with d'Orsay to dominate his succession-planning, Blessington doomed his family to extinction. He also made his heiress, in terms both of material wealth and of personal happiness, the poorest little rich girl to be encountered in this study.

In more general terms, too, the d'Orsay-Gardiner mis-match highlights some important things. It shows what an 'arranged' marriage really was like, and is a warning against calling other marriages 'arranged' which essentially were not. It shows the importance of mutual attraction for the future success of a dynastic marriage: unless it was and remained to some extent a marriage of affection, it was in danger of going seriously wrong. Finally, it shows that in spite or because of marriage settlements, the sensational could still happen. The irony is that an arranged marriage should have had more injurious consequences than any of the *mésalliances* and the elopements and clandestine marriages in the sample.

SEVEN

'Speculations and castle-buildings'[527]

THE IDENTIFICATION
OF AN HEIRESS

The element of chance, speculation and risk in any marriage to a known or suspected heiress has been implicit, and often explicit, in every chapter of this book. But the theme is of fundamental importance and requires a chapter in its own right. The element of speculation was often unresolved for long years after the date of the marriage. Some of the greatest heiresses, indeed, were not even suspected of being heiresses at the time of their marriage, and a significant few were retrospective heiresses, whose transmission of the estates of their family into the family of their husbands did not take place until after they were dead – sometimes not until after they were long dead. The element of speculation could therefore extend to the very identification of the heiress. As for the element of risk: it has so far been discussed in its legal aspect – how the ambitions of a husband could be dashed and even turned to loss by the provisions of a marriage settlement. But the risk may also have been of a genetic nature. Genetics, because they have an obvious bearing on unexpected developments and on speculation, are the first issue which the present chapter will explore.

In 1542, the dying King James V of Scotland, whose heiress was a newly born daughter, famously observed that the House of Stuart's title to the crown had 'come with a lass and will pass with a lass'. (Actually, it did not; for, the 'lass', who was Mary Queen of Scots, married her cousin, Henry Stuart, Lord Darnley, by whom she had King James VI and I.) Nancy Mitford stated the case for genetic risk more strongly in 1956: 'Heiresses have caused the extinction as well as the enrichment of many a … family, since the heiress, who must be an only child if she is to be really rich, often comes of barren or enfeebled stock.'[528] This is a perhaps surprising pronouncement on the part of a member of a famous, or infamous, clan of sisters (who did, however, have an only brother, killed in the Second World War). It also appears to confound two different things: 'a barren and enfeebled stock' and a genetic propensity to produce female children. This study has already featured at least two sons of heiresses who behaved with a folly bordering on feeble-mindedness – the 2nd Earl of Massereene and the 2nd Earl Grandison. But it would be pushing the evidence too far to suggest that their follies were genetic in origin. A propensity to produce female children is a different matter. Then as now, it was exhibited by particular families in one, two or three generations, but was unlikely to be a permanent feature of family demography. Certain of the families whose history has been discussed in these pages repeatedly failed to maintain a father-to-son succession: the Fitzgerald, Fitzgerald Villiers and Mason Villiers family of Dromana produced three heiresses in the period 1662–1800; and the Montagus made two false starts in creating a cadet line of Montagu of Beaulieu between 1723 and 1867. But in both cases, these difficulties were overcome.

Other families and estates which passed through a series of female successions did not emerge so unscathed. A case in point is the Aungier family and estates. After the death in 1705 of Ambrose Aungier, 2nd and last Earl of Longford, his estates in counties Longford and Cavan and in Dublin City passed, eventually, to the son and daughter of his sister, Alice, wife of James Cuffe. The son, Michael Cuffe (1694–1744), died leaving an only child and sole heiress, Elizabeth, the wife (1740) of Thomas Pakenham of Pakenham Hall, Castlepollard, Co. Westmeath, who was created Baron Longford in 1756. The daughter, another Alice, married (c.1690) James Macartney (d.1727), a judge of the Common Pleas, and had a son, James Macartney junior (1694–1770). Meanwhile, the Aungier estates had been partitioned, the Longford (and Cavan) in 1719 and the Dublin City in 1724. (The latter ceases to count because its two halves were then sold to wipe out Aungier encumbrances on the other estates.) The manor of Longford, with which went control of the corporation and parliamentary borough of Longford, went to Cuffe, and the manor of Granard, the borough of Granard and the lands in Co. Cavan went to James Macartney senior.[529]

At the death of James Macartney junior in 1770, the male line of the Aungier/Cuffe/Macartney family failed for the third time. Macartney was succeeded by two surviving daughters and co-heiresses, Frances (d.1789), wife of Fulke Greville of Wilbury, Wiltshire, and Mary (d.1765), wife of Sir William Henry Lyttleton, 7th Bt, who was created Lord Westcote in the peerage of Ireland and Lord Lyttleton in the peerage of Great Britain. This meant that the Macartney half of the property was further divided and passed into the possession of absentee Englishmen. Meanwhile, the Aungier/Cuffe/Pakenham family successfully maintained a father-to-son succession and avoided further fragmentation of their half. Elizabeth Cuffe/Pakenham, Lady Longford, was created countess of Longford in her own right in 1785, with remainder to her son, the 2nd Baron Longford (who in the event pre-deceased her). At her death in 1794, her grandson, the 3rd Baron, succeeded as 2nd Earl of Longford, and this re-creation of the honours of the extinct Aungiers is still extant today. The late (7th) Earl was called Francis Aungier Pakenham.

Another family which sustained two breaks in the male succession in the course of the eighteenth century, and whose estates passed through an heiress in 1725 and to three co-heiresses in 1796, was the Langford, later Langford Rowley, family of Summerhill, Co. Meath. In 1725, Hercules Rowley, son of the Langford heiress, succeeded her childless brother, Sir Henry Langford, 3rd and last Bt, in the Langford estates in Meath and round Crumlin, Co. Antrim. He died in 1742. His son, heir and (apparently) only child, the Rt Hon. Hercules Langford Rowley, represented Co. Londonderry (where the dwindling Rowley estates were situated), 1743–60, and Co. Meath, 1761–94 (when he died). His wife, who was created Viscountess Langford in 1766, bore him five children: Hercules, 2nd Viscount Langford, his heir, who died unmarried in 1796; Clotworthy, who died in 1781, leaving one daughter, Frances; Arthur, who died (unmarried?) in 1779; Jane, who married the 1st Earl of Bective in 1754 and had five sons and two daughters; and Catherine, who married the recently mentioned 2nd Baron Longford in 1768 and had five sons and four daughters.[530]

By 1796, thanks to the failure of the three Langford Rowley brothers to produce a male heir, the succession went once more down the female line, but this time seems to have been shared among their two sisters, Lady Bective and Lady Longford, and Frances, the daughter of the only brother who produced a child. A marriage between cousins simplified the ensuing partition: in 1794 Frances had married the Hon. Clotworthy Taylour, fourth son of Lord and Lady Bective. So, when Hercules Langford Rowley, 2nd Viscount Langford, died unmarried in 1796, the Meath estates went to the Taylours and the less valuable northern estates to Lady Longford, who settled them on her second surviving son in 1815.[531] Meanwhile, Clotworthy Taylour had been created Baron Langford in 1800. Both families are still going strong, though now dissociated from Ireland, and have experienced no further breaks in the male line.

Earlier in the century, another family provides a striking example of how female succession could spell total eclipse. This is the Rogerson family, established (or seemingly so) by Sir John Rogerson (1676–1741), lord chief justice of the King's Bench, 1727–41. Rogerson had four daughters, and at his death divided his very considerable property equally among them. As a result, the name Rogerson has disappeared, except for its survival as a Dublin City place-name, Rogerson's Quay.[532]

A near-contemporary contrast to the Rogersons is provided by the happier (from the dynastic point of view) story of Lady Blayney's four daughters. Lady Blayney, on inheriting the Cairnes estate in Monaghan in 1743, settled it on all four of them, but with the intention – as she graphically put it – of making 'one of my daughters an eldest son'. In the meantime, she gave up all thought of returning to live in England (where she had been born and spent her youth), because nobody in London would know anything about her daughters or their fortunes if she did so. 'Here [Ireland] it was known, and they had a chance of being much better settled than in England. So, I sighed, I gulped, and I remained.' Her strategy, as has been seen, was 'to give the estate to the eldest, with good fortunes however to the others' amounting to £4,000 apiece or its equivalent in land.[533] The eldest made a highly satisfactory marriage (in 1752) to a man with a large estate of his own conveniently situated in an adjoining county, which he represented in parliament. He made no demur at using the return for the parliamentary borough of Monaghan, which went with the Cairnes estate, for the benefit of his brothers-in-law, and all worked together for the ultimate advantage of the male heir to the estate.

Perhaps the Cairnes stock really was both 'barren' and 'enfeebled'? For whatever reason, Lady Blayney's first and second daughters were childless; her third daughter had one son, who died in adolescence; only the fourth daughter, Harriet Westenra, produced two sons who survived to adulthood. The hopes of the whole family connection were now concentrated on the elder of these. Lady Blayney's second daughter was married to General Robert Cuninghame, the commander-in-chief in Ireland, and he obtained a retirement peerage for himself (the barony of Rossmore) in 1796 with a special remainder in favour of the issue male of his wife's sisters. Eventually, although it took almost eighty years from the inception of Lady Blayney's succession-planning in 1743, a male heir in the person of Warner William Westenra, the 2nd Lord Rossmore, inherited the Cairnes estate.[534]

Essentially, though the outcomes were very different, the situations of Sir John Rogerson and Lady Blayney were the same: each had no son and four daughters. It is possible that genetics contributed to this situation (and to its continuation into the next generation of the Cairnes/Murray family). But skilful planning, and a clever and considerate settlement strategy, could avert the 'extinction' of families thus circumstanced. The real threat posed by female inheritance was not so much that of a 'barren or enfeebled stock', as that of fragmentation of estates and major loss of wealth and consequence. A sole heiress would cause little harm but, unless the tendency to treat all daughters equally were resisted (as it was by Lady Blayney), co-heirship could indeed cause the division or fragmentation of estates – as, for example, would have happened in the case of the two daughters and co-heiresses of the 2nd Viscount Allen, but for the accident that the younger of them, Lady Newhaven, produced no children. If there were enough co-heiresses, and they were all treated alike, the result would indeed be the extinction of the family (to the enrichment, of course, of the families into which

Frances Murray Cairnes (1734?–1820), eldest daughter and principal heiress of Lady Blayney, and wife of Willim Henry Fortescue, MP for Monaghan borough, 1761–70, created earl of Clermont; from a non-contemporary mezzotint after a painting by Sir Joshua Reynolds of c.1775

AUTHOR'S COLLECTION

the co-heiresses married). However, if the family estate was neither fragmented nor crippled with cash payments to the daughters who did not inherit it, co-heirship was not a terminal condition. The eldest or otherwise selected daughter would have to be married on terms which preserved the family name (something which Lady Blayney among her other preoccupations actually failed to do); and though the family peerages (if there were any) might expire, it was always probable that they would be recreated for the benefit of the heiress, her husband or their son, so long as the family had not suffered a major loss of wealth and consequence in the interim. There was, indeed, one positive advantage in transmitting an estate through an heiress: it was possible to choose or at any rate vet a son-in-law, but not possible to have any say in the matter of a son.

Some of the examples recently cited bear out these tentative conclusions. The House of Dromana sustained three female successions in 150 years, and survived mainly because there was only one heiress at a time. Moreover, the worst depredations on the family estate were committed under the male proprietorship of the 2nd Earl Grandison. By contrast, the Langford Rowley and the Aungier families were beset with co-heirships; they allowed themselves to be 'enfeebled' by partition; and the Macartney side of the Aungier family further enfeebled itself by a second partition. The Cuffe/Pakenham side of the Aungier family was more fortunate and/or more skilful. In 1781, the 2nd Lord Longford deliberately glossed over the fragmentation of the inheritance when lobbying George III for a re-creation of the earldom of Longford in the person of his mother, whom he described as 'the immediate representative and descendant of the last Earl of Longford, who died in 1706 [*sic* – 1705] and whose estate she now possesses'.[535] This was at best a half-truth, since she only possessed half (actually less than half) the estate, and controlled only one of the Aungier boroughs. She was, however, in a financial position to support the higher title because her husband's Pakenham estates were more than equivalent to the other half of the Aungier inheritance, and because husband and wife had resisted the temptation to practise cadet inheritance.

Marrying into a family whose estate had passed through two heiresses in three generations did not have the effect of 'enfeebling' the Pakenhams, of rendering them 'barren', or of inclining them towards an over-production of females. There was some doubt about the 3rd Earl of Longford (1817–60), known in the family as 'fluffy', who died unmarried and in a seedy and probably syphilitic state in lodgings in London.[536] Otherwise, the Pakenhams more than reproduced themselves in the male line, and even provided male heirs for two other families, the Conollys of Castletown as well as the Langford Rowleys. Besides, heiresses were far from being the only cause, real or imaginary, for genetic concern: the Irish and other upper classes were very considerably in-bred, not particularly for reasons connected with inheritance, but more simply because, in the restricted circles in which young, aristocratic men and women moved, cousins were apt to be the focus of early and often permanent attachments. To this

'SPECULATIONS AND CASTLE-BUILDINGS'

potential source of barrenness and enfeeblement must be added the perennial factors (which may or may not be genetically derived) of alcoholism and homosexuality. These particularly affected the behaviour, and sometimes the judgement,[537] of men (simply because men were freer agents than women). And men were also exclusively liable to be killed unexpectedly in battle, by assassins,[538] in duels and in riding accidents. Under the best of demographic circumstances, families have always found it difficult to sustain an unbroken male descent for longer than a few generations: among aristocratic families in Ireland in the period 1740–1840 there were plenty of additional causes militating against a father-to-son succession.[539]

All this gave much encouragement to 'speculations and castle-buildings' – the main theme of the present chapter. These were of two broad kinds: speculations inspired in an aristocratic bridegroom by the demographic circumstances of his bride's family; and speculations inspired in any aristocrat by the possibility of a windfall inheritance from the family of his father, his mother or his wife. Mention has already been made, in other contexts, of a number of marriages which, at the time of their making, seemed to the bridegrooms to hold out possibilities of future advantage beyond the scope of the current negotiation. These include the marriage of Lord Blayney and Mary Cairnes in 1724, the marriage of William Conolly junior and Lady Anne Wentworth in 1733, the marriage of Lord Tyrone and Elizabeth Monck in 1769, and the marriage of Thomas Henry Foster and Lady Harriet Skeffington in 1810. From the bridegroom's point of view, the first of these speculations was a failure, the second ended up costing more than it was worth, and the third and fourth were unqualified successes (the fourth was actually scarcely a speculation, granted the near-certainty and imminence of the lady's inheritance). Another marriage which is worth considering under the heading of 'speculation' is the ill-fated union of Lord Belmore and Lady Henrietta Hobart in 1780.

There was not much ground for speculation about Lord Belmore's circumstances – though the bride's father, Lord Buckinghamshire, was at pains to represent them as being more favourable than they actually were, presumably to emphasise his own cleverness in engineering the marriage. To his brother-in-law Buckinghamshire reported joyfully

> Harriet has made a conquest of Mr Corry,[540] member for the county of Tyrone, who is, from every account, the best match in this kingdom. His property is immense ... £6,000 per annum [unsettled, plus £5,000 per annum] ... settled upon a child by a former wife, to whom his behaviour was amiable to a proverb. He is universally esteemed, acknowledged to be generous without profusion, honourable upon the most correct line. He is rather well in his figure. His age, thirty-two. And, in addition to these capital points, his nose resembles mine.[541]

As all this blague suggests, Buckinghamshire acted foolishly throughout this negotiation. He not only forced his daughter into a marriage which was contrary to her inclination, but considerably exaggerated the desirability of it from a dynastic and financial point of view. Lady Henrietta was an earl's daughter with a fortune of £20,000 (£15,000 of it to come at a future date). Belmore was then a commoner; he became a peer soon afterwards mainly because Buckinghamshire recommended him for ennoblement. The 'child' by his previous marriage was a son, so Lady Henrietta was unlikely to be the mother of the heir. Finally, it was no big deal for a woman endowed as she was with fortune and rank to obtain the settlement terms conceded to Lady Henrietta: £500 a year pin money and £2,000 a year jointure for herself, £6,000 a year in land for the eldest son of the marriage and £20,000 as a provision for younger children.

It was in fact Belmore who had good reason to speculate on the future advantages which might accrue from the marriage (which may explain his willingness to sacrifice the interests of his son by his former wife). In 1780, Buckinghamshire's immediate family consisted of three daughters (of whom Henrietta was the eldest) by his late first wife, and one by his second; his second wife was much younger than him and had many years of child-bearing left to her; but, significantly, three male children born to her had died in infancy. How much Belmore was anticipating in 1780 is difficult to judge. But it is significant that, in the deed of separation which was agreed upon in 1781, he asserted his 'rights ... [to] any estates or personal property which shall vest in Lady Belmore'.[542] His tenacity was well judged. In 1794, when her father died without surviving issue male, she – as his eldest daughter – succeeded to Blickling Hall and the accompanying Hobart estate in Norfolk. By then, however, she was divorced and had ceased to be Lady Belmore. So, this great inheritance passed to her son by her second marriage. Meanwhile, Belmore was still footing the bill for the first. Prior to their separation, the Belmores had had one daughter, who in due course received the £20,000 earmarked for younger children (and the equivalent of the portion which Belmore received with Lady Belmore). From 1781 to Belmore's death in 1802, Lady Belmore drew from his estate an allowance of £1,000 a year, and from 1802 until her own death three years later, a jointure of £2,000 a year. When to these outings are added the costs (of c. £3,000) he incurred in divorcing her, it is obvious that his speculation was an expensive failure. But it narrowly missed being a huge success.[543]

There were matters of birth and death and of legal presumption that marriage settlements could not cover; they could not, for example, presume that children would not be born while those theoretically capable of bearing them were still

John Hobart, 2nd Earl of Buckinghamshire (1722–93), from a print after a portrait by Gainsborough painted c.1780
AUTHOR'S COLLECTION

'SPECULATIONS AND CASTLE-BUILDINGS'

alive. In other respects, however, marriage settlements were designed to be as comprehensive as possible. This meant that most speculation was of the second kind, as already defined: it arose out of events subsequent to the marriage and unforeseeable at that time.

For example, William Bury of Shannongrove, Co. Limerick, could not have foreseen in 1724, when he married the Hon. Jane Moore, elder sister of the future Earl of Charleville, that Lord Charleville (who was not even married at the time) would die childless, in 1764, and that the Burys' eldest son would succeed to the Charleville estate.[544] Similarly, William Henry Dawson, the grandfather of the 2nd Earl of Portarlington, could not have foreseen in 1737, when he married Mary Damer, that only one of her three brothers would have children; that the three (unborn) sons of that brother would all die childless, one of them by suicide; that the one (unborn) daughter of that brother, Lady Caroline, would never marry; and that on Lady Caroline's death in 1828, nearly 100 years after the marriage, Lord Portarlington and his younger brother would between them succeed her in the Dorchester estates.[545] Nor could the 2nd Earl of Lanesborough have foreseen in 1754, when he married Lady Jane Rochfort, only daughter of the 1st Earl of Belvedere, that her three brothers would die either childless or unmarried, and that in 1814, when she was 77 and he had been dead for 35 years, she would inherit the settled part of the Belvedere estates, amounting to roughly one-half of the total. (It was probably a misfortune from the point of view of subsequent earls of Lanesborough that he was dead at the time, since Lady Lanesborough settled her Rochfort inheritance, not on her Lanesborough grandson, the 4th Earl, but on the son of one of her daughters, George Marlay [1791–1831].) It is worthy of note that two of these unforeseeable heiresses were old women by the time they inherited, and one was long dead.

Essentially, inheritance of this remote description, if it came to pass, had as little to do with marrying an heiress as had Thomas Roberts's windfall inheritance from Jane Roberts, Duchess of St Albans, or Percy Wyndham O'Brien's inheritance of the Thomond estates of his mother's sister's husband.[546] William Pitt the Elder, subsequently 1st Earl of Chatham, had been the beneficiary of a similar windfall in 1765; this was the estate of Burton Pynsent in Somerset, bequeathed to him by an admirer who was not even a distant relation and whom he scarcely knew. Perhaps this windfall caused Pitt to speculate on his contingent expectations under the settlements of the estates of his Irish cousins, who were none other than the Grandisons. In 1766, when Earl Grandison died, only his ageing daughter, Countess Grandison, and her fifteen-year-old son, George Mason Villiers, Viscount Villiers, stood between Pitt and the Grandison inheritance worth c.£9,000 a year. The gossips hastened to comment that Lord Villiers 'is inclined to be wild and has not had the smallpox, and Pitt is lucky.... Everyone concludes the boy is to die.'[547] In the event, he lived until 1800, and Pitt died in 1778.

To what extent Pitt himself entered into this wishful thinking, is unknown. It

THE PURSUIT OF THE HEIRESS

does, however, seem likely that the 9th Lord Cathcart allowed himself to be drawn into speculation on the future destination of the fortune salvaged from Maguire by Cathcart's stepmother. In 1770, it was intimated to him by an intermediary who may well have been just a busybody, that 'her Ladyship was at a loss for a particular friend to open her mind to', that she was 'forlorn and destitute of friends by being so long gone from her own country', and that she had 'a vast affection and regard ... for your Lordship and family'.[548] Accordingly, Lord Cathcart began to act as her unofficial adviser (not that his advice was necessarily taken) in her various lawsuits with Maguire's heirs and agents. By 1776, when he died, they were subscribing their letters to each other as 'your most affectionate' mother and son.[549] In 1789, when she in turn died, it is obvious from the way in which the principal beneficiary of her will, Philip Cosgrave, explained its provisions to Cathcart's son and successor, the 10th Lord, that the latter had entertained hopes of succeeding to much of her remaining fortune.[550]

Disappointments of the kind experienced by Lord Cathcart, and possibly by Pitt, so often occurred that it must surely have been an article of aristocratic training that no one should presume too far on the strength of presumptive inheritance? Hence Lady Portarlington's coldly realistic (and, as things turned out, prophetic) advice to her son not to count his Dorchester chickens while Lady Caroline Damer ruled the roost.[551] Hence also the philosophical sentiments expressed by the 2nd Earl of Rosse (of the second creation)[552] to his uncle's widow, the Dowager Lady Rosse, after the 2nd Earl had discovered that his family was not going to inherit the Harman estate:

I have really never looked to the possibility of my possessing your estates. I had in truth no selfish wish about them, except as far as self is concerned in the future comfort of my children. I never was so unkind or so unwise as to calculate on my succeeding you in becoming the proprietor of them. Indeed, I hold all these speculations and castle-buildings on the property of another very culpable, because they at last lead to coveting another person's goods.[553]

Lord Rosse stressed the moral dimension of such speculations, but there was a practical dimension, too. Anyone who allowed himself to become fixated on an inheritance which might never happen, was in danger of neglecting or procrastinating over the affairs of the estates which were already in his possession, of living extravagantly and perhaps – consciously or subconsciously – of borrowing on the strength of his prospective but putative inheritance. Thomas Conolly did all these things. He had good reason to hope for much more than the c.£115,000 which he eventually drew from the

William Schaw Cathcart, General the 10th Lord, later 1st Earl, Cathcart (1755–1843), caricatured by Gillray, 11 June 1800. Cathcart was 'Gold Stick', or colonel of the 2nd regiment of Life Guards.

AUTHOR'S COLLECTION

'SPECULATIONS AND CASTLE-BUILDINGS'

Strafford inheritance of his mother, Lady Anne Wentworth, and acted accordingly. An old friend, who saw what was going on and knew him well enough to be forthright, warned him in 1794: 'It is essential to the happiness of your life to give up the (vain) pursuit of Lord Strafford's fortune and to render your own, which is a noble one, more easily manageable by selling a part to pay off debt.'[554]

Though Conolly's hopes were to be dashed, and though his mother in the end cost him more in jointure than she brought him in landed property and cash, he had more ground to go upon than William Bury, Lord Lanesborough and William Henry Dawson; and most slow-burning heiresses took as long as Jane Bury and Lady Lanesborough to be recognisable as such or, like Mary Damer, were only posthumously recognisable. Other heiresses of this type who have featured in earlier chapters and different contexts include the women who inherited – or whose sons inherited – the Thomond estate in counties Clare and Limerick (1741), the Dutton estate in Gloucestershire (1743), the Petty estate in Co. Kerry (1751), the Grandison in Co. Waterford (1766), the Conyngham in counties Donegal and Meath (1781), and the Harman in Co. Longford (1784 and 1838).

The third of these heiresses, Anne Petty, Countess of Kerry, repays closer study in the present context. She was the only daughter of the famous Sir William Petty (d.1687), surveyor-general of Ireland, and she founded fifteen years after her demise the famously double-barrelled family of Petty-Fitzmaurice, earls of Shelburne and marquesses of Lansdowne. She had two brothers, who succeeded in turn to the 'immense estate'[555] of their father, mainly in Co. Kerry. When she married in 1692, she was no more than a handsomely portioned woman who brought £10,000 to her husband, Thomas Fitzmaurice, 21st Lord of Kerry, later created earl of Kerry.[556] The Earl and Countess of Kerry had two sons, William and John, and three daughters. He died in 1741 and she in 1737.

Meanwhile, her father's Petty estates had devolved on the second of her brothers, Henry Petty, Earl of Shelburne (c.1675–1751), whose

Jane, Countess Dowager of Rosse: a silhouette of 1838 reproduced from the original at Birr Castle

COURTESY OF THE EARL AND COUNTESS OF ROSSE

> wife and children all pre-deceased him. On his death in 1751, the Kerry property (and vast family assets in England) passed to ... [her] *second* son, John Fitzmaurice, then MP for Co. Kerry and manager of ... [Lord Shelburne's]

affairs in Ireland; Fitzmaurice promptly changed his name and had the Shelburne title revived within two years.[557]

In his trenchant autobiography, William Petty-Fitzmaurice, 2nd Earl of Shelburne (1737–1805), who was created marquess of Lansdowne in 1784, described his grandmother, Anne Countess of Kerry, as 'a very ugly woman who brought into … [our] family whatever degree of sense may have appeared in it or whatever wealth is likely to remain in it'. Later, in 1772, 'upon settling his affairs … [and adding up] all the different rentrolls', he calculated the landed element in that wealth to be 'a good £40,000 a year'.[558] Yet, throughout her life and for some years after her death, there had been no inkling that she was going to occupy this pivotal position in family history.

Luke Gardiner, the founder of the ill-fated Gardiner family, Viscounts Mountjoy, married in 1711 Anne Stewart (1697–1753), daughter of Capt. the Hon. Alexander Stewart (d.1702). Capt. Stewart was the dissolute and penniless brother of the 2nd Viscount Mountjoy (of the first creation), who died in 1728. The 2nd Viscount Mountjoy was succeeded, as 3rd and last viscount and as one and only earl of Blessington (of the first creation), by a son who died childless in 1769, when all the Stewart honours became extinct. Lord Blessington's estates passed, under the terms of his will, in various directions (some being sold to pay his debts). But one of them, the estate in Co. Tyrone (which had a rental of £4,333 a year in 1788, rising sharply thereafter), passed first to Admiral the Hon. John Forbes, a closer relative than the very distant Gardiners, and then, when Forbes died without issue male, to Luke Gardiner's grandson, the 1st Viscount Mountjoy of the second creation. Lord Mountjoy inherited it in 1797, forty-four years after the death of the heiress who now brought it into the Gardiner family.[559]

Another example of remote inheritance from a long-dead heiress likewise relates to an estate in Co. Tyrone. This was the Castlegore or manor of Hastings estate, located in and around Castlederg, which had belonged to Hugh Edwards of Castlegore (d.1743?). Under the terms of Edwards' will, dated 1737, his estate passed to his (only?) daughter, Olivia, and her issue, with remainder (should there be no surviving issue) to Edwards' brothers and sisters in order of seniority. (In practice, this remainder became vested in the issue of his eldest sister, Margaret, who had married in 1722, Robert Stuart of Eary, Co. Tyrone).[560] The heiress, Olivia Edwards (1731–1820) married twice. Both her husbands were in a position to devote themselves to their inheritance, because they had little or none of their own: her first husband, the 2nd and last Earl of Rosse of the first creation (d.1764), possessed only a remnant of a once large patrimonial estate, and her second, John Bateman, was the landless younger brother of Rowland Bateman (1737–1803) of Oak Park, Tralee, Co. Kerry.[561] She had issue by neither of them, and spent a lonely and uncomfortable widowhood in Castlegore,

> a woman who had long outlived her generation, her eyesight, and all her passions except that one which increases with age [avarice]. She lingered in this her

ancient castle until the floors cracking under her feet and the ceilings tumbling on her head admonished her to tardy and reluctant flight; for, the trifle it would have taken to have averted this calamity, she could not bear to part with. She would perhaps have been a wonder in any country but she was an especial wonder in this one, where profusion is the defect of the gentry, and parsimony the only fault which the poor do not forgive.[562]

This frightful description of Olivia Edwards, Countess of Rosse, lends reality to Nancy Mitford's view of the heiress. At Lady Rosse's death in 1820, the 2nd Earl Castle Stewart, grandson of Margaret Edwards and Robert Stuart of Eary, succeeded to the Castlegore estate under the remainder established eighty-three years previously by the will of Hugh Edwards in 1737.[563] With a rental in 1829 of almost £2,000 a year rising to £3,308 by 1862,[564] it was a welcome addition to Lord Castle Stewart's existing estates, all of them likewise located in Tyrone, though in a different part of the county.

Long before 1820, and following a succession of deaths among those with claims to the Castlegore estate which had priority over those of Margaret Edwards, the ultimate destination of the inheritance was known. But this was not the case – at any rate up until the last minute – with most other remote inheritances of this kind. In 1733, the Hon. Mary Fitzwilliam, eldest daughter of the 5th Viscount Fitzwilliam of Merrion, had married the Wiltshire magnate, the 9th Earl of Pembroke. Over sixty years later, in 1816, her great-nephew, the 7th Viscount Fitzwilliam, decided to by-pass the brother who was to succeed him in the family titles, and bequeathed his very valuable property in/and around Dublin to the 11th Earl of Pembroke, her grandson. According to a tradition preserved in the Pembroke family, the 7th Viscount Fitzwilliam invited both Lord Pembroke and his brother's son to tea, and chose Lord Pembroke as his heir because his Fitzwilliam nephew drank the tea out of a saucer. The saucer is also preserved in the Pembroke family.[565] Obviously, this was a decision and a disposition of property which could not have been foreseen until just before it took effect.

On the 7th Viscount Fitzwilliam's death, Lord Pembroke set off for Dublin to inspect his inheritance. From there, he wrote his wife an amusing account of his reception and particularly of his triumphal entry on

> a jaunting car…, which is on two wheels over one of which the passenger hangs his legs.… Having signed my name at the Custom House office, built mind you on my estate, a just mark of consideration and respect took place immediately; so much so that a crowd of blackguards without soon discovered that I was a big lord. These fellows … were all a little more [? saucy] than I liked in the offer of their services, in return for which I gave two or three well-rounded oaths; and happening at the same time to raise my umbrella that I might get out my

The 7th Viscount Fitzwilliam of Merrion, after a painting by H. Howard of pre-1816 – the year of the 7th Viscount's death.

AUTHOR'S COLLECTION

pocket handkerchief, they thought ... that I was going to make my way through them by clearing my course with blows. For, upon one fellow hallowing out, 'Your honour, lash them well, do', 'Aye, do, do, do' repeated a number of them, laughing and welcoming the big lord to the dear little isle.[566]

The Fitzwilliam estate had been producing, at least nominally, almost £14,000 a year at the end of the eighteenth century; Lord Pembroke was supposed to be in financial difficulties at the time he inherited it; and, as his letter makes plain, he had no previous association with or interest in Ireland. It was therefore assumed that he would obtain authority to sell all or part of his immense Irish windfall.[567] In fact, he did neither. Instead, he and his successors maintained the Fitzwilliam tradition of combining absenteeism with efficient and enlightened landlordism. Meanwhile, the disinherited Fitzwilliam brother, who had succeeded as 8th Viscount in 1816, died in 1830, and was succeeded briefly by another brother, with whom the title died in 1833. The saucer-wielding nephew, unless he is a figment of family imagination, must have been a son of the 9th Viscount and must have predeceased his father. For present purposes, however, the material circumstance is that the heiress who carried the Fitzwilliam estate into the Pembroke family had died in 1769, forty-seven years before this unexpected event took place.

In the case of the heiress who carried the Loftus of Monasterevan estate into the Moore family in 1725, the time-lag was seventy-six years. She was Jane Loftus, wife of Charles Moore, 2nd Viscount Moore, whose great-grandson, Henry Moore, 4th Earl of Drogheda, succeeded to the estate as remainderman under the Loftus family settlements on the death of his distant cousin, Adam Loftus, 3rd Viscount Loftus. The estate was located in and around Monasterevan, Co. Kildare, with a large overspill (the manor of Rosenalis) into the Mountmellick area of Co. Laois. Years later, in 1767, it had a rental of £5,425 a year. By 1725, when the Moores inherited it, their patrimonial estates, deriving originally from a generous grant of ex-monastic lands in north Dublin and in counties Louth and Meath, was greatly reduced in size and hopelessly encumbered by debt. The Loftus windfall came, therefore, in the nick of time. It made it possible for the 5th Earl of Drogheda, who succeeded to the Moore titles and debts in 1727, to sell virtually all his patrimonial property and fall back on the Loftus seat and estate as his only remaining means of supporting his rank and lifestyle. There were now no remaining Loftuses of that branch of the far-flung Loftus family, and no one to police the inheritance and preserve the Loftus name. Lord Drogheda did not double-barrel himself to Loftus-Moore; and when, in the late 1760s, his son and successor, the 6th Earl of Drogheda, remodelled the old seat of the Loftuses at Monasterevan in Strawberry Hill Gothic (he had married a daughter of Horace Walpole's first cousin), he called it Moore Abbey. This signalled the final absorption of the Loftuses into the Moores. But it was not a case of 'retrieving yourself by marrying', since nobody had married an heiress and the heiress concerned was long dead.[568]

A yet more strikingly posthumous heiress was Margaret Fortescue, daughter of Thomas Fortescue of Reynoldstown, Co. Louth, who married the already-mentioned Sir Arthur Brooke, Bt, in 1751. She had two brothers, one of whom was created Lord Clermont and was succeeded in the Fortescue estates and as 2nd Viscount Clermont in 1806 by the son of her second brother. When the 2nd Lord Clermont died without issue in 1829, he established by his will a series of contingent remainders. Under the last of these, which came into operation in 1898, a share of the Clermont estates of Ballymascanlon, Carlingford and Ravensdale, Co. Louth, and at Newry, Co. Armagh, passed to the 4th Viscount de Vesci, the descendant of Margaret Fortescue's daughter, Selina Elizabeth Brooke, wife of the 1st Lord Knapton and mother of the 1st Viscount de Vesci.[569] Margaret Fortescue herself had died in 1756, so the inheritance transmitted via her came to pass 142 years after her death.

By contrast, another heiress who was roughly contemporary with Margaret Fortescue almost lived to see the transmission of her inheritance to her son. She was Caroline Paget, only child of General Thomas Paget (c.1685–1741) and niece of the 6th Lord Paget of Beaudesert, Staffordshire. She belonged to a branch of the Pagets which was partly domiciled in Ireland, and married in 1737 a husband who was similarly situated – Sir Nicholas Bayly, 2nd Bt, of Plas Newydd, Anglesey, and Mount Bagenal, Carlingford, Co. Louth. The Baylys had three sons, Henry, Thomas and Paget, while the senior line of the Paget family failed to reproduce itself in the male line. Following the death of the 8th Baron Paget in 1769, the Paget estates passed to the Baylys' eldest son, Henry, who also succeeded as 9th Lord Paget (that being a barony in fee and so transmissible through a woman). Sir Nicholas Bayly died in 1782, cadet inheritance was eschewed, and Henry Bayly/Paget, Lord Paget, inherited his father's Welsh and Irish estates in addition to his mother's Paget estates in Staffordshire. In 1784 he was created earl of Uxbridge (a title previously borne by the head of the Paget family). He was succeeded in 1812 by the eldest of his numerous sons, Henry William Paget, 2nd Earl of Uxbridge, who was created marquess of Anglesey in 1815 in recognition of the part he played as commander of the British cavalry at the battle of Waterloo. Appropriately, in view of his Irish connections and large Irish estate in the Cooley peninsula, Co. Louth, he was twice (1828–9 and 1830–33) lord lieutenant of Ireland.[570] All this was inconceivable to the heiress, Caroline Paget, who had died in 1766. But she had lived to within three years of her son's inheritance of the Paget estates and barony.

The history of the Hill family, marquesses of Downshire and Viscounts Dungannon, furnishes two instances of unexpected inheritance – one remote and the other fairly immediate. In the 1690s, when William Hill of Hillsborough, Co. Down, married the eldest daughter of Michael Boyle, Archbishop of Armagh, he could not have foreseen that nearly a century later, in 1779, his great-grandson, the 1st Marquess of Downshire, would inherit part of Archbishop Boyle's extensive possessions, the Blessington estate, Co.

Wicklow.[571] (A more valuable part of Archbishop Boyle's possessions – the future Longford/de Vesci estate in counties Dublin, Cork and Limerick and in Hampshire, with a gross rental of £5,000 a year in 1778 – passed at the same time to the descendants of a slightly earlier marriage: in the 1st Viscount de Vesci's case, the marriage was that of an ancestor called Denny Muschamp, to another of Boyle's daughters, and had taken place in 1661.)[572]

Likewise, another great-grandson of William Hill, the Hon. Arthur Hill (1739–70), son and heir of the 1st Viscount Dungannon, could not have foreseen in 1762, when he married Letitia Morres, elder daughter of the 1st Viscount Mountmorres, that she would become the co-heiress of her only brother, the 2nd Viscount. The 2nd Viscount Mountmorres was childless and was due to be succeeded as 3rd Viscount by their half-brother, with whom he was on bad terms. Against this background, the 2nd Viscount settled his family seat, Castlemorres, Co. Kilkenny, and as much of the family estate as he could (4,000 Irish acres, valued at £125,000 in 1818) on his two sisters and their issue male in 1782 and confirmed these dispositions by will at his death in 1797. They were unsuccessfully contested in the courts by the unfortunate 3rd Viscount, who understandably was aggrieved that family estates, including the family seat, should have been sundered from the family name and title. In this instance, insult was added to injury. The 2nd Viscount Dungannon, son and heir of the elder sister and Arthur Hill, showed unseemly eagerness to sell his half of the Mountmorres inheritance, including his half of Castlemorres. He complained: 'Its outward appearance is rather grand, but the inside is nothing – small rooms – fit for nothing but a barrack.' He did at least sell his half of the house to the co-heir who owned the other half.[573]

Two other co-heiresses became recognisable as such over approximately the same time-scale as the Morres sisters; these were Jane Countess of Bective and Catherine Lady Longford, sisters of the already-mentioned Hercules Langford Rowley, 2nd Viscount Langford. Lord Bective married Jane Rowley in 1754 and Lord Longford married Catherine Rowley in 1768, at both of which dates three Rowley brothers were living. One died in 1779 and one in 1781. From that point onwards – but not until then – it began to look increasingly likely that the two sisters would each inherit at least one-third of the estates. However, this outcome was not certain until Lord Langford died unmarried in 1796.

Other heiresses, although alive at the time they inherited, had not been identifiable as heiresses at the time of their marriage. The purely English example of Lady Grenville has already been given: she married in 1792 and became an heiress only because her brother, Thomas Pitt, 2nd Lord Camelford, was killed in a duel in 1804. In the case of one fortunate Irishman, his intended, who was not an heiress at the time of their engagement in 1797, had become one by the time of their marriage in 1799. He was Thomas Lefroy (1776–1869), the future lord chief justice, and she was Mary, only surviving child and eventual heiress of Jeffry Paul of Silverspring, Co. Wexford. Lefroy had been a TCD contemporary

'SPECULATIONS AND CASTLE-BUILDINGS'

and close friend of her only brother, the Rev. Thomas Paul, via whom he first met Paul's sister. As Lefroy's father, a retired army officer with some – but not a great deal of – property in Limerick, was still alive, and as Lefroy's ability to support a wife depended on how well he did at the bar, it appears to have been agreed that the couple might become officially or unofficially engaged, but that the marriage must await developments. By June 1798 Lefroy was an accepted member of the Paul family. Later in that year, however, 'Tom Paul, a vigorous young man in robust health…, died suddenly. Mary now became heiress of the Paul estates and, eventually, a moderately wealthy woman.'[574] Only this unforeseeable accident, combined with Lefroy's early-displayed promise as a barrister, permitted Mary Paul and him to marry as soon as they did.

Because the timing of these events was tight and is crucial to an understanding of them, his motives have generally been misrepresented. The myth, fostered somewhat surprisingly by his descendants (presumably because it makes a good story), has grown up that he had formed an attachment to Jane Austen, whom he then jilted in order to marry an heiress. The connection with Jane Austen is accurate enough: her father's parish of Steventon was next-door to the Hampshire parish of Lefroy's uncle, the Rev. Peter Isaac Lefroy, vicar of Ashe. But, if an attachment ever existed, it was ended by Lefroy's engagement to his best friend's sister, who was not an heiress at the time.

Another category of heiress was one who was alive at the time of her marriage, was recognised as being an heiress, but in the end turned out to be much richer than had been imagined. Ireland was blessed with few buried treasures of this type. The value of land held no great surprises, unless it was suddenly inflated by mineral discovery or urban development, neither of which was an event of common occurrence in Ireland. There were no Irish equivalents of the famous Mary Davies, who brought the manor of Ebury, alias Belgravia, into the possession of the ancestor of the dukes of Westminster in 1677; or of that other great London heiress, Lady Rachel Wriothesley, who – through a marriage which 'on both sides was also a passionate love match' – brought Bloomsbury and Covent Garden into the possession of the dukes of Bedford in 1669.[575] However, a few fortunate Irishmen married non-Irish ladies who bore some resemblance to these archetypal heiresses.

One such was the 3rd Earl of Rosse and the English heiress, or rather co-heiress, whom he married in 1836, Mary Field. Over and above her marriage portion of £20,000, Lady Rosse received in the fullness of time £8,700 in cash and the Yorkshire estates of Heaton and Shipley, near Bradford, valued c.1840 at £88,000, subject to a mortgage of £10,000. This meant that she was worth c.£100,000 – a wonderful windfall for the earls of Rosse, who were not rich enough to support an earldom predicated on the unfulfilled assumption that it would be accompanied by the Harman estate. Lady Rosse's younger sister and co-heiress, Delia Duncombe, had been endowed with cash and property to an equivalent value. But all her Yorkshire land was and remained rural, whereas

THE PURSUIT OF THE HEIRESS

Heaton and Shipley, though rural c.1840 and valued accordingly, were increasingly absorbed into the urban outgrowth of Bradford. Whatever the relativities of c.1840, Lady Rosse became, for reasons unforeseeable then, the richer co-heiress of the two,[576] just as the dukes of Bedford – on a hugely grander scale – had been fortunate in Lady Rachel Wriothesley's share of the supposedly rural estates of her father.

One Irishman who married into great English mineral wealth was, obviously, Lord Stewart, later the 3rd Marquess of Londonderry. This was obvious at the time of his marriage to Frances Anne Vane-Tempest in 1819. However, if she was a rich mine-owner in 1819, she was a great deal richer by the time of his death in 1854. His own efforts, it should be said, and not just luck, had a good deal to do with this happy development.[577]

Another Irishman who married the heiress to great, but in this case wholly unrecognised, mineral wealth was the Hon. Windham Quin, later 2nd Earl of Dunraven, whose wife was Caroline Wyndham, heiress to Clearwell Court, Gloucestershire, and Dunraven Castle, Glamorganshire, and their accompanying estates. She was an heiress whose riches were (in a different sense from that intended by Katherine Conolly) 'all to come'; as has been seen, Windham Quin had wondered, before he finally committed himself, if he might not be better-off with a wife whose 'fortune would be *present*'. In spite of these reservations, the marriage went ahead in 1810.[578] In 1815, after his wife's father had died, Windham Quin confusingly double-barrelled his surname, becoming Windham Wyndham-Quin; and when his own father was advanced to an Irish earldom in 1822, he confusingly took his title from Mrs Wyndham-Quin's Welsh estate (though Dunraven actually sounds like a name straight out of Maria Edgeworth).

At this stage, the Welsh and English estate was only beginning 'to recover from its former bad management' and was still crippled with debts incurred by the wildly extravagant Wyndhams.[579] Money was short, and there were wrangles with Mrs Wyndham-Quin's mother over the furniture, china and linen at Dunraven Castle, and the financial responsibility for the upkeep of the place. Early in 1817, however, relations temporarily took a sufficiently affectionate turn for Mrs Wyndham to offer her heiress-daughter a present of £50 to enable her to attend a ball at Dublin Castle.[580] Caroline Wyndham-Quin was hardly the Cinderella which this episode would suggest. But the disposable income out of her estate seems to have been only of the order of £1,500 a year. And although the potential of the Welsh estate was already recognised as being greater than that of the Gloucestershire, this was because the former was 'chiefly on old leases and underlet', not because anyone seems yet to have realised that Dunraven Castle was, almost literally, perched upon a coalmine.

The discovery of coal transformed the situation and the magnitude of Caroline Wyndham-Quin's, now Lady Dunraven's, inheritance. No longer did Lady Dunraven have to stay away from the ball, or Lord Dunraven have to invest money saved out of his Irish rental 'in the improvement of the [Welsh] estates and of your income'.581 Henceforth, the Welsh estate subsidised the Irish, particularly during the Famine (just as the 3rd Earl of Rosse's Yorkshire estates financed his employment schemes and other acts of benevolence on his Co. Offaly estate during the same period of crisis). As has been seen, the income of the Welsh estate eventually became so large in relation to that of the Gloucestershire that the latter, along with Clearwell Court, could be hived off on a younger son without significant loss to the head of the family. None of this could have been foreseen in 1810. At that stage, Caroline Wyndham was recognisable as an heiress, but the scale of her inheritance was not understood. Had it been, her trustees might well have driven a hard bargain and ensured that the whole of her estate would pass to a younger son, who would of course have been called Wyndham, not Wyndham-Quin.

From this, it would be logical to infer that, when the size of an inheritance was completely underestimated at the time of an heiress's marriage, or if the inheritance itself came much later and out of the blue, there were unlikely to be strings attaching it to a second son. This was literally and legally true. But the idea of cadet inheritance died hard: partly because of the ingrained predisposition to perpetuate the heiress's name in conjunction with her estate; partly because of the convenience of providing in land for a second son who would otherwise have to be provided for in (probably borrowed) money; and partly because of the natural desire of fond parents, aunts and uncles to give a second son, who had had none of the luck so far, the benefit of any windfall which occurred. These considerations help to explain why the Fitzwilliam and part of the Dorchester estates passed to second sons of the fortunate families who inherited them. It was purely by chance that they were subsequently reunited or united to the Pembroke and Portarlington estates through the succession of scions of the cadet line to the earldoms of Pembroke and Portarlington. The same thing had already happened in the case of the Thomond estate – only the other way round. In that case, it was the failure of the cadet line of Percy Wyndham O'Brien, Earl of Thomond, coupled with his intestacy, which united the Thomond estate in Ireland to the earldom of Egremont.

The Conyngham family, by contrast, kept their Burton and Conyngham inheritances separate – or almost entirely so – forever. When Henry Conyngham, only Earl Conyngham, died in 1781, he was succeeded by special remainder in the barony of Conyngham by his sister's elder son, Francis Pierpont Burton of Buncraggy (d.1787), who assumed the additional surname of

The 12th Earl of Pembroke, from an engraving of c.1840 by Holl after a portrait by Chalon of c.1830. On the death of his father, the 11th Earl, in 1827, the Pembroke estates in England passed to the 12th Earl, while the Fitzwilliam estates in Ireland passed to the 12th Earl's half-brother, the Hon. Sidney Herbert. They were reunited in 1862 when the 12th Earl died without issue and Sidney Herbert's son succeeded as 13th Earl.

AUTHOR'S COLLECTION

Conyngham. He was left the Conyngham estates in Co. Limerick and in Kent. But the Conyngham estates at Slane, Co. Meath, and in Co. Donegal, passed to her second son, William Burton, who also assumed the additional surname of Conyngham. When William Burton Conyngham died unmarried in 1796, the Meath and Donegal estates went to the elder son of the late F.P. Burton Conyngham, 2nd Lord Conyngham. (He had succeeded as 3rd Lord Conyngham in 1787, and was created Earl Conyngham in 1797 and Marquess Conyngham in 1816.) But they were again kept separate from the Burton patrimonial estate in Co. Clare, which had gone to the second son, Francis Nathaniel Burton, at his father's death in 1787.

This separation of the Clare estate from the Donegal and Meath made some geographical as well as genealogical sense: Donegal and Meath lie some distance apart, but Slane at least lies on the route (or on a possible route) between Donegal and Dublin. It might be expected that accidental inheritance through a woman would in most other instances produce nonsenses in geographical terms (as marriage to a known heiress often did).[582] But this was not always so. Two successive instances of such an inheritance, which took place in two successive generations of the one family, were so geographically convenient that they give a misleading impression of strategic planning. The family concerned is the Creighton family, Earls Erne, of Crom Castle, Newtownbutler, Co. Fermanagh, and the two inheritances, which took effect in 1792 and 1829 respectively, were of substantial estates which virtually adjoined the Crom estate of the Creightons (itself acquired through a marriage of 1655).[583]

The first of these acquisitions through marriage was the Knockballymore estate, Magheraveely, Co. Fermanagh, just over the county boundary from Clones, Co. Monaghan, and located between Clones and Newtownbutler. In 1742, Meliora Creighton (1706–92), sister of the 1st Lord Erne, married Nicholas Ward of Knockballymore. Nicholas Ward's parents were Bernard Ward, great-uncle of Judge Michael Ward of Castle Ward, Strangford, Co. Down (father of the 1st Viscount Bangor), and Jane, *née* Davys, heiress of her brother, Edward Davys of Knockballymore, who died without issue at some date post-1701. Nicholas Ward had succeeded to Knockballymore by 1718; so he must have been considerably older than Meliora Creighton, his wife. Their son was called Bernard Smith Ward because of an inheritance from a family called Smith of Knockneshamer, Co. Sligo, who may also have been related to the Wards via Jane Davys. From the Smiths came the Ward estates in Connaught (comprising, in 1750, at least 1,300 Irish acres in Co. Mayo and 1,200 in Co. Sligo).

Nicholas Ward died in 1751 and Bernard Smith Ward in 1770. Under the latter's will, the Ward estates were to belong to his widowed mother, Meliora, for her life and then pass to her brother's son, the 1st Earl Erne. The bequest took effect at her death in 1792. Years later, from 1874 to the early 1880s, the 3rd Earl Erne was to employ Capt. Charles Cunningham Boycott as his agent for the Mayo estate, at Lough Mask, near Cong, with consequences which added a word to the English language. The 1st Earl's inheritance from the Wards, particularly of Knockballymore, had two unusual features. First, it was distinctly uncommon for aristocrats to marry their county neighbours. Secondly, it was equally uncommon for a collateral relation in the female line to be preferred to a collateral relation in the male, particularly when healthy, male Wards were in abundant supply. On both counts, the Creightons were very lucky. But their good luck could not have been foreseen in 1742 or until 1770.

In 1797 they did it again. This time the estate concerned, which was called Aghalane and was near Crom but on the opposite side of the lough, had previously belonged to another, and the senior, branch of the Creighton family. It had passed out of family possession in 1738, when John Creighton of Aghalane and Killynick died without a son, and in his will directed that his estate should be sold and the proceeds divided among his six daughters. The purchaser was Samuel Cooke, later Sir Samuel, alderman of the city of Dublin. Cooke's daughter, Anne, married Walter Weldon, a member of the Weldon family of Rahenderry, Co. Laois, and by 1784 Aghalane was owned jointly by Mrs Anne Weldon, now a widow, and her son by Walter Weldon, Samuel Cooke Weldon. Then, by an extraordinary coincidence, one of the Weldons' two daughters, Jane, married in 1797 Colonel the Hon. John Creighton, second son of the 1st Earl Erne and father of the 3rd. At this stage, Jane Weldon was simply a well-portioned wife (she brought the large sum of £17,000 to John Creighton as her portion). But soon afterwards, her only brother, Samuel Cooke Weldon, died leaving as his co-heiresses Jane and his other sister. In 1816, the Weldon estates (of which only Aghalane was in Co. Fermanagh) were partitioned between the co-heiresses, the Aghalane estate going (for obvious reasons) to Jane Creighton. From 1829, it became part of what was called in mid-nineteenth-century Erne estate records 'the Killynick estate'. Following a purchase of additional land to the value of £19,382 in the period 1842–52, this combined Killynick estate had a total acreage of 1,798 (Irish). No planning, however careful, could have produced a more satisfactory outcome than the addition of Knockballymore and Killynick to the Creighton portfolio. And, yet, no planning had been involved.

Another heiress whose estate was geographically convenient to the relation to whom it passed, was Grace Boyle, Countess of Middlesex. She was the only child and heiress of Field-Marshal the 2nd Viscount Shannon (1675–1740) of Ashley Park, Surrey, and Shannon Park, Carrigaline, near Cork City. His first wife had been an illegitimate member of the Sackville family, and Grace, his daughter by his second marriage, made a prestigious marriage in 1744 to the Sackville heir, Charles Sackville, Earl of Middlesex, later (1765) 2nd Duke of Dorset. Although Grace Boyle's father was dead and the marriage grand enough to turn most people's heads, her guardians or trustees took good care of her interests. In the event of the marriage proving childless, which it did, she was to retain control of her own inheritance. When she died in 1763 (before her husband succeeded to the dukedom of Dorset), she left her Shannon Park, Co. Cork, estate to a Boyle kinsman, subject only to a life interest which seems to have expired in or by 1778.

The Boyle kinsman, appropriately, was called Lord Shannon (an earldom of that name having be re-created for his father in 1756), and his smallish patrimonial property was located elsewhere in the same county, at Castlemartyr, Clonakilty and Courtmacsherry. In 1740, the rental of the Shannon Park estate had stood at £2,300 which by 1820 had risen to £4,800. The importance of this windfall to Lady Middlesex's Boyle kinsman, the 2nd Earl of Shannon, can be gauged by the fact that in 1791 his total landed income (Shannon Park included) was just over £6,000, according to his own calculation. The Shannon Park inheritance relieved him from the serious financial difficulties he was then experiencing. It also reunited in the person of a Boyle two sections of the vast Munster estate built up by his and Lady Middlesex's common ancestor, the 'Great' Earl of Cork.[584] The Boyle motto is 'God's providence mine inheritance'. But there was in fact more planning than providence in this happy outcome because it derived from testamentary selection, not from the accidents of marriage.

Geographical (and genealogical) appropriateness gave added value to any windfall inheritance. So, too, did opportunities vouchsafed to the heir apparent for future planning or current management prior to his actual succession to the estate. Obviously, this last desideratum could not be realised until his inheritance was assured, and often not even then. This, for example, was the bitter experience of Thomas Conolly, whose Wentworth inheritance via his mother materialised well within his own lifetime, but sourced his last years with interfamilial disputes and lawsuits, running from 1795 almost until his death in 1803. More generally, if the heir apparent were the remainderman under a family settlement, the current possessor of the estate might resent his very existence or might be unwilling to accept the fact of his own childlessness. (An heir apparent chosen by him and named in his will was much more likely to be welcome than an heir apparent chosen for him by a previous settlement.) Equally obviously, the heir apparent could have no involvement with the running of the estate if his identity – like that of Lord Pembroke – were unknown until the last minute. The Petty-Fitzmaurice inheritance was a freak in this latter respect. Henry Lord Shelburne's last child (a second son) died in 1750, so his nephew, the Hon. John Fitzmaurice, was not the recognised heir apparent until then. Fitzmaurice remained on this footing for only a year, at the end of which Lord Shelburne died and Fitzmaurice succeeded. However, for some time prior to 1750 he had been acting (as has been noted) as manager of the absentee Shelburne's affairs in Ireland. So, by coincidence, he already possessed long experience of the estate by the time he came into it.

Clearer examples of this are the fairly long-expected inheritance by the 2nd Earl of Roden of the Clanbrassill estate in 1802 and the inheritance by Colonel Charles Vereker of the Prendergast Smyth estate in 1817.

James Hamilton, 1st Viscount Limerick and later (1756) 1st Earl of Clanbrassill, had married in 1729. There were two children: James, his only son and successor (as 2nd Earl of Clanbrassill in 1758), b.1729; and Anne, b.1730. In 1752 she married the Hon. Robert Jocelyn, later 1st Earl of Roden (1731–97). Her brother, James, the 2nd Earl of Clanbrassill, married much later, in 1774. Prior to this, speculation had been rife as to the future destination of his estate. In 1772, it had been noted that he was 'forty-five, an English member [of parliament], has an employment of £3,000 a year and an estate of £7,000, a most domestic man, the last of his family and yet will not marry, so that Lord Roden has a good chance'. In the event, Clanbrassill's marriage proved childless, and Lord Roden's 'good chance' became a probability. Whether his sister became his heiress presumptive because of the provisions of their parents' marriage settlement or because of a personal decision made by Clanbrassill, is unclear. The more important consideration is that Clanbrassill and his heirs, the Jocelyns, worked together for their mutual advantage. Clanbrassill returned his Jocelyn nephews for his borough of Dundalk, Co. Louth, and his electoral influence there and in Co. Louth was exercised to obtain offices and emoluments for the by-no-means affluent Jocelyns.

When he died in 1798, his estates passed for the remainder of her life to his sister, Anne Countess of Roden, on whose death in 1802 they devolved on her eldest son, the 2nd Earl of Roden (1752–1820). By then they had been reduced, by enforced sales for the payment of debt, to the Dundalk estate, Co. Louth, and the Tollymore estate, Bryansford, Co. Down, on both of which there were modest family seats. Most of the small and scattered Roden estates further south, mainly in Co. Tipperary, were also sold (the Roden seat of Brockley Park, Stradbally, Co. Laois, passed to a younger brother of the 2nd Earl). After the Union, an English property and, preferably, seat were desirable adjuncts to any major Irish family. Clanbrassill's English estate at Mentmore in Buckinghamshire had long since been sold. But, in 1778, the 1st Earl of Roden had inherited the English baronetcy and English seat of Hyde Hall, Sawbridgeworth, Hertfordshire, which up to then had been enjoyed by the senior line of the Jocelyn family. Hyde Hall more than compensated for Mentmore; and the combined, if depleted, Clanbrassill and Roden estates were now geopolitically rationalised and disencumbered of debt. Dundalk survived, though as a single-member constituency, and a Jocelyn sat at Westminster for Co. Louth. So, family influence was still considerable, and the 3rd Earl of Roden was created a UK baron in 1821. He took Clanbrassill as his title.[585]

The Prendergast Smyth and Vereker families represented the coming together of three estates.[586] Sir Thomas Prendergast, 2nd Bt (c.1700–1760), of Gort Castle, Co. Galway, died without issue male and chose as his principal heir John Prendergast Smyth (1742–1817), the second son of his sister, Elizabeth. The Smyths were a family prominent in Limerick City and County, particularly the former (where they were the major property-owners in the old 'Englishtown').

THE PURSUIT OF THE HEIRESS

Charles Smyth, Elizabeth Prendergast's husband, was the son of a former bishop of Limerick who had prospered exceedingly. Charles Smyth represented Limerick City in parliament, 1731–76, and was succeeded in the representation by his eldest son, Thomas, 1776–85, and then by his second son, John, 1785–97. It was originally intended that the eldest son should inherit the Smyth estates and the second the Prendergast. But Thomas Smyth died young and unmarried in 1785, a third brother also died young, and both inheritances merged in John, who was created Baron Kiltarton in 1810 and Viscount Gort in 1816.

John Prendergast Smyth seems to have been a confirmed, sybaritic bachelor. In 1782 he was described as 'a gentlemanlike, drawing-room man', and in 1802 (by a Dublin Castle official who was fed up with his alarmist accounts of the state of Co. Limerick) as 'a respectable, elegant and amiable man, ... [whose] judgement, and particularly ... nerves, I have no opinion of. He is the very man to be [thrown] into consternation by the idea of the town in which he lives being sacked: his china would be broken and his favourite ladies all – Lord knows what!'[587] From 1785 onwards, it looked increasingly likely that Smyth's combined inheritance would pass to or through his sister, Juliana (d.1811), wife of their cousin, Thomas Vereker (d.1801) of Roxborough, in the liberties of Limerick City. Thomas and Juliana Vereker had married in 1759, at a time when this seemed a most improbable eventuality, because she then had three brothers living. Thomas Vereker is thus yet another example of a man who married an heiress who was unrecognisable as such at the time of the marriage. He himself was not in a position to contribute much to the Smyth and Prendergast amalgam of estates because he had run through most of his own through improvidence. But the Roxborough property was at least a useful adjunct to the Smyth political interest in Limerick City.

The Verekers had, among other children, two sons. Henry, the heir apparent, was killed in a duel in 1792. So, the succession devolved on the second son, Charles (1768–1842). 'A handsome, vulgar, forward Irishman',[588] Charles Vereker was the antithesis of his elegant uncle, John Prendergast Smyth. He had served in the army, and so was appointed to succeed his uncle as colonel of the Limerick City Militia, in which capacity he outwitted General Humbert at Collooney, Co. Sligo, in September 1798, and diverted the French from marching into Ulster. He replaced his uncle as the Smyth representative for Limerick City (1794–1800 and 1802–17), and in 1817 succeeded by special remainder to his uncle's peerages and to estates nominally worth nearly £18,000 a year. In anticipation of this event, he had commissioned John Nash to build a Gothick castle on the Lough Cutra part of the Gort estate, which John Prendergast Smyth had made over to him in 1810.

Charles Smyth, MP for Limerick (1731–76), and his daughter Juliana, wife of Thomas Vereker and mother of the 2nd Viscount Gort, by Hugh Douglas Hamilton, c.1770

AUTHOR'S COLLECTION

'SPECULATIONS AND CASTLE-BUILDINGS'

At the time of John Prendergast Smyth, 1st Viscount Gort's, death in 1817, it looked as if harmonious family relationships and timely succession-planning had safely tided the family over the two successive breaks in the male succession which had recently occurred. However, it was then discovered that, in addition to the settlement and other charges which were known to affect the estate, the late Lord Gort had run up personal debts to the astonishing amount of £60,000, and that these too were now a lien upon it. Charles Vereker, the 2nd Viscount, had incurred debts of his own in building Lough Cutra, fighting Limerick City elections and salvaging Roxborough and other parts of the Vereker estate which his father had not alienated irretrievably. He had intended to recoup himself for this laudable expenditure out of the cash he assumed he would inherit from his uncle, but instead of cash was faced with further and unexpected debt. He sold outlying portions of the Smyth, Prendergast and Vereker estates, but still found it a struggle to keep up the interest payments. The Famine more-or-less ended the struggle. Soon after the 2nd Viscount Gort's death, his son, the 3rd Viscount, whose estates were still valued at £150,000, fell victim to a punitive clause in the Encumbered Estates Act which brought down many landowners similarly situated on the margins of solvency. Despite heroic efforts to save it, the Gort estate was sold up in 1851.[589]

In this instance, advance notice of the future destination of the estates, and advance planning for their exploitation, rationalisation and administration, all went for nothing because of the day-to-day mismanagement (a major theme of the concluding chapter) and personal extravagance of John Prendergast Smyth, 1st Viscount Gort. In the next, and final, instance of a female inheritance which took effect time enough for forward planning to be possible, the results were mixed. The modest success of the Clanbrassill-Roden handover was not replicated, but the financial collapse of the Gorts was not replicated either. One principal obstacle to forward planning and dynastic success in this instance was that the heir apparent, the Hon. Charles Dillon (1745–1813), was not made aware of his expectations until surprisingly late in the day, and not until he had involved himself in an unascertainable but crippling amount of debt, which, for the rest of his life, disabled him from making the most of his inheritance.[590]

Charles Dillon's mother, Lady Charlotte Lee, eldest sister of the 3rd Earl of Lichfield, had married his father, Henry Dillon, 11th Viscount Dillon, in 1744; and in 1772, when Lord Lichfield died childless, he left the Lichfield estates to his eldest sister's eldest son, Charles Dillon, subject to a life-interest to a

'A handsome, vulgar, forward Irishman', Colonel Charles Vereker, 2nd Viscount Gort: engraved by J. Heath in 1811 from a drawing from life by John Comerford which was then in the possession of Sir Jonah Barrington.

AUTHOR'S COLLECTION

childless, elderly uncle who succeeded as 4th and last earl of Lichfield and died in 1776. The Lee/Lichfield estates were located at Ditchley in Oxfordshire and Quarendon in Buckinghamshire, and with them came a great house, Ditchley Park, built for the 2nd Earl of Lichfield by James Gibbs.[591] Lady Charlotte's situation as the mother of the eventual heir was unrecognisable in 1744, because her brother, the 3rd Earl, had not yet married at the time and other collateral male Lees (besides the future 4th Earl) were waiting in the wings and might have produced sons. Until the 3rd Earl died in 1772, his intentions were unclear. All the *Peerages* state that it was Lady Charlotte who inherited the estates in 1776, and imply that this was the effect of some previous settlement and that she was her brother's heir presumptive. None of this is correct. The two obstacles to forward planning for the combined Lee and Dillon inheritances in the period 1744–76 were that the ultimate destination of the Lee estates was unknown until 1772, and that Lady Charlotte and the 11th Viscount Dillon almost certainly resented the fact that the 3rd Earl had by-passed her in favour of their son, with whom they were not on good terms.

Apart from the fact that the Lee estate was in England and the Dillon in Ireland, the Dillons were in some major respects suitable heirs. Both families were long-established: the Dillons were the more ancient, but the Lees could boast royal, though illegitimate, descent from Charles II. The tradition of both families was Roman Catholic and Jacobite, though the 3rd Earl of Lichfield became a Hanoverian Tory under George III and, more surprisingly, the 11th Viscount Dillon also became a frequenter of the latter's Court.[592] Originally, Lord Dillon had been colonel of Dillon's Regiment in the service of the King of France, and had lived in France until 1744. In that year, which was also the year in which he married Lady Charlotte Lee, he deemed it prudent to leave France and take up residence in England. This did not betoken a shift in his allegiance (although such a shift did gradually take place): it was a prudential move, designed to protect the extensive Irish estates in counties Mayo and Roscommon which Lord Dillon had inherited in 1741, from the provisions of the Penal Laws passed by the Irish parliament, particularly a recent act of 1738 by which the estates of those in foreign service were automatically forfeited.[593] In religion, there certainly was no shift of allegiance: both Lord Dillon and Lady Charlotte, his wife, remained staunch Roman Catholics for the rest of their days.

Not so Lord Lichfield. Probably as a result of his marriage to a Protestant in 1745, he changed his religion – to the indignation of his mother and his sister, Lady Charlotte. The Dillons' son, Charles, followed his example in 1767. This may have had a bearing on Lord Lichfield's choice of heir. It certainly caused great bitterness within the Dillon family, provoking his parents to accuse Charles Dillon of 'changing my religion upon interested motives', which he stoutly denied.

> I conformed in September 1767; my uncle died in September 1772. I never knew he intended to leave me his estate, nor did he know at the time that it was

in his power. My father was the first person who apprised me of the disposition he had made, after his death...; and so far from paying any court to him [Lord Lichfield] or using any means to induce him to make me his heir, I neglected him shamefully, ... which I have often been sorry for since, and had not seen him [more than?] twice for a twelvemonth before his death.[594]

Technically, though Charles Dillon also stoutly denied that he had the slightest intention of doing this, his change of religion put it in his power, under the Irish Penal Code, to gain immediate possession of the Dillon estates in Ireland (to which he was heir), and 'put it out of my father's power to make the least provision for my younger brothers and sisters' (who remained Catholics).[595]

The further cause of dissension between Charles Dillon and his parents, which ante-dated the 3rd Earl of Lichfield's bequest, was that Charles Dillon had got himself into serious financial difficulties through racing and gambling – 'dissipation and extravagance', as he acknowledged that it had been – which necessitated his living abroad in Brussels. He reckoned his debts at £30,000–£35,000.[596] But this fell very far short of the gross amount: rather, it was what he called

> a reasonable composition.... My creditors hold their demands upon me by a tenure which is very precarious with any man – I mean my own life. The bargains I have made with them are almost all illegal, being usurious in the highest degree. A court of equity would set them aside by compelling those who have advanced the money to take back their principal with the legal interest of five per cent; and although I would not upon any consideration avail myself of such a remedy, which I hold to be dishonourable, yet the intimation of such an intention ... could not fail of producing the desired effect.... I have not received one-third of the money which constitutes the nominal debt, and in many cases not one-fifth.[597]

This implies that the gross amount of his debts was of the order of £100,000–plus. It also suggests that Lord Lichfield can have known nothing about his nephew's improvidence when he made him his heir. Had he known, and had he still wanted to settle the Lee estates on the Dillons, Lord Lichfield could have left them to Charles Dillon's mother or to trustees, instead of to Charles Dillon himself, and they might then have been kept clear of the latter's debts.

The matter of the debts became pressing in March–July 1776, because Charles Dillon was in hot negotiation to marry.[598] He had not yet come into the Lichfield estates because the elderly 4th Earl with a life interest in them did not die until November. So he had no alternative but to persuade his father to re-settle the Dillon estates in Ireland. As part of this deal, Charles Dillon had hoped to be able to raise £30,000 off the estates for the satisfaction of at least the most pressing claims (or perhaps for the payment of a percentage to all the claimants?). In the end, it seems to have been agreed that the sum should be

£20,000.[599] On this basis, a reconciliation between his parents and him was patched up and his marriage went ahead.

On the death of the 4th Earl of Lichfield, Charles Dillon double-barrelled his name to Dillon-Lee. This not only signalled his succession to the estates of the Lees but also his intention of embarking on a dynastic quest to get the 'honours ... now extinct' of the Lee family revived in his own person.[600] Actually, this quest had begun immediately after the death of the 3rd Earl in 1772, when the 4th Earl had requested that 'Mr Dillon (upon whom he [the 3rd Earl] has entailed his estate) might be allowed to accompany ... [the 4th Earl to an audience with George III], in hopes that it might possibly prove an introduction of the young gentleman to a peerage one day or other.'[601] The extinction of the Lichfield honours in 1776, Dillon-Lee's reconciliation with his father, who had some influence with the government and at Court, and Dillon-Lee's choice of wife, strengthened his claims to be promoted to at least a British barony of Lichfield. Mrs Dillon-Lee was the Hon. Henrietta Phipps, sister of the 2nd Lord Mulgrave (1744–92) and of his successor, the 3rd Lord and 1st Earl of Mulgrave (1755–1801), who were (from 1777) increasingly prominent members of the British government. In June 1779, Dillon-Lee was assured by his father 'that, if I had not been in the situation I am [i.e. crippled by debt], I should certainly before this time have been a peer of England, that he knew that the K[ing] had a personal regard for me, and that he [George III] had expressed it upon several occasions'.[602]

In 1787 his pretensions to a British peerage were strengthened by his father's death and his succession as 12th Viscount Dillon and to the Irish estates. In the interim, his much-loved wife, Henrietta Phipps, had died (in 1782), but as she had borne him a daughter and a son and heir, Henry Augustus (1777–1832), her influential Phipps relations still had a strong vested interest in the success of his application for a British peerage. According to the Dillon entry in *Burke's Peerage*, which no doubt was based on family information, he was twice offered an (Irish) earldom, in 1789 and 1800, and on both occasions refused it. These dates coincide with the political crises over the Regency and the Union respectively. Dillon's influence in the Irish parliament was too trifling for any such offer to have been made to him as an inducement to support the Dublin Castle line on the Regency; but, when numerous creations of peers and promotions in the peerage were made after the event, he might well, as the holder of an ancient viscountcy, have been offered a step to preserve his seniority. If so, he presumably refused it in order to make it clear that he wanted a British peerage, or nothing. In 1794, he applied direct to Pitt for a re-creation of at least the most junior title of the Lee family, but without success.

In 1797, he tried again, this time via the Lord Lieutenant of Ireland, who received a stern rebuff from the Home Secretary, the 3rd Duke of Portland:

> I must not ... omit to represent to you that the character he bears in this kingdom [England], as well in the country as in town, was such as to occasion his

society to be shunned by those who wished to be well thought of; ... and I have always understood that his setting up his residence in Ireland was owing partly ... to the greater facility with which an introduction is obtained into the best company and first circle in that than in this country.[603] With that impression upon my own mind, ... you will not blame me for the averseness I feel to support his wishes for an English peerage.[604]

It is interesting to speculate about what Dillon had done to 'occasion his society to be shunned'. It is possible that his second marriage in 1787 to his mistress, a Belgian actress called Marie Rogier, harmed him socially. However, the three children she bore him, one of them a son, were born in wedlock, and his heir was the son of his previous marriage to Henrietta Phipps. It is possible that he had done something during his racing and gambling days which was sufficiently damaging to character to cause the *élite* of the turf to proscribe him. Perhaps, for all his professions of 1776 to the contrary, he really had tried to wriggle out of his debts in a manner which was considered 'dishonourable'? Whatever the precise explanation, it was – essentially – his debts which militated against his aspirations to a British peerage.

A further obstacle was that, for reasons unconnected with Dillon's personal improvidence, both the Lee and the Dillon estates were encumbered and/or unproductive at the respective times when he inherited them. These embarrassments were rooted in family history. In 1674, when Sir Edward Henry Lee, 5th Bt, was created earl of Lichfield in contemplation of his marriage to Charles II's natural daughter, Lady Charlotte Fitzroy, the patent of peerage stated that Lee was worthy of a more ample estate than he had inherited from his ancestors. The deficiency in his inherited estate was made up to him by a marriage portion of £20,000 and a series of pensions and sinecures. One of the latter, the office of custos brevium in the Court of Common Pleas which yielded an erratic, average nett income of c.£1,250 a year, appears to have been annexed to the earldom, and was held by the earls of Lichfield from 1700 to 1776. This office was an important adjunct to a smallish landed income which amounted to no more than c.£7,000 a year gross as late as c.1800: it was an asset which Lord Dillon did *not* inherit.[605] What he did inherit was the debts of the 3rd Earl of Lichfield, who had spent heavily on supporting the Tory cause in Oxfordshire elections (notably that of 1754) and on the prestigious chancellorship of the Tory stronghold of Oxford University which he held from 1762 to his death in 1772. Lord Dillon also inherited the jointures of two dowager countesses of Lichfield, the second of whom lived until 1784.[606] Under these circumstances, he was advised in 1783 to let Ditchley Park, which he could not afford to live in and the rent from which would increase his income out of the Lee estates by £700 a year.[607] He seems to have lived at Ditchley from 1776 until c.1787, after which it may have been intermittently let to strangers.[608]

The Dillon estates in Ireland were also unproductive in the short term, though rents were rising as old leases fell in. It is probable that, during the Penal Era, the

THE PURSUIT OF THE HEIRESS

Dillons had deliberately let some lands on favourable terms to Protestant tenants, in order to give themselves an insurance against Protestant 'discovery'. (Something similar may have been done by the earls of Westmeath, who did not conform to the Established Church until 1751, and many of whose leases were for three lives dating from 1736.)[609] While Dillon's father lived, Dillon received nothing out of the estates except the present maintenance provided under his marriage settlement. It was even suggested that, 'contrary to your idea of the agreement made on your marriage, ... instead of £20,000 you have not power to charge your [father's] estate with a single shilling'.[610] Because of his debts, Dillon was in constant fear of arrest and had to remain in Brussels. Under the impression (probably false) that no debt 'can affect an Irish estate but what is registered in Ireland', he contemplated moving to Ireland in 1783. But he was warned that 'your person will be as much in danger in Dublin as in London, and [that] £1,500 would not put Loughglinn [Charlestown, Co. Roscommon, the Dillon seat] in a proper situation for your reception'.[611] Dillon's financial situation improved or at any rate his borrowing power increased, when his father died in 1787 and he succeeded to the estate; and under his personal superintendence, the gross rental of the estate improved also, and dramatically so, until by 1805 it stood at over £20,000 a year.[612]

This had much to do with his own presence on the spot and personal exertions. He must have moved to Ireland and restored Loughglinn in or before 1787, the year of his father's death, as he served as sheriff of Co. Mayo for that year.[613] In 1788, he successfully established his legal right to sit in the Irish House of Lords – a right which, from a combination of outlawry and absence, no Lord Dillon had exercised for at least a hundred years.[614] In the same year, 1788, he was appointed a governor of Co. Mayo, and in 1796 he raised a yeomanry corps, the Loughglinn Cavalry, on his Mayo and Roscommon estates. In Co. Mayo, he opposed the monopoly of representation and patronage long established by the Brownes of Westport and their then head, the 3rd Earl of Altamont (created marquess of Sligo in 1801 for his services in promoting the Union in Connaught). This may have made him lukewarm in the cause of the Union, which he probably supported, though he is not named among its supporters except by implication.[615] But an offer of an (Irish) earldom is likely

Detail from a portrait of Charles Dillon-Lee, 12th Viscount Dillon, in peer's robes and therefore painted from 1787 onwards; the artist appears to have been Edward Mawbrye

PRIVATE COLLECTION

214

enough to have been made at this time. When Catholic Emancipation did not follow the Union, he annoyed the government by addressing an 'incendiary' letter to the Irish Catholics in February 1801.[616] However, the government could not afford to quarrel with him because at the 1802 general election, he 'frightened' Lord Sligo 'out of *one half* of the County Mayo' and secured one of the county seats for his son, Henry Augustus Dillon.[617] The younger Dillon was four times elected for Co. Mayo, and continued to represent it until he succeeded as 13th Viscount Dillon on his father's death in 1813.

What of course mattered more than Dillon's increased Irish rental and political clout was the *nett* income which he enjoyed from all sources, English as well as Irish, and whether or not it was sufficient to support a British or UK peerage and particularly earldom. There is one good reason for thinking that he did not receive, after the payment of interest charges, more than a fraction of his gross rental. In 1799, when negotiating the marriage settlement of his only daughter by Henrietta Phipps (who was also the only younger child of his first marriage), he stated that her marriage portion of £10,000 could not be paid until after his death.[618] For a man with, nominally, £27,000 a year, who had probably received at least £10,000 with Henrietta Phipps in 1776, this was a remarkable admission. It suggests that he was still crippled by his debts, and implies that, while he had found no way of repudiating them, he was in hopes that his son and successor might be able to do so.

By 1802, however, this optimism had evaporated and he had come to the realisation that only a massive sale of land could free him from his difficulties. Land in England sold in this period for ten or so years' purchase more than land in Ireland, so the Lichfield estate in Buckinghamshire was the one selected for sale. Its rental in 1763 (£4,211 a year) had been liable to deductions totalling about 20 per cent for Land Tax, tithes, and parish dues.[619] Deducting 20 per cent from the gross rental of c.£5,000 forty years on, and assuming that the estate sold for thirty one years' purchase in 1802, it would have realised c.£115,000. This may all have gone to the paying-off of Dillon's debts. It certainly left him with no land in England except the Ditchley estate, which had a rental of only £2,418 gross, plus a house and park which Dillon was currently occupying but which he had sometimes been obliged to let. After 1802, it was more than doubtful if, with his reduced landownership and consequence in England, he was any longer qualified for a UK peerage. His newly established political influence in Ireland strongly reinforced his claims to promotion in the Irish peerage (the very thing which he seems already to have declined), but not to a revival of the English honours of the Lichfields.

The truth was that his (very considerable) effectiveness as an agent of dynastic revival had been blighted in advance by his huge personal debts, to say nothing of the probably unreasonable prejudice which operated against him in government circles on account of 'the character he bears'. Indeed, it is arguable that in 1772, when the 3rd Earl of Lichfield's decision was made, the Lees and the

Dillons were not really 'circumstanced for each other'. Lord Lichfield had acted for the best and at least had concentrated everything on the one inheritor whom he did indeed make 'an eldest son'. Because the break in the male line of the Lees and the extinction of their peerages could not have been anticipated, none of his sisters had married with a view to becoming the family's future heiress; and the eldest, Lady Charlotte, had certainly made the best marriage of them all. The only thing which Lord Lichfield might have done to facilitate forward planning was to have declared his intentions in favour of Charles Dillon-Lee some years sooner than he did (thus causing a family row on the vexed subject of conversion). Because Charles Dillon's position as heir-apparent was unknown and undeclared until the last minute, he had had no idea of what was at stake when he plunged recklessly into debt. Whether he would have behaved differently if he had known that he was heir to more than a cash-strapped Irish viscountcy is open to doubt. But at least there was a possibility that he might.

More generally, it is perhaps not going too far to say that, in the nature of things, and with some partial exceptions like the Roden-Clanbrassill succession, inheritance through an heiress was always compromised by being to some extent unplanned and unplannable. Although the circumstances of the Dillon-Lee case were unusual, they are typical in the sense that they contained a large element of the unexpected. Nobody knew that Lord Lichfield was going to leave the Lee estates to Charles Dillon-Lee, and Lord Lichfield (almost certainly) did not know that Dillon-Lee was a 'ruined' man before the bequest was made, and therefore could not have foreseen that Dillon-Lee's youthful improvidence would preclude him from making a dynastic success of the inheritance. Dillon-Lee was an unexpected *heir*: more usually, the unexpectedness related to an heiress, whether alive or – as was often the case – dead. Marrying an heiress may appear, with hindsight, to have been a simple matter: with the knowledge available at the time of the marriage, it was actually more a matter of 'speculations and castle-buildings'.

EIGHT

The safer and surer routes to riches

The importance of good management, thrift and economy as ingredients in dynastic success has become obvious from a number of the case studies already outlined. The absence of these virtues in the cases of the Earl of Blessington, the 1st Viscount Gort and the 12th Viscount Dillon compromised the dynastic future of their respective families, the first two to the point of ruination. Their presence in the cases of the 3rd Marquess of Londonderry and the 2nd Earl of Dunraven suggests that even the most fortunate of marriages did not, on its own, assure dynastic success. Lord Londonderry's successful exercise of 'entrepreneurial paternalism' has already been mentioned. It was he who took the bold decision to gain for his wife's collieries an export outlet by buying the Seaham estate, Co. Durham, and creating Seaham town and harbour. This was not brought effortlessly to fruition, and involved high risk and heavy borrowing. Indeed, the Londonderrys had to a weather a 'prolonged crisis in their resources', and were 'frequently on the verge of bankruptcy'.[620] The Dunraven collieries, too, were not developed without effort; and Lord Dunraven, like Lord Londonderry, seems to have been a hard-working and conscientious manager of this and his other financial concerns. He even seems to have been able to indulge in the most expensive 'hobby'[621] of all, architecture, without running himself into debt, as witness the sanctimonious inscription carved into the masonry of Adare Manor, which informs the visitor that not a penny of the money expended on its construction was borrowed.

Lord Dunraven has left a more detailed testimonial to his own good management. In 1848, two years before his death, he wrote a long letter to his solicitor in which he contrasted the prudence of his own and Lady Dunraven's behaviour with the imprudence of that of their elder son and daughter-in-law. The letter, like Lord Mark Kerr's, reveals the serious and self-denying aspect of marriage to an heiress:

> My poor friend, Serjeant Goold [the father of Lord Dunraven's daughter-in-law], said to me, 'If my daughter does not bring your son a large fortune, she will save him one, for she is the most economical creature in the world!!' Alas, this all remains to be proved. They are consuming their income with interest,

while their children are of course becoming more expensive every day....

The second season after I married, my sensible wife, finding that the London life was beyond our income, gave it up, and we got rid of our house; and, though a great heiress, she was content to remain in the country when I had to be in London attending parliament. My son and his wife might have done the same. Where should we have been now, if my wife's heart ... had been set upon being a fine lady in London, and I had encouraged her, and it had brought me every year deeper in debt? ... Our course led upwards, theirs leads downwards, and it is very easy to go downhill....

I find that, out of landed property alone, unaided by commerce or by a profession, enough is not yielded to enable one generation to raise the family greatly and firmly, as I wished to do. It requires the concurrence of two generations, and I little thought my successor would begin to undermine what I had built up with such self-denial. It is with great pain I see them following a course where they will sink step by step, till their little boy will be the sacrifice, doomed like so many sons of fine London ladies to cut off entails and pay for their parents' recklessness.

And he concluded by (incorrectly) quoting Juvenal: 'True it is in worldly affairs that *Nullum numen abest* [*recte*: habes] *si sit prudentia*.'[622]

Though his Latin may have been rusty, he was correct in saying that nothing – advantageous marriage included – signified unless accompanied by prudence. Indeed, because of the speculative nature of advantageous marriage, it could itself be regarded as a threat to common prudence. Thomas Conolly was deflected from managing his 'noble' patrimonial estate properly because of the expectation of a great inheritance from his mother; the young, giddy and utterly self-indulgent Kingsboroughs were so carried away by the vastness of Lady Kingsborough's inheritance that they heavily encumbered it by riotous living in the first decade or so after their marriage; Henry Cecil and Emma Vernon reacted similarly, seriously reducing the nett income from her estate as a consequence; and the financially embarrassed 2nd Earl of Glengall was so blown off-course by his marriage to a great heiress that he bankrupted himself and postponed the rationalisation of his affairs for another twenty years and until after he himself was safely dead.

It must also be strongly suspected that the 1st Earl of Clanwilliam never recovered from the delusions of affluence brought on by his marriage in 1765 to the great heiress, Theodosia Magill. By the mid-1790s the couple had run up debts to the tune of £46,250, to which would soon be added the need to provide an annual allowance for their recently married eldest son, £30,000 for portions for their younger children, and a jointure of £3,500 for Lady Clanwilliam in the extremely likely event of her surviving her debauched and dropsical husband. Most of the extravagance which had brought them to this pass had been the fault of Lord Clanwilliam. But Lady Clanwilliam had been extravagant also – for example, commissioning wedding portraits of herself from both Gainsborough and Reynolds (and presumably passing the bill to her husband). Nevertheless,

Wedding portraits of Lady Clanwilliam by Gainsborough and Reynolds, 1765. Lady Clanwilliam had a hook nose, which Gainsborough mitigated by painting her almost full-face: Reynolds accentuated it by painting her more nearly in profile (see p.220). Soon afterwards Reynolds was persuaded to straighten the nose, but not – unfortunately – until after a tell-tale mezzotint had been published.

ULSTER MUSEUM

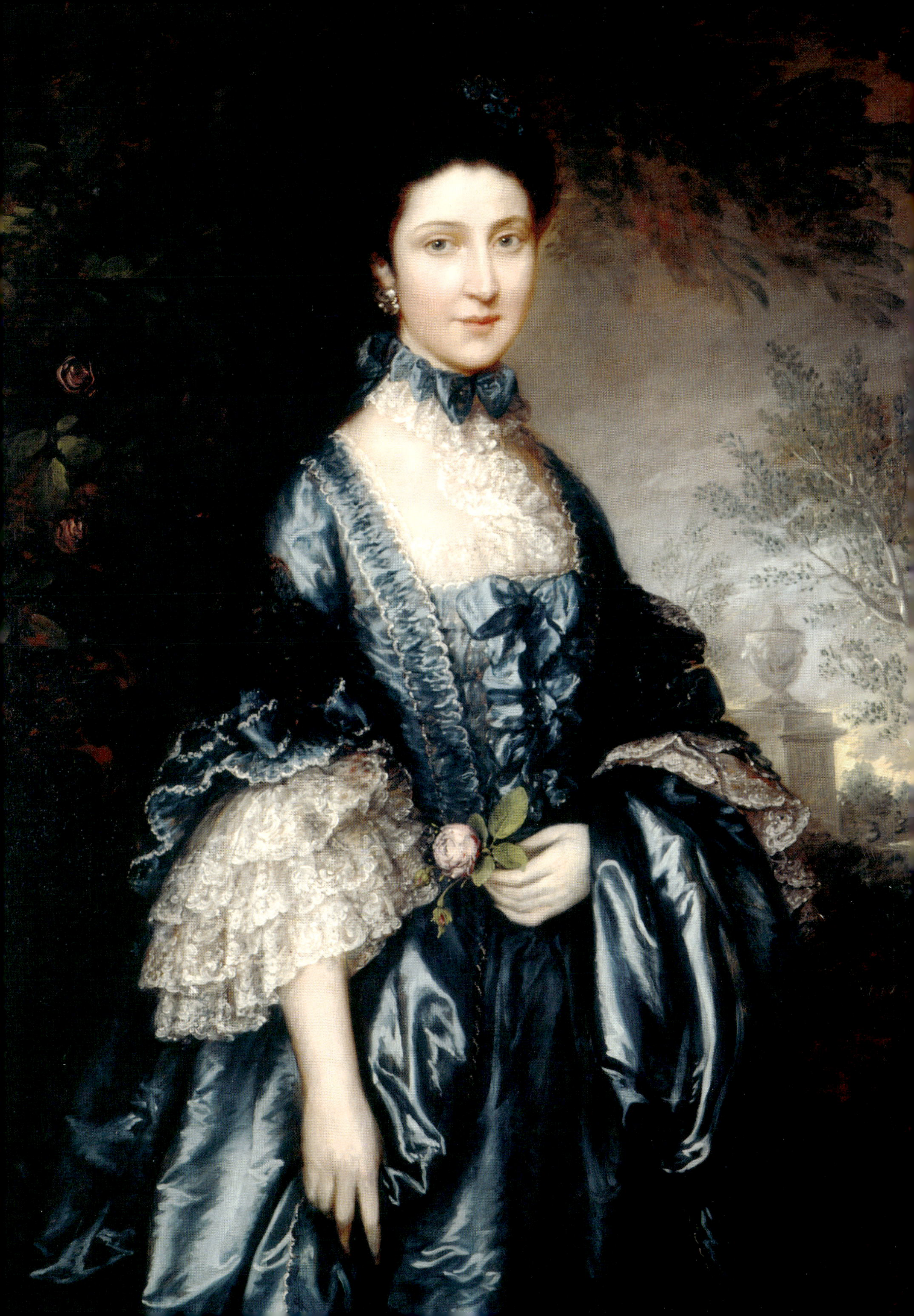

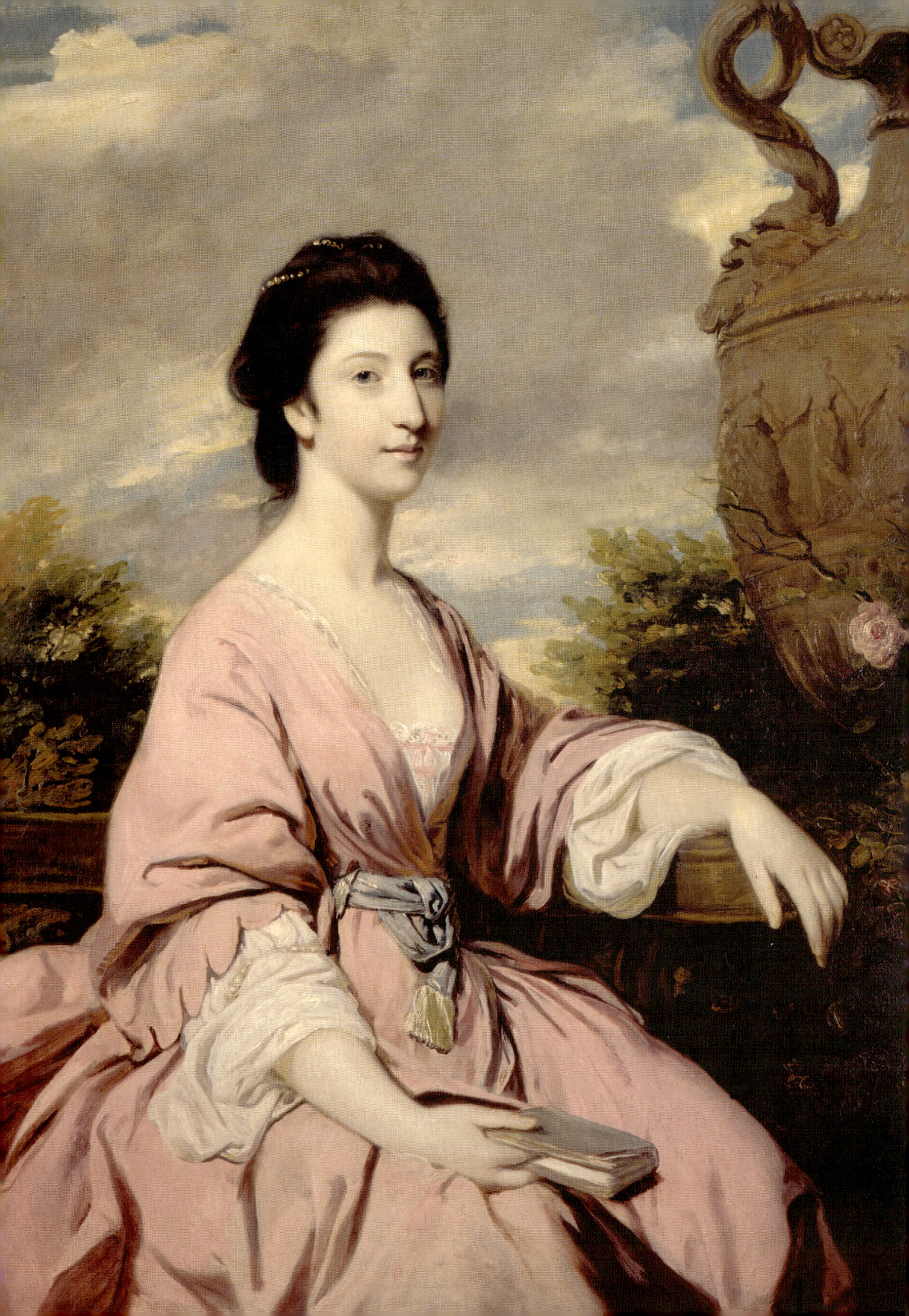

she now made sure that in the two re-settlements of their estates which took place in rapid succession, in 1794 and 1795 respectively, her estate survived intact (subject to some additional charges) and that the income which she personally would draw from it for the rest of her life would be greatly increased. As for Lord Clanwilliam's estate, producing in excess of £11,000 a year in 1793, it was to be sacrificed *in toto* to the re-establishment of their finances. He died in 1800, without having 'one action to look back upon which can give him comfort', and by 1805 not an acre of his patrimonial estate was left. Want of prudence and good management, exacerbated in his case by a natural disposition to vice and extravagance and the *hubris* brought on by marriage to a rich woman, had led to this catastrophe.[623]

Another Irishman brought to destruction because the gods answered his prayers was William Wellesley Pole (1788–1857), son and heir of an elder brother of the Duke of Wellington. Wellesley Pole's father had added the latter name following his inheritance of the Pole estate of Ballyfin, Co. Laois, via a long-dead heiress, his great-aunt, Anne Pole, *née* Colley (d.1745–50?); and Wellesley Pole married a live heiress in 1812 who brought with her a substantial part of the estates and assets of three major English families. These were: the Child family of Wanstead, Essex (a great house re-modelled for the Childs by Colen Campbell in the 1720s); the Tylney family of Rotherwick, Hampshire (whose heiress had married a Child); and the Long family, baronets, of Draycot, Wiltshire, one of whom, Sir James, succeeded in 1784 to all the estates of his maternal uncle, John Child Tylney, 2nd and last Earl Tylney in the peerage of Ireland. Sir James Long Tylney (as he now became) died in 1794, leaving a son and three daughters. The son died, young and unmarried, in 1805; two of the daughters did not marry; and William Wellesley Pole's heiress-wife was the only one who did.

Following the marriage, he changed his name to Pole-Tylney-Long-Wellesley (curiously, the name of Child had long since been dropped, although the bulk of the fortune had originated with this branch of the well known banking family); and in right of his wife, he came into possession of an income variously reckoned at £25,000 and £39,000 a year, 'ready cash' of c.£300,000, the great Palladian mansion of Wanstead and the lesser country house of Rotherwick. He proved incapable of managing this huge accession of wealth, which quite simply turned his head. Initially, his wife's trustees stepped in to curb the inroads he was making into her fortune. But by some legal device their efforts were frustrated, and they failed to preserve the entail of the estates and protect the interests of the two sons and a daughter born to the Long-Wellesleys. Wanstead was demolished in 1822 (the carved supporters from Earl Tylney's arms in the pediment are preserved on gate piers at Castle Forbes, Co. Longford). Long-Wellesley 'died a pauper through his extravagance' in 1857, and his unfortunate wife many years previously, in 1825. She would no doubt have concurred with the obituary notice which stated that he 'was redeemed by no single virtue, adorned by no single grace'.[624]

Wedding portrait of Lady Clanwilliam by Reynolds

ULSTER MUSEUM

THE PURSUIT OF THE HEIRESS

Francis Rawdon, later Rawdon-Hastings (1754–1826), 1st Lord Rawdon (1783), 2nd Earl of Moira (1793) and 1st Marquess of Hastings (1817), was not a graceless, squalid wastrel like Long-Wellesley (and Lord Clanwilliam). In fact, he was a high achiever. But, like them, he was a living demonstration of the truth of *'Nullum numen habes si sit prudentia'*. As the elder son and heir of the 1st Earl of Moira, he had been in line from birth for the Rawdon estates in counties Down and Meath, and inherited these in 1793. Prior to that, in 1789, he had succeeded to the Leicestershire, Warwickshire and other estates of his mother's childless brother, Francis Hastings, 10th Earl of Huntingdon.[625] Lord Huntingdon had three younger brothers and two sisters; but the brothers had all pre-deceased him and only one of his sisters, Lady Elizabeth, Lord Rawdon's mother, had married. Having come into this major English inheritance via his heiress-mother, Lord Rawdon, now 2nd Earl of Moira, himself proceeded to marry, in 1804, a considerable Scottish heiress, Lady Flora Mure Campbell, daughter and heiress of the 5th Earl of Loudon (d.1786), and Countess of Loudon in her own right. With these two inheritances via women came two major seats as well as estates: Donington Hall, Loughborough, and Loudon Castle, Mauchline, Ayrshire.

Moira was a distinguished soldier, and he later acquitted himself with distinction as governor-general of India (1812–22). As a party politician, however, he was not a success, partly because of a magniloquence of manner and speech which verged on the ridiculous, and partly because he attached himself devotedly to the Prince of Wales, who led him a merry dance which ultimately led nowhere. His mother had foreseen this as long ago as 1803, when she had remarked drily that she did not expect 'the sunshine of prosperity to enliven and cheer my family from that constellation'.[626] The fruitless attachment to the Prince was also baneful in a financial sense, since it encouraged Moira's natural propensity to extravagance. At Donington, for example, he pulled down the existing house and rebuilt it in 1793–5,

> utterly regardless of cost, in the ... 'Strawberry Hill Gothic' style of architecture, with Gothic hall, imposing dining-room and immense library, and an entrance designed by himself. It was a magnificent house of 203 rooms, costing far more than he could afford.... The new [Donington] ... was completed in 1795, and one of his first acts as host was to invite the Bourbon family, who were in exile from France, to stay as his guests for as long as they wished. His

Lord Moira, from an engraving published in October 1804 after an original potrait in the possession of his sister. He was commander of the forces in Scotland at this time (note the view of Edinburgh Castle in the background), which was how he met his heiress-wife, the Countess of Loudon.

AUTHOR'S COLLECTION

THE SAFER AND SURER ROUTES TO RICHES

hospitality to his royal visitors was said to be so lavish that it included an open cheque on Coutts' Bank laid discreetly on each bedroom dressing-table.[627]

It was no coincidence that in the same year, 1795, he sold for £62,000 his recently inherited patrimonial estate in Meath (brought to the Rawdon family by a late 17th-century heiress) in order, as he claimed, to meet the 'great and unavoidable expense of my situation'. In 1800, his two Co. Down estates, at Moira and Ballynahinch, went the way of the Meath; of these, the Ballynahinch estate, on which the Rawdon family seat of Montalto was located, comprised c.12,445 statute acres at a rental of c.£4,000 a year.[628] When his mother, who was entitled to live in Moira House, Ussher's Island, Dublin, died in 1808, it too was sold, and with its sale the Rawdon family ceased to have any territorial connection with Ireland. In the meantime, his marriage to Lady Loudon in 1804 had brought him effective control over her estate in Ayrshire, and might have been expected – in conjunction with the sales of Irish assets – to have brought stability to his finances. Not so. At the end of 1805, Lady Loudon and he commissioned an architect called Archibald Elliot to design a massive enlargement of the originally fifteenth-century Loudon Castle. Work on this went on until 1811, at a reputed cost of c.£100,000 (which is believable), and having absorbed and then anticipated the revenues of the Loudon estate, was left unfinished for lack of further funds. The new Loudon Castle, which can still be seen today in spite of a major fire in 1941, was a fanciful Gothick pile with classical internal features, like Donington. It has also been described as 'the Scottish Windsor',[629] which is apt, because of its stylistic affinity to the alterations and additions made to Windsor Castle by the Prince Regent/George IV, and because of the personal affinity of Moira to the Prince Regent.

Following this new extravaganza and his financial difficulties of older date, Moira was forced to acknowledge in 1812 that he could not afford to live any longer at either Loudon or Donington. Under these circumstances, the offer of the governorship-general of India (made by the government to get rid of him and of his presumed influence on the Prince Regent) proved irresistible. As Moira put it to his favourite sister, Lady Granard, India held out the prospect of 'the re-establishment of our finances'. The post carried with it a salary and emoluments out of which he reckoned sufficient could be saved, 'without niggardliness of living', to enable Moira and Lady Loudon 'to make provision for younger children, which we cannot now do'. In an earlier attempt to explain to Lady Granard how he had got himself into this financial mess, he had referred, with characteristic magniloquence (and vagueness), to 'a petty but most galling perversity of fortune which, operating with a gaudy show of prosperity, has silently gnawed my spirits'. India, needless to say, provided no remedy for his financial difficulties.[630] Moreover, his notion of 'the great and unavoidable expense' appropriate to his 'situation' must have been inflated by his promotion to the marquessate of Hastings in 1817. The East India Company voted him a grant of £60,000 in 1819 in recognition of the success of his most recent military campaign, but when he resigned the governorship-general in 1822, he still could not make ends meet and in 1824 was glad to accept the ludicrously inferior governorship of Malta because he needed the money. He died, still governor of Malta, in 1826, when the East India Company generously voted a further £20,000 for the support of his widow and children.

It was of course absurd for a man who had inherited a good paternal estate, who was both the son and the husband of an heiress, and who had held remunerative regimental and/or military offices all his life and the governorship-general of India for ten years, to complain of a 'most galling perversity of fortune'. The truth was that Hastings was utterly incapable of managing his financial affairs. He was hyperbolically described as 'the Timon of the present age, whose chivalrous spirit, impelled by a magnificent temper, has completely exhausted a splendid fortune'.[631] Imprudence was the plain English for a 'chivalrous spirit'; and imprudence on the Hastings scale would have made heavy in-roads into any number of inheritances.

In other cases the imprudence was unrelated to fortunate marriage and not off-set by windfall inheritance from an heiress. The 1st Earl Annesley was a threat to his family's fortune solely because of dangerously *imprudent* marriage, and the 2nd Earl of Massereene partly for that reason and partly because of the general imprudence and gullibility which had marked his whole career. The affairs of the Damer estate were 'deranged' in 1808 and the debts of John Damer and his younger brother, the 2nd Earl of Dorchester, 'enormous', because they 'trusted everything to ... agents' and could not be got 'to look at an account'. On the death of the 7th Earl of Westmeath in December 1814, it was reported (optimistically) that with him 'have died, as I understand, all his debts, and Lord Delvin comes into an estate of £11,000 a year and which will soon be £14,000'. Although the 2nd Marquess of Donegall dodged his creditors and evaded the payment of most of his debts from his succession in 1799 until his death in 1844, the estates became liable for the enormous sum of almost £400,000 at the latter date.[632] The 6th Lord Farnham, who succeeded his childless elder brother on 20 September 1838 and died on 19 October, was within a month of bringing similar ruin down upon the Farnham family. He had

> early made away with an excellent income, and raised considerable sums of money by post obits on his elder brother's life. These would have assigned the rental of his estates to the Jews, and they no doubt would have cut the woods where they could. All this the short period of his possessing the title has prevented, and the speculations of those money-lending gentlemen fell with his life.

No marriage, however advantageous, could have been a happier event for the Farnham family and estate than the death of the 6th Lord Farnham. A similar reflection occurred to Katherine Conolly in 1736 when her feckless and altogether unsatisfactory nephew, Williams Conyngham of Slane, was reported to be

THE SAFER AND SURER ROUTES TO RICHES

dying (he did not actually die until 1738): 'It's a sad consideration ... that [the death of] one that should have been the head of his family ... should be the means to preserve a family.'633

Another welcome demise was that of Henry O'Brien, 7th Earl of Thomond (1688–1741). His death has so far been discussed solely in the context of his testamentary dispositions and the future ownership of the Thomond estate. But its most important consequence was, actually, that it relieved the estate of his feckless mismanagement and reckless expenditure (almost all of it in England, where he resided nearly all of the time). The property was no doubt encumbered when he inherited it, as an infant, in 1691: debt always had a longer history than at first sight appears. He also inherited no less than three dowagers and their jointures, one of which ran until 1702, another until 1715 and the last until 1746. On the other hand, the estate enjoyed the recuperative effect of his own minority, which ran from 1691 until 1707 (he married two years before he came of age), and was burdened by him with no settlement charges, since he had no children and was pre-deceased by his wife.

His first major depredation took place in 1720, when he unguardedly sold the manor and castle of Carlow and other lands

> in the counties of Carlow and Queen's County ... to James Hamilton Esq., his then agent, for £20,900, which sale not long before Lord Thomond's death (1741) was set aside by the court of Chancery in Ireland as having been obtained by fraud and imposition, and it was decreed to stand as a security only for the purchase money and interest, and Hamilton to account for the rents and profits.

This decree, however, was reversed long years later, and the Hamilton family's title to the lands was confirmed. Thomond also sold to Hamilton in the following year, 1721, the Thomond estate of Holmpatrick, Co. Dublin (from which Hamilton's descendant later took his peerage title). This transaction was never challenged in the courts and may not have been the result of 'fraud and imposition'. Nevertheless, the Co. Dublin estate was another major loss to the Thomond portfolio.

Moreover, in spite of raising large capital sums and putting paid to his landownership in Leinster, Thomond still left at his death debts to the fantastic amount of £101,900. The trustees of his will, followed by his Wyndham successors, paid as much of this debt as they could out of income over a long period of time, and though forced to sell land, made sure that as far as possible it was land which was effectively out of the economic control of the landlord and static in its rental. Between 1741 and 1749, £49,171 was raised by what came to be called 'Lord Thomond's loppings', and a further £18,509 in the early nineteenth century.634 Needless to say, the income from the Clare and Limerick estate was impaired for more than half a century, and its capital value forever, by the need to pay off debts on this staggering scale. It was as well that Thomond died at the comparatively early age of fifty-three.

These are all examples of the ruin or near-ruin brought down on families by the imprudence of individual family members (though imprudence seems almost to have become a family failing among the Damers). In the case of the Ponsonby family, earls of Bessborough, a pattern of imprudence was established over three or more generations as a result of almost uninterrupted absenteeism from their Irish estates. It is no longer believed that absenteeism *per se* on the part of an Irish landowner was synonymous with neglect. But it was so in the case of the Bessboroughs. On a visit to Ireland and to his friend, Lord Duncannon, son and heir of the 3rd Earl of Bessborough, in 1828, the English Whig diarist, Thomas Creevy, reflected:

> The history of this family may be said to be the history of ill-fated Ireland. Duncannon's great-grandfather began building this house [Bessborough, Pilltown, in south Kilkenny] in 1745. He finished it in 1755, and lived in it till 1757 (two years), when he died. His son left Ireland when 18 years old, and having never seen it more, died in 1792. Upon that event his son, the present Lord Bessborough, made his first visit to the place and he is not certain whether it was *two* or *three* days he stayed here, but it was one or the other. In 1808, he and Lady Bessborough came a tour to *the Lake of Killarney*, and having taken their own house in their way either going or coming, they were so pleased with it as to stay here a *week*, and once more in 1812, having come over to see the young Duke of Devonshire at Lismore, when his father died, they were here a month. So from 1757 to 1825, 68 years, the family were [here] five weeks and two days.... My dears, it is absenteeism on the part of landlords, and the havoc that middlemen make with their property, that plays the very devil.

In 1785, Lady Portarlington had made a similar comment, though she differed from Creevy in her chronology. According to her, Bessborough was 'a very good house ... [which] felt as warm and comfortable as if the family had left it the day before, and has not been inhabited these 40 years.'[635]

Some of this was exaggerated or wrong. Bessborough was habitable, and had been inhabited by the 1st Earl, long before 1755; he had also maintained a Dublin town house in Henrietta Street, in which he frequently resided up to his death in 1758 (not 1757). However, in essence, the comments on the Bessborough family's indifference to their Irish seat and property were just. In 1793 (not 1792), when the 3rd Earl inherited them, his report of what he found on 'his first visit' does reveal complete ignorance of the most elementary facts about his inheritance:

Brabazon Ponsonby, 2nd Viscount Duncannon and 1st Earl of Bessborough, painted by Charles Jervas? in 1727? on the occasion of George II's coronation?

AUTHOR'S COLLECTION

> I came here [Bessborough] yesterday and am indeed very much pleased with the place.... I hope I may be able to make a sketch for you before I go, [but] I mean to confine myself to the three days [i.e. to stay for only that time].... The house is large and very comfortable but, as you may suppose, very old-fashioned. There are several good pictures ... – I have just discovered a Claude Lorrain[e. In church, I was] entertained with my prayer book, near 100 years old, which prayed for Queen Anne and the Princess Sophia.... The extent of the estate is very great. There are 27,000 English acres all lying near together here belonging to me, but a good deal of it in long leases, and you must not from that suppose me very rich.[636]

Prudence and good management are not uppermost in the popular conception of the aristocratic values, so it may seem perverse to single them out as the deciding factor in the rise and fall of great Irish families. Yet, in the course of this study, a number of individuals have been mentioned who may fairly be regarded as the personification of good, and in some cases self-denying and dynastically driven, management. These include Lady Blayney, Henry Monck, Grace Boyle, Countess of Middlesex, the 1st and 3rd Marquesses of Londonderry, the 2nd Earl of Dunraven, Harriot Mellon, and so on. Others may at least be credited with good intentions: Lords Henry Stuart, Mark Kerr and, surprisingly enough, Aldborough. In 1794, the last-named peer smugly admonished his newly married nephew, George Hartpole of Shrule, Co. Laois:

> I'm glad ... you have got some hundreds towards your wedding expenses, [and] hope, as Mrs Hartpole's fortune was so extremely small, that you have run into no unnecessary ones.... Better suit one's coat to their [sic] cloth and be managing at first than retrench afterwards instead of getting forward. We have both been ill-used by our parents and forced to live on a little. I have never since exceeded my income..., and shall now, I daresay, lay by £3,000 or £4,000 every year, my estates now producing me £9,600 and upwards yearly, and my outgoings, jointure, chief and crown rents and other expenses never exceeding £5,000; not even this year though I ... am engaged in a very costly building in this city [Dublin – Aldborough House, Amiens Street].[637]

Clearly, Lord Aldborough's plans for economising, like everything else he did, were on the grand scale. It may also be significant that the figure he quotes for his gross rental does not tally with the evidence, two years earlier, of his own pocket-book.[638] The meticulously detailed accounts kept by the 1st Marquess of Londonderry[639] are more convincing proof of good management than Lord Aldborough's good intentions.

Good management on the part of an Irish landowner usually expressed itself at a fairly strategic level: decisions as to when property was to be bought or sold (e.g. Lord Londonderry's – or his father's – acquisition of a half-share of the Salters' Proportion), decisions as to the size of holding and nature of lease which were the desideratum on tenanted land, etc, etc. The Irish tenurial system, to say nothing of the general position of Irish agriculture in the Irish, British and imperial economy, did not leave the Irish landlord with a great deal of opportunity for management of a more positive and interventionist kind. Investment in the long-term improvement of his own estate was not much practised (until, perhaps, towards the end of the period under review, when the calling-in of expert 'agriculturists', who were usually Scottish, became fashionable),[640] and nor would it have been expected, understood or necessarily welcomed by the tenants. 'In the pre-Famine era, one of the most constructive things that Irish landlords could have done was to help more of their poorest tenants to emigrate – as several of their Scottish counterparts did. Those who did so in Ireland were a tiny minority.'[641] This was a form of investment which was particularly likely to be misunderstood, and possibly to provoke attempts to assassinate the landlord or his agent. But even the more obvious and seemingly uncontroversial modes of improvement were not attempted. As Lady Blayney, with her youthful experience of English practice, remarked in 1787: 'Repairs for tenants' houses is not practised in Ireland, [although] in many places it would not cost much. They build a mud cottage as some would raise paste [i.e. pastry] for a goose-pie, and say it is warmer than stone walls.'[642]

There were exceptions to this pattern of non-investment in permanent improvements to the tenanted parts (always the vast majority) of Irish estates. The dukes of Devonshire, for example, were a notable exception, no doubt because they applied English practice and experience to Ireland. On the large estate in counties Cork and Waterford which had been brought to the family by the Burlington heiress in the middle of the eighteenth century, the 6th Duke of Devonshire spent between 1816 and 1859 some 11 per cent of his rent receipts on capital improvements (drainage, new farm buildings, urban renewal and roads). It must however be said that, while this policy was commendable and produced good results in the medium term, it was expensive and when continued and extended into the railway age ultimately led to a huge deficit. On the Thomond estate in counties Clare and Limerick, Colonel George Wyndham, eldest illegitimate son and principal heir of the 3rd Earl of Egremont (d.1837), spent heavily on improvements, and was one of the 'tiny minority' of landlords who gave controversial assistance to tenants to emigrate and so reduce the overcrowding on the estate. In his own defence, he carefully documented this expenditure. His figures show that between 1838 and 1843 he spent £3,354 on assisted emigration, and distributed £1,615 among those who preferred to receive money rather than have their passage paid for them. Over the same period he contributed £2,386 to hospitals, dispensaries, loan funds, etc, and spent £7,597 on improvements, excluding those improvements which were still in progress on 1 July 1843. Between 25 March 1839 and 25 March 1843 six hundred and twenty-one families were removed from his estates. In 1843 his rent receipts were reduced by £1,072, probably as a result of his outlay on the draining of tenanted land. In September 1842 he had written: 'I have no intention of diminishing the rental of the Irish estate, but am prepared to lower those farms that are too high and to add rent to those that are too low.... I think it will be better to lay out money in draining the lands than in reducing rents.'[643]

In Ireland, the greatest deterrent to landlord investment in tenanted farms was the almost universal prevalence of leases rather than more flexible tenurial arrangements, and long leases at that; for, although the general trend of the period 1740–1840 was towards shorter leases, a short lease by Irish standards was still one of twenty one years' duration. The length of the leases on the Thomond estate (exclusive of the fee farms and perpetuities which accounted for nearly half of it) had appalled Percy Wyndham O'Brien, an Englishman with no previous experience of Ireland, when he inherited it in 1741. Between 1749 and his death in 1774, he 'tried the expedient of replacing leases by yearly tenancies, a change justly deprecated by Knox [the agent] as damaging to the land'. (His more realistic successor, Lord Egremont, reversed this policy as fast as he could find tenants of suitable calibre.) As has been seen, Lord Bessborough – though he did not over-react as Percy Wyndham O'Brien had done – was immediately struck in 1793 by the length of 'a good deal' of his leases, and (rightly) saw this as an impediment to his becoming 'very rich' overnight. Like a marriage settlement, a lease was a contractual obligation. As long as it lasted, and as long as the tenant adhered to its terms, the landlord could no more re-enter the farm for the good purpose of spending money on improving it, than he could for the bad purpose of evicting the tenant. The result was that an improving landlord had to work through and in co-operation with the tenant, if anything was to be achieved; and often little was accomplished by even the best of landlords. Instead, what improvements were made, were made by the tenants themselves, who calculated the amount of money they could prudently spend in this way according to the length of the unexpired term of their lease.

The landlord, on his side, unless he was in the exceptional category to which the Devonshires and Colonel Wyndham belonged, ploughed next-to-none of the income from his estate back into it on a regular, annual basis. Rather, assuming that he improved at all, he did so in specialised and often geographically intensive ways, by reclaiming untenanted marginal land (such as that 'great improver', Anthony Foster, reclaimed at Collon, Co. Louth, in the 1750s and 1760s), or by getting surveys made of remote parts of his estate, expelling squatters and forming properly delimited leaseholds (as Henry Villiers-Stuart's trustees and Henry Villiers-Stuart himself did, c.1817–1826, on a mountainous part of the Dromana estate called Slievegrine, and as the earls of Leitrim did over a much longer period on their backward Kilmacrenan estate, Co. Donegal).[644] Other profitable and prestigious activities for the more energetic landlord were the establishment of a model farm or an estate town or village. The first three Marquesses of Downshire were the greatest town-planners of the period; but Lord Aldborough, too, founded an estate village, Stratford-upon-Slaney, and numbered another among his good intentions.[645] Such a settlement would occupy an area much smaller than a townland: the 1st Earl Grandison's Villierstown, founded in the years 1750–52, occupied only part of the townland of Ballingown, beside Dromana, and consequently, required minimal re-negotiation of existing tenurial arrangements;[646] the near-contemporary Dromana village required none, because the site of it was part of the Dromana demesne. In other cases, the disruption of existing tenurial arrangements and sitting tenants was immense, as when the 1st Viscount de Vesci flattened, c.1770, the then village of Abbeyleix (the site of which was added to his enlarged demesne), and established his new town of Abbeyleix on parts of the nearby townlands of Knocknamoe and Rathmoyle.[647]

There was also in some of these ventures an overtly 'protestantising' dimension which must have given the locals additional reason to be suspicious of them. Lord Grandison, for example, deliberately imported from elsewhere, particularly Ulster, a colony of protestant linen-weavers to get his new Villierstown off to a good start, and Nathaniel Clements did the same at Glenboy, Co. Leitrim, in 1768–73.[648] At various times foreign protestants – Huguenots, Palatines, Moravians and Genevese – were also much sought-after for similar purposes. Granted that in the period 1704–93 only Protestants had the vote in county elections, there was political as well as protestantising rationale behind these importations. Political influence was an important factor in another respect: it would enable the landlord to promote his foundation at very little cost to himself – the fees on a patent obtained from the crown granting him the right to hold fairs and markets in the new town.[649] Though sectarian and electioneering motives cannot be discounted, the impetus behind these enterprises was generally and genuinely economic, and if they prospered – which Abbeyleix did and Villierstown and especially Glenboy did not – the benefits of that prosperity were diffused among the inhabitants without regard to religious denomination. Many of the benefits, as was the intention, centred on the landlord himself.

Among Ireland's landlord-inspired towns, one of the best-preserved is Tyrellspass, which is of particular interest in the present context because it was laid out by an heiress, Jane, Countess of Belvedere. The half of the Rochfort/Belvedere estate which she inherited in 1814 from her late husband, the 2nd and last Earl of Belvedere, had no residence or obvious focal point on it or near it. Gaulstown had been sold in 1784, partly because of its unhappy associations with the imprisonment of the 1st Earl of Belvedere's wife, and partly because money had had to be raised wherever it could be got to pay his enormous debts. Belvedere itself was unavailable because it was located on the half of the estate settled on Jane, Countess of Lanesborough. So Jane, Lady Belvedere (who died in 1836) and her second husband, Abraham Boyd (who died in 1822), made their home in Tyrellspass. There they laid out a rather English-looking village green, at one end of which they built themselves a pleasant, unpretentious house which is now The Village Hotel. They must have subscribed heavily to the new Board of First Fruits parish church, within which

THE SAFER AND SURER ROUTES TO RICHES

Lady Belvedere erected in 1816 a very expensive and over-the-top funeral monument to her late husband and benefactor. In the semi-circle of buildings clustered round one side of the green are to be found, in addition to the church, a couple of charitable institutions built or endowed by Lady Belvedere, including 'a place of worship for Wesleyan Methodists'. At her death, and in no small measure thanks to her, the town contained 537 inhabitants and 82 mostly well-built houses, and had assumed its present tasteful and pleasing appearance. It was obviously intended to be a place of genteel residence and resort, rather than a commercial centre. To that extent, it is untypical of the economically driven genesis of most other landlord villages and towns.[650]

Lady Belvedere is presumably remembered with gratitude and affection in Tyrrellspass, and Lord Grandison is certainly recorded in local history as the 'good' Earl mainly on the strength of his building of Villierstown. (He had also speculated, not very successfully, in the 1730s in a patent manure,[651] some whiff of which may have lingered on.) Generally speaking, if a landlord acquired the epithet 'good' at all, he did so on foot of a sort of remote benevolence which most often expressed itself in town-planning, fairs, markets, churches (or the granting of free sites for churches) and charitable foundations. Landlords were also remembered kindly for helping deserving tenants, for respecting 'tenant right' (defined in 1840 as 'the paramount claim which by old custom every tenant in possession considers himself to a renewal in preference to any other person'), and for administering manorial and other forms of regulation and justice of which he was the local agent with efficiency and impartiality. 'Every generation, new landowners [i.e. landowners who had just succeeded to their family estates] … tried to improve or at least maintain the status and finances of their own families, while they and their agents struggled to deal with problems presented by tenants and their families. The prosperity of whole communities was dependent on positive leadership and shrewd management'[652] – but, inevitably, at a strategic and paternalistic level. In more pragmatic respects, the landlord's relationship to his own land bore some resemblance to that of the top-soil upon it.

For landed magnates who, like Lord Dunraven, wished to make a positive contribution to their family's greatness, and who were precluded by the Irish tenurial system from investing money in the most obvious way, the improvement of their own estates, other outlets were still open. As Lord Dunraven suggested, they could pursue 'commerce or … a profession'. As has been noted, commerce was not much pursued by the landed *élite* – not even by their younger sons – with the exception of banking. The wine business was another exception: the Hon. Price Blackwood (1760–1816), younger brother of the 2nd Lord Dufferin, was a wine-merchant in the early nineteenth century, as was Nathaniel Sneyd of

Life-size plaster bust of the 2nd Earl of Belvedere – probably a rejected model for the Tyrellspass funeral monument – by Thomas Kirk, 1816.

AUTHOR'S COLLECTION

Bawnboy, Co. Cavan, MP for that county, 1801–26.[653] Pursuing a profession was, however, a different matter, and many landed estates were founded or augmented by professional earnings, particularly from the Law.[654] Moreover, existing landed magnates were more active than is commonly supposed in buying yet more land. This is particularly true of the second half of the period under review, by which time the return on investment in land had become more than economic, provided only that the purchase money was not borrowed. The 1st Earl Erne, for example, seems in the 1810s and 1820s to have added, by purchase, 8,700 Irish acres to his inherited 5,759 in Co. Fermanagh; and his grandson, the 3rd Earl, continued the process by spending between 1842 and 1862 £93,108 on Fermanagh land with a rental of £4,601 by 1875. The Erne estate in that county seems to have been roughly trebled by purchases made from 1810 onwards.[655] At all times, existing landowners were usually prepared to pay over the odds for 'contiguity' – or a bit of land, large or small, which would plug a gap in, or straighten a boundary of, their inherited estate. Purchase of additional land by existing landlords was always a more effective, because selective, mode of increasing landed wealth than marriage could pretend to be.

In other ways, too, landlords were prepared and often eager to put their money to enterprising and entrepreneurial use. Prospecting for and extracting the mineral resources of their own estates were a favourite landlord activity. In 1760 Lord Conyngham claimed proudly, but unspecifically, that he had 'discovered some valuable mines on my estate', presumably in Donegal.[656] In that and the previous and succeeding decades, the almost adjoining collieries of Creenagh and Drumglass, near the optimistically named Coalisland, Co. Tyrone, were worked enthusiastically by syndicates of local landlords, who included Andrew Thomas Stuart, later 1st Earl Castle Stewart, and Richard Robinson, archbishop of Armagh, 1765–94, who was a temporal as well as spiritual peer of Ireland. (The results were mixed, and Creenagh seems to have been distinctly less successful than Drumglass.)[657] The 2nd Earl of Leitrim was not only interested in the mineral potential of his wife's Rosshill estate,[658] but in 1802–12 allowed himself to be drawn into much more active exploration of the Kildrum mine, near Dunfanaghy, on his patrimonial estate in Co. Donegal.

The Wandesford family, Viscounts Castlecomer, and their successors, the Southwell-Wandesfords and the Prior-Wandesfords, did well for a long period stretching from the seventeenth to the twentieth century out of the famous Castlecomer collieries, Co. Kilkenny.[659] But it was more usual for mineral wealth to be an *ignis fatuus* which dazzled and ultimately blinded those who followed it. Irish coal seams were in general thin and fractured and could not be worked without disproportionate extraction costs.[660] This was the experience of the syndicate which had attempted to work the Creenagh mine in Co. Tyrone. Over the period 1752–6, the first five years in which it was in operation, 864 tons of coal were extracted; but they were sold for only £205, and the total operating loss was £1,616.[661] The visionary English expert who had encouraged and advised Lord

Leitrim about the Kildrum enterprise eventually came clean: 'I wish I could announce to you that the mine was in a flourishing state. I have long since informed you that, though like other miners I existed upon hopes, yet that it must soon cease to be a matter of profit except some new discovery took place. I will take care that not much is lost.'[662] This was the story of most coal-mining ventures in Ireland. None flourished like Castlecomer, although it should also be said that none, or at any rate few, flopped so completely as Sir Vere Hunt, 1st Bt's, experiment in 1813–18 at Glengoole, alias New Birmingham, on his family estate in Co. Tipperary.[663]

Generally speaking, Irish peers and landed magnates had to look beyond their Irish estates for investment and entrepreneurial opportunities. Within Ireland, as has already been suggested,[664] investment in office was a widespread activity at least up to the 1780s. Beyond Ireland, government securities and money-raising schemes, and the stock market, offered a handsome return for those with surplus cash or at least a temporary command of money. Sir George Macartney, Earl Macartney, the proprietor of a small north Antrim estate and a high earner as a diplomat and proconsul, actually borrowed £1,600 in 1781 in order to invest it in government securities which, because of the American War, yielded a higher return than the interest he had to pay on the loan. Investing money in this manner also had the advantage 'that I may command it at a moment's warning, as I know not how soon I may' require it. In 1794, he invested a further £6,000 (this time of his own money) in the Funds, which once again were at a wartime premium. In c.1800, he was drawing an income of at least £2,400 a year from government securities, as compared to (an only recently achieved) rental income of c.£1,500 from his north Antrim estate.[665] He was exceptional in his professional earnings and in the smallness of his landed property. But further research into investment patterns will almost certainly show that enterprising landed magnates in Ireland significantly supplemented their rentals in this way.

This of course is to equate good management with at least some degree of enterprise; but even if it is interpreted in Lord Aldborough's limited sense of careful budgeting and housekeeping, it was still of crucial importance, and provided scope for considerable divergence of performance. For example, a difference of one per cent in the rate of interest paid on borrowed money, or the difference between remitting money to England at times of the year when the exchange was most and least favourable, meant a loss or saving of hundreds or even thousands of pounds a year.[666] In any annual budget, household and personal expenditure was a major, probably the major, item. For this reason the proverbially rich William Hare, later 1st Earl of Listowel, was described in 1797 as 'the possessor of £25,000 a year ... and a man of no expense.'[667] Where two aristocratic families are roughly on a par in terms of rental income, size of wife's portion, number of children, and so on, and there is yet a striking difference between the financial circumstances of the two, that difference is probably to be accounted for by sheer bad management on the part of the less affluent.

The 2nd Earl Grandison, for instance, was roughly on a par with his wife's brother-in-law, the 1st Marquess of Londonderry, in all the important respects (except that Lord Londonderry had nine surviving children and Lord Grandison only one). Yet, Lord Londonderry was painstakingly founding a dynasty, while Lord Grandison was immersed in 'difficulties'. Lady Portarlington wondered in 1785 if Grandison had 'extricated himself from some of ... [them] at least, as he is building a fine house at Dromana and is living in a great style. He pays his cook a hundred a year. We are to pay him a visit ... to see his house, as it is to be *built for nothing*.' The very next in this run of letters from Lady Portarlington reveals that other peerage families, including the Portarlingtons themselves, were also in 'difficulties':

> [Lord and Lady de Vesci] talk of going to Bath very soon, and propose staying for two years. Lady de Vesci told me very plainly it was on a saving scheme, as they owe money, and find the same difficulty raising money as we do, though he has his estate in his own power. They told me Lady Welles, who is a sister of Lord de Vesci's, has lived there till they have made their circumstances quite easy.... I shall get my mother ... to send me information with regard to the expense of living there...; and I can't say I should be at all ashamed. However, for the present I see no prospect of our going anywhere, as there's no rents paid, so that we are as much distressed at home as if we were in a strange country; for everything we have received has gone to pay the fees and the interest.[668]

The reference to interest requires no comment. The fees referred to were those (of some £400) which had to be paid for the various heraldic and other formalities connected with the promotion of her husband to the earldom of Portarlington.[669] Her unashamed acceptance of their need to economise clearly did not extend to turning down an accession of rank, even though living like an earl was a more serious and long-term commitment than paying the fees on an earldom. Nevertheless, the Portarlington estate in Co. Laois, with a statute acreage of over 18,000, ought to have been more than adequate to the support of that rank; and in 1785 Lord and Lady Portarlington's cripplingly large family of four younger sons and four daughters was still in its early stages.[670] There is therefore, in this as in the case of Lord Grandison, no obvious reason for the financial difficulties being experienced, although in both the cost of rebuilding the family seat may have been a factor.

In striking contrast to these two cases of bad management is the record of the 8th Earl of Abercorn – arguably the most skilful manager of the period under review. Lord Abercorn combined generosity and prudence, magnificence and economy. He built or rebuilt a number of houses in England, Ireland and Scotland, in the last of which kingdoms he also scored the signal dynastic success of buying back, in the mid-eighteenth century, a good part of the family estates which a seventeenth-century ancestor had lost through adherence to the Catholic faith during a time of religious persecution and confiscation.[671] Unlike

Lord Aldborough, Lord Abercorn was a man of deeds rather than words; indeed, of few of the latter. In 1761, when George III's German bride spent her first night on English soil at Lord Abercorn's house near the Essex coast, Horace Walpole quipped: 'If she judged by her host, [she] must have thought she was coming to reign in the land of taciturnity.'[672] In spite of the bad press which he has been given by Walpole and others, Lord Abercorn emerges from his own correspondence as a man of succinctness rather than mere taciturnity. His letters to his agents bristle with good sense, pithily and amusingly expressed. 'I beg leave to suggest that tenants sometimes exaggerate their difficulties with a view to depreciating their farms.' 'It can by no means be worthwhile to lay out £500 upon a bleachgreen in order to let it for £40.' 'I thought you made too much concession ... in the former contests, and it seems you did not purchase peace.' 'Caution the tenants that, if they claim for more trees than shall appear to have been planted, they will be charged a shilling for each that is deficient.' 'What is called indulgence to the tenants is in the end cruelty.'[673] The last remark is a reminder that Lord Abercorn was humane as well as hard-headed. His letters, if they do not display the kind of eloquence which would have appealed to

The 8th Earl of Abercorn, painted c.1760 in Van Dyck costume by John Giles Eckhardt

COURTESY OF THE TRUSTEES OF THE ABERCORN HEIRLOOMS SETTLEMENT

Walpole, are as eloquent of good management as Lord Londonderry's accounts.

The example of Lord Abercorn is particularly significant in the context of the present study, because so far from sharing Lord Dunraven's good fortune in marrying an heiress, he was a life-long bachelor. Indeed, if the perspective is widened to take in the Abercorn family as a whole, from its early-seventeenth century beginnings in Ireland to its ultimate dynastic achievement in attaining a dukedom in the second half of the nineteenth, what is noteworthy is that over that long period it only once, in 1660, enjoyed that species of good fortune. The future importance of the Donegal estate which the heiress concerned brought into the family may be gauged from the fact that by 1832 its rental, at £9,000 a year, was approximately half that of the patrimonial estate in Tyrone.[674] All the same, the bachelor Lord Abercorn's contribution, in the form of the reacquired family property in Scotland, was even greater. Moreover, bachelorhood had the advantage over all but the most advantageous marriage, in that it saved an estate one generation of settlement charges. By Lord Abercorn's day, the Abercorn estate needed the rest, because his father and in particular his grandfather had been prolific. For the same reason, his bachelorhood did not endanger the succession. As a result of this rest, Lord Abercorn was able to treat his brothers and their children handsomely during his lifetime and at his death in 1789;[675] which he would either not have been able to do, or which the estate would have suffered from his doing, if he had had children of his own. In terms of day-to-day expense, too, his household was the cheaper to run for the fact that it contained neither boudoir nor nursery.

It would have been cheaper still if Lord Abercorn himself had been lacking: in other words, if the head of the family had been a minor as well as a bachelor. Later, in the period of post-1815 and post-war depression, when the rental of the Abercorn estate in Ireland made its dramatic descent from £37,000 to £26,000 a year, it was extremely fortunate for the family that the 2nd Marquess of Abercorn, its then head, was indeed a minor, who did not come of age until 1832, after the painful adjustment to a realistic level of rent had been effected on his behalf. Obviously, special circumstances applied to this instance of minority. But it is generally speaking true that, from the second half of the seventeenth century onwards, when minorities in private families ceased to be exploited for the financial advantage of the crown and of royal favourites, minorities became matters for rejoicing instead of regret.[676]

So, under certain conditions, did lunacies. They were a menace if they imperilled the marriage prospects of current and future members of the lunatic's family;[677] also if they fell short of being lunacies within the legal meaning of the term, and left weak-minded individuals like Lords Massereene and Sydney at liberty to alienate or attenuate the family estate. If, however, the lunacy was of a non-hereditary kind, and if the sufferer were certifiable, 'confined' and under the jurisdiction of the lord chancellor, lunacies, like minorities, by reducing personal and household expenditure to comparatively small amounts, provided an opportunity for financial recuperation or the accumulation of savings. In one respect, lunacies were more beneficial than minorities; they generally lasted longer. In the case of the already-mentioned Lord Creighton, later the 2nd Earl Erne, the lunacy lasted from 1798, when he was certified, until 1842, when he died. From 1828 until 1842 he bore the family titles, but during even that period he subsisted on a modest annual allowance of £780.[678] In the case of his neighbour, an untitled and much smaller landowner, George Montgomery of Ballyconnell, Co. Cavan, who inherited his family's estate in 1787, died in 1841 and was 'confined' for all of that time, the annual allowance was £600 in 1804.[679] This latter must have included the upkeep of the house and demesne at Ballyconnell, which was where the lunatic lived: Lord Erne's £780 did not relate to the family seat, since Lord Erne lived in London.

In another instance, that of the 2nd Viscount Bangor, who was certified in 1785 and died in 1827, the only allowance about which information survives was that appropriated to the upkeep of the family seat, Castle Ward, Strangford, Co. Down. This was set by the Court of Chancery in 1789 at £300 a year – a sum which proved to be 'pitiful' in relation to the needs of Castle Ward and its extensive and scenic demesne. In 1806, a visiting friend of the family was 'sorry to see the place in great *déshabillé*. It will take a large sum to put in perfect repair the offices and demesne.' Later in the interregnum created by the lunacy, one of Lord Bangor's younger brothers removed him from Castle Ward into cheaper accommodation elsewhere, and allegedly sold much of the furniture in the house.[680] This is all hard to reconcile with usual practice in such cases. Generally speaking, the allowances and financial *régime* laid down by the Court of Chancery were realistic and had been agreed in advance with the next of kin. These latter normally constituted the 'committee of lunacy' (as indeed they did in Lord Bangor's case) which the Court appointed to look after the lunatic and his affairs. So, it was not usual for the long-term interests of the family to be neglected and the family seat reduced to *désabillé*. Perhaps the Court had been compelled to impose drastic economies because Lord Bangor's financial situation was dire? His father, the already-mentioned 1st Viscount, had had a large family and had spent a good deal of (probably borrowed) money building Castle Ward and buying additional land. His wife, who had been a woman of independent means when they married, had cost the estate c.£1,000 a year in maintenance from the time of their separation in 1766 or 1767 to her death in 1789. Finally, the heir apparent to the title, Lord Bangor's brother, Edward Ward, had incurred heavy expenditure on electioneering for Co. Down. If, as seems probable, Lord Bangor's finances were at a low ebb, it is reasonable to suggest that land, rather than just furniture, would have had to be sold had the estate not enjoyed the respite of a 40-year-long lunacy.

Lunacies came by law under the supervision of the Court of Chancery: minorities could be so supervised if the guardians of the minor decided that this was appropriate, and debt-burdened estates could be placed – voluntarily or compulsorily – under Chancery supervision whether or not the beneficial owner was a minor. The heavily encumbered Granard estates in counties Longford, Leitrim and Westmeath, for example, lay under Chancery receivership from c.1833 to the 1850s because the creditors had obtained a Chancery decree to that effect, not because the 7th Earl of Granard (1833–89) was a minor for almost all of the period concerned. In other instances, the transfer of responsibility to the Court of Chancery was voluntary. In 1808, shortly before he himself caused a minority by dying, Lord Henry Stuart remarked: 'My [wife's] trustees, from their situation in life, cannot give much attention to the business, and I have lately thought of putting the whole of the property in Chancery.' By 'Chancery' he presumably meant the Irish Court (although the English one could have assumed responsibility for the whole Grandison estate because a part of it was in England); certainly, it was the Irish Court of Chancery which supervised the management of the estate during the minority of his son, 1809–24.[681]

Others did not share Lord Henry's confidence in the Court's efficiency. Sir John Browne, 7th Bt, of The Neale, Co. Mayo (soon to be created Lord Kilmaine), complained very bitterly in the 1780s that the agent and receiver appointed by Chancery to run his estate until debts to the tune of £45,000 had been paid off, had failed to settle accounts regularly and properly with Browne; the latter, who claimed almost to have cleared the estate of debt, was taking legal proceedings to get the receiver sacked.[682] Nor was the Court's record of stewardship in the Granard case at all impressive. In 1843, it enforced a sale of household effects at Castle Forbes, Co. Longford, many of them mundane and valueless; the proceeds amounted to c.£400, but it was reckoned that Lord Granard would have to spend £2,000 replacing what had been sold when he came of age. In 1834, the capital debt affecting the Granard estates was £175,000; the gross rental was £11,200 a year; and the yearly accumulation of debt was therefore £3,178. By 1852, the situation was worse, with the capital debt now amounting to something between £210,000 and £225,000 (the imprecision of the figure does not inspire confidence).[683] Eventually, solvency was restored by the sale in 1858 of the whole of the estate in Co. Westmeath – a solution which could surely have been found sooner?

Inevitably, debtors who had been placed under Chancery supervision against their will were harsh – and unreliable – critics of the workings of the Court. However, Thomas Lefroy, who was well qualified to judge of such matters and had no obvious axe to grind, strongly advised Lady Osborne in 1821 not to put her son's estate under the jurisdiction of Chancery. He argued that the management of the estate would in practice be delegated to attorneys, who would trump up lawsuits in order to increase their fees; and that tenants might be reluctant to travel from Co. Waterford (where the Osborne, like the Dromana, estate was situated) to Dublin to make proposals for leases, with the result that some farms would remain unlet.[684] Due to lack of surviving evidence, the performance of the Irish Court in this respect cannot be examined, as the performance of its

English counterpart can. It is likely that privately appointed trustees, if they were capable men and in a position to give 'much attention to the business', would do a better job than court officials.

Be that as it may, either form of impersonal management would be able to fulfil the managerial, though not the social and political, responsibilities of landlordism as efficiently as most landlords and at next-to-no cost to the estate. By contrast, even a notably efficient landlord like Lord Abercorn could make little impression on the Irish tenurial system and, bachelor though he was, cost the estate a good deal on account of the various households and establishments which his rank required him to maintain. There was also the worrying possibility that a bachelor landlord would go and spend £60,000 on 'china ... and ... favourite ladies'.[685]

Prudence, good management, well targeted purchases of land, skilful outside investments, bachelorhood, minority, lunacy – these were all sure ingredients of prosperity among the landed *élite,* and generally speaking more beneficial than the speculative rewards, if any, of matrimony. However, it is tolerably clear that the biggest single factors in landlord prosperity in the period under review were the rate at which old leases fell in, and the possibility or otherwise of raising rents to the new economic level when the old leases did fall in. Landlords whose leases fell in slowly were correspondingly slow to benefit from the boom which occurred in the last third of the eighteenth century: landlords whose ancestors had been prodigal with the kind of leases which were peculiarly prevalent in Ireland and which were in effect a concealed form of sale – fee farm grants and leases for lives renewable forever – had the misfortune not to benefit at all. 'Prodigal' is perhaps a harsh word: seventeenth- and early eighteenth-century landlords had found it extremely difficult to attract tenants, and thereby obtain income, except on disadvantageous terms.[686] In consequence, the leases they had been obliged to grant, if they were not in perpetuity, were at any rate long. Nor, until a situation of rising rental capacity came into being, was there any practical, monetary difference between the rent reserved in a perpetuity lease and the going rentable rate for land.

The assumption that rents were going to rise on the re-letting of lands begins to be made only from the mid-1760s, and even then mainly in Leinster and Munster. In 1765, for example, Lord Kildare was looking forward to a 'likely' increase in his Co. Kildare rental of '£2,000 a year by the rise of land which must come into my hands in a few years, as the lives [named in the leases] are above *seventy and eight*' years of age.[687] This optimism was not universal even in those two provinces. In 1772–3, for example, rents were reported to be falling in counties Louth and Meath and, next door to Leinster, in Co. Cavan.[688] In Connaught and Ulster the future was generally less clear. At the end of 1779, Lord Kildare's son and successor, the 2nd Duke of Leinster, who wanted to sell his heiress-wife's estate in Co. Roscommon, took the view that, 'if we can possibly weather another year, I think the purchase of lands ... must rise, for though we shall not feel the immediate benefit, yet those that look forward must see that this country must flourish'.[689] In Ulster, his uncle, Thomas Conolly, the leading landholder in Co. Londonderry, was only now, in the 1780s and 1790s, experiencing the rental difference between his perpetuity and his determinable leases in that county.[690]

Conolly had once been probably the richest landlord in Ireland. The *nouveaux riches* of the late eighteenth century were the luckier members of the existing landed aristocracy, those who now rose from its ranks (in Lady Bracknell's famous phrase) as a result of the leasing policy pursued by their ancestors. In Ireland, there may well have been no rise of great estates at the beginning of the century; but, as in England, there certainly was a realisation of great rental incomes at the end. It was those in possession of these great rental incomes rather than those married to or descended from heiresses (though numerous landowners would have been in both categories) who were the new rich among the old aristocracy.

Conclusion

During the period 1740–1840, general demographic trends, applicable to the aristocracy of the British Isles as a whole, tended to reinforce the long pre-existing shift in property law in the direction of the collateral male heir, and to reduce the chances of a woman becoming an heiress. Statistically, there was less likelihood of a daughter inheriting from her father at the end than at the beginning of the eighteenth century. 'The generations born between 1650 and 1724, who were fathering children from the early 1670s onwards … [failed] to maintain their numbers by an increasing margin.… This tendency towards extinction was reversed around the middle of the century…, and from the 1770s onwards seven sons were being born to every five males.'[691]

> [General] mortality fell during the second half of the eighteenth century at an unprecedented rate. The expectation of life at birth rose by 20 per cent in a single generation, comparing the cohorts born 1725–49 and 1750–74. The rate of child mortality … fell by 30 per cent over this period, and this was responsible for most of the effect, since the expectation of life at the age of five rose by only five [per cent] at the same epoch. Child mortality continued to fall rapidly, and dropped another 20 per cent by the next cohort [1775–99].

What demographic distinction there was between the sexes on the whole militated against female inheritance. Although middle-aged men (40–64) came during this period to have a markedly shorter expectation of life than middle-aged women, 'male mortality in the age-group 15–39' (a much more significant age-group in the present context) fell 'very considerably', and this in spite of the fact that Britain was at war for over forty of the hundred years between 1740 and 1840. In the younger age-group, the under-fifteens, there was a slightly higher rate of mortality among girls than among boys.[692] So, regardless of whether the male heir were a son or a cousin, the outlook was still bleak for a daughter. The main difference was that, if he were a cousin, she was in with a chance because her father might be at liberty, and disposed, to give the preference to her. To that extent, a demographic change which increased the likelihood of father-to-son succession was very bad news indeed.

Other statistics suggest – at least at first blush – that the change had affected the marriage market, because by the latter half of the period under review, there were not very many heiresses among the wives of Irish peers. This admittedly simplistic conclusion is based on an examination of William Playfair's *British Family Antiquity* (11 vols., London, 1809–11), volumes four and five of which, the volumes relating to the peerage of Ireland, were published in 1810. According to Playfair, there were two hundred and seventeen Irish peers in existence in 1810 (when the Irish peerage was at or near its maximum size). This includes those who also held titles in the peerage of England, Scotland, Great Britain and the United Kingdom. Of these two hundred and seventeen, fifty-three can be excluded as irrelevant to the present exercise on the ground that they had no connection with Ireland, in terms of either residence or property. Another thirty-three have to be excluded because they were unmarried – five on account of minority, and one on account of lunacy. Two special cases have then to be excluded, the Countess of Antrim and Viscountess Newcomen (still alive and well, in spite of her adventure back in 1772),[693] because they were heiresses themselves as well as peeresses in their own right. This leaves a total of one hundred and twenty-nine impeccably, though not exclusively, Irish peers; for example, the 2nd Marquess of Hertford is included, although his marquessate was British, on the strength of his subsidiary title in the peerage of Ireland, and his Co. Antrim estate. Also included in the hundred and twenty-nine are peeresses in their own right who had been so created in consideration of their husbands' claims and services, not their own; if they were heiresses they are so categorised, and if not, as non-heiresses. Peers who were widowers are treated as if their wives were still alive, rather than as unmarried; and peers who had been twice married are treated as if their second was their only wife.

The resulting figures for the peers' wives are: 17 heiresses, 18 'doubtful' heiresses and 94 non-heiresses. It should be stressed that, in categorising borderline cases, the bias has been towards over-, not under-, enumeration of the heiresses. Every woman described by Playfair as an 'heiress' features among either the 17 or the 18, on the ground that this must have been the description given by her husband in the return which he furnished to the author; because of the difficulty in ascertaining the size of fortunes in cash, a husband's categorisation is as good as any. In cases where it is known that a lady became an heiress subsequently to 1810 (the 2nd Marquess of Waterford's wife is a case in point), or where it is thought that Playfair was incorrect in not describing her as such at that date, she is included among the 17 heiresses. No attempt has been made to apply the rigorous, but surely sensible, definition of heiress propounded elsewhere in this book – 'a bride who brought with her assets which far outweighed any return that her husband's family was obliged to make'; so that if, for example, it is known that an heiress's estate passed before or after 1810 to a second son, with the effect that she was not really an heiress at all, she is still categorised as one. Finally, the 'doubtful' heiresses are so doubtful that it would not do much violence to the truth if they were transferred en bloc to the category of the non-heiresses, making a total of 112 of the latter, against the existing figure for the heiresses of seventeen. The 'doubtful' category is mainly composed of ladies described by Playfair as the heiresses or even co-heiresses of obscure squireens: in practical terms of hard cash, a well-portioned non-heiress was probably more desirable than the co-heiress of an obscure squireen.

On the twin, but large, assumptions that most of the leading Irish landowners were peers of Ireland, and that most of the Irish peers of 1810 had been heirs apparent at the time of their marriage, these figures suggest that the Irishmen best-qualified to marry heiresses had had very little success in so doing – or perhaps had made very little effort so to do. Even if they had had a preview of Hollingsworth's statistics, they would have known from personal experience that there were numerous exceptions to the general trend away from female inheritance. After all, the present study has documented the existence in 1810 of a number of very important heiresses (some of them, admittedly, becoming marriageable well before or well after that date, and not all of them Irish and/or married to Irishmen): Baroness Nugent (Lady Buckingham), Sarah Child (Lady Westmorland), Lady Frances Susan Wandesford (Lady Ormonde), Mary Sandys (Lady Downshire), Frances Nixon/Hely-Hutchinson, Juliana Warter-Wilson (Lady Rous), Charlotte Boyle Walsingham (Lady Henry Fitzgerald), Susan Watson (Lady Carbery), Lady Henrietta Hobart (Lady Belmore), Lady Emily Hobart (Lady Castlereagh), Anne Pitt (Lady Grenville), the Countess of Bective and Lady Longford, the Countess of Antrim and Lady Mark Kerr, Mary Paul (Mrs Thomas Lefroy), Mary and Anne Bermingham (Ladies Leitrim and Charlemont), Lady Gertrude Villiers, Lady Caroline Damer, the Countess of Loudon, the Countess of Dunraven, Lady Harriet Skeffington, Frances Anne Vane-Tempest, Lady Jane Rochfort (Lady Lanesborough), Lady Harriet Gardiner, Margaret Lauretta Mellish (Lady Glengall), Mary Field (Lady Rosse),[694] Lady Rosa Nugent and Catherine Osborne. These are clear cases of daughters inheriting great or considerable estates from their fathers or brothers in the period c.1780–1840 (i.e. after the new demographic trends had had time to make themselves felt).

Moreover, the new trends could not and did not have retrospective effect; they could not override the demographic pattern of an earlier age, or interrupt the transmission of property through an heiress long dead. This consideration accounts for the number of great or considerable estates which men inherited during the period c.1780–1840 from their mothers, sisters, aunts, grandmothers, great-aunts or other remote female forebears. (Inheritance from mothers is excluded from the list which follows, if the mothers are already included among the heiresses in the previous paragraph.) The male inheritors who fall into this category are: the 2nd and 3rd Lords Conyngham, John Prendergast Smyth (1st Viscount Gort), Laurence Harman (1st Earl of Rosse of the second creation), the 2nd Earl of Moira, the 1st and 3rd Earls Erne, Thomas Conolly, the 2nd Earl of Roden, the 11th Earl of Pembroke, Colonel Charles Vereker (2nd Viscount Gort), the 2nd Lord Rossmore, the 2nd Earl Castle Stewart and the Hon. Laurence Harman King-Harman.

So, although there was less scope, statistically speaking, during the period c.1780–1840 for inheritance by or via a woman, it still happened in a considerable number of cases, and account of it has to be taken in any assessment of the extent to which heiresses were the object of deliberate pursuit. Actually, if the deaths of children under five are left out of the reckoning – events which can hardly be described as unexpected during the earlier era of high infant mortality – the scope for unexpected developments in the form of death was not so very much abridged in the second half of the eighteenth and first quarter of the nineteenth century. The Buckinghamshire family is an example of heavy, male infant mortality at a time when it was a demographic aberration, and the Paul, Blessington, Westmeath and Osborne families are all examples of a daughter inheriting because her only brother died.

Perhaps the Irish peers of 1810 had been averse to 'speculations and castle-buildings'? For whatever reason, they made a sensible and predictable choice of marriage partners and were content to marry the averagely portioned daughters of other Irish aristocratic families. In this respect, their marriage pattern mirrors that of their forerunners of 1783,[695] whose sons and grandsons many of them of course were. Such ladies were, after all, an obvious choice – their cousins, their childhood sweethearts, the daughters of their parents' friends, and the girls whom they met at 'routs' and 'assemblies' during the Dublin season. Nor was this in financial terms an entirely sentimental and senseless choice. For one thing, a marriage portion, like a deposit, was usually non-returnable, and would remain with the husband's family even if the marriage were childless or the wife died young.[696] Moreover, it must be remembered that even the £10,000 which was all Lord Abercorn was offering with his daughters, would if put out at compound interest, yield roughly £34,000 twenty-five years later. The money was not likely to be drawn upon for a younger child's portion until then; but even if the first child of the marriage was a daughter, lived to marry, and married below the median age (for aristocratic women) of twenty-four,[697] it would still have time to treble.

It was of course optimistic to imagine that anything of the kind would happen. In practice, probably only a tiny minority of husbands or fathers of husbands used the wife's portion for the purpose for which it was intended. Even if they used it for the comparatively sensible purpose of liquidating existing debt, or avoiding the contraction of additional debt, this was still an abuse of the system; money which should have been set apart to gain compound interest could not economically be employed in the discharge or avoidance of debts on which only simple interest was payable. To this abuse of the system, for which husbands and their fathers were to blame, were added the complications of demographic change, for which they were not. A portion of £10,000, rightly employed, would provide portions of the same amount for three younger children, and a jointure of £1,000 a year for their mother for several years; and this would more than suffice in most mid-eighteenth century circumstances, in view of the then expectation of life and mean family size. It would not, however, suffice at the end of the century and later, when a fourth younger child was a strong possibility, and a widowhood of ten or twenty years' duration almost a probability. Compounding these unforeseeable difficulties were delusive wartime prosperity, inflation of prices and inflation of peerage honours.

It may well be that around 1800 it was actually necessary to marry an heiress (again according to the rigorous definition of 'a bride who brought with her assets which far outweighed any return that her husband's family was obliged to make'), in order to avoid marrying *disadvantageously,* because at that epoch a standard marriage portion, properly employed, would be insufficient for the purpose expected of it. However, contemporaries were oblivious of the striking demographic change in which they were caught up. The basis of calculating settlement provision did not change; and families did not perceive and act upon the new importance of seeking out a wife who had more to offer than a portion calculated on the time-honoured basis. Admittedly, such women were in shorter supply in 1800 than they had been in 1750. But if the eldest sons who were Irish peers by 1810 had consciously and deliberately pursued those that remained, their success-rate in catching them would surely have been more impressive than it was?

Conscious and deliberate pursuit was lacking because aristocratic bridegrooms did not and could not entertain very serious expectations that dynastic aggrandisement would ensue from the marriages they made. Dynastic aggrandisement was sometimes – though much less often than has been imagined – the accidental result of marriage, or the incidental result of a match which had been made on personal grounds at least as much as from ambitious motives. But all this was speculative to the point of clairvoyancy: good management was the only safe and sure route to riches. If luck were to contribute to dynastic aggrandisement, it would be more likely to take the form of bachelorhood, minority, lunacy, death or – the luckiest circumstance of all – an inherited leasing structure which conduced to rising rentals. Heiresses were probably not a danger from the genetic point of view; but known heiresses bristled with dangers of another kind: cadet inheritance, a crippling jointure, and a settlement proviso that their estates would revert to their own right heirs if the marriage did not produce a son. Potential heiresses were likely to be much less well protected. But marrying one was a matter of chance not calculation.

The popular assumption that people, and particularly husbands, expected to do well out of marriage, is inherently implausible, since the calculation brought to bear on any marriage negotiation and settlement was 'collateral', not unilateral. Security, insurance and an 'equality of fortune' and burdens were the main aims of most families when negotiating a marriage, even the marriage of their eldest son. This was for the quite fundamental reason that the system was designed not just for the benefit of the eldest son and future family head, but for that of the younger children as well. Its object was to make primogeniture possible by reconciling it to parental affection for the younger children. It did not seek to extend the principle of primogeniture at their expense, and any subsequent variations and inflations of the original settlement provision which were made, almost invariably benefited the younger children (and/or their mother) at the expense of the eldest son.[698] The same was true when cadet inheritance was practised, except that in that event the beneficiaries were the mother and the second son, to the exclusion of the eldest son and the rest of the younger children.

In the many case-studies discussed in the course of this book, the contracting parties to a settlement seem generally to have been actuated by considerations of insurance and security rather than of advantage and aggrandisement. These latter might subsequently accrue to the husband's family and estate if something happened which could not have been clearly foreseen at the time of the marriage. If so, they were a bonus. But they were seldom an objective from the outset. The only suitor in this book who used the word 'pursuit' in connection with an heiress was Windham Quin in 1810 and he used it to describe – far from accurately – his half-hearted courtship of Caroline Wyndham which had begun two years previously.[699] It was subsequent historians, not contemporary suitors, who fixed upon heiresses as an object of pursuit: contemporary suitors seem to have recognised that, since marriage held out small hope of dynastic aggrandisement, a 'marriage of affection' was a more sensible aim.

NOTES

NOTES TO CHAPTER ONE

1. Quoted in T.U. Sadleir ed. 'Letter from Edward, 2nd Earl of Aldborough, to his agent at Belan', in *Co. Kildare Archaeological Journal*, VII (1912–14), pp. 333–4.
2. III, pp. 173–80. Unless otherwise attributed, the references in the succeeding paragraph are also taken from this source. In these notes, standard genealogical works of reference like *The Complete Peerage, Burke's Peerage, Burke's Landed Gentry of Ireland* and, most recently, *Burke's Irish Family Records*, will be taken as read, and only more off-beat works like the *New Peerage* of 1784 will be particularly cited.
3. A.P.W. Malcomson, 'Absenteeism in Eighteenth-Century Ireland' (hereafter, 'Absenteeism'), in *Irish Economic and Social History* (hereafter *IESH*), I (1974), pp. 16–17. The opportunity of the present study will be taken to correct a number of such misunderstandings in the former.
4. National Library of Ireland (hereafter NLI) Fingall Papers, MS 8021/10, Robert Harrison to 7th Earl of Fingall, 7 March 1767; Claude Chevasse, *The Story of Baltinglass* (Kilkenny, 1970), p. 41.
5. NLI Stratford Papers, MS 19,144, notes made by Aldborough in an *Almanack* for 1792.
6. British Library (hereafter BL) Holland House Papers, Add. MS 51,682, ff. 146–8, Lord Wycombe to Lady Holland, 8 May 1798.
7. Quoted in D. Dickson, *Old World Colony: Cork and South Munster, 1630–1830* (Cork, 2005), p. 85.
8. R.B. McDowell, *Ireland in the Age of Imperialism and Revolution, 1760–1800* (Oxford, 1979), p. 122.
9. H.J. Habbakuk, 'English Landownership, 1680–1740', in *The Economic History Review*, 1st ser., X (1940), and 'Marriage Settlements in the Eighteenth Century', in *Transactions of the Royal Historical Society* (hereafter *TRHS*), 4th ser., XXXII (1950). The debate is both summarised and extended in P. Roebuck, *Yorkshire Baronets, 1640–1760: Families, Estates and Fortunes* (hereafter *Yorkshire Baronets* – Oxford, 1980), pp. 3–16, 251-6, and 294–316, and in J. Cannon, *Aristocratic Century: the Peerage of Eighteenth-Century England* (Cambridge, 1984), pp. 132–47.
10. C. Clay, 'Marriage, Inheritance and the Rise of Large Estates in England, 1660–1815' (hereafter, 'Marriage and Large Estates'), in *The Economic History Review*, 2nd ser., XXI (1968), pp. 504–7.
11. Malcomson, 'A Lost Natural Leader: John James Hamilton, 1st Marquess of Abercorn (1756–1818)', in *Proceedings of the Royal Irish Academy* (hereafter *Proc. RIA*), vol. 88, sec. C, no. 4 (1988), pp. 68–9.
12. For examples of such casual, gossipy letters, see 237*n* and 290*n* below.
13. Malcomson, *Nathaniel Clements: Government and the Governing Elite in Ireland, 1725–75* (Dublin, 2005), pp.413–14.
14. Public Record Office of Northern Ireland (hereafter PRONI) Clanmorris Papers, D/4216/F/1, copy will and codicils, 1779–81. This comes from the papers of one branch of Lord Bangor's descendants; there is another copy in PRONI Londonderry Estate Office Papers, D/654/Y1/11.
15. Registry of Deeds, Dublin (hereafter ROD), vol. 320, p. 524, memorial 219,940, conveyance from the 2nd Earl of Carrick [and 8th Viscount Ikerrin], 4 May 1779.
16. D.W. Hayton ed. *Letters of Marmaduke Coghill, 1722–1738* (Irish Manuscripts Commission [hereafter IMC], Dublin, 2005), p. 31, Coghill to Edward Southwell, 30 November 1725.
17. Coghill Papers (in the possession of Lady Coghill, Sourden, Rothes, Moray), Lord Charleville's will, 1762/4. See also p. 193.
18. Killadoon Papers (papers of the Clements family, earls of Leitrim, in the possession of Mr and Mrs Charles Clements, Killadoon, Celbridge, Co. Kildare), Q/3/16, Colonel H.T. Clements (the heir) to his wife, April 1878. Other wills of the period 1740–1840 which disposed of smaller, but still sizeable, amounts of real estate include those of Hugh Edwards (d.1743?), the 3rd Viscount Mountjoy and only Earl of Blessington (d.1769), Acheson Moore (d.1770), the 3rd Earl of Lichfield (d.1772), the only Lord Callan (d.1815) and the 2nd Lord Castle Coote (d.1823). For the first five, see pp. 196, 20, 250, 210–11, 171 and 173 above, and for the last the Cosby Papers, Stradbally Hall, Stradbally, Co. Laois, B/2, copy of Lord Castle Coote's will and codicils, 1822.
19. PRONI Foster/Massereene Papers, D/562/2227, copy of a letter from John to J.L. Foster, 30 September 1810; Malcomson, *John Foster: the Politics of the Anglo-Irish Ascendancy* (Oxford, 1978), p. 23 and Appendix, Table Two; Malcomson ed. *The Extraordinary Career of the 2nd Earl of Massereene, 1743–1805* (Belfast, 1972), passim.
20. Malcomson, 'The Fall of the House of Conolly, 1758–1803', in A. Blackstock and E. Magennis eds. *Politics, People and Society: Essays in Honour of P.J. Jupp* (UHF, Belfast; 2007).
21. Quoted in Malcomson, *Lord Massereene*, p. 121.
22. PRONI Foster/Massereene Papers, D/4084/1/2/1/10, marriage settlement of the 5th Viscount (later 1st Earl of) Massereene and Anne Eyre, 24 November 1741; ibid., D/4084/1/1/1/30, copy recovery of the Co. Antrim estate, Trinity 1770. Presumably there was a contemporary recovery of the Co. Monaghan estate as well.
23. Quoted in Malcomson, *Lord Massereene*, p. 129.
24. PRONI Annesley Papers, D/1503/3/5/45, Chancery bill filed by Martin Connor, the gardener [3 July 1805];

D/1503/3/6/1, draft statement of the 2nd Earl Annesley's case, [pre 22 April 1803]; D/1503/3/8/19, letter from the 1st Earl Annesley to the future 2nd Earl, 1 June 1798; D/1503/3/ 5/72, minute of a conversation with 'Sophy', 30 December 1819; and D/1503/3/8/33, copy of the death certificate of 'Sophia Kelley ... widow of Lord Annesley', 21 February 1850.

25 History of Parliament transcript from the unpublished part of the diary of Joseph Farington, 29 September 1804, kindly placed at my disposal by Professor P.J. Jupp.

26 Surrey History Centre, Woking: Midleton Papers, MS 1248/20/75, Rev. George Chinnery to Viscountess Midleton, 18 August 1762; PRONI Tighe Papers, D/2685/14, typescript family history entitled 'The Tighe Story' by Rear-Admiral W.G.S. Tighe, p. 21.

27 NLI Wicklow Papers, MS 4811 (duplicated in MS 38,601/2), 'Reminiscences of Mrs [Caroline] Hamilton', née Tighe, [c.1800].

28 University of Limerick (hereafter UL) Special Collections, Dunraven Papers, D/3196/D/3, Mrs Eleanor Edwin to Mrs Anna Maria Wyndham, [c. 7 January 1792].

29 P & B. Rowan (antiquarian booksellers), Belfast: file and folder of letters from Lord Conyngham (of Slane Castle, Co. Meath) to his attorney, Joshua Sharpe of Lincoln's Inn (hereafter Conyngham-Sharpe Letters), letter of 5 September 1759. For the question of parental control over the portions of younger children, see pp. 125–7 above, and for marriage settlements more generally, see Chapter Two.

30 When an estate was vested in trustees (as all settled estates had to be), its legal owner was the trustees: its beneficial owner was the person for whose benefit the trustees held the estate.

31 PRONI Donoughmore Papers (originals in Trinity College, Dublin – hereafter TCD), T/3459/D/48/154, Hon. Francis Hely-Hutchinson to 1st Earl of Donoughmore (his brother), 31 January 1820.

32 Malcomson, 'The Fall of the House of Conolly' (loc. cit.).

33 See p. 132 above.

34 Hatchlands Park, East Clandon, Surrey: Dillon Papers (in the possession of Mr and the Hon. Mrs Alec Cobbe [née Dillon], William Sheldon, Gray's Inn, to Lord Dillon's lawyer or man of business, 1 January 1799. I am grateful to Mr Cobbe for sending me a photocopy of this letter.

35 For these two wills, see respectively 69n and p. 180, and for a joke about 'old maids on annuities' (cracked by the English Whig, Joseph Jekyll, in October 1822), see L. Mitchell *The Whig World, 1760–1837* (London, 2005), p. 71.

36 Glin Castle, Co. Limerick: photocopy of 'Notes on the Gort family collected and copied for his nephew, Vereker M. Hamilton, by [the 4th] Viscount Gort', 1879–80 (kindly made available to me by the Knight of Glin), pp. 178–9. The reason for the build-up of arrears of interest is not hard to seek. The £2,000 was a charge on the Gort estate, Co. Galway, which between 1742 and 1770 was the subject of protracted and ruinously expensive litigation launched against Lady Meath's brother, Sir Thomas Prendergast, 2nd Bt, by representatives of a previous, forfeiting, Jacobite proprietor (ibid., pp. 180–90). In the end, Sir Thomas and his successors defeated this legal challenge, but in order to do so they had to raise nearly £20,000 by selling the ancestral Prendergast estate of Newcastle, near Clonmel, Co. Tipperary. For the subsequent history of the Gort family, see pp. 207–9 above.

37 NLI Smythe of Barbavilla (Collinstown, Co. Westmeath) Papers, MS 41,589/36, James Stopford to William Smyth (the Smyths of Barbavilla did not assume the additional 'e' until c.1810), 24 June [1726]; Shelfield House, Shelfield, Alcester, Warwickshire, Kilmaine Papers, 4P, paper drawn up by John Browne, 1764; Dillon Papers, Hon. Charles Dillon-Lee (later 12th Viscount Dillon) to [John] Needham (his former companion on the Grand Tour, currently his go-between with his father, the 11th Viscount), 16 July 1776, and [Sir] Neale O'Donel [1st Bt] to Dillon-Lee, 29 October 1783; Elton Hall, Peterborough, Cambridgeshire, Proby (Carysfort) Papers, MS copy of the act of Parliament, 1784 (to be found in a chest received from the family's Dublin solicitors, Messrs Orpen, Franks & Co.).

38 Conyngham-Sharpe Letters, 5 September 1759; PRONI Foster/Massereene Papers, D/4084/1/2/1/13, deed of re-arrangement, 14 May 1774; ibid., D/1939/3/15, brief in Massereene v Ferrard, 1838; NLI Killadoon Papers (papers of the Clements family, earls of Leitrim, transferred to NLI from Killadoon, Celbridge, Co. Kildare), MS 36,066/1, correspondence on the subject between Ferrard and the 2nd Earl of Leitrim, 1835–41.

39 TCD volume of printed Irish House of Lords appeals papers, 1711–39, pp. 142–3; E.M. Johnston-Liik, *History of the Irish Parliament, 1692–1800: Commons, Constituencies and Statutes* (6 vols., UHF, Belfast, 2002), III, p. 326.

40 Annaly/Clifden Papers (in the possession of James King Esq., Rock's Chapel Road, Crossgar, Co. Down), A/1, deeds of 1, 9 and 23 May 1769; J. Brown and T.E. Tomlins eds. *Reports of Cases, upon Appeals and Writs of Error, in Parliament, from 1701 to ... 1800* (2nd. ed., 8 vols., London, 1803), VII, pp. 388–96.

41 PRONI Emly Papers, T/3052/81, Luttrell to E.S. Pery, 18 October 1774.

42 Annaly/Clifden Papers, A/2, two deeds from Luttrell to Henry Thompson of the City of London, 25 March 1771.

43 Ibid., Irnham and Luttrell to Samuel Wegg, 29 April 1772.

44 TCD Conolly Papers, MS 3977/627a, Irnham to Thomas Conolly, 6 January 1780.

45 Annaly/Clifden Papers, A/2, release to Carhampton (formerly Irnham) and Irnham (formerly Luttrell), 27 June 1785.

46 NLI Heron Papers, MS 13,047/1, Thomas Barnard, Bishop of Killaloe, to 2nd Earl of Buckinghamshire, 20 January [1787].

47 J. Cannon ed. *The Letters of Junius* (Oxford, 1978), p. 317.

48 PRONI Emly Papers, T/3052/81 and 80, Luttrell to E.S. Pery, 18 October 1774, and Irnham to Pery, 12 October 1774.

NOTES

49. Undated letter printed in E.M. Richardson ed. *Long-forgotten Days ... [an Aldborough family history]* (London, 1928), p. 231.
50. Quoted in D. Large, 'The Wealth of the greater Irish Landowners, 1750–1815', in *Irish Historical Studies* (hereafter, *IHS*), XV, no. 57 (March 1966), p. 37.
51. NLI positive microfilm 5553, Dorchester rental, 1787–98; The National Archives, Kew (hereafter TNA), Chancery Masters Account Books, C.101/2617, Dorchester rental, 1848.
52. Mrs Godfrey Clark ed. *Gleanings from an Old Portfolio* (3 vols., Edinburgh, 1895–8), III, pp. 234–6, obituary notice in *The Gentleman's Magazine*, [post 6 March 1808], and letter from the Dowager Lady Portarlington to Lord Portarlington, 6 March 1808. The Dorchester inheritance also included a valuable English estate in and around Dorchester itself. What in the end happened was that Lady Caroline Damer, who died in 1828, divided the Tipperary from the Dorset property and 'left all her Irish estates (£18,000 a year) to Lord Portarlington ... [and] her English estates, Milton Abbey [Dorchester] and all her personal property to his brother, Henry Dawson' – NLI Killadoon Papers, MS 36,034/14, 2nd Earl of Leitrim to Lady Leitrim, 9 December 1828. The estates were soon reunited: Lord Portarlington died unmarried in 1845, and his nephew, Henry Dawson's son, succeeded as 3rd Earl of Portarlington.
53. See p. 79 above and 256n below.
54. PRONI Encumbered Estates Court Rentals, D/1201/81, 59, 47 and 67–8, Portarlington sale rentals, 1849, 1852, 1855 and 1858; NLI calendar of the Irish Land Commission Papers (for access to which I am indebted to its compiler, the late Mr Edward Keane), sub LC 1785 and LC 2639.
55. For the Burlington and Fitzwilliam inheritances, see pp. 105, 138–9, 197–8 and 203 above.
56. See 637n and p. 227. See also: NLI Smythe of Barbavilla Papers, MS 41,580/4, Mrs Jane Bulkeley to Mrs Jane Bonnell, 9 April 1728 (lamenting that the 'fortunes' of the 1st Viscount Midleton's daughters 'are but small'); and Hatchlands Park, Dillon Papers, Lady Catherine Skeffington to Hon. Mrs Dillon-Lee, 9 October [1780], lamenting that Lady Harriet Skeffington's 'fortune was but small'.
57. K.W. Nicholls, 'Irishwomen and Property in the sixteenth Century', in M. MacCurtain and M. O'Dowd eds. *Women in early modern Ireland* (Edinburgh, 1991), pp. 20–21.
58. Sometimes this was formally recognised by the conversion of the portion into an annuity: see p. 00 below, and PRONI Abercorn Papers, D/623/B/5, deed of annuity from the 8th Earl of Abercorn to his sister, Lady Ann Hamilton, 17 May 1744.
59. These quotations are taken from Betty Rizzo, *Companions without Vows: Relationships among Eighteenth-Century British Women* (University of Georgia Press, 1994), pp. 31, 33 and 34, and the argument from Chapter Two ('Socio-economics') generally.
60. NLI Killadoon Papers, MS 36,034/44, 2nd Earl of Leitrim to his wife, 27 July 1836.
61. Author's collection, Blessington Deeds, conveyance from Margaret, Dowager Viscountess Mountjoy, to 2nd Viscount Mountjoy, 6 June 1804. For Lady Mountjoy's arrears of jointure, see p. 9 above, and for the Mountjoy/Blessington family and its dynastic *débâcle*, pp. 178–85.
62. L. Stone, *Broken Lives: Separation and Divorce in England, 1660–1857* (Oxford, 1993), pp. 13–14 and 25–6. The classic example of a wife caught in an incompatible marriage to a husband who would not agree to a separation is Lady Elizabeth Foster in the period c.1780–82. See C. Chapman and J. Dormer, *Elizabeth and Georgiana: the Duke of Devonshire and his two Duchesses* (London, 2002), pp. 13–24. For examples of private deeds of separation, see 39n and 517n, and for correspondence about two such private separations, those of Lord and Lady Tyrawley in 1774–5 and Lord and Lady Rancliffe in 1822, see Granard Papers, Castle Forbes, Newtownforbes, Co. Longford, J/F/3 and K/1/1–2.
63. L. Stone, *Road to Divorce: England, 1530–1987* (Oxford, 1990), pp. 263–7 and 347–92.
64. C. Hicks, *Improper Pursuits: the scandalous Life of Lady Di Beauclerk* (London, 2001), p. 175. A woman could obtain release from her marriage if she could prove that her husband was impotent or suffered from some other physical or from mental incapacity, in which case an ecclesiastical court would pronounce the marriage null; there would then be no need for a divorce, because the marriage had never existed. See p. 75 and 257n, and Stone, *Road to Divorce*, p. 191. For further discussions of divorce, see pp. 75 and 257n, 43–4, 118–19, 142–54 and 192 above.
65. E. Spring, *Law, Land and Family: Aristocratic Inheritance in England, 1300–1800* (Chapel Hill and London, 1993), pp. 80–87.
66. Spring, 'Law and the Theory of the Affective Family', in *Albion*, XVI (Appalachian State University, 1984), p. 5.
67. NLI, Killadoon Papers, MS 36,064/9, Sir Richard Hardinge, 1st Bt, to Lord Clements, [post 6 October 1802?]; Jonathan Cherry, 'An Historical Geography of the Farnham Estates in Co. Cavan, 1650–1950' (unpublished Ph.D. thesis, NUI Dublin, 2004), p. 682. I am grateful to Dr Cherry for his help with this matter, and also for the information that no version of the marriage settlement seems to survive in the Farnham Papers in NLI. Lord Farnham had had two daughters by a previous marriage. But the only one of them who married did so when he was still only heir presumptive and had not succeeded to his elder brother's estate.
68. Killruddery, Bray, Co. Wicklow, Meath Papers, A/1/418, the marriage settlement, 6 January 1868, and J/2/20, account of a total sum of £172,000 put at Lord Meath's disposal for estate improvement by Lady Meath by 1906. Her marriage portion had been £50,000. Obviously, this example falls well outside the period 1740–1840, but it is hard to think of a more striking one of the wealth which could still inure to a by-passed heiress.

69 NLI Farnham Papers, D.20,463, will of the 3rd Lord and 1st Earl of Farnham, made 29 September 1798, proved 3 November 1800. Again, my thanks to Jonathan Cherry. This is an unusually informative will, which gives very full information about Farnham's first marriage settlement and other anterior transactions.

70 PRONI Staples Papers, D/1567/13/15, informatively annotated copy of Lord Pery's will, 8 December 1802, and codicils, 18 January and 16 June 1804.

71 A.E. (Mrs Warenne) Blake ed. *An Irish Beauty of the Regency…, the Hon. Mrs Calvert [née Pery] (1767–1852)* (London, 1911), p. 5.

72 *The Complete Peerage*, sub 'Pery'.

73 PRONI Brookeborough Papers, D/3004/A/3/19, abstract of title reciting the terms of Sir Arthur's marriage settlement, 10 June 1842; NLI De Vesci Papers, MS 38,748/21, draft settlement of Elizabeth Selina Brooke on her marriage to Lord Knapton [later 1st Viscount de Vesci], 1769, and letter to Lord de Vesci from Francis Brooke, 4 December 1786; R.F. Brooke, *The brimming River* (Dublin, 1961), pp. 15–16. The passage about Sir Arthur's alleged 'blowing' of his inheritance from Lord Ranelagh is incorrect. See Malcomson, 'The Enniskillen Family, Estate and Archive', in *Clogher Record* (1998), pp. 90 and 92.

74 Birr Castle, Co. Offaly, Rosse Papers, C/1/8, Hercules Langrishe to Henry Flood, 26 April 1774. The will was disputed by the daughters and was litigated over for five years. In the end, Stuart was bought off by a cash payment. See: PRONI Castle Stewart Papers, D/1618/8/17, will of Acheson Moore, 3 February 1770, and D/1618/7/1/1–67, case papers and correspondence relating to the litigation, c.1768–82; PRONI Annesley Papers, D/1854/4/6, pp. 43–62, law student's notes by the Hon. Richard Annesley on the case; and Johnston-Liik, *History of the Irish Parliament, 1692–1800*, V, pp. 289–90.

75 Spring, 'Law and the Theory of the Affective Family', pp. 8–9.

76 NLI Smythe of Barbavilla Papers, MS 41,580/24, Alderman Thomas Pearson to Mrs Jane Bonnell, 12 March 1719[/20]; Hayton ed. *Letters of Marmaduke Coghill*, p. 72, Coghill to Southwell, 12 August 1729 (Coghill was the Judge of the Prerogative Court); PRONI Foster/Massereene Papers, D/4084/1/2/1/10, marriage settlement, 24 November 1741; NLI MS 38,748/21.

77 See, for example, E.H. Coleridge, *The Life of Thomas Coutts, Banker* (2 vols., London, 1920), II, pp. 312–14, settlement on Coutts's marriage to his (Irish) second wife, 17 January 1815; and Birr Castle, Rosse Papers, E/39, settlement on the marriage of Lord Oxmantown and Mary Field, 13 April 1836.

78 J. Gwyn, *The enterprising Admiral: the personal Fortune of Admiral Sir Peter Warren* (Montreal, 1974), pp. 132–3 and 140; Castle Forbes, Co. Longford, Granard Papers, J/11/1, Elizabeth Countess of Moira to her grandson, Viscount Forbes, March 1803; Malcomson, 'The Fall of the House of Conolly', (loc. cit.); Spring, 'Law and the Theory of the Affective Family', pp. 8–2.

79 NLI Leinster Papers, MS 41,552/49, Thomas Coutts to 2nd Duke of Leinster, 20 December 1798.

80 PRONI Chatsworth Papers, T/3158/428 and 691, Lady Burlington to Marquess of Hartington [her son-in-law], 2 January 1754 and 31 May 1755, T/3158/760, Hartington to Lady Burlington, 11 July 1755, T/3158/665, William Conner to Hartington, 12 May 1755, and T/3158/737, Sir Anthony Abdy to Hartington, 28 June 1755.

81 *The Complete Peerage,* sub 'Nugent'; C. Nugent, *Memoir of Robert, Earl Nugent; with Letters, Poems and Appendices* (London, 1898), passim.

82 Longford-Westmeath Library, Mullingar: Boyd Rochfort Papers, survey of the estate of Abraham Boyd and the Countess of Belvedere (note how the husband's name comes first, though the estate was the wife's) at Tyrellspass, Milltown[pass], etc, Co. Westmeath, 1818; NLI Reports on Private Collections, no. 112 (the Boyd Rochfort Papers), rentals of the Westmeath estate of Lady Belvedere and (from 1836) [her son], George Augustus Rochfort Boyd, 1822–44. For Lady Belvedere's rebuilding of the town of Tyrrellspass, see pp. 230–31 above. In 1876, Lady Lanesborough's great-grandson, Charles Brinsley Marlay of Belvedere, who had inherited the settled estates, owned c.9,000 statute acres in Westmeath worth c.£5,750 a year. This suggests that the settled estates had a higher acreage than Lady Belvedere's half, but that Lady Belvedere's half had the higher valuation per acre and perhaps was less rural.

83 Birr Castle, Rosse Papers, D/7/149, Langlois Lefroy of Carrigglas, Co. Longford, to 6th Earl of Rosse, 20 February 1949. For an example of a modern historian's view, see 113n below.

NOTES TO CHAPTER TWO

84 For the significance of this expression, see 374n below.

85 Dickson, *Old World Colony,* pp. 87 and 91; Large, op. cit., pp. 37–8. See also: Malcomson, *John Foster,* pp. 32–5; J.P. Cooper, 'Patterns of Inheritance and Settlement by great Landowners from the fifteenth to the eighteenth Centuries', in J. Goody, J. Thirsk and E.P. Thompson eds. *Family and Inheritance: Rural Society in Western Europe, 1200-1800* (Cambridge, 1976), pp. 200, 210 and 223.

86 Anon., *The Irish Register, or a List of the Duchess Dowagers, Countesses, … Widows and Misses of large Fortunes in England …* (London, 1742), p. 11. (I am indebted for this reference to the Knight of Glin.) The background to the writing of the pamphlet is discussed on pp. 102–4 above.

87 NLI Smythe of Barbavilla Papers, MS 41,582/12, William Smyth to his brother, [Archdeacon James Smyth?], 20 December 1738.

88 Ibid., MS 41,597/2, Ralph Smyth to John Cooke, [no day or month] 1780.

89 PRONI Donoughmore Papers, T/3459/F/13/88, Lord Hutchinson to Hon. Francis Hely-Hutchinson, 25 March 1824. Confusingly, there were Hutchinsons on both sides of this negotiation. But Sir Samuel Synge Hutchinson, 3rd Bt, was the head of a different (though probably

90 NLI De Vesci Papers, MS 38,899, Handcock to Knapton, 18 May 1751.
91 PRONI Foster/Massereene Papers, D/562/5112. The Fosters were not at this stage an aristocratic family, but they were ennobled less than fifty years later.
92 Large, op. cit., pp. 38–40; Dickson, *Old World Colony*, p. 91. For further particulars of this grand alliance, see pp. 49–50 above.
93 Stone, *Broken Lives*, pp. 284–386, especially pp. 284, 286 and 333. His grandfather, the 6th Earl, had remarked wistfully in 1763 that the estate, 'though not very considerable for the income, contains a great many acres' – PRONI Sheffield Papers, T/3465/4, Westmeath to John Holroyd, 5 October 1763. In the same year, Westmeath had applied to the Lord Lieutenant for a pension to augment his 'small fortune' (PRONI Alnwick Papers, T/2872/20, Westmeath to 2nd Earl of Northumberland, [1763?]), and by 1767 was in receipt of a pension of £800 a year.
94 NLI Farnham Papers, D.20,463, Farnham's will, 1798.
95 Dickson, *Old World Colony*, p. 528.
96 PRONI Foster/Massereene Papers, D/562/14614, case of Frederick Hamilton, claimant to the viscountcy of Boyne, 1772.
97 Dickson, *Old World Colony*, p. 528.
98 BL Strafford Papers, Add. MS 22,229, ff. 13–14, D[enis] Kelly to 1st Earl of Strafford, 6 March 1725; NLI ILB 340, printed House of Lords appeal papers in Thynne v Glengall, [c.1850] (for this marriage and settlement, see pp. 78–9 above); Elton Hall, Peterborough (Messrs Orpen, Franks & Co. chest), Proby Papers, settlement on the marriage of Lord Carysfort and Elizabeth Grenville, sister of the 1st Marquess of Buckingham, 11 April 1787.
99 PRONI Belvedere Deeds, T/3468/4, copy of Lord Belvedere's will, 2 June 1774; BL Aberdeen Papers, Add. MS 43,227, ff. 163–4, 1st Viscount Melville to 4th Earl of Aberdeen, 15 November 1808; PRONI Foster/Massereene Papers, T/2519/4/1659, Hon. Chichester Skeffington to John Foster, 25 September 1810; PRONI Londonderry Estate Office Papers, D/654/F/25, settlement on the second marriage of the 3rd Marquess of Londonderry, 27 March 1819; PRONI Donoughmore Papers, T/3459/D/48, Hon. Francis Hely-Hutchinson to Lord Donoughmore, 18 January 1820; Stone, *Broken Lives*, p. 286. This last is a recital of the terms of the Westmeath-Cecil marriage settlement of 1812, by which Lady Emily's portion of £15,000 was strictly settled on the younger children, with the £500 a year interest on £10,000 of it reserved for her pin money.
100 Spring, 'Law and the Theory of the Affective Family', p. 19.
101 For a discussion of delays in the payment of portions, see pp. 9–10 above.
102 PRONI Shannon Papers, D/2707/A/1/5/35, 4th Viscount Strangford to 1st Earl of Shannon, 5 December 1760; PRONI typescript copies of a few items from the Wicklow Papers in NLI, MIC/146, Lord Chief Justice Henry Singleton to Ralph Howard, 4 June 1751; Sheffield Archives Wentworth Woodhouse Muniments (photocopies in PRONI, reference T/3302), T/3302/2/78, Ludlow to 4th Earl Fitzwilliam, 24 September 1794; History of Parliament transcripts from the Chatham Papers, TNA 30/8/118, Bute to Pitt the Younger, 6 December 1799; PRONI Liverpool Papers (photocopies of some strays from the archive in BL, which have since been reunited with that archive), T/2593/36, Ranelagh to 2nd Earl of Liverpool, 6 January 1819.
103 PRONI Strutt Papers, T/3092/1/4, Leinster (then Lord Kildare) to his wife, 10 June 1766. For the question of the Duchess's portion, see 136*n* below.
104 PRONI Downshire Papers, D/671/D/14/2/20, Prerogative will of the 2nd Marquess of Downshire, made 24 November 1797 and proved 7 October 1801. I am grateful to Dr Deborah Wilson, who completed a QUB doctoral thesis in 2003 entitled 'Women and Property in wealthy landed Families in Ireland, 1750–1850', and to Mr and Mrs Alan Dalton of Waimauku, West Auckland, New Zealand, for drawing this passage to my attention. For the settlement provision made for the younger children, see also 698*n* below.
105 PRONI Lord Robert Fitzgerald Papers, D/3151/11, Lord Robert to 3rd Duke of Richmond, 6 November 1790; *Gleanings from an Old Portfolio*, II, pp. 233–4, Lady Louisa Stuart to Lady Portarlington, 1 May 1796.
106 Hatchlands Park, Surrey, Dillon Papers: Hon. Charles Dillon-Lee to his wife, 17 June 1779. Needless to say, his diplomatic career never got off the ground. For the point about 'ruined' men seeking diplomatic posts in order to evade their creditors back home, see same to John Needham, 16 July 1776. For the sizeable sums which two of the 1st Duke of Leinster's sons made out of civil and diplomatic office, see p. 42, and for the naval prize money received by the younger son of another family, p. 99.
107 Rizzo, *Companions without Vows*, p. 337.
108 BL Anglesey peerage case papers, Add. MS 31,889, ff. 35-50, *Case of Ann, Countess of Anglesey, lately deceased … and of her three Surviving Daughters* (1766).
109 NLI Pakenham-Mahon Papers, MS 10,711, H.M. Sandford to Maurice Mahon, 16 April 1799; West Sussex Record Office Petworth House Archives, PHA/57/24, Bishop Cleaver to Lord Egremont, 1 May [1799]; A.L. King-Harman, *The Kings of King House* (Bedford, 1996), pp. 26–9; W. Power, *White Knights, Dark Earls: the Rise and Fall of an Anglo-Irish Dynasty* (Cork, 2000), pp. 40–46; J. Todd, *Rebel Daughters: Ireland in Conflict, 1798* (London, 2003), pp. 205–49 and 263–9.
110 PRONI Belvedere Deeds, T/3468/2, Rochfort's will, 5 April 1730.
111 Malcomson, 'The Fall of the House of Conolly' (loc. cit.); NLI Smythe of Barbavilla Papers, MS 41,585/6, Michael Clarke (the head agent for the Conolly estate) to William Smyth, 7 October 1752.
112 PRONI Abercorn Papers, D/623/A/144/9, Sir John Stewart, 1st Bt, to Abercorn, 7 January 1816, and

/A/85/89, copy of a letter from Abercorn to Sir James Galbraith, 1st Bt, 2 February 1816.

113 Large, op. cit., p. 38. See also p. 136 above and 395*n*. Mary Cairnes, Lady Blayney, widow of the 7th Lord Blayney, survived her husband for the same period (1732–90). However, the classic examples of the long-lived dowager are actually: Lady Sophia Osborne, widow of Donough, Lord O'Brien, who survived her husband's drowning in 1682 by 64 years, dying in 1746; and – in recent times – Frances Lois, widow of the 5th Earl of Rosse, who survived him by 66 years (1918–84), and from 1958 to her death also drew a jointure from the estate of a second husband, the 5th Viscount de Vesci. For the Leeson family, earls of Milltown, see also pp. 44 and 79 above.

114 See pp. 20–21 above.

115 By T.H. Hollingsworth, in *Population Studies: Supplement to Volume XVIII, no. 2* (London, 1964); for the material on which most of this paragraph is based, see pp. 85 and 65.

116 Malcomson, 'The Irish Peerage and the Act of Union, 1800–1971', in *TRHS*, 6th ser., X (2000), pp. 293–303.

117 For guidance on the general economic situation described in this paragraph, I am indebted to Dr T.R. McCavery.

118 Malcomson, *John Foster*, pp. 25 and 13. For the 'affective', as opposed to the inflation-related, motives behind the provision for Lady Ferrard, see pp. 123–4 above.

119 PRONI Villiers-Stuart Papers, T/3131/C/17/1–2, papers about securing the payment of Lady Grandison's fortune, 1715 and [1720?], J/12/4, copy of Lady Elizabeth Villiers's marriage settlement, 12 June 1739, and C/5/18, Maurice Ronayne (the agent) to Grandison, 16 September 1728.

120 See pp. 68–70 above.

121 Hollingsworth, op. cit., pp. 51 and 96.

122 Ibid. p. 36; Large, op. cit., p. 41.

123 UL Dunraven Papers, D/3196/E/3/66, Lord to Lady Dunraven, post-marked 24 December 1825.

124 Cannon, *Aristocratic Century*, p. 89, quoting Horace Walpole to Sir Horace Mann, 8 July 1784; Gwyn, *Admiral Sir Peter Warren*, pp. 132–3 and 140; Annaly/Clifden Papers, A/10, deeds relating to the sale of Lady Southampton's (*née* Warren) Irish property, 1773, 1790 and 1801–9.

125 NLI Smythe of Barbavilla Papers, MS 41,580/24 and 31, Alderman Thomas Pearson to Mrs Jane Bonnell, 12 March 1719[/20], and King to Mrs Bonnell, 25 January 1723/4.

126 Birr Castle, Rosse Papers, E/39, settlement of the fortune of Mary Field, 13 April 1836.

127 Large, op. cit. p. 40; BL Egmont Papers, Add. MS 46,988, f. 4, copy of a letter from Egmont to William Taylor, 15 January 1736/7; Dickson, op. cit., p. 108.

128 PRONI Belmore Papers, D/3007/H/6/4, Thomas Townshend to Belmore, 5 May 1817.

129 Malcomson, '1st Marquess of Abercorn', p. 168.

130 See pp. 50–52 above.

131 PRONI Castlereagh Papers, D/3030/P/145, Lord Castlereagh to Lord Stewart, November 1816.

132 BL Egmont Papers, Add. MS 46,988, f. 2, Egmont to Taylor, 6 January 1736/7.

133 PRONI Abercorn Papers, D/623/A/249, draft affidavit in the handwriting of Sir James Galbraith, [c.1819], and D/623/C/4/10–11, Tyrone and Donegal estate rent-books, 1832–8.

134 E. Wakefield, *An Account of Ireland, Statistical and Political* (London, 1812), I, p. 276; see 268*n* below.

135 Dickson, *Old World Colony*, p. 94.

136 B. Fitzgerald ed. *The Correspondence of Emily, Duchess of Leinster* (Dublin, 1949–57), I, 130; PRONI Leinster Papers, D/3078/3/2, notes by the 1st Duke of his debts and annual outgoings, 31 December 1766 and 1772; NLI Leinster Papers, MS 631, ff. 101 and 104, 2nd Duke to his mother and step-father, 13 May 1779 and 13 October 1791; J. Greig ed. *The Farington Diary by Joseph Farington, R.A.* (London, 9 vols., 1922–8), I, pp. 103–4, and II, pp. 148–9, cited in Large, op. cit., p. 38; West Sussex Record Office Goodwood (Richmond) Papers, MS 1083, marriage settlement of the 1st Duke and Lady Emily Lennox, 6 February 1746/7 (I am grateful to Mr Timothy J. McCann of the West Sussex RO for examining the marriage settlement and the related correspondence [Goodwood Papers, MS 102, ff. 59–64] on my behalf). The wags of the day, whose comments are quoted in *The Complete Peerage*, sub 'Leinster', said that the Duchess received no portion at all – an impossibility. No information about the marriage settlement exists in the Leinster Papers (PRONI D/3078); and the Registry of Deeds memorial of the settlement (PRONI MIC/311/61, vol. 126, p. 32, 3 March 1747) does not give figures for portion and jointure. Memorials of such deeds generally omit intrusive details of this kind which were not basic to title; for guidance on this last point, I am indebted to Mr John McCabe.

137 PRONI Macartney Papers, D/572/5/56, Robert Waller to Sir George Macartney, 23 November 1773.

138 S. Tillyard, *Aristocrats: Caroline, Emily, Louisa and Sarah Lennox, 1740–1832* (London, 1994), pp. 299–301 and 308–10. Tillyard achieves what might have been thought mission impossible – a sensitive and sympathetic account of Ogilvie and of the Duchess's relationship with him (pp. 245–51, 310–32, 343–4 and 424–6). The epilogue (pp.424–6) is an elegiac account of his last years. See also F. Campbell, 'The elusive Mr Ogilvie (1740–1832)', in *Familia: the Ulster Genealogical Review* (hereafter *Familia*), II, no. 9 (1993).

139 Keele University Library Sneyd Papers (photocopies in PRONI reference, T/3229), T/3229/1/4, Attorney-General FitzGibbon to William Eden, 22 August 1785, printed in D.A. Fleming and Malcomson eds. *'A Volley of Execrations': the Letters and Papers of John FitzGibbon, Earl of Clare, 1772–1802* (IMC, Dublin, 2005), no. 44.

140 PRONI Strutt Papers, T/3092/4/5, Mrs Ann Lynch to Lady Lucy Foley, 28 December 1790; the Duchess of Sermoneta, *The Locks of Norbury …* (London, 1940), pp. 3 and 97–9.

141 TNA Home Office Papers, HO 100/72, ff. 308–9, 2nd Earl Camden to 3rd Duke of Portland, 18 October 1797; PRONI Martin & Henderson Papers, D/2223/M11; manor of Ardglass maps, 1768; PRONI Ardglass estate letter book, T/1546/1, memo. by Ogilvie, 27 June 1808. Up

NOTES

to her death in 1780, the Lecale estate was in jointure to the 1st Duke's mother.
142 NLI Leinster Papers, MS 41,552/19, 2nd Duke to James Spencer (his agent), March 1784; PRONI Foster/Massereene Papers, D/562/1488, rental of the property forfeited by Lord Edward Fitzgerald, [c.1798]. Farington (see 136*n* above) states that Ogilvie subsequently acquired this estate (as he did Lord Lecale's); but this was in trust for Lord Edward's children.
143 PRONI Lord Robert Fitzgerald Papers, D/3151/19, Lord Robert to Duke of Richmond, 21 February 1801.
144 NLI Leinster Papers, MS 631, f. 104, 2nd Duke to Ogilvie, 13 October 1791.
145 Irish Architectural Archive, Dublin, Castletown Papers, A/10/6: 2nd Duke to Thomas Conolly of Castletown, Co. Kildare (his uncle-by-marriage), 26 July 1798.
146 PRONI Leinster Papers, D/3078/3/13, E. Tickell to 3rd Duke, 18 October 1821, and D/3078/2, rent-book for the 3rd Duke's estate, 1822.
147 PRONI Downshire Papers, D/607/I/103, Dowager Marchioness of Downshire to Thomas Handley, 21 February 1809.
148 NLI Leinster Papers, MS 41,552/58, Ogilvie to 3rd Duke, 14 May 1814.
149 Birr Castle, Rosse Papers, H/41, 2nd Lord Walsingham to Lady Saye and Sele, 21 December 1798. However, the House of Commons – which in most respects played a very subsidiary part to the House of Lords in the framing of divorce acts – often intervened to ensure 'that a clause providing … for the divorced wife was inserted in the act' – Stone, *Broken Lives*, p. 278.
150 Hicks, *Lady Di Beauclerk*, p. 194; P. Marson, 'The Lowry Corry Families of Castle Coole, 1646–1913' (UHF, 2007) – I am most grateful to Mr Marson for letting me see and draw upon an early draft of his text; E. Inglis-Jones, *The Lord of Burghley* (London, 1964), pp. 54–102, 104–12 and 145–7. 'The Lord of Burghley' was Henry Cecil, who succeeded in 1793 as 10th Earl of Exeter, and his divorced first wife was Emma Vernon of Hanbury Hall, Worcestershire. Though a great heiress, she was the worst-treated of the four divorcees in this sample. For her case, and for divorce more generally, see pp. 142–54 above.
151 BL Egmont Papers, Add. MS 47,029, f. 66, Philip Perceval to Lord Perceval, 8 July 1721.
152 Large, op. cit., p. 41.
153 Quoted in H. Pearson, *'Labby': the Life and Character of Henry Labouchere* (London, 1936), pp. 168–9.
154 Malcomson, *Nathaniel Clements*, pp. 352–7, 362–4 and 383.
155 For the Glengall and Carbery marriages, see pp. 78–9 and 70–71 above.
156 *Leinster Correspondence*, III, p. 211, Lady Louisa Conolly to Emily, Duchess of Leinster, 11 July [1776]; Annaly/Clifden Papers, A/1, settlement on Irnham's marriage to Judith Maria Lawes, 14 January 1735, and re-settlement of his estates and his wife's reversionary interest in the Jamaican plantations, 9 May 1769; A/4, deeds relating to charges on the Jamaican property 1789–97 (Judith Maria, Dowager Countess of Carhampton, died in 1798); and A/2, settlement on Colonel Luttrell's marriage to Jane Boyd, 20 June 1776. In 1752, Peter Browne, later 2nd Earl of Altamont, married the only daughter and heiress of Denis Kelly, chief justice of Jamaica. Like Irnham's marriage of 1735, this endogamic union brought in its wake the commercial assets of plantations and slaves.
157 For these quotations and transactions, see Conyngham-Sharpe Letters, 2 February and 27 October 1761, 5 and 27 June 1768 and 3 February 1781, and for Conyngham more generally *The Complete Peerage*, sub 'Conyngham', and pp. 169–70 above.
158 Malcomson, 'Fall of the House of Conolly' (loc. cit.).
159 Large, op. cit., p. 41; Cannon, *Aristocratic Century*, pp. 6–8, 72, 76 and 78–92. For a further discussion of endogamic marriage see pp. 127–8 and 244 above.
160 NLI Smythe of Barbavilla Papers, MS 41,598/2, Michael Clarke to Ralph Smyth, 29 January 1774.
161 Ibid., MS 41,581/13, Arthur Blennerhassett to William Smyth, 26 December 1738.
162 PRONI Miscellaneous autograph collection T/2534/5, Richmond to William Adair, 19 December 1758; Branscombe, Seaton, Devon: Tickell Papers (in the possession of Major-General M.E. Tickell), A/78, Jane Lehunte to Mrs Clothilda Tickell, 9 December 1758.
163 The converse seems not to have applied. It certainly did not apply in the case of Lady Charlotte Fitzgerald, one of the sisters of the 2nd Duke of Leinster, who married an English commoner, J.H. Strutt of Terling Place, Essex; see PRONI Strutt Papers, T/3092/11, Mrs Ann Strutt and 2nd Duke of Leinster to Lady Charlotte, 3 October and 19 November 1788.
164 Large, op. cit., pp. 39–40.
165 PRONI Londonderry Estate Office Papers, D/654/F/10, settlement on the marriage of Robert Stewart (later 1st Marquess of Londonderry) and Lady Sarah Seymour-Conway, 3 June 1766; PRONI Villiers-Stuart Papers, T/3131/J/19/1, draft settlement on the marriage of Viscount Villiers (later 2nd Earl Grandison) and Lady Gertrude Seymour-Conway, 31 October 1771. In the case of these two sisters, the size of the portion varied between £6,500 and £6,000; but this is almost certainly to be attributed to the difference between Irish and British currency, and to the presence and absence of a clause stipulating that the bride was to receive a lump sum of £300 at the time of her widowhood.
166 BL Egerton (Hertford) Papers (photocopies in PRONI, reference T/3076/2), T/3076/2/30–31, 2nd Earl Grandison to Hertford, and Hertford to Grandison, 7 and 13 August 1785. The social inferior was Robert Stewart.
167 PRONI Strutt Papers, T/3092/1/3, 1st Duke of Leinster to his wife, 31 May 1766.
168 Hull University (Brynmor Jones Library) Hotham Papers (photocopies in PRONI, reference T/3429), T/3429/1/63, 2nd Earl of Buckinghamshire (the Lord Lieutenant) to Sir Charles Hotham-Thompson, 8th Bt, 6 August 1780.
169 TNA Chatham Papers, 30/8/102, f. 230, draft of a letter from Pitt to Sackville about Herbert, 29 December 1783.

170 PRONI Castlereagh Papers, D/3030/24, Hertford to [Robert Stewart?], 25 September 1766.

171 PRONI Hertford Papers, T/3076/2/34 and 55, Castlereagh to 2nd Marquess of Hertford, 21 September [1797] and 27 June 1811.

172 H.M. Hyde, *The Rise of Castlereagh* (London, 1933), pp. 9–11, and passim. See also 266n below.

173 PRONI Londonderry Estate Office Papers, D654/F/11, marriage settlement of Stewart and Lady Frances Pratt, 6 June 1775; see 131n above.

174 PRONI Londonderry Estate Office Papers, D/654/H/1/1, pp. 4–6, Lord Londonderry's (then Robert Stewart) account book, 1781–6, and D/654/H/1/3, pp. 1, 3, 16, 21–2, 28, 53, 189 and 356, idem, 1791–1803; PRONI Ker of Portavo Papers, D/2651/2/102, Stewart to David Ker, 26 January 1786. The estate was the Salters' Proportion in and around Magherafelt. The Stewarts acquired a half-share in the lease (the rental figures are for this half-share only), their partners in it being Thomas, followed by Sir Robert, Bateson. For the information that the Stewarts' involvement dated from as early as 1779, and for the entry in D/654/H/1/1, I am indebted to Ms Joanne Stone and Dr Anne Casement.

175 See 171n and, for the information on which the rest of this paragraph is based, 131n and 172n.

176 History of Parliament transcript from the Althorp (Spencer) Papers, Spencer to William Elliot, 31 December 1806, and Duke of Bedford to Spencer, 2, 6 and 18 January 1807.

177 Malcomson ed. *Irish Official Papers in Great Britain: Private Collections, Volume One* (Belfast, 1973), p. 35; hereafter, *I.O.P.: Private Collections I*.

178 A. Cobbe, 'The Cobbe Family of Hampshire and Ireland' in A. Laing ed. *Clerics and Connoisseurs: an Irish Art Collection through three Centuries* (London, 2001), pp. 37–46; also pp. 98–104. For Newbridge House and its building, see pp. 27–36 and, particularly, A. Cobbe and T. Friedman, *James Gibbs in Ireland: Newbridge, his Villa for Charles Cobbe, Archbishop of Dublin* (Hatchlands, Surrey, 2005), passim.

179 Abstract of the settlement, kindly made available to me by Mr Alec Cobbe. The original, dated 24 April 1755, is among the family papers at Newbridge, Donabate, Co. Dublin.

180 NLI Fingall Papers, MS 8021/10, Robert Harrison to 7th Earl of Fingall, 12 February 1767.

181 Norfolk Record Office Hobart of Blickling Papers, MC 3/294, 3rd Marquess of Londonderry to Emily, Marchioness of Londonderry, 25 August 1822.

182 PRONI Wentworth Woodhouse Muniments T/3302/2/79, 2nd Marquess of Hertford to Lord Fitzwilliam, 3 October 1794. This letter refers to George Hatton of Clonard, Co. Wexford.

NOTES TO CHAPTER THREE

183 BL Egmont Papers, Add. MS 46,988, f. 4, copy of a letter from Egmont to Taylor, 15 January 1737; BL Strafford Papers, Add. MS 22,229, Lady Lucy Wentworth to 1st Earl of Strafford (her father), 18 January 1737.

184 Quoted in Malcomson, 'The Newtown Act: Revision and Reconstruction', in *IHS*, XVIII, no. 71 (March 1973), p. 318; but *cf.* 266n below. Dr Anne Casement has pointed out to me that Mary Cowan was actually 24 at the time of her marriage, and so was unlikely to have been in the state of innocence described. The best example of a lucky or shrewd bridegroom who captured a considerable heiress when she was very young and her fortune ill-protected legally, was the 18th Earl of Ormonde, who married the 15-year-old Anna Maria Clarke, only daughter of Job (or Joseph) Hart Pryce Clarke of Sutton Hall, Derbyshire, and Aldershot, Hampshire, in March 1805.

185 Marquess of Kildare ed. *The Earls of Kildare, 1057–1773: Second Addenda [to 1804]* (Dublin, 1872), pp. 163–5, C.J. Fox to Marquess of Kildare, February 1768; NLI King-Harman Papers, MS 8810/3, Caroline FitzGerald to Lady Jane King, 4 October 1769; NLI MS 3275, printed depositions in a lawsuit between [the 3rd] Earl of Kingston and Caroline, Countess of Kingston, his mother, [c.1818].

186 See p. 9 and 27–9 above.

187 Coleridge, *Thomas Coutts*, II, p. 313.

188 The three daughters, all of whom had married men of title, seem to have received marriage portions of £25,000 each and well over £100,000 each thereafter – ibid., II, pp. 4 and 369–72.

189 Ibid., pp. 363–72 and 391–400; C.E. Pearce, *The jolly Duchess: Harriot Mellon …* (London, 1915), pp. 190–316; E. Healey, *Coutts & Co., 1692–1992: the Portrait of a private Bank* (London, 1992), pp. 231–49, 256–61 and 270–86. For the subsequent history of Angela Burdett-Coutts, see pp. 166–7 above.

190 For examples of an heiress's estate settled on the surviving partner, see pp. 66 and 183 above. For the legal background to 'contingent remainders', see L. Bonfield, 'Marriage Settlements and the "Rise of Great Estates": the Demographic Aspect', in *The Economic History Review*, 2nd ser., XXXII, no. 4 (1979), pp. 484–5.

191 J. Kelly, 'Belvedere House: Origins, Development and Residents, 1540–1883', in J. Kelly ed. *A History of St Patrick's College, Drumcondra* (Dublin, 2006), pp. 33–5 L.B. Namier and J. Brooke, *The History of Parliament: the House of Commons, 1754–90* (3 vols., London, 1964), II, p. 232; Coghill Papers (loc. cit.), will of Hester, Dowager Countess of Charleville, 26 April 1784. I am most grateful to Dr Kelly for the light he has shed on Hester, Countess of Charleville.

192 For a discussion of the subsequent history of the Shelburne and Conyngham families and of the complicated descent of their estates, see pp. 89, 195–6 and 203–4 above.

193 Dickson, *Old World Colony*, p. 90, in part quoting from the Betham Papers, NAI M 749, p. 156; Sir J.B. Burke,

193 *Vicissitudes of Families* (new ed., 2 vols., London, 1883), II, pp. 405–6.
194 See pp. 102–4 above.
195 B. Falk, *The Way of the Montagus: a Gallery of Family Portraits* (London, c.1955), pp. 281–2; Cannon, *Aristocratic Century*, p. 126.
196 See pp. 27 above.
197 PRONI Donoughmore Papers, T/3459/D/49/72, 145, 152, and /F/13/88, Francis Hely-Hutchinson to Lord Hutchinson, 24 December 1822 and 24 March and 22 April 1824, and Lord Hutchinson to Francis Hely-Hutchinson, 25 March 1824.
198 Richardson ed. *Long-forgotten Days*, pp. 245–6 and 251–2, quoting letters from Lady Blayney to her cousin, Mrs Lavington, 24 January 1743/4 and 22 April 1786.
199 PRONI Armagh Diocesan Registry Papers, DIO 4/13/10/4/1, memo by Monck, 20 June 1765; DIO 4/13/10/4/2, memo and calculations by Monck, post 1 August 1769.
200 DIO 4/13/10/4/13, account of Lady Tyrone's inheritance from her late father, February 1789.
201 Tempered, however, by the more judicious W.E.H. Lecky, *History of Ireland in the Eighteenth Century*, I (cabinet ed., London, 1919), p. 371.
202 By James Kelly in *Eighteenth-Century Ireland*, IX (1994), pp. 7–43.
203 The legislation, as documented by Kelly (pp. 11–12 and 24), comprised: an ineffectual act of 1634 against the 'tak[ing] away ... and deflower[ing] ... maydens'; an act of 1707 'for the more effectual preventing the taking away and marrying children [women under 18 and men under 21] against the wills of their parents and guardians' *(6 Anne, cap.16)*; an act of 1725 providing that 'a Catholic priest or degraded clergyman who married two Protestants or a Protestant and a Catholic was guilty of a felony punishable by death' *(12 George I, cap.3)*; an act of 1735 'for the more effectual preventing of clandestine marriages' *(9 George II, cap.11);* and two further acts of 1745 and 1749 for the same purpose *(19 George II, cap 13; 23 George II, cap.10).* The acts of 1707-49 anticipated the provisions of Lord Hardwicke's famous Marriage Act of 1753, which therefore needed no Irish counterpart *(*Stone, *Road to Divorce*, p. 128).
204 UL Dunraven Papers, D/3196/L/5/1, typescript copy of a letter from Mrs S[arah] Colvill to her husband, Robert Colvill, 1 October 1772. Unless otherwise attributed, the information about the Newcomen case is taken from this source.
205 For some memorable anecdotes about the couple, see the Knight of Glin, 'James Gandon's Work at Carrigglas, Co. Longford', in *The Country Seat: Studies in the History of the British Country House* (London, 1970), pp. 185–8 and 191–2 (hereafter, *The Country Seat*).
206 NLI Smythe of Barbavilla Papers, MS 41,599/7, John Agnew, Longford, to Ralph Smyth, 3 March 1772.
207 Kelly, 'Abduction of Women of Fortune', pp. 20–21 and 35-6; PRONI Abercorn Papers, D/623/A/35, Archdeacon Hamilton to Abercorn, 1 December 1761; Rev. George Hill, 'Gleanings in Family History from the Antrim Coast: the Macnaghtens and MacNeills', in *The Ulster Journal of Archaeology,* 1st ser., VII (1860), pp. 134–6 (I am indebted for this reference to Mr Ian Montgomery); PRONI Sneyd Papers, T/3229/1/38, Lord Chancellor Clare to 1st Lord Auckland, 19 September 1801, printed in Fleming and Malcomson, '*A Volley of Execrations',* no. 515.
208 T.C. Barnard, *The Abduction of a Limerick Heiress: social and political Relations in mid-Eighteenth-Century Ireland* (Maynooth Studies in Local History, Dublin, 1998), passim. This monograph was researched (heroically) when the Smythe of Barbavilla Papers in NLI, the major source for it, were in an unsorted state in the 'aluminiums' familiar to the more intrepid NLI readers. I have since sorted and listed that archive. The part of it relating to the Ingoldsbys and the abduction now bears reference MS 41,581/1–37.
209 Egmont Papers BL Add. MS 46,999, f. 139, Philip Perceval to Sir John Perceval, 29 October 1709.
210 Kelly, 'Abduction of Women of Fortune', p. 30
211 See 109*n*.
212 W.A. Maguire, 'Castle Nugent and Castle Rackrent: Fact and Fiction in Maria Edgeworth', in *Eighteenth-Century Ireland,* XI (1996), pp. 146–59; Rizzo, *Companions without Vows*, pp. 175–84 and 357–61; *The Gentleman's Magazine for August 1789*, pp. 766–7; E. Ford, *Tewin Water, or the Story of Lady Cathcart ...* (privately printed, Enfield, 1876), passim; PRONI, Nugent of Farrenconnell Papers, D/3835/E, 'Memoir of the celebrated Lady Cathcart...'.
213 Author's collection, letters to her stepson, the 9th Lord Cathcart (d.1776) and to his son, the 10th Lord Cathcart, 1770–89, about Lady Cathcart and her proceedings against Maguire's executors (hereafter Cathcart Letters), James Russell to 9th Lord Cathcart, 25 April 1770; W.J. Hardy, 'Lady Cathcart and her Husbands', in *St Albans and Herts Architectural and Archaeological Society [Journal]* (1898), p. 125. The title deeds to her various properties are apparently in the Hertfordshire RO, D/EP, T/2341–7.
214 Quoted in Rizzo, *Companions without Vows*, p. 177.
215 Cathcart Letters, Gregg & Potts, Skinners' Hall, London, to 9th Lord Cathcart, 23 May 1775.
216 Maguire, 'Castle Nugent', p. 152.
217 See 215*n*.
218 Maguire, 'Castle Nugent', p. 148.
219 R. Sedgwick, *The History of Parliament: the House of Commons, 1715–54* (2 vols., London, 1970), II, p. 520.
220 Cathcart Letters, James Russell to 9th Lord Cathcart, 25 April 1770.
221 Ibid., Lady Cathcart to George Meares, her Dublin attorney, June 1775.
222 Maguire, 'Castle Nugent', pp. 152–3; Cathcart Letters, Gregg & Potts to Cathcart, 23 May 1775.
223 Gregg & Potts to Cathcart, 23 May 1775.
224 Maguire, 'Castle Nugent', pp. 149 and 156–7; Rizzo *Companions without Vows*, pp. 175–82.
225 Cathcart Letters, Cathcart to George Meares, 3 June 1775.
226 Maguire, 'Castle Nugent', p. 152.
227 Cathcart Letters, James Russell to Cathcart, 25 April 1770.
228 Maguire, 'Castle Nugent', pp. 151–4.

229 Ibid. These – and the fact that she was actually imprisoned for a much shorter part of her time in Ireland than had hitherto been imagined – are the major revisions made by Dr Maguire to the story. I am indebted to him for these ideas and most grateful for his help while I was working on this section of the book.
230 Ibid., p. 148.
231 Cathcart Letters, Lady Cathcart to Carthcart, 24 May 1775.
232 Ibid., Mr Sutton, Basinghall Street, to 10th Lord Cathcart, and Philip Cosgrave, Tewin Water, to Cathcart, both 4 August 1789.
233 Rizzo, *Companions without Vows*, p. 182.
234 PRONI Villiers-Stuart Papers, T/3131/J/12/4, copy of the marriage settlement, 12 June 1739.
235 T/3131/D/3, letters from Mrs Richard Butler to Grandison, 1734 and 1746; /F/9, scrappy calculations of Grandison and Mason rentals and financial affairs, 1738–c.1746 and 1765; and /J/13-14, bundle of settlement documents and copy of the patent creating the Grandison viscountcy, 1747–8, 1750–52 and 1761–2.
236 T/3131/B/5/3, Dean Alexander Alcock to Mason, 9 July 1739.
237 PRONI Bedford Papers, T/2915/7/29, Primate Stone to Duke of Bedford, 27 March 1759.
238 PRONI Villiers-Stuart Papers, T/3131/E/ 10/1–2, two formal documents about the name change, October–November 1771.
239 National Archives of Ireland (hereafter NAI), Pembroke Estates Management Ltd. (Dublin) Papers, 97/46/1/2/7 and 97/46/1/2/6, Hon. William Fitzwilliam to 6th Viscount Fitzwilliam, 26 December 1758, and Carbery to Lord Fitzwilliam, 25 March 1760. I am grateful to Ms Aideen Ireland of NAI for providing me with the reference numbers of these letters, which I last saw in the offices of Pembroke Estates Ltd long prior to the deposit of the archive in NAI.
240 Carbery Papers (in the possession of Mr Robert Boyle, Bisbrooke Hall, Glaston, Rutland), C/3/26, David Roche to 4th Lord Carbery, 11 December 1795, and D/1, bundle of c.175 documents about the Watson fortune and the ensuing disputes over it, 1794–1831.
241 NAI, D.20,487, the marriage settlement, 11 August 1792.
242 Carbery Papers, C/3/27, Roche to Carbery, 30 December 1795.
243 C/3/50, Roche to Carbery, 12 March 1802, and D/11, G.F. Evans to Baxendale & Co., and reply, 18 and 25 April 1829; TNA Chancery Masters' Accounts, C.108/77, attested rental of the estate of Edward Hartopp, 1815.
244 NAI D.20,487, the marriage settlement, 20 January 1806, and D.20,500, deed of mortgage, 26 March 1805.
245 See Malcomson, List, with introduction, of the Springfield Castle (Muskerry) Papers in PRONI's Register of Irish Archives, particularly A/3/3, assignments from the 1st Lord Lyttleton (of the second creation) to Sir Brodrick Chinnery, 1st Bt, of mortgages on the estate, 1802. I am grateful to Mr and the Hon. Mrs Jonathan Sykes (*née* Deane) for making the compilation of this list possible and for their hospitality at Springfield Castle. Lord Muskerry's grandfather had succeeded in 1747 to a patrimonial estate worth c.£2,500 a year, much of it a 'rising' property (NLI Smythe of Barbavilla Papers, MS 41,581/12, Arthur Blennerhasset to William Smyth, 8 June 1734); so the previous family record of the Deanes was one of extreme fecklessness.
246 NLI Killadoon Papers, MS 36,065/8: Robert Livingston (surveyor) to 2nd Earl of Charlemont (husband of the other co-heiress), 16 September 1807.
247 Killadoon Papers at Killadoon, G/1, wills of William Bermingham of Rosshill, 1790 and [1798?], and G/4, epitome of the Bermingham-Clements marriage settlement, 24 July 1800 (a full copy of the settlement will be found in NLI Leitrim Papers, MS 33,850/1); NLI, MS 33,850/5, counsel's opinion, 1 August 1828, on the title to the Rosshill estate, which recites the Rosshill settlement of 24 July 1800.
248 Killadoon Papers at Killadoon, C/2: accounts current for the half-year's rent of the Rosshill estate, 1804 and 1816; PRONI, Landed Estate Court Rentals (printed), D/1201/61, sale rental of the Rosshill estate, 1860.
249 Killadoon Papers at Killadoon, G/1, will of William Bermingham, [1798?].
250 NLI Killadoon Papers, MS 36,031/3, Lady Leitrim, Rosshill, to Mrs Bermingham (her mother), Cheltenham, 29 September 1825, MS 36,031/5, Lord Leitrim to Mrs Bermingham, 1 October 1835, and MS 36,032/10, Lady Charlemont to Lord Leitrim, 19 October and 5 November [1843?]. Although strongly attached to Rosshill and ardent in her testamentary injunctions of 1825 that her daughters should live there periodically, Mrs Bermingham showed no inclination to do so herself but, like most dowagers (see pp. 17–18 above), took up her abode somewhere where there was a nucleus of similarly situated ladies – in her case Cheltenham. For her will and testamentary papers, 1825–7, see Killadoon Papers at Killadoon, G/2.
251 NLI Killadoon Papers, MS 36,064/10, letters to Lord Leitrim from Arthur Lynch and Arthur P. Lynch of Petersborough Castle, Ballinrobe, about mining on the Rosshill estate, 1805–12.
252 Ibid., MS 36,032/11, Charlemont to Leitrim, [c.1804], and MS 36,065/8, James Williamson (surveyor) to Leitrim, 16 June 1806; Killadoon Papers at Killadoon, C/2, printed copy of an *Act for vesting the real, freehold and chattel estates and lands of William Bermingham late of Rosshill in trustees, 1808*.
253 Ibid., MS 36,032/1, Mrs Bermingham, Clifton, to Leitrim, 20 December [1807?].
254 Ibid., MS 36,031/3, Lady Leitrim to Mrs Bermingham, 29 September 1825, MS 36,032/11, Charlemont to Leitrim, [c.1804], MS 36,032/10, Lady Charlemont to Leitrim, 7 September 1843, MS 36,032/9, Lady Charlemont to Leitrim, 8 May 1830, and MS 36,069/4, Lady Charlemont to Hon. W.S. Clements, 6 September [1838].
255 Ibid., MS 36,032/10, Leitrim to Lady Charlemont, 2 October [1840].
256 Ibid., Lady Charlemont to Leitrim, 23 September [1840]; NLI MS 3813, rental of the 3rd Earl of Leitrim's Rosshill

estate, 1867. This shows that, using the Landed Estates Court for the purpose, Lord Leitrim had bought outright 18,690 of the former undivided acreage of 22,453, with a rental of £1,904 a year.
257 PRONI Perceval-Maxwell Papers, D/1556/17/4, statement of Mrs Grace Maxwell's case, 12 February 1779, and opinion of Lloyd Kenyon on it, 2 June 1779. Kenyon became chief justice of the King's Bench in 1788, and presumably knew what he was talking about. However, it was the usual procedure in cases of impotence for an ecclesiastical court to annul the marriage, in which case the question of divorce did not arise because the marriage was deemed never to have taken place.
258 See 28*n* above.
259 PRONI Annesley Papers, D/1503/3/5/72, minute of a conversation with 'Sophy' (the alleged Lady Annesley), 30 December 1819.
260 Clay, 'Marriage and Large Estates', p. 505. Clay argues that in England the gap between the two if anything widened from the last third of the eighteenth century, because the fall which then took place in the interest rate was more than counteracted by a rise in the purchase price of land. In Ireland the price of land probably did not rise so significantly as in England; but the interest rate did not fall so significantly either.
261 Dickson, op. cit., pp. 97 and 106–7; PRONI Caledon Papers, D/2433/A/1/92, deed of sale of the Caledon estate by [the 7th] Earl of Orrery to James Alexander [later 1st Earl of Caledon], 18 January 1776.
262 PRONI Foster/Massereene Papers D/207/19/77, John Stratford to Anthony Foster 4 June 1747; PRONI Arran Papers (originals in TCD), T/3200/1/43, Hon. Richard Gore to 2nd Earl of Arran, 22 January 1788.
263 PRONI Miscellaneous British Records Association deposit, D/585/34, deed between Rev. Thomas Ross, Viscount Caulfeild, etc., 14 May 1799.
264 See 200*n* above.
265 PRONI Armagh Diocesan Registry Papers, DIO 4/13/10/4/15, financial calculations by Elizabeth, Lady Waterford, [1801?].
266 PRONI Londonderry Estate Office Papers, D/654/F/6, marriage settlement of Alexander Stewart and Mary Cowan, 30 June 1737.
267 See p. 38 above; PRONI Donoughmore Papers, T/3459/F/13/87, Lord Hutchinson to Francis Hely-Hutchinson, 19–20 December 1823
268 D.J. Butler, *Cahir: a Guide to Heritage Town and District* (Cahir, 1999), pp.7–8; NLI ILB 340, printed House of Lords appeal papers in Thynne v Glengall, [c.1850]; W.E. Vaughan, *Landlords and Tenants in mid-Victorian Ireland* (Oxford, 1994), pp. 223–4; NLI printed Encumbered Estates Court Rentals, vol. 18 (August–November 1853), Glengall sale rental, 11 November 1853, with contemporary newspaper commentary stuck to the front endpaper of the volume; 'Rental of the estate of the trustees of Lady Margaret Charteris, 1864' (courtesy of Dr D.J. Butler). *The Complete Peerage*, sub 'Glengall', reports a story that Lady Glengall's fortune was £1,500,000.

269 PRONI Granard Papers, J/9/2/2, Countess of Moira to her daughter, the Countess of Granard, 3 May 1792. For the tendency of the Irish aristocracy to eschew marriage into the commercial classes, see pp. 44–8, 127–8 and 244 above.
270 Malcomson, *Nathaniel Clements*, pp. 206–88.
271 For some comment on these, see ibid., pp. 244–5 and 406–7.
272 East Sussex Record Office, Abergavenny Papers, ABE/25C, settlement on the Robinson-Nevill marriage, 29 September 1781, and ABE/20X, will of John Robinson, 29 April 1802. I am indebted for these references to Mr Christopher Whittick of ESRO.
273 Abergavenny (John Robinson) Papers (in the possession of the Marquess of Abergavenny, Eridge Castle, Tunbridge Wells), C/18, Robinson to Hon. Henry Nevill, 6 July 1782. This Lord Maitland, later 8th Earl of Lauderdale (d.1839), was a cousin of the immensely rich by-passed heiress, Lady Mary Maitland, who married the 12th Earl of Meath in 1868 (see p. 19 above).
274 See pp. 38 and 19 above.
275 For the financial collapse of his predecessor, Sir Ralph Gore, 6th Bt, one and only Earl of Ross, see Malcomson, 'Belleisle and its Owners', *Clogher Record* (1998), pp. 9–31, and Malcomson, *Nathaniel Clements,* pp. 290–300.
276 NLI Killadoon Papers, MS 36,064/9, Sir Richard Hardinge, 1st Bt, to Lord Clements (later 2nd Earl of Leitrim), [post 6 October 1802?].
277 See p. 42 above.
278 NLI Leinster Papers, MS 41,552/30, Emily, Duchess of Leinster to her son, the 2nd Duke, 12 June [1791].
279 Marson, 'The Belmores of Castle Coole'.
280 PRONI Londonderry Estate Office Papers, D/654/F/1–4, the marriage settlement, 7 June 1794; Hyde, op.cit., pp. 115-9. See also 131*n* above.
281 Killadoon Papers at Killadoon, C/2, volume entitled 'Valuation of the estate of the Rt Hon. The Earls of Leitrim and Charlemont situated in [the] counties of Galway and Mayo, 1857'. See also 248*n* above.

NOTES TO CHAPTER FOUR

282 See the frontispiece. Nugent himself owed almost everything he possessed to his three marriages – see pp. 23–4.
283 PRONI Foster/Massereene Papers, D/562/719, Thomas Burgh to John Foster, 5 January 1775; Northamptonshire RO Stowe (Nugent/Grenville) Papers (photocopies in PRONI, ref. T/3503), T/3503/2 and 3A–C, proposal by Lord Nugent for the marriage settlement, and the component deeds of settlement themselves, 14–15 April 1775; *Historical Manuscripts Commission* (hereafter, *HMC*) *Report ... on the Dropmore Papers*, I (London, 1892), pp. 358 and 360, Marquess of Buckingham to W.W. Grenville, 18 and 29 October 1788; Nugent, *Memoir of Earl Nugent,* pp. 26–7; TNA W.D. Adams Papers, 30/58/1, Buckingham to Pitt, 16 October 1794. In this case, the estates were initially settled on the eldest son, but must subsequently have

been re-settled, by internal family arrangement, on the second. The authority for Lord Grenville's self-styled 'stewardship' is Grenville to Thomas Coutts, 29 October 1804, quoted in P.J. Jupp, *Lord Grenville, 1759–1834* (Oxford, 1985), p. 301. Initially, Lady Grenville had been just the sort of well portioned young woman who, it was argued in Chapter Three, was a particularly desirable acquisition: her portion at marriage in 1792 was £20,000 with £11,000 more to come on her father's death, and no strings or stewardship attached (Jupp, *Grenville*, p. 108).

284 Malcomson, 'Absenteeism', pp. 28–30.
285 Dickson, *Old World Colony*, pp. 85–94, especially pp. 88–9.
286 PRONI Downshire Papers, D/607/C/5, draft of a letter from Lord Downshire to Lady Clanwilliam, [3–26 October 1793]; PRONI Clanwilliam/Meade Papers, D/2044/F/13, reminiscences of the 3rd Earl of Clanwilliam, c.1870, pp. 1–3.
287 Malcomson, 'A Woman Scorned?: Theodosia, Countess of Clanwilliam (1743–1817)', *Familia,* no. 15 (1999), pp. 1–25.
288 PRONI Templemore Papers, T/3303/1/6, marriage settlement of Lord Spencer Chichester and Lady Harriet Stewart, 7 August 1795. I am grateful to the present Marquess of Donegall for drawing my attention to the existence (and the terms) of this settlement, the original of which is in his possession. See also W.A. Maguire, *Living like a Lord: the 2nd Marquess of Donegall, 1769–1844* (UHF, Belfast, 1984), pp. 12–18, and RIA Charlemont Papers, 2nd ser., IX, f. 59, Dr Alexander Haliday to 1st Earl of Charlemont, 15 January 1799.
289 Dickson, *Old World Colony*, p. 89.
290 *The Complete Peerage,* sub 'Thomond' and 'Inchiquin'; Hon. H.A. Wyndham, *A Family History, 1688–1837: the Wyndhams of Somerset, Sussex and Wiltshire* (Oxford, 1950), pp. 108–9, 225, 255–7; Malcomson, 'Absenteeism', pp. 19 and 30–31; Namier and Brooke, *House of Commons, 1754–90,* III, pp. 667–8; The Petworth House Estate Office Archive, Petworth, West Sussex, PHA/MC/6/19A, Edmond Hogan to Richard Lahy, Gray's Inn, 21 April 1741 and 10 April 1744, MC 7/35, Hogan to Robert French (executor and trustee of 7th Earl of Thomond), 5 October and 11 December 1745, MC 7/32, letters from G.J. Guidott, Inner Temple, to French, 1741–5, some of them about a Chancery suit between Percy Wyndham O'Brien and Lord Inchiquin, and MC 7/27, letters from Percy Lord Thomond to Richard Lahy, 1763–4, about the late Lord Thomond's bequests to Jacobite O'Briens in France, the Shortgrove estate, etc. For the sale of Shortgrove, see Smith Papers, Moot Farm, Downton, Wiltshire: John North to Joseph Smith, 29 October 1801 (Smith, Pitt's private secretary from 1787 to 1806 and a wealthy multiple sinecurist, had rented Shortgrove for some, or many, years prior to his purchase of it in 1801). For the 4th and 5th Earls of Inchiquin, see p. 8 above. The latter was created marquess of Thomond in 1800, but of course owned none of the former Thomond estates and had not inherited any of the earlier Thomond titles, all of which had expired in either 1741 or 1774.

291 PRONI Darnley Papers, T/2851/2, Hugh to Ralph Howard, 14 September 1784; NLI Reports on Private Collections, no. 12, survey of the Stoyte/Darnley estate in the parish of Street, Co. Westmeath, 1767. For the Petty case, see pp. 195–6 above, and for other examples of cadet inheritance in defiance of geography, see Malcomson, 'Absenteeism', p. 29.
292 Malcomson, *Archbishop Charles Agar: Churchmanship and Politics in Ireland, 1760–1810* (Dublin, 2002), pp. 107 and 118–19.
293 The Creighton family, Earls Erne, annexed two adjoining estates to their core estate in Co. Fermanagh as a result of two different marriages. But only one of these was a marriage to a neighbour, and neither was a deliberate attempt at annexation. See pp. 204–5 above.
294 PRONI Abercorn Papers, D/623/B/S, deeds of purchase by the Colepeper family from the representatives of the Duke of Lennox of the manors of Magavlin and Lismoghry, 26–7 January 1678; and D/623/A/1, copy of an epitaph on Elizabeth Hamilton [*née* Colepeper, mother of the 6th Earl of Abercorn, c.1709].
295 Dickson, op. cit., p. 110.
296 History of Parliament transcripts from the Chatham Papers, TNA 30/8/149, 1st Earl of Kingston to Pitt, 18 November 1789 and 2 February 1790.
297 Cambridge University Library, Pitt/Pretyman Papers (photocopies in PRONI, reference T/3319), T/3319/13, 10th Earl of Westmorland to Pitt, 4 April 1792; PRONI Abercorn Papers, D/623/A/134/24, Thomas Knox to Abercorn, 3 June [1792].
298 Malcomson, 'Absenteeism', p. 24.
299 TNA Home Office Papers, HO 100/94, ff. 279–80, Oxmantown to Duke of Portland, 14 December 1800; Rosse Papers, D/7/97 and 99, 2nd Earl of Rosse to the 1st Earl's widow, 30 September 1818, and reply, 'Received 15 November'.
300 History of Parliament transcripts from the Melville Papers, National Library of Scotland, MS 15, f. 81, Colonel Charles Craufurd to Henry Dundas, 5 March 1800.
301 PRONI Villiers-Stuart Papers, T/3131/E/67, Pierse Barron to Grandison, 11 June 1782.
302 Quoted in Cannon, *Aristocratic Century*, p. 127.
303 T/3131/G/1/3, schedule of Lord and Lady Henry Stuart's debts, [c.1802]. See also 383*n* below.
304 T/3131/L/2/11, copy of the Stuarts' marriage settlement, 30 June 1802.
305 T/3131/G/1/8, Stuart to [Coutts Trotter?], 6 November 1802.
306 E.M. Johnston[-Liik] ed. 'The State of the Irish House of Commons in 1791', in *Proc. RIA,* LIX, sec. C, no. 1 (1957), pp. 42 and 53.
307 *Gleanings from an Old Portfolio*, II, pp. 43–5, Lady Portarlington to Lady Louisa Stuart, 10 October 1785. See also 199*n* above.
308 See 305*n* above; PRONI Villiers-Stuart Papers, T/3131/G/2, Stuart to Sir William Homan, 26 February 1808.

309 T/3131/I/1/7, newspaper cutting of the 1880s rhapsodising on the 1826 election.

310 Malcomson, *John Foster*, p. 251.

311 Unless otherwise attributed, the information on which the next three paragraphs are based is taken from my introduction to PRONI D/1735, the McGildowny Papers; Edmund McGildowny was the principal agent for the Antrim family, particularly for Lord and Lady Mark Kerr, c.1800–1832.

312 See pp. 7–27 above.

313 Angela, Countess of Antrim, 'The quarrelling Countesses' (typescript of a talk given to the Larne Historical Society on 8 October 1979, kindly made available soon afterwards to me by the late Lady Antrim), p. 11, and passim. The text has since been edited and published by Mr Ian Montgomery (the PRONI archivist who has catalogued the massive Antrim Estate Office Archive) in *The Glynns: the Journal of the Glens of Antrim Historical Society* (2002), pp. 24–36. In the published version, the reference to Edmund Phelps is at pp. 30–31.

314 PRONI Antrim Estate Office Papers, D/2977/7B/85 and 88-9, rentals of the respective shares in the estate which Lord Antrim, Edmund McDonnell and Frances Anne owned in 1839.

315 All these quotations are taken from two letters: D/2977/5/1/6/1 and 17, Kerr to Edmund McDonnell, 3 April 1821 and 2 January 1838.

316 See p. 28 above.

317 The main source of information about 'the wars of the Westmeaths' and the background to Lady Rosa's inheritance is Stone's brilliant 'Westmeath v Westmeath', in *Broken Lives,* pp. 284–346. But see also: Castle Forbes, Co. Longford, Granard Papers, K/2/8, Greville to Viscountess Forbes, 6 February 1852, K/4/18, rental of the Mullingar estate, 1852, and K/4/12, estate and financial correspondence, 1847–54, of Viscountess Forbes, mother and guardian of the 7th Earl of Granard (mentioning a good offer of £125,000 for the Mullingar estate made in 1854); and PRONI Howard Bury Papers, T/3069/K/5 and 6, printed letters from Lord Westmeath to the editor of *The Westmeath Guardian*, 20 July and 10 August 1865. The Greville motto is a snippet from a longer Latin quotation, and may make better sense in context: in isolation, it means 'I scarcely call these things our own'.

318 See p. 59 above.

319 Cunningham ed. *Letters of Horace Walpole,* I, p. 171, Walpole to Mann, 26 May 1742. I am indebted for this reference to the Knight of Glin.

320 In the copy of the pamphlet which I have used (and which belongs to the Knight of Glin), and possibly in all copies, there is bound in at the end a second title, a spoof *English Register…*, also printed in 1742. This lists all the available English bachelors and widowers, mostly with addresses, and argues that an importation of Irishmen is unnecessary and an insult.

321 PRONI Villiers-Stuart Papers, T/3131/D/8/2.

322 The petition is printed in *The Complete Peerage*, sub 'Manchester'. The original is BL Add. MS 32,726, f. 158.

323 Young, *A Tour in Ireland …* (Dublin, 1780), II, p. 83; NAI M.2077, Beaulieu estate map, 1766; PRONI Knight of Kerry Papers, MIC/639/10/54, Judge Day to 2nd Earl of Glandore, 27 May 1810.

324 *The Complete Peerage*, sub 'Londonderry'. Londonderry had been a widower since 1812 and had been involved in numerous notorious *liaisons* with women, particularly while ambassador to Vienna from 1814 onwards. It would have been less alliterative but more accurate if Moore had said 'old *roués*', not 'old dandies'. Londonderry's private life undoubtedly added to the prejudice against him.

325 See 131*n* above. See also PRONI Londonderry Estate Office Papers, D/654/F/25, the marriage settlement, 27 March 1819.

326 A. Heesom, 'Entrepreneurial Paternalism: the 3rd Lord Londonderry (1778–1854) and the Coal Trade', in *Durham University Journal*, new ser., XXXV (1973–4), pp. 238–56.

327 A. Casement, 'William Vitruvius Morrison's Scheme for Mount Stewart, Co. Down: was it ever realised', in *Irish Architectural and Decorative Studies*, VII (2004), pp. 33–4 and 39; and idem, 'The Management of the Londonderry Estates in Ulster during the Great Famine', in *Familia*, no. 21 (2005), pp. 18–19 and 41–2.

328 For other examples of such reunification, see Malcomson, 'Absenteeism', pp. 28–9.

329 For the Dunravens, see pp. 339–41 and 202–3 above.

330 NLI Lismore Papers, MS 6914, rental of the Burlington/Devonshire estates in Ireland, 1798.

331 Malcomson, 'The Gentle Leviathan: Arthur Hill, 2nd Marquess of Downshire, 1753–1801', in P. Roebuck ed. *Plantation to Partition: Essays in Ulster History in Honour of J.L. McCracken* (hereafter, *Plantation to Partition* [Belfast, 1981]), pp. 102–17; PRONI Pollock Papers, T/3346/6, Downshire to John Pollock, [early August 1801].

332 See 199*n* above.

333 PRONI Donoughmore Papers, T/3459/B/1, copy of the marriage settlement, 19 April 1751, and /Z/25, Knocklofty estate rental 1789-98.

334 Elton Hall, Peterborough, Proby Papers, volume of c.1930 typescript copies titled 'Miscellaneous 1', containing (p. 133) a copy of the will of the 2nd Viscount Allen, 25 June 1730, Messrs Orpen, Franks & Co. chest, copy of the will of Margaret Viscountess Allen, 20 July 1754, MS 53, volume (1799–1802) containing an Irish estate rental, 1799, Book 18 (MS 488), assignment of mortgage, 22 February 1810, and unnumbered and untitled volume containing a Huntingdonshire estate rental, 1823; PRONI Bedford Papers, T/2915/3/42, 1st Lord Carysfort to 4th Duke of Bedford, 11 December 1757; History of Parliament transcripts from the Dropmore Papers, 1st Earl of Carysfort to Lord Grenville, [c.1 January 1790] and 13 January 1799; PRONI Shannon Papers, D/2707/A3/3/29, 2nd Earl of Shannon to Lord Boyle, 31 May [1797]; PRONI Liverpool Papers, T/2593/47, 3rd Earl Talbot [the Lord Lieutenant] to Liverpool, 27 February 1821, printed in *IOP: Private Collections*, I, p. 267; R.F. Foster, *Charles Stewart Parnell: the Man and his Family* (Hassocks, 1976), pp. 119, 206 and 208.

335 See p. 73 above.

336 History of Parliament transcripts from the Chatham Papers, TNA 30/8/174, Rous to Pitt, 18 April 1800; Suffolk RO (Ipswich branch) Stradbroke Papers (microfilm of the Irish estate material in PRONI, ref. MIC/253), MIC/253/50, statement of case concerning the lands of Cullen, Co. Tipperary [1800], and MIC/253/14, A. Coates to 2nd Earl of Stradbroke, 11 March 1840. The question of the extent and value of the estate is complicated by the fact that an unascertainable proportion of it was sold in 1830 – see M. Lenihan, *Limerick: its History and Antiquities* (Dublin, 1866), p. 744.

337 PRONI Donoughmore Papers, T/3459/C/2/149–50, Francis Hely-Hutchinson and Rev. Christopher Harvey to the Provost, 17 October 1785; /F/2, Robert Pigott to Francis Hely-Hutchinson, 6 May 1814; and /D/48-9, Francis Hely-Hutchinson to his eldest brother, the 1st Earl of Donoughmore, 18 January 1820 and 22 April 1824.

338 See pp. 81–2 above.

339 Norfolk and Norwich RO, Hobart of Blickling (Buckinghamshire) Papers (photocopies in PRONI, ref. T/3110/1–13), rentals, etc, 1817–42, relating to the share of the Vintners Proportion owned by Lady Castlereagh/Londonderry, 1817–29, and left by her in 1829 to the representatives of her eldest half-sister, Lady Henrietta Hobart, Marchioness of Lothian (formerly Lady Belmore, who had died in 1805).

NOTES TO CHAPTER FIVE

340 For the source of this quotation, see 374n.

341 Stone, *The Family, Sex and Marriage in England, 1500–1800* (New York, 1977); R. Trumbach, *The Rise of the Egalitarian Family: Aristocratic Kinship and Domestic Relations in Eighteenth-Century England* (New York, 1978); Bonfield, 'Marriage Settlements', (op. cit., 1979) and Bonfield, *Marriage Settlements, 1601–1740* (Cambridge, 1983); Spring, 'Law and the Theory of the Affective Family', *Law, Land and Family* (ops. cit., 1983 and 1993) and 'A Comment on Payling's "Economics of Marriage"', *The Economic History Review*, LVI, no. 2 (2003); S.J. Payling, 'The Economics of Marriage in late Mediaeval England: the Marriage of Heiresses', and '…A Reply to Spring', ibid., LIV (2001), and LVI (2003). This is only a selection from a more voluminous literature.

342 Cannon, *Aristocratic Century*, p. 79.

343 Malcomson 'Fall of the House of Conolly', op. cit.; BL Strafford Papers, Add. MS 22, 229, ff. 427–8, 1st Earl of Strafford to Lady Strafford (Lady Anne's parents), 23 May 1729, and Add. MS 22,228, f.77, Conolly to Strafford, 2 May 1733. For the Conolly marriage settlement and its consequences, see pp. 6, 34 and 194–5 above.

344 Add. MS 22,228, ff. 126 and 131, Lady Anne to Strafford, 30 May and 17 August 1734; NLI Smythe of Barbaville Papers, MS 41,578/11, Mrs Conolly to her sister, Mrs Bonnell, 22 April 1738.

345 H.C. Lawlor, *A History of the Family of Cairnes or Cairns and its Connections* (London, 1906), pp. 82–106; P. Collins ed. *County Monaghan Sources in PRONI* (Belfast, 1998), pp. 26–7; Richardson ed. *Long-forgotten Days*, pp. 245–6 and 251–2, Lady Blayney to Mrs Lavington, 24 January 1743/4 and 22 April 1786.

346 N.P. Canny, *The upstart Earl: a Study of the social and mental World of Richard Boyle, 1st Earl of Cork (1566–1643)* (Cambridge, 1982), pp. 119 and 123; S.J. Connolly, 'Family, Love and Marriage in early modern Ireland', in M. MacCurtain and M. O'Dowd eds. *Women in early modern Ireland* (Edinburgh, 1991), pp. 278 and 288. For telling examples of affective marriages in the first third of the eighteenth century, see Conolly, pp. 280–82 and 286–7.

347 NLI Smythe of Barbavilla Papers, MS 41,585/6, Michael Clarke to William Smyth, 1 December 1750.

348 Ibid., MS 41,578/7 and 9, Mrs Conolly to Mrs Bonnell, 9 December 1734 and 25 May 1736.

349 Ibid., MS 41,579/9, Francis Burton to Mrs Bonnell, 9 November and 9 December 1729.

350 Ibid., MS 41,577/1–5, Mrs Mary Jones to her sister, Mrs Bonnell, 11 May [1734?], and MS 41,378/11, Mrs Conolly to Mrs Bonnell, 22 April 1738.

351 Quoted in B. Falk, *The Way of the Montagus*, p. 281. For the Duchess of Manchester, see pp. 59 and 102–4 above.

352 For this act, see pp. 156–7 above.

353 Dickson, *Old World Colony*, pp. 526–7.

354 L. Mitchell, *The Whig World*, p. 44; TCD Conolly Papers, MS 3977/706, Byng to Thomas Conolly (his brother-in-law), 6 Dec. 1780.

355 Chapman and Dormer, *Elizabeth and Georgiana*, pp. 13–24. After his succession to the earldom of Bristol and its attendant wealth in 1779 and after the final collapse of the marriage in 1780, he still refused to allow his daughter more than a 'scanty' and irregularly paid 'pittance' of £300 a year.

356 These quotations are insertions made by Lady Belmore herself in a paper drawn up at the time of her divorce in 1793 – Marson, 'Belmores of Castle Coole'.

357 Quoted in Tillyard, *Aristocrats*, p. 187.

358 PRONI Sneyd Papers, T/3229/1/32, Clare to Auckland, 19 June 1800, printed in Fleming and Malcomson eds. *A Volley of Execrations*, no. 464. These sentiments go far to disprove the scurrilous contemporary stories that Lady Clare was an adulteress and Clare a cuckold – see: A. Kavanaugh, *John FitzGibbon, Earl of Clare: Protestant Reaction and English Authority in late Eighteenth-Century Ireland* (Dublin, 1997), pp. 125, 203–5 and 313; and '*A Volley of Execrations*', pp. 145–6, 238n and 404n. Lady Clare was pretty and fashion-crazed and came from a family noted for its volatility. It is probable that her conduct was light and flirtatious and nothing worse.

359 Anon., *Letters on Love, Marriage and Adultery addressed to the Rt Hon. The Earl of Exeter* (London, 1789: reprinted, New York and London, 1984), pp. 63, 86 and 97.

360 T.C. Barnard, 'A Tale of three Sisters: Katherine Conolly of Castletown', in idem, *Irish Protestant Ascents and Descents, 1641–1770* (Dublin, 2004), pp. 266–87.

361 NLI Smythe of Barbavilla Papers, MS 41,582/6, Rev. James Smyth to his brother, William Smyth, 24 May 1728; NLI Wicklow Papers, MS 38,601/2 (part), typescript copy of Caroline Hamilton's 'Reminiscences', [c.1800].

362 F.F. Moore, *A Georgian Pageant* (London, 1908), pp. 105 and 110–12. See also I. Gantz, *The Pastel Portrait: the Gunnings of Castle Coote …* (London, 1963), pp. 21–65.

363 NLI Smythe of Barbavilla Papers, MS 41,581/12, Arthur Blennerhassett to William Smyth, 8 June 1734, and MS 41,598/2, Michael Clarke to Ralph Smyth, 29 January 1774. For the other references to the importance of education, see pp. 133–4 above. For the musical component of the education of young women of rank, see R.A. Richey, 'Landed Society in mid-Eighteenth-Century Co. Down' (unpublished Ph.D. thesis, QUB, 2000), p. 137.

364 Tullynally Castle, Castlepollard, Co. Westmeath: Pakenham Papers, P/21-2, notes by Thomas Pakenham on the Tullynally and other Irish country-house libraries for a lecture on that subject to the London Chapter of the Irish Georgian Society, c.1975; Sotheby's sale catalogue of *The Library of the Rt Hon. The Earl of Granard, 21 July 1993*. For Lady Moira, see also Richey, op. cit., pp. 137–43.

365 PRONI Donoughmore Papers, T/3459/F/13/88, Lord Hutchinson to Hon. Francis-Hutchinson, 23 March 1824. For George Rochfort's will, see p. 32 above.

366 See p. 36 above.

367 Tullynally Castle, Pakenham Papers, N/1, journal of the 2nd Lord Longford, 1777-81. See also p. 200 above and, for the de Vesci instance, 73*n*.

368 See 29*n* above.

369 PRONI Villiers-Stuart Papers, T/3131/B/4/2, copy of a letter from Mason to Lord Grandison, 8 February 1739; NLI Farnham Papers, D.20,463, will of Lord Farnham, 29 September 1798.

370 See 104*n* above.

371 UL Dunraven Papers, D/3196/C/1/9, Viscount Mountearl to his son, Hon. Windham Wyndham Quin, 16 December 1816.

372 Richardson ed. *Long-forgotten Days,* pp. 245–6 and 251–2.

373 Cannon, *Aristocratic Century,* p. 90; Hicks, *Lady Di Beauclerk,* pp. 72–3. See also A. Foreman, *Georgiana, Duchess of Devonshire* (London, 1998), pp. 14–21.

374 *The Complete Peerage*, sub 'Richmond'; R.W. Ketton-Cremer, *Horace Walpole: a Biography* (London, 1964), p. 208; PRONI Chatsworth Papers, T/3158/376 and 381, copy of a letter from the Duchess to the Duke, [May?] 1748, and Rev. Dr Thomas Cheyney to the Duke, 28 June 1748; Foreman, *Georgiana, Duchess of Devonshire*, p. 17; BL Wellesley Papers, Add. MS 37, 308, f. 222, Downshire to 2nd Earl of Mornington, 20 March 1799.

375 See pp. 157–61 above.

376 PRONI Foster/Massereene Papers, D/562/2783, copy of a letter from Lady Massereene to Lord Roden, 12 May [1780]; Hatchlands, Surrey: Dillon Papers, Lady Catherine Skeffington to Hon. Mrs Dillon Lee, 9 October [1780].

377 NLI Killadoon Papers, MS 36,034/29, Lord to Lady Leitrim, 5, 12 and 28 February 1833. In 1838, however, Burges did in fact fall heir to almost all Lady Poulett's wealth, including '£34,992 at one dash' as her residuary legatee – MS 36,041/6, Lady Leitrim to Hon. W.S. Clements, 1 June 1838.

378 Tillyard, *Aristocrats,* pp. 9–10. This is not the English example which it sounds. Richmond at this stage was a large Irish landowner in Co. Limerick (UL Dunraven Papers, D/3196/K/4, rental and valuation of the Richmond estate at Adare, 23 December 1721), and Cadogan was the son and heir of Henry Cadogan (1642–1714) of Liscarton, Co. Meath.

379 Maguire, *Living like a Lord,* pp. 26–8.

380 History of Parliament transcripts from the Chatsworth Papers, Duchess of Devonshire to Dowager Lady Spencer, 7 January 1799.

381 Rizzo, *Companions without Vows,* p. 334.

382 PRONI Abercorn Papers, D/623/A/81/57–8, copies of letters from Abercorn to the Dowager Lady Waterford and to Lord Waterford, 2 and 30 April 1803; Waterford Papers, Curraghmore, Co. Waterford, C/4/1-6, Northumberland estate rentals, 1833–59; BL Aberdeen Papers, Add. MS 43,227, f. 17, 1st Viscount Melville to 4th Earl of Aberdeen, 29 June [1805].

383 History of Parliament transcripts from the Camden Papers, 2nd Earl of Chatham to Camden, 15 September 1796.

384 NLI De Vesci Papers, MS 38,899, Handcock to Knapton, 18 May 1751.

385 NLI Leinster Papers, MS 41,552/49, Leinster to Ross, 26 December 1798, MS 41,552/53, Ross to Leinster, 3 July 1799, and MS 41,552/49, Coutts to Leinster, 20 December 1798. This last supposition, that an estate which 'came by the female line' might go to a daughter, is significant in the context of the present study.

386 Cannon, *Aristocratic Century,* pp. 73 and 90. See also 183*n* above and for the similar reaction of Sarah Fownes, p. 8.

387 Quoted in Malcomson, 'The gentle Leviathan', p. 103; author's collection, Hillsborough to 1st Earl of Moira, 20 May 1786; Hayton ed. *Letters of Marmaduke Coghill,* p. 31, Coghill to Southwell, 30 November 1725.

388 See 104*n* above; PRONI Pollock Papers, T/3346/11, Dowager Lady Downshire to John Pollock, 3 December [1801]; TNA Chatham Papers, 30/8/130 (part 2), Dowager Lady Downshire to Pitt, 10 September 1804. The mother of his son was one Sarah Dore. The other two children, both girls, had a different mother, Elizabeth Russell of Hillsborough. The son for whom Lady Downshire applied, and on whose behalf the Downshire family continued to take an active interest, was called William Arthur Dorehill, Arthur being the late Lord Downshire's Christian name, and Dorehill being an anagram of Dore and Hill, the Downshire family name. The two daughters had been given the surname 'Russhill', which was not so much an anagram as a weak pun.

389 Tillyard, *Aristocrats,* pp. 400–02; Malcomson, 'Fall of the House of Conolly' (loc. cit.).

390 See 25*n* above.

391 Quoted in Connolly, 'Family, Love and Marriage', p. 280; PRONI FitzGerald (Knight of Kerry) Papers,

MIC/639/1/12, Mullins to Robert FitzGerald, 4 June 1747.

392 NLI Killadoon Papers, MS 36,034/29, Lord to Lady Leitrim, 28 February 1833. Lady Poulett was Margaret Burges, daughter and heiress of Ynyr Burges (d.1792), a director and sometime governor of the East India Company, and widow of Sir John Smith Burges, Bt (he had double-barrelled his name in consideration of the wealth she had brought him), of Havering Bower, Essex. Lady Poulett possessed both money and the East Ham and Shoebury estates in Essex.

393 Centre for Kentish Studies, Camden Papers, U840/0.200/9, Massy to 2nd Earl Camden, 18 August 1798. Ultimately, he settled for a peerage for himself rather than for her, and for the title of Clarina – a village on his Co. Limerick estate – instead of Niagara, which (according to family tradition recounted by the Knight of Glin) she claimed she could neither pronounce nor spell.

394 PRONI Macartney Papers, D/572/5/77, Robert Waller to Macartney, 31 January 1774; *The Complete Peerage*, sub 'Sydney'; Stradbally Hall, Cosby Papers: D/1, particulars of Lord Sydney's debts (of over £27,000 secured on the estate, plus unspecified 'private debts', [1774], A/11, MS copy of an act for vesting part of his Co. Laois estate in trustees for the purpose of selling it to clear the debts, [1784?], and D/2, rental of the lands for sale (1,160 Irish acres producing £1,976 a year), [1784?]. All or most of these lands were bought by Henry Grattan out of the £50,000 voted him in 1782 by a grateful Irish parliament. Earlier in his career, in 1765, Sydney had been obliged to quit his post as minister resident at Copenhagen on account of some form of temporary insanity (Cosby Papers, H/4, Syndey's diplomatic letter-book, 1765–6). So, the onset of a young wife may simply have resurrected an old problem.

395 See p. 34 and 113*n* above and, for general conclusions about the ages at which aristocrats married, Hollingsworth, op. cit., pp. 16 and 22.

396 Maguire, *Living like a Lord*, pp. 41–2; RIA Charlemont Papers, 12 R. 20, f. 59, Dr Alexander Haliday to 1st Earl of Charlemont, 15 January 1799. For the outmoded popular view of the 1st Marquess as a tyrannical landlord, see Malcomson, 'Absenteeism', pp. 17 and 20, and for a modern reinterpretation, W.A. Maguire, 'Lord Donegall and the Hearts of Steel', *IHS*, XXI, no. 84 (September 1981), passim.

397 UL Dunraven Papers, D/3196/K/2/5, marriage settlement, 9 June 1777, /B/6/1, heads of a deed of separation between Lord and Lady Mountearl, 2 January 1817, and /B/6/5–6, copy of a letter from Lord Mountearl to Colonel [Edmund] Coghlan [Governor of Chester], 26 August 1819, and memo by Mountearl on the letter, [26 August 1819].

398 Quoted in Malcomson, 'Speaker Pery and the Pery Papers' in *North Munster Antiquarian Journal*, XVI (1973–4), p. 54, 41*n*.

399 NLI Killadoon Papers, MSS 36,033/1 and 36,034/1-4, correspondence between Lord and Lady Clements/Leitrim, c.1800–1809, and MS 36,031/2-3, letters to Mrs Bermingham from Lady Clements/Leitrim, 1800–02 and 1825; F. Gerard, *Some fair Hibernians …* (London, 1897), pp. 59–85 (her account relies heavily on the contemporary testimony of Lady Morgan); K. Garlick, *Sir Thomas Lawrence: a Catalogue of the Paintings* (Oxford, 1989), pp. 166–7 and 223.

400 NLI Killadoon Papers, MS 36,034/35, Lord to Lady Leitrim, 3 February 1836.

401 PRONI Chatsworth Papers, T/3158/366, the playing cards, and T/3158/427, Hartington to Lady Burlington, [post 8 December 1754].

402 UL Dunraven Papers, D/3196/B/1, Hon. Windham Quin to 1st Lord Adare, 6 March 1810, and D/3196/E/3/6, 61 and 145, Lord to Lady Dunraven, 28 June 1810, 2 January 1825, 2 May 1830, and 24 June 1840.

403 See 204*n* above.

404 NLI Leinster Papers, MS 41,552/30, Emily, Dowager Duchess, to Leinster, 12 June [1791], and MS 41,552/39, Duchess to Duke, endorsed '1795'.

405 'The de Ros Papers', in the *Annual Report of the Public Record Office of Northern Ireland for 1993–4* (Belfast, 1995), Appendix I, pp. 51–62.

406 Inglis-Jones, *Lord of Burghley*, pp. 88–109, and passim.

407 Chapman and Dormer, *Elizabeth and Georgiana*, p. 23; Stone, *Road to Divorce*, pp. 320, 325, 359 and 255; Hicks, *Lady Di Beauclerk*, pp. 185–90.

408 I am grateful to Dr John Bergin of the Eighteenth-Century Legislation Project in the School of History and Anthropology, QUB, for information about the number of divorce acts passed by the Irish parliament, and more generally for his guidance on the question of divorce.

409 There would have been at least one more if Arthur Annesley, 4th Lord Altham, had not contented himself with rough justice and a judicial separation: in February 1717, finding his wife in bed with a lover, he cut the lover's ear off 'with part of the adjoining cheek, after which he turned madam out in her shift and had her howled some miles by the servants, crying "A whore, a whore!"' – BL Egmont Papers, Add MS. 47,028, f. 181, Philip Perceval to Lord Perceval, 12 February 1717.

410 Cannon, *Aristocratic Century*, p. 84; *The Complete Peerage*, sub 'Westmeath'.

411 Stone, *Broken Lives*, p. 299.

412 Ibid., pp. 284–326. *The Complete Peerage*, sub 'Westmeath', states erroneously that the couple were divorced.

413 Stone, *Road to Divorce*, p. 255.

414 Malcomson, *Archbishop Charles Agar*, p. 131.

415 Chapman and Dormer, *Elizabeth and Georgiana*, pp. 114–28; Stone, *Broken Lives*, pp. 137–8; M.S. Lovell, *A scandalous Life: the Biography of Jane Digby [Lady Ellenborough]* (London, 1995), pp. 49–57.

416 Quoted in Malcomson, 'The Erne Family, Estate and Archive', c.1610–c.1950', in E.M. Murphy and W. Roulston eds. *Fermanagh History and Society* (Dublin, 2004), p. 213.

417 For Lord Clare's caustic remark about the portions of £10,000 apiece which the 2nd Duke of Leinster 'had the honour to pay' to his illegitimate siblings, see p. 41 above.

For the provision made for the illegitimate children of aristocratic men, see pp. 170–72.

418 Malcomson ed. *Irish Official Papers*, I, p. 187, Major R. [?T.] Wilson to Lord William Bentinck, 4 July 1798.

419 *The Trial of Viscountess Belmore (formerly Lady Henrietta Hobart and Daughter to John, Earl of Buckinghamshire) for Adultery with the Earl of Ancram* (London, 1792), p. 11 and passim. For access to this source I am indebted to Dr John Bergin.

420 NLI Smythe of Barbavilla Papers, MS 41,585/5, Darby Clarke to William Smyth, 23 April 1742 [*sic* - 1743].

421 There was a contemporary English precedent for this: in 1736 Robert Knight, Lord Luxborough (afterwards Earl of Catherlough), an Irish peer with no connection with Ireland except his peerages, repudiated his wife for adultery with the poet, John Dalton, who was her son's tutor (Horace Walpole claimed that she had been caught in bed with the doctor). Lord Luxborough (presumably relying on the fact that she had borne him a son and heir) did not obtain either a separation or a divorce, but banished her to his decrepit and isolated seat in Warwickshire, Barrels, where she created a notable garden. Her confinement, unlike Lady Belvedere's, was not close. She was allowed to make and receive visits, and carried on a brisk correspondence with horticulturists and society ladies – see *Letters written by the late Rt Hon. Lady Luxborough to William Shenstone, etc* (1st Irish ed., Dublin, 1776). She died in 1756, and Lord Luxborough, by now earl of Catherlough, in 1772. Unfortunately for him, their son and heir had pre-deceased him (1762).

422 For the often conflicting evidence about Lady Belvedere's alleged adultery and subsequent incarceration, see: J.C. Lyons, *The Grand Juries of the County of Westmeath … [1772]–1853], with an historical Appendix* (privately printed, Ledestown, 1853), pp. 273–85; D. Guinness and W. Ryan, *Irish Houses and Castles* (London, 1971), pp. 295–6; M. Girouard, 'Belvedere House, Co. Westmeath…', in *Country Life*, 22 June 1961, pp. 1480–83; PRONI Belvedere Deeds, T/3468/3 and 4, copy of the Belvederes' marriage settlement, 5 August 1736, and Lord Belvedere's will, 2 June 1774; PRONI Chatsworth Papers, T/3158/1529 and 1531, Arthur Rochfort to Devonshire, [c.20? May? 1757?] and 25 May 1757. At Belvedere, Lord Belvedere built c.1760 a mock ruin designed to block out the view of his brother's house, then called Rochfort but subsequently re-named Tudenham. The wall is known as 'the jealous wall', which is quite misleading as Tudenham belonged to another brother, George Rochfort, with whom Belvedere had quarrelled, but for reasons unconnected with jealously or Lady Belvedere.

423 Malcomson, 'Theodosia, Countess of Clanwilliam', pp. 1–9; idem, Introduction to the Castle Ward Papers in PRONI (D/2092); Richey, 'Landed Society in Co. Down', pp. 186 and 193.

424 H.G. Hutchinson ed. *Letters and Recollections of Sir Walter Scott by Mrs Hughes of Uffington* (London, 1904), p. 261; Johnston-Liik, *History of the Irish Parliament*, V, p. 196; S. Lynam, *Humanity Dick: a Biography of Richard Martin, MP, 1754–1834* (London, 1975), pp. 75–81 and 93.

425 Stone, *Road to Divorce*, pp. 262 and 264.

426 Malcomson, '1st Marquess of Abercorn', pp. 69–70.

427 C. Phillips, *Curran and his Contemporaries* (4th ed., London, 1841), pp. 385–6 (the quotation is from John Philpot Curran's speech, as Cloncurry's counsel, at the trial for crim. con. on 19 February 1807); D. Phelan, *Lyons Demesne: a Georgian Treasure restored to the Nation* (privately printed, 1999), pp. 29-30 and 48; Betjeman, *Collected Poems … compiled with an Introduction by the Earl of Birkenhead* (enlarged ed., London, 1970), pp. 74–85; Cloncurry, *Personal Recollections …* (Dublin, 1849), pp. 253–4. There was a four-year gap in this instance between the successful proceedings for crim. con. and the divorce for two reasons: (1) the Cloncurrys had been married twice, once by a Roman Catholic priest and once by a Protestant clergyman, and the first marriage proved difficult to annul (NLI Cloncurry Papers, MS 8492, Cloncurry to his agent, Thomas Ryan, 17 March 1811); and (2) because Cloncurry had not wanted to re-marry until c.1810. The divorce proceedings before the UK House of Lords had the accidental effect of proving Cloncurry's succession to his father's peerage – 'the first time a man's *having a whore* as his wife was of service to him in the proof of his pedigree' (Killadoon Papers at Killadoon, Q/2/5, 2nd Earl of Charlemont to 2nd Earl of Leitrim, 11 July 1811).

428 C. Costello, *A Class apart: the Gentry of County Kildare* (Dublin, 2005), pp. 40–44.

429 Stone, *Broken Lives,* pp. 15–16.

430 Kelly, 'Abduction of Women of Fortune', p. 13; Hicks, *Lady Di Beauclerk*, p. 73; Stone, *Broken Lives,* pp. 13, 137 and 161.

431 See 165*n* above.

432 M. Duprée, review of the 1982 version of *The Pursuit of the Heiress* in *The Economic History Review*, XXXVI, no. 4 (November 1983).

433 The nearest thing to a marriage between an aristocrat and a milkmaid was that between the already-mentioned Henry Cecil, 10th Earl of Exeter (when still Henry Cecil, and incognito), and Sally Hoggins, 'the cottage Countess', in 1791. See Inglis-Jones, *Lord of Burghley,* pp. 88–107 and, for a mention of two other morganatic marriages of similar, but non-bucolic, type, p. 131.

NOTES TO CHAPTER SIX

434 Cannon, *Aristocratic Century*, p. 75; Rosse Papers, H/41, Lady Saye and Sele to Lady Hawke, 25 and 29 January 1790.

435 Cannon, *Aristocratic Century*, pp. 74–5. For the Irish statutes, see 203*n* above.

436 Stone, *Road to Divorce*, pp. 121–30, especially p. 129; Maguire, *Living like a Lord*, p. 67.

437 Maguire, *Living like a Lord*, pp. 62–74; History of Parliament transcripts from the Chatsworth Papers, entry in the 6th Duke of Devonshire's diary dated 12 December 1821.

438 Stone, *Road to Divorce*, pp. 130–31; Maguire, *Living like a Lord*, p.69.

439 PRONI Castle Ward Papers, D/2092/1/10, [Hon. Edward Ward to his wife], Lady Arabella Ward, 17 May 1808. According to *The Complete Peerage*, this was only the start of a 'career of reckless indulgence', which landed Lord Glentworth in prison for 'the greatest part of his time after he became of age'. He pre-deceased his father, dying in 1834, so Lady Glentworth never became countess of Limerick. Presumably a jointure charged on the estate had been settled retrospectively upon her, in which case she lived to draw it for thirty-four years. She died in 1868.

440 See pp. 12–14 and 136 above and, for the expressive word 'squeezing', used by the Countess of Moira in 1796, see Malcomson, 'Theodosia, Countess of Clanwilliam', p. 12. In 1760, the father of Dudley Alexander Cosby, later Lord Sydney (see pp. 135–6 above), wrote to Cosby begging him 'most earnestly and in the most friendly and cordial manner not to go to law with me…. Suppose you were successful and able to exonerate the estate, you cannot undo my actions' – Stradbally Hall, Cosby Papers, H/3, Pole Cosby to D.A. Cosby, 1 January 1765.

441 See pp. 90–91 and 194; Rosse Papers, D/7/140, 'Abstract of the will and codicils of the late Jane, Countess Dowager of Rosse…', [1838].

442 NLI Killadoon Papers, MS 36,035/33, Lord Clements to Lady Leitrim (his mother), 4 July 1836.

443 The original is no. 10.4 in the Conroy Papers in Balliol College Library, Oxford (the Conroys' son, Sir John Conroy, 3rd and last Bt, was a Fellow of Balliol). A very full modern transcript, made by Mrs Katherine Jessel in 1981, is in J/30 of the Rosse Papers.

444 The 10th Earl of Westmorland had made a very daring dash to Gretna in 1782 with Sarah, daughter and heiress of the very rich banker, Robert Child of Osterley Park, Middlesex. But, although Westmorland outran his pursuers and married the heiress, Child made sure that Westmorland gained as little as possible from his 'bold act'. The Westmorlands had one son (the future 11th Earl) and three daughters. Child tied up his fortune for the benefit of the eldest daughter, Sarah, who married George Villiers, 5th Earl of Jersey, in 1804. Lord Jersey double-barrelled his name to Child-Villiers, and his wife and he inherited Child's famous seat, Osterley Park, Middlesex, and everything else which Child could bestow upon them. This is therefore another example of 'cadet inheritance', not one of a runaway marriage which paid off.

445 Even Queen Victoria, who hated Sir John Conroy, seems to have forgotten the 'escapade'. In an entry in her journal (Royal Archives, Windsor, Z431) for 8 July 1837, she refers to Lady Alicia as 'a very pretty young person…, the daughter of the Earl of Rosse, and married Mr Conroy about a month or three weeks ago'. I am indebted for this reference to Mrs Catherine Jessel.

446 This was Arthur Edward Knox of Castlerea, Co. Mayo. Much of the Knoxes' marriage settlement, which was dated 1835, is recited in J/31 of the Rosse Papers.

447 A. Plowden, *The young Victoria* (London, 1981), pp. 150 and 161–2.

448 *Balliol College Library: the Conroy Papers – a Guide* (Oxford, 1987), pp. 18–19.

449 Ibid., p. 2.

450 PRONI T/1005, typescript copy of entries relating to Irish men and women, 1720–1846. I am indebted for this reference to Dr W.H. Crawford.

451 NLI Killadoon Papers, MS 36,069/3, Mrs Caulfield to W.S. Clements, Lord Clements, 15 April 1833 and May 1847.

452 Quoted in E.B. Mitford, *Life of Lord Redesdale* (London, 1939), p. 155.

453 See p. 38 above; Cannon, *Aristocratic Century*, p. 89.

454 G. de Diesbach, *Secrets of the Gotha* (London, 1964), pp. 254–5.

455 PRONI Hotham Papers, T/3429/1/42, Buckinghamshire to Hotham Thompson, 13 March 1779.

456 The following paragraphs are taken from my list of, and introduction to, the Villiers-Stuart Papers, PRONI T/3131. They have also been informed by the researches and theories of the late James Villiers-Stuart, who was keenly interested in his family's history and intrigued by the Stuart de Decies peerage case. The reconstruction of events presented here met with his concurrence, as the best attempt so far to reconcile all the known facts. But there remain elements of speculation in what follows.

457 Mrs Frederick Sullivan, an English visitor to Dromana in September 1836, noted various oddities, but attributed them to Irishness not to the want of harmonising feminine influence. At the time of her visit, Henry Villiers-Stuart seems to have been in residence, although it is possible that she mistook William for his elder brother. She wrote: 'Dromana is quite beautiful!…, the views lovely in every direction. The house is (like all things in Ireland) full of contrasts – such a grand drawing-room, such tumble-down offices, sixteen lamps in the chandelier, and pack-thread for bell-ropes; a beautiful gold paper, and no curtains to the six windows; an eagle before the windows, a stuffed seal in the hall, some great elk horns over the staircase, lots of family pictures, an old theatre turned into a workshop, the remains of what must have been very fine hanging gardens, connected by stone steps, down to the river, a lovely new garden from whence are extensive and rich romantic views. Nothing could be more hospitable than Mr Villiers Stuart, nothing more Irish than the spirit of himself and his place!' See G. Lyster ed. *A Family Chronicle …* (London, 1908), p. 131.

458 It is commonly said that the Hindu-Gothic bridge leading from Cappoquin into the Dromana demesne was a triumphal arch built to mark her arrival as a newly-wed. In fact, it was not built until 1849.

459 Cannon, *Aristocratic Century*, p. 91, and more generally pp. 76–8 and 90–92.

460 PRONI Annesley Papers, D/1503/3/8/10, John Pollock's narrative, 5 November 1797.

461 PRONI Dufferin Papers, D/1071/H/B/D/78/86 and 87,

Lady Dartrey to 1st Earl of Dufferin, 6 and 21 August 1880.
462 E. Healey, *Lady Unknown: the life of Angela Burdett-Coutts* (London, 1978), pp. 203–5.
463 Lyons, *Grand Juries of Co. Westmeath*, pp. 198–202.
464 Malcomson, '1st Marquess of Abercorn', pp. 69–70. For Ladies Downshire and Louisa Conolly, see p. 134 above.
465 Conyngham-Sharpe Letters, 9 July 1768.
466 Ibid., 20 August 1768.
467 Ibid., 9 September 1768. Conyngham's letters often complain about Sharpe's delays and challenge his advice. But usually Conyngham climbs down and defers. Sharpe was an eminent conveyancer, stood high in his profession (the Reynolds portrait was commissioned by a client and admirer), and also stood up to his clients, however aristocratic.
468 Ibid., 9 September 1768.
469 Ibid., 27 November 1768 and N.D. Conyngham states that he would like to seek 'a verdict by my peers', which must presumably mean the Irish House of Lords.
470 Ibid., 8 January 1771.
471 And very satisfactorily as to rank and connections: his wife was Lady Emma Georgiana Lygon, daughter of the 1st Earl Beauchamp of Madresfield Court, Worcestershire.
472 Tullynally Castle, Pakenham Papers, G/1/9–10, letters to 2nd Earl of Longford about his brother's and his own illegitimate children, 1815–22, and H/1/12, letters and papers about the annuities payable to two of the 2nd Earl's illegitimate children, 1859.
473 R. Whitworth, *Field-Marshal Lord Ligonier: a Story of the British Army, 1702–1770* (Oxford, 1958), pp. 49–50, 53 and 169.
474 Whitworth, *Ligonier*, passim; Malcomson, *Nathaniel Clements*, pp. 38–42 and 265–6; *The Complete Peerage*, sub 'Ligonier'.
475 Malcomson, *Archbishop Charles Agar*, p. 113.
476 PRONI Donoughmore Papers, T/3459/F/13/144, Lord Hutchinson to Hon. Francis Hely-Hutchinson, 14 October 1825.
477 Ibid, and T/3459/F/13/31, Hutchinson to Hely-Hutchinson, 26 October 1821.
478 NLI Smythe of Barbavilla Papers, MS 41,578/12, Mrs Conolly to Mrs Bonnell, 15 January 1738/9.
479 Whitworth, *Ligonier*, pp. 173 and 388–90.
480 P. Mackesy, *The Coward of Minden: the Affair of Lord George Sackville* (London, 1979), p. 226.
481 Greig, *The Farington Diary*, III, pp. 75–6. The comments quoted are those of the painter, James Northcote.
482 Malcomson, *Archbishop Charles Agar*, p. 425.
483 Castle Forbes, Co. Longford, Granard Papers, K/3/1, Capt. John Hart to Viscountess Forbes, 17 September [1834].
484 Inglis-Jones, *Lord of Burghley*, pp. 131–9.
485 In Henry Monck's terminology – see p. 60 above.
486 C.I. Osborne ed. *Memorials of the Life and Character of [her Mother] Lady Osborne and some of her Friends* (2 vols., Dublin, 1870), I, p. xii, and I, p. 6, Lady Osborne to her aunt, 10 May 1816.
487 Ibid., I, pp. 53–5, Lady Osborne to her aunt, 28 May [1821].
488 Stone, *Broken Lives*, p. 291.
489 Unless otherwise attributed, the information about Bernal Osborne which appears in this and the next two paragraphs is taken from the *New Oxford DNB* entry for him by Derek Beales.
490 *Memorials of Lady Osborne*, I, pp. 225–6, 232 and 246, Lady Osborne to Catherine Bernal Osborne, 1846–7.
491 Quoted in Lady D. Nevill, *Reminiscences* (London, 1906), p. 120. For the virtual worthlessness of Bernal Osborne's West Indian property, see pp. 109-10.
492 Ibid., p. 111, Bernal Osborne to Lady Dorothy Nevill, 23 December 1865. She lived at Dangstein on the Hampshire-Sussex border, just outside the small town of Rogate.
493 *Memorials of Lady Osborne*, I, p. 316, Lady Osborne to Catherine Bernal Osborne, 21 July [c.1855].
494 Ibid., I, p. xiii.
495 Lady V. Greville, *Vignettes of Memory* (London, c.1920), pp. 111–12. She puts no date on this unpleasant experience; but as she had no obvious connection with Ireland before she married the son and heir of Lady Rosa Nugent and the 1st Lord Greville in 1863, it is reasonable to place it in the 1860s or 1870s.
496 In recognition of which, he had been christened 'Osborne' and was nicknamed 'Obby'.
497 The surviving Osborne archive is now at Hatfield House, Hertfordshire. Mr Robin Harcourt-Williams, Lord Salisbury's librarian and archivist, tells me that it does not contain wills, settlements and estate material. It has the appearance of being a nineteenth-century selection of letters kept for their autographic rather than historical interest, and considerably 'weeded'. It presumably includes the originals of the letters printed in the *Memorials of Lady Osborne*.
498 Malcomson, *Nathaniel Clements*, pp. 23–30 and 132–6.
499 Johnston-Liik, *History of the Irish Parliament*, IV, pp. 256–62.
500 See p. 18 above.
501 The best, single source of information on the Blessingtons is still M. Sadleir, *Blessington-d'Orsay: a Masquerade* (London, 1933), a splendid book and a good read. It examines the complex personalities of Lord and Lady Blessington and d'Orsay and the interrelationship among them. Its principal shortcoming is that Sadleir seems not to have studied the text of the Blessington Estate Act of 1846 and therefore is reduced to guesswork (usually good) when certainty was obtainable. Unless otherwise attributed, the information in this and the ensuing paragraphs is drawn from Sadleir or, to a much lesser extent, from W. Connely, *Count d'Orsay* (London, 1954).
502 PRONI Abercorn Papers, D/623/A/144/14, Sir John Stewart, 1st Bt, to Abercorn, 6 January 1817.
503 TCD Conolly Papers, MS 3978/412, Conolly to 2nd Earl of Strafford, 19 November 1786.
504 These are the figures given for the respective rentals in 1846 in *An Act for vesting the real Estates of Charles John, Earl of Blesinton [a variant of Blessington] ... in Trustees for Sale for the Payment of his Debts and for other Purposes* (9 Victoria, cap. 1, 18 June 1846), schedules 1 and 2, and

summarised in R.R. Madden, *The literary Life and Correspondence of the Countess of Blessington* (3 vols., London, 1855), I, pp. 460–61. The estates had been worth c.£30,000 a year in 1798, but had been considerably reduced in value by sales made in Blessington's lifetime, notably of land in Tyrone in 1814.

505 The will is recited in the *Blessington Estate Act*, pp. 6–8, and in Sadleir, *Blessington-d'Orsay*, pp. 371–2.

506 *Blessington Estate Act*, schedule 4. The debts are greatly under-stated by Sadleir (*Blessington-d'Orsay*, p. 318). Among the annuities which had fallen in by 1846 was the jointure of £1,000 per annum payable to Blessington's step-mother, the Dowager Viscountess Mountjoy, who died in 1839.

507 *The Blessington Papers, from the Collection of autograph Letters and historical Documents formed by Alfred Morrison..., printed for private Circulation, 1895*, p. 47, Thomas Farrer to Luke Norman, 21 May 1832.

508 Sadleir, *Blessington-d'Orsay*, pp. 169 and 177.

509 *Blessington Estate Act*, pp. 27–9 and 32.

510 Ibid., p. 17.

511 Sadleir, *Blessington-d'Orsay*, pp. 284–5; J. Fyvie, 'The most gorgeous Lady Blessington', in the *Anglo-Saxon Review*, vol. 10 (September 1901), pp. 20–21. Worn out by money worries and literary hack-work, Lady Blessington died of heart failure in 1849.

512 *Blessington Estate Act*, p. 32 and schedule 5.

513 PRONI Donoughmore Papers, T/3459/D/48/153–4, Francis Hely-Hutchinson to 1st Earl of Donoughmore, 18 and 31 January 1820.

514 *Blessington Papers*, pp. 45–6, Thomas Farrer to John Hely-Hutchinson, 18 April 1832.

515 Sadleir, *Blessington-d'Orsay*, pp. 180–81.

516 *Blessington Papers*, pp. 44–5, John Hely-Hutchinson to Thomas Farrer, 12 April 1832.

517 Author's collection, Blessington Deeds: deed of separation ('the Count and Countess d'Orsay and their trustee to Charles, Viscount Canterbury and others'), 16 February 1838; *Blessington Estate Act*, pp. 14–27.

518 Sadleir, *Blessington-d'Orsay*, p. 320. D'Orsay acknowledged debts to the tune of c.£120,000 (Fyvie, 'Lady Blessington', pp. 21–2), but his true indebtedness was probably greater.

519 Author's collection, Blessington Deeds: indenture between Lady Harriet and Thomas Henry Baker, 23 November 1836.

520 Ibid., conveyance (actually, a deed incorporating arrears of interest amounting to £6,000 in a mortgage of part of the Dublin estate for £10,800) from Lord Mount Temple [elder brother and trustee of the late Charles Spencer Cowper] to Frederick H. Janson and another (mortgagees), 10 November 1882.

521 The date is sometimes given as September 1852, not quite a month after d'Orsay's death – see Connely, *Count d'Orsay*, pp. 544 and 561. This is incorrect, although they may have announced their engagement in September 1852. The marriage took place on 4 January 1853 and the marriage settlement was dated 3 January.

522 He sold this house and its 7,000-acre estate for £220,000 in 1861, the purchaser being the Prince of Wales, who enormously enlarged the house and moved in in 1863. Conservative Norfolk society had been unwilling to accept into its rank a wife who had previously been a mistress, so the Cowpers had decided to settle permanently on the Continent. See G. Brook-Shepherd, *Uncle of Europe [Edward VII]* (reprint, 1975), pp. 41–2. The royal family's acquisition of Sandringham is perhaps the least-known consequence of the Blessington disaster.

523 Loc. cit., conveyance of 10 November 1882.

524 Madden, *Lady Blessington*, I, p. 55.

525 Quoted in L. McKinstry, *Rosebery: Statesman in Turmoil* (London, 2005), p. 45.

526 PRONI, T/1282/1, pp. 4–6, diary of John Ynyr Burges of Parkanaur, Castlecaulfield, Co. Tyrone, 1818–55.

NOTES TO CHAPTER SEVEN

527 For the source and significance of this quotation, see p. 194 above.

528 N. Mitford, *Noblesse oblige: an Enquiry into the identifiable Characteristics of the English Aristocracy* (reprint, Harmondsworth, 1965), p. 41. See also 630*n*.

529 Pakenham Papers, A/6/5, deed partitioning the Aungier estates in counties Longford and Cavan, 25 November 1719; A/6/6, settlement on the marriage of Thomas Pakenham and Elizabeth Cuffe, 19 March 1739/40; A/6/7, deeds settling the Aungier/Cuffe estate on the issue of Thomas Pakenham and Elizabeth Cuffe, 1746–7; and C/2, deeds relating to these settlements, 1734, 1769–70 and 1774.

530 Pakenham Papers, C/2/1, settlement on the marriage of the 2nd Long Longford and the Hon. Catherine Rowley, 24 June 1768.

531 Pakenham Papers, Z/2/4, settlements of and case papers about the Langford and Rowley estates and the debts charged upon them, 1791–7 and 1815.

532 Malcomson, 'The Erne Family, Estate and Archive', p. 212.

533 Richardson ed. *Long-forgotten Days*, pp. 246 and 251–2, Lady Blayney to Mrs Lavington, 24 January 1743/4 and 22 April 1786.

534 Malcomson, 'The Earl of Clermont: a long-forgotten Co. Monaghan Nobleman of the late eighteenth Century', in *Clogher Record*, VII (1973), passim; Collins ed. *County Monaghan Sources in PRONI*, pp. 121–5.

535 Hon. Sir J.W. Fortescue ed. *The Correspondence of King George III from 1760 to December 1783 ...* (6 vols., London, 1927–8), vol. V, no. 3272, 2nd Lord Longford to the King, 26 February 1781.

536 Pakenham Papers, H/1/2A-B, letters to Henry Hamilton (brother-in-law and an executor to the 2nd Earl of Longford and a guardian of the 3rd), 1835–47, and D/3/2, doctor's bill for the (enormous) cost of attending the 3rd Earl at the end of his life, with related correspondence, 1860. I am grateful to Ms Eliza Pakenham for help with this latter reference.

537 Lord Blessington is a notable case in point.

538 The obvious exception is Miss Knox of Prehen; but, then, she was almost certainly shot in mistake for her father, just as Mrs Smythe was shot over a century later, in 1882, in mistake for her brother-in-law, William Barlow Smythe of Barbavilla.

539 Statistically and demographically, however, the chances of a father-to-son succession were improving during this period; see p. 241 above.

540 This is hard to reconcile with her subsequent statement that, until the marriage negotiations were too far advanced for it to be practicable for her to retract, she did not even know Armar Lowry-Corry by sight (see p. 118 above). Buckinghamshire presumably meant that Corry had taken a great fancy to Lady Henrietta.

541 See 168*n* above.

542 Marson, 'Belmores of Castle Coole'.

543 Ibid.

544 See pp. 4–5 above.

545 See pp. 14–15 above.

546 See pp. 58 and 86–7 above.

547 Quoted in Cannon, *Aristocratic Century*, p. 127.

548 Cathcart Letters, James Russell to Cathcart, 25 April 1770.

549 Ibid., Cathcart to Lady Cathcart, 6 June 1775, and reply, 12 June 1775.

550 Ibid., Cosgrave to Cathcart, 4 August 1789.

551 See 52*n* above.

552 The earldom of Rosse was successively held by two different branches of the Parsons family. The senior branch died out in 1764 with the death of Olivia, Countess of Rosse's husband. The earldom was revived for the junior branch in 1806.

553 Rosse Papers, D/7/18, Rosse to Lady Rosse, 30 September 1818.

554 Quoted in Malcomson, 'Fall of the House of Conolly' (loc. cit.)

555 PRONI Wicklow Papers, MIC/146, Lord Chief Justice Henry Singleton to Ralph Howard, 4 June 1751.

556 Springfield Castle (Muskerry) Papers, Drumcollogher, Co. Limerick: E/1/2, marriage settlement, 13 January 1692.

557 Dickson, *Old World Colony*, p. 88.

558 Quoted in Lord Fitzmaurice, *Life of William, Earl of Shelburne …* (2 vols., London, 1912), I, p. 2; W.H.G. Bagshawe, *The Bagshawes of Ford: a biographical Pedigree* (privately printed, London, 1886), p. 331, diary of Colonel Samuel Bagshawe, 12 November 1772.

559 PRONI Granard Papers: T/3765/J/3/4 letters to St George McCarthy from Luke Gardiner (later 1st Viscount Mountjoy) about Gardiner's wish to raise a mortgage for £3,000 off his reversionary interest in the Mountjoy estate in Tyrone (Newtownstewart, Aughentaine and Mountjoy), 1788; and J/3/8–19, case papers and correspondence over the manors of Mountjoy and Newtownstewart, 1796–c.1805.

560 PRONI Castle Stewart Papers, D/1618/2/8, settlement on the marriage of Robert Stuart and Margaret Edwards, 18 April 1722, and D/1618/2/21, copy extracts from the will of Hugh Edwards of Castlegore, dated 12 October 1737 and proved 4 February 1744.

561 Rosse Papers, B/15, memorial of the marriage settlement of Lord Rosse and Olivia Edwards, 15 February 1754. See also PRONI Castle Stewart Papers, D/1618/2/2–42, leases of farms on the Castlegore estate, 1757–1819, in most of which Lord Rosse or Bateman are joined with Olivia Edwards; this was because, even though the estate belonged to her, she could not perform any legal act without the concurrence of her husband.

562 J. Gamble, *Views of Society and Manners in the North of Ireland …* (London, 1819), pp. 216–21.

563 D/1618/2/24, deed whereby the 2nd Earl Castle Stewart made a tenant to the praecipe of the Castlegore estate, 8 May 1820.

564 D/1618/5/3 and D/1618/6/1, rentals of the Tyrone estates of the Earls Castle Stewart, 1829 and 1862.

565 I am indebted for these details to the late Patricia, Viscountess Hambleden (*née* Lady Patricia Herbert).

566 Calendar of the Irish material at Wilton House, Wiltshire (compiled for PRONI by Professor D.W. Hayton), Lord to Lady Pembroke, 9 June 1816.

567 NAI Pembroke Estates (Dublin) Papers, 97/46/3/1, letter-book of Mrs Barbara Verschoyle, 1796–1820, pp. 115–6, Mrs Verschoyle to Lord Fitzwilliam, 19 May 1798; *The Complete Peerage*, sub 'Pembroke'. I am grateful to Ms Aideen Ireland of NAI for providing me with the reference number for this manuscript.

568 Malcomson, 'A House divided: the Loftus Family, Earls and Marquesses of Ely, c.1600–c.1900', in D. Dickson and C. O'Grada eds. *Refiguring Ireland: Essays in Honour of L.M. Cullen* (Dublin, 2002), pp. 185–6; Malcomson, *Nathaniel Clements*, p. 33; Malcomson, *John Foster*, pp. 12–13, 112 and 114–15.

569 Malcomson ed. *The De Vesci Papers* (IMC, Dublin, 2006), pp. 8–9.

570 The Irish estate and viceregal archive of the Anglesey family is in PRONI, ref. D/619.

571 *The De Vesci Papers*, pp. 8 and 109.

572 Ibid., pp. 4, 8 and 15–16. See also Malcomson, 'Absenteeism', p. 24.

573 PRONI Dungannon Papers, D/778/634 and 641, particulars of the cost of valuing the Castlemorres estate, [c.1818], and Richard Jebb to Dungannon, 15 May 1820.

574 Sir J.H. Lefroy, *Loffroy of Cambray* (privately printed, 1868), and J.A.P. Lefroy, *Loffroy of Cambray[: a Supplement]* (privately printed, 1961), quoted in Malcomson's introduction to his list of the Lefroy Papers formerly at Carrigglas Manor, Co. Longford, in PRONI's Register of Irish Archives. See also Lefroy Papers, H/1, Jeffry Paul to his wife, 26 June [1798].

575 C.T. Gatty, *Mary Davies and the Manor of Ebury* (2 vols., London, 1921), passim; G. Scott Thomson, *The Russells in Bloomsbury, 1669–1771* (London, 1940), pp. 13–18 and 58; L. Stone, 'The Wriothesleys, 1530–1667', in *Family and Fortune: Studies in Aristocratic Finance in the sixteenth and seventeenth Centuries* (Oxford, 1973), pp. 236–41; Cannon, *Aristocratic Century*, pp. 72 and 76. Lady Rachel was one of three sisters and co-heiresses, and had drawn Bloomsbury and Covent Garden by lot in 1667 when the

estates of her father, the 4th and last Earl of Southampton, were divided among them. At that stage, no particular premium was set on the London property.

576 Rosse Papers, E/39, deeds constituting the marriage settlement of Lord Oxmantown and Mary Field, 13–14 April 1836, and G/62, letters, accounts and valuations, 1837–52, relating to the estates of the late John Wilmer Field of Heaton Hall, subsequently the property of his two daughters and co-heiresses.

577 See p. 217 above.

578 UL Dunraven Papers, D/3196/K/2/17, the marriage settlement, 11 December 1810.

579 Ibid., D/3197/E/3/61, Lord to Lady Dunraven, 2 January 1825. For the history of one of the Wyndham extravagances, see A. Rowan, 'Clearwell Castle, Gloucestershire', in *The Country Seat*, pp. 145-9.

580 UL Dunraven Papers, D/3197/E/4/9, Mrs Wyndham to Mrs Wyndham-Quin, 21 February 1817.

581 D/3196/E/4/7, financial calculations of Mrs Wyndham, [5 August 1816?], /E/4/5, Mrs Wyndham to Mrs Wyndham-Quin, 21 July [1816?], and /E/3/61, Lord to Lady Dunraven, 2 January 1825.

582 Malcomson, 'A House divided: the Loftus Family', passim. The division alluded to in the title is that between the Loftus estate in Co. Wexford and the Hume estate at the diagonally opposite end of Ireland in Co. Fermanagh, Nicholas Loftus, 2nd Viscount Loftus, having married the Hume heiress in 1736.

583 Malcomson, 'The Erne Family, Estate and Archive', pp. 205–7, 209 and 211–12.

584 Malcomson, Introduction to E. Hewitt ed. *Lord Shannon's Letters to his Son: a Calendar of the Letters of the 2nd Earl of Shannon to his Son, Viscount Boyle, 1790–1802* (Belfast, 1982), p. xlviii.

585 Bagshawe, *Bagshawes of Ford*, p. 326, diary of Colonel Samuel Bagshawe, 12 October 1772; 10th Earl of Roden, *Tollymore: the Story of an Irish Demesne* (Belfast, 2005), pp. 93–101; Malcomson, 'The Struggle for Control of Dundalk Borough, 1782–92', in *County Louth Archaeological Journal*, XVII (1970), passim.

586 Glin Castle, Co. Limerick: 'Notes on the Gort family collected … by Viscount Gort', 1879–80, pp. 191, 251, 288, 297–303, 306 and 311–12; R.S. Rait, *The Story of an Irish Property [the Lough Cutra Estate, Gort]* (Oxford, 1908), pp. 66–89; M. Potter, *The Government and the People of Limerick: the History of Limerick Corporation/City Council, 1197–2006* (Limerick, 2006), pp. 196–203 and 252–78.

587 Hampshire RO Wickham Papers (photocopies in PRONI, ref. T/2627/5), T/2627/5/183, William Wickham (the Chief Secretary) to Henry Addington (the Prime Minister), 18 December 1802, quoted in Malcomson, 'Speaker Pery and the Pery Papers', p. 52. For the Smyth interest in Limerick City, see ibid., pp. 49–50.

588 Quoted in Johnston-Liik, *History of the Irish Parliament*, VI, p. 466.

589 For the clause in the Encumbered Estates Act, see Vaughan, *Landlords and Tenants*, p. 133, and Casement, 'Management of Ulster Estates', pp. 54–5. The enforced sale of the estate roused such widespread sympathy for the 3rd Viscount Gort that a petition was organised in 1852 by Anthony Lefroy of Carrigglas, Co. Longford, from the nobility and gentry of Ireland to the Prime Minister, Lord Aberdeen, soliciting a government pension for Lord Gort (PRONI Register of Irish Archives: Lefroy Papers, J/44).

590 This account of a key instance of female inheritance is based on the Dillon (and Lee) Papers at Hatchlands Park, Surrey, where I have received boundless help from Isabel Cobbe (*née* Dillon).

591 A. Cobbe and T. Friedman, *James Gibbs in Ireland*, pp. viii, 3, 33 and 77.

592 Dillon Papers, Hon. Charles Dillon-Lee (later 12th Viscount Dillon) to his wife, 17 June 1779.

593 J. Bailey 'The Dillon Family in France, 1690-1794' (unpublished typescript, 1972, kindly made available to me by Isabel Cobbe), pp. 34–9 and 59.

594 Dillon Papers, Dillon (later Dillon-Lee and 12th Viscount) to John Needham (his go-between with his father), 16 July 1776.

595 Ibid.

596 Dillon Papers, Dillon to Needham, [mid-March] and 12 and 16 July 1776.

597 Ibid., Dillon to Needham, 9 July 1776.

598 Ibid., Dillon to 2nd Lord Mulgrave (his prospective brother-in-law), 12 March 1776, and Dillon and Dowager Lady Mulgrave to Needham, 28 June 1776.

599 Ibid., Christopher Palles (Irish agent or man of business to the 11th Viscount Dillon) to Charles Dillon-Lee, 21 March 1783.

600 History of Parliament transcripts from the Chatham Papers, TNA 30/8/129, 12th Viscount to Pitt, 7 August 1794.

601 Fortescue ed. *Correspondence of George III*, II, nos. 1138, 1140 and 1142, 12th Earl of Suffolk [Secretary of State for the Northern Department] to the King, 4 and 6 October 1772. In the end, Dillon-Lee went alone, the 4th Earl being 'a total cripple'.

602 Dillon Papers, Dillon-Lee to his wife, 'Hariot' [i.e. Henrietta], 17 June 1779.

603 In spite of Portland's condescending comments, 'the best company and first circle' in Ireland *were* discerning and selective. Some of them found Dillon noisy and vociferous in both private company and the Irish House of Lords (Hewitt ed. *Lord Shannon's Letters to his Son*, pp. 49, 74 and 102, Shannon to Boyle, 31 May [1797] and 4 April and 23 May [1798]). But no objection arose in 1798 when he was made a knight of St Patrick, Ireland's highest order of chivalry, to which admission was carefully guarded.

604 History of Parliament transcripts from the Pelham Papers, Portland to Thomas Pelham (Chief Secretary), 9 August 1797.

605 *The Complete Peerage*, sub 'Lichfield'; Oxfordshire RO Dillon Papers, DIL XVIII/M/111r, rentals of the Ditchley estate, Oxfordshire, and Quarendon estate, Buckinghamshire, c.1800; Hatchlands Dillon Papers, account book, 1710-40, in which the 1st and 2nd Earls of Lichfield recorded their earnings as custos brevium. The tenures of Charles II's grants to the *male* Fitzroys were more open-ended; see Stone, *Broken Lives*, p. 158. For

prompt and great assistance with the Oxfordshire RO Dillon Papers, I should like to thank Ms Hannah Jones, Archives Assistant.
606 Hatchlands Dillon Papers, 11th Viscount Dillon to his son, Charles Dillon-Lee, 31 March 1784.
607 Ibid., Christopher Palles to Charles Dillon-Lee, 5 February 1783.
608 He was certainly back in residence in October 1801. After his death, Ditchley was continuously let from 1815 to 1829 to a fellow-Irishman (who was busy anglicising himself), the 2nd Earl of Normanton.
609 Stone, *Broken Lives,* p. 286.
610 Hatchlands Dillon Papers, Palles to Dillon-Lee, 5 February 1783.
611 Ibid., Dillon-Lee (then Dillon) to John Needham, 2 July 1776, and Palles to Dillon-Lee, 21 March 1783.
612 N. Ó Muraíle, 'Local Names from the Dillon Rental, 1805', in M. Comer and N. Ó Muraíle eds. *Béacán/Bekan: Portrait of an East Mayo Parish* (Castlebar, 1986), p. 179. I am grateful for this reference to Mrs Brigid Clesham. The original rental is among the Dillon Papers in the Oxfordshire RO.
613 Most of the Irish estate (83,750 statute acres) was in Co. Mayo, but Loughglinn and 5,435 acres were in Co. Roscommon. The two counties are contiguous, as was the Dillon estate in each.
614 NLI Joly MS 39, 13th Lord Trimlestown to Marquess of Buckingham (the Lord Lieutenant), 1 January 1789.
615 *Lord Shannon's Letters to his Son,* pp. 154–5, Shannon to Boyle, 13 September [1798]; PRONI Castlereagh Papers, D/3030/811, Altamont to [Robert Marshall, 5 June 1799; NLI Talbot-Crosbie Papers, PC 188, Anselm Nugent [Dillon's attorney?] to 2nd Earl of Glandore, 3 October 1801.
616 3rd Marquess of Londonderry ed. *Memoirs and Correspondence of Viscount Castlereagh ...* (first ser., 4 vols., London, 1848–9), IV, pp. 29–33, Alexander Knox to Castlereagh, 9 February 1801.
617 PRONI Wickham Papers, T/2627/5/D/21, William to Henry Addington, 23 August 1802.
618 See p. 10 above.
619 Oxfordshire RO introduction to the Dillon Papers (which states that the Buckinghamshire estate was sold in 1802); Hatchlands Dillon Papers, Quarendon account book, [1759–65?] (no total is given, so this is my slightly conjectural calculation); *Return of Owners of Land in England and Wales in 1873, exclusive of the Metropolis* (2 vols., London, 1875), II, Oxfordshire, p. 7.

NOTES TO CHAPTER EIGHT

620 Heesom, op. cit., p. 239, and Heesom, 'Problems of Church Extension in a Victorian New Town: the Londonderrys and Seaham Harbour', in *Northern History,* XV (1979), pp. 138-55, especially p. 149.
621 D/3196/J/3, Dunraven to the architect, James Pain, 21 February 1842.
622 UL Dunraven Papers, D/3196/C/12, Dunraven to Sir Matthew Barrington, 2nd Bt, 14 June 1848. I am grateful to the late Mrs Anne Warren for identifying the misquotation.
623 Malcomson, 'Theodosia, Countess of Clanwilliam', pp. 7–15.
624 The two last quotations are taken from P. McCarthy and K.V. Mulligan, 'New Light on Ballyfin...', in *Irish Architectural and Decorative Studies*, VIII (2005), p. 121. See also *The Complete Peerage* sub 'Castlemaine' [a most unlikely place to find Earl Tylney of Castlemaine], and Thorne, *House of Commons, 1790–1820,* IV, pp. 847–9.
625 Castle Forbes, Granard Papers, C/10, copy will and probate of Lord Huntingdon, 1789, and J/8/11 and M/4/8/1, Moira to his mother, Elizabeth, Countess Dowager of Moira, 13 January 1799, and 13 September 1807. The Hastings estates had a rental of £7,000 a year in 1789, which doubled to £14,000 by 1807.
626 Ibid., J/11/1, Elizabeth Lady Moira to her grandson, Lord Forbes, March 1803. For Moira's magniloquence of speech and overestimate of the extent of his influence over the Prince, see East Sussex RO, Petworth House Archives, PHA/55, Moira to 3rd Earl of Egremont, 9 June 1812.
627 H. Blyth, *The pocket Venus [Lady Florence Paget, wife of the 4th Marquess of Hastings]* (London, 1966), p. 12; Sir N. Pevsner, *The Buildings of England: Leicestershire and Rutland* (reprint, Harmondsworth, 1973), p. 84. Pevsner notes some 'entirely classical' features inside the house, and records it as an early work by the architect, William Wilkins, without mentioning the personal contribution allegedly made by Moira.
628 Johnston-Liik, *History of the Irish Parliament,* VI, pp. 146–8; PRONI constituency history notes in connection with the same project, ENV/5/HP/8/1, Co. Down; PRONI Granard Papers, T/3765/M/4/5/16, Moira to Elizabeth Lady Moira, 11 January 1795, and T/3765/J/9/2/19, Lady Moira to her daughter, the Countess of Granard, 4 December 1800.
629 Anon., *Loudon Castle: the ancestral Home of the Campbells of Loudon* (Loudon Castle, 1995), pp. 3–13 and 22. I am most grateful to Mrs John Grieve for tracking down this guidebook for me.
630 PRONI Granard Papers T/3765/M/4/9/2, Moira to Countess of Granard 21 October 1812, and T/3765/M/4/8/33, Moira to Lady Granard, 4 January 1810; Castle Forbes, Granard Papers, J/8/11, letters and papers of Lady Granard about Moira's plans to sell Hastings lands in England in 1814.
631 Quoted, without clear attribution, in Johnston-Liik, *History of the Irish Parliament*, VI, p. 148. It could also be argued that the family was afflicted with genetic as well as financial exhaustion. Lord Huntingdon's three brothers had all died young pre-1789, and so did Hastings' only son to survive infancy, followed by the two sons of that son; they were the 2nd, 3rd and 4th Marquesses of Hastings respectively, and the marquessate died with the last in 1868. They all died from natural causes, and their respective ages at death were 34, 18 and 26. Hastings himself, a tall, athletic, healthy man, had lived to 71 (in spite of being the son of the Hastings heiress). If any family is to be adduced as

corroboration of Nancy Mitford's 'enfeebled stock' argument it is the Rawdon-Hastings-Loudon family.

632 See 52*n* above; PRONI Hertford Papers, T/3076/2/63, H.A.S. Harvey to 2nd Marquess of Hertford, 2 January 1815 (this may have been true in regard to some of Lord Westmeath's debts, but a lot remained as a charge upon the estate – see pp. 28–9 above); Maguire, *Living like a Lord*, pp. 95–7.

633 NLI Killadoon Papers, MS 36,066/1, 2nd Viscount Ferrard to 2nd Earl of Leitrim, 17 November 1838; NLI Smythe of Barbavilla Papers, MS 41,578/8, Mrs Conolly to Mrs Bonnell, 3 August 1736.

634 Petworth House Estate Office Archive, MS catalogue, compiled c.1806-c.1814, of the Irish estate records; Wyndham, *The Wyndhams*, pp. 255–60.

635 J. Gore ed. *Creevy* (London, 1949), p. 298, entry in Creevy's diary for 19 September 1828; *Gleanings from an Old Portfolio*, II, p. 45, Lady Portarlington to Lady Louisa Stuart, 10 October 1785.

636 9th Earl of Bessborough and A. Aspinall eds. *Lady Bessborough and her Family Circle* (London, 1940), p. 98, 3rd Earl to his wife, 21 July [1793].

637 TCD Hartpole Papers, MS 1933/140, Aldborough to Hartpole, 25 January 1794. I am indebted for this reference to Professor L.M. Cullen.

638 See 5*n* above.

639 See 174*n* above.

640 For example, George Duffus, who was called in to advise by the head agents for the Pakenham/Longford estates in counties Longford and Westmeath – see Pakenham Papers, H/2/4, letters from Duffus to Stewart & Kincaid, 1840–46.

641 C. O'Grada, *Ireland: a new economic History, 1780–1939* (Oxford, 1994), p. 129, quoted in W.H. Crawford's review of M. Dowling, *Tenant Right and agrarian Society in Ulster, 1600–1870*, in *Familia*, no. 15 (1999), pp. 106-7.

642 Richardson ed. *Long-forgotten Days*, p. 252, Lady Blayney to Mrs Lavington, 12 June 1787.

643 L. Proudfoot, 'The Management of a Great Estate: Patronage, Income and Expenditure on the Duke of Devonshire's Irish Property, c.1816 to 1891', in *IESH*, XIII (1986), pp. 32–55; West Sussex RO, Petworth House Archives, PHA/1720, Colonel Wyndham's 'Memorandum book', 1842–4; Wyndham, *The Wyndhams*, pp. 256–60.

644 Malcomson, *John Foster*, pp. 14–16; PRONI Villiers-Stuart Papers, T/3131/H/5/1–68, lists of tenants, mainly on Slievegrine, c.1817; Boole Library UCC, Villiers-Stuart Papers (formerly NLI MS 24,685), lists of 633 Slievegrine tenants, 1826; Malcomson, *Nathaniel Clements*, pp. 307–8. For the general point about marginal land, I am indebted to Professor B.M.S. Campbell.

645 See 637*n* above.

646 PRONI Villiers-Stuart Papers, T/3131/K/10/1–45, series of leases whereby Grandison established a Protestant linen colony at Villierstown, 1750, 1754 and 1760.

647 Malcomson ed. *The de Vesci Papers*, p. 20.

648 Malcomson, *Nathaniel Clements*, p. 306.

649 NLI De Vesci Papers, MS 38,742, patent authorising the 1st Viscount de Vesci to hold fairs and markets at Abbeyleix, 1800; PRONI Villiers-Stuart Papers, T/3131/J/15/1, patent authorising Grandison to hold fairs and markets at Villierstown, 1751; PRONI Rossmore Papers, T/2929/37/4, patent authorising the Earl of Clermont (husband of Lady Blayney's eldest daughter) to hold a weekly market in Monaghan, 14 January 1792.

650 S. Lewis, *A topographical Dictionary of Ireland ...* (2 vols., 1837), II, pp. 669–70; H. Potterton, *Irish Church Monuments, 1750–1880* (Belfast, 1975), p. 35.

651 PRONI Villiers-Stuart Papers, T/3131/C/15/1-24, miscellaneous correspondence about the manure, 1725–33 and 1742, and /C/5/59, Maurice Ronayne to Grandison, 19 June 1730.

652 W.H. Crawford, 'Landlord-Tenant Relations in Ulster, 1609–1820', in *Irish Economic and Social History*, II (1975), pp. 5–22; idem, review of M. Dowling's *Tenant Right* (loc. cit.), p. 106. See also Large, op. cit., pp. 29 and 33–5.

653 Malcomson ed. *Eighteenth-Century Irish Official Papers in Great Britain: Private Collections, Volume Two* (Belfast, 1990), pp. 85 and 108, Richard Ryder (the Home Secretary) to 4th Duke of Richmond (the Lord Lieutenant), 18 February 1811, and W.W. Pole (the Chief Secretary) to Ryder, 8 January 1811; Thorne ed. *The House of Commons, 1790–1820*, V, pp. 220–21.

654 See 608*n* above; Malcomson, *John Foster*, pp. 13–14.

655 PRONI Erne Papers, D/1939/2/3A and C, estate surveys, 1862, /2/17, Lisnaskea estate rental, 1815, and /21/7/3, memorandum book about family finances, [c.1878].

656 Conyngham-Sharpe Letters, 1 February 1760.

657 PRONI Castle Stewart Papers, D/1618/15/6/26, Creenagh colliery accounts, 1752–6; PRONI Armagh Diocesan Registry Papers, DIO 4/13/5/1–7, Drumglass colliery accounts with Davis Duckart, 1769–78. Drumglass and Creenagh were parallel rather than rival concerns, since Andrew Thomas Stuart, the principal lay landlord in the area, was involved in Drumglass, just as Primate Robinson was involved in Creenagh. However, it was later claimed by an English mining expert (with a name which inspired confidence) that the interests of Creenagh had been subordinated to those of Drumglass – D/1618/15/6/32, Isaac Newton, London, to A.T. Stewart, 20 March 1766.

658 See p. 72 above.

659 Malcomson, *Archbishop Charles Agar*, pp. 107–8.

660 I am indebted for this point to B.M.S. Campbell.

661 PRONI D/1618/15/6/26.

662 NLI Killadoon Papers, MS 36,064/1–3, letters to Leitrim from John Walker, 1802–12, especially MS 36,064/3, letter of 30 February 1812.

663 W. Nolan, '"A public Benefit": Sir Vere Hunt, Bt, and the Town of New Birmingham, Co. Tipperary, 1800–18', in H.B. Clarke, J. Prunty and M. Hennessy eds. *Surveying Ireland's Past: multidisciplinary Essays in Honour of Anngret Simms* (Dublin, 2004), pp. 415–53, especially 436–9.

664 See pp. 79–80 above.

665 P. Roebuck ed. *Macartney of Lisanoure (1737–1806): Essays in Biography* (UHF, Belfast, 1983), pp. 282–3 and 292–5.

666 For illustrations of the importance of both interest and exchange rates, see PRONI Villiers-Stuart Papers,

T/3131/C/8/2, John Kennedy to Grandison, 23 February 1740, and /C/5/5 and 8, Ronayne to Grandison, 11 October 1725 and 30 December 1726. The last two letters show that the exchange rate varied from 6$^{1}/_{2}$ to 11$^{1}/_{2}$ per cent. Though variable, it was always adverse, and so fulfilled the deterrent, though not the fiscal, function of an absentee tax.

667 PRONI Abercorn Papers, D/623/A/108/17, James Galbraith to Abercorn, 25 December 1797.

668 *Gleanings from an old Portfolio,* II, pp. 7–8 and 33–4, Lady Portarlington to Lady Louisa Stuart, [1785] and 4 August 1785.

669 BL Add. MS 23,711, Schedule of fees charged on Irish patents, 1752–83.

670 See 54*n* above; History of Parliament transcripts from the Chatham Papers, TNA 30/8/118, Lord Bute to Pitt, 6 December 1799.

671 G. Jackson-Stops, 'Baronscourt, Co. Tyrone', in *Country Life,* 12 July 1979, pp. 36–8.

672 Cunningham ed. *Letters of Horace Walpole,* III, p. 433.

673 PRONI Abercorn Papers, D/623/A/26/40, 42, 64, 94 and 124, copies of letters from Abercorn to Lady Hamilton, 3 August 1784, James Hamilton, 3 November 1784, Walter Scott, 10 June 1785, and James Hamilton, 23 February 1786 and 15 August 1787. See also W.H. Crawford, *The Management of a major Ulster Estate in the late eighteenth Century: the 8th Earl of Abercorn and his Irish Agents* (Maynooth Studies in Local History, Dublin, 2001), passim.

674 See 133*n* and 294*n* above.

675 See 11*n* above.

676 P. Roebuck, 'Post-Restoration Landownership: the Impact of the Abolition of Wardship', in *The Journal of British Studies* (Connecticut, Fall 1978), pp. 67–85.

677 For the case of the 2nd Earl Erne and Lady Caroline Creighton see pp. 129–30 above.

678 Malcomson, 'The Erne Family, Estate and Archive', p. 214.

679 Killadoon Papers at Killadoon, E/10, rental of the Montgomery estate, 1803. This is present at Killadoon because the 1st Earl of Leitrim was Montgomery's uncle and one of Montgomery's committee of lunacy.

680 Malcomson, Introduction to the Castle Ward Papers in PRONI (D/2092).

681 PRONI Villiers-Stuart Papers, T/3131/G/2, Stuart to Homan, 22 October 1808; Boole Library, University College Cork: Villiers-Stuart Papers (formerly NLI MS 24,614/2), bill of costs taxed by Thomas Ball, a Master in the Irish Court of Chancery, 1812–27. Irish Court of Chancery accounts relating to the estates of minors (and lunatics) existed for the period 1787–1874, but were destroyed in the Four Courts fire of 1922. I am indebted for this information to Professor S.J. Connolly.

682 Shelfield House, Shelfield: Kilmaine Papers, 4P, Browne to [John] Cromie, [pre-September 1789, when Browne became Lord Kilmaine].

683 Castle Forbes, Granard Papers, K/1/3C, letters and papers of Hamilton Fitzgerald (uncle and trustee of the minor), 1834, N/2, marked up, printed sale catalogue of the contents of Castle Forbes, 7 June 1843, K/3/6, copy of a letter from Viscountess Forbes (the minor's mother), to the Chancery-appointed receiver, Robert F. Rynd, 26 October 1844, and K/4/18, calculation of the income and charges, 1852.

684 *Memorials of Lady Osborne,* I, pp. 55–8, Lady Osborne to her aunt, 28 May and 23 June [1821].

685 See pp. 208–9 above.

686 Crawford, 'Landlord and Tenant Relations', pp. 7–12; P. Roebuck, 'Rent Movement, proprietorial Incomes and agricultural Development, 1730–1830', in *Plantation to Partition,* pp. 82–101.

687 BL Holland House Papers, Add. MS 51,426, ff. 214–15, Lord Kildare to Lord Holland, 'Received' 20 June 1765. For Munster examples, see: PRONI Shannon Papers, D/2707/A/2/3/25, Lord Shannon to James Dennis, 19 February 1773; and PRONI Armagh Diocesan Registry Papers, DIO 4/13/10/4/4, Lord Tyrone to Henry Monck, 11 November 1777.

688 PRONI Additional Sheffield Papers, T/3465/14 and 26, Rev. Dr Thomas Foster to John Baker Holroyd, 10 July 1772 and 21 October 1773.

689 NLI Leinster Papers, MS 41,552/19, Leinster to his agent, James Spencer, 26 December 1779.

690 E.A. Currie, 'Fining down the Rents: the Management of the Conolly Estates in Ireland, 1734–1800', in *Derriana* (1979), pp. 26–7 and 36.

NOTES ON THE CONCLUSION

691 Clay, 'Marriage and Great Estates', p. 517; Roebuck, *Yorkshire Baronets,* pp. 271–88.

692 Hollingsworth, op. cit., pp. 61, 64 and 96.

693 See 204*n* above.

694 It should be noted that Rosse family history and the Birr Castle archive (Sections G and H) contain two fairy-tale cases of marriages to heiresses which run counter to Hollingsworth and to the general thesis of this study. These were the marriages of Lord Oxmantown (later 3rd Earl of Rosse) to Mary Field, and of their son, the 4th Earl of Rosse, in 1870 to Cassandra, daughter and heiress of the 4th Lord Hawke. Both marriages were entirely to the satisfaction and advantage of the husband and his family. The person who had much reason for dissatisfaction was the collateral male heir who succeeded to the barony of Hawke.

695 See 159*n* above.

696 Clay, op. cit., p. 507.

697 Hollingsworth, op. cit., pp. 16 and 22.

698 For the immense provision made for all the younger children of the marriage of the 2nd Marquess of Downshire and Mary Sandys, see: PRONI Downshire Papers, D/671/V/451, English Court of Chancery account of the application of £179,887 raised through sales of Downshire property, 1800–11; and W.A. Maguire, *The Downshire Estates in Ireland, 1801–1845 …* (Oxford, 1972), pp. 85–9. See also 104*n* above.

699 See p. 139 above.

BIBLIOGRAPHY

MANUSCRIPT SOURCES
(arranged alphabetically according to repository):

Boole Library, University College, Cork
Villiers-Stuart papers (unsorted archive, of which approximately two-thirds was previously sorted, listed and selectively photocopied by PRONI [ref. T/3131]).

British Library, London
Aberdeen Papers, Add. MS 43,227.
Anglesey peerage case papers, Add. MS 31,889.
Egmont Papers, Add. MS 46,988, 46,999 and 47,028–9.
Holland House Papers, Add. MS 51,426 and 51,682.
Miscellaneous manuscripts, Add. MS 23,711.
Strafford Papers, MS 22,228–9.
Wellesley Papers, Add. MS 37,308.

East Sussex Record Office, Lewes
Abergavenny Papers, ABE/25C, ABE/20X.

History of Parliament Trust, London
Typescript transcripts of material from the following archives:
Althorp (Spencer) Papers.
Camden Papers (*see also under* Centre for Kentish Studies).
Chatham Papers (*see also under* The National Archives, Kew).
Chatsworth Papers (*see also under* Public Record Office of Northern Ireland).
Dropmore (W.W. Grenville) Papers.
The Farington Diary (*see also* Greig, J., ed. *The Farington Diary*).
Melville Papers in the National Library of Scotland.
Pelham Papers.

Irish Architectural Archive, Dublin
Castletown Papers, A/10/6.

Centre for Kentish Studies, Maidstone
Camden Papers, U840.

Limerick University Library, Special Collections
Dunraven Papers, D/3196/A, B, C, D, E, K and L.

Longford-Westmeath Library, Mullingar
Survey of the Co. Westmeath estate of Abraham Boyd and Jane, Countess of Belvedere, 1818.
Howard Bury Papers (see PRONI, T/3069).

The National Archives, Kew
W.D. Adams Papers, 30/58.
Chancery Masters Account Books, C.101, and C.108.
Chatham Papers, PRO 30/8/102, 118 and 130.
Home Office Papers, HO 100/72 and 94.

The National Archives of Ireland, Dublin
Miscellaneous Carbery Deeds, D.20,487 and D.20,500.

Beaulieu estate map, M.2077.
Pembroke Estates Management Ltd. (Dublin) Papers, 97/46.

The National Library of Ireland, Dublin
Cloncurry Papers, MS 8492.
De Vesci Papers, MS 38,742, 38,746/12, 38,746/20, 38,748/21, 38,899 and 39,073.
Dorchester rental, p. 5553.
Encumbered Estates Court rentals (printed), vol. 18, August–November 1853, with newspaper cutting and rental relating to the Glengall estate sale, 11 November 1853.
Farnham Papers, D.20,463.
Fingall Papers, MS 8021/10.
Heron Papers, MS 13,047.
Irish Land Commission Papers (calendar by the late Mr Edward Keane), LC 1785 and 2639.
Joly MS 39 (letter from Lord Trimlestown to Lord Buckingham, 1789).
Killadoon Papers, MSS 36,031/2–3, 36,031/5, 36,032/1, 36,032/9–11, 36,033/1, 36,034/1–4, 36,034/29, 36,034/44, 36,035/33, 36,041/6, 36,064/1–3, 36,064/9–10, 36,065/8, 36,066/1 and 36,069/4.
King-Harman Papers, MS 8810/3.
Kingston case paper, MS 3275.
Leinster Papers, MSS 631 and 41,552 (*see also under* Public Record Office of Northern Ireland).
Leitrim Papers, MSS 3813 and 33,850.
Lismore Papers, MS 6914.
Pakenham-Mahon Papers, MS 10,711.
Reports on Private Collections, nos. 12 and 112.
Smythe of Barbavilla Papers, MSS 41,577–41,582, 41,585, 41,589 and 41,597–9.
Stratford Papers, MS 19,144.
Talbot Crosbie Papers, PC 188.
Thynne v Glengall printed case paper, [c.1850], ILB 340.
Villiers-Stuart Papers, MSS 24,614 and 24,685 (now re-located to the Boole Library, UCC: *see also* PRONI, T/3131).
Wicklow Papers, MSS 4811 and 38,601/2.

Norfolk Record Office, Norwich
Hobart of Blickling (Buckinghamshire) Papers, MC 3/294.
Lothian (Buckinghamshire) Papers (photocopies in PRONI, T/3170/1–13).

Oxfordshire Record Office
Dillon Papers, DIL XVIII/M/111r.

Private Collections
(Those marked with an asterisk have been catalogued by PRONI and the catalogue placed in the PRONI Register of Irish Archives – q.v.)

Abergavenny (John Robinson) Papers (in the possession of the Marquess of Abergavenny, Eridge Castle, Tunbridge Wells), C/18.
Annaly/Clifden Papers, incorporating title-deed material, 1735–88, deriving from the Luttrell family, earls of Carhampton (in the possession of James King Esq., Rock's Chapel Road, Crossgar, Co. Down), Section A.
Butler, Dr D.J., Cahir, Co. Tipperary: 'Rental of the estate of the trustees of Lady Margaret Butler Charteris, 1864' (photocopy).
Carbery Papers* (in the possession of Robert Boyle Esq., Bisbrooke Hall, Glaston, Rutland), Sections C–D.
Cobbe Papers (in the possession of Hugh Cobbe Esq., Newbridge, Donabate, Co. Dublin).

Coghill Papers (in the possession of Lady Coghill, Sourden, Rothes, Moray).
Cosby Papers* (in the possession of Adrian Cosby Esq., Stradbally Hall, Stradbally, Co. Laois), A/11, B/2, D/1–2 and H/3–4.
Dillon Papers (in the possession of Mr and the Hon. Mrs Alec Cobbe [née Dillon], Hatchlands Park, East Clandon, Surrey). See also Oxfordshire RO.
FitzGerald, Desmond, Knight of Glin, Glin Castle, Glin, Co. Limerick: 'Notes on the Gort family', compiled 1879–80 (photocopy).
Granard Papers* (in the possession of Lady Georgina Forbes, Castle Forbes, Newtownforbes, Co. Longford, K/3. See also under PRONI.
Killadoon Papers* (in the possession of Mr and Mrs Charles Clements, Killadoon, Celbridge, Co. Kildare), C/2, E/10, G/1, 2 and 4, and Q/2.
Kilmaine Papers* (in the possession of Lord Kilmaine, Shelfield House, Shelfield, Alcester, Warwickshire), 4P.
Lefroy Papers* (in the possession of Major and Mrs Jeffry Lefroy, formerly of Carrigglas Manor, Longford, Co. Longford), H/1 and J/44.
Malcomson, A.P.W., Belfast: Blessington Deeds, 1785–1882, Cathcart Letters, 1770–89, and Letter from Lord Hillsborough to Lord Moira, 20 May 1786.
Meath Papers* (in the possession of the Earl and Countess of Meath, Killruddery, Bray, Co. Wicklow), A/1 and J/2/20.
Pakenham Papers* (in the possession of Thomas Pakenham Esq., Tullynally Castle, Castlepollard, Co. Westmeath), A/6, C/2, G/1, H/1, N/1, P/21–2 and Z/2.
The Petworth House Estate Office Archive* (in the possession of Lord Egremont at Petworth, and separate from the Petworth House Archive in the West Sussex RO [q.v.]), PHA/MC/6/19A, MC/7/27, 32 and 35, and MS catalogue of Irish estate records compiled c.1806–14.
Proby Papers* (in the possession of Sir William Proby, Bt, Elton Hall, Peterborough, some of them formerly in the office of his Dublin solicitors, Messrs Orpen, Franks & Co.).
Rosse Papers* (in the possession of the Earl and Countess of Rosse, Birr Castle, Co. Offaly), B/15, C/1, D/7, E/39, G/62, H/41 and J/30–31.
Rowan, P & B. (antiquarian booksellers, Belfast): letters from Henry Conyngham, Baron, Viscount and Earl Conyngham, to Joshua Sharpe.
Smith of Shortgrove, Newport, Essex, Papers (in the possession of Mrs Ian Campbell, Moot Farm, Downton, Wiltshire).
Springfield Castle (Muskerry) Papers* (in the possession of Mr and the Hon. Mrs Jonathan Sykes, Springfield Castle, Drumcollogher, Co. Limerick).
Tickell Papers* (in the possession of Major-General M.E. Tickell, Branscombe, Seaton, Devon), Section A.
Waterford Papers (in the possession of the Marquess of Waterford, Curraghmore, Portlaw, Co. Waterford), C/4.

Public Record Office of Northern Ireland, Belfast
Abercorn Papers, D/623/A, B and C.
Alnwick (2nd Earl of Northumberland Irish viceregal) Papers (in the possession of the Duke of Northumberland, Alnwick Castle, Northumberland), T/2872.
Annesley Papers, D/1503/3 and D/1854/4.
Antrim Estate Office Papers, D/2977/5/1/6 and D/2977/7B.
Ardglass estate letter-book, T/1546.
Armagh Diocesan Registry Papers, DIO 4/13/5 and 10.
Arran Papers (photocopied selection from the originals in TCD), T/3200.
Autograph collection, T/2534/5.
Bedford Papers, T/2915.
Belmore Papers, D/3007/H.
Belvedere Deeds, T/3468.
British Records Association miscellaneous deposit, D/585.
Brookeborough Papers, D/3004/A/3/19.

Burges diary, T/1282.
Caledon Papers, D/2433/A/1 and 13.
Castle Stewart Papers, D/1618/2, 5, 6–8 and 15.
Castle Ward Papers, D/2092/1/10.
Castlereagh Papers, D/3030.
Chatsworth Papers (photocopies of most of the Irish material, 1693–1812, at Chatsworth, Bakewell, Derbyshire), T/3158.
Clanwilliam/Meade Papers, D/2044/F.
Clanmorris Papers, D/4216/F/1.
Darnley Papers, T/2851.
Donoughmore Papers (photocopies of the originals in TCD), T/3459/B, C, D and F.
Downshire Papers, D/607/C and I, D/671/D/14/2/20 and D/671/V.
Dufferin Papers, D/1071/H/B/D/78.
Dungannon Papers, D/778.
Dunraven Papers, D/3196 (now transferred to Limerick University Library).
Egerton (Hertford) Papers (photocopies of the originals in BL), T/3076/2.
Emly (E.S. Pery) Papers, T/3052.
Encumbered and Landed Estates Court printed rentals (incomplete set), D/1201.
Erne Papers, D/1939/2 and 21.
FitzGerald (Knight of Kerry) Papers, MIC/639.
Fitzgerald (Lord Robert) Papers, D/3151.
Foster/Massereene Papers, D/207, D/562, D/1739, D/4084 and T/2519/4.
Glenarm sketch book: volume containing architectural drawings and miscellaneous sketches of Glenarm Castle and the Glenarm vicinity, c. 1820–c. 1860, D/3560/1
Granard Papers, T/3765/J/3 and 9, L and M. See also PRONI Register of Irish Archives.
Hotham Papers (photocopied selection from the originals in the Brynmor Jones Library, University of Hull), T/3429.
Howard Bury Papers, T/3069/K.
Ker of Portavo Papers, D/2651/2.
Leinster Papers D/3078/2 and 3.
Liverpool Papers (photocopies of some strays from the archive in BL, which have since been reunited with that archive), T/2593.
Londonderry Estate Office Papers, D/654/F and H and D/654/Y1/11.
Lothian (Buckinghamshire) Papers (originals in the Norfolk Record Office), T/3170.
Macartney Papers, D/572.
McGildowny Papers, D/1375.
Martin & Henderson Papers, D/2223/M.
Nugent of Farrenconnell, Co. Cavan, Papers, D/3835/E.
Pembroke Papers: calendar of the Irish material in the possession of the Earl of Pembroke at Wilton House, Wiltshire.
Perceval-Maxwell Papers D/1556/17.
Pitt/Pretyman Papers (photocopied selection from the originals in the Cambridge University Library), T/3319.
Pollock Papers, T/3346.
Portpatrick marriage register: typescript copy of entries relating to Irish people, T/1005.
Registry of Deeds Papers (microfilm copies of the originals in Henrietta Street, Dublin), MIC 311, vol. 126, p. 32, and vol. 320, p. 524.
Rossmore Papers, T/2929/37.
Shannon Papers, D/2707/A.
Sheffield Papers (additional), T/3465.
Sneyd Papers (photocopied selection from the originals in Keele University Library), T/3229.
Staples Papers, D/1567/13/15.
Stowe (Nugent/Grenville) Papers (photocopied selection from the originals in the Northamptonshire Record Office), T/3503.
Stradbroke Papers (microfilm of the Irish estate material in the Suffolk RO, Ipswich), MIC 253.

Strutt Papers, T/3092.
Templemore Papers, T/3303.
Tighe Papers, D/2685/14.
Villiers-Stuart Papers, T/3131, B, C, D, E, G, I, J and L.
Wentworth Woodhouse Muniments (small photocopied selection from the originals in the Sheffield Archives), T/3302.
Wickham Papers (originals in the Hampshire RO), T/2627/5.
Wicklow Papers (microfilm copies of a folder of typescripts of eighteenth- and early nineteenth-century correspondence in NLI), MIC/146.

Public Record Office of Northern Ireland Register of Irish Archives
(Lists/calendars of archives in private possession outside NI which PRONI has reported on but not photocopied/microfilmed in their entirety or at all):

Cosby Papers, Stradbally Hall, Stradbally, Co. Laois.
Granard Papers, Castle Forbes, Newtownforbes, Co. Longford. See also PRONI, T/3765.
Kilmaine Papers, Shelfield House, Shelfield, Alcester, Warwickshire. (The PRONI contribution is an add-on to a previous NRA list.)
Lefroy Papers, formerly at Carrigglas Manor, Longford, Co.Longford.
Meath Papers, Killruddery, Bray, Co. Wicklow.
Pakenham Papers, Tullynally Castle, Castlepollard, Co. Westmeath.
Rosse Papers, Birr Castle, Co. Offaly.
Springfield Castle (Muskerry) Papers, Springfield Castle, Drumcollogher, Co. Limerick.

Royal Irish Academy, Dublin
Charlemont Papers, 12 R. 20.

Surrey History Centre, Woking
Midleton Papers, MS 1248/20.

Trinity College, Dublin
Conolly Papers, MS 3977, 3978.
Hartpole Papers, MS 1933.

West Sussex Record Office, Chichester
Goodwood (Richmond) Papers, MS 102 and MS 1083.
Petworth House Archive, PHA/55, 57 and 1720. See also under Private Collections – Petworth House Estate Office Archive.

PRINTED AND SECONDARY SOURCES
(arranged alphabetically according to author/editor)

Anon., *The Irish Register, or a List of the Duchess Dowagers, Countesses, … Widows and Misses of Large Fortunes in England …* (London, 1742)
Anon., *Letters on Love, Marriage and Adultery addressed to the Rt Hon. The Earl of Exeter* (London, 1789: reprinted, New York and London, 1984)
Anon., *Loudon Castle: the ancestral Home of the Campbells of Loudon* (Loudon Castle, 1995)
Bagshawe, W.H.G., *The Bagshawes of Ford: a biographical Pedigree* (privately printed, London, 1886)
Bailey, J., 'The Dillon Family in France, 1690–1794' (unpublished typescript, 1972)
Balliol College Library: the Conroy Papers – a Guide (Oxford, 1987)
Barnard, T.C., *The Abduction of a Limerick Heiress: social and political Relations in mid-Eighteenth-Century Ireland* (Maynooth Studies in Local History, Dublin, 1998)
Barnard, T.C., 'A Tale of three Sisters: Katherine Conolly of Castletown', in idem, *Irish*

Protestant Ascents and Descents, 1641–1770 (Dublin, 2004)

Belmore: *The Trial of Viscountess Belmore (formerly Lady Henrietta Hobart and Daughter to John, Earl of Buckinghamshire) for Adultery with the Earl of Ancram* (London, 1792)

Bessborough, 9th Earl of, and Aspinall, A., eds. *Lady Bessborough and her Family Circle* (London, 1940)

Betjeman, Sir J., *Collected Poems* ... (enlarged ed., London, 1970)

Blake, A.E. (Mrs Warenne) ed. *An Irish Beauty of the Regency ... the Hon. Mrs Calvert [née Pery] (1767–1852)* (London, 1911)

The Blessington Estate Act (9 Victoria, cap. 1), 1846

Blyth, H., *The pocket Venus [Lady Florence Paget, wife of the 4th Marquess of Hastings]* (London, 1966)

Bonfield, L., 'Marriage Settlements and the "Rise of Great Estates": the Demographic Aspect', in *The Economic History Review*, 2nd ser., XXXII, no. 4 (1979)

Bonfield, L., *Marriage Settlements, 1601–1740* (Cambridge 1983)

Borenius, T., and Hodgson, Rev. J.V., *A Catalogue of the Pictures at Elton Hall in Huntingdonshire* ... (London, 1924)

Brook-Shepherd, G., *Uncle of Europe [Edward VII]* (reprint, 1975)

Brooke, R.F., *The brimming River* (Dublin, 1961)

Brown, J., and Tomlins, T.E., eds. *Reports of Cases, upon Appeals and Writs of Error, in Parliament, from 1701 to ... 1800* (2nd ed., 8 vols., London, 1803)

Burke, J.B. *Dormant, Abeyant, Extinct and Forfeited Peerages of the British Empire* (London, 1883)

Burke, J.B., *Vicissitudes of Families* (new ed., 2 vols., London, 1883)

Burke, J.B., *The Landed Gentry of Ireland* (1899, 1904, 1912 and 1958 eds.)

Burke, J.B., *Peerage and Baronetage* (1933 ed.)

Butler, D.J., *Cahir: a Guide to Heritage Town and District* (Cahir, 1999)

Campbell, F., 'The elusive Mr Ogilvie (1740–1832)', in *Familia: the Ulster Genealogical Review*, II, no. 9 (1993)

Cannon, J., ed. *The Letters of Junius* (Oxford, 1978)

Cannon, J., *Aristocratic Century: the Peerage of Eighteenth-Century England* (Cambridge, 1984)

Canny, N.P., *The upstart Earl: a Study of the social and mental World of Richard Boyle, 1st Earl of Cork (1566–1643)* (Cambridge, 1982)

Casement, A., 'William Vitruvius Morrison's Scheme for Mount Stewart, Co. Down: was it ever realised?', in *Irish Architectural and Decorative Studies,* VII (2004)

Casement, A., 'The Management of the Londonderry Estates in Ulster during the Great Famine', in *Familia: Ulster Genealogical Review*, no. 21 (2005)

Chapman, C., and Dormer, J., *Elizabeth and Georgiana: the Duke of Devonshire and his two Duchesses,* (London, 2002)

Cherry, J., 'An Historical Geography of the Farnham Estates in Co. Cavan, 1650–1950' (unpublished Ph.D. thesis, NUI, Dublin, 2004)

Chevasse, C., *The Story of Baltinglass* (Kilkenny, 1970)

Clark, Mrs G., ed. *Gleanings from an old Portfolio* (3 vols., Edinburgh, 1895–8)

Clay, C., 'Marriage, Inheritance and the Rise of Large Estates', in *The Economic History Review*, 2nd ser., XXI (1968)

Cobbe, A., 'The Cobbe Family of Hampshire and Ireland', in A. Laing ed. *Clerics and Connoisseurs: an Irish Art Collection through three Centuries* (London, 2001)

Cobbe, A. and Friedman, T., *James Gibbs in Ireland: Newbridge, his Villa for Charles Cobbe, Archbishop of Dublin* (Hatchlands, Surrey, 2005)

C[ockayne], G.E., *The Complete Peerage*, ed. Vicary Gibbs and others (13 vols., London, 1910–40)

Coleridge, E.H., *The Life of Thomas Coutts, Banker* (2 vols., London, 1920)

Connely, W., *Count d'Orsay* (London, 1954)

Connolly, S.J., 'Family, Love and Marriage in early modern Ireland', in M. MacCurtain and M. O'Dowd eds. *Women in early modern Ireland* (Edinburgh, 1991)

Cooper, J.P., 'Patterns of Inheritance and Settlement by Great Landowners from the Fifteenth to the Eighteenth Centuries', in J. Goody, J. Thirsk and E.P. Thompson (eds.), *Family and Inheritance: Rural Society in Western Europe, 1200–1800* (Cambridge, 1976)

Costello, C., *A Class apart: the Gentry Families of County Kildare* (Dublin, 2005)

Crawford, W.H., 'Landlord-Tenant Relations in Ulster, 1609–1820', in *Irish Economic and Social History*, II (1975)

Crawford, W.H., review of M. Dowling, *Tenant Right and agrarian Society in Ulster, 1600–1870*, in *Familia*, no. 15 (1999)

Crawford, W.H., *The Management of a major Ulster Estate in the late eighteenth Century: the 8th Earl of Abercorn and his Irish Agents* (Maynooth Studies in Local History, Dublin, 2001)

Cullen, L.M., *The Emergence of Modern Ireland* (London, 1981)

Cunningham, P., ed. *The Letters of Horace Walpole, Earl of Orford* (9 vols., London, 1857)

Currie, E.A., 'Fining Down the Rents: the Management of the Conolly Estates in Ireland, 1734–1800', in *Derriana* (1979)

Debrett J., *The New Peerage...,* III [Ireland] (London, 1784)

'The de Ros Papers', in the *Annual Report of the Public Record Office of Northern Ireland for 1993–4* (Belfast, 1995), Appendix I

Dickson, D., 'The Economic History of the Cork Region in the Eighteenth Century', (Ph.D. thesis, University of Dublin, 1977)

Dickson, D., *Old World Colony: Cork and South Munster, 1630–1800* (Cork, 2005)

Diesbach, G. de, *Secrets of the Gotha* (London, 1964)

Duprée, M., review of the 1982 version of *The Pursuit of the Heiress* in *The Economic History Review* (November 1983)

Falk, B., *The Way of the Montagus: a Gallery of Family Portraits* (London, c.1955)

Ferguson, A.H., 'The lasting Legacy of a bigamous Duchess: the Benchmark Precedent for medical Confidentiality', in *Social History of Medicine*, vol. 19, no. 1 (2006)

Fitzgerald, B., ed. *The Correspondence of Emily, Duchess of Leinster* (3 vols., Dublin, 1949–57)

Fitzgerald, C.W. (Marquess of Kildare), ed. *The Earls of Kildare, 1057–1773: Second Addenda* [to 1804] (Dublin, 1872)

FitzGerald, D. (Knight of Glin), 'James Gandon's Work at Carrigglas, Co. Longford', in *The Country Seat: Studies in the History of the British Country House* (London, 1970)

Fitzmaurice, Lord, *Life of William, Earl of Shelburne ...* (2 vols., London, 1912)

Fitzpatrick, L., and Teevan, R., 'Caricature at Churchill', in W. Laffan ed. *A Year at Churchill* (Churchill Press, Tralee, 2003)

Fleming, D.A., and Malcomson, A.P.W., eds. *'A Volley of Execrations': the Letters and Papers of John FitzGibbon, Earl of Clare, 1772–1802* (IMC, Dublin, 2005)

Ford, E., *Tewin Water, or the Story of Lady Cathcart ...* (privately printed, Enfield, 1876)

Foreman, A., *Georgiana, Duchess of Devonshire* (London, 1998)

Fortescue, Hon. Sir J.W., ed. *The Correspondence of King George III from 1760 to December 1783 ...* (6 vols., London, 1927–8)

Foster, R.F., *Charles Stewart Parnell: the Man and his Family* (Hassocks, 1976)

Froude, J.A., *The English in Ireland in the Eighteenth Century* (3 vols., London, 1881)

Fyvie, J., 'The most gorgeous Lady Blessington', in *The Anglo-Saxon Review*, vol. 10 (September 1901)

Garlick, K., *Sir Thomas Lawrence: a Catalogue of the Paintings* (Oxford, 1989)

Gantz, I., *The Pastel Portrait: the Gunnings of Castle Coote ...* (London, 1963)

Gatty, C.T., *Mary Davies and the Manor of Ebury* (2 vols., London, 1921)

The Gentleman's Magazine, August 1789

Gerard, F., *Some fair Hibernians ...* (London, 1897)

Girouard, M., 'Belvedere House, Co. Westmeath...', in *Country Life*, 22 June 1961

Gore, J., ed. *Creevy* (London, 1949)

Greig, J., ed. *The Farington Diary*, by Joseph Farington, R.A. (8 vols., London, 1922–8)

[Grenville, W.W.] *Historical Manuscripts Commission Report ... on the Dropmore Papers*, I (London, 1892)

Greville, Lady V., *Vignettes of Memory* (London, c.1920)

Guinness, D., and Ryan, W., *Irish Houses and Castles* (London, 1971)

Gwyn, J., *The enterprising Admiral: the personal Fortune of Admiral Sir Peter Warren* (Montreal, 1974)

Habbakuk, H.J., 'English Landownership, 1680–1740', in *The English Historical Review*, 1st ser., X (1940)

Habbakuk, H.J., 'Marriage Settlements in the Eighteenth Century', in *Transactions of the Royal Historical Society*, 4th ser., XXXII (1950)

Hardy, W.J., 'Lady Cathcart and her Husbands', in *The St Albans and Herts. Architectural and Archaeological Society Journal* (1898)

Hayton, D.W., ed. *Letters of Marmaduke Coghill, 1722–1738* (IMC, Dublin, 2005)

Healey, E., *Lady Unknown: the Life of Angela Burdett-Coutts* (London, 1978)

Healey, E., *Coutts & Co., 1692–1992: the Portrait of a private Bank* (London, 1992)

Heesom, A., 'Entrepreneurial Paternalism: the 3rd Lord Londonderry (1778–1854) and the Coal Trade', in *Durham University Journal*, new ser., XXXV (1973–4)

Heesom, A., 'Problems of Church Extension in a Victorian New Town: the Londonderrys and Seaham Harbour', in *Northern History*, XV (1979)

Hewitt, E., ed. *Lord Shannon's Letters to his Son: the Letters from the 2nd Earl of Shannon to his Son, Viscount Boyle, 1790–1802* (Belfast, 1982)

Hicks, C., *Improper Pursuits: the Scandalous Life of Lady Di Beauclerk* (London, 2003)

Hill, Rev. G., 'Gleanings in Family History from the Antrim Coast: the Macnaghtens and Macneills', in *The Ulster Journal of Archaeology*, 1st ser., VII (1860)

Hollingsworth, T.H., 'The Demography of the British Peerage', in *Population Studies*: Supplement to Volume XVIII, no. 2 (London, 1964)

Hyde, H.M., *The Rise of Castlereagh* (London, 1933)

Inglis-Jones, E., *The Lord of Burghley* (London, 1964)

Jackson-Stops, G., 'Baronscourt, Co. Tyrone', in *Country Life*, 12 July 1979

Johnston[-Liik], E.M., ed. 'The State of the Irish House of Commons in 1791', in *Proceedings of the Royal Irish Academy*, LIX, sec. C, no. 1 (1957)

Johnston-Liik, E.M., *History of the Irish Parliament, 1692–1800: Commons, Constituencies and Statutes* (6 vols., UHF, Belfast, 2002)

Jupp, P.J., *Lord Grenville, 1759–1834* (Oxford, 1985)

Kavanaugh, A., *John FitzGibbon, Earl of Clare: Protestant Reaction and English Authority in late Eighteenth-Century Ireland* (Dublin, 1997)

Kelly, J., 'Abduction of Women of Fortune', in *Eighteenth Century Ireland*, IX (1994)

Kelly, J., 'Belvedere House: Origin, Development and Residents, 1540–1883', in J. Kelly ed, *A History of St Patrick's College, Drumcondra* (Dublin, 2006)

Ketton-Cremer, R.W., *Horace Walpole: a Biography* (London 1964)

King-Harman, A. L., *The Kings of King House* (Bedford, 1996)

Laffan, W., (ed.), *Painting Ireland: topographical Views from Glin Castle* (Churchill House Press, Tralee, 2006)

Large, D., 'The Wealth of the Great Irish Landowners, 1750–1815', *in Irish Historical Studies*, XV, no. 57 (March 1966)

Lawlor, H.C., *A History of the Family of Cairnes or Cairns and its Connections* (London, 1906)

Lecky, W.E.H., *History of Ireland in the Eighteenth Century* (cabinet ed., 5 vols., London 1919)

Lefroy, Sir J.H., *Loffroy of Cambray* (privately printed, 1868)

Lefroy, J.A.P., *Loffroy of Cambray [a Supplement]* (privately printed, 1961)

Lenihan, M., *Limerick: its History and Antiquities* (Dublin, 1866)

Lewis, S., *A topographical Dictionary of Ireland ...* (2 vols., London, 1837)

Londonderry, 3rd Marquess of, ed. *Memoirs and Correspondence of Viscount Castlereagh ...* (first ser., 4 vols., London, 1848–9)

Lovell, M.S., *A scandalous Life: the Biography of Jane Digby [Lady Ellenborough]* (London, 1995)

Luxborough, Lady, *Letters ... to William Shenstone* (1st Irish ed., Dublin, 1776)

Lynam, S., *Humanity Dick: a Biography of Richard Martin, MP, 1754–1834* (London, 1975)

Lyons, J.C., *The Grand Juries of the County of Westmeath ... [1727–1853], with an historical Appendix* (privately printed, Ledestown, 1853)

Lyster, G. ed. *A Family Chronicle ...* (London, 1908)

McCarthy, P., and Mulligan, K.V., 'New Light on Ballyfin [Co. Laois]…', in *Irish Architectural and Decorative Studies…*, VIII (2005)
McDonnell, A. (Countess of Antrim), 'The quarrelling Countesses' (typescript of a talk given to the Larne Historical Society, 1979)
McDowell, R.B., *Ireland in the Age of Imperialism and Revolution*, 1760–1800 (Oxford, 1979)
Mackesy, P., *The Coward of Minden: the Affair of Lord George Sackville* (London, 1979)
McKinstry, L., *Rosebery: Statesman in Turmoil* (London, 2005)
Madden, R.R., *The literary Life and Correspondence of the Countess of Blessington* (3 vols., London, 1855)
Maguire, W.A., 'Lord Donegall and the Hearts of Steel', in *Irish Historical Studies*, XXI, no. 84 (September 1981)
Maguire, W.A., '*Living like a Lord: the 2nd Marquess of Donegall, 1769–1844*', (UHF, Belfast, 1984)
Maguire, W.A., 'Castle Nugent and Castle Rackrent: Fact and Fiction in Maria Edgeworth', in *Eighteenth-Century Ireland*, XI (1996)
Malcomson, A.P.W., 'The Struggle for Control of Dundalk Borough, 1782–92', in *County Louth Archaeological Journal*, XVII (1970)
Malcomson, A.P.W., *The Extraordinary Career of the 2nd Earl of Massereene, 1743–1805* (Belfast, 1972)
Malcomson, 'The Earl of Clermont: a forgotten Co. Monaghan Magnate of the late eighteenth Century', in *Clogher Record*, VII (1973)
Malcomson, A.P.W., ed. *Eighteenth-Century Irish Official Papers in Great Britain: Private Collections, Volume One* (Belfast, 1973), and Volume Two (Belfast, 1990)
Malcomson, A.P.W., 'The Newtown Act: Revision and Reconstruction', *in Irish Historical Studies*, XVIII, no. 71 (March 1973)
Malcomson, A.P.W., 'Speaker Pery and the Pery Papers', in *North Munster Antiquarian Journal*, XVI (1973–4)
Malcomson, A.P.W., 'Absenteeism in Eighteenth-Century Ireland', in *Irish Economic and Social History*, I (1974)
Malcomson, A.P.W., *John Foster: The Politics of the Anglo-Irish Ascendancy* (Oxford, 1978)
Malcomson, A.P.W., 'The Gentle Leviathan: Arthur Hill, 2nd Marquess of Downshire, 1753–1801', in P. Roebuck ed. *Plantation to Partition: Essays in Ulster History in Honour of J.L. McCracken* (Belfast, 1981)
Malcomson, A.P.W., 'A lost natural Leader: John James Hamilton, 1st Marquess of Abercorn (1756–1818)', in *Proc. RIA,* vol. 88, sec. C, no. 4 (1988)
Malcomson, A.P.W., 'The Enniskillen Family, Estate and Archive', in *Clogher Record* (1998)
Malcomson, A.P.W., 'A Woman Scorned?: Theodosia, Countess of Clanwilliam (1743–1817)', in *Familia*, no. 15 (1999)
Malcomson, A.P.W., 'The Irish Peerage and the Act of Union, 1800–1971', in *The Transactions of the Royal Historical Society,* 6th ser., X (2000)
Malcomson, A.P.W., '*Archbishop Charles Agar: Churchmanship and Politics in Ireland, 1760–1810',* (Dublin, 2002)
Malcomson, A.P.W., 'A House divided: the Loftus Family, Earls and Marquesses of Ely, c.1600–c.1900', in D. Dickson and C. O'Grada eds. *Refiguring Ireland: Essays in Honour of L.M. Cullen* (Dublin, 2003)
Malcomson, 'The Erne Family, Estate and Archive, c.1610–c.1950', in E.M. Murphy and W. Roulston eds. *Fermanagh History and Society …* (Dublin, 2004)
Malcomson, A.P.W., *Nathaniel Clements: Government and the Governing Elite in Ireland, 1725–75* (Dublin, 2005)
Malcomson, A.P.W., ed. *The De Vesci Papers* (IMC, Dublin, 2006)
Malcomson, A.P.W., 'The Fall of the House of Conolly, 1758–1803', in A. Blackstock and E. Magennis eds. *Politics, People and Society: Essays in Honour of P.J. Jupp (*UHF, Belfast, 2007)
Marson P., 'The Lowry Corry Families of Castle Coole, 1646–1913' (UHF, Belfast, 2007)
Massingberd, H.M., ed. *Burke's Irish Family Records* (London, 1976)

Mitchell, L., *The Whig World, 1760–1837* (London, 2005)
Mitford, E.B., *Life of Lord Redesdale* (London, 1939)
Montomgery, I., ed. 'The quarrelling Countesses', in *The Glynns: the Journal of the Glens of Antrim Historical Society* (2002)
Moore, F.F., *A Georgian Pageant* (London, 1908)
Morrison, A., *The Blessington Papers, from the Collection of autograph Letters and historical Documents formed by …* (1895)
Namier, L.B., and Brooke, J., *The History of Parliament: the House of Commons, 1754–90* (3 vols., London, 1964)
Nevill, Lady D., *Reminiscences* (London, 1906)
Nicholls, K.W., 'Irishwomen and Property in the sixteenth Century', in M. MacCurtain and M. O'Dowd eds. *Women in early modern Ireland* (Edinburgh, 1991)
Nolan, W., '"A public Benefit": Sir Vere Hunt, Bt, and the Town of New Bermingham, Co. Tipperary, 1800–18', in H.B. Clarke, J. Prunty and M. Hennessy eds. *Surveying Ireland's Past: multidisciplinary Essays in Honour of Anngret Simms* (Dublin, 2004)
Nugent, C., *Memoir of Robert, Earl Nugent; with Letters, Poems and Appendices* (London, 1898)
Ó Muraile, N., 'Local Names from the Dillon Rental, 1805', in M. Comer and N. Ó Muraile eds. *Béacán/Bekan: Portrait of an East Mayo Parish* (Castlebar, 1986)
Payling, S.J., 'The Economics of Marriage in late Mediaeval England: the Marriage of Heiresses', in *The Economic History Review (2003)*
Pearce, C.E., *The jolly Duchess: Harriot Mellon …* (London, 1915)
Pearson, H., *'Labby': the Life and Character of Henry Labouchere* (London, 1936)
Pevsner, Sir N., *The Buildings of England: Leicestershire and Rutland* (reprint, Harmondsworth, 1970)
Phelan, D., *Lyons Demesne: a Georgian Treasure restored to the Nation* (privately printed, 1999)
Plowden, A., *The young Victoria* (London, 1981)
Potter, M., *The Government and the People of Limerick: the History of Limerick Corporation/City Council, 1197–2006* (Limerick, 2006)
Potterton, H., *Irish Church Monuments, 1570–1880* (Belfast, 1975)
Power, W., *White Knights, Dark Earls: the Rise and Fall of an Anglo-Irish Dynasty* (Cork, 2000)
Proudfoot, L., 'The Management of a Great Estate: Patronage, Income and Expenditure on the Duke of Devonshire's Irish Property, c.1816 to 1891', in *Irish Economic and Social History*, vol. XIII (1986)
Rait, R.S., *The Story of an Irish Property [the Lough Cutra Estate, Gort]* (Oxford, 1908)
Return of Owners of Land in England and Wales in 1873, exclusive of the Metropolis (2 vols., London, 1875)
Richardson, E.M. ed. *Long-forgotten Days … [Family History of the Stratfords, Earls of Aldborough]* (London, 1928)
Richey, R.A., 'Landed Society in mid-Eighteenth-Century Co. Down', (unpublished Ph.D. thesis, QUB, 2000)
Rizzo, B., *Companions without Vows: Relationships among eighteenth-century British Women* (University of Georgia Press, 1994)
Roden, 10th Earl of, *Tollymore: the Story of an Irish Demesne* (Belfast, 2005)
Roebuck, P., 'Post-Restoration Landownership: the Impact of the Abolition of Wardship', in *The Journal of British Studies* (Connecticut, Fall 1978)
Roebuck, P., *Yorkshire Baronets, 1640–1760: Families, Estates and Fortunes* (Oxford, 1980).
Roebuck, P., 'Rent Movement, proprietorial Incomes and agricultural Development, 1730–1830', in *Plantation to Partition …* (Belfast, 1981)
Roebuck, P., ed. *Macartney of Lisanoure (1737–1806): Essays in Biography* (UHF, Belfast, 1983)
Rowan, A., 'Clearwell Castle, Gloucestershire', in *The Country Seat …* (London, 1970)
Sadleir, M., *Blessington-d'Orsay: a Masquerade* (London, 1933)
Sadleir, T.U., ed. 'Letter from Edward, 2nd Earl of Aldborough, to his agent at Belan', in *Co. Kildare Archaeological Journal*, VII (1912–14)
Sedgwick, R., *The History of Parliament: the House of Commons, 1715–54* (2 vols., London, 1970)

Sermoneta, Duchess of, *The Locks of Norbury: the Story of a remarkable Family in the eighteenth and nineteenth Centuries* (London, 1940)

Sotheby's sale catalogue of *The Library of the Rt Hon. The Earl of Granard, 21 July 1993*

Spring, E., 'Law and the Theory of the Affective Family', in *Albion* (Appalachian State University, 1984)

Spring, E., *Law, Land and Family: Aristocratic Inheritance in England, 1300–1800* (Chapel Hill and London, 1993)

Stone, L., 'The Wriothesleys, 1530–1667', in idem, *Family and Fortune: Studies in Aristocratic Finances in the sixteenth and seventeenth Centuries* (Oxford, 1973)

Stone, L., *The Family, Sex and Marriage in England, 1500–1800* (New York, 1977)

Stone, L., *Road to Divorce: England, 1530–1987* (Oxford, 1990)

Stone, L., *Broken Lives: Separation and Divorce in England, 1660–1857* (Oxford, 1993)

Thomson, G. Scott, *The Russells in Bloomsbury, 1669–1771* (London, 1940)

Thorne R.G., ed. *The History of Parliament: the Commons, 1790–1820* (5 vols., London, 1986)

Tillyard, S., *Aristocrats: Caroline, Emily, Louisa and Sarah Lennox, 1740–1832* (London, 1994)

Todd, J., *Rebel Daughters: Ireland in Conflict, 1798* (London, 2003)

Trumbach, R., *The Rise of the Egalitarian Family: Aristocratic Kinship and Domestic Relations in Eighteenth-Century England* (New York, 1978)

Vaughan, W.E., *Landlords and Tenants in mid-Victorian Ireland* (Oxford, 1994)

Wakefield, E.G., *An Account of Ireland statistical and political* (2 vols., London, 1812)

Whitworth, R., *Field-Marshal Lord Ligonier: a Story of the British Army, 1702–1770* (Oxford, 1958)

Wilson, D., 'Women and Property in wealthy landed Families in Ireland, 1750–1850' (unpublished Ph.D. thesis, QUB, 2003)

Wyndham, Hon. H.A., *A Family History, 1688–1837: the Wyndhams of Somerset, Sussex and Wiltshire* (Oxford, 1950)

Young A., *A Tour in Ireland …* (2 vols., Dublin, 1780)

INDEX

Abbeyleix, Co. Laois, 230
abduction, 32, 62–7, 155, 255
Abercorn, Earl, Marquess, Marchioness and Duke of:
    see under Hamilton
Abergavenny, Earl of: see Nevill
absentee landlordism, 87, 102, 108–9, 198, 206, 225–227
absentee tax, 87, 271
acts of parliament (private), 11, 21, 43, 73, 143, 164,
    182–3, 253, 256, 262
acts of parliament (public), 18–9, 117, 122, 143, 156–7,
    165, 178, 183, 209–10, 255
Adare, Lord and Lady: see under Quin
Adare Manor, Co. Limerick, 141, 217
Adderley, Elizabeth: see Ross
adultery: see infidelity
'affectiveness': see love-matches
Agar, George, Lord Callan, 171–3, 247
Agar, Welbore, 2nd Earl of Normanton, 269
Aghalane, Co. Fermanagh, 205
agriculture: see under expenditure (estate)
alcoholism: see drunkenness
Aldborough, Earl and Countess of: see under Stratford
Aldborough House, Amiens Street, Dublin, 1, 227
Alexander, James, 1st Earl of Caledon, 79
alimony: see under divorce and separation
Allen, Hon. Elizabeth, Lady Carysfort (wife of the
    1st Lord),107–9, 175
Allen, Hon. Frances, Lady Newhaven, 108, 189
Allen, Joshua, 2nd Viscount Allen, 107, 189
Allen, Joshua, 5th Viscount Allen, 108
Allen, Margaret, Viscountess Allen (widow of the
    2nd Viscount), 108–9
Allsop, Henry, 1st Lord Hindlip, 45
American War of Independence, 75, 233
Amiens, viscountcy of, 1
Amiens Street, Dublin, 1
Anglesey, Earl of: see Annesley, Richard, 6th Earl of
    Anglesey
Annaly, Lord: see Gore, John
Annesgrove, Co. Cork, 76
Annesley, Arthur, 4th Lord Altham, 262
Annesley, General Arthur Grove, 75, 88
Annesley, Francis Charles, 1st Earl Annesley, 7–8, 75, 166,
    224
Annesley, Mary, Countess Annesley (first wife of the
    1st Earl), 75, 88
Annesley, Richard, 6th Earl of Anglesey, 32
Annesley, Richard, 2nd Earl Annesley, 7–8, 250
Annesley, Sophia, Countess Annesley (second wife of the
    1st Earl), 7–8, 166
annuities, 7, 8, 10, 13, 32, 108, 143, 169–71, 173,
    180–81, 184, 249
    see also jointures

Antrim, County, 5–7, 96–8
Antrim, Earl, Countess, Marchioness and Marquess of:
    see McDonnell
architecture and building, 39, 44, 52, 60–61, 95, 97, 100,
    124, 133, 149, 178–9, 198, 200, 208, 214, 217, 221–3,
    229–31, 269
Ardglass Castle, Co. Down, 43
Arklow, Co. Wicklow, 108
army, 31, 42, 99, 165
Arran, Earl of: see under Gore
Ashmead Bartlett, William: see Bartlett
attainder: see under forfeiture
Aungier, Ambrose, 2nd Earl of Longford, 187, 190
Aungier, family of, earls of Longford, 187–190
Austen, Jane, 201
Austria, 163–166

bachelors, 109, 208, 236, 245, 259
Ballingown, near Dromana, Co. Waterford, 230
Ballyconnell House, Co. Cavan, 237
Ballyfin, Maryborough, Co. Laois, 221
Ballyhimmock, Co. Cork: see Annesgrove
Ballynahinch, Co. Down, 222–3
Banbury borough, Oxfordshire, 164
Bangor, Co. Down, 3–4
Bangor, Viscounts: see Ward, Bernard, and under Ward,
    Nicholas
Bank of Ireland, 35
bankruptcy, 11–12, 79, 181, 217
banks and bankers, 12, 35, 45–6, 55–6, 58, 60, 166–7,
    221, 223, 231
Barker, Ann (mistress of Earl Conyngham), 170
Barker, Rev. Thomas, late of Grettleton, Wiltshire, 170
Barralet, John James, 123, 124
Barrington, Sir Jonah, 62
Barry, James, of Newtownbarry (Bunclody), Co. Wexford,
    85
Barry, Colonel John Maxwell, 5th Lord Farnham:
    see Maxwell Barry
Barry, Judith, Mrs John Maxwell, 85
Bartlett, William Ashmead, 166–7
Bateman, John, 196
Bateman, Rowland, of Oak Park, Co. Kerry, 196
Bateson, Sir Robert, 1st Bt, 254
Bateson, Thomas, 254
Bath, 17, 234
Bath, Marquess of: see under Thynne
Bayley, Martha, Mrs Joseph Leeson, 79
Bayly, Caroline, Lady Bayly: see Paget
Bayly, John, of Castlemore, Co. Cork, 85
Bayly, Sir Nicholas, 2nd Bt, 199

285

Bayly, family of, of Plas Newydd, Anglesey, and Mount Bagenal, Carlingford, Co. Louth, baronets, 199
Beauclerk, Lady Di (née Churchill; formerly Viscountess Bolingbroke), 43
Beauclerk, Rev. Lord Frederick, 57
Beauclerk, George, 3rd Duke of St Albans, 58
Beauclerk, Jane, Duchess of St Albans: see Roberts
Beauclerk, Osborne de Vere, 12th Duke of St Albans, 178
Beauclerk, William Amelius, 10th Duke of St Albans, 178
Beauclerk, William Aubrey de Vere, 9th Duke of St Albans, 56–7
Beaulieu, Hampshire, 102–3
Beaulieu, Earl of: see Hussey-Montagu, Edward
Beaulieu, Lord Montagu of: see Montagu-Douglas-Scott
Bedford, dukes of: see Russell
Belfast, Lady: see Chichester, Anna, Marchioness of Donegall
Belfast, Lord: see Chichester, George, Augustus, 2nd Marquess of Donegall
Belgravia, London, 201
Bell, Edward (trooper in the carbineers, c.1760), 168
Bellaghy, Co. Londonderry, 110
Bellew, John, 4th Lord Bellew, 29
Belmore, Earl and Countess: see Corry
Belvedere, Mullingar, Co. Westmeath, 149, 230, 263
Belvedere, Earl and Countess of: see under Rochfort
Bentinck, William Henry Cavendish, 3rd Duke of Portland, 212
Beutley, Richard (designer and engraver), 117
Beresford, Elizabeth, Marchioness of Waterford (née Monck; wife of the 1st Marquess), 60–2, 77, 131, 191
Beresford, Lady Elizabeth: see Cobbe
Beresford, George de la Poer, 2nd Earl of Tyrone and 1st Marquess of Waterford, 52–3, 60–2, 78, 95, 131, 191
Beresford, Henry de la Poer, 2nd Marquess of Waterford, 131
Beresford, Henry de la Poer, 3rd Marquess of Waterford, 95
Beresford, Susanna, Marchioness of Waterford (wife of the 2nd Marquess), 131, 242
Beresford, family of, marquesses of Waterford, 53
Berkeley, James, 3rd Earl of Berkeley, 134
Berkshire: see Easthampstead Park, Berkshire
Bermingham, Anne, Countess of Charlemont (wife of the 2nd Earl), 72–4, 109, 137
Bermingham, Francis, 18th Lord Athenry, 48
Bermingham, Mary, Mrs William Bermingham, 72–4, 82, 109, 137–8, 256
Bermingham, Mary, Lady Clements and Countess of Leitrim (wife of the 2nd Earl), 72–4, 82, 109
Bermingham, William, of Rosshill, Cong, Co. Mayo, 72
Bernal, Ralph: see Bernal Osborne
Bernard, James, of Castle Bernard, Co. Cork, 117
Berwick-upon-Tweed, 131
Bessborough, earls of: see under Ponsonby
Bessborough, Pilltown, Co. Kilkenny, 226
Betham, Sir William, 58
Betjeman, Sir John, 151

bigamy, 7, 143, 164–5
Bilboa, Co. Limerick, 109
Bingham, (Charles) Barry, 2nd Lord Clanmorris, 162
Bingham, Lady Lavinia: see Spencer, Lavinia, Countess Spencer
Bingham, Richard, 2nd Earl of Lucan, 52
birth-rate: see under demography
Blackburn, Elizabeth (alias Lane): see Skeffington, Elizabeth
Blackrock, Co. Dublin, 11, 41, 108, 164
Blackwood, Joyce (daughter of Joseph Leeson senior and wife of Robert Blackwood), 44
Blackwood, Hon. Price, 231
Blackwood, Robert, of Ballyleidy, Co. Down, 44
Blake, Eliza, of Ardfry, Co. Galway, 162
Blaquiere, Hon. Peter Boyle, 162
Blatherwycke, Northamptonshire, 70
Blayney, Cadwallader, 7th Lord Blayney, 60, 113–4, 153, 191
Blayney, Edward, 3rd Lord Blayney, 113
Blayney, Henry Vincent, 5th Lord Blayney, 113
Blayney, Mary Cairnes, Lady Blayney: see Cairnes
Blessington/Blesinton, earls of: see Stewart, William, and Gardiner, Charles John
Blessington, Co. Wicklow, 199–200
Blickling Hall, Norfolk, 148, 192
Bligh, Lady Anne: see Ward
Bligh, John, 3rd Earl of Darnley, 8, 89
Bligh, Mary, Countess of Darnley (wife of the 3rd Earl), 89
Bloomsbury, London, 201, 267–8
Blundell, family of, Viscounts Blundell, 105
borrowing: see debts
Bourbon, family of (exiled members of the French royal family), 222–3
Bourke, Hon. Bridget, Mrs John Gunning of Castle Coote, Co. Roscommon, 121
Boycott, Capt. Charles Cunningham, 204–5
Boyd, Abraham, KC, 24, 230
Boyd, George, of Dublin, merchant, 46
Boyd, Jane, Countess of Carhampton, 46
Boyd Rochfort, family of: see Rochfort Boyd
Boyle, Lady Charlotte: see Cavendish, Charlotte, Marchioness of Hartington
Boyle, Dorothy, Countess of Burlington, 23, 139
Boyle, Eleanor: see Hill, Eleanor
Boyle, Grace, Countess of Middlesex, 205–6, 227
Boyle, John, 5th Earl of Cork and Orrery, 2, 76–7, 106, 135, 191–2
Boyle, Margaret, Countess of Cork and Orrery (second wife of the 5th Earl), 76–7, 106
Boyle, Michael, Archbishop of Armagh, 199–200
Boyle, Richard, 1st Earl of Cork, 115, 206
Boyle, Richard, 3rd Earl of Burlington (and 4th Earl of Cork), 23
Boyle, Richard, Field-Marshal the 2nd Viscount Shannon, 205
Boyle, Richard, 2nd Earl of Shannon, 90, 206
Boyle, family of, earls of Cork and Burlington, 15

INDEX

Boyle Walsingham, Charlotte, Lady Henry Fitzgerald, Baroness de Ros in her own right, 81, 141
Brabazon, Chaworth, 6th Earl of Meath, 10
Brabazon, Edward, 7th Earl of Meath, 10
Brabazon, Juliana, Countess of Meath: see Prendergast
Brabazon, Mary, Countess of Meath, 19, 249
Brabazon, Reginald, Lord Brabazon and 12th Earl of Meath, 19, 249
Bradshaw: see Cavendish Bradshaw
Branden, Lord: see Crosbie, Maurice
Bristol, earls of: see Hervey, Frederick, and Hervey, Frederick William
British peerage: see peerage of England/Great Britain/the United Kingdom
Brockley Park, Stradbally, Co. Laois, 207
Brooke, Sir Arthur, Bt, of Colebrooke, Co. Fermanagh, 20, 250
Brooke, Francis, of Colebrooke, 20
Brooke, Letitia Charlotte, later Lady Parnell, 20
Brooke, Margaret, Lady Brooke (née Fortescue): see Fortescue
Brooke, Selina Elizabeth, later Viscountess de Vesci: see Vesey
Brown, W.H. (artist), 154
Browne, Dodwell, of Rahins, Co. Mayo, 162
Browne, Elizabeth, Countess of Altamont (née Kelly): see Kelly
Browne, Hon. John, 162
Browne, Sir John, 7th Bt, 1st Lord Kilmaine, 11, 238
Browne, John Denis, 3rd Earl of Altamont and 1st Marquess of Sligo, 214
Browne, Margaret Elizabeth, Mrs Henry Caulfeild, 214
Browne, Peter, 2nd Earl of Altamont, 253
Brussels, 31
Brydges, Elizabeth, Duchess of Chandos (widow of the 2nd Duke), 1
Buckingham, dukes of: see under Villiers
Buckingham, Marquess, Marchioness and Duke of: see Grenville
Buckinghamshire, Earl and Countess of: see Hobart
building: see under architecture and building
Bulstrode, Elizabeth (mistress of Earl Conyngham), 169–70
Bunbury, Lady Sarah: see Lennox
Bunclody, Co. Wexford: see Newtownbarry
Burdett-Coutts: see Coutts
Burges, Lady Caroline: see Clements
Burges, Sir John Smith, Bt, 262
Burges, John Ynyr, of Parkanaur, Castlecaulfield, Co. Tyrone, 128, 261
Burges, Margaret, Countess Poulett: see Poulett
Burges, Ynyr (d.1792), sometime governor of the East India Company, 262
Burgh, Margaretta: see Foster
Burke, Honora, of Glinsk, Co. Galway: see Taaffe
Burke, Sir John Bernard, 58
Burlington, earls of: see Boyle, Richard, and Cavendish, George Augustus

Burrell, Elizabeth: see Fitzgibbon, Elizabeth, Countess of Clare
Burrell, Peter, 1st Lord Gwydyr, 80
Burrell, Priscilla Barbara (née Bertie), Lady Gwydyr and Baroness Willoughby of Eresby in her own right, 80
Burton, Catherine, Viscountess Netterville, 4, 12
Burton, Francis, of Buncraggy, Co. Clare, 21, 38, 58
Burton, Francis Nathaniel, of Buncraggy, 203–4
Burton, Francis Pierpont, 2nd Lord Conyngham: see Conyngham
Burton, Mary: see Conyngham
Burton, Samuel, of Burton Hall, Co. Carlow, 4, 12
Burton's Bank, 12
Burton Pynsent, Somerset, 193
Bury, Jane (wife of William Bury of Shannongrove, Co. Limerick), 5, 193–5
Bury, John, of Charleville Forest, Co. Offaly, and Shannongrove, Co. Limerick, 5, 193
Bury, William, of Shannongrove, Co. Limerick, 5, 193–5
Bute, Countess and Marquesses of: see under Stuart
Butler, Anna Maria, Countess of Ormonde: see Clarke
Butler, Brinsley, 2nd Earl of Lanesborough, 193–5
Butler, Brinsley, 4th Earl of Lanesborough, 193
Butler, Frances Susan, Countess of Ormonde: see Wandesford, Lady Frances Susan
Butler, James, 19th Earl and 1st Marquess of Ormonde, 89
Butler, Jane, Countess of Lanesborough: see Rochfort
Butler, John, 17th Earl of Ormonde, 89
Butler, Margaret Lauretta, Countess of Glengall (wife of the 2nd Earl), 46, 78–9, 218, 257
Butler, Margaret, Viscountess Ikerrin: see Hamilton, Margaret
Butler, Richard, 1st Earl of Glengall, 39
Butler, Richard, 2nd Earl of Glengall, 29, 39, 78–9, 83, 218
Butler, Thomas, 6th Viscount Ikerrin, 4
Butler, Walter, 18th Earl and only (of that creation) Marquess of Ormonde, 89, 254
Butler, family of, earls and marquesses of Ormonde, 1, 89
Butler Charteris, Lady Margaret, 79
Byng, George, of Wrotham Park, Barnet, 118, 127

cadet inheritance, 83–91, 103–6, 188, 195–6, 199, 203, 246, 264
Cadogan, Henry, of Liscarton, Co. Meath, 261
Cadogan, Lady Sarah: see Lennox, Sarah, Duchess of Richmond
Cadogan, William, 1st Lord, and Earl, Cadogan, 129
Cahir town and estate, Co. Tipperary, 46, 78–9
Cairnes, Sir Alexander, 1st Bt, 60, 113–4
Cairnes, Sir Henry, 2nd Bt, 60, 114
Cairnes, Mary, Lady Blayney, 59–60, 113–4, 126–7, 137, 153, 188–9, 228
Cairnes, William (d.1706), 60, 113
Calcutta habour, 70
Caledon estate, Co. Tyrone, 77, 109

287

Callan, Lord: *see* Agar, George
Camden, Earl and Marquess: *see* Pratt
Camelford, Lord: *see* Pitt, Thomas
Campbell, Charles, of Dublin, 4, 12
Campbell, Lady Flora Mure, Countess of Loudon (wife of the 2nd Earl of Moira), 222–3
Campbell, James Mure, 5th Earl of Loudon, 222
Campbell, Mary, Viscountess Mountjoy: see Gardiner
Cannon, John, 166
Canny, Nicholas, 115
Capua, Charles, Prince of, 163
Carbery, Lord and Lady: *see under* Evans and Evans-Freke
Cardiff, 164–5
Carlingford, Co. Louth, 199
Carlow, 'manor and castle' of, Co. Carlow, 225
Carlow, Viscount and Viscountess: *see under* Dawson
Carlyle, Jane Walsh (Mrs Thomas Carlyle), 179
Carpenter, George, 2nd Earl of Tyrconnel, 143
Carpenter, Margaret (portrait-painter), 98
Carpenter, Lady Susanna: *see* Beresford
Carra, Magheraveely, Co. Fermanagh, 65
Carton, Co. Kildare (seat of the dukes of Leinster), 31, 41
Cary, barony of, Co. Antrim, 96
Carysfort borough and estate, Co. Wicklow, 108–9
Carysfort, Lord and Lady, and Earl and Countess of: *see* Proby
Cashel petty sessions, Co. Tipperary, 172
Castleblayney, Co. Monaghan, 113
Castlecomer collieries, Co. Kilkenny, 89, 232
Castle Coote, Lord: *see* Coote, Charles Henry
Castle Forbes, Co. Longford, 122, 221, 238
Castlegore, Castlederg, Co. Tyrone, 196–7
Castlemorres, Co. Kilkenny, 200
Castle Nugent, Edgeworthstown, Co. Longford, 65–6
Castle Rackrent, 67
Castlereagh, Lord and Lady: *see under* Stewart
Castletown, Celbridge, Co. Kildare, 120
Castle Ward, Strangford, Co. Down, 149, 237
Cathcart, General Charles Schaw, 9th Lord Cathcart, 194
Cathcart, Elizabeth, Lady Cathcart, 65–7, 114, 135, 155, 193–4
Cathcart, General William Schaw, 10th Lord and 1st Earl Cathcart, 193–4
Catholic Association, 95
Catholic Emancipation, 95, 163, 178
Caulfeild, Anne, Countess of Charlemont: *see* Bermingham
Caulfeild, Francis William, 2nd Earl of Charlemont, 72, 162
Caulfeild, Hon. Henry, 162
Caulfeild, James Molyneux, 3rd Earl of Charlemont, 162
Caulfield, Margaret Elizabeth: *see* Browne
Cavan, County, 19, 239
Cavendish, Catherine, Duchess of Devonshire (wife of the 3rd Duke), 127
Cavendish, Charlotte, Marchioness of Hartington (wife of the future 4th Duke), 23, 105, 127, 138–9, 228
Cavendish, George Augustus, 1st Earl of Burlington, 105

Cavendish, Georgiana, Duchess of Devonshire, 117, 145
Cavendish, William, 3rd Duke of Devonshire, 52
Cavendish, William, 4th Duke of Devonshire, 105, 127, 138–9
Cavendish, William, 5th Duke of Devonshire, 117, 145
Cavendish, William George Spencer, 6th Duke of Devonshire, 226, 228
Cavendish Bradshaw, Hon. Augustus, 150
Cecil, Brownlow, 9th Earl of Exeter, 142
Cecil, Lady Catherine: *see* Perceval, Catherine, Countess of Egmont
Cecil, Elizabeth, Marchioness of Salisbury (wife of the 5th Marquess), 178
Cecil, Lady Emily: *see* Nugent, Emily, Marchioness of Westmeath
Cecil, Emma, Mrs Henry Cecil, 43, 142–3, 146, 174, 218
Cecil, Henry, 10th Earl and 1st Marquess of Exeter, 142–3, 146, 174, 218
Cecil, James, 6th Earl of Salisbury, 133
Cecil, James, 7th Earl and 1st Marquess of Salisbury, 28
Cecil, Robert, 7th Marquess of Salisbury, 178
Cecil, Sarah, Countess of Exeter: *see* Hoggins
Cecil, family of, marquesses of Salisbury, 152
Chancery, Court of, 71, 77, 96–7, 225, 237–8, 271
Chandos, Duchess of: *see* Brydges, Elizabeth
Charlemont, earls of: *see under* Caulfeild
Charles II, King, 213, 268–9
Charleville, Earl of: *see* Moore, Charles
Charlotte, Princess Royal of England, 16
Charlotte, Queen, 16, 235
Cheltenham, 17
Chichester, Anna, Marchioness of Donegall (wife of the 2nd Marquess), 129, 136, 156, 175
Chichester, Arthur, 5th Earl and 1st Marquess of Donegall, 21, 86–88, 136, 156–7
Chichester, Barbara, Marchioness of Donegall (third wife of the 1st Marquess), 21
Chichester, George Augustus, 2nd Marquess of Donegall, 42, 86, 129, 136, 156, 163, 175, 224
Chichester, Lord Spencer, 86
Chichester, family of, earls and marquesses of Donegall, 88
Child, Robert, of Osterley Park, Middlesex, 264
Child, Sarah, Countess of Westmorland (daughter and heiress of Robert Child), 243, 264
Child, family of, of Wanstead, Essex, 221
Child-Villiers, George, 5th Earl of Jersey: *see* Villiers
children (younger):, 27–33, 36–44, 49–52, 64, 68, 72, 77–8, 83–9, 93–4, 96, 98–9, 100, 105, 122–8, 192, 223, 233–4, 244–6, 251, 271
see also cadet inheritance
Chiswick Villa, London, 105
Chudleigh, Elizabeth, Duchess of Kingston, 24
church: *see* ecclesiastical profession
churches, 231
Churchill, Lady Diana: *see* Beauclerk, Lady Di
Churchill, family of, of Henbury, Dorset, 15
cities: *see* Dublin city; London; urban property

INDEX

Clanbrassill, earls of: *see* Hamilton
Clanmorris, Lord: *see* Bingham, (Charles) Barry
Clanwilliam, Earl and Countess of: *see under* Meade
Clare, County, 86–7, 225, 228
Clare, Earl and Countess of: *see* Fitzgibbon
Clare, Viscount: *see* Nugent, Robert Craggs, Earl Nugent
Clarina, barony of, 136, 262
Clarina, Co. Limerick, 262
Clarina, Lord and Lady: *see under* Massy
Clarke, Anna Maria, Countess of Ormonde (wife of the 18th Earl), 254
Clarke, Job/Joseph Hart Pryce (father-in-law of the 18th Earl of Ormonde), 254
Clearwell Court, Gloucestershire, 105, 202
Clements, Lady Caroline, 128
Clements, Elizabeth, Countess Dowager of Leitrim, 17–8
Clements, Lady Elizabeth, 17
Clements, Lady Louisa, 17
Clements, Lady Maria, 138
Clements, Mary, Lady Clements and Countess of Leitrim: *see* Bermingham
Clements, Rt Hon. Nathaniel, 3, 4, 80, 230
Clements, Nathaniel, Lord Clements and 2nd Earl of Leitrim, 72–4, 82, 109, 128, 137–8, 229, 232
Clements, Robert, 1st Earl of Leitrim, 229
Clements, Robert Bermingham, Lord Clements, 109
Clements, William Sydney, 3rd Earl of Leitrim, 74
Clifton (Bristol), 17
Clinton, Pelham-: *see* Pelham-Clinton
Clonmel, Co. Tipperary, 171, 179
Clonyn Castle, Delvin, Co. Westmeath, 100, 174
coal: *see* mineral wealth
Coalisland, Co. Tyrone, 232
Cobbe, Charles, Archbishop of Dublin, 52–3
Cobbe, Lady Elizabeth, 52–3
Cobbe, Thomas, of Newbridge, Donabate, Co. Dublin, 52–3
Coghill, Hester, Countess of Charleville, 57
Coghlan, Colonel Edmund, 136
Coghlan, Margaret Mary: *see* Quin, Margaret Mary, Viscountess Mountearl
Cole, Sir Arthur, 2nd Bt, Lord Ranelagh, 250
Colepeper, Elizabeth: *see* Hamilton, Elizabeth
Colley, Anne, Mrs Pole, of Ballyfin, Maryborough, Co. Laois, 221
Collon, Co. Louth, 123, 229
Collooney, Co. Sligo, battle at, 208
Comerford, John, 90, 209
Common Law (women's entitlements under), 16, 18–25, 122, 241
commerce: *see* mercantile wealth
'The Cong estate', Co. Mayo, 73
Connemara, Co. Galway, 149
Connolly, S.J., 115
Connor, Sophia: *see* Annesley, Sophia, Countess Annesley
Conolly, Lady Anne, 6, 34, 112–3, 116, 120, 137, 191, 207

Conolly, Caroline: *see* Hobart, Caroline, Countess of Buckinghamshire
Conolly, Mrs Katherine, of Castletown, Co. Kildare, 32, 112–6, 120, 172, 202, 224
Conolly, Katherine (later Lady Gore), 32
Conolly, Lady Louisa, 48, 118, 122, 134
Conolly, Thomas, of Castletown, Co. Kildare, 10, 34, 47–9, 122, 134, 179, 194, 206, 218, 240
Conolly, William (Speaker), 6, 116, 120
Conolly, William, junior, 6, 32, 34, 112–3, 116, 120, 137, 191
Conolly, family of, of Castletown, Co. Kildare, 191
Conroy, Sir Edward, 2nd Bt, 128, 157–61
Conroy, Sir John, 1st Bt, 158–161
conspicuous consumption: *see* expenditure (building; personal)
Conway, Seymour-: *see* Seymour-Conway
Conyngham, Ellen, Countess Conyngham: *see* Merrett
Conyngham, Francis Pierpont (*né* Burton), 2nd Lord Conyngham, 58, 195, 203–4
Conyngham, Brigadier Henry, 58
Conyngham, Henry, Baron, Viscount and Earl Conyngham (d.1781), 9, 11, 47, 58, 169–71, 173, 203, 232
Conyngham, Henry, 3rd Lord and 1st Earl and Marquess Conyngham, 58, 203
Conyngham, Mary (mother of the 2nd Lord Conyngham), 58
Conyngham, Mary, Lady Shelburne: *see* Williams
Conyngham, William Burton (*né* Burton), of Slane Castle, Co. Meath, 195, 203
Conyngham, Williams (of Conyngham Hall, alias Slane, Co. Meath), 58, 172, 224–5
Cooke, Alderman Sir Samuel (of Dublin), 205
Coolure, Castlepollard, Co. Westmeath, 125
Coote, Charles Henry, 2nd Lord Castle Coote, 247
Coote, Thomas, Judge of the King's Bench, 64
Copley, Catherine: *see* Hamilton, Catherine, Marchioness of Abercorn
Copley, Sir Joseph, 3rd Bt (brother of the foregoing), 150
Cork City, 106–7
Cork, County, 55, 85, 90, 147, 205–6, 228
Cork (North) Militia, 147
Cork and Burlington, earls of: *see under* Boyle
Cork and Orrery, Earl and Countess of: *see under* Boyle
Cornwall, County, 130
Cornwallis, Charles, 1st Marquess Cornwallis, 130
Cornwallis, Charles, 2nd Marquess Cornwallis, 130
Cornwell, Miss (niece of Mr Webster of Longford, Co. Longford), 63
Corry, Armar Lowry-, 1st Earl Belmore, 43, 81, 118, 143, 148, 191, 267
Corry, Grace: *see* Maxwell
Corry, Henrietta Lowry-, Countess Belmore (second wife of the 1st Earl), 43, 81, 118, 143, 148, 191, 267
Corry, Lady Louisa Lowry-, 147–8, 191
Corry, Somerset Lowry-, 2nd Earl Belmore, 39

289

Cosby, Dudley Alexander, Lord Sydney, 135, 236, 262, 264
Cosby, Isabella, Lady Sydney, 136
Cosgrave, Philip (Lady Cathcart's steward), 67, 194
Cotter, Sir James, 62
Court of Chancery: *see* Chancery, Court of
Court of Wards: *see* Wards, Court of
Coutts, Angela-Burdett-, Baroness Burdett-Coutts, 56, 166–7
Coutts, Clara, Mrs Money, 167
Coutts, Harriot, Mrs Thomas Coutts: *see* Mellon
Coutts, Thomas, 55–6, 132–3
Coutts' Bank, 167, 223
Covent Garden, London, 201, 267
Cowan, Mary: *see* Stewart, Mary
Cowan, Sir Robert (half-brother of Mary Cowan/Stewart), 55
Cowper, Hon. Spencer, of Sandringham Hall, Norfolk, 183
Craufurd, General Sir Charles (second husband of the Dowager Duchess of Newcastle), 91
Creenagh colliery, Co. Tyrone, 232, 270
Creevy, Thomas, 226
Creighton, Abraham, 2nd Earl Erne, 129, 228
Creighton, Jane (*née* Weldon), the Hon. Mrs John Creighton, 205
Creighton, Lady Caroline: *see* Wortley, Caroline Stuart-, Lady Wharncliffe
Creighton, John, 1st Earl Erne, 129, 146, 153, 204–5, 232
Creighton, John, 3rd Earl Erne, 204, 232
Creighton, John, of Aghalane and Killynick (d.1738), 205
Creighton, Colonel the Hon. John, 205
Creighton, Lord: *see* Creighton, Abraham, 2nd Earl Erne
Creighton, Mary, Countess Erne, 146, 153
Creighton, Meliora, Mrs Nicholas Ward, 204
criminal conversation ('crim. con.'): *see under* divorce and separation
Crofton, Hon. Hamilton Ralph, 162
Crom Castle and estate, Co. Fermanagh, 204–5
Crosbie, Lady Anne: *see* Talbot, Lady Anne
Crosbie, Diana, Countess of Glandore (wife of the 2nd Earl), 28, 39, 50, 175
Crosbie, John, 2nd Earl of Glandore, 28, 39, 50, 175
Crosbie, Lyne, Miss, 162
Crosbie, Maurice, 1st Earl of Glandore, 28
Crosbie, Hon. and Rev. Maurice, 3rd Lord Branden, 162
Crump, Mrs Dorothea: *see* Pery, Dorothea, Lady Glentworth
Cuffe, Alice (*née* Aungier), wife of James Cuffe, 187
Cuffe, Elizabeth: *see* Pakenham
Cuffe, James, of Ballinrobe, Co. Mayo, 187
Cuffe, James, Lord Tyrawly, 249
Cuffe, Mary, Lady Tyrawly, 249
Cuffe, Michael, of Ballinrobe, Co. Mayo, 187
Cuninghame, General Robert, 1st Lord Rossmore, 189
Curraghmore, Co. Waterford (seat of Lord Waterford), 61, 95
currency, 233–4, 253

Dalton, John, 263
Damer, Lady Caroline, 15, 193–4, 249
Damer, Dawson-: *see* Dawson-Damer
Damer, George, 2nd Earl of Dorchester, 15, 193, 224
Damer, Hon. John, 15, 193, 224
Damer, Joseph, 1st Earl of Dorchester, 15, 193
Damer, Hon. Lionel, 193
Damer, Mary: *see* Dawson, Mary, Viscountess Carlow
Darnley, Earl and Countess of: *see* Bligh
daughters: *see under* children (younger)
Davies, Mary (heiress of Belgravia), 201
Dawson, Augusta, Countess of Dartrey, 167
Dawson, Caroline, Countess of Portarlington (wife of the 1st Earl), 15, 30, 194, 226, 234
Dawson, John, 2nd Viscount Carlow and 1st Earl of Portarlington, 234
Dawson, John, 2nd Earl of Portarlington, 15, 193–4, 234, 249
Dawson, Mary, Viscountess Carlow, 15, 193
Dawson, Thomas, 1st Lord Dartrey and only Viscount Cremorne, 46
Dawson, William Henry, 1st Viscount Carlow, 193–5
Dawson, family of, of Dawson's Grove, Co. Monaghan, 46
Dawson-Damer, Hon. Henry, 193, 249
Dawson-Damer, Henry John, 3rd Earl of Portarlington, 15, 193, 203
Davys, family of, of Knockballymore, Co. Fermanagh, 204
Deane, Anne, Lady Muskerry: *see* Fitzmaurice
Deane, Sir Matthew, 4th Bt, of Dromore, Co. Cork, 256
Deane, Sir Robert Tilson, 6th Bt, 1st Lord Muskerry, 71
debts, 5, 8–12, 20, 27–30, 36–7, 42, 46–7, 49, 50, 53–5, 57, 59, 68–9, 79, 88, 95, 110, 126–9, 143, 146–59, 162, 165, 167–8, 172, 211
Decies, Co. Waterford: *see under* Waterford, County
Decies, Lord Stuart de: *see* Villiers-Stuart, Henry
De Freyne, Lord: *see* French, Arthur
Delvin, Lord: *see* Nugent, George Thomas
demography, 34–7, 190–1, 241–6, 267
De Ros, barony of, 142
Derry, bishopric of, 118
De Vesci, Viscount and Viscountess: *see under* Vesey
Devonshire, Duke and Duchess of: *see under* Cavendish
Dickson, David, 85
Digby, Simon, of Landenstown, Co. Kildare, 27
Dighton, Richard, 82
Dillon, Lady Charlotte, Viscountess Dillon (wife of the 11th Viscount), 209–12, 216
Dillon, Henry, 11th Viscount Dillon, 209–12, 214
Dillon, Henry Augustus, 13th Viscount Dillon, 212, 214
Dillon's Regiment (in French service), 210
Dillon-Lee, Charles, 12th Viscount Dillon, 31, 209–17
Dillon-Lee, Hon. Henrietta (*née* Phipps): *see* Phipps
Dillon-Lee, Marie (*née* Rogier): *see* Rogier
diplomatic service, 31, 42, 233
disease: *see under* medicine and disease
Ditchley Park, Oxfordshire, 210, 213, 215, 268–8

INDEX

divorce and separation, 18, 43–4, 74–5, 119, 136, 142–53, 182–3, 192, 236–7, 249, 262, 263
Donegal, County, 47, 89, 204, 229, 236
Donegal Militia, 137
Donegall, Marquess and Marchioness of: *see under* Chichester
Doneraile, 1st Viscount: *see* St Leger, Arthur
Donington Hall, Loughborough, Leicestershire, 222–3
Donoughmore, Baroness, and earls, of: *see under* Hely-Hutchinson
Dorchester, earls of: *see under* Damer
Dorchester, town and estate of, 249
Dore, Sarah (mother of the 2nd Marquess of Downshire's illegitimate son), 134, 261
Dorehill, William Arthur (the illegitimate son), 134, 261
D'Orléans, Duc: *see* Ferdinand-Louis-Charles
D'Orsay, Alfred, Count d'Orsay: *see* Grimaud
Dorset, County, 249
Dougherty, Owen (accomplice in the abduction of Miss Newcomen), 63
dowagers: *see under* jointures
dower, 16, 20–1
dower houses, 17
Down, County, 50–1, 105, 149, 207, 237
Downshire, Marquess and Marchioness of: *see under* Hill
dowries: *see* portions
Dromana, Co. Waterford (seat of Lord Grandison), 93–5, 163–5, 229, 234, 264
Drumcondra Lane school, Dublin, 120
Drumglass colliery, Co. Tyrone, 231–2, 270
drunkenness, 127, 194
Dublin, archbishopric of, 52–3
Dublin Castle, 48
Dublin City, 15, 48, 62, 178–184, 197–8
Dublin, County, 107, 178–84
Dublin, County, militia of, 178
Duckart, Davis, 270
duelling, 67, 136, 191, 200, 208
Duffus, George (Scottish agriculturist), 270
Dunbrody Park, Co. Wexford, 86
Duncombe, Delia: *see* Field
Dundalk borough, Co. Louth, 207
Dungannon, Viscounts: *see under* Hill-Trevor
Dunluce, barony of, Co. Antrim, 96
Dunluce, Viscount: *see* McDonnell, Charles
Dunraven Castle, Glamorganshire, 105, 202
Dunraven, Earl and Countess of: *see under* Quin
Dunraven, earldom of, 202
Durham, County, 96, 104–5, 217
Dutton, James (formerly Naper), 1st Lord Sherborne, 88, 167–8
Dutton, Sir John, 2nd Bt, 88
Dysart, Countess of: *see* Tollemache, Charlotte

Easthampstead Park, Berkshire, 105
East India Company, 223–4

Ebury, manor of, 201
eccentricity: *see under* insanity
ecclesiastical profession, 31, 164
Eckhardt, John Giles (portrait-painter), 235
Edgeworth, Maria, 67
Edgeworth, Richard Lovell, 142
Edgeworth, family of, of Edgeworthstown, Co. Longford, 67
education, 120–21
Edward, Prince of Wales, later King Edward VII, 266
Edwards, Hugh, of Castlegore (Castlederg), Co. Tyrone, 196, 247
Edwards, Margaret: *see* Stuart, Margaret
Edwards, Olivia, Countess of Rosse, 196–7
Edwards, William (accomplice in the abduction of Miss Newcomen), 62–3
Egmont, Earl and Countess of: *see under* Perceval
elections (parliamentary), 51–2, 80, 87, 94–5, 101, 137, 149, 163–4, 176–7, 187, 189-90, 207–9, 213–5, 230, 237
electoral influence: *see under* political influence
Elliot, Archibald (Scottish architect), 223
elopements, 71, 112, 118–9, 155–63, 264
see also abduction
Elton Hall and estate, Huntingdonshire, 38, 107–8
emigration (landlord-assisted), 160–61
Emo Court, Co. Laois (seat of the earls of Portarlington), 234
Encombe Castle, Somerset, 133
Encumbered Estates Act: *see under* Encumbered/Landed Estates Court
Encumbered/Landed Estates Court, 15, 79, 183, 209, 258
encumbrances: *see under* debts
English peerage: *see* peerage of England/Great Britain/the United Kingdom
ennoblement: *see under* peerages
Erne, Earls: *see under* Creighton
Essex, County, 23, 83, 86–7
see also Gosfield, Essex; Harwich, Essex; Shortgrove, Essex; Wanstead, Essex; Witham Place, Essex
estate acts: *see under* acts of parliament (private)
estate villages, 229–231
Evans, George, 2nd Lord Carbery, 70
Evans, George, 3rd Lord Carbery, 71
Evans, George, 4th Lord Carbery, 46, 70, 175
Evans, George Freke-, 71
Evans, John, 5th Lord Carbery, 71
Evans, Susan, Lady Carbery (wife of the 4th Lord), 46, 70–1, 175
Evans-Freke, John, 6th Lord Carbery, 71
exchange rates (between British and Irish currency), 233, 270–1
expenditure (building), 31, 60–1, 72, 100, 208–9, 222–3, 234
expenditure (election), 51, 53, 80, 209, 237
expenditure (estate), 51, 78–9, 99, 227–33, 249
expenditure (personal), 39–41, 53, 93, 98-9, 116, 180–1, 209, 217–25, 234, 239

Eyre, Anne, of Row Tor, Derbyshire, Countess of Massereene, 6–7, 12, 21, 84, 128
Eyre, Henry, of Row Tor, 84

fairs and markets, 230–1
Famine, The, 37, 72, 79, 181, 203, 209, 228
Fane, John, 10th Earl of Westmorland, 160, 264
Fane, Sarah, Countess of Westmorland: *see* Child, Sarah
Fane, Lady Sarah, Countess of Jersey, 264
Farnham estate, Co. Cavan, 85
Farnham, Lords and earls of: *see under* Maxwell
Featherstone, Robert (accomplice in the abduction of Miss Newcomen), 62–3
fee farm grants: *see under* leases
fees of honour, 234
Ferdinand II, King of Naples, 163
Ferdinand-Louis-Charles, Duc d'Orléans, 182
Fermanagh, County, 204–5, 232
Ferrard, Viscountess: *see* Foster, Margaretta
Ffrench, Thomas, 2nd Lord Ffrench, 46
Field, Delia, the Hon. Mrs Arthur Duncombe, 201
Field, Mary, Countess of Rosse (wife of the 3rd Earl), 38, 201, 271
'fine and recovery': *see under* 'recoveries'
Fitzgerald, Ann, 'Mrs William Naper', 168
Fitzgerald, Augustus Frederick, 3rd Duke of Leinster, 43, 52
Fitzgerald, Caroline: *see* King, Caroline, Countess of Kingston
Fitzgerald, Lord Charles, Lord Lecale, 41–3
Fitzgerald, Charlotte, Lady Henry Fitzgerald: *see* Boyle Walsingham
Fitzgerald, Lady Charlotte, Baroness Rayleigh, 253
Fitzgerald, Lord Edward, 42, 251
Fitzgerald, Emilia-Olivia, Duchess of Leinster (wife of the 2nd Duke), 41, 141
Fitzgerald, Emily, Duchess of Leinster (wife of the 1st Duke), 40–3, 48, 81, 118, 121–2
Fitzgerald, Lord Henry, 41–2, 81, 141
Fitzgerald, James, 20th Earl of Kildare and 1st Duke of Leinster, 31, 41–3, 48, 122, 239
Fitzgerald, Mary, Countess of Kildare (mother of the 1st Duke of Leinster), 41
Fitzgerald, Lady Mary (second wife of Sir Charles Ross), 132
Fitzgerald, Lord Robert, 42
Fitzgerald, William Robert, 2nd Duke of Leinster, 10, 37, 43, 132, 141, 239
Fitzgerald, Lord William, 152
Fitzgerald, family of, of the Decies, Co. Waterford, 68, 95, 187, 190
Fitzgerald-Villiers, Katherine, Viscountess Grandison: *see* Villiers
Fitzgibbon, Anne, Countess of Clare (wife of the 1st Earl), 260
Fitzgibbon, Elizabeth, Countess of Clare (wife of the 2nd Earl), 38, 80

Fitzgibbon, John, 1st Earl of Clare, 41, 64, 118–20, 127, 135, 142, 145, 153
Fitzgibbon, John, 2nd Earl of Clare, 38, 80
Fitzmaurice, Anne, Countess of Kerry: *see* Petty, Anne
Fitzmaurice, Anne, of Springfield Castle, Drumcollogher, Co. Limerick, Lady Muskerry, 71
Fitzmaurice, Thomas, 1st Earl of Kerry, 89, 195
Fitzmaurice, Petty-: *see* Petty-Fitzmaurice
Fitzroy, Anne, Duchess of Grafton (wife of the 3rd Duke): *see* Liddell, Anne
Fitzroy, Anne, Lady Southampton (wife of the 1st Lord): *see* Warren, Anne
Fitzroy, General Charles, 1st Lord Southampton, 39
Fitzroy, Lady Charlotte, Countess of Lichfield, 213
Fitzroy, George Ferdinand, 2nd Lord Southampton, 162
Fitzroy, families of, dukes of Cleveland and Grafton, 268–9
Fitzwilliam, John, 8th Viscount Fitzwilliam of Merrion, 198
Fitzwilliam, Hon. Mary: *see* Herbert, Mary, Countess of Pembroke
Fitzwilliam, Richard, 7th Viscount Fitzwilliam of Merrion, 197
Fitzwilliam, Thomas, 9th Viscount Fitzwilliam of Merrion, 198
Fitzwilliam, family of, Viscounts Fitzwilliam of Merrion, 15, 197–8
Forbes, Arthur Hastings, 7th Earl of Granard, 100, 238
Forbes, Lady Elizabeth Mary: *see* Parkyns
Forbes, Hon. Frederick, 162
Forbes, George, 5th Earl of Granard, 62
Forbes, George, 6th Earl of Granard, 122
Forbes, Admiral the Hon. John, 196
Forbes, Selina, Countess of Granard, 21, 122, 223
Ford Castle, Co. Northumberland, 131
forfeiture, 42, 210, 248, 253
Fortescue, Margaret, Lady Brooke (wife of Sir Arthur, Bt), 199
Fortescue, William Charles, 2nd Viscount Clermont, 199
Fortescue, William Henry, 1st Viscount and only Earl of Clermont, 189, 199, 270
fortune-hunters, 8, 26, 62–7, 102–4, 166–7
fortunes: *see* portions
Forward, Isabella, 1st Countess of Wickow, 84
Forward, William, of Castle Forward, Co. Donegal, 84
Forward-Howard, William, 3rd Earl of Wicklow: *see* Howard
Foster, Anthony, Chief Baron of the Exchequer, 229
Foster, Lady Elizabeth, afterwards Duchess of Devonshire, 117, 145, 153, 249, 260
Foster, Harriet: *see* Skeffington, Harriet, 9th Viscountess Massereene
Foster, John, of Dunleer, Co. Louth, 28
Foster, John, 1st Lord Oriel, 5, 36, 123–4
Foster, John Thomas, of Stonehouse, Dunleer, Co. Louth, 118, 153
Foster, Margaretta, Viscountess Ferrard, 36, 123–5, 177–8
Foster, Thomas (portrait-painter), 158

INDEX

Foster, Thomas Henry, 2nd Viscount Ferrard: *see* Skeffington
Fownes, Lady Elizabeth, 120–21
Fownes, Sarah, Mrs William Tighe, 8
Fownes, Sir William, 2nd Bt, 8
Fox, Caroline, Lady Holland: *see* Lennox, Lady Caroline
Fox, Charles James, 117
Fox, Elizabeth Vassall, Lady Holland, 145
Fox, Henry, 1st Lord Holland, 118
Fox-Strangways, Lady Muriel: *see* Quin, Muriel, Lady Adare
Fox-Strangways, Lady Susan, 118
Frederick Charles William, Hereditary Prince, later King, of Wurttemberg, 16
Freemasons, 171
Freke, Percy, 162
Freke-Evans: *see* Evans/Evans-Freke
French, Arthur, 1st Lord de Freyne, 162
French Revoluntionary War, 35, 233
Frescati, Blackrock, Co. Dublin, 41
Freyne, Lord de: *see* French, Arthur
Froude, J.A., 62
'The Funds': *see under* stockmarket

Gabrielli, Gaspar, 151
Gainsborough, Thomas, 14, 22, 192, 219
Galway, County, 62, 72–4, 207–9
gambling, 129, 211–3
Gardiner, Mrs Anne: *see under* Stewart
Gardiner, Charles (d.1769), 178
Gardiner, Charles John, 2nd Viscount Mountjoy and only Earl of Blessington (of the second creation), 10, 178–85, 217
Gardiner, Charles John (illegitimate son of the Earl of Blessington), 178–84
Gardiner, Hon. Miss Harriet, 10, 181
Gardiner, Lady Harriet, Countess d'Orsay, 153, 178, 180–5
Gardiner, Rt Hon. Luke, 178, 196
Gardiner, Luke, 1st Viscount Mountjoy (of the second creation), 18, 178, 196
Gardiner, Luke Wellington, Viscount Mountjoy (d.1823), 196
Gardiner, Margaret, Viscountess Mountjoy (second wife and widow of the 1st Viscount), 9, 18, 178, 181, 266
Gardiner, Marguerite, Countess of Blessington, 179–81, 184, 266
Gardiner, Mary, Viscountess Mountjoy (first wife of the 2nd Viscount), 179–80
Gardiner, Mary (illegitimate daughter of the Earl of Blessington), 180, 182–3
Gardiner, Mrs Mary: *see* Perfect
Gardiner, family of, Viscounts Mountjoy, etc, 178, 183
Gaulstown Park, Rochfortbridge, Co. Westmeath, 149, 230
genealogy, 1–2, 44–5, 87–8
genetics, 186, 189–90, 245, 269–70
Genevese, 230
George II, King, 103

George III, King, 16, 171, 191, 212, 235
George, Prince of Wales and Prince Regent, later King George IV, 223-3
Germain, Lord George: *see* Sackville, Lord George
Gersch, Emil, 164
Gersch, Leopold, 164
Gersch, Leopoldine, 164–6
Gibbs, James, 210
Gilford, Co. Down, 85–6
Gill Hall, Gilford, Co. Down, 86
Gillray, James, 101, 194
Glamorganshire: *see* Dunraven Castle, Glamorganshire
Glandore, Earl and Countess of: *see under* Crosbie
Gleadowe, William, of Killester, Co. Dublin: *see* Newcomen, Sir William Gleadowe, 1st Bt
Glenarm, barony of, Co. Antrim, 96
Glenarm Castle, Co. Antrim, 96–8
Glenboy, Co. Leitrim, 230
Glengall, Earl and Countess of: *see under* Butler
Glengoole, alias New Birmingham, Co. Tipperary, 233
Glentworth, Lord and Lady: *see under* Pery
Gloucestershire: *see* Clearwell Court, Gloucestershire; Sherborne, Gloucestershire
Godfrey, Barbara: *see* Chichester, Barbara, Marchioness of Donegall
Goold, Augusta: *see* Quin, Augusta Wyndham-, Countess of Dunraven
Goold, Serjeant Thomas, 217
Gordon, Alexander, 4th Duke of Gordon, 130
Gordon, Jane, Duchess of Gordon, 130
Gordon, Lady Louisa, Marchioness Cornwallis, 130
Gore, Arthur Saunders, 2nd Earl of Arran, 77
Gore, Arthur Saunders, 3rd Earl of Arran, 77
Gore, Katherine, Lady Gore: *see* Conolly, Katherine
Gore, John, 1st Lord Annaly, 62
Gore, Sir Ralph, 7th Bt, 80
Gort town and estate, Co. Galway, 208, 248
Gort, Viscounts: *see* Smyth, John Prendergast, and Vereker, Colonel Charles
Gosfield, Essex, 23, 83
Granard, earls of: *see under* Forbes
Granard, Co. Longford, 187
Grandison, Viscountess, Earl and Countess: *see under* Villiers
Granville, Anne, Mrs Dewes, 117
Grattan, Henry, 262
Great Glemham, Suffolk, 1, 74
Grenville, Anne, Lady Grenville: *see* Pitt, Anne
Grenville, Elizabeth: *see* Proby, Elizabeth, Countess of Carysfort
Grenville, George Nugent, 1st Marquess of Buckingham, ii, 83–4
Grenville, Lord George Nugent, 2nd Lord Nugent, 84
Grenville, Mary Elizabeth, Marchioness of Buckingham (wife of the 1st Marquess), ii, 83–4
Grenville, Richard, 2nd Earl Temple, 83
Grenville, Richard, 2nd Marquess and 1st Duke of Buckingham, ii, 257–8

293

Grenville, William Wyndham, Lord Grenville, 84
Gretna Green, 157–63, 264
Greville, Charles, 170
Greville, Frances (née Macartney), wife of Fulke Greville, 187
Greville, Fulke, of Wilbury, Wiltshire, 187
Greville (later Greville-Nugent), Fulke Southwell, 1st Lord Greville, 100
Greville, Lady Rosa, Baroness Greville: *see* Nugent
Greville, family of, earls of Warwick, Lords Greville, etc, 259
Grimaud, Alfred, Count d'Orsay, 153, 178–85
Grosvenor, family of, dukes of Westminster, 201
Grove, Mary: *see* Annesley, Mary, Countess Annesley
Grove, family of, of Annesgrove, alias Ballyhimmock, Co. Cork, 75, 91
guardianship, 26, 48, 60, 156, 175, 181, 237–8
Gunning, Hon. Bridget, Mrs John Gunning: *see* Bourke
Gunning, Elizabeth, successively Duchess of Hamilton and Argyll, 121
Gunning, John, of Castle Coote, Co. Roscommon, 121
Gunning, Maria, Countess of Coventry, 121
Gwydyr, Lord and Lady: *see* Burrell

Habbabuk, Professor Sir John, 2–3, 18
Hamilton, Anne, Countess of Orkney: *see* O'Brien, Anne, Countess of Inchiquin
Hamilton, Lady Anne, Countess of Roden (sister and heiress of the 2nd Earl of Clanbrassill), 207
Hamilton, Anne, of Bangor, Co Down, 3–4
Hamilton, Mrs Caroline (née Tighe), of Hamwood, Co. Meath, 121
Hamilton, Catherine, Marchioness of Abercorn (first wife of the 1st Marquess), 150
Hamilton, Lady Catherine Elizabeth (future wife of the 4th Earl of Aberdeen), 131
Hamilton, Cecil, Marchioness of Abercorn (second wife of the 1st Marquess), 150, 153
Hamilton, Lady Cecil: *see* Howard, Cecil, Countess of Wicklow
Hamilton, Elizabeth (mother of the 6th Earl of Abercorn), 89–90
Hamilton, Emma, Lady Hamilton, 170
Hamilton, Lady Harriot Margaret (fiancée of the 2nd Marquess of Waterford), 131
Hamilton, Hugh Douglas, 20, 28, 48, 96, 130, 208
Hamilton, James, 6th Earl of Abercorn, 236
Hamilton, James 7th Earl of Abercorn, 236
Hamilton, James, 8th Earl of Abercorn, 3, 234, 239
Hamilton, James, 2nd Marquess and 1st Duke of Abercorn, 236
Hamilton, James (the 7th Earl of Thomond's agent), 225
Hamilton, James, 1st Viscount Limerick and 1st Earl of Clanbrassill, 207
Hamilton, James, 2nd Earl of Clanbrassill, 207
Hamilton, John James, 9th Earl and 1st Marquess of Abercorn, 33, 39, 131, 143, 150, 153, 169, 172, 179, 244
Hamilton, Margaret, of Bangor, Co. Down, Viscountess Ikerrin, 3–4
Hamilton, Margaret, of Caledon, Co. Tyrone: *see* Boyle, Margaret, Countess of Cork and Orrery
Hamilton, Sir William, 170
Hamilton, family of, earls of Abercorn, 89–90, 234–6
Hamilton, Miss ('an Irish heiress'), 134
Hammersmith, London, 47
Hampshire, 200, 201
see also Beaulieu, Hampshire
Hanbury Hall, Worcestershire, 142
Handcock, Hon. Mrs Elizabeth: *see* Vesey, Hon. Miss Elizabeth
Handcock, Gustavus, of Waterstown, Co. Westmeath, 27, 131
Handcock, Robert, 27, 132
Lord Hardwicke's Marriage Act: *see* Marriage Act (Lord Hardwicke's)
Hare, William, 1st Earl of Listowel, 233
Harman, Anne, Lady Parsons (second wife of the 3rd Bt), 90
Harman, Jane, Countess of Rosse (wife of the 1st Earl), 90–91, 158, 194
Harman, Laurence, 1st Earl of Rosse (of the second creation), 90–91, 194
Harman, Hon. Laurence King-: *see* King-Harman
Harman, family of, of Newcastle, Co. Longford, 90–91
Hart, Emma: *see* Hamilton
Hartpole, George, of Shrule, Co. Laois, 16, 227
Hartpole, Mrs (wife of George Hartpole), 16, 227
Harwich, Essex, 80
Hastings, Lady Elizabeth: *see* Rawdon, Elizabeth
Hastings, Francis, 10th Earl of Huntingdon, 222
Hastings, family of, earls of Huntingdon, 269–70
Hastings, Rawdon-: *see* Rawdon-Hastings
Hatch, Dorothy, Lady Hutchinson: *see* Hutchinson, Dorothy
Hatch, John, of Lissen Hall, Co. Dublin, 59
Hatton, George, of Clonard, Co. Wexford, 53, 154, 254
Hawke, Cassandra Harvey-, Countess of Rosse (wife of the 4th Earl), 271
Hawke, family of, Lords Hawke, 271
Hawkins, William (Ulster King of Arms), 64
Hayes, Sir Henry, 62–4
Headford, Co. Galway, 42
Hely, John, of Gortroe, Co. Cork: *see* Hely-Hutchinson, Rt Hon. John
Hely-Hutchinson, Christian, Baroness Donoughmore, 107, 110
Hely-Hutchinson, Frances Wilhelmina, Hon. Mrs Frances Hely-Hutchinson, 110
Hely-Hutchinson, Hon. Francis, 27, 30, 59, 110
Hely-Hutchinson, Rt Hon. John, 106, 110
Hely-Hutchinson, General John, Lord Hutchinson and 2nd Earl of Donoughmore, 27, 59

INDEX

Hely-Hutchinson, John, 3rd Earl of Donoughmore, 110, 171
Hely-Hutchinson, John (illegitimate son of the 1st Earl of Donoughmore), 171
Hely-Hutchinson, Richard, 1st Earl of Donoughmore, 171
Henniker, Anne, Lady Henniker (wife of the 1st Lord), 1
Henniker, Anne-Elizabeth: *see* Stratford, Anne-Elizabeth, Countess of Aldborough
Henniker, John, Sir, 1st Lord Henniker, 1
Henrietta Street, Dublin (the 1st Earl of Bessborough's house in), 226
Herbert, Anne, Hon. Mrs Nicholas Herbert, 1
Herbert, Hon. Mrs Elizabeth, of Muckruss, Co. Kerry: *see* Sackville, Hon. Elizabeth
Herbert, George Augustus, 11th Earl of Pembroke, 197, 206
Herbert, George Robert, 13th Earl of Pembroke, 197, 203
Herbert, Henry Arthur, of Muckruss, Co. Kerry, 50
Herbert, Mary, Countess of Pembroke (wife of the 9th Earl), 197
Herbert, Robert Henry, 12th Earl of Pembroke, 197, 203
Herbert, Sidney, Lord Herbert of Lea, 203
Hertford, Earl, Marquess and Marchioness of: *see under* Seymour-Conway
Hertfordshire, 65, 67–70
Hervey, Lady Elizabeth: *see* Foster
Hervey, Frederick, Bishop of Derry and 4th Earl of Bristol, 118, 153–4, 260
Hervey, Frederick William, 5th Earl and 1st Marquess of Bristol, 146, 179
Hervey, Mary, Countess Erne: *see* Creighton
Hill, Arthur, 2nd Marquess of Downshire, 31, 105, 126–7, 134, 153, 229, 271
Hill, Lord Arthur, 2nd Lord Sandys: *see* Sandys
Hill, Arthur Blundell Sandys, 3rd Marquess of Downshire, 229
Hill, Eleanor (wife of William Hill of Hillsborough, Co. Down), 199
Hill, Lord George, 121, 236
Hill, Jane, Lady George Hill: *see* Knight
Hill, Mary, Marchioness of Downshire: *see* Sandys, Mary
Hill, William, of Hillsborough, Co. Down, 199
Hill, Wills, 1st Marquess of Downshire, 134, 199, 229
Hilll-Trevor, Arthur, 1st Viscount Dungannon, 200
Hill-Trevor, Hon. Arthur, 200
Hill-Trevor, Arthur, 2nd Viscount Dungannon, 200
Hill-Trevor, Letitia, Hon. Mrs: *see* McDonnell, Letitia Marchioness of Antrim
Hoare, William, of Bath, 84
Hobart, Caroline, Countess of Buckinghamshire (second wife of the 2nd Earl), 10, 81
Hobart, Lady Emily: *see* Stewart, Emily, Marchioness of Londonderry
Hobart, Lady Henrietta: *see* Corry, Henrietta Lowry-, Countess Belmore
Hobart, John, 2nd Earl of Buckinghamshire, 48–9, 81, 118, 163, 191, 244, 267

Hobart, Mary Anne, Countess of Buckinghamshire (first wife of the 2nd Earl), 192
Hobart, family of, earls of Buckinghamshire, 191–2, 244
Hogan, Edmond (Lord Thomond's head agent), 87
Hogarth, William, 45
Hoggins, Sarah, Countess of Exeter, 143, 174
Hollingsworth, T.H., 34, 243
Holmes, James? (portrait-painter), 179
Holmpatrick, Co. Dublin, 225
Homan, Sir William, Bt, 94
homosexuality, 79, 179–80, 191
Hoppner, John, 11
House of Commons (British), 253
House of Lords (British), 253
House of Lords (Irish), 170, 214, 265
House of Lords (UK), 157, 165–6, 263
House of Lords (British, Irish and UK): *see under* divorce and separation
Howard, Cecil, Countess of Wicklow (wife of the 4th Earl), 33
Howard, H. (portrait-painter), 197
Howard, Ralph, 1st Viscount Wicklow, 84
Howard, Robert, 2nd Earl of Wicklow, 84
Howard, William Forward-, 3rd Earl of Wicklow, 33, 84
Howard, William Forward-, 4th Earl of Wicklow (son and heir of the 3rd Earl), 33
Hudson, Thomas (follower of), 68
Huguenots, 171, 230
Hume, family of, of Castle Hume, Churchill, Co. Fermanagh, baronets, 268
Huntingdonshire, 108
Hunt, Sir Vere, 1st Bt, 233
Hussey-Montagu, Edward, Earl of Beaulieu, 102–3, 155
Hussey-Montagu, Isabella: *see* Montagu, Isabella, Duchess of Manchester
Hutchinson, Dorothy (*née* Hatch), Lady Hutchinson, 59
Hutchinson, Hely-: *see* Hely-Hutchinson
Hutchinson, Richard, of Knocklofty, Co. Tipperary, 106
Hutchinson, Sir Samuel, 3rd Bt, 27, 59
Hyde Hall, Sawbridgeworth, Hertfordshire, 207

illegitimacy, 8, 42, 58, 134, 145–6, 148–9, 156, 164–74, 213, 228, 261
immigration (landlord- and/or government-assisted), 230
impotence, 74, 249, 257
imprisonment, 6, 65–6, 149, 156, 214, 264
improvement (agricultural): *see* expenditure (estate)
Inchiquin, Earl and Countess of: *see under* O'Brien
income: *see* interest rates; jointures; professions; rentals; stock-market
India: *see* Calcutta harbour; East India Company; Nabobs
India, governorship-general of, 223
industry: *see* estate villages; mineral wealth
infidelity, 17–8, 116–19, 129–31, 135, 141–54, 260, 262–3
inflation, 35, 39, 244

influence (political): *see* political influence
Ingoldsby, Catherine (Mrs James Naper), 54, 64
Ingoldsby, Frances (later Mrs Hugh Fitzjohn Massy), 48, 54, 64
Ingoldsby, Henry, of Carton, Co. Kildare, and Ballybricken, Co. Limerick, 54, 64
Ingoldsby, General Sir Richard, 64
inheritance: *see* children (younger); partible inheritance; primogeniture; settlements (marriage and other); wills
insanity, 6, 8, 73–4, 129, 135–6, 137–8, 142, 149, 236, 245, 249, 262
interest rates, 10, 17, 21, 77–8, 180–1, 211, 233, 257
Itchingham, family of, of Dunbrody, Co. Wexford, 86

Jacobites, 20, 66, 210, 248, 258
Jamaica, 13, 46, 79, 253
James V, King of Scotland, 186
James VI of Scotland and I of England, King, 186
Jeffereyes, Marianne, Countess of Westmeath (divorced first wife of the 7th Earl), 142–3, 150
Jervas, Charles, 226
Jocelyn, Anne, Countess of Roden: *see* Hamilton, Lady Anne
Jocelyn, Lady Harriet: *see* Skeffington
Jocelyn, Robert, 1st Earl of Roden, 128, 207
Jocelyn, Robert, 2nd Earl of Roden, 207
Jocelyn, Robert, 3rd Earl of Roden, 207
Johnson, Dr Samuel, 18
Johnston, Thomas (abductor of Miss Newcomen), 62–3
jointures, 9, 17, 20–1, 27–9, 33–7, 41, 43–4, 58–9, 72, 74, 82, 93, 104, 111, 113, 122–5, 136, 142, 174, 180–1, 192, 213, 218, 225, 236, 244–6, 252, 266
see also widows
Jones, Thomas, 6th Viscount Ranelagh, 30
Joyce Country, Co. Galway, 72–4, 82
'Junius', 13

Kauffman, Angelica, 93, 123
Kelly, Denis, Chief Justice of Jamaica, 253
Kelly, Elizabeth, Countess of Altamont (wife of the 2nd Earl), 79
Kemmis, Thomas, 15
Kent, County, 58
see also Minster-in-Thanet, Kent; Ramsgate, Kent; Sandwich, Kent
Kenyon, Lloyd, Chief Justice of the King's Bench in England, 1st Lord Kenyon, 157
Keppel, Hon. and Rev. Frederick, Bishop of Exeter, 162
Kerr, Charles, Viscount Dunluce: *see* McDonnell, Charles
Kerr, Lady Charlotte: *see* McDonnell, Lady Charlotte
Kerr, Hugh Seymour, 4th Earl of Antrim: *see* McDonnell
Kerr, Admiral Lord, Mark, 96–100, 148, 217, 227
Kerr, William, Earl of Ancram and 5th Marquess of Lothian, 96, 148
Kerry, County, 89, 195–6

Kilcommon demesne, Cahir, Co. Tipperary, 79
Kildare, County, 239
see also Kilrush, Co. Kildare; Monasterevan, Co. Kildare; Punchestown, Co. Kildare
Kildare, Earl and Countess of: *see under* Fitzgerald
Kildrum mine, Dunfanaghy, Co. Donegal, 232
Kilkenny, County, 89, 226–7
Killadoon, Celbridge, Co. Kildare, 18
Killough, Co. Down, 3
Kilmacrenan estate, Co. Donegal, 229
Kilrush, Co. Kildare, 42
King, Caroline, Countess of Kingston, 55, 147, 148–9, 218
King, Edward, 1st Earl of Kingston, 91
King, Frances, Viscountess Lorton (wife of the 1st Viscount), 91
King, George, 3rd Earl of Kingston, 55
King, Colonel [Henry?], 91
King, Sir Henry, 3rd Bt, 38
King, James, 4th Lord Kingston, 55
King, Jane, Countess of Rosse: *see* Harman, Jane
King, Lady Mary, 32, 65
King, Robert, 2nd Earl of Kingston, 32, 55, 65, 147, 148–9, 218
King, Hon. Robert, 1st Viscount Lorton, 91
King-Harman, Hon. Laurence, 91
Kingston, Lord, and Earl and Countess of: *see under* King
Kingston, Duchess of: *see* Chudleigh
Kirk, Thomas (sculptor), 231
Knapton, Lord: *see* Vesey, John Denny
Knight, Edward, of Godmersham Park, Kent, 174
Knight, Hon. Henrietta, Lady Luxborough, 263
Knight, Jane, Lady George Hill, 174
Knight, Robert, Lord Luxborough and Earl of Catherlough, 263
Knockballymore, Co. Fermanagh, 204–5
Knocklofty, Co. Tipperary, 106
Knox, Andrew, of Prehen, Londonderry, 64, 267
Knox, Anne, Lady Welles, 234
Knox, Arthur Edward, of Castlerea, Co. Mayo, 160, 264
Knox, Lady Jane: *see* Parsons, Lady Jane
Knox, Miss Mary Anne, of Prehen, Co. Londonderry, 63–4, 267

Lamb, Elizabeth, Viscountess Melbourne, 117
Lamb, William, 2nd Viscount Melbourne, 183
Landed Estates Court: *see* Encumbered/Landed Estates Court
Landownership, 2–3, 14, 19, 26, 52, 83, 105, 123, 148–9, 227–32, 238–9
see also absentee landlordism; sales of land
Lanesborough, Countess of: *see* Rochfort, Jane
Langford Rowley, Catherine: *see* Pakenham, Catherine, Lady Longford
Langford Rowley, Hercules, 2nd Viscount Langford, 188, 200
Langford Rowley, Jane: *see* Taylour, Jane, Countess of Bective

INDEX

Langford Rowley, family of, of Summerhill, Co. Meath, and Langford Lodge, Co. Antrim, Viscounts Langford, 188, 190
Laois, County, 104
  see also Abbeyleix, Co. Laois; Ballyfin, Maryborough, Co. Laois; Brockley Park, Stradbally, Co. Laois; Rosenalis, Mountmellick, Co. Laois; Stradbally, Co. Laois
Large, David, 2
Latouche, family of, of Marlay, Co. Dublin, Bellevue, Co. Wicklow, Harristown, Co. Kildare, etc, 46
Lauderdale, earls of: see under Maitland
Laxton Park, Northamptonshire, 70–71
Law: see Chancery, Court of; legal profession; litigation
Lawes, Judith Maria, Lady Irnham and Countess of Carhampton, 13, 46, 79
Lawes, Sir Nicholas (Governor of Jamaica), 46
Lawless, Elizabeth Georgiana, Lady Cloncurry (first-wife of the 2nd Lord), 151–2
Lawless, Nicholas, 1st Lord Cloncurry, 44
Lawless, Valentine, 2nd Lord Cloncurry, 151–2
Lawrence, Sir Thomas, 33, 137–8, 172–3, 179
leases, 11–4, 126, 213–4, 227–9, 238–40
Lecale, barony of, Co. Down, 42–3, 81
Lecale, Lord: see Fitzgerald, Lord Charles
Lee, Lady Charlotte, Countess of Lichfield: see Fitzroy
Lee, Lady Charlotte: see Dillon, Lady Charlotte, Viscountess Dillon
Lee, Dillon-: see Dillon-Lee
Lee, Sir Edward Henry, 5th Bt, 1st Earl of Lichfield, 213
Lee, George Henry, 2nd Earl of Lichfield, 209
Lee, George Henry, 3rd Earl of Lichfield, 209–13, 215, 247
Lee, Robert, 4th Earl of Lichfield, 210, 211, 268–9
Leeds, dukes of: see under Osborne
Leeson, Elizabeth, Countess of Milltown (third wife and widow of the 1st Earl), 34, 136
Leeson, Joseph, senior, 44
Leeson, Joseph, 1st Earl of Milltown, 34
Leeson, Joseph, 2nd Earl of Milltown, 79
Leeson, Joseph, junior (nephew of the 2nd Earl of Milltown), 79
Leeson, Joyce (fourth daughter of Joseph Leeson senior): see Blackwood
Leeson, Mrs Martha: see Bayley
Leeson, family of, earls of Milltown, 44
Lefroy, Anthony, of Carrigglas, Co. Longford, 268
Lefroy, Mary (née Paul), 200–01
Lefroy, Rev. Peter Isaac, 201
Lefroy, Thomas (Lord Chief Justice of Ireland), 175, 200, 238
legal profession, 31, 232
Leigh, James Henry, of Stoneleigh, Warwickshire, 155–6
Leigh, Julia (née Twistleton), Hon. Mrs James Henry Leigh, 155–6
Leinster, dukes and duchesses of: see under Fitzgerald
Leinster, province of, 62, 239
Leinster House, Dublin, 41
Leitrim, countesses of: see Bermingam, Mary; Clements, Elizabeth
Leitrim, earls of: see under Clements
Lennox, Charles, 2nd Duke of Ricmond, 129
Lennox, Lady Caroline, 118
Lennox, Lady Louisa: see Conolly, Lady Louisa
Lennox, Sarah, Duchess of Richmond (wife of the 2nd Duke), 129
Lennox, Lady Sarah, 118, 145
libraries (country house), 122
Lichfield, earls of: see Lee
Liddell, Anne, Duchess of Grafton, 43
Ligonier, Edward, 2nd Viscount, and Earl, Ligonier, 143, 171
Ligonier, Francis, 171
Ligonier, Field-Marshal Sir John, 1st Visocunt, and Earl, Ligonier, 171–2
Limavady, Co. Londonderry, 47
Limerick City, 207–8
Limerick City Militia, 208
Limerick, County, 70–1, 86–7, 105, 109–110, 225, 228, 261
Limerick, Earl of: see Pery, Edmond Henry
linen: see under estate villages
Lisburn, Co. Antrim, 50
Liscarrol, manor of, Co. Cork, 85
Listowel, Earl of: see Hare, William
litigation, 7–8, 10–4, 67, 71, 96–100, 181, 206, 238, 248, 250, 264
Lloyd, Alicia, Countess of Rosse: see Parsons
local government, 95, 231
Lock, Charles, 43
Lock, family of, of Norbury Park, Mickleham, Surrey, 42
Loftus, Adam, 3rd Viscount Loftus, 198
Loftus, Jane, Viscountess Moore (wife of the 2nd Viscount), 198
Loftus, family of, of Loftus Hall, Fethard, Co. Wexford, Viscounts Loftus and earls and marquesses of Ely, 268
Lombard, Rev. Edmond, 117, 125
London, 17–18, 46–8, 78, 105, 201, 218
Londonderry, County, 50–3, 110, 227, 240
Londonderry, Marquess and Marchioness of: see under Stewart
Long, Mary (illegitimate daughter of the 1st Earl of Donoughmore), 171
Long, family of, of Draycot, Wiltshire, baronets, 221
Long-Tylney, Catherine (wife of William Pole-Tylney-Long-Wellesley), 221
Long-Tylney, Sir James, 7th Bt, 221
Long-Wellesley, William Pole-Tylney-, 4th Earl of Mornington, 221
Longford, Co. Longford, 62–3, 187–8, 190
Longford, County, 62, 65–7, 90–91, 238
Lord Lieutenancy of Ireland, 50–52, 199
Lords Chancellor: see under Chancery, Court of
Lorraine, Claude, 227
Lorton, Viscount and Viscountess: see under King
Lothian, Marquess of: see Kerr, William
Loudon Castle, Mauchline, Ayrshire, 222–23

Loughcrew, Oldcastle, Co. Meath, 88
Lough Cutra Castle, Gort, Co. Galway, 208
Loughglinn, Charlestown, Co. Roscommon, 214
Loughglinn Yeoman Cavalry, 214
Lough Mask, Cong, Co. Mayo, 204
Louth, County, 198–9, 207, 229, 239
love-matches, 47–8, 57, 59, 113, 116–20, 123, 127–8, 129–42, 148–54, 201
Lowry-Corry: *see* Corry
Lucan, Earl of: *see under* Bingham
Ludlow, Peter, 1st Earl Ludlow, 30
lunacy: *see* insanity
Luttrell, Colonel the Hon. Henry Lawes, Lord Irnham and 2nd Earl of Carhampton, 12–13, 46, 157
Luttrell, Jane, Countess of Carhampton: *see* Boyd
Luttrell, Judith Maria, Lady Irnham and Countess of Carhampton: *see* Lawes
Luttrell, Simon, 1st Lord Irnham and Earl of Carhampton, 12–13, 46, 157
Luttrellstown, Co. Dublin, 13
Lygon, Lady Emma Georgiana, Countess of Longford (wife of the 2nd Earl), 265
Lyons, Co. Kildare, 151
Lyttleton, Mary (*née* Macartney), Lady Westcote, etc, 187
Lyttleton, William Henry, 1st Lord Westcote and 1st Lord Lyttleton (of the second creation), 187

Macartney, Alice (*née* Cuffe), wife of Judge James Macartney, 187
Macartney, Sir George, Earl Macartney, 233
Macartney, James (Judge of the Common Pleas), 187
Macartney, James, junior, 187
Macartney, family of, of Granard, Co. Longford, 190
The Macdermots of Ballycloran, 109
McDonnell, Lady Anne Catherine, Countess of Antrim, 96–8, 127, 242
McDonnell, Charles, Viscount Dunluce, 98
McDonnell, Lady Charlotte, Countess of Antrim, 96–100
McDonnell (formerly Phelps), Edmund, 97–100
McDonnell, Hugh Seymour, 4th Earl of Antrim, 98
McDonnell, Letitia, Marchioness of Antrim (wife of the 6th Earl, and Marquess), 99, 200
McDonnell, Lady Letitia, 96
McDonnell, Randal, 6th Earl, and Marquess, of Antrim, 96–8
McGildowny, Edmund (agent for Lord and Lady Mark Kerr), 259
Mackay, Rev. James, of 'Phipsborough', Co. Dublin (father of Jane, Countess of Belvedere), 54
Mackenzie, Hon. James Stuart-, 129
Macnaghten, John, of Benvarden, Co. Antrim, 64
Magherafelt, Co. Londonderry, 227, 254
Magill, Lady Anne: *see* Ward, Lady Anne, Viscountess Bangor
Magill, Robert Hawkins, 149
Magill, Theodosia: *see* Meade, Theodosia, Countess of Clanwilliam

Magill, family of, of Gill Hall, Co. Down
Maguire, Frances Augusta (mistress of the 1st Marquess of Abercorn), 172, 173
Maguire, Colonel Hugh, 65–7, 194
Maguire, W.A., 255–6
Maitland, Eleanor, Countess of Lauderdale: *see* Todd
Maitland, James, 7th Earl of Lauderdale, 80
Maitland, James, Lord Maitland and 8th Earl of Lauderdale, 80
Maitland, Lady Mary: *see* Brabazon, Mary, Countess of Meath
Maitland, Admiral Thomas, 11th Earl of Lauderdale, 19
Manchester, Duke and Duchess of: *see under* Montagu
manor courts, 231
Marlay, Charles Brinsley, of Belvedere, Mullingar, Co. Westmeath, 252
Marlay, George, of Belvedere, 193
marriage, passim, and *see* especially elopements; love-matches; *mésalliances*
Marriage Act (Lord Hardwicke's), 117, 156, 255
marriage registers, 160–62
marriage settlements: *see* settlements (marriage and other)
Married Women's Property Acts, 17–8, 55–7, 65–6
Martin, Elizabeth (*née* Vesey), Mrs Richard Martin, 150
Martin, Richard, of Ballynahinch, Co. Galway, 149–52
Mary, Queen of Scots, 186
Mason, Aland, of Waterford City, 68, 125
Mason, family of, of Waterford City, 68
Massereene, earls of, and Viscountess: *see* Skeffington
Massy, Catherine, Lady Clarina (wife of the 1st Lord), 135
Massy, General Eyre, 1st Lord Clarina, 135
Massy, Hon. George, 162
Massy, Hugh, 1st Lord Massy, 135
Massy, Hugh, 3rd Lord Massy, 162
Massy, Hugh Fitzjohn, 64
Mawbrye, Edward (portrait-painter), 214
Maxwell, Barry, 3rd Baron and 1st Earl of Farnham, 10, 19, 21, 29, 125, 250
Maxwell, Grace, Countess of Farnham, 21, 29, 80, 125
Maxwell, Lady Grace, 19, 80
Maxwell, Mrs Grace (wife of Colonel John Maxwell of Falkland, Co. Monaghan), 74–5
Maxwell, Hon. and Rev. Henry, later 6th Lord Farnham, 85, 224
Maxwell, Henry, 7th Lord Farnham, 85
Maxwell, John, of Farnham, Co. Cavan, 85
Maxwell, Colonel John, of Falkland, Co. Monaghan, 74–5
Maxwell, Mrs Judith: *see* Barry
Maxwell Barry, Colonel John, 5th Lord Farnham, 85, 224
May, Anna: *see* Chichester, Anna, Marchioness of Donegall
May, Sir Edward, 2nd Bt, 129, 156
Mayne, Frances, Lady Newhaven: *see* Allen, Hon. Frances
Mayne, Capt. John, 57
Mayo, County, 52, 210, 213–4, 218–9, 269
Meade, John, 1st Earl of Clanwilliam, 85, 147
Meade, General the Hon. John, 85–6

INDEX

Meade, Richard, 3rd Earl of Clanwilliam, 147
Meade, Robert, 2nd Earl of Clanwilliam, 86, 218
Meade, Theodosia, Countess of Clanwilliam (wife of the 1st Earl), 85, 147–9, 218–21
Meade, family of, Earls of Clanwilliam, 86
Meath, County, 88–9, 239
medicine and disease, 137–8, 186, 190, 228, 266, 269–70
see also insanity
Mellish, Elizabeth: *see under* Thynne
Mellish, Margaret Lauretta: *see* Butler, Margaret Lauretta, Countess of Glengall
Mellish, William, of Woodford, Essex, 46, 78
Mellon, Harriot, Mrs Thomas Coutts, later Duchess of St Albans, 55–7, 166, 227
Mentmore, Buckinghamshire, 207
mercantile wealth, 44–7, 64, 113, 218, 231
Merrett, Ellen, Countess Conyngham, 47–8
Merrett, Mrs Rebecca (*née* Savage), 47
Merrett, Solomon, of St Olave's, Hart Street, London, merchant, 47–8
mésalliances, 7–8, 97, 102–4, 118, 143, 154, 162–75, 259
Milltown, Earl and Countess of: *see under* Leeson,
Milton Abbey, Dorchester, 249
mineral wealth, 72, 89, 96, 104–5, 201–2, 217, 232
minority, 118, 156–7, 162, 172, 180–1, 225, 236–8, 245, 254
Minster-in-Thanet, Kent, 47, 58
Mitford, John, 1st Lord Redesdale (Lord Chancellor of Ireland), 162
Mitford, Nancy, 186, 197, 269–70
model farms, 229
Moira, Co. Down, 222–3
Moira House, Ussher's Island, Dublin, 223
Molesworth, Richard, 3rd Viscount Molesworth, 148
Molesworth, Hon. Mary: *see* Rochfort, Mary, Countess of Belvedere
Monaghan, Co. Monaghan, 60, 113–14, 188, 270
Monasterevan, Co. Kildare, 198
Monck, Charles Stanley, 1st Viscount Monck, 106
Monck, Elizabeth: *see* Beresford, Elizabeth, Marchioness of Waterford
Monck, Henry, of Charleville, Co. Wicklow, 60–62, 106, 227
Monck, Henry Stanley, 2nd Viscount Monck, and Earl of Rathdowne, 106
Moneylenders, 129, 224
Montagu, Isabella, Duchess of Manchester (wife of the 2nd Duke), 59, 102–3, 117
Montagu, John, 2nd Duke of Montagu, 59, 102
Montagu, family of, dukes of Montagu, 187
Montagu, William, 2nd Duke of Manchester, 59, 102, 117
Montagu-Douglas-Scott, Henry John, 1st Lord Montagu of Beaulieu, 103, 187
Montalto, Ballynahinch, Co. Down, 223
Montgomery, George, of Ballyconnell, Co. Cavan, 237
Moore Abbey, Monasterevan, Co. Kildare, 198
Moore, Acheson, of Ravella, Aughnacloy, Co. Tyrone, 20, 247

Moore, Charles, 2nd Lord Moore of Tullamoore, and Earl of Charleville, 5, 57, 193
Moore, Charles, 2nd Viscount Moore, 198
Moore, Charles, 6th Earl and 1st Marquess of Drogheda, 198
Moore, Edward, 5th Earl of Drogheda, 198
Moore, Henry, 4th Earl of Drogheda, 198
Moore, Hester, Countess of Charleville: *see* Coghill
Moore, Jane, Viscountess Moore: *see* Loftus
Moore, Hon. Jane: *see* Bury, Jane
Moore, Thomas, 104
Moravians, 230
Morgan, Elizabeth Georgiana: *see under* Lawless
morganatic marriages: *see under mésalliances*
Morres, Francis Harvey, 3rd Viscount Mountmorres, 200
Morres, Harvey, 1st Viscount Mountmorres, 200
Morres, Harvey Redmond, 2nd Viscount Mountmorres, 200
Morres, Hon. Letitia: *see* McDonnell, Letitia, Marchioness of Antrim
Morrison, William Vitruvius, 97
mortality: *see under* demography
mortgages: *see under* debts
Mountjoy Forest, Co. Tyrone, 179, 184
Mountmorres, Viscounts: *see* Morres
Mount Stewart, Co. Down (seat of Lord Londonderry), 39
Mullingar, Co. Westmeath, 100, 168, 238
Mullins, Frederick, 135
Mullins, Thomas, 1st Lord Ventry, 135
Munster, province of, 62, 86, 90, 239
murder, 63–4
Murphy, Mr (Irish clergyman, 1808), 157
Murray, Frances Cairnes, Countess of Clermont (wife of William Henry Fortescue, Earl of Clermont), 199, 189
Murray, Colonel John, 60, 113, 137
Muschamp, Denny, 200

Nabos: *see* Alexander, James, 1st Earl of Caledon; Cowan, Sir Robert; Watson, Colonel Henry
Namier, L.B., 108
Naper, Ann, 'Mrs William Naper': *see* Fitzgerald, Ann
Naper, Catherine (wife of James Dutton Naper): *see* Ingoldsby, Catherine
Naper, James Dutton, of Loughcrew, Co. Meath, and Sherborne, Gloucestershire, 88, 167, 195
Naper, William, of Loughcrew, 89
Naper, William, of Littleton, Co. Westmeath, 168
Naper, Major-General William, of Littleton, 168
Napier, Lady Sarah: *see* Lennox
Nash, John, 208
Nash, Rev. Dr Treadwell, 142
navy, 31, 35, 42
Netterville, Catherine, Viscountess Netterville: *see* Burton, Catherine
Netterville, Nicholas, 5th Viscount Netterville, 12
Nevill, Henry, Lord Nevill and 2nd Earl of Abergavenny, 80

299

Nevill, Mary, Countess of Abergavenny: *see* Robinson
New Birmingham, alias Glengoole, Co. Tipperary, 233
Newbridge, Donabate, Co. Dublin, 52
Newcastle, Ballymahon, Co. Longford, 90
Newcastle, Clonmel, Co. Tipperary, 248
Newcastle, Duke and Duchess of: *see under* Pelham-Clinton
Newcomen, Charlotte, Viscountess Newcomen, 62–3, 141, 242
Newcomen, Thomas Gleadowe-, 2nd Lord Newcomen, 46
Newcomen, Sir William Gleadowe-, 1st Bt, 63, 141
Newhaven, Lady: *see* Allen, Hon. Frances
Newtown Anner, Clonmel, Co. Tipperary, 175–8
Newtownbarry, Co. Wexford, 84–5
Newtownstewart, Co. Tyrone, 178–83
Niagara, intended barony of, 135, 262
Nickson, Christian: *see* Hely-Hutchinson, Christian, Baroness Donoughmore
Nimmo, Alexander, 72
Nixon, Frances Wilhelmina: *see* Hely-Hutchinson, Frances Wilhelmina
Nixon, family of, of Belmont, Co. Wexford, 110
Norfolk, County: *see* Blickling Hall, Norfolk; Sandringham, Norfolk
North, Anne: *see* Herbert, Anne, Hon. Mrs Nicholas Herbert
Northcote, James (painter), 265
North, Dudley, of Great Glemham, Suffolk, 1
Northamptonshire, 70–1
Northumberland, County, 131
Nugent, Anna Craggs (wife of the future Earl Nugent), 23–4
Nugent, Emily, Marchioness of Westmeath, 28, 100, 143–44, 152–3, 175, 251
Nugent, George Frederick, 7th Earl of Westmeath, 28, 142–3, 150, 224, 270
Nugent, Lord: *see* Grenville, Lord George Nugent; Nugent, Robert Craggs
Nugent, George Thomas, Lord Delvin, 8th Earl and only Marquess of Westmeath, 28, 100, 143–4, 152–3, 174, 224
Nugent, Marianne, Countess of Westmeath: *see* Jeffereyes
Nugent, Mary Elizabeth: *see* Grenville, Mary Elizabeth, Marchioness of Buckingham
Nugent, Robert Craggs, Viscount Clare and Earl Nugent, 23–4, 83
Nugent, Lady Rosa, Baroness Greville, 100
Nugent, Thomas, 6th Earl of Westmeath, 214, 251
Nugent, family of, earls of Westmeath, 214
Nugent-Grenville: *see* Grenville

O'Brien, Anne, Countess of Inchiquin (wife of the 4th Earl), *suo jure* Countess of Orkney, 8
O'Brien, Donough, Lord O'Brien (uncle of the 7th Earl of Thomond), 252
O'Brien, Henry, 7th Earl of Thomond, 86, 193, 225

O'Brien, Mary, Countess of Inchiquin (first wife of the 5th Earl), *suo jure* Countess of Orkney
O'Brien, Murrough, Lord O'Brien (d.1741), only surviving son of the 4th Earl of Inchiquin, 87
O'Brien, Murrough, 5th Earl of Inchiquin and 1st Marquess of Thomond, 8, 258
O'Brien, Percy Wyndham, and O'Brien, George Wyndham: *see* Wyndham O'Brien
O'Brien, Lady Sophia, widow of Donough, Lord O'Brien, 225, 252
O'Brien, William, 4th Earl of Inchiquin, 8, 87
O'Brien, family of, princes of Thomond, earls of Inchiquin, earls of Thomond, etc, 87
O'Donel, Sir Neale, 1st Bt, 11
Offaly, County, 105
office-holding and 'venality', 79–80, 104, 128, 207, 212–13
Ogilvie, Cecilia, 42
Ogilvie, William, 41–3, 118, 122, 253
O'Keefe, William (caricaturist), 103
Ombersley Court, Worcestershire, 105
O'Neill/Oneal, family of, kings of Ulster, 1
Orford, Earl of: *see* Walpole, Horace
Oriel, Lord: *see* Foster, John
Oriel Temple, Collon: *see* Collon, Co. Louth
Orkney, Countesses of: *see under* O'Brien
Ormonde, earls of: *see under* Butler
Orrery, Earl and Countess of: *see under* Boyle
Osborne, Catherine, Lady Osborne (*née* Smith; wife of the 9th Bt), 175–7, 238
Osborne, Catherine, Mrs Bernal Osborne, 176–7
Osborne, Francis Godolphin, 5th Duke of Leeds, 93
Osborne, Sir Francis, 15th Bt, 177
Osborne, George William, 6th Duke of Leeds, 93, 131
Osborne, Sir Henry, 11th Bt, 175
Osborne, Sir Peter George, 17th Bt, 178
Osborne, Ralph Bernal, 176–7
Osborne, Lady Sophia: *see* O'Brien
Osborne, Thomas, 4th Duke of Leeds, 134
Osborne, Sir Thomas, 9th Bt, 175
Osborne, Sir William, 10th Bt, 175
Osterley Park, Middlesex, 264
O'Toole, Rt Hon. Lady Catherine, 162
Ott, Pauline Theresia: *see* Villiers-Stuart
Oxford, university of, 213
Oxfordshire, 213
see also Ditchley Park, Oxfordshire
Oxmantown, Lord: *see* Harman, Laurence, 1st Earl of Rosse

Paget, Caroline, Lady Bayly, 199
Paget, Henry William, 2nd Earl of Uxbridge and 1st Marquess of Anglesey, 199
Paget, family of, of Beaudesert, Staffordshire, Lords Paget, earls of Uxbridge and marquesses of Anglesey, 199
Pakenham, Catherine (*née* Langford Rowley), Lady Longford (wife of the 2nd Lord Longford), 187, 200

INDEX

Pakenham, General the Hon. Sir Edward, 171
Pakenham, Edward Michael, 2nd Lord Longford, 125, 187, 190, 200
Pakenham, Edward Michael, 3rd Earl of Longford, 190
Pakenham, Elizabeth (née Cuffe), Countess of Longford, 122, 187
Pakenham, Emma Georgiana, Countess of Longford: see Lygon
Pakenham, Francis Aungier; 7th Earl of Longford, 187
Pakenham, Thomas, 1st Lord Longford, 187
Pakenham, Admiral the Hon. Thomas, 125
Pakenham, Thomas, 2nd Earl of Longford, 170–71, 187
Pakenham Hall, Co. Westmeath, 122
Palatines, 230
Paris, 6, 8
'Parker's daughter' (mistress of the 1st Earl of Donoughmore), 171
Parkyns, Elizabeth, Lady Rancliffe (wife of the 2nd Lord), 249
Parkyns, George Augustus, 2nd Lord Rancliffe, 249
Parnell, Letitia Charlotte, Lady Parnell (wife of the 2nd Bt): see Brooke
Parsons, Alicia (née Lloyd), Countess of Rosse (wife of the 2nd Earl), 128, 158–61
Parsons, Lady Alicia (younger daughter of the 2nd Earl of Rosse), 128, 158–61, 163, 264
Parsons, Anne, Lady Parsons: see Harman, Anne
Parsons, Cassandra, Countess of Rosse: see Hawke
Parsons, Frances Lois, Countess of Rosse (widow of the 5th Earl), 136, 252
Parsons, Lady Jane (elder daughter of the 2nd Earl of Rosse), 160
Parsons, Sir Laurence, 3rd Bt, 90
Parsons, Laurence, 1st Earl of Rosse: see Harman, Laurence
Parsons, Sir Laurence, 5th Bt, 2nd Earl of Rosse (of the second creation), 38, 90, 128, 158–61, 194
Parsons, Laurence, 4th Earl of Rosse, 271
Parsons, Mary, Countess of Rosse: see Field
Parsons, Richard, 2nd Earl of Rosse (of the first creation), 196
Parsons, William, Lord Oxmantown, later 3rd Earl of Rosse, 38, 160, 201–3, 271
Parsons, Sir William, 4th Bt, 90
Parsons, family of, earls of Rosse of two different creations, 267
partible inheritance, 95–6, 188–9, 201–2, 205, 267
patronage: see office-holding and 'venality'; pensions (from the Crown); political influence
Paul, Jeffry, of Silverspring, Co. Wexford, 200
Paul, Colonel Joshua, 77
Paul, Mary, Mrs Thomas Lefroy: see Lefroy
Paul, Rev. Thomas, 201
pedigrees: see genealogy
peerage of England/Great Britain/the United Kingdom, 34, 37, 47, 241–2
peerage of Scotland, 34, 37, 65, 241

peerages (creation, re-creation and extinction of), 2, 35, 44–6, 50, 53, 58, 60, 62, 66, 68, 84, 87, 90–1, 95, 101–06, 108–10, 135, 142–3, 165–6, 180, 187–92, 202, 208, 212–15, 241–4, 258, 262, 263
Pelham-Clinton, Anna Maria, Duchess of Newcastle (widow of the 3rd Duke), 91
Pelham-Clinton, Henry, 4th Duke of Newcastle, 91
Pelham-Clinton, Henry, Earl of Lincoln, 154
Pembroke, Earl and Countess of: see under Herbert
Penal Laws: see under Roman Catholics
pensions (from the Crown), 30, 108, 161, 213, 251, 268
Perceval, Catherine, Countess of Egmont (first wife of the 2nd Earl), 55, 127, 133–4
Perceval, Lady Helena, 39
Perceval, John, 1st Earl of Egmont, 39, 55, 133
Perceval, John, 2nd Earl of Egmont, 39, 133–4
Perfect, Rev. Henry (Bedfordshire clergyman), 169
Perfect, Mary (mistress of Earl Conyngham), 169–70, 173
perpetuities: see under leases
Pery, Annabella, Lady Glentworth (wife of the eldest son of the 1st Earl of Limerick), 157, 162, 264
Pery, Dorothea, Lady Glentworth (second wife of the 1st Lord), 136–7
Pery, Edmond Henry, 2nd Lord Glentworth and 1st Earl of Limerick, 19, 157, 174
Pery, Edmond Sexten, Viscount Pery, 19–20
Pery, Henry Hartstronge, Lord Glentworth (eldest son of the 1st Earl of Limerick), 157, 162, 264
Pery, William Cecil, 1st Lord Glentworth, 136–7
Petrie, William (seducer of Mrs Richard Martin), 150
Petty, Anne, Countess of Kerry, 89, 195–6
Petty, Henry, Earl of Shelburne, 195–6, 206
Petty, John, Lord Shelburne, 58, 195
Petty, Mary, Lady Shelburne: see Williams
Petty, Sir William, 195
Petty-Fitzmaurice, John, 1st Earl of Shelburne, 89, 195–6, 206
Petty-Fitzmaurice, William, 2nd Earl of Shelburne and 1st Marquess of Lansdowne, 196
Phelps, Edmund: see McDonnell, Edmund
Phillips, Samuel, of Foyle, Co. Kilkenny, 64
Phillips, Thomas (portrait-painter), 59, 141
Phipps, Constantine John, 2nd Lord Mulgrave, 212
Phipps, Hon. Henrietta, Mrs Charles Dillon-Lee, 212, 215
Phipps, Henry, 3rd Lord, and 1st Earl of, Mulgrave, 212
Piers, Sir John, 6th Bt, 151
Pike, Mary (abducted Quaker heiress), 64
pin money, 27, 28, 44, 72, 142, 182, 192, 251
Pitt, Anne, Lady Grenville, 84, 200–01, 258
Pitt, Thomas, 2nd Lord Camelford, 200
Pitt, William, the Elder, 1st Earl of Chatham, 193
Pitt, William, the Younger, 16, 212
Playfair, William, 241–2
Plunket, Hon. Randal, 162
Pole, family of, of Ballyfin, Maryborough, Co. Laois, 221
political influence, 36, 42, 50–55, 60, 64, 90, 108–9, 125, 230

301

Ponsonby, Brabazon, 1st Earl of Bessborough, 52, 226
Ponsonby, Lady Elizabeth: *see* Fownes
Ponsonby, Frederick, 3rd Earl of Bessborough, 226–9
Ponsonby, Henrietta Frances, Countess of Bessborough (wife of the 2nd Earl), 117
Ponsonby, Hon. John, Speaker of the Irish House of Commons, 52, 55
Ponsonby, John William, Viscount Duncannon and 4th Earl of Bessborough, 226
Ponsonby, William, 2nd Earl of Bessborough, 226
population: *see under* demography
Portarlington, Earl and Countess of: *see under* Dawson; Dawson-Damer
Portarlington, earldom of, 234
portions, 2, 5–6, 9–12, 16–20, 27–38, 41–53, 60–64, 72, 74, 80–81, 104, 106, 111–13, 116–18, 123–5, 130, 132, 136, 146–8, 151–2, 166, 174, 176, 180–3, 188–9, 192, 213–15, 218, 244–5, 249, 252, 254, 257–8
Portland, Duke of: *see* Bentinck
Portpatrick, Wigtonshire, 161
Poulett, John, 4th Earl Poulett, 135
Poulett, Margaret (*née* Burges), Countess Poulett, 129, 135, 261
Power, John, 2nd Earl of Tyrone, 95
Power, Marguerite, Countess of Blessington: *see* Gardiner
Pratt, Charles, 1st Earl Camden, 51
Pratt, Hon. Frances: *see* Stewart, Frances, Marchioness of Londonderry
Pratt, John Jeffreys, 2nd Earl and 1st Marquess Camden, 51
Prendergast, Elizabeth, Mrs Charles Smyth, 207
Prendergast, Juliana, Countess of Meath, 10
Prendergast, Sir Thomas, 1st Bt, 10
Prendergast, Sir Thomas, 2nd Bt, 207, 248
'present maintenance', 27, 27, 33, 55, 143, 214, 218–21
primogeniture, 26–7, 55, 77–8, 110, 122, 245
  see also cadet inheritance; children (younger)
Primrose, Archibald, 5th Earl of Rosebery, 183
Prior-Wandesford, family of, of Castlecomer, Co. Kilkenny, 232
prize money, 19, 31, 99
Proby, Elizabeth, Lady Carysfort: *see* Allen, Hon. Elizabeth
Proby, Elizabeth, Countess of Carysfort (*née* Grenville; second wife of the 1st Earl), 29, 38, 109
Proby, Granville Leveson, 3rd Earl of Carysfort, 109
Proby, John, 1st Lord Carysfort, 108, 174–5
Proby, John Joshua, 2nd Lord and 1st Earl of Carysfort, 11, 29, 38, 108–9
Proby, family of, earls of Carysfort, 108
professions, 31, 165, 218, 231
Punchestown, Co. Kildare, 108
purchases (of land): *see* sales (of land)

Quarendon estate, Buckinghamshire, 210, 215
Quin, Augusta Wyndham-, Countess of Dunraven (wife of the 3rd Earl), 217

Quin, Caroline Wyndham-, Countess of Dunraven (wife of the 2nd Earl), 23, 105, 139, 202, 246
Quin, Edwin Wyndham-, 3rd Earl of Dunraven, 217
Quin, Margaret Mary, Viscountess Mountearl (second wife of the 1st Earl of Dunraven), 136
Quin, Muriel, Lady Adare (first wife of the 1st Earl of Dunraven), 136
Quin, Richard, 1st Lord Adare, Viscount Mountearl and Earl of Dunraven, 126, 136, 139, 141, 202
Quin, Windham Wyndham-, 2nd Earl of Dunraven, 105, 139, 202, 217–18, 227, 231, 246

Ramsgate, Kent, 47
Rancliffe, Lord and Lady: *see* Parkyns
Ranelagh, Lord: *see* Cole, Sir Arthur
Ranelagh, 6th Viscount: *see* Jones, Thomas
rape: *see under* abduction,
Rash, Co. Tyrone, 18, 179, 183–4
Rathdowne, Earl of: *see* Monck, Henry Stanley
Rathfriland, Co. Down, 85–6
Rathmolyon, Co. Meath (the 2nd Earl of Moira's estate of), 157
Ratisbon (alias Regensburg), 31
Rawdon, Elizabeth (*née* Hastings), Countess of Moira (third wife of the 1st Earl), 122, 222–3
Rawdon, John, 1st Earl of Moira, 122, 222
Rawdon, Lady Selina: *see* Forbes
Rawdon-Hastings, Francis, 1st Lord Rawdon, 2nd Earl of Moira and 1st Marquess of Hastings, 222, 269–70
Rawdon-Hastings, family of, 2nd, 3rd and 4th Marquesses of Hastings, 269–70
Rayleigh, Baroness: *see* Fitzgerald, Lady Charlotte
reclamation (land), 229
'recoveries', 7, 15
Redesdale, Lord: *see* Mitford, John
Reed, John (surveyor), 76
Registry of Deeds memorials, 252
remittances (of money to England), 233
rentals, 1–8, 14–15, 19–21, 24, 28, 33, 36, 39–42, 51–2, 59, 60–9, 64, 68–74, 78, 82, 84, 89, 93–4, 98–100, 104, 107–9, 125, 133–4, 147, 152, 171, 175, 180, 190, 196–200, 206, 208, 213–15, 221–4, 227–9, 232–3, 236, 238, 244–5, 249, 250, 256, 265–6, 269
replacement rates: *see under* demography
Reynolds, Sir Joshua, ii, 40, 106–7, 108, 133, 170, 189, 218, 220
Richmond, Duke and Duchess of: *see under* Lennox
Ricketts, Edward Jervis, later 2nd Viscount St Vincent (husband of Hon. Cassandra Twistleton), 155–6
Roberts, Jane, Duchess of St Albans, 58, 193
Roberts, Thomas, of Cork City, banker, 58, 193
Roberts, Sir Walter, 6th Bt, of Glassenbury, Kent, 58
Robinson, John, 80
Robinson, Mary, Countess of Abergavenny, 80
Robinson, Richard, Archbishop of Armagh and 1st Lord Rokeby, 232, 270

Rochfort, Alice, 32
Rochfort, Anne, 32
Rochfort, Hon. Arthur, 148–9
Rochfort, George, of Gaulstown, Co. Westmeath, 32, 123, 148
Rochfort, George, of Rochfort (alias Tudenham), Co. Westmeath, 263
Rochfort, George Augustus, 2nd Earl of Belvedere, 24, 30, 230
Rochfort, Jane, Countess of Belvedere (second wife and widow of the 2nd Earl), 24, 54, 230–31
Rochfort, Jane, Countess of Lanesborough, 24, 193, 230
Rochfort, Mary, Countess of Belvedere (second wife of the 1st Earl), 148–9, 153, 230
Rochfort, Robert, 1st Earl of Belvedere, 30, 148–9, 153, 230
Rochfort, Tomasine, 32
Rochfort, alias Tudenham, Co. Westmeath, 263
Rochfort Boyd, George Augustus, 24
Rochfort Boyd, family of (of Tudenham, Co. Westmeath), 24
Roden, Countess of: *see* Hamilton, Lady Anne
Rogerson, Sir John (Chief Justice of the King's Bench), 188
Rogerson's Quay, Dublin, 188
Rogier, Marie (Belgian actress who was mistress and then second wife of the 12th Viscount Dillon), 213
Rokeby, Lord: *see* Robinson, Richard
Roman Catholics, 163, 210, 213–15, 234–5, 255, 263
Roscommon, County, 42, 210, 213–14, 239, 269
Rosenalis, Mountmellick, Co. Laois, 198
Ross, Sir Charles Lockhart, 7th Bt, 132
Ross, Elizabeth, Mrs David Ross of Rostrevor, 77
Ross, Elizabeth, Lady Ross (widow of Sir John Lockhart Ross, 6th Bt), 132
Rosse, Earl and Countess of: *see* Harman, Laurence, and under Parsons
Rosshill estate, Cos. Galway and Mayo, 72–3, 82, 109, 232, 256
Rosshill House and demesne, Co. Mayo, 72–3, 82
Rous, Lady Frances, 110
Rous, Sir John, 6th Bt, 1st Earl of Stradbroke, 110
Rous, John Edward, 2nd Earl of Stradbroke, 110
Rous, Juliana, Lady Rous (first wife of the 6th Bt), 110
Rousseau, Jean Jacques, 122
Rowley: *see* Langford Rowley
Roxborough, Limerick City, 208–9
Royal Academy, The, 172
Royal Marriage Act (1772), 117
runaway marriages: *see under* elopements
Russborough, Co. Kildare, 44
Russell, Elizabeth, of Hillsborough, Co. Down (mother of the 2nd Marquess of Downshire's illegitimate daughters), 261
Russell, family of, dukes of Bedford, 201
Rutland, County, 70

Sackville, Charles, Earl of Middlesex and 2nd Duke of Dorset, 205
Sackville, Hon. Elizabeth, Mrs Herbert of Muckruss, Co. Kerry, 49–50
Sackville, Lord George, 1st Viscount Sackville, 49–50
Sackville, Grace, Countess of Middlesex (*née* Boyle): *see* Boyle, Grace, Countess of Middlesex
Sadleir, Michael, 179, 182, 265
St Albans, dukes and duchesses of: *see under* Beauclerk
St George, Emilia-Olivia: *see* Fitzgerald, Emilia-Olivia, Duchess of Leinster
St George, St George Ussher, Lord St George, 42
St John, Diana, Viscountess Bolingbroke: *see* Beauclerk, Lady Di
St John, Hon. Henrietta: *see* Knight, Hon. Henrietta, Lady Luxborough
St Lawrence, Lady Isabella: *see* Cosby, Isabella, Lady Sydney
St Leger, Arthur, 1st Viscount Doneraile, 29, 85
St Leger, Hon. Hayes, 29, 85
St Mawes borough, Cornwall, 23
St Patrick, Order of, 268
sales (of land), 6, 15, 42–3, 73–4, 77, 80, 83, 123, 181–4, 196, 198, 205–6, 221–5, 232, 238–9, 265–6
Salisbury, Earl, Marquess and Marchioness of: *see under* Cecil
Salters' Proportion, Magherafelt, Co. Londonderry, 227, 254
Sandringham, Norfolk, 266
Sandwich, Kent, 47
Sandys, Arthur, 2nd Lord Sandys (of the second creation), 105
Sandys, Edwin, 2nd Lord Sandys (of the first creation), 134
Sandys, Mary, Marchioness of Downshire (wife of the 2nd Marquess), 23, 105, 134, 153–4, 174, 271
Savage, Charles, of St Olave's, Hart Street, London, 'packer', 47
Scotland, 156–7, 228, 236
Scottish Peerage: *see* peerage of Scotland
Seaham, Co. Durham, 217
Seaton Sluice, Co. Northumberland, 131
separate maintenance: *see* pin money
separation: *see* divorce and separation; and *under* settlements (marriage and other)
Seringapatam, storming of, 31
settlements (marriage and other), 3, 5–14, 17–23, 26–86, 93, 99, 106–10, 112–15, 122–34, 142, 152–3, 155–6, 169–70, 174–5, 180, 182–5, 191–2, 192, 211–12, 221, 229, 245, 251, 258
Seven Years' War, 135, 168
Seymour, Lady Elizabeth, Countess of Thomond, 87
Seymour-Conway, Lady Frances, Countess of Lincoln, 153
Seymour-Conway, Francis, 1st Earl and Marquess of Hertford, 49–50, 154
Seymour-Conway, Francis Ingram, 2nd Marquess of Hertford, 242
Seymour-Conway, Lady Gertrude: *see* Villiers, Gertrude, Countess Grandison

Seymour-Conway, Isabella Anne, Marchioness of Hertford (second wife of the 2nd Marquess), 50
Seymour-Conway, Lady Sarah: *see* Stewart, Lady Sarah
Shannon, Earl of: *see* Boyle, Richard
Shannon, Viscount: *see* Boyle, Field-Marshal Richard
Shannon Park and estate, Carrigaline, Co. Cork, 205–6
Sharpe, Joshua, of Lincoln's Inn (attorney), 169–70, 265
Shee, Martin Archer (portrait-painter), 132
Shenstone, William, 263
Sherborne, Gloucestershire, 88
Shortgrove, Newport, Essex, 87, 258
Shrule Castle, Co. Laois, 227
single men/women: *see* bachelors; spinsters
Singleton, Henry, Chief Justice of the Common Pleas, 30
Skeffington, Anne, Countess of Massereene: *see* Eyre
Skeffington, Lady Catherine, 128
Skeffington, Chichester, 8th Viscount, and 4th Earl of, Massereene, 5, 128
Skeffington, Clotworthy, 5th Viscount, and 1st Earl of Massereene, 6–7, 21
Skeffington, Clotworthy, 6th Viscount, and 2nd Earl of Massereene, 6, 12, 166, 187, 224, 236
Skeffington, Elizabeth, Countess of Massereene, 6, 166
Skeffington, Harriet, 9th Viscountess Massereene, 5, 191
Skeffington, Lady Harriet (*née* Jocelyn), later Countess of Massereene, 128
Skeffington, Henry, 7th Viscount, and 3rd Earl of, Massereene, 5–7
Skeffington, John, 10th Viscount Massereene and 3rd Viscount Ferrard, 12, 157
Skeffington, Thomas Henry, 2nd Viscount Ferrard, 12, 122–3, 157, 178, 191
slaves, 46, 253
Slievegrine, Co. Waterford, 229
Smith, Miss Catherine: *see* Osborne, Catherine, Lady Osborne
Smith, Joseph, of Shortgrove, Essex, 258
Smith, family of, of Knockneshamer, Co. Sligo, 204
Smyth, Miss Anne, 120
Smyth, Charles, MP for Limerick City, 208
Smyth, Elizabeth (*née* Prendergast): *see* Prendergast
Smyth, Rev. James (Co. Antrim clergyman), 120
Smyth, John Prendergast, 1st Baron Kiltarton and Viscount Gort, 208–9, 217
Smyth, Juliana, Mrs Thomas Vereker, 208
Smyth, Penelope, Princess of Capua, 163
Smyth, Ralph, of Barbavilla, Co. Westmeath, 63
Smyth, Thomas, MP for Limerick City, 208
Smythe, Maria, Mrs Henry Matthew Smythe, 267
Smythe, William Barlow, of Barbavilla, Co. Westmeath, 267
Sneyd, Nathaniel, of Bawnboy, Co. Cavan, 231–2
Sneyd, Rev. William, 142
sons: *see* cadet inheritance; children (younger); partible inheritance; primogeniture
Southampton, Earl of: *see* Wriothesley, Thomas
Southampton, Lord and Lady: *see* Fitzroy, General Charles; Warren, Anne

Southwell, Agnes Elizabeth, Countess Wandesford, 89
Spencer, George John, 2nd Earl Spencer, 52
Spencer, Lavinia, Countess Spencer (wife of the 2nd Earl), 52
spinsters, 10, 16–17, 31, 102, 221
Steuart, General William (step-father of the 1st Earl Grandison), 36–7, 68
Stewart, Alexander (father of the 1st Marquess of Londonderry), 53, 55
Stewart, Anne (wife of the Rt Hon. Luke Gardiner), 196
Stewart, Capt. the Hon. Alexander (d.1702), 196
Stewart, Charles, 3rd Marquess of Londonderry, 53, 82, 98, 104–05, 110, 155, 202, 217, 227, 259
Stewart, Emily, Viscountess Castlereagh and Marchioness of Londonderry (wife of the 2nd Marquess), 82, 110
Stewart, Frances, Marchioness of Londonderry (second wife of the 1st Marquess), 50, 53
Stewart, Frances Anne Vane-Tempest-, Marchioness of Londonderry (second wife of the 3rd Marquess), 23, 98, 104–05, 202, 217
Stewart, Frederick, 4th Marquess of Londonderry, 105
Stewart, George Vane-Tempest-, 2nd Earl Vane and 5th Marquess of Londonderry, 105
Stewart, Mary (mother of the 1st Marquess of Londonderry), 50, 55, 78, 254
Stewart, Robert, 1st Marquess of Londonderry, 39, 50–53, 78, 82, 217, 227, 234
Stewart, Robert, Viscount Castlereagh and 2nd Marquess of Londonderry, 50–53, 82, 110
Stewart, Lady Sarah (first wife of the 1st Marquess of Londonderry), 50, 53
Stewart, William, 3rd Viscount Mountjoy and only Earl of Blessington (of the first creation), 196, 247
Stewart, family of, Viscounts Mountjoy and one and only Earl of Blessington, 179, 184
Stillorgan, Dublin, 11, 107
stock-market, 56, 80, 85, 233
Stone, Lawrence, ix, 112, 115, 175
Stopford, James, 1st Earl of Courtown, 10
Stoyte, Mary, of Street, Co. Westmeath: *see* Bligh, Mary, Countess of Darnley
Stradbally, Co. Laois, 262
Stradbroke, Earl of: *see under* Rous
Strafford, earls of: *see* Wentworth, Frederick Thomas, Wentworth, Thomas, and Wentworth, William
Strangford, Co. Down, 3, 81, 141
Strangways, Fox-: *see* Fox-Strangways
Stratford, Anne-Elizabeth, Countess of Aldborough (second wife of the 2nd Earl), 1, 34
Stratford, Barabara, Countess of Aldborough (first wife of the 2nd Earl), 1
Stratford, Edward, 2nd Earl of Aldborough, 14, 16, 34, 74, 227, 229, 233
Stratford, Lady Hannah, 14
Stratford, Martha, Countess Dowager of Aldborough, 14
Stratford, family of, earls of Aldborough, 1, 14
Stratford-upon-Slaney, Co. Wicklow, 229

INDEX

Strutt, Charlotte, Baroness Rayleigh: *see* Fitzgerald, Lady Charlotte
Strutt, J.H., of Terling Place, Essex, 253
Stuart, Andrew Thomas, 1st Earl Castle Stewart, 20, 196–7, 232, 270
Stuart, Lady Caroline: *see* Dawson, Caroline, Countess of Portarlington
Stuart, Lady Gertrude Amelia: *see* Villiers, Lady Gertrude Amelia
Stuart, Lord Henry, 93–5, 227, 238
Stuart, John, 2nd Marquess of Bute, 164
Stuart, John, 4th Earl and 1st Marquess of Bute, 30, 93
Stuart, Margaret (*née* Edwards), wife of Robert Stuart of Eary, Co. Tyrone, 196–7
Stuart, Mary, Countess of Bute (wife of the 3rd Earl), 234
Stuart, Robert, of Eary, 196–7
Stuart de Decies, Lord: *see* Villiers-Stuart, Henry
Stuart-Mackenzie: *see* Mackenzie
Stuart, Villiers-: *see* Villiers-Stuart
Stuart-Wortley: *see* Wortley
Suffolk, County, 1, 74
  see also Great Glemham, Suffolk,
Sullivan, Arabella, Mrs Frederick Sullivan, 264
surveying, 72–3, 97–9, 104, 110, 229
Swayne, Mary (wife of Matthew Swayne), 168
Swayne, Matthew (trooper in the carbineers, c.1760), 168
Swords borough, Co. Dublin, 53
Sydney, Lord and Lady: *see* Cosby

Taaffe, Christopher, of Rookwood, Co. Galway, 152
Taaffe, Honora (*née* Burke), Mrs Christopher Taaffe, 152
Taaffe, Mr (trustee of Lady Cathcart's marriage settlement), 66
Tait, Archibald Campbell, Archbishop of Canterbury, 167
Talbot, Lady Anne (daughter of the 1st Earl of Glandore), 39
Taylour, Hon. Clotworthy, 1st Lord Langford (of the second creation), 188
Taylour, Jane (*née* Langford Rowley), Countess of Bective (wife of the 1st Earl), 188, 200
Tempest, Vane-: *see* Vane-Tempest
Temple, Earl: *see* Grenville, Richard
Temple, Henry John, 3rd Viscount Palmerston, 183
Tempo, Co. Fermanagh, 66
tenant right, 231
Tewin Water, Hertfordshire, 67
Thomond, earls and Marquess of: *see* O'Brien, Henry, Murrough and Percy Wyndham
Thynne, Alexander, 7th Marquess of Bath, 169
Thynne, Elizabeth, Lady Edward Thynne (*née* Mellish), 79
Tighe, Caroline: *see* Hamilton
Tighe, Mrs Sarah: *see* Fownes
Tighe, William, of Rosanna, Co. Wicklow, 8
Tipperary, County, 15, 86, 110, 147, 171, 176, 218–19, 249
title deeds: *see* 'recoveries'; Registry of Deeds memorials; settlements (marriage and other); wills

titles (hereditary): *see* peerages
Todd, Anthony, 80
Todd, Eleanor, Countess of Lauderdale, 80
Tollemache, Charlotte, Countess of Dysart: *see* Walpole, Charlotte
Tollymore Park, Bryansford, Co. Down, 207
towns: *see* estate villages; urban property
trade: *see* mercantile wealth
Trevor, Hill-: *see* Hill-Trevor
Trollope, Anthony, 109
Trumbach, Randolph, 112
Trumbull, family of, of Easthampstead Park, Berkshire, 105
Tudenham, Co. Westmeath: *see* Rochfort
Tullamore, Co. Offaly, 4
Tunbridge Wells, 17
Turner, Mary (the 1st Earl of Belvedere's 'housekeeper'), 149
Twistleton, Hon. Cassandra, 155
Twistleton, Elizabeth, Lady Saye and Sele (widow of the 13th Lord), 155
Twistleton, Hon. Julia: *see* Leigh
Tylney, John Child, 2nd Earl Tylney, 221
Tylney, family of, of Rotherwick, Hampshire, 221
Tyrawly, Lord and Lady: *see* Cuffe
Tyrconnel, Earl of: *see* Carpenter
Tyrone, County, 18, 39, 89–90, 178–84, 191, 196–7, 232, 265–6, 270
Tyrone, Earl and Countess of: *see* Power, John, and under Beresford
Tyrrellspass, Co. Westmeath, 231

Union (between Ireland and Great Britain), 35–6, 109–10, 207, 212, 214
United Kingdom peerage: *see under* peerage of England/Great Britain/the United Kingdom,
unmarried sons/daughters: *see* bachelors; spinsters
urban property, 11, 15, 78–9, 201–02, 230–31

Vane, earldom of, 104
Vane-Tempest, Sir Henry, 2nd Bt, 96–7, 104, 127
Vane-Tempest-Stewart: *see* Stewart
'venality': *see* office-holding and 'venality'
Ventry, Lord: *see* Mullins, Thomas
Vereker, Colonel Charles, 2nd Viscount Gort, 207–09
Vereker, Henry, 208
Vereker, John Prendergast, 3rd Viscount Gort, 209, 268
Vereker, Juliana (*née* Smyth): *see* Smyth
Vereker, Thomas, of Roxborough, Limerick City, 208
Vernon, Emma, Mrs Henry Cecil: *see* Cecil
Vernon, Mrs (*née* Cornwell, of Berrington Hall, Herefordshire), 142
Vesey, Hon. Anne: *see* Knox, Anne, Lady Welles
Vesey, Hon. Miss Elizabeth (m. firstly Robert Handcock and secondly Viscount Pery), 27, 131
Vesey, Hon. Miss Jane, 125
Vesey, John Denny, 1st Lord Knapton, 27, 131, 199

Vesey, John Robert, 4th Viscount de Vesci, 199
Vesey, Selina Elizabeth, Viscountess de Vesci (wife of the 1st Viscount), 20, 199, 234
Vesey, Thomas, 1st Viscount de Vesci, 125, 199–200, 230, 234
Victoria, Duchess of Kent, 158–61
Victoria, Queen, 158–61, 264
villages: *see* estate villages
Villiers, Brigadier Edward, 95
Villiers, Elizabeth, Countess Grandison, 36–7, 68, 93, 193–4
Villiers, George Mason, 2nd Earl Grandison, 49, 68–70, 93, 187, 190, 193, 234
Villiers (later Child-Villiers), George, 5th Earl of Jersey, 264
Villiers, Gertrude, Countess Grandison (wife of the 2nd Earl), 49
Villiers, Lady Gertrude Amelia, 93–4, 131
Villiers, John, 5th Viscount and 1st Earl Grandison, 36, 68, 95, 193, 230–31
Villiers, Katherine Fitzgerald-, Viscountess Grandison, 36, 94, 94–5
Villiers, family of, dukes of Buckingham, earls of Jersey Viscounts Grandison, etc, 68
Villiers-Stuart, Henry, Lord Stuart de Decies, 95, 163–6, 175, 229, 264
Villiers-Stuart, Henry John, 166
Villiers-Stuart, Pauline, Lady Wheeler-Cuffe, 164
Villiers-Stuart, Pauline Theresia, Lady Stuart de Decies, 163–5, 175
Villiers-Stuart, William, 163–6, 264
Villierstown, Co. Waterford, 230–31, 270
Vincent, Richard, of London, merchant, 113

Wakefield, Edward Gibbon, 15
Wallace Collection, The, 179
Walpole, Charlotte, Countess of Dysart (niece of Horace Walpole), 127
Walpole, Horace, 4th Earl of Orford, 24, 87, 102, 117, 121, 127, 145, 198, 235, 263
Wandesford, Agnes Elizabeth, Countess Wandesford: *see* Southwell Wandesford, Charles Butler Southwell Clarke, of Castlecomer, Co. Kilkenny (fourth son of the 17th Earl of Ormonde), 89, 232
Wandesford, Lady Frances Susan, Countess of Ormonde (wife of the 17th Earl), 89
Wandesford, John, 5th Viscount Castlecomer and only Earl Wandesford, 89, 232
Wandesford, Prior-: *see* Prior-Wandesford
Wanstead, Essex, 221
Ward, Lady Anne, Viscountess Bangor (wife of the 1st Viscount), 149, 237
Ward, Bernard, 1st Viscount Bangor, 3–4, 149, 237
Ward, Bernard Smith, of Knockballymore, Co. Fermanagh, 204–5
Ward, Hon. Edward, 237

Ward, John, 15th Lord Ward and 1st Viscount Dudley, 66
Ward, Meliora (*née* Creighton): *see* Creighton
Ward, Nicholas, 2nd Viscount Bangor, 149, 237
Ward, Nicholas, of Knockballymore, Co. Fermanagh, 204
Ward, Colonel the Hon. Robert, 3–4, 237
Ward, family of, Viscounts Bangor, 3–4
Warren, Anne, Lady Southampton, 21, 38–9, 162, 174
Warren, Admiral Sir Peter, 21
Wards, Court of, 236
Wards in Chancery: *see under* Chancery, Court of
Warter Wilson: *see* Wilson
Waterford, County, 68, 93–5, 163–6, 175–7, 228, 238
  see also Dromana, Co. Waterford; Villierstown, Co. Waterford
Waterford, Marquess and Marchioness of: *see under* Beresford
Watson, Colonel Henry, 70–71
Watson, Susan: *see* Evans, Susan, Lady Carbery
Wax, Mary (abducted heiress), 64
wealth: *see* landownership; mercantile wealth; mineral wealth; rentals; stock-market; urban property
Webster, Mr, of Longford, Co. Longford, 62–3
Webster, Thomas (son of the foregoing), 62–3
Weldon, Ann (*née* Cooke), 205
Weldon, Jane (the Hon. Mrs John Creighton): *see* Creighton
Weldon, Samuel Cooke, 205
Welles, Lady: *see* Knox, Anne
Wellesley, Arthur, 1st Duke of Wellington, 144
Wellesley Pole, William, 1st Lord Maryborough, 221
Wellesley, William Pole-Tylney-Long: *see* Long-Wellesley, William Pole-Tylney-
Welwyn, Hertfordshire, 67
Wentworth, Lady Anne: *see* Conolly, Lady Anne
Wentworth, Eliza, Countess of Strafford (widow of the 3rd Earl), 21
Wentworth, Frederick Thomas, 3rd Earl of Strafford (of the 1711 creation), 21
Wentworth, Thomas, 1st Earl of Strafford (of the 1711 creation), 6, 113
Wentworth, William, 2nd Earl of Strafford (of the 1711 creation), 6, 194–5
Westenra, Mrs Harriet (*née* Cairnes Murray), 189
Westenra, Warner William, 2nd Lord Rossmore, 189
West Indies, 79, 149, 176
  see also Jamaica
Westmeath, County, 24–5, 27, 83, 89, 100, 168, 238, 250, 251
Westmeath, earls and Marquess of: *see* Nugent, George Frederick, Nugent, George Thomas, and Nugent, Thomas
Westminster, dukes of: *see* Grosvenor
Westmorland, Earl of: *see* Fane
Wexford, County, 110
Whaley, Anne, Countess of Clare: *see* Fitzgibbon
Whaley, family of, of Whaley Abbey, Co. Wicklow, 260
Wharncliffe, Lord and Lady: *see* Wortley

INDEX

The Whigs, 117, 145, 176
Wicklow, Countess of: *see* Forward
Wicklow, Earl of: *see* Howard
Wicklow, County, 84, 107–8
widows, 17–18, 20–24, 34, 65-8, 102–3, 122, 133, 196–7, 244
  see also jointures
Wilkins, William, 269
William IV, King, 158–61
Williams, Sir Charles Hanbury, 102
Williams, Sir John, of Minster-in-Thanet, Kent, 58
Williams, Mary, Lady Shelburne, 58
wills, 3, 17–18, 20–24, 30, 31–2, 41, 46–8, 56–7, 67, 71, 75–6, 87–9, 96–8, 123, 126, 149, 166, 175, 180–84, 194–9, 204–6, 209–10, 247, 249
Wilson, Edward Warter, of Bilboa, Co. Limerick, 109–10
Wilson, Juliana Warter: *see* Rous, Juliana, Lady Rous
Windsor, family of, Viscounts Windsor, 165
Witham Place, Essex (seat of the 8th Earl of Abercorn), 235
Worcestershire: *see* Hanbury, Hall, Worcestershire; Ombersley Court, Worcestershire
Wortley, Caroline Stuart-, Lady Wharncliffe (wife of the 1st Lord), 129–30, 146
Wortley, Hon. James Archibald Stuart-, 129–30
Wortley, James Stuart-, 1st Lord Wharncliffe, 129–30
Wriothesley, Lady Rachel (heiress of Bloomsbury and Covent Garden), 201, 267–8
Wriothesley, Thomas, 4th Earl of Southampton, 267–8
Wyndham, Anna Maria (wife of Thomas Wyndham), 202
Wyndham, Caroline (daughter of Thomas Wyndham): *see* Quin, Caroline Wyndham-, Countess of Dunraven
Wyndham, Charles, 2nd Earl of Egremont, 87
Wyndham, Colonel George, 1st Lord Leconfield, 228
Wyndham, Hon. Percy Charles, of Shortgrove, Essex, 88
Wyndham, Thomas, of Clearwell Court, Gloucestershire, and Dunraven Castle, Glamorganshire, 202
Wyndham, Sir William, 3rd Bt, 87
Wyndham O'Brien, George, 3rd Earl of Egremont, 88, 117–18, 203, 225, 228–9
Wyndham O'Brien, Percy, one and only Earl of Thomond (d.1774), 87–8, 193, 203, 225, 229

Yorke, Philip, 1st Earl of Hardwicke: *see* Marriage Act (Lord Hardwicke's)
Yorkshire, 201
Young, Arthur, 104